DATA AND TELECOMMUNICATIONS
SYSTEMS AND APPLICATIONS

Charles N. Thurwachter, Jr.
DeVry Institute of Technology

PRENTICE HALL
Upper Saddle River, New Jersey   *Columbus, Ohio*

Library of Congress Cataloging-in-Publication Data
Thurwachter, Jr., Charles N.
   Data and telecommunications : systems and applications / Charles
N. Thurwachter, Jr.
      p.   cm.
   ISBN 0-13-793910-8
   1. Data transmission systems.   2. Computer networks.   I. Title.
TK5105.T48   2000
004.6—dc21   99-17286
                                                                CIP

Publisher: Charles E. Stewart, Jr.
Associate Editor: Kate Linsner
Production Editor: Rachel Besen
Copyeditor: Roaring Mountain Editorial Services
Design Coordinator: Karrie Converse-Jones
Cover Designer: Thomas Mack
Cover Image: International Stock
Production Manager: Deidra M. Schwartz
Marketing Manager: Ben Leonard

This book was set in Palatino and Helvetica Light Condensed by Maryland Composition and was printed and bound by R.R. Donnelley & Sons Company. The cover was printed by Phoenix Color Corp.

©2000 by Prentice-Hall, Inc.
Pearson Education
Upper Saddle River, New Jersey 07458

Printed in the United States of America

10 9 8 7 6 5 4 3 2 1

ISBN: 0-13-793910-8

Prentice-Hall International (UK) Limited, *London*
Prentice-Hall of Australia Pty. Limited, *Sydney*
Prentice-Hall of Canada, Inc., *Toronto*
Prentice-Hall Hispanoamericana, S. A., *Mexico*
Prentice-Hall of India Private Limited, *New Delhi*
Prentice-Hall of Japan, Inc., *Tokyo*
Prentice-Hall (Singapore) Pte. Ltd., *Singapore*
Editora Prentice-Hall do Brasil, Ltda., *Rio de Janeiro*

To Sean and Evan

Preface

The philosophy of this treatment of communications systems and networking is to present the subjects in such a way that they are understandable for students who have a limited mathematical background. Whenever possible, and this is for most topics, differential and integral calculus have been avoided. In those few cases where they were required for understanding, in most situations they appear in an appendix at the end of the book. This will allow presenters to choose to include those discussions or not without altering the flow of topic selection.

The main themes of *Data Communications: Systems and Applications* are the following:

1. The units and terminology of the subject area are introduced. This includes a thorough treatment of the decibel unit of relative magnitude along with the clear distinction between the decibel as a unitless number and the units of physical measurement, volts, watts, and so forth that can be used to express physical quantities.

2. The three types of media that are used in communications, metallic, optical, and atmospheric, are treated in separate chapters. In addition to describing how they are used, attention is paid to the various effects material considerations have on the performance of the first two. Extensive discussion is included on troubleshooting and grounding issues where appropriate. The antenna chapter features an application study on frequency modulation antennas.

3. The treatment of Fourier analysis focuses on accomplishing four goals:
    a. Showing that the shape and duty cycle of a wave affects only the relative magnitude of the fundamental frequency and harmonics

    b. Showing that the frequency of the waveform affects only the location of the fundamental frequency and harmonics and not the amplitudes

    c. Explaining how the shape of a wave or the line code selected affects the power inherent in the waveform

    d. Explaining that any waveform can be described by its amplitude and frequency components and the equivalence of looking at signals in the time or frequency domain

4. The treatment of analog modulation techniques is done in a unified way. Amplitude and angle modulations are treated in separate chapters with a focus on bandwidth and power considerations and how the form of the modulating signal changes the modulated spectrum. Special attention is given to how amplitude and frequency information are conveyed in both forms. This emphasis is an effective instructional tool.

5. Pulse modulation is contrasted with analog modulation, again focusing on bandwidth and power considerations. Pulse code modulation is developed and explored in detail with particular focus on how it is used in the telephone system, including framing. Other forms of pulse modulation are briefly reviewed.

6. Coding is explored and examples are used to explain how source and channel coding is applied in communications systems. Many examples are used to clearly illustrate how these mechanisms work. Students may find this chapter to be one of their favorites; information theory is demystified and made very approachable.

7. Analog modulation is extended to include digital modulation forms and how these techniques are used for most terrestrial- and space-based data communications. Again, the focus is on bandwidth and power considerations. Additionally, extensive treatment of error rate calculations and how bandwidth of the channel affects these calculations are provided.

8. Nomenclature for discussing networking and telecommunications is covered in a single chapter. The OSI model is used as a framework for breaking the discussion up into functional blocks that combine to get a message from source to destination. The focus of this chapter is on the communications functionality contained in the lower three layers of the model. Special attention is paid to the protocol and service aspects of each layer and the difference between a protocol and a network.

9. One chapter discusses the modern telephone system and how it is architecturally composed, with a focus on how signaling changes with technology. In-band and out-of-band signaling are contrasted using POTS and ISDN. This leads into a discussion of the interoffice network signaling SS7. Line types and several components particular to the telecommunications industry are described. Additionally, an introduction to how various services are provided and priced out to the consumer is provided.

10. The remaining discussion on networking is broken up into two additional chapters. The first concerns itself exclusively with a description of various networking components and how they work and make up the other half of

the combination of protocols and network hardware that are jointly commonly referred to as the network. The second chapter is an overview of three protocols, FieldBus, Ethernet, and TCP/IP, that illustrate three different approaches to fit three different networking application areas.

11. Links of understanding are made with earlier material whenever possible. This serves to reinforce earlier subject matter and tie together a large amount of material for the student. Further, the writing style is directed to the practically oriented practitioner and student. Therefore, the material is structured and written in a more conversational style than is traditionally used in a textbook.

AUDIENCE

Some reviewers may be concerned with the depth of treatment of some subjects and wonder who the prospective audience is for this book. This book is designed for readers who need an understanding of this subject area but who are not mathematically inclined. This does not preclude a discussion of areas where an understanding can be achieved without mathematical rigor. The IEEE has addressed this distinction between technicians, technologists, and engineers in a Draft IEEE Position Paper on Engineering Technology, which was approved by the IEEE Educational Activities Board (EAB) in 1991. This document is reprinted below. Note that the comments concerning design and application expertise and responsibility overlap. The primary audience and intended reader of this text is the four-year engineering technologist.

The IEEE recognizes the need to properly integrate the graduates of bachelor level (four-year or equivalent) engineering technology programs (technologists) in the technical community, to identify the position in the industry for which their educational preparation is best suited, and to identify educational opportunities available subsequent to graduation.

Engineers and technologists are often assigned to the same project team to effectively utilize their complementary knowledge, experience, and skills. In a typical scenario, engineers use theory and design principle to develop problem solutions, products, or systems with Technologists transforming the engineers' design concepts into actual prototypes or products. Technicians (associate degree engineering technology graduates and holders of an equivalent degree from various countries) are often supervised by engineers and/or technologists in the development, fabrication and testing of devices and systems. In actual practice the technical contribution and responsibilities of the team members often overlap and can vary considerably.

The professional responsibilities of engineers and technologists may vary in relationship to the amount and content of their academic preparation. A technologist's work ranges from design to sales and typically incorporates application of well documented concepts, analysis using established mathematical procedures, and design using established guidelines.

Engineering technology programs emphasize both technical and practical proficiency, and almost every technical course includes a laboratory component. Courses in engineering technology programs, compared with similar courses in engineering programs, tend to be more oriented toward applications with less emphasis on underlying science.

Graduates of four-year engineering technology programs can be admitted directly into a master's degree program in engineering technology or into equivalent programs in various countries. Those who wish to pursue a graduate program in engineering or computer science may need to take additional undergraduate courses as required by their individual college or university.

As is suggested by the above statement, a technologist may be called upon to function as a senior technician or in a nonanalytic engineering position. For that reason material is included that might normally not be covered in a text intended for this population.

When this book is adopted for a course at the technician level, the subject areas omitted would still provide a useful guide for them as they mature on the job and need to extend their skills. Further, after being introduced to some subject areas in brief, the barriers to their understanding are significantly reduced when they use a book with which they are already familiar.

It may also be appropriate for an introductory course at the engineering level, where the focus is on a survey of several aspects of communications. This might be followed by a more in-depth treatment in a subsequent course or with supplementary material provided by the instructor. The text is not designed to address the analytical needs of the advanced student.

Having worked for many years in the data communications industry, I have often found that a practical understanding of how networking and telecommunications work in the modern environment is lacking in some employees, both young and old. The last four chapters of this book make a good survey of the current environment. The absence of mathematical rigor also make it accessible to nontechnical professionals who need a general understanding of networking or telecommunications hardware. As a technical professional, I have often found that the material in these chapters was more valuable to me in day-to-day business operations than the in-depth understanding that I obtained elsewhere.

I have used this text for several semesters with students who fit the description of a technologist, and I have had good success with this approach. The employers who hire these students have expressed their appreciation of the understanding of the basics with which they come to the job. This is for me validation enough that the choice of topics and depth of coverage is appropriate. The coverage is sufficient for a fast-paced two-semester sequence or a more measured three-semester pace.

When used in a two-semester course, I suggest omitting Chapters 4, 5, 8, and 17, Optical Media, Antennas, Amplitude Modulators, and Demodulators (except for the envelope detector section), and Three Protocols. Further, Chapters 14 through 16 may be covered only selectively.

ANCILLARIES

A companion laboratory manual, defining several experiments, is available. The laboratory manual describes a group of experiments that are coupled with the text. Therefore, the number of experiments in this text is relatively small, but focused. These experiments have been chosen with two things in mind. First, they complement the main thrusts of the text and emphasize the same points critical to understanding that are emphasized in the text. Having both the text and laboratory manual written by the same author offers certain advantages to the adopter of both. I have used them together extensively in a two-semester sequence on communications and have had good success. Second, no great economic burden is placed on the student when purchasing the components required. Additionally, the experiments also do not call for exotic test equipment that would make the adoption of them economically prohibitive to the instructional organization.

ACKNOWLEDGMENTS

This book would be a very different one without the interaction with the students that have participated in its refinement. Their input has been invaluable in forming how best to present certain material. Additionally, I am appreciative of Prentice Hall and the entire staff with whom I worked; without their contributions, this book also would never have seen the light of day. I especially want to thank Charles E. Stewart, Jr., Kate Linsner, and Rachel Besen. In addition, several reviewers offered valuable feedback during the earlier stages of manuscript preparation. I would particularly like to acknowledge the following individuals at DeVry Institute of Technology for their assistance and support: Robert Diffenderfer, William Lin, Robert Morris, James Ronca, and Lowell Tawney.

I encourage any interested reader to write with any comments about the material or coverage. Clearly not every topic that could be covered has been. I have tried to be selective in those included; others may have other opinions. Please convey these to me, and I will make an effort to reflect those opinions in subsequent editions. Additionally, although I have made every effort to weed out any misstatements, I learned long ago that occasional errors are part of the human condition. The best way I can see for uncovering these is to elicit comments from you, the reader. Please be assured that any and all kudos, comments, or criticisms will be received with interest and attention.

Contents

1

Fundamental Concepts

The field of data communications is a vast and exciting one. It also is one of the fastest growing fields of engineering technology. The explosion of the Internet, wireless telephones, multiple telephone service providers is creating an infrastructure that requires skilled people to help it grow. When the word *data* in the phrase *data communications* is used, *data* is a general term that includes analog signals such as voice along with digital data streams. Although voice-only systems have some special considerations, generally a study of communications systems that will support digital data will also yield an understanding of those systems designed to support only voice, video, and so forth. The basic idea is that the information that is to be sent should not be restricted in any way.

Communications systems have had many different implementations throughout history, but they all used the best technology of the time to accomplish the same basic task: to send information from one place at one time to another place and time. As technology has moved forward, the two places have gotten farther apart and the time has shrunk. Additionally, the amount of information per signal sent has gotten denser. Although many of these approaches are compelling to study, only systems using electromagnetic signals sending data across a variety of channel types will be explored here. Semaphore, smoke signals, underwater lasers, and the use of diplomatic language as an encryption code will be excluded.

In this first chapter, several important terms are defined. Although definitions sound boring, the field of communications, like any specialized field, has its own vocabulary. This vocabulary must be captured before an understanding of the field can be achieved. For example, to someone totally unfamiliar with the sport of baseball, the terms *suicide squeeze* and *stealing* might have very different interpretations than is intended. Decibels and interface standards are also explored.

■ DATA COMMUNICATIONS EQUIPMENT, DATA TERMINAL EQUIPMENT, AND COMMUNICATIONS CHANNEL

A discussion of communications systems will be used to define some terms. All data communications systems, independent of manufacturer, use the general terminology of data communications equipment (DCE) and data terminal equipment (DTE). Each pair of DCEs communicates through the block-designated communications channel (CC). See Figure 1.1. Note the interaction points between these two classes of equipment, the DTE-DCE and the DCE-DTE interfaces. Just below each of the boxes is an example of each piece of equipment. In this figure, the personal computer (PC) is using its modem to place a call through the telephone system to another modem connected to a remote printer. Once the connection is established, the personal computer can send files to be printed at the remote site. Note that each DTE connects through a DCE to a communications channel, through another DCE to another DTE. In another example, a data entry keyboard might be remotely situated from the computer in which the data is stored and it communicates through a communications channel. This is a common situation in which large amounts of data are collected and stored on a central computer. Often billing and customer service centers are implemented in this manner.

This text will focus on the DCE and the CC blocks shown in Figure 1.1, that is, the communications components only. To facilitate this discussion, see Figure 1.2. These three subsystems of a communications system are the three most basic components. They feature a transmitter, where the information input is applied. The transmitter impresses, or modulates, the carrier signal with the information source. A carrier signal is simply the specific frequency that we would tune the receiver to pick up the broadcast.

For example, the carrier signal of your favorite radio station is the frequency that you tune your radio to to listen to it. In the case of a radio station, the information input is the music and/or voice of the announcer. The receiver is the radio itself, and the transmitter is the radio station transmitter. The communications channel is the area around the transmitter antenna location where the signal has sufficient power to be received by your radio.

Figure 1.1
DTE-DCE connection diagram.

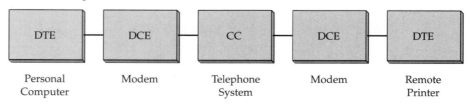

| DTE | DCE | CC | DCE | DTE |
| Personal Computer | Modem | Telephone System | Modem | Remote Printer |

Figure 1.2
Communication components.

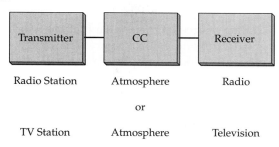

Assume that the radio station is broadcasting a clean signal, your radio is a good one, and it does not distort the signal that it receives. Then all the noise, distortion, and interference you hear on your radio came from the communications channel. This is the general case. We will examine communications systems in this way. The transmitter prepares the signal that is sent, the effects of transmission through the channel are modeled as additions to the signal caused by the nonideal channel, and the receiver extracts the signal from the communications channel. By the way, nothing says that the interference of the communications channel has to remain fixed over time. In soft channels especially, it generally does not.

■ HARD AND SOFT COMMUNICATIONS CHANNELS

The communications channel that will be discussed fall into two broad groups, hard and soft channels. Those channels that you can touch, such as coaxial cable, wire, and fiber optic cable, are hard. All other channels such as air, space, and seawater, are soft.

The central difference between them is that in hard channels the signal travels a known, confined, physical path (e.g., the path is well defined: it is hard). In a soft channel, the signal radiates and although the path length may be determined, the actual path is not confined (e.g., the path is "soft"). Typically, hard channels also contain some inherent shielding from interference due to the way they are constructed, whereas soft channels do not have any built-in shielding from interference.

Soft channels are often called unguided channels because the signal does not take a single path through the channel over time. Similarly, hard channels are often referred to as guided channels because the signal is guided along the same path again and again.

■ ANALOG AND DIGITAL SIGNALS

The input signals to be examined are arbitrary in nature and include examples of both analog and digital data. Analog data sources are defined as those data sources that take on any value in the range of values that the source spans. The microphone used in the telephone system is a good example of an analog input signal and device. Ideally, the microphone output can take on any value of frequency and amplitude that is produced by the speaker.

A digital data source is any source that can take on only a limited set of values, sometimes only two (0 and 1) for a binary data source such as a flip-flop. The keyboard on your computer is a good example of a generalized digital data source. The output of the keyboard is a discrete set of values.

Many communications systems are also inherently analog and digital. Generally, the term analog communications system applies to those communications systems that are used to transfer analog or digital information from one place to another, but always in an analog manner. Digital communications system applies to those communications systems that are used to transfer analog or digital information, but always in a digital manner. The critical distinction is the form of the modulated signal in the channel.

Analog data source: An input signal that has continuous values with no abrupt breaks. Virtually all naturally produced signals are analog data sources.

Digital data source: An input signal that has values with "squarelike" edges; in the ideal world, these would be discontinuous with a single point taking on more than one amplitude value. Any ideal pulsed or square wave is an example.

Analog component: A component that operates with continuous signals applied to its input and produces a continuous signal on its output. Typically, any non-clocked component is an analog component. Examples include amplifiers, transformers, and capacitors.

Digital component: A component that operates with digital signals on at least one of its inputs or outputs. Typically, the component will require a clock source. Examples include flip-flops, microprocessors, and analog-to-digital (A/D) and digital-to analog (D/A) converters.

Analog communications system: A communications system that transfers an analog or digital data source from source to destination. While the signal is in the communications channel, it remains continuous. Analog communications systems often require a carrier signal, and most are broadband. Examples include broadcast radio, television, and cable television. The analog modem hooked up to your PC is another good example of an analog communications system. It is sending a digital data source in an analog way, but only for a short distance. In most parts of the United States, the signal is very quickly translated into a digital pulse sequence for transmission.

Digital communications system: A communications system that transfers an analog or digital data source from source to destination. While the signal is in the communications channel, it is digital in nature but may be analog or digital at either end. Examples include pulse code modulation (PCM) systems used in the telephone system and integrated services digital network (ISDN) modems. These all use some kind of PCM or a variant, and they will be discussed in Chapter 10. Today, the terms *digital communications system* and *pulse modulation system* are virtually synonymous.

Table 1.1 summarizes the difference between sources and the form the signal takes while it is in the channel. Always classify the communications system by the form the signal takes while it travels from the source to destination: If the signal is analog in the channel, you have an analog communications system.

Cellular telephones are good examples of why these definitions tend to break down in the real world. Often advanced systems combine elements of all of the above distinctions. Cellular telephones transmit an analog data source by converting it to a digital sequence and then modulate and multiplex that sequence in an analog manner. At the other end, the process is reversed. Both transmitter and receiver contain analog and digital components. Additionally, digital data sources are also possible if a modem is hooked up to the cellular telephone. Cellular telephone systems will be discussed further in Chapter 10.

The modern trend is toward digital communications systems because they have many advantages over analog communications systems. Some of these advantages are a result of the technology in use today; others result from the inherent digital nature of digital data sources. Modern integrated circuits (ICs) make digital design inexpensive and reliable compared to analog design. Encoding the data stream into a digital sequence offers many advantages, including greater dynamic range and error detection and recovery by the use of coding.

Additionally, once encoded into digital streams, many sources may be combined and sent; for example, voice, video, and data may be combined and sent over the same communications system. To see the great advantages of this last point, imagine how the growth of the Internet would have been restrained if it had been necessary to build a new telephone system, to exchange data. The advantage of being able to use the existing telephone system and combining the digitized voice and data produced by modems over one communication system was critical to that growth.

Digital communications systems also have some disadvantages over analog communications systems. The major one has to do with something called bandwidth. This term has not yet been defined, and an exact definition will be given in the next chapter. For now, think of bandwidth as just width. The wider the band, the more space it takes up. Generally, it takes more bandwidth to transmit a digital signal than an analog one at the same data rate or information capacity.

Table 1.1
Analog and Digital Communication Classifications

Source/Channel	Analog Channel	Digital Channel
Analog source	Broadcast radio Television	Traditional telephone
Digital source	Modem I Facsimile	ISDN telephone

Generally, the advantages of digital communications systems outweigh their disadvantages except in soft or unguided channels. In hard or guided channels, digital communications systems are the dominant technology.

■ SIMPLEX AND DUPLEX SYSTEMS

To this point communications systems have been discussed implicitly assuming the information transfer is in one direction only. This is not generally true; many times it is an advantage or a requirement to have two-way communication. Try to imagine telephone conversations if the telephone communications system was one-way. We will therefore divide all communications systems into one of three types.

Simplex (SX) communications systems are those systems where information is transferred in one direction, all the time. Broadcast radio is an example of simplex communications. The radio station's transmitter sends a signal to your radio. Your radio does not communicate back to the transmitter. Broadcast TV is also a familiar example of a simplex communications system.

Half-duplex (HDX) communications systems are those systems where information is transferred in two directions, but only in one direction at one time. These systems usually alternate communication flow, first in one direction and then in another. Today, voice conversations over the Internet are one example of half-duplex communications; only one person can speak at a time.

Another good example of a half-duplex communications system is a walkie-talkie. One person presses the transmit button, speaks, says "over," and then the other person presses the transmit button, speaks, and says "over" to transfer the communication channel back to the first speaker. Each person can speak, but that transfer can only take place in one direction at a time.

Full-duplex (FDX) communications systems are those systems where information is transferred in both directions at the same time. The traditional telephone system is a good example of a full-duplex system. Both users can speak at the same time; even if this reduces the intelligibility of the conversation, the communications system features that capability. For an illustration of the three modes of communication, see Figure 1.3.

■ BASEBAND AND BROADBAND SIGNALS

So far, two ways to partition communications systems have been used to talk about them. First was the distinction of analog versus digital. Second was the three classifications of "exness" (simplex, half-duplex, and full-duplex.) There is one other big picture way of dividing these systems, using the distinction between baseband and broadband communication systems.

The terms *baseband* and *broadband* are used to describe signals in terms of where they lie in the frequency spectrum. When we use the term baseband, as in baseband signal, we are speaking of a signal whose spectrum extends down to 0 frequency, or nearly so. Broadband signals are those signals where the frequency spectrum does not

Figure 1.3
Simplex and duplex communication.

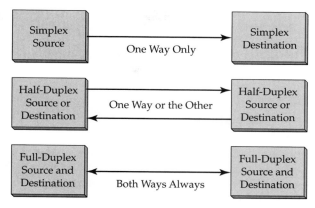

lie close to 0 frequency. This means that the signal is confined to some frequency band centered about some carrier signal frequency. See Figure 1.4.

In both of the drawings in Figure 1.4, the horizontal axis is frequency. The vertical axis is amplitude or voltage. This is a little different from what you are used to seeing on an oscilloscope, where the horizontal axis is time. This kind of display is called a spectral display, representing the frequency spectrum of the signal that is examined. In both drawings, the shaded area represents the presence of a signal.

In the first drawing, the shaded area extends from 0 hertz (Hz) to 1 kilohertz (kHz). This is an example of what is meant by baseband. The frequency spectrum extends from 0 frequency to some higher frequency, here 1 kHz. In the second drawing, the shaded area extends from 2 to 3 kHz. Note that both occupy the same bandwidth, 1 kHz. The frequency spectrum does not lie close to 0 frequency. Recall that when analog communications systems were defined, it was stated that they require a carrier signal. In the ra-

Figure 1.4
Baseband and broadband signals.

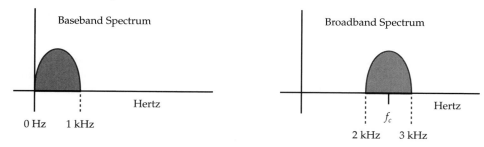

dio example, the carrier signal frequency is that frequency that you tune your radio to. In the broadband case, this is shown at the center of the drawing.

Examples of baseband systems include major elements of the telephone system and two dominant local area network (LAN) systems, Ethernet and Token Ring. Other than LAN networks and the telephone system, most communications systems around us are broadband, including broadcast and cable TV, broadcast amplitude modulation (AM) and frequency modulation (FM) radio, satellite systems, cellular telephones, and pagers.

■ HERTZ AND RADIANS

Two equivalent units represent frequency of sinusoidal signals. The traditional unit to use is hertz, or cycles per second, as the unit of frequency, which uses the variable f. However, as will be seen in the next section and many times throughout this book, sinusoidal signals are written using the variable w to represent frequency rather than f. The units of w are radians per second (rad/sec).

This notation is used because sinusoidal signals are also described by the term angular frequency. Angular frequency is the frequency expressed in radians per second. Both units are equivalent. The practice that will be followed is to use frequency in problems statements and most figures. Most modulation formula will be expressed in radians per second; w, can be replaced by hertz using the following formula for conversion:

$$w = 2\pi f \qquad (1\text{-}1)$$

■ EXAMPLE 1.1

Express a frequency given as 100 Hz and 100 rad/sec in the alternate units:

$$w = 2\pi f = 2\pi(100 \text{ Hz}) = 628 \text{ rad/sec}$$

$$f = \frac{w}{2\pi} = \frac{100 \text{ rad/sec}}{2p} = 15.9 \text{ Hz}$$

■ MODULATE

This section introduces you to the word *modulate,* one of the most fundamental concepts of communications. This text uses this word and its various tenses to describe how communications systems work and to identify what signals are inputs, outputs, etc.

Sometimes, it may seem as if a lot of time is spent talking about the definitions of words. This is because the study of communications systems is often hampered by lack of familiarity with the terms used. It is also true that communications has too many acronyms and terms that have special meanings. Many of these terms may mean something entirely different when used in a discussion that is unrelated to the technology of communications. This can be confusing even to those brought up with the English language.

The basic definition of *modulate* is to adjust or adapt in some proportion or to regulate in some manner. An example is 'We will modulate the heat flow in order to properly temper this metal.' Often the term is used to describe or characterize a singing voice or to describe the pitch, intensity, or tone of music. In electronics, especially communications, it has had the traditional meaning of varying the amplitude, frequency, or phase of a carrier wave. Modern use of the term in communications extends the concept to include those systems where a carrier wave is not required. Both of these types of systems will be discussed below.

Often when modulation is discussed, it will mean multiplication of one term by another. For example, when it is stated that $a(t)$ is modulating a carrier wave, mathematically what is meant is shown in equation 1-2. It can be clearly seen that $a(t)$ is multiplying a sinusoid. Further, the function $f(t)$ is referred to as the modulated signal. The modulated signal results from the act of modulation.

$$f(t) = a(t)\cos(w_c t) \qquad \textbf{(1-2)}$$

Note that the carrier signal in equation 1-1 is characterized by the argument of the cosine function. For all analog communications systems, this is where it appears. Equations of the form of equation 1-2 will be used to describe the three types of analog communications systems discussed. Figure 1.5 should help you identify how these terms combine and are used with those of the next two sections.

■ MODULATING SIGNAL AND MODULATED SIGNAL

In every communications system, there are always two basic signals that will be identified. The first of these is the modulating signal, which is the signal that contains the information that is to sent to the destination from the source. In any communications system, this would be the input signal. For example, in an AM or FM broadcast, the modulating signal might be music, talk, sports, or a commercial, depending on the station.

Figure 1.5
Basic communications terms.

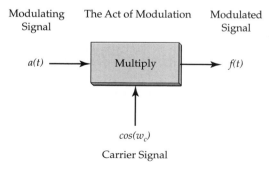

Digital signals can be modulating waves as well; examples include the data from your computer sent to a modem, a fax machine, and digitized data from a remote location. The modulating signal can have any form, and for the most part, there will be little distinction made between analog and digital modulating signals. The modulators that will be explored can handle many forms of data.

The second signal, which every communications system produces, is the modulated signal. This signal may be analog or digital in nature and is the signal that actually is present in the communications channel. This is the signal actually sent from source to destination. When the modulated signal is analog in nature, those communications systems are referred to as analog communications systems. When the modulated signal is digital in nature, those communications systems are referred to as digital communications systems. Always classify communications systems by the nature of the signal in the channel, called the modulated signal.

Most digital communications systems are implemented using pulse modulation techniques. In communications, sometimes it is desirable to have "digital" waveforms take on more than two amplitude values. Instead of just 0 or 1, leading to the term *digital*, which has come to mean binary, you might use 0, 1, 2, and 3. A multileveled waveform such as this cannot be properly referred to as digital, so the preferred practice is to call all such waveforms pulsed, regardless of how many amplitude levels they may have.

It is interesting to note that before the explosion of binary computers into our society, the word *digital* could have been used to discuss multilevel waveforms with no confusion. However, since that technological revolution, the language has changed a bit and now to most people digital and binary mean the same thing. Therefore, to avoid confusion and to specify that more than two amplitude levels are possible, the term *pulsed waveform* will be taken to mean any noncontinuous waveform of any number of amplitude levels. When pulsed waveforms are used as modulated signals, they are often referred to as a pulse train (e.g., a "train" of pulses, hooked up like cars in a train riding on a railroad).

■ CARRIER WAVE

The third waveform that may be present in a communications system, if it is an analog communications system, is the carrier wave or carrier frequency or carrier signal, which all mean the same thing. It is called a carrier wave because it is the wave that the information is "carried on." Close examination of equation 1-1 shows a subscript c on the w term in the argument of the cosine. This subscript stands for carrier. The frequency is given by w radians.

In analog communications systems, a high-frequency carrier wave is modulated by the modulating signal. Essentially, the modulating signal information is impressed onto the high-frequency carrier wave. This can be done in three fundamental ways; all three will be studied. The three fundamental characteristics of any data source are amplitude, frequency, and phase.

Modulating signals change one or more of these three quantities of the carrier wave to create the modulated signal. Remember, only analog communications systems make use of a carrier wave. Go back and examine Figure 1.4, which showed baseband and broadband spectrums. Note that the broadband spectrum is centered on f_c, the carrier frequency. In Figure 1.5, the carrier signal is shown multiplying the modulating signal.

■ MODULATORS AND DEMODULATORS

Now, some of you are probably a little confused by all the different ways the root word *modulate* has been used in the above paragraphs; hang in there, there are only two more. A modulator is the actual circuitry that is used to create the modulated signal. It has one or two inputs and one output. If the communications system is an analog one, it has two inputs and one output. The inputs are the modulating signal and the carrier wave. The output is the modulated signal.

If the communications system is digital, it has one input and one output. The input is the modulating signal and the output is the modulated signal. See Figure 1.6. Below each signal is a practical example with which you should be familiar. Note that in the example shown, the output of the digital communications system is being used as the source for the analog communications system. Today, this is often the case.

Modulators are the critical piece of a communications system's transmitter. Other than filtering, amplification, and so forth, all the interesting stuff that goes on in a communications system happens in the modulator. The type of modulators used differentiates communications systems. As mentioned previously, there are three fundamental types of communications systems, the type of modulator distinguishes them, and they make use of, amplitude, frequency, and phase. Digital communications systems are also distinguished by the type of modulator they use, although most commercially important ones are of the same type, amplitude, with varying degrees of precision.

Demodulators operate inversely from the modulator. Modulators are used at the source to generate the modulated signal; demodulators are used at the destination to retrieve the modulating signal from the modulated signal that passed through the communications channel. Modulators and demodulators are the inverse of each other. In all applications, whatever the modulator does, the demodulator must undo at the other end. Again, they either have two inputs and one output or one input and one output depending on whether they are classified as analog or digital communications systems. See Figure 1.7; as in the previous figure, an illustrative example is listed below each signal.

It is instructive to examine Figures 1.6 and 1.7 and compare the modulated and modulating signals in each case. Be sure that they make sense to you. Sometimes it is confusing to think of these signals both as radio transmissions and as things as familiar as a music CD. The only difference between the two for our purposes is that one is "of the moment" and the other is "on the shelf."

It is not appropriate to leave you with the impression that demodulators are not interesting, too. In the transmitter, all the interesting stuff goes on in the modulator; in the receiver, all the interesting stuff goes on in the demodulator. Although it can be said that the demodulator is the inverse of the modulator, the demodulator is actually more com-

Figure 1.6
Two types of modulators.

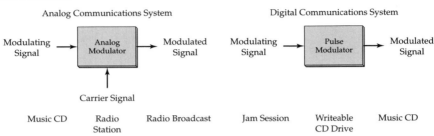

plex. If you think about it, it usually is easier to change something than figure out how it was changed and remove the change. For example, it is possible to change your automobile's finish with a hammer and almost no work. It is not as easy to remove the dent and then paint the finish so that the fender looks new.

■ TRANSMITTERS AND RECEIVERS

A transmitter is that device that combines the modulator with the necessary power amplification and circuitry to place the modulated signal into the communications channel. The receiver combines the demodulator with amplification and the circuitry to both acquire the signal from the communications channel and present it to the user at the destination. Some common examples of transmitters are an AM, FM, or TV broadcast center and a cellular telephone when you are talking, etc.

Some common examples of receivers are a car radio, pager, and cellular telephones when you are listening to someone else speak. Transmitters and receivers are sometimes separate, as in the radio station and your radio and sometimes combined, as in your cellular telephone. It does not matter whether they are distinct or colocated; they have separate functions and will be discussed as if they were separate. Whether they are separate

Figure 1.7
Two types of demodulators.

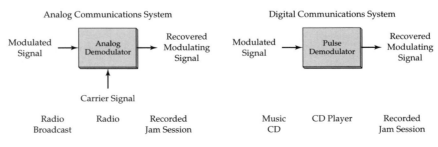

or combined is usually determined by whether the communications system is designed to be simplex or duplex, respectively.

■ SIGNAL-TO-NOISE (S/N) RATIO

Signal-to-noise (S/N) is the ratio of signal strength, or power, to noise power. Both quantities must always be measured in the same bandwidth for the ratio to have meaning: Whatever the bandwidth of the signal, you must measure the noise in that same bandwidth to get an accurate result. This should not come as a surprise to you; a simple example from everyday life will help make this clear.

Imagine you were asked to estimate how many leaves a particular tree in your backyard has. One way would be to cut the tree down and just count them, but you rather like the tree. Further, it seems a shame to kill it just to answer a question, so you try to come up with another way. You decide that because the tree loses all its leaves in the fall, you will just wait until they have all fallen down and count them then; this method is a little boring, but at least it saves the tree.

After fall comes and goes, you go out one winter day to count the leaves on the ground; they are all off now, and the tree is completely bare. You look around and start picking up and counting leaves; surprisingly, you are done rather quickly; there were only about 200 leaves in the whole yard. You think to yourself, that was not so bad, I sure thought there were more leaves than that on such a big tree. Well, the mistake is pretty clear. In an open yard some of the tree leaves blew away before they could be counted, so the "bandwidth" of the measurement was too narrow. You needed to count each leaf as it fell, from the time the first leaf fell to the time the last leaf fell.

In the analogy above, the signal was the leaves on the tree, the bandwidth was the time it took for all the leaves to fall, and the noise was the wind, blowing away leaves before they could be counted. To accurately measure the signal, you must account for the bandwidth of the noise. The result was incorrect because the signal was not measured across the entire bandwidth of the signal. As each leaf fell, some of the signal was transmitted to the ground, where the leaf could be counted.

Think of the travel of the leaf from the tree to the ground as the communications channel and the time it took for all the leaves to fall as the bandwidth of the signal. To get an accurate reconstruction of the signal at the destination, you need to measure the entire signal, not just some convenient part of it.

In communications systems, we are concerned with power, not leaves, but the analogy holds. Even though you may not understand how a transmitter or receiver works, it is possible to measure a key performance figure of the receiver using S/N measurements. The S/N ratio is a key performance parameter of any communications system.

The S/N ratio is only strictly defined after reception; therefore, it is a good way of talking about the performance of the receiver. One would ask what is the signal-to-noise performance of the receiver? The S/N ratio measures the relative power of the signal and the noise. It is defined as

$$\frac{S}{N} \text{ (dB)} = 10 \log \frac{S \text{ (W)}}{N \text{ (W)}} \qquad \textbf{(1-3)}$$

Whenever you see a log function on one side of an equation, the other side is being expressed in decibels.

■ DECIBELS, PART 1

The decibel is a base 10 logarithmic measure. This means that the decibel is just the power of 10. For example, 1000 represents 30 decibels (dB). That is 10 times 3; the power of 10 that represents 1000. The factor of 10 comes from the definition of a decibel:

$$y(dB) = 10 \log(x) \qquad \qquad \textbf{(1-4)}$$

■ EXAMPLE 1.2

Find the number of decibels represented by 10,000:

$$y(dB) = 10 \log(10,000)$$
$$y(dB) = 10 \log(10^4) = 10(4) = 40 \text{ dB}$$

Although Example 1.2 illustrates the concept of a decibel, in electronics this concept is used to relate one value to another. A more suitable, precise definition is

$$y(dB) = 10 \log \left(\frac{P_1}{P_2} \right) \qquad \qquad \textbf{(1-5)}$$

Usually, decibels are applied when relating one power to another. Inside the parentheses above are two powers, P_1 and P_2. The decibel represents the *value of the ratio* of the two powers. This is an easy way to talk about two powers by the value of their ratio without regard to the actual values. This is an important concept and is used throughout communications.

■ EXAMPLE 1.3

System 1 has an input power of 1 W and an output power of 100 W. System 2 has an input power of 5 mW and an output power of 0.5 W. Compare the two systems power gains using the decibel:

$$\text{System: } 1{:}10 \log \left(\frac{100 \text{ W}}{1 \text{ W}} \right) = 20 \text{ dB} \qquad \text{System: } 2{:}10 \log \left(\frac{0.5 \text{ W}}{0.005 \text{ W}} \right) = 20 \text{ dB}$$

Example 1.3 illustrated the use of the decibel to compare the gain of two systems without using the actual input and output values. Gain and a related concept, attenuation, are introduced in the next section. After that, more will be said about decibels and how they are used.

■ GAIN AND ATTENUATION

As stated earlier, one of the objectives of this introductory chapter is to introduce you to terms that are used to discuss communications systems. Being able to express by how much a signal is increasing or decreasing when it passes through a communications system is a very important concept; it is a way to talk about how much power was used to transmit the information and how much power was received. The gain (rise) and attenuation (loss) of a system are defined by the ratio of the output power over the input power, respectively. This power gain or loss is measured in units of the decibel:

$$\text{gain (dB)} = 10 \log \frac{P_{out}}{P_{in}} \qquad \textbf{(1-6)}$$

$$\text{attenuation (dB)} = 10 \log \frac{P_{in}}{P_{out}} \qquad \textbf{(1-7)}$$

Note that the two definitions in equations 1-6 and 1-7 are very similar. The gain and attenuation are found by just inverting the ratio of average powers. This is because the convention is to always talk about a positive gain or a positive attenuation. When the output power is greater than the input power, the system exhibits gain. When the reverse is true, the system exhibits attenuation. Once this is defined, apply the appropriate equation, 1-6 or 1-7. An example or two will illustrate how these formulas are applied.

■ EXAMPLE 1.4

A communications system has a specified transmit power of 10 W. At the receiver, the measured received power is 1 mW. First, is gain or attenuation occuring? Second, what is the amount of gain or attenuation? Remember to always express the answer as a positive number of decibels.

Because the part of the communications system under consideration is the channel, and the input power to the channel is larger than the output power of the channel, attenuation is occuring. Therefore, apply equation 1-7:

$$P_{in} = 10 \text{ W} \qquad P_{out} = 0.001 \text{ W}$$

$$\text{attenuation} = 10 \log \left(\frac{P_{in}}{P_{out}} \right) = 10 \log \left(\frac{10^1}{10^{-3}} \right) = 10 \log (10^4) = (10)(4) = 40 \text{ W}$$

■ EXAMPLE 1.5

A communications system has a specified gain of 30 dB. You have measured the output power of the system with a power meter and have determined its value to be 100 W. What is the input power being applied?

$$30 \text{ db} = 10 \log \frac{100W}{P_{in}} \rightarrow \frac{30}{10} = \log \frac{100}{P_{in}} \rightarrow 10^3 = \frac{100}{P_{in}} \rightarrow P_{in} = \frac{100}{10^3} = 0.1 \text{ dB}$$

■ EXAMPLE 1.6

Find the S/N ratio of a system where you have measured the signal level at 10 W and the noise level at 1 mW:

$$\frac{S}{N}\,(\text{dB}) = 10\log\left(\frac{S}{N}\right) = 10\log\left(\frac{10}{0.001}\right) = 40\;\text{dB}$$

Usually, you do not have such measurements. Often it is necessary to infer one signal, usually the noise level, from two measurements of the signal, as Example 1.7 illustrates.

■ EXAMPLE 1.7

In a certain communications system, when no input signal is applied, the output power is measured at 1 mW. After applying the input signal at appropriate levels, the output power is measured at 3 W. What is the S/N ratio of the communications system?

  The proper approach to this problem is to recognize that the first measurement is only finding the noise power contributed by the communications system. The second, after applying the input signal, is the power of the signal plus the noise. To understand this, think about your home stereo system. Turn the input selector to the CD input and do not place a CD in the player. When you turn up the volume with no signal applied, you hear static, or noise, from the speakers. After placing a CD in the player, what is heard from the speakers is the signal plus the noise. This is expressed in equation 1-8:

$$\frac{S}{N} = 10\log\left(\frac{P_{S+N} - P_N}{P_N}\right)$$
$$\frac{S}{N} = 10\log\left(\frac{3 - 0.001}{0.001}\right) = 34.8\;\text{dB}$$

(1-8)

  The larger the S/N ratio is, the better it is. Virtually all communication systems are ranked by their S/N ratios. Designers try to maximize the S/N ratio of the products they design. Users often make their purchase decisions partly based on the performance of the communications system. The S/N ratio is an important measurement of performance in the marketplace of communications systems.

  Because these expressions use powers (the product of voltage and current or voltage squared over resistance by Ohm's law), it is assumed that the source and load resistance are equal. If they are not, or if you are given or have measured the quantities in voltage across some resistance, equation 1-6 must be modified as shown in equation 1-9. Equation 1-7 is modified in a similar way.

$$\text{gain (dB)} = 20\log\frac{V_{\text{rms out}}}{V_{\text{rms in}}} + 10\log\frac{R_{\text{in}}}{R_{\text{load}}}$$

(1-9)

Note the similarity between the terms, and observe the inversion of quantities of the arguments of the logarithms. The 20 multiplying the voltage ratio comes from the expression of Ohm's law, where power can be represented by the voltage squared over the resistance. The inversion of in and out in the voltage and resistance terms comes from the fact that the resistance is dividing the voltage. This results in the inversion. Also, note that the expressions all use root mean square (rms) values; this is always the case when calculating average powers.

■ DECIBELS, PART 2

Everyone should be familiar with some common numerical values of decibels. They are used frequently as a kind of shorthand in discussing power ratios generally. See Table 1.2. You may want to check these values with your calculator, using equation 1-5. Note that the decibel value is *not* linear with power ratio.

It is also important to realize that the decibel is a dimensionless number, like radian and degree. Values of power, voltage, and current have dimensions and units because they are all physical quantities, not just numbers describing a ratio of two physical quantities.

Because it is just a form of number, a decibel can be converted to a pure number using the antilogarithm. You can always use this to convert back and forth between the ratios shown in Table 1.2 and the decibel values. Because the decibel is an expression of the power of 10, it is converted back to a pure number from a decibel by taking the decibel value and evaluating it as a power of 10. Example 1.8 illustrates this.

■ EXAMPLE 1.8

Confirm that the power ratio of 2 is given by 3 dB.

$$3 \text{ dB} = 10 \log \left(\frac{2}{1}\right) \rightarrow \frac{3}{10} = \log (2) \rightarrow 10^{(3/10)} = 10^{\log (2)} \rightarrow 1.995 = 2$$

That is very close to the value in Table 1.2. It illustrates that many of the values in Table 1-2 are approximate. For most calculations that you will do, the accuracy is acceptable.

Table 1.2
Common Decibel Values

Power Ratio	Decibel Value	Power Ratio	Decibel Value
1	0	8	9
2	3	10	10
3	5	100	20
4	6	1000	30

There are three other common expressions using the decibel concept. In these three, it is assumed that the resistance of the source and load are exactly equal. They are specialized expressions where the reference power is predetermined.

In the first expression, dBm is used where the reference power is defined as 1 mW. This unit is usually used to rate the output power of instruments and systems. It is also a common rating on power meters. The dBm, a logarithmic measurement of power referenced to 1 mW and expressed as decibels per milliwatt, is defined as

$$\text{dBm} = 10 \log \frac{\text{power level (W)}}{10^{-3}} = 30 + 10 \, L_y \, [\text{power level (w)}] \qquad \textbf{(1-10)}$$

■ EXAMPLE 1.9

The power measured at the output of a certain communication system is 15 W. What is the output power expressed in dBm?

$$P_o^{(\text{dBm})} = 10 \log \frac{15}{0.001} = 41.8 \text{ dBm}$$

The second common expression is sometimes used in the telephone system. It states that the noise power levels are very small and uses only a picowatt as a reference power. The dBrn, a logarithmic measurement of power referenced to 1 pW and expressed as decibels per picowatt, is defined as follows:

$$y(\text{dBrn}) = 10 \log \frac{\text{power level (W)}}{10^{-12}}$$

$$y(\text{dBrn}) = 120 + 10 \log[\text{power level (W)}] \qquad \textbf{(1-11)}$$

The measures of dBm and dBrn are related. As can be seen from the definitions above, 0 dBm is equal to 90 dBrn.

■ EXAMPLE 1.10

When measuring the input power to a communications system, you find that the equipment has been calibrated in dBrn. Unfortunately, the computer program you have to enter the data into requires the measurements to be stated in dBm. But you quickly realize that it is possible to convert from one to the other with your calculator. The meter yields a value of 150 dBrn. Find the value in dBm.

$$150 \text{ dBrn} = 10 \log \frac{P}{10^{-12}} \rightarrow \frac{150}{10} = \log \frac{P}{10^{-12}} \rightarrow 10^{15} = \frac{P}{10^{-12}} \rightarrow P = 10^{15} \, 10^{-12} = 10^3 \text{ W}$$

$$y(\text{dBm}) = 10 \log \frac{P}{10^{-3}} = 10 \log \frac{10^3}{10^{-3}} = 60 \text{ dBm}$$

To check your calculations, check that 90 added to the calculation of dBm equal the value of dBrn? The answer is checked and correct; the shortcut mentioned above does work.

The third common expression is used in the CATV industry and certain broadband LAN systems. It expresses the voltage of the waveform across a 75 Ω load. It uses voltage because in these widely standardized systems the resistance is fixed and known. All CATV systems use 75 Ω components, so this is a natural choice for this industry. The dBm V, a logarithmic measurement of voltage referenced to 1 mV across a 75 Ω load, expressed as decibels per millivolt, is

$$\text{dBm V} = 20 \log \frac{V_{\text{rms}}}{10^{-3}} \tag{1-12}$$

The dBmV also can be related back to dBm; if the source and load resistance are kept at 75 Ω, 0 dBm = 48.75 dBmV.

When using equipment to measure or drive communications systems, make sure you know the units in which the powers are calibrated. One of the frustrating things when measuring waveforms on an oscilloscope and relating them to power and dBm is that you always have to have the conversions written down somewhere. Then you need to fire up your calculator to compute them. Table 1.3 does this conversion for you for one particular case. That case is where the measurement impedance is 50 Ω. Most high-frequency test equipment is terminated in this impedance. Note in Table 1.3 that negative values of dBm do not indicate negative voltages or powers, just small magnitude signals.

Before the subject of decibels is complete, it is important to realize that the decibel and dBm can be combined in ways to describe gain and attenuation of any system. This means that sometimes you can combine the two quantities directly and obtain a measure of the gain or attenuation of a system. To understand when you can do this, it is necessary to explore a little deeper into just how these quantities are used to describe power amplification.

Any quantity, voltage, current, or power, can be amplified. Power amplification means that the power applied to an input of an amplifier is increased by some amount when it appears on the output. Power amplification is usually described in dBm in a discussion of input and output powers. When the power amplification of an amplifier is being described, the decibel is usually used. Therefore, it is permissible to add the dBm and decibel together to describe gain and to subtract them to describe attenuation. This is shown in equations 1-13 and 1-14 and illustrated in Example 1.11.

$$\text{gain (dBm)} = \text{dBm} + \text{dB} \tag{1-13}$$

$$\text{attenuation (dBm)} = \text{dBm - dB} \tag{1-14}$$

■ **EXAMPLE 1.11**

A certain communications system has an input power of 2 dBm. The gain of the system is 5 dB. What is the out put power?

Table 1.3
Decibels to Volts to Watts Conversion Table, 50 Ω Termination

dBm	Vrms (*V*)	Vpp (*V*)[a]	Power (mW)
+30	7.10	20.0	1000
+20	2.25	6.36	100
+15	1.15	3.25	25
+10	0.71	2.01	10
+5	0.40	1.13	3.2
0	0.225	0.64	1.0
−5	0.125	0.35	0.32
−10	0.071	0.20	0.10

[a] Vpp = Volts peak to peak.

$$\text{gain (dBm)} = 2\text{ dBm} + 5\text{ dB} = \text{dBm}$$

As can be seen, this is a handy way of quickly finding the output power once the input power is known. Often in figures in later chapters when implementations of communications systems are explored, the symbol shown in Figure 1.8 will be used. It is used to represent power gain as a shorthand way to describe voltage or current gain. When calculating system performance, a particular decibel value is assigned to it.

Finally, it is not always correct to add and subtract decibels and dBm freely, but it is always permissible to add or subtract two quantities expressed in decibels from each other. The resulting unit is the decibel. It is always correct to add and subtract two quantities expressed in decibels and dBm from each other; the resulting unit is dBm. Although it is permissible to subtract two quantities in dBm from each other, never add two quantities expressed in dBm to each other. In the first case the resulting units are decibels and express a comparison between two powers. In the second case the operation has no meaning. The best rule of thumb is if at least one of the quantities is expressed in decibels, addition or subtraction can be performed.

Figure 1.8
Power amplification.

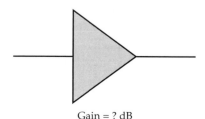

Gain = ? dB

■ INTERFACE STANDARDS

In this section, four interface standards will be introduced; they are widely used throughout the communications industry. Interface standards are specifications, which in the United States are jointly standardized by the American National Standard Institute (ANSI) and the Electronic Industries Association (EIA). They are published by the EIA as EIA standards with a number and revision letter to identify the particular interface standard. For example, EIA-232-D is EIA standard number 232 revision D. The interface standards are all for connecting the DCE to the DTE.

Interface standards are designed to specify the assignment of signals to specific pins and to define the mechanical specifications of the connector, allowing many vendors to make equipment with agreed-upon interface connections. Without these standards, the field of communications would be chaotic; every manufacturer would have its own "pet" interface and require you to buy the cables only from them at high prices. Today, whenever standard connectors are not specified, this situation rules the day.

If you have ever tried to hook up a personal computer or stereo system, you have encountered and worked with an interface standard. Even more basically, when you plug in a lamp or other electrical appliance, the plug always matches the socket or jack. This is also an example of an interface standard.

The four most widely used interface standards in communications systems, outside the telephone system, are discussed in the following sections. As stated earlier, standard interface cables are used to connect the DTE to the DCE almost universally. Because a personal computer can be viewed as having DTE and DCE interfaces, often RS-232 cables are used to attach the printer (DCE device) to the parallel output port of the computer (DTE device). This is usually a fully pinned cable.

Often you will have at least one additional serial port on the back of the computer, and this as well is designed to be used with a RS-232 cable, but the 9 pin version. These two versions are discussed in the next section. If you have an external modem, it would also be connected with an RS-232 cable. However, for most new systems, the modem is mounted directly on the computer's bus, and no external cable is required for communications between the DCE and DTE devices. The only cable then used is the telephone cord connecting the modem to the telephone system.

■ TROUBLESHOOTING INTERFACE STANDARDS

Often students wonder why interface troubleshooting material is of importance. After all, often you just buy the proper cable, attach it to both devices, and from there on it is software. The importance of the descriptions of the interface standards that follow is that to fix a problem, one must first locate it. Often the easiest way to do this is to isolate on which side of the communications channel the problem is occurring. Then at least you know where the problem lies. To do this, it is necessary to understand what signals are on what lines of the interface and from which direction they are sourced.

One of the most useful things about an interface standard is that the definition of the standard tells you from which end system the signal is originating. If you test that line and see no signal, you know that the problem is on the end that is supposed to be generating that signal. This is a very useful troubleshooting technique. In the descriptions below, the tables always clearly indicate which device, DCE or DTE, is generating the signal.

Of course, it is also possible that the cable itself is bad. This condition is easily determined by removing the cable from one piece of equipment and monitoring the signals present at the connector. If the signal is present at the connector but is not reaching the other end of the cable, the problem lies in the cable itself and not the end systems. To perform this analysis, it is critical to understand which pins should be active on the connector; the interface standard gives you this information.

Two important rules also concern interface standards and the cables that implement them:

1. The male connector is always associated with the DTE, and the female connector always associated with the DCE.
2. The DTE is normally required to supply the cable to use for interconnection. When you purchase a DTE device, make sure the proper cables are shipped with it. DCE devices rarely comes with cables.

■ EIA-232-D

The title of standard 232 is Interface Between Data Terminal Equipment and Data Circuit-Terminating Equipment Employing Serial Binary Data Interchange, but everyone just refers to it as 232. EIA-232-D specifies the familiar 25-pin connector, which has 13 pins on the top row and 12 pins on the bottom row.

When looking at an EIA-232-D connector for the first time, it is hard to know where to start counting the pins. Which is pin 1 and how does the rest of the numbering go? When you hold a connector in front of you with the longer side up (the top side is considered the row with 13 pins), the upper left-hand corner is pin 1. Pin 2 is the next pin on the same row to the right and so on to pin 13 at the extreme upper right-hand corner. The bottom row of 12 pins is numbered from pin 14 at the lower left-hand corner to pin 25 at the lower right-hand corner. See Figure 1.9.

The cable length is set at a maximum of 50 ft, but if the load capacitances are lower than those specified, longer-distance cables are acceptable. Cable lengths of 100 ft are typically no problem if you purchase good-quality cables and do not try to push the speed up too much above the stated maximum data rate. The maximum data rate is specified to be 20 kbps, but, as with any interface specification, length can be traded off for speed. With cables shorter than 10 ft, speeds of up to a few megabits per second (Mbps) are possible.

It is also common to not fully pin EIA-232-D cables. Many manufacturers use only 14 or fewer of the 25 circuits specified in the standard. Typically, when you purchase such a cable, it is wired with only 14 pins connected. The other pins may or may not be present in the connector. This situation occurs because most systems make no use of several of the possible circuits, and as such, it is a waste of money to always wire them. Some equipment does require a full set of circuits. When this is the case, make sure that

Figure 1.9
The 25-pin EIA-232-D connector.

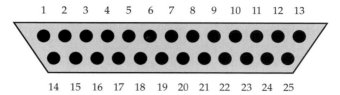

the cables you are using are of the right pin count to pass all the required signals that the particular piece of equipment requires.

Interface specifications talk about connections between DCE and DTE devices in terms of interface circuits. EIA-232-D describes four types of interface circuits that apply to virtually all systems. They are ground or common return, data, control, and timing circuits. When the standard speaks of circuits, it means only the connection between the DCE and DTE that flows through that pin assignment. There is no standardization on how the circuitry in the respective DCE or DTE equipment is actually implemented. It is just a way of speaking that is particular to people who work in the field of interface standards.

Of the 25 circuits possible in an EIA-232-D interface, 22 are specified to carry only one of the four circuit types. The remaining three sets of pins are left unassigned and are available for whatever purposes a manufacturer may choose. However, no manufacturer is required to use any of those circuits in the same way. In practice, if they are used, they are rarely accessible to the user. Internal connectorized components may send special signals on those lines.

Each circuit has a two- or three-letter designation that is a short-hand way of identifying the circuit and its intended function. As each of the four circuit types identified above is examined, the designation and pin assignments are identified. The common signal name for each circuit as used in the field is also provided.

The voltage ranges for EIA-232-D for the high and low states are symmetric about ground. High state voltages are defined as more positive than +3 V. Low state voltages are defined as more negative than −3 V. Maximum voltages are ±15 V. Because EIA-232-C uses the voltage range of 5 to 15 V and EIA-232-D and EIA-232-C are commonly connected together, most interfaces are designed to the older specification, EIA-232-C. This means that output voltages are between +5 and +15 for a ON, which is defined as a logical 0, and between −5 and −15 for an OFF, which is defined as a logical 1. Be careful of this; most of us associate positive voltages with logical 1s and negative voltages with logical 0s. It is the opposite case with 232.

Ground Circuits

Two pin sets are assigned to ground circuits. They are pin 7, Signal Ground/Common Return, and pin 1, Protective Ground. In 14 pin cables, only pin 7 is wired, this is the ground connection between the DCE and the DTE. Its abbreviation is AB. See Table 1.4.

Table 1.4
EIA-232-D, Ground Circuits

Pin Number	Function	Signal Name	Circuit
7	Signal Ground	Ground	AB

Data Circuits

There are two types of data circuits, primary and secondary. If there is only one set of data being sent or received, it will be on the primary data circuit, pins 2 and 3. In a primary data circuit the signals traveling along it are operating at the maximum data rate of the interface. A secondary data circuit is one where a slower signal is connected when there is more than one data rate in the interface. Further, each secondary data circuit is defined as one of two types, auxiliary and backward.

In auxiliary secondary data circuits, the direction of transmission is independent of the primary channel. In a backward secondary data circuit, the data transfer is in the reverse direction of the primary data circuit(s). Both types of secondary data circuits are controlled by an individual set of secondary control circuits. Table 1.5 shows the data circuits implemented in a 14 pin cable.

Note that the DTE is defined as the data source; not only does this equipment come with the cable, but it is defined as the transmit location of the data. This is exactly right; data communications equipment is not the source of the data; it is just the technology that enables the data to travel from source to destination.

Control Circuits

The control circuits are used primarily to start and stop data flow. They also function to indicate the status and condition of the DTE and DCE. Each set of data circuits has an associated set of control circuits. In addition, each DTE and DCE has two control circuits associated with it to indicate status and condition. See Table 1.6.

Pin 8, the Received Line Signal Detector, used to be known as Carrier Detect; hence the signal name CD. Before pulse modulation techniques became common, all communications systems were implemented as analog communications systems, so there was always a carrier to detect. Today, this situation has changed, and the circuit has been given a more general name that indicates a received signal at the DCE.

Table 1.5
EIA-232 Data Circuits

Pin Number	Function	Signal Name	Circuit	Data Signal Source
2	Transmitted Data	TD	BA	DTE
3	Received Data	RD	BB	DCE
14	Secondary Transmitted Data	STD	SBA	DTE
16	Secondary Received Data	SRD	SCA	DCE

Because control circuits are used to control the flow of the "conversation" over the interface, it is important to identify what each of the signals in Table 1.6 actually does. In the discussion below, it will be assumed that there is a terminal that is the source of the data and a modem that is used to send the transmission. On the other end, a similar situation exists; there is a modem to receive the transmission and a terminal to sink the data. In general terms, the terminal is the DTE and the modem is the DCE. The following signals are used to send data:

DSR—Data Set Ready: The signal that the modem sends to the terminal that says, "I am powered up and ready to listen to your commands."

RTS—Request to Send: The signal that is sent from the terminal to the modem to tell it to get ready to start data transmission.

CTS—Clear to Send: The signal that the modem sends to the terminal that says, "My data port is now clear, I have received your RTS signal and am now ready to send data."

DTR—Data Terminal Ready: The signal that the terminal sends to the modem to tell it to connect to the telephone line.

The following signals are used to receive data:

RI—Ring Indicator: The signal that the modem sends to the terminal that tells the terminal that the modem has detected that the telephone line it is connected to is ringing. Actually, this signal just toggles in the presence of a ring; it is in high state for a ring and in low state for no ring. Therefore, if we see activity on this line, we know the telephone is ringing and someone is trying to call the modem.

CD—Carrier Detect: The signal that the modem sends to the terminal that tells the terminal that the modem has detected a valid carrier signal on the telephone line and expects data transmission to begin.

These six control signals are used by modems and PCs everywhere to handle the "handshaking" required in managing connections to the telephone system.

Table 1.6
EIA-232-D Control Circuits

Pin Number	Function	Signal Name	Circuit	Control Signal Source
4	Request to Send	RTS	CA	DTE
5	Clear to Send	CTS	CB	DCE
6	Data Set Ready	DSR	CC	DCE
20	Data Terminal Ready	DTR	CD	DTE
8	Received Line Signal Detector	CD	CF	DCE
22	Ring Indicator	RI	CE	DCE

Timing Circuits

So far, 12 of the 14 line cables often encountered have been defined; there are only two remaining lines and they are both designated for timing circuits. These are used to provide timing information across the circuit. The first, Transmitter Signal Element Timing, pin 15, is used to provide timing information to the transmitting element, the DCE, from the DTE. The second, Transmit Signal Element Timing, pin 24, is used to provide timing information to the signal source, the DTE, from the DCE. Both circuits use a transition from high to low, centered in the middle of the data bit. Only synchronous communications utilize the timing or clocking lines. Most data communications devices designed for RS-232 connectors are asynchronous and hence do not use these pins. See Table 1.7.

A complete circuit listing for all 25 pins is available from any manufacturer of the cables or the EIA. Most 232 cables manufactured have a maximum of 14 lines; for many it is less. Remember that the EIA-232-D is an interface standard. It defines the pin assignments and physical and mechanical specifications and suggests length and data rate maximums for guaranteed performance. Cables made to this standard provide communication channels for many types of signals.

There is no relationship between the interface standard and what kinds of data it can carry. It is just an agreement among manufacturers for a standard jack and plug configuration. This is no different from the standard telephone jack and plug or the standard power cord jack and plug. They are standardized by different industries for different purposes, but they are just interface standards, not restrictions on what information can be sent on them.

Finally, some of you may be wondering why this discussion has referred to DCE as data communications equipment, whereas the EIA standards refer to DCE as data circuit-terminating equipment. This is because today there are many pieces of communications equipment that do not act as both a DCE and a DTE. Traditionally, they were in the same box; today this is not always true, but generally, a DTE always connects to a DCE and vice versa.

■ EIA-449

The title of EIA-449 is General Purpose 37-Position and 9-Position Interface for Data Terminal Equipment and Data Circuit-Terminating Equipment Employing Serial Binary Data Interchange. It is otherwise known as 449. This standard extends 232 to faster speeds and longer distances, providing a transition path from 232. It provides for 10 new

Table 1.7
EIA-232-D Timing Circuits

Pin Number	Function	Signal Name	Circuit	Timing Signal Source
15	Transmission Signal Element Timing (DCE)	?	DB	DCE
24	Transmit Signal Element Timing (DTE)	?	DA	DTE

interchange circuits, mostly to provide for new applications and diagnostics, especially remote diagnostics. Standard 449 is designed to operate at speeds of 2 Mbps at distances of up to 200 ft. Again, these can be traded off for longer distances at lower speeds and vice versa. The four types of circuits remain the same.

The 37 pin option is used primarily by expensive, specialized equipment and is not commonly seen because the connectors themselves are expensive. The 37 pin option contains all the circuits that are present in 232, although on different pins, and several new circuits are added, primarily control circuits. The 37 pin connector is arranged in two rows with 19 pins on the top row and 18 on the bottom row. Just as in the 25 pin 232 connector, the pin positions are numbered from left to right on the top and then across bottom row. In addition, just as in the 25 pin connector, the pins are staggered to prevent incorrect connection.

Interestingly, the 37 pin standard has two options in 449, balanced operation and unbalanced. The highest speeds are obtainable only when using the 26 out of the 37 pins that are assigned as the A option. When some of these signals are reassigned to other pins in the B option, lower top speeds are possible. The B option uses only 10 of the 37 pins and is seldom implemented. Higher-speed transmissions are possible in the A option because each interface circuit is balanced. Balanced means that each signal has its own dedicated ground pin. The B option uses a single, shared ground for all signals, just like the 232 interface standard. Both of these are referred to as unbalanced interfaces. Therefore, the 449 can be pinned out as either a balanced or an unbalanced interface.

The 9 pin 449 interface is widely implemented; it is cheaper to buy 9 pin connectors than 25 or 37 pin connectors. Also, and sometimes more important, space is at a premium, and the space savings of a 9 pin connector are critical. Because it has a much wider acceptance, the 9 pin version circuits are identified in Table 1.8 just as was done for the 14 pin version of the 232 interface. These two interfaces will be most common ones in your work. Note that the 9 pin option is designated for secondary traffic only. Do not let this concern you; it is commonly used for primary data traffic, but the standard stresses the 37 pin option as the primary one.

■ EIA-530

High Speed 25-Position Interface for Data Terminal Equipment and Data Circuit-Terminating Equipment is the title of EIA-530 standard. EIA-530 gives the 25 pin connector the balanced capability present in the 37 pin connector version of 449. Additionally, because the 37 pin connector is expensive and big, 530 was developed to replace the 37 pin version of 449. The four circuit types are still here but most of the data, timing, and control circuits are now balanced, having their own dedicated ground wire.

Due to the balanced nature of the circuits in 530, the way the individual wires are bundled in the cable is important. Each circuit and its respective ground are an individually twisted pair. This significantly increases the noise immunity of the circuits and allows differential sensing at the receive end, which allows faster data rates and longer runs. Unlike the 232 standard and the 37 pin version of the 449 standard, 530 interfaces are usually completely pinned and wired. For that reason, the entire pinout is presented Table 1.9.

Table 1.8
Nine-pin EIA-449 Circuit Assignments

Pin Number	449 Function	232 Function	Circuit (449)	Circuit (232)	Direction
1	Shield	Protective Ground	Shield	AA	N/A
2	Secondary Receiver Ready		SRR	SCF	From DCE
3	Secondary Send Data	Secondary Transmitted Data	SSD	SBA	To DCE
4	Secondary Receive Data	Secondary Received Data	SRD	SBB	From DCE
5	Signal Ground	Signal Ground or Common Return	SG	AB	To DCE
6	Receive Common	N/A	RC	N/A	From DCE
7	Secondary Request to Send	Secondary Request to Send	SRS	SCA	To DCE
8	Secondary Clear to Send	Secondary Clear to Send	SCS	SCB	From DCE
9	Send Common	N/A	SC	N/A	To DCE

Except as noted in the table, all circuits are balanced in nature and have individual dedicated grounds. The circuit mnemonics, AA, BA, CA, DA, etc, have the following meanings. Those that start with an A are common grounds. A 'B' indicates a data circuit; a 'C', a control circuit; and a 'D', a timing circuit. Some control circuits also start with other letters, but the rule for data and timing is followed closely.

■ V.35

Standard V.35 is called Data Transmission at 48 kbps Using 60–108 kHz Group-Band Circuits. This standard was originally developed by AT&T for use with high-speed digital data service (DDS) offerings. It is, however, capable of being used at higher data rates than inferred from the title. Its intended use to link high-speed digital signals between DTE and DCE devices makes it applicable for a variety of high-speed links.

This interface is used widely in a variety of networking equipment, such as routers. It features both balanced and unbalanced circuits. Typical usage for this interface involves speeds of up to 128 kbps for distance runs of 1000 m. V.35 connectors are typically wired with 16 pins connected. Adapter modules are available to translate this interface to EIA-232 and EIA-530 interface connectors. Table 1.10 lists the pins normally wired and their names and functions.

V.35, just like the other interface standards we have reviewed, divides up the signals into the same four classes. The three timing circuits are U, V, W, X, Y, and AA. Similarly, there are data, control, and ground circuits as well. The identification of these is left as an exercise.

Table 1.9
EIA-530 Circuit Pin Assignments

Pin Number	Function	Circuit	Type	Direction
1	Signal Ground	Shield	N/A	N/A
2	Transmitted Data	BA	Data	To DCE
3	Received Data	BB	Data	From DCE
4	Request to Send	CA	Control	To DCE
5	Clear to Send	CB	Control	From DCE
6	DCE Ready	CC	Control	From DCE
7	Signal Ground	AB	N/A	N/A
8	Received Line Signal Detector	CF	Control	From DCE
9	Receiver Signal Timing Ground (DCE)	DD	Timing	From DCE
10	Received Line Signal Detector Ground	CF	Control	From DCE
11	Transmit Signal Timing Ground (DTE)	DA	Timing	To DCE
12	Transmit Signal Timing Ground (DCE)	DB	Timing	From DCE
13	Clear to Send Ground	CB	Control	From DCE
14	Transmitted Data Ground	BA	Data	To DCE
15	Transmit Signal Timing (DCE)	DB	Timing	From DCE
16	Received Data Ground	BB	Data	From DCE
17	Receiver Signal Timing (DCE)	DD	Timing	From DCE
18*	Local Loopback	LL	Control	To DCE
19	Request to Send Ground	CA	Control	To DCE
20	DTE Ready	CD	Control	To DCE
21*	Remote Loopback	RL	Control	To DCE
22	DCE Ready Ground	CC	Control	From DCE
23	DTE Ready Ground	CD	Control	To DCE
24	Transmit Signal Timing (DTE)	DA	Timing	To DCE
25*	Test Mode	TM	Control	From DCE

*These pins are the only circuits that operate in unbalanced mode in this interface standard and they are all control circuits.

The connector itself is bulky and is easily recognized once encountered. It has 34 pins, as shown in Figure 1.10. Note that the pin number is designated by a letter of the alphabet instead of a number. V.35 connectors are often used when the data are in a synchronous form. A clue to this is that there are several clocking pins assigned. Asynchronous communication has no need for these pins.

■ TROUBLESHOOTING INTERFACE CABLES

Tables 1.4 through 1.10 provide a decided advantage when troubleshooting communication systems. Knowing where a signal originates, source or destination, often allows you to identify problems quickly and easily. This section will review practices that will be useful in locating the source of the problem.

It is easy to identify at a glance which device is acting as the DTE and which is acting as a DCE if you recall that all interface cables use the male connector to attach to the DTE device and the female connector to attach to the DCE device. In any communica-

Table 1.10
V.35 Pin Out

Pin	Function	Circuit	Direction
A	Protective Ground	FG	N/A
B	Signal Ground	SG	N/A
C*	Request to Send	RTS	To DCE
D*	Clear to Send	CTS	From DCE
E*	Data Set Ready	DSR	From DCE
F*	Received Line Signal Detector	RLSD	From DCE
H*	Data Terminal Ready	DTR	To DCE
J*	Ring Indicator	RI	To DCE
P	Transmitted Data (A)	TD	To DCE
R	Received Data (A)	RD	From DCE
S	Transmitted Data (B)	TD	To DCE
T	Received Data (B)	RD	From DCE
U	Serial Clock Transmit Ext. (A)	SCTE	To DCE
V	Serial Clock Receive (A)	SCR	From DCE
W	Serial Clock Transmit Ext. (B)	SCTE	To DCE
X	Serial Clock Receive (B)	SCR	From DCE
Y	Serial Clock Transmit (A)	SCT	From DCE
AA	Serial Clock Transmit (B)	SCT	From DCE

* These circuits are unbalanced.

tions system, there is always a source and destination for each signal pin on an interface connector. This can be determined by using the tables provided if you know which device is the DTE and which is the DCE. Remember, except in very rare instances, there is always one of each attached to the interface cable.

If you have a problem, identify the two ends of the communication system and make sure that, indeed, something is broken and the system is not functioning properly. You then have three places to check:

1. Is the source machine is malfunctioning?
2. Is the destination machine malfunctioning?
3. Is the interface cable broken?

The first and second situations require replacement of the device. The third one requires a replacement of the interface cable. To identify the cause of the problem, disconnect one

Figure 1.10
V.35 Connector.

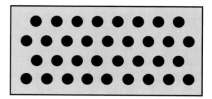

end of the cable and use a signal probe or similar device to examine important pins to get a quick idea if the proper signals are arriving at their destination. Typically, it is easier to disconnect the DCE end, the female connector on the cable or the male connector on the device.

Assuming the signals are arriving properly, check the signals that are to be sent to the DCE from the DTE device. Specifically, check pin 2 on an EIA-232 cable. If you do not see any activity on this pin, either the DTE device or the cable is bad. If you see activity on this pin, it is very likely that the DCE device is malfunctioning. Typically, you can swap it out with a spare unit off the shelf.

In the case where you do see activity on pin 3, you need to identify where the failure is. The most efficient procedure here is to swap out the cable because the DTE rarely fails; it is very likely that the interface cable is the problem. If, after swapping out the DCE device and the interface cable, the communications system is still not functioning, it is likely that the DTE device has failed.

Similar procedures work for any of the interface standards discussed above; in general, find the pin the transmitted data is carried on and check it at the DCE device end.

PROBLEMS

1. Find the number of decibels represented by each of the following numbers:

   (a) 10   (c) 10,000
   (b) 1000   (d) 1,000,000

2. Find the gain or attenuation exhibited by a communications system that has the following input and output powers (in, out):

   (a) 10 mW, 10 W   (d) 5 V at 50 Ω, 10 V at 50 Ω
   (b) 10 μW, 10 W   (e) 10 V at 100 Ω, 5 V at 50 Ω
   (c) 1 W, 1 mW   (f) 10 V at 1 mA, 1 W

   is the measured output with an appropriate input signal level applied.

   (a) 10 mW, 10 W   (c) 5 V at 50 Ω, 10 V at 50 Ω
   (b) 10 μW, 10 W   (d) 10 V at 1 mA, 1 W

3. A communications system has a 30 dB gain. Find the output power for each of the following input powers:

   (a) 1 W   (d) 5 V at 50 Ω
   (b) 1 mW   (e) 50 V at 600 Ω
   (c) 1 μW   (f) 10 V at 1 mA

6. For a 1 W input power, find the power ratios expressed in decibels for the following output powers:

   (a) 2 W   (c) 10 W
   (b) 5 W   (d) 100 W

4. Find the S/N ratios for the following pair of signal and noise levels (S, N):

   (a) 1 W, 1 mW   (c) 1 mW, 10 W
   (b) 100 W, 1 mW   (d) 1 V at 50 Ω, 25 V at 50 Ω

7. Translate the following values into 50 Ω dBm:

   (a) 100 dBrn   (d) 3.25 V (pp)
   (b) 20 dBrn   (e) 2 dB
   (c) 0.4 V$_{rms}$ (f) -10 dB

5. Find the S/N ratios for the following pairs of output powers. The output powers are first measured with zero input signals applied. The second output power

8. Find the output power in dBm for each input power; assume the gain of the circuit is 3 dB.

   (a) 10 dBm   (b) -10 dBm

9. Which device always has the male connector, DTE or DCE?

10. Which device always has the interface cable shipped with it, DTE or DCE?

11. How many data circuits exist in each of the following interface standards?
    (a) 14 pin 232   (c) 530
    (b) 9 pin 449   (d) V.35

12. Which data circuits are used for the higher-speed data sources, primary or secondary?

13. Transmitted data from the DTE device are always on what pin of the RS-232 interface?

14. Received data from the DCE device are always on what pin of the RS-232 interface?

15. Express the following frequencies in units radians per second:
    (a) 100 Hz   (c) 1 kHz
    (b) 500 Hz   (d) 1 MHz

16. Express the following frequencies in units hertz:
    (a) 100 rad/sec   (c) 1 kilo rad/sec
    (b) 500 rad/sec   (d) 1 mega rad/sec

Electromagnetic Signals

As stated in Chapter 1, our discussion of communications will be limited to those communications systems that make use of the electromagnetic spectrum. This discussion will include a chapter on optical media because one can view optical wavelengths as an extension of the electromagnetic spectrum, which will be made clear below. Except for brief mention, such fascinating areas as communication by semaphore, smoke signals, and sign language will be ignored. Thus, there is a clear need to understand what is meant by the term *electromagnetic spectrum.*

When a modulator is constructed from electronic components, its output is an electric signal that is characterized by its voltage and frequency. Any signal that has these properties is classified under the general label electromagnetic signal. The term *electromagnetic spectrum* refers to the entire group of electromagnetic signals. Each electromagnetic signal is propagated through some communications channel to its destination. Because electromagnetic signals are used to send the signal through the communications channel, we need to have a basic understanding of what they are and how they are related to one another and the environment.

In the following sections the relationships between wavelength and frequency and constructive and destructive interference and how the material affects the velocity of propagation of electromagnetic waves will be explored. This last effect can be used to troubleshoot communication systems with a device called a time domain reflectometer (TDR). In this chapter the meaning of the term *bandwidth* as applied to communications systems will be clarified. Finally, frequency standardization, the systems that operate in each frequency band, and the propagation mode of electromagnetic waves in each of those bands will be discussed.

■ ELECTROMAGNETIC SPECTRUM

To begin, the word *electromagnetic* is a compound word: electro and magnetic. The first part of this word is short for electrical, and the second clearly has something to do with magnets or magnetism. Rest assured, we will not be extending our study to those communications systems that work by reversing the poles on magnets. We will, however, need to understand how the two terms interrelate.

One of the most basic effects of any electrical current is that a magnetic field is created by the simple act of current flow. Therefore, a study of the field of communications using electronics must include the magnetic effects of the changing electric fields produced. Electronic components are used to construct communications systems. Some of the components that are used in constructing these systems are inherently magnetic. For example, inductors and transformers both make use of coils, which focus and concentrate magnetic fields. That is the story behind the word *electromagnetic*.

The word *spectrum* literally means a range of values or a set of related quantities; both meanings apply here. The electromagnetic spectrum is usually represented as a chart similar to the one shown in Figure 2.1. This chart shows the first meaning clearly; there is a range of values of frequencies extending from 30 Hz to 300 GHz. The electromagnetic spectrum extends both below and above the chart in Figure 2.1, but the range shown spans the range of frequencies that virtually all communications systems use today. Next to the frequency spans is a two- or three-letter abbreviation for the band; these are defined later in the chapter.

It is also useful to have a chart that will show where in these bands certain common communications systems that will be studied here lie. Figure 2.2, gives this information. You will recognize several of the systems. The frequency ranges are approximate, designed to give a general idea where they lie with respect to each other. Each of the frequency ranges listed below will be discussed:

Figure 2.1
Electromagnetic spectrum.

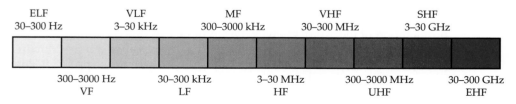

Figure 2.2
Communications system operating frequencies.

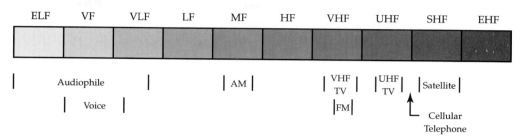

Audiophile band	30–20,000 Hz
Voice band	300–3400 Hz
Broadcast AM radio	540–1710 kHz
LF cordless telephone	43–50 MHz
Broadcast VHF TV	54–216 MHz, channels 2–13
Broadcast FM radio	88–108 MHz
Broadcast UHF TV	470–800 MHz, channels 14–69
Analog cellular telephone	824–894 MHz, Old UHF channels 73–83
ISM bands	902–928 MHz, 2.4–2.48 GHz, and 5.7–5.85 GHz
Digital telephone (DCS)	1710–1880 MHz
Satellite links	4–8 GHz, C-band with 1-m-diameter dishes
	12–18 GHz, Ku-band with ½-m-diameter dishes

■ FREQUENCY AND WAVELENGTH

The second meaning of electromagnetic spectrum, a range of related values, also applies. It is easy to see that a higher frequency must be related in some way to a lower frequency. For example, 20 Hz is exactly twice 10 Hz. But exactly how is this relationship worked out, and is there a relationship to anything else that depends on the frequency or will change in some way as it is changed? The answer is yes; frequencies are related to each other and inversely related to their wavelengths. Equation 2-1 defines this relationship:

$$c = \lambda f \tag{2-1}$$

where c = speed of light = 3×10^8 m/sec
λ = wavelength
f = frequency

Before exploring this equation in more detail, let us be sure we recognize the relationships between frequency, wavelength, and period or cycle time. Figure 2.3 details these relationships. There are different ways to refer to the wavelength, as one period or one cycle of the signal. They are equivalent and inversely related to the frequency. In your

Figure 2.3
Frequency, wavelength, period, and cycle time.

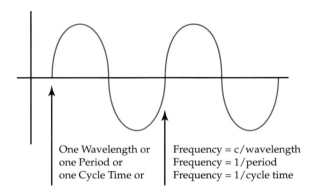

One Wavelength or
one Period or
one Cycle Time or

Frequency = c/wavelength
Frequency = 1/period
Frequency = 1/cycle time

study of technical matters, you will discover that different ways of speaking about something arise in different fields of study, depending on the orientation or goals of the field. In this text, both period and cycle time will be used, depending on the point to be made.

Using equation 2-1, if the wavelength or frequency of any electromagnetic signal is known, the other can be found. Some common frequencies and their wavelengths are shown in Table 2.1. Just for review, if you study Table 2.1, you may be surprised at the length of some of the waves that are encountered every day. Did you imagine that when you are talking to a friend on the telephone that the average length of the electromagnetic wave that generates the sound wave you hear is 300,000 m long? That is 3000 football fields placed end to end. For those rusty in converting football fields to miles, that is about 185 miles long.

In your telephone conversation you hear many wavelengths per second, say 1000; this should give you some idea of how fast they are moving. Remember, in each second of conversation, you hear 1000 waves each averaging 3000 football fields long, or put an-

Table 2.1
Common Wavelengths

Band	Approximate Center	Wavelength (m)
Voice	~1 kHz	300,000
Audiophile	~10 kHz	30,000
Broadcast AM	~1000 kHz	300
Broadcast FM	~100 MHz	3
Satellite	~10 GHz	0.03

other way, waves placed end to end stretch over 3,000,000 football fields. Put still another way, in each second of a telephone conversation, the total length of electromagnetic waves would go around the earth about seven and a half times. This is not to say that the sound waves entering your ear are that long, only that the electromagnetic energy that produces those sound waves is of that length.

■ **EXAMPLE 2.1**

What is the shortest carrier wavelength used in the broadcast AM radio? The shortest wavelength would be associated with the highest frequency, which is given as 1710 kHz:

$$\lambda = \frac{c}{f} = \frac{3 \times 10^8}{1710 \times 10^3} = 175 \text{ m}$$

On the other hand, the average length of the carrier wave for broadcast FM is only about 3 m long, or just under 10 ft. Because this is so short, moving a few feet can make a difference in what part, or phase, of the wave you encounter. This short wavelength explains why moving the car a few feet when listening to FM radio makes a difference in the reception heard from the radio when listening to FM. It also explains why there is no similar effect when listening to AM.

This effect is caused by a reflected radio wave being received simultaneously with a wave received directly from the transmitter. The reflected wave can add to or cancel the amplitude of the original wave. This process is called interference and forms patterns defined by the buildings around you. Because the wavelength, or period, of the carrier wave is so short, the interference patterns created by the environment you are in are also short. Therefore, a movement of a few feet takes you out of an interference pattern where destructive interference is occurring and the signal strength is greatly reduced to a location where the interference is less destructive.

Interference has two meanings, one specific to communications. This meaning refers to extraneous power interfering with the signal transmission or reception. This is an important subject in communications systems but is not the meaning that we will explore now.

The second meaning relates to waves. This interference is a variation in the wave amplitude due to the superposition of two or more waves. This variation in amplitude results in some degree of interference. If the amplitudes add in such a way that the result is larger than either original wave, it is called constructive interference. If the result is smaller than either original wave, it is called destructive interference. The first is a specific case of variation that is particularly nice, whereas the other, destructive interference, is the cause of poor FM reception and is much more commonly encountered. Three cases of interference are shown in Figure 2.4, note the variation in amplitudes and shapes.

As can be seen in Figure 2.4, something close to the second case (Figure 2.4b) is what is happening when you lose the radio station in your car. Suppose that two signals, taking different paths to your car antenna, arrive 180° out of phase; this means 100% destructive interference. In this situation, very little power is coupled to your antenna, and you lose the signal.

Because of the short wavelengths of broadcast FM radio, moving the car a few feet forward can change the phase relationship between the two signals and move you into case 3 (Figure 2.4c). Here, although the energy looks distorted, enough is being coupled to the antenna, often enough, so that you hear the station clearly. Before you try to find the location shown in case 1 (Figure 2.4a), you should realize that for all practical purposes it does not exist. Even if you could locate such a place, all that would happen is that the station would come in clear, and you have that already in any situation except case 2. So it is a fruitless quest; there will be no noticeable difference in how you hear the radio station.

Figure 2.4
Constructive and destructive interference.

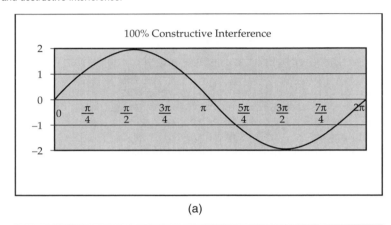

(a)

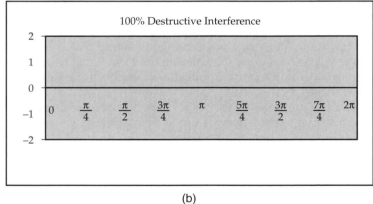

(b)

Figure 2.4
(*Continued*)

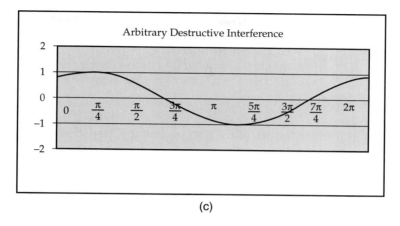

(c)

You should also realize that the wavelength of a signal makes a difference in how the antenna designed to receive it is constructed. It should make sense to you that an antenna designed to receive wavelengths thousands of meters long would be different from an antenna designed to receive wavelengths just a few meters long. In your experience, you have probably seen many different kinds of antennas; the frequency that they are designed to receive determines the shape of the antenna. For example, all television antennas are alike, all cellular telephone antennas are alike, and so on. Chapter 5 discusses this topic further.

■ DIELECTRIC CONSTANT, VELOCITY FACTOR, AND VELOCITY OF PROPAGATION

To explore these topics it is necessary to return to an examination of equation 2-1, shown again here:

$$c = \lambda f \tag{2-1}$$

where c = speed of light = 3×10^8 m/sec
λ = wavelength
f = frequency

The constant c, or the speed of light, relates the frequency and wavelength. This is because *all* electromagnetic waves move at the speed of light when moving through what physicists call free space. This observation was one of Albert Einstein's greatest insights. *Free space* is just a term that defines space free of any perturbations that would affect the electric or magnetic field strength. Just like any material, free space has an impedance. The characteristic impedance of free space is defined by the square root of the ratio of the magnetic permeability to the electric permittivity, as shown in equation 2-2:

$$Z_{fs} = \sqrt{\frac{\mu_0}{\varepsilon_0}} = \sqrt{\frac{1.26 \times 10^{-6}\,\text{H/m}}{8.85 \times 10^{-12}\,\text{F/m}}} = 377\,\Omega \tag{2-2}$$

where

Z_{fs} = characteristic impedance of free space
μ_0 = magnetic permeability of free space (Henrys/meter)
ε_0 = electrical permittivity of free space (Farads/meter)

For review, electrical permittivity is more commonly referred to as the dielectric constant. When used in that way, *dielectric constant* is defined by taking the ratio of a material's permittivity to the permittivity of free space. The dielectric constant is defined as 1.0 for free space.

$$\varepsilon_r = \frac{\varepsilon_m}{\varepsilon_0} \tag{2-3}$$

where

ε_r = dielectric constant of a material
ε_m = electrical permittivity of a material
ε_0 = electrical permittivity of free space

Because the dielectric constant is a more easily available and familiar number, the values of it for a few common materials are presented in Table 2.2.

Because frequency and wavelength are related through equation 2-1, this relationship must be modified for the material that you are using. For free space, the relationship is as given in equation 2-1. However, the dielectric constant changes the velocity of propagation (reduces the observed speed of light, or any electromagnetic wave, in materials), and so it must be accounted for when determining the observed velocity of electromagnetic waves in a material. This relationship is presented in equation 2-4:

$$c = \lambda f \sqrt{\varepsilon_r} \tag{2-4}$$

Again, by definition, electromagnetic (EM) waves travel at the speed of light in free space. In all other materials the observed speed is somewhat reduced. Equation 2-4 allows one to compute this reduction based on the dielectric constant of the material.

Table 2.2
Dielectric Constant

Material	Dielectric Constant
Free space (vacuum)	1.0
Air	1.0006
Metallic conductors	1.2–1.6
Rubber	3.0
Glass	7.5

Table 2.3
Velocity Factor

Material	Velocity Factor
Free Space (vacuum)	1.0
Air	0.975–0.95
Metallic Conductors	0.90–0.80
Rubber	0.65–0.55
Glass	0.365

Equation 2-5 relates the velocity of propagation of an electromagnetic wave in any material to dielectric constant and a new term called the velocity factor. The velocity factor is a dimensionless number:

$$v_f = \frac{1}{\sqrt{\varepsilon_r}} = \frac{v_p}{c} \tag{2-5}$$

where v_f = velocity factor
v_p = velocity of propagation (m/sec)

As can be seen from an examination of the Tables 2.2 and 2.3, the dielectric constant and the velocity factor are related inversely. That is as one goes up, the other must go down. The exact relationship is explored in the next paragraphs. It is important that you recognize this physical principle.

Example 2.2 and 2.3 illustrate the application of these equations.

■ EXAMPLE 2.2

Find the velocity factor and velocity of propagation for rubber. Use Table 2.2 to find the dielectric constant.

$$v_f = \frac{1}{\sqrt{\varepsilon_r}} = \frac{1}{\sqrt{3}} = 0.58$$

Notice that the result is a number that is in the range shown in Table 2.2. Because materials are made in a variety of different ways, the exact velocity depends on the exact chemical content. This is because there are many different kinds of things that are referred to as rubber, from the natural plant to sophisticated compounds. Given this fact, it should not be surprising that ranges are the order of the day when talking about this subject.

To find the actual velocity of electromagnetic waves in the material rubber, find the velocity of propagation in that material:

$$v_f = \frac{v_p}{c} \rightarrow v_p = cv_f = (3 \times 10^8)(0.58) = 1.74 \times 10^8 \text{ m/sec}$$

Here, the speed is reduced by exactly the value of the velocity factor. From this observation, it is clear that the velocity factor can be defined as a percentage of the speed of light in free space. This percentage yields the actual velocity of any electromagnetic wave in the particular material for which it is calculated.

■ EXAMPLE 2.3

For an electromagnetic wave moving in a metallic conductor, with a dielectric constant of 1.15, what is the velocity factor and how much longer would it take to travel 1,000,000 m than the same wave traveling in free space?

$$v_f = \frac{1}{\sqrt{1.15}} = 0.9325$$

Applying the familiar relationship distance equals rate times time, we can find an expression for the time as show below.

$$d = rt \rightarrow t = \frac{d}{r}$$

For conductor

$$t = \frac{10^6}{0.9325 * 3.00 \times 10^8} = 3.57 \times 10^{-3} \text{ sec}$$

For free space,

$$t = \frac{10^6}{3.00 \times 10^8} = 3.33 \times 10^{-3} \text{ sec}$$

So, conductor path takes

$$t = 3.57 \times 10^{-3} - 3.33 \times 10^{-3} = 0.24 \times 10^{-3} \text{ sec longer}$$

From examination of the tables and examples above and the discussion so far, you should have concluded that the type of material that the electromagnetic wave moves through can change its characteristic impedance and hence its velocity. Pay special attention to Table 2.3, which lists some common materials and their respective velocity factors, to explore this relationship. It is important to understand how the material that the electromagnetic spectrum you are using to communicate in affects the perceived velocity of the speed of light.

As far as anyone knows, Einstein is correct; the speed of light is the same everywhere we can observe. The results that could be interpreted as light somehow slowing in materials is actually correctly viewed as light taking a longer path through materials due to the gravitational effects of its mass. The velocity remains the same, but the path length differs, so in effect, a longer time elapses for the two paths, where one is slightly "longer" than the other.

This length cannot be measured macroscopically; if you use a ruler, the length is the same in both cases. However, during the travel in the metallic conductor used as an example, the light must bend somewhat to get around obstacles and so takes a longer path from one end to the other. It is kind of like weaving through traffic instead of staying in your lane. Unless one speeds up, it takes longer to arrive at your destination. Of course, virtually everyone who does this weaving does speed up, so your experience may not match this example.

◼ FREQUENCY STANDARDIZATION

Because communications systems operate in many different wavelengths, it should come as no surprise that there is government standardization of names and frequency bands. Each frequency band or wavelength range has certain types of transmissions licensed to operate there. Typically, there is also a maximum power limit set for each type of transmission as well, but that is outside the scope of this discussion. Several governmental agencies exist to meet and discuss what services are allowed in what frequency bands.

In the United States, the body that controls this activity is the Federal Communications Commission (FCC). Most other countries have similar bodies with similar names. These bodies have authority to set standards only within their own boundaries. However, as is easily imagined, when dealing with wavelengths longer than some countries are big, coordination is important. Economic considerations, regional-based content, and interference issues resulting from electromagnetic energy leaking into other countries' boundaries are big issues.

Worldwide standardization makes sense if the goal is to have a portable telephone or radio that works anywhere in the world. Similarly, if country A is concerned that country B's television transmissions are interfering with its own, this also is of great interest to both governing bodies and individual consumers. Consequently, these governmental bodies get together every 10 years to work this kind of problem out. Actually individual working groups meet much more often, and working papers and draft standards are issued quite regularly, but the official documents are issued at these meetings. Companies that manufacture communication gear are very interested in the outcomes of these meetings. Therefore, they contribute a lot of technical and legal talent to try to make the outcomes favorable to the particular line of products or services they offer. This can be an interesting area to work in if you are very patient and like to travel and can both read and write long, laborious, very detailed technical and legal documents.

For those interested in exploring this area, one good place to start is the Institute of Electrical and Electronic Engineers (IEEE). This organization has national committees that write standards for submission to other national and international committees. Joining a working group or committee that is writing a communication standard is generally dependent on having corporate sponsorship to pay for the time, energy, and travel necessary to contribute to and have an effect on the effort.

Any IEEE member can attend and anyone can vote once they have satisfied certain attendance requirements. However, to actually influence the technical content of the standard, you must contribute, and this takes significant effort and time, hence, the typical requirement for corporate or institutional sponsorship to succeed.

Other ways to participate also exist, depending on the specific area where you or your organization wants to have an impact. For example, the EIA is run in very much the same way. At the next level up, the North American submissions are often coordinated through the American National Standards Institute (ANSI). Just understanding what committee has an impact on what standards often takes some time. Many committees share responsibility with other committees under other standards organizations. This means coordination and communication are critical to success in this field.

■ BANDWIDTH

One of the most fundamental concepts of the electromagnetic spectrum that is important to communications is bandwidth. In Chapter 1, it was suggested that you think of bandwidth as width. Bandwidth is defined as the range of frequencies that are used to send the information from the source to the destination. Sometimes it is also defined as that portion or band of the electromagnetic spectrum occupied or required by a signal. The bandwidth of a signal is found by subtracting the lower frequency value from the upper frequency value:

$$\text{bandwidth} = f_{\text{upper}} - f_{\text{lower}} \qquad \text{(2-6)}$$

As can be seen, the "width" of frequencies is captured by the bandwidth calculation. It should be clear that the wider the bandwidth, the more frequency space that is used to send the information and hence the more information that can be sent.

■ EXAMPLE 2.4

What is the bandwidth of the voice band?

$$\text{bandwidth} = 3400\,\text{Hz} - 300\,\text{Hz} = 3100\,\text{Hz}$$

■ BANDWIDTH AND INFORMATION CAPACITY

Sometimes bandwidth can be confused with the information capacity. Information capacity is defined as the amount of information that can be sent from a source to a destination. As a general principle, the more bandwidth used by a communications system, the more information content that can be sent and the larger the information capacity. Just how much more information can be sent for a given amount of increased bandwidth depends on the modulation technique.

In normal usage, the information capacity of a communications system or device is referred to as the speed of that system or device. This distinction, however, is often lost in the marketing of products in the communications area. To see an example of this, think for a moment about the telephone modem that would be used with a personal computer. When the speed of a modem is discussed, what one really means is the amount of information capacity it has. Because all electromagnetic waves travel at the same speed regardless of their wavelength or frequency, how is the speed of the modem expressed in bits per second?

The answer is that what is being expressed is the information capacity of the modem. The larger the information capacity, the larger the speed specification in bits per second. It is also true that all of the modems designed to work with the telephone system use the same bandwidth. The bandwidth of the telephone system, which is 300 to 3400 Hz, is fixed. As you are aware, modems of many different speeds are available; these are examples of many different information capacities operating in the same bandwidth.

■ BANDWIDTH AND CARRIER FREQUENCY

Accepting as a general principle that the wider the bandwidth, the more information that can be sent leads one to ask why not just keep increasing the bandwidth again and again. Higher information capacity modems (faster modems) seem easy when looked at from this perspective. Because more information is being sent, paying more money for the modems would be justified if higher information capacity was needed. This is the case, in every area, and is limited primarily by one of two factors: Either the frequency bandwidth is fixed, or there is limited frequency bandwidth that is economically profitable to utilize.

A fixed-frequency bandwidth means that the bandwidth cannot be expanded by any means. Usually this results from the limitations of the media that are used for the communications channel; the best example of this is the traditional telephone system. Without an entire retrofit, the traditional telephone system has a limited bandwidth, determined by the components used to construct it. The physical nature of the components limits the bandwidth.

The other possibility is that the communications channel is fixed by law. Television broadcasts and AM and FM radio currently have bandwidths determined by law. Law, unlike physical reality, can be changed. A good example of this is the plight of UHF TV channels 73 to 83. Prior to about 1975, these stations believed that the frequencies they were assigned by the FCC would always be theirs, by law. Around that time, cellular telephone systems were a gleam in the eye of several telecommunications companies, but no appropriate frequency space was available. Those companies lobbied for changes in the law and won; today this frequency band is, by law, theirs.

If the frequency bandwidth is fixed, one must look to modulation techniques or coding techniques to increase the information capacity. Because, as mentioned above, the frequency bandwidth of the telephone system is fixed, both of these techniques have been exploited to achieve the high information capacity modems currently offered for voice-grade telephone lines.

Although there are many reasons why some additional frequency bandwidth might be economically unprofitable to exploit. The primary one is that the higher the carrier frequency selected, the higher the cost of the system because high-frequency components are generally more costly than low-frequency components. The pressure to make the best economic use of the limited usable spectrum tends to keep the channel bandwidth allocations narrow. Thus, it is up to clever engineers to figure out how to pack in more information using less bandwidth.

This approach keeps open areas for future innovation and also helps with international standardization (e.g., the less spectrum that is needed to dedicate to some new service, the less chance that some other system is already using that spectrum). Different countries allocate the electromagnetic spectrum differently within their borders; because an international service must cross these boundaries, careful selection of carrier frequencies and bandwidth used must take place to give the system a chance to succeed.

Although using a higher carrier frequency results in higher system cost, there are some advantages. The first is that as in most industries, new technology frees up new resources. Only since the 1970s could cost-effective systems operating at carrier frequencies above a few hundred megahertz be built. Earlier, the technology simply could not produce the components necessary to construct devices that operated at these frequencies. This illustrates a general rule: The higher the carrier frequency, the fewer systems there are that can exist to compete for available spectrum. This means fewer competitors, easier competition, and fewer previously licensed spectrum "off limits signs."

It is also an advantage that there are more available channels of a given bandwidth at a higher carrier frequency than at a lower in a given percentage bandwidth of the carrier. For example, FM broadcast radio uses a carrier frequency 100 times higher than AM broadcast radio (100 MHz versus 1000 kHz). This allows 100 times more 10 kHz channels in the FM band than are possible in the AM band.

■ EXAMPLE 2.5

Calculate how many 10 kHz channels are possible for a 20% bandwidth around the center frequency of the broadcast AM and FM bands. This calculation will illustrate how the choice of carrier frequency can affect how many channels can be placed in the same percentage bandwidth around the carrier frequency. Take the center of the AM band to be 1000 kHz and the center of the FM band to be 100 MHz.

First, find the bandwidths for the two bands. This gives us something that is called the system bandwidth. This is because it yields a number that defines the total bandwidth of the system. Then find the number of 10 kHz channels in that system bandwidth, and divide the two system bandwidths found by the channel bandwidth, here 10 kHz, to determine the number of channels:

$$\text{AM:} \quad (20\%)(1000 \text{ kHz}) = 200 \text{ kHz}$$

$$\text{FM:} \quad (20\%)(100 \text{ MHz}) = 20 \text{ MHz}$$

The number of 10 kHz channels possible is given by

$$\text{number of channels} = \frac{\text{system bandwidth}}{\text{channel bandwidth}}$$

$$\text{AM:} \quad \frac{200 \times 10^3}{10 \times 10^3} = 20 \text{ channels} \tag{2-7}$$

$$\text{FM:} \quad \frac{20 \times 10^6}{10 \times 10^3} = 2000 \text{ channels}$$

As can be seen, the choice of the carrier frequency can have a dramatic impact on the number of channels possible in the same percentage bandwidth. The higher the carrier frequency, the more channels of a given bandwidth are possible. Sometimes this is expressed as a percentage that relates the percentage of bandwidth of the channel to the carrier frequency. This is shown in equation 2-8:

$$\text{percentage of bandwidth} = \left(\frac{\text{channel bandwidth}}{\text{carrier frequency}} \right) 100\% \tag{2-8}$$

It can be easily seen that these two relationships are saying the same thing from different perspectives. The final major advantage in using a higher carrier frequency is that higher bandwidth services are possible. Again looking at the AM broadcast band as compared to the FM broadcast band, it is clear that it is possible to have a service that uses 2 MHz of bandwidth in the FM band but not in the AM band. In the AM band the modulating signal's bandwidth would exceed the carrier frequency. In the FM band, although the service might not be practical, it is at least physically possible.

To review, in guided or hard channels, it is also often true that the physical constraints of the communications channel sometimes restrict the bandwidth available. For example, the telephone systems bandwidth is 3100 Hz; this bandwidth cannot be changed without a very great investment and a long time. This situation leads engineers to find ways to stretch the information bandwidth (information capacity) beyond the frequency bandwidth. The frequency bandwidth is what we defined earlier, the range of frequencies used; the information bandwidth (information capacity) is the data rate that can be sent in a specific frequency bandwidth. Much of modern communications design is about increasing the information bandwidth (information capacity) without increasing the frequency bandwidth.

Again, bandwidth has two meanings, but usually the context makes the meaning clear. When one talks about a communications channel, frequency bandwidth is usually meant; when one talks about data rate or information transfer, information capacity, or information bandwidth, is what is usually meant.

■ FREQUENCY BANDS

Table 2.4 summarizes the 10 frequency bands or ranges that are defined and will be discussed here. Note that each is designated to be an entire decade of frequencies. They all use numbers divisible by 3, so wavelength calculations end up as integer powers of 10 m because the speed of light is 30,000,000 m/sec. Table 2.4 is also used to introduce the concept of propagation mode that will be discussed below. The band names are uninspired but should be easy to remember because of the simple naming. The primary applications of each band are listed below:

ELF—Extremely Low Frequency, 30–300 Hz: These are the power line frequencies and the lower end of human hearing. Certain home control systems use the power line frequencies of 50 Hz (Europe) and 60 Hz (United States) to communicate with "smart" lamps, toasters, home security systems, and so forth.

VF—Voice Frequency, 300–3000 Hz: This is essentially the same frequency band that is used by the telephone system (300–3400 Hz) and contains 95% of the frequency content of human speech. The so-called audiophile band (30–20,000 Hz) is the extreme limit of human hearing. Human voice transmissions are contained in a much narrower band, primarily the band discussed here.

Table 2.4
Frequency Bands and Propagation Mode

Band	Frequency Range	Wavelength Range (m)	Propagation Mode	Nickname
ELF	30–300 Hz	10,000,000–1,000,000	GW	ELF
VF	300–3000 Hz	1,000,000–100,000	GW	VF
VLF	3–30 kHz	100,000–10,000	GW	
LF	30–300 kHz	10,000–1,000	GW	
MF	300–3000 kHz	1,000–100	GW	
HF	3–30 MHz	100–10	SW	Shortwave
VHF	30–300 MHz	10–1	LOS	VHF
UHF	300–3000 MHz	1–0.1	LOS	UHF
SHF	3–30 GHz	0.1–0.01	LOS	Microwave
EHF	30–300 GHz	0.01–0.001	LOS	Millimeter

VLF—Very Low Frequency, 3–30 kHz: The upper range of human hearing, although most people by the time they are 25 have lost all hearing above 15 kHz. The only technological use for this band of frequencies today is for communicating with submarines covertly over very long ranges.

LF—Low Frequency, 30–300 kHz: Not used widely because it is less effective for long-range communication than the VLF band.

MF—Medium Frequency, 300–3000 kHz: The most common application is broadcast AM radio, which uses the frequency band, 540–1660 kHz.

HF—High Frequency, 3–30 MHz: This band is widely used for long-range communication, making use of the sky wave propagation effect. Military (long-distance aircraft), political (Voice of America, BBC), commercial (CB radio), and amateur radio (ham radio) users all make use of this frequency band, made unique by the composition of our own earthly atmosphere. If we had a different atmosphere, the sky wave propagation mode might move to a different frequency band. If no atmosphere, there would be no sky wave propagation mode. The sky wave propagation effect is entirely controlled by the chemical composition of the atmosphere.

VHF—Very High Frequency, 30–300 MHz: Broadcast FM radio uses this band (88–108 MHz), as do the traditional VHF TV channels (channels 2–13). Traditional two-way FM radios also use this band, and of course, it has applications in the military sector as well.

UHF—Ultra High Frequency, 0.3–3 GHz: Many new services are appearing that make use of this band. Traditional users were the UHF TV channels (14–83). Today many new uses are emerging, including cellular telephones and all kinds of paging systems.

SHF—Super High Frequency, 3–30 GHz: The lower end of this range is used by microwave ovens to heat food, but the primary use of this band is for satellite communications. There are two major systems in use: the C band (4–6 GHz) and the Ku band (14–16 GHz). Terrestrial microwave links, used in a variety of private and public communications systems, also use this band for line-of-sight (LOS) transmission over a range of about 40 miles.

EHF—Extremely High Frequency, 30–300 GHz: This is the next frontier for communications. Active experimentation is ongoing in this band, but component costs are extremely high, so any widespread commercial use is some time away. The nickname for this band, millimeter, comes directly from the wavelength range; it is measured in millimeters. At the time this nickname was first applied, the use of wavelengths of these lengths was considered remarkable.

Above 300 GHz, one enters into the so-called optical spectrum: infrared, visible spectrum, and ultraviolet. Although communications systems use these frequency bands, they are chiefly optical systems that make use of fiber optic cable. These frequencies are not good choices for unguided or soft channel transmissions because of the interference caused by the environment, namely, the sun.

The infrared band is used inside buildings for communications; some optical wireless LAN systems use reflected infrared signals to connect PCs together. Virtually all hand-held remote control units use infrared frequencies to control various appliances in the home. Examples include the remote control(s) for audio-visual systems (television, home theater, CD player, etc.). Additionally, infrared wavelengths mean heat. A heat lamp uses an infrared lamp; these are often used to relax muscle aches or in a bathroom ceiling lamp. The lamps that keep fast-food hamburgers hot until the customer arrives are also infrared lamps. Infrared wavelengths are not the same as the ultraviolet radiation that tans you on a summer day at the beach.

The visible spectrum is used by human beings to communicate naturally. We have special receptors that can see these high frequencies, eyes, and we use them in many different ways to communicate. Visible light wavelengths are used in fiber optic hard channels, and rarely in soft channels, by lasers. Even setting aside the issue of interference from the sun, the use of these frequencies in soft channels is not considered a good choice because of the danger of anyone who looks into the laser.

A safe situation is the so-called laser light shows that are becoming increasingly popular. The lasers used to produce the images are always pointed very carefully and, most importantly, not in the direction of the audience. As a technical person, you may someday be involved in operating these systems; make sure you do not take it as an opportunity to damage your vision. As a member of the audience, you have nothing to fear.

Finally, the ultraviolet spectrum is not generally used to communicate. For us, ultraviolet wavelengths mean radiation. A tanning studio uses ultraviolet lamps; you get a sunburn from the ultraviolet waves from the sun. Fluorescent lamps such as those in the ceiling of the classroom you attend also emit a fair amount of ultraviolet light, as do computer monitor screens. Sometimes special glasses are used by those especially sensitive to light in this frequency range. Ultraviolet light is not visible, but specific lens materials can be manufactured to block that portion of the spectrum above visible light to protect sensitive eyes.

Frequencies above the ultraviolet region are interesting physical phenomena but are not usable today in communications systems. As technology improves, however, it seems likely that the usable upper band will increase and these bands will come into use.

■ PROPAGATION MODES

The propagation characteristics listed in the Table 2.4 show how in soft channels the electromagnetic waves propagate through the atmosphere in different ways. There are three modes of propagation that waves can take: ground wave (GW), sky wave (SW), and line of sight (LOS). These are depicted in Figure 2.5. We will examine each of these modes of propagation and do some simple calculations.

Ground Wave Propagation

In the GW mode of propagation, the electromagnetic waveform essentially follows the contour of the earth. This is the way all transmissions below about 3 MHz use to travel from source to destination. The most common example is broadcast AM radio, which uses the frequency band 540 to 1710 kHz.

This propagation mode can be used to communicate over long distances if both the source and destination are on the earth. Because electromagnetic waves in this frequency band are scattered by the atmosphere, they do not penetrate the upper atmosphere. Therefore, these frequencies are not used for earth-to-space (or vice versa) communications.

This propagation mode uses the diffraction properties of the lower atmosphere to propagate from source to destination. The diffraction can be thought of as scattering the electromagnetic wave. This frequency band also has the dubious distinction of being the one most susceptible to variation due to the time of day or presence of the sun. Because it is most dependent on the characteristics of the atmosphere, it diffracts through it; a change in the atmosphere will affect how the waves travel. The sun has a profound effect on the upper atmosphere, so different behaviors of transmission in the frequency band during the day and evening are observed.

Sky Wave Propagation

The second mode, SW, makes use of the reflecting properties of the earth's atmosphere at altitudes from 100 to 250 miles for frequencies in the band, 3–30 MHz. When an electromagnetic wave reflects, or bends, part of its energy passes through the atmosphere and is lost in space. However, most of it is bent back toward the surface of the planet. The wave essentially "skips" along, jumping over large areas, only to appear again several hundred miles away. The areas that are skipped over have a special name, the skip zone. This propagation mode allows waves transmitted in this frequency range to be heard on the other side of the globe from where they were transmitted and explains why this band is so popular for long-distance communications.

Figure 2.5
GW, SW, and LOS modes.

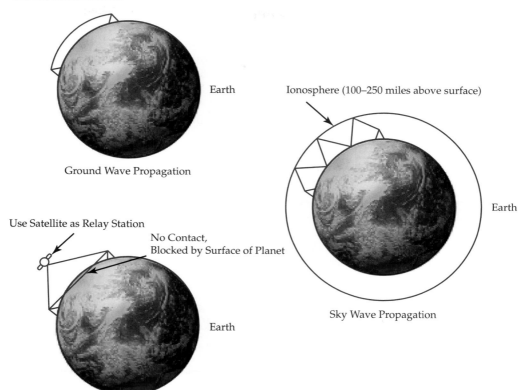

Ground Wave Propagation

Earth

Ionosphere (100–250 miles above surface)

Use Satellite as Relay Station

No Contact,
Blocked by Surface of Planet

Earth

Earth

Sky Wave Propagation

Line-of-Sight Propagation

The third mode, LOS, is used by frequencies above 30 MHz. Here the atmosphere of our planet does not refract, or bend the electromagnetic wave much; typically less than 1% of the power is reflected down toward the surface of the planet. Therefore, these waves travel in a straight line and pass through any portion of the atmosphere easily.

This phenomenon is both an advantage and disadvantage, depending on with whom you are trying to communicate. When communicating with someone in space, this is a good band to use. When communicating with someone on the surface of the planet, because the wave travels in a straight line, the transmit and receive antennas both must be able to see each other. This is not a problem when both antennas are relatively close, but the curvature of the earth prevents any long-distance communication using LOS propagation unless one or both antennas are extremely tall.

Because of this phenomenon, the concept *LOS radio horizon* has been developed, which allows the calculation of how tall an antenna must be. Either just the transmit antenna can be raised or both transmit and receive antennas. For most consumer applications, it is impractical to require the consumer to raise a tower. Thus, the transmit antennas for broadcast FM, broadcast TV, cellular telephones, and others who transmit using these frequencies for their carrier waves need to use tall towers; the receivers must be able to see the transmitters. To see how tall they must be, use equation 2-9:

$$d = \sqrt{2h} \qquad \text{(2-9)}$$

where d = LOS radio horizon (miles)
         h = antenna height (feet)

This equation does not use the same units for both sides. It is a handy rule, but be careful about the units when applying it.

■ EXAMPLE 2.6

You have been asked to calculate how tall an antenna must be raised for a new TV station. The only data you can get is from the marketing department, and they say it must reach customers up to 50 miles away. You get out your calculator and do the following calculation:

$$d = \sqrt{2h} \qquad \text{or} \qquad h = \frac{d^2}{2}$$

$$50 = \sqrt{2h} \rightarrow h = \frac{50^2}{2} = 1250 \text{ ft}$$

■ EXAMPLE 2.7

Another question appears in your in-basket. The problem is that due to local ordinances, the highest tower possible on this site is 1000 ft. What is the impact and are there any other solutions that will let the original viewing area be maintained? You get out your trusty calculator and make the following calculation:

$$d = \sqrt{2(1000)} = 44.7 \text{ miles}$$

Not so good, but hardly surprising; you told them that 1250 ft were required. You ask yourself, What if the viewers all used antennas on the top of the roofs? Assuming a roof height of 3 m and the antenna mounted on a pole adding another 1 m, what difference will this make? You get out your calculator and remembering that 3.2 ft equals 1 m, produce the following:

$$d_1 = \sqrt{2(1000)} = 44.7 \text{ miles}$$

$$d_2 = \sqrt{2(4)(3.2)} = 5.1 \text{ miles}$$

$$d_{\text{total}} = d_1 + d_2 = 49.8 \text{ miles}$$

It is not quite up to specification of 50 miles, but it is close. Maybe some people on the fringe will build their antennas just a little higher or maybe add a preamplifier because they are at the extreme limit of reception anyway. You make it clear in your presentation to your manager what the engineering trade-offs were; your manager can decide how to present it to marketing.

■ EXAMPLE 2.8

Another good question to ask is, How much lower can you make a transmit antenna if you use a receive antenna? Assume the transmit antenna has an initial height of 100 m. Then compute the new height if a receive antenna of height 10 m is added to the communications system.

$$d = \sqrt{2h} = \sqrt{2(100)(3.2)} = 25.3 \text{ miles}$$

$$25.3 \text{ miles} = \sqrt{2h_{tx}} + \sqrt{2h_{rx}} \rightarrow \sqrt{2h_{tx}} = 25.3 - \sqrt{2(10)(3.2)} = 25.3 - 8 = 17.3$$

$$h_{tx} = \frac{(17.3)^2}{2} = 149.6 \text{ ft} = 46.8 \text{ m}$$

As can be seen, the addition of a 10 m receive antenna saved $100 - 46.8 = 53.2$ m in height for the transmit antenna. This savings illustrates that where possible it is always more efficient to construct two smaller towers, one for transmit and one for receive, than it is to construct just one big transmit tower.

■ POWER RADIATION

The following equation is taken directly from the inverse square law of physics for radiation in an isotropic medium (isotropic means the same everywhere you look). This assumption is only strictly true for free space, but it is a good assumption to determine the maximum distance that a transmitter and receiver can be separated and still expect to communicate. This calculation always gives a maximum distance.

$$P_{rx} = \frac{P_{tx}}{4\pi r^2} \tag{2-10}$$

where $\quad P_{rx}$ = power arriving at receiver
$\qquad\quad P_{tx}$ = power transmitted
$\qquad\qquad r$ = distance from transmitter

To better understand equation 2-10, recall that the surface area of a sphere is given by the equation

$$SA_{\text{sphere}} = 4\pi r^2$$

If the power is radiating isotropically, that is in the same way in every direction, it should expand out in a sphere. If that is true, the power should fade away as the volume of the sphere grows because the same power must now "cover" a larger surface area. If this equation still does not seem intuitive to you, imagine it is a day at the beach and your son wants the beach ball inflated. There are two balls that you can choose to inflate, one small and the other larger. Which is easier, or requires less power to inflate? The small ball is easier to inflate because when it is completely inflated, its surface area is smaller. Make the analogy between the power radiating and your breath, where the surface area of the beach ball is the "surface" of the energy radiating out from an antenna. The smaller the radius of the beach ball, the less power is required to inflate it.

■ EXAMPLE 2.9

How far away can the receiver be from a transmitter when the transmitted power is 1000 W and the minimum receive power necessary is 1 mW?

$$P_{rx} = \frac{P_{tx}}{4\pi r^2} = 10^{-3} \text{ W} = \frac{1000 \text{ W}}{4\pi r^2} \rightarrow r = \sqrt{\frac{1000}{4\pi 10^{-3}}} = 282 \text{ m}$$

Remember, this is a maximum distance; for most applications it will be significantly less because of the relatively bad assumption that your locality is as free from obstruction as free space. This may also be a bad assumption if you do not use an isotropically radiating antenna at the transmitter. Some types of antennas direct more of their power in one direction than another. Consequently, the receiver can be farther away in some directions than others. For more detail on this subject, refer Chapter 5.

■ EXAMPLE 2.10

It is often interesting to understand just how far specific transmit powers will carry. The following example will illustrate how far an isotropically radiating antenna will carry for a typical low-power radio station. Although different receivers need different amounts of power to operate well, the estimate below is what one would need for a typical situation.

Assume a receiver sensitivity of 100 μV, an antenna resistance of 100 Ω and a transmit power of 1 kW. With this information calculate the necessary receive power and radius as follows:

$$P_{rx} = \frac{E^2}{R} = \frac{(100 \times 10^{-6})^2}{100} = 1 \times 10^{-10} \text{ W} \rightarrow r\sqrt{= \frac{1000}{4\pi 10^{-10}}} = 9 \times 10^5 \text{ m} = 540 \text{ miles}$$

Remember, this is a maximum radius; in most cases, the signal will not reach nearly this far.

■ FIELD INTENSITY

Recall that all signals are electromagnetic in composition. That means that they are composed of both electric and magnetic fields. Because the power of something must come from combining its parts, we can write the expression

$$P = EH \tag{2-11}$$

where P = electromagnetic power density (W/m²)
  E = electric field intensity (V/m)
  H = magnetic field intensity (A/m)

Note that the units are just what one would expect, watts for power, volts for electrical quantities, and amperes for current or magnetic field quantities. Of course, because the subject is densities and intensities, these must be expressed per unit distance; that is where the meters comes in. Earlier, the result for the characteristic impedance of free space was developed, and it was stated that it was equal to the ratio of the magnetic permeability to the electric permittivity. The value that was obtained was 377 Ω. Using Ohm's law, one can write

$$P = EH = \frac{E^2}{Z} = \frac{E^2}{377} \rightarrow E = 377H \tag{2-12}$$

Now, to obtain an expression for the electric field intensity one can combine equations 2−10 and 2−12 in the following way by setting the powers equal to each other:

$$P_{rx} = \frac{P_{tx}}{4\pi r^2} = \frac{E^2}{377} \rightarrow E^2 = \frac{377 P_{tx}}{4\pi r^2} \rightarrow E = \frac{\sqrt{30 P_{tx}}}{r} \tag{2-13}$$

Equation 2−13 gives a way to calculate the electric field intensity for any power transmission if you know only the power transmitted and the distance from the transmitting location. Note that by combining equation 2−13 with equation 2−12, you can also find the magnetic field intensity at any distance. The next example illustrates how this is done.

■ EXAMPLE 2.11

For a radio station with a transmitting power of 1000 W, find the power density, electric field intensity, and magnetic field intensity at a distance of 2 km from the antenna:

$$P_{rx} = \frac{P_{tx}}{4\pi r^2} = \frac{1000}{4\pi(2000)^2} = 2.0 \times 10^{-5} \, \text{W/m}^2$$

$$E = \frac{\sqrt{30 P_{tx}}}{r} = \frac{\sqrt{(30)(1000)}}{2000} = 8.7 \times 10^{-2} \, \text{V/m}$$

$$H = \frac{E}{Z} = \frac{0.0866}{377} = 2.30 \times 10^{-4} \, \text{A/m}$$

To summarize, because electromagnetic waves travel at different speeds in different materials, you might infer that the three types of propagation are caused by changes in how different frequencies move through different materials. Our atmosphere is made up of several layers; these layers have different reflectivity for different wavelengths. Below 3 MHz, the wave will pass through the lower atmosphere easily but is bent (refracted) continuously by the upper atmosphere, so the waves are seen to follow the earth's curvature. Above 30 MHz, both the lower and upper atmosphere are transparent to the waves, and you get waves that pass right through the upper atmosphere and appear to go in straight lines.

In between these two limiting situations is a narrow band of frequencies where the upper atmosphere reflects the wave sharply. Any ham radio operator will tell you that this reflection varies with time of day, weather, and the sunspot cycle of the sun. The percentage of reflection will vary, but some always occurs, and this is the second type of propagation, SW. In this frequency range, waves essentially bounce around the earth, reflecting from the upper atmosphere and the surface of the earth. On good nights, it is common to be able to pick up a surprising low-power broadcast from the other side of the globe.

The HF range is very valuable for long-range communications using no other hardware than an earth-based transmitter and receiver. Of course, LOS frequencies are replacing them but their use comes at a cost, placing a satellite in orbit to "catch" the LOS wave as it exits the upper atmosphere and "reflect" it down to earth. Satellites are expensive and were not technically possible before about 1950, so again we see the effect of technology opening new uses for the electromagnetic spectrum.

■ SUMMARY

In this chapter, the electromagnetic spectrum has been explored. The frequency bands and application systems that use those bands have been identified. The relationship between frequency and wavelength has been reviewed along with how interference effects transmissions. The effect of the material in which the electromagnetic wave travels has been described through the use of the dielectric constant, and this has been expressed in two different ways, the velocity factor and the velocity of propagation. Bandwidth was defined and its relationship to the information capacity of a communications system was explored. The three propagation modes that are used in atmospheric communications were defined, and the impact on antenna height was explored. Finally, calculations of field intensities were made, and the electric and magnetic fields were related to the impedance of free space.

PROBLEMS

1. Find the wavelength of each of the following frequencies:
   (a) 10 Hz   (c) 10 MHz
   (b) 1 kHz   (d) 1 GHz

2. Find the frequency of each of the following wavelengths:
   (a) 1 cm   (c) 1 km
   (b) 1 m   (d) 1 mile

3. Find the perceived speed of light in each of the following materials:
   (a) Free space
   (b) Velocity factor = 0.90
   (c) Dielectric constant = 1.20
   (d) Dielectric constant = 4.0

4. Find the bandwidth for each of the following pairs of signal frequencies (lower, upper):

(a) 1 kHz, 10 kHz   (c) 0 Hz, 3 kHz

(b) 10 MHz, 20 MHz   (d) 1 GHz, 1.1 GHz

5. For each of the following bandwidths, find the upper frequency given the lower frequency (BW, lower):

(a) 1 kHz, 1 kHz   (c) 10 kHz, 1 GHz

(b) 1 kHz, 1 MHz   (d) 60 Hz, 0 Hz

6. Find the percentage bandwidth for a 10 kHz bandwidth signal at each of the following center frequencies:

(a) 20 kHz   (c) 1 MHz

(b) 50 kHz   (d) 1 GHz

7. What happens to the information capacity for each of the following situations?

(a) Channel bandwidth doubles

(b) Channel bandwidth halves

8. What frequency band and propagation mode does each of the following services use?

(a) Cellular telephone

(b) Broadcast AM radio

(c) Broadcast VHF-TV

(d) Broadcast FM radio

(e) Long-range terrestrial communications

(f) Satellite communications

9. How high would a transmitting tower have to be for each of the following distances from the tower? Assume no receive antenna height.

(a) 1 mile   (c) 40 miles

(b) 25 miles   (d) 200 miles

10. For each of the distances below, calculate the new height of the transmit antenna required with the addition of a 50 ft receive antenna:

(a) 1 mile   (c) 40 miles

(b) 25 miles   (d) 200 miles

11. Find the power density, electric field intensity, and magnetic field intensity for each of the following radiated powers and distances from the transmitting antenna:

(a) 100 W, 1 km   (c) 2 kW, 1 km

(b) 1 W, 1 m   (d) 2 W, 1 cm

3

Metallic Media

In this chapter, several aspects of metallic media, sometimes called transmission lines, will be explored. Two types of wire geometry, coaxial and parallel wire, will be explored in detail. This detail will include physical properties, construction techniques, shielding, connectorization, cross talk, grounding issues, and standards. How a metallic media attenuates with distance and frequency will be discussed. Standing waves, voltage standing wave ratio (VSWR), reflection coefficient, and the use of a time domain reflectometer (TDR) will be introduced. The use of balanced signaling and differential amplifiers as an effective noise reduction technique will be discussed. Next a brief discussion on using a TDR to troubleshoot metallic media is included. Finally, a discussion on LAN wiring standards, baluns, and the various category types of twisted pair cable will conclude the chapter.

▆ METALLIC CONDUCTORS

Metallic transmission lines provide important links in virtually all communications systems such as telephone lines, and cable TV lines. This discussion will be broken up into three sections, coaxial cables, parallel conductors, and twisted pairs. Before talking about what is unique about each type of metallic cable, however we will discuss what is the same.

First, all metallic conductors functioning as transmission lines exhibit a change in the way current flows in a conductor that is dependent on the frequency of the signal. What happens is that the current flows move to the outer edge, or skin of the wire, as the frequency of the signal on the metallic conductor increases. This effect is known as the skin effect, which is that at high frequencies the current flows in a conductor moves to the edge, or skin, of the wire. This effect is so dominant that at high frequencies 99% of all the current flows in the outside 5% of the wire diameter. The falloff as you move inward toward the center of the wire is inversely as the square root of the frequency and given by equation 3-1. It defines skin depth as the point at which the current density falls to 1 / e of its initial value. The skin effect is shown in the shaded area of Figure 3.1. It is interesting to note that this effect is responsible for the design of transmission lines where the line is constructed of, for example, a hollow square. Because at high enough frequencies, all the current is conducted near the edge of the conductor, a hollow shape can serve just as well as a solid conductor would, but at considerable weight and cost savings.

The second common attribute that all metallic conductors share is that there are four basic parameters that control the behavior of metallic transmission lines. These are the line geometry, the dielectric medium, the series resistance, and the series inductance. Some may be wondering what happened to capacitance; surely that must be important. It is, but the shunt capacitance is defined by the first two parameters listed. They are more fundamental because they determine the capacitance; therefore they will be used to describe the capacitance. Although the equations that describe capacitance, equations 3-4 and 3-8, will be given, it is important to understand that the capacitance exhibited by a metallic conductor is a consequence of the wire geometry and dielectric constant.

The third common attribute is that electric power propagates down a metallic conductor, just as it does through free space, by electromagnetic waves. The particular type of wave that is seen in metallic conductors is called a transverse electromagnetic (TEM) wave. This term arises because as a transverse wave travels down the conductor, or propagates down a conductor, the direction of displacement is perpendicular to the direction of propagation. This means that both the electric and magnetic fields that make up any electromagnetic wave move down the cable perpendicular to each other and parallel to the long axis of the cable.

Figure 3.1
Skin effect.

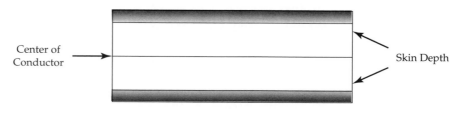

Shaded area indicates current density

■ SKIN DEPTH

Skin depth is the point at which the current density flowing in the wire falls to $1/e$ of its initial value. The falloff is inversely as the square root of frequency as you move inward toward the center of the wire and is given by equation 3-1. This equation includes as factors the conductivity, σ, of wire, here taken to be copper, and the relative permeability of the wire, again here taken to be copper. Recall that conductivity is just the reciprocal of resistivity. Permeability, μ, is a measure of the current density per unit of field intensity; the relative permeability of copper is approximately 1. The equation defining these properties and relating them to skin depth can be reduced to the form shown below for wires composed primarily of copper:

$$\text{skin depth} = \frac{1}{\sqrt{\pi f \mu_r \sigma}} = \frac{0.066}{\sqrt{f}}\ \text{m} \tag{3-1}$$

One would say that at high frequencies the current is flowing within a skin depth of the surface. To give you some sense of what the skin depth is for various frequencies, Table 3.1 lists the skin depth for copper wire at various frequencies. Noting that most copper wire in use in communications lines is on the order of 1 mm or less in diameter, it can be seen that above 1 MHz the effect is pronounced. It is also of interest to see that the transition occurs in the audio band. From Table 3.1, at 10 kHz, the center of the audiophile band (20 to −20 kHz) the skin depth is half of the diameter of 18 gage wire. For audiophiles, this is one big reason why high-quality audio systems often use very thick wire.

Table 3.2 lists wires with a single solid conductor and relates the American Wire Gauge (AWG) to the wire diameter and resistance per kilometer. Very often, hookup wire is not made of a single, solid conductor but is stranded or constructed of a bundle of wire strands for a conductor. Table 3.3 shows how the resistance per unit length varies for AWG of stranded wires. By the way, there are several ways to make stranded wire of a certain gauge; you can use more strands of thinner diameter or fewer strands with a larger diameter. Table 3.3 represents a typical compromise of these two factors.

As can be seen from a comparison of the Tables 3.2 and 3.3, there seems to be very little difference in resistance between the two types of wires, solid conductor and stranded. This is true at DC for which these tables are compiled. At high frequencies, however, the situation changes and solid conductor wire is preferred.

Table 3.1
Skin Depth at Various Frequencies

Frequency	Skin Depth
100 Hz	6.6 mm
10 kHz	0.66 mm
1 MHz	0.066 mm

Table 3.2
Solid Conductors

American Wire Gauge	Solid Conductor Diameter (mm)	Resistance/Km (Ω)
12	2.05	5.5
18	1.02	22
24	0.511	88
30	0.255	338

If you recall your early circuit classes, you will remember that the resistance of a wire depends on its cross-sectional area and the larger the diameter, the lower the resistance. This has a bearing on the effect of where the current travels in a conductor. Often the analogy was with a pipe of water; the thicker the pipe, the more water that can flow and so the lower the resistance. So, if all the current is flowing in the outside half of the conductor, you really have a conductor with a reduced effective diameter. You cannot include that part of the wire where no current flows when computing resistance.

Therefore, the high-frequency resistance of a metallic conductor is not dominated by the cross-sectional area but by the length of the perimeter because it is only on the perimeter of the conductor that the current is flowing. This resistance is measured by the parameter called surface resistance. Thick wire is preferred for high-quality audio applications because of its larger diameter, and hence larger perimeter. Thus, it lowers the resistance for all signal frequencies in the audio band, both those not subject the skin effect through the larger diameter and those that are through the larger perimeter.

The physical reason this occurs is that at higher frequencies, the magnetic field near the center of the conductor increases. This increase makes current flow "harder" for the charge carriers, electrons, because they have to "break" the magnetic field lines to conduct, so they move to the edge where the magnetic field is weaker. The effective thickness of this edge is called the skin depth. Therefore, at high frequencies, the electromagnetic forces within the metallic conductor force the current towards the surface and thus the skin effect raises the effective resistance.

The other related effect caused by the skin effect is a small decrease in the wire inductance as frequency increases. This effect is not significant unless very high frequencies are reached, so it will not be discussed further here.

Table 3.3
Stranded Wire

American Wire Gauge	Number and Diameter of Strands (mm)	Resistance/Km (Ω)
12	19 × 0.45	5.5
18	19 × 0.25	18
24	19 × 0.13	69
30	7 × 0.25	338

■ WIRE GEOMETRY AND FIELDS

The four basic parameters that define metallic transmission lines have different results when applied to each wire type because the geometry is different. It is beyond the scope of this book to go into the derivations of these results, but some of the more important results will be summarized. Because the geometry of the coaxial line leads to relatively simple forms for the electromagnetic (that is the electric and magnetic) fields, this arrangement will be examined first. Such a cable is shown in Figure 3.2. As can be seen, the electric field is radial, it extends out perpendicularly from the center, and the magnetic field forms a series of concentric circles around the center conductor.

The four factors that characterize the performance of any metallic conductor are

1. Characteristic impedance of the conductor—dominated by the wire geometry
2. Capacitance of the conductor—dominated by the wire geometry
3. Inductance of the conductor—dominated by the wire geometry
4. Velocity of propagation in the metallic conductor—dominated by the material choice

Careful readers are probably wondering what the difference is between characteristic impedance and the familiar impedance. Characteristic impedance is defined as the square root of the inductance divided by the capacitance, or more generally, the ratio of voltage to current. Characteristic impedance is sometimes called the surge impedance and represents the impedance for a wave traveling down the line.

Characteristic impedance is of interest in characterizing transmission lines as long as the diameter of the conductor is significantly smaller than the wavelength. A good rule of thumb is that as long as the diameter is less than three times the wavelength of the signal, the results of this chapter apply. This rule is always true for any type of commonly encountered metallic conductor operating at signal frequencies of less than 1 GHz, and often much higher.

Hence, small metallic conductors work fine as long as the wavelength of the signal does not get too small. For example, AWG 18 gauge wire has a diameter of about 1 mm.

Figure 3.2
Coaxial cable electric field.

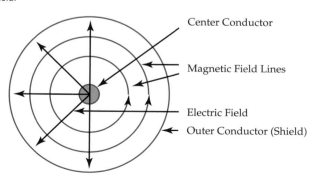

Center Conductor

Magnetic Field Lines

Electric Field
Outer Conductor (Shield)

The rule above would indicate that as long as the wavelength of the signal on that wire is more than 3 mm, characteristic impedance can safely be used to measure the impedance of the conductor. A 3 mm wavelength is exhibited by a frequency of 10 GHz.

The characteristic impedance for a line depends on the geometry; for a coaxial cable, as the outside diameter of the coaxial line increases as a ratio to the center conductor, the characteristic impedance will increase. Now, unfortunately, that leads one to the wrong conclusion, namely, that large coaxial lines would generally have higher impedance and hence higher attenuation per unit distance. Actually, the opposite is true because as coaxial lines increase in outside diameter, the center conductor is increasing faster. This acts to reduce the impedance, not increase it, which can be observed in Table 3.5, shown later in this chapter. Take note of this fact when examining the graph in Figure 3.3.

The capacitance and inductance for a metallic conductor are determined from the equations shown below. An intuitive feel for the results they will yield, however, can be obtained by noting how the geometry of the line effects their magnitude and hence their contribution. Because the inductance depends linearly on the ratio of the outside diameter to the inside, it should grow larger as this ratio increases. Alternately, because the capacitance depends inversely on the same ratio, it should grow smaller as this ratio increases.

Both these effects along with how the impedance changes with this ratio are shown in Figure 3.3. Note that this graph is valid only for coaxial lines; however, similar curves can be drawn for any type of cable using the equations shown below. Note that the curve for the inductance has been scaled down by a factor of 2 to make the graph more compact.

The velocity of propagation for any electromagnetic wave in free space is just the velocity of light, but the coaxial cable is not free space. The relative permittivity of the dielectric reduces this velocity as shown in the equations below. Recall the discussion in Chapter 2 concerning how the perceived speed of light changes in a material. There the

Figure 3.3
Coaxial line performance curves.

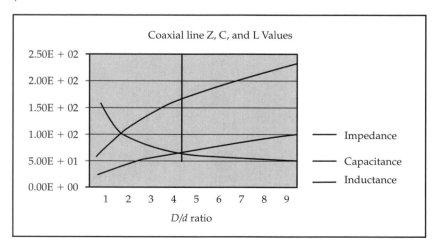

effect of relative permeability was not accounted for explicitly; this is shown in the equations below. Referring to Figure 3.4 and using equations 3-2 through 3-5, the variables that are important to designers selecting cable for systems can be defined.

$$Z_o = \sqrt{\frac{L}{C}} = \frac{1}{2\pi}\sqrt{\frac{\mu_r}{\varepsilon_r}}\log\left(\frac{D}{d}\right) = 138\sqrt{\frac{\mu_r}{\varepsilon_r}}\log\left(\frac{D}{d}\right)\Omega = \frac{138}{\sqrt{\varepsilon_r}}\log\left(\frac{D}{d}\right)\Omega \quad \textbf{(3-2)}$$

$$L = 460\mu_r\log\left(\frac{D}{d}\right)\text{nH}/\text{m} \quad \textbf{(3-3)}$$

$$C = \frac{24.1\varepsilon_r}{\log\left(\frac{D}{d}\right)}\text{pF}/\text{m} \quad \textbf{(3-4)}$$

$$v_p = cv_f = \frac{c}{\sqrt{\mu_r\varepsilon_r}} = \frac{3\times10^8}{\sqrt{LC}}\text{ m}/\text{s} \quad \textbf{(3-5)}$$

Typical relative permittivity (dielectric constant) is $\varepsilon_r = 2$.

Typical relative permeability is $\mu_r = 1$.

For 50 Ω coaxial cable, $C \approx 90$ pF/m, $L \approx 0.25$ μH/m.

To summarize, for the coaxial line case only, the geometry of the coaxial line can be used to get a good approximation of the characteristic impedance knowing only three quantities and assuming the metallic conductor is copper. These quantities are

1. The outside diameter of the coaxial cable (D)
2. The outside diameter of the inside conductor (d)
3. The relative permittivity, or as it is more commonly known, the dielectric constant of the foam sheath that insulates the center conductor from the braided shield.

Figure 3.4
Inner and outer radius.

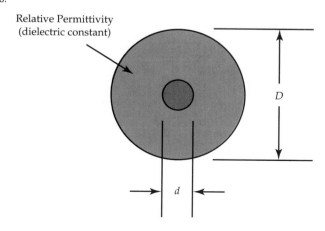

Relative Permittivity
(dielectric constant)

D

d

The expressions for parallel wires or shielded pair of parallel wires are almost the same. There is a small difference between the multipliers shown in equations 3-2 through 3-4 and those in equations 3-6 through 3-8. This is because the formulas must correspond to the different geometries of the two conductor types.

It is important to understand that the equations for a parallel wire are only applicable if the distance D, shown in Figure 3.5 between the parallel lines, is large with respect to the diameter of the individual wires. This is a good assumption for wires that are separated at distances easily visible to the eye. Examine closely equations 3-2 through 3-4 and compare them to equations 3-6 through 3-8.

$$Z_o = 276 \sqrt{\frac{\mu_r}{\varepsilon_r}} \log\left(\frac{D}{r}\right) \Omega = \frac{276}{\sqrt{\varepsilon_r}} \log\left(\frac{D}{r}\right) \Omega \qquad (3\text{-}6)$$

$$L = 921\mu_r \log\left(\frac{D}{r}\right) nH/m \qquad (3\text{-}7)$$

$$C = \frac{12.1\varepsilon_r}{\log\left(\frac{D}{r}\right)} pF/m \qquad (3\text{-}8)$$

$$v_p = cv_f = \frac{c}{\sqrt{\mu_r\varepsilon_r}} = \frac{3 \times 10^8}{\sqrt{LC}} \ m/s$$

Typical relative permittivity (dielectric constant) is $\varepsilon_r = 2$.

Typical relative permeability is $\mu_r = 1$.

For 600 Ω cable flat parallel cable, $C \approx 6pF/m$, $L \approx 2\ \mu H/m$.

These equations are not as good an approximation for shielded parallel wires but will do for a first approximation of the results; if you need to be very accurate, consult other sources. They are not as accurate because for twisted pair cables, the separation D is not large with respect to the wire radius r. Similar equations can also be generated for single wires above ground, for example, power lines on a pole above ground and for microstrip lines used in very high frequency design.

Figure 3.5
Geometry diagram for parallel wires.

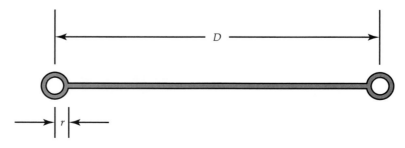

■ EXAMPLE 3.1

You are asked to choose among three wire choices for a LAN installation. The first wire is a parallel wire arrangement that has a high D/r ratio. The second choice is a parallel wire arrangement that has a small D/r ratio. The third choice is a coaxial cable. You are told only that it is important to keep the impedance low and that the wire must run under carpet in a heavy traffic area. Which choice do you make?

The key to understanding this example lies in first realizing that the coaxial cable would not work well under the carpet. It would create a bump that might trip someone. This leaves us with two choices, the high D/r parallel wire or the low D/r parallel wire. Examining equation 3-6, you recognize that as the separation of the parallel wires grows, the impedance increases. Because a low impedance is desired, you choose the smaller D/r ratio parallel wire.

After reading the rest of the chapter, you will realize there is another good reason why coaxial cable would not be a good choice. (Hint: When someone steps on a cable, the geometry changes and the standing wave ratio, or SWR, increases.)

■ EXAMPLE 3.2

Equations 3-2 through 3-8 are very useful for those who are involved in the manufacture of cables. This example will illustrate how to apply equation 3-2. A certain coaxial cable has the following dimensions: The center conductor is 1 mm in diameter, the outside diameter of the cable is 4 mm, and the polyvinyl chloride (PVC) sheath, or jacket surrounding and protecting the outside shield, is 0.5 mm in diameter. As always, the dielectric constant of the foam dielectric is taken to equal 2. This results in the following values:

$$D = 4 - 0.5 = 3.5 \text{ mm}$$

$$d = 1 \text{ mm}$$

$$\varepsilon_r = 2$$

$$Z_o = \frac{138}{\sqrt{2}} \log\left(\frac{3.5}{1}\right) = 53 \ \Omega$$

The only tricky thing about applying this equation is that the outside diameter must be the diameter of the shield, not the outside jacket.

■ EXAMPLE 3.3

Review equations 3-6 through 3-8 and verify the following statements for parallel wires with a fixed conductor radius. As the distance between the conductors of a parallel wire arrangement increases,

1. The characteristic impedance increases.
2. The inductance increases.
3. The capacitance decreases.

■ **EXAMPLE 3.4**

Do the same thought experiments as in Example 3.3 for coaxial lines; refer to equations 3-2 through 3-4. As the outside diameter of a coaxial cable increases,

1. The characteristic impedance *decreases.*
2. The inductance increases.
3. The capacitance decreases.

The first item in Example 3.4 deserves some additional explanation. Looking at equation 3-2, one would expect that for a fixed center conductor diameter, as the outside diameter increased, the characteristic impedance would also increase. However, the manufacture of coaxial cables is such that the shield diameter is only increased when the center conductor is increased even more. As stated earlier, you get the opposite result that you might expect; as a general rule as the outside diameter of a coaxial cable increases, the impedance actually goes down.

Shielded cables, like the coaxial cable and shielded pair, are widely used to reduce interference on small signal circuits or radio frequency (RF) transmission lines. Consider how noise enters a coaxial line. Any noise results from a current flow in a conductor. In any shielded cable there are actually two components of current flow, the desired signal and the noise current. Of course, the noise current is not impressed on the cable by design; rather it is induced by the noise environment, but it still is a current.

Considering just the noise current, some fraction will flow on the shield and some fraction will flow on the conductor inside the shield. Therefore, the objective of shielding is to cause most of the current to flow on the shield so that little current and voltage are induced in the conductors inside the shield. This varies, as you might expect, with frequency and the type of shield. The better the shield, the higher the percentage of induced noise current that will flow in the shield and not in the conductor(s) that lie inside the shield.

Although shields may be solid metal, most practical cables use some kind of braided or taped wire as the shield. Note that flexible conduit, if conductive, will work as a shield. A good rule of thumb is that the smaller the visible "leaks" in the wire braid used for the shield are, the better the shield. By better, it is meant that it will work to a higher frequency and will exhibit smaller leakage capacitance. Sometimes several shields are used; coaxial cable is available with up to three shields, each shield adding about 20 dB of additional protection against leakage currents.

There are at least three disadvantages of adding additional shields:

1. Higher cost
2. Lower flexibility
3. Higher weight per unit length

These factors tend to limit applications that can use multiple shielded cable. For example, a very rigid cable would have a large radius of curvature. If bent to route around corners, the cable may be crimped, which can severely alter the impedance of the cable.

This causes problems due to increased SWR (SWR will be discussed further later in this chapter). This fact can be seen in a general way by looking at the above equations for characteristic impedance. The impendence depends on the radius of the shield; by crimping, or sharply bending, a coaxial or any shielded cable, this value will change. When the impedance changes, the matching between source and load changes and you get reflections, leading to less power transferred from source to destination.

To illustrate how much the impedance of a coaxial line can change due to a bend or crimp in the outer shield, the following example is provided.

■ EXAMPLE 3.5

A particular coaxial cable has an outer shield diameter of 5 mm. Someone steps on the cable and it is crimped down to 3 mm as a result. What affect will this crimp have on the impedance of the cable at the point of impact?

$$Z_o = \frac{138}{\sqrt{2}} \log\left(\frac{D}{d}\right) = 97.6 \log\left(\frac{5 \text{ mm}}{1 \text{ mm}}\right) = 68.2 \ \Omega \quad Z_{o(crimp)} = 97.6 \log\left(\frac{3 \text{ mm}}{1 \text{ mm}}\right) = 46.5 \ \Omega$$

As can be seen, the crimp changes the impedance by almost 20 Ω, or over 30%. Later, when SWR is discussed, it will be seen that the impact this crimp has can be calculated in another way.

■ BRAIDED SHIELD

Because the most common type of shield is the braided shield, it is instructive to examine the braided wire shield and develop an equation that will tell how good a shield it is. Recall the rule of thumb stated above that the smaller the visible leaks are, the better the shield. This lack of leaks is called the shield coverage. Shield coverage depends on several characteristics of the braided wire shield, such as

1. Number of bands of wires that make up the shield
2. Number of strands of each wire band
3. Number of wire crossings per unit length
4. Weave angle—the angle between the bands of wires and the center conductor
5. Shield radius
6. Wire strand diameter

Another aspect of shielding is the fill factor, F; this component describes the relative density of the wire braid, or shield. The effectiveness of a cable design is often measured by how effective the shielding is; shield coverage is used to describe this. However, the efficiency of a particular braid is often characterized by how little fill is required for a particular shield coverage. The lower the fill factor for a particular shielding coverage, the more efficient the braid design. Lower fills usually indicate lower material costs and lower weight, both desirable factors. Figure 3.6 illustrates these components, and exam-

Figure 3.6
Coaxial cable construction.

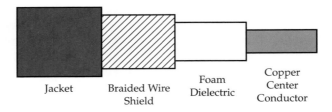

Jacket   Braided Wire   Foam   Copper
             Shield   Dielectric   Center
                                     Conductor

Exploding Braided Wire Shield

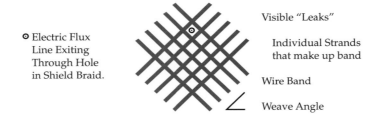

⊘ Electric Flux
Line Exiting
Through Hole
in Shield Braid.

Visible "Leaks"

Individual Strands
that make up band

Wire Band

Weave Angle

ple 3.6 illustrates the equations necessary to determine shield coverage and shows how they work together to characterize the shielding coverage.

■ EXAMPLE 3.6

A certain coaxial cable is constructed in the following way; determine the fill and shield coverage.

r_{shield} = shield radius   = 0.1 cm

r_{strand} = strand radius   = 0.02 cm

θ = weave angle   = 25°

N_b = number of bands   = 5

N_s = number of strands in each band = 10

$$F = \text{fill} = \frac{N_s r_{\text{strand}} N_b}{4\pi r_{\text{shield}}\cos\theta} = \frac{(5)(0.02)(10)}{4\pi(0.1)\cos(25)} = 0.878 \qquad \textbf{(3-9)}$$

$$K = \text{shield coverage} = 2F - F^2 = (2)(0.878) - (0.878)^2 = 98.51\% \quad \textbf{(3-10)}$$

Note that shield coverage is determined by the fill factor. A reasonable number for shield coverage is 95%. The physical parameters of a few common coaxial cables are

Table 3.4
Common Coaxial Cable Shielding Coverage

Cable Type	N_s	r_{strand}	N_b	r_{shield}	θ	Fill	Coverage (%)
RG-6	16	0.0160	9	0.256	25.0	0.790	95.61
RG-11	24	0.0180	8	0.388	27.5	0.799	95.96
RG-58	12	0.0127	9	0.165	27.7	0.746	93.57
RG-59	16	0.0160	7	0.206	27.6	0.780	95.14

listed in Table 3.4 to give you a feel for the numbers. The radius numbers are given in centimeters.

Another commonly used measurement for the effectiveness of the shield is defined by

$$S = \text{shield effectiveness} = 20 \log \left(\frac{I_o}{I} \right) \tag{3-11}$$

Here I_o is the current in the shield, and I is the current in the conductor inside the shield. This equation can be used when you have direct measurements of the current flows but do not have access to the physical data on the cable construction. For this equation to be applicable, both ends of the cable must be terminated in the characteristic impedance of the cable.

Sometimes, increased flexibility of the shielded cable is a requirement. Where increased flexibility is important, often so-called tape-wound shields are used instead of wire strands or in combination with them. If a good, flexible shield is required, both types of shield are used in appropriate ratios. Where the shield quality is less important and flexibility is critical, only tape-wound shields are used, but the shielding effectiveness of this type of coaxial cable is relatively poor. When flexibility is undesirable, usually for physical protection, flexible conduit is used as a shield. For highly protective applications, flexible armor is also available.

■ CABLE CONNECTORS

Interestingly, and something most people tend to ignore, for the cable to be of use, it generally must connect something to something else. For most applications, this is done with connectors attached to each end of the cable. These connectors are an integral part of the cable, and the noise coupling through their shields can be an important part of the overall effectiveness of the shield.

The best example that comes to mind to illustrate this is the cable-TV cable. Usually, the connector has been crimped on and the center conductor is just the wire of the cable sticking out. This has a much greater resistance and leakage current than a cable designed with a connector that mates with its counterpart socket.

It is much cheaper to just carry a cable spool and cut cables to length in the field. "Connectors" are then crimped on, with all the damaging effects of altering the cable geometry. The other alternative is to bring prepared cables with finished connectors for every application likely to be found in the field. Which approach would you choose if you were the owner of the cable-TV system, the engineer in charge, the technician in the field, or an informed customer (subscriber)? Each might have a unique perspective on this issue.

Three good questions to ask to roughly evaluate the shielding effectiveness of a connector and how good the system design is with respect to noise immunity of the cable are

1. Are the connectors finished or crimped on?
2. Does the connector used have the shield extending beyond the center conductor?
3. How good is the ground on the shield?

These questions are really system design issues and depend on the length of the cable and the frequency used. The connector issues will be explored further at the end of the chapter. Cable grounding is a critical system design issue and is discussed in the following section.

■   CABLE GROUNDING

To begin with there are really only two issues that determine the appropriate techniques for grounding cables. These are the length of the cable and the frequency of operation. A single ground connection can work for short cables; for longer ones multiple grounds may be required. Short in this case is defined as a cable length of less than 5% of the wavelength of the lowest frequency being applied to the cable. It is usually best to ground both ends of the cable for best resistance to noise coupling. Except when using frequencies below 1 MHz. For best noise immunity in that situation, it is actually preferable to have only one end of the cable shield grounded. Shielded cable is rarely needed or used at low frequencies, and so this exception to the rule is not as applicable as it might once have been. Example 3.7 illustrates these ideas.

■   EXAMPLE 3.7

A cable is being run between two systems. The distance between the two systems is 10 m. The center frequency of the signal to be carried on the coaxial cable is 1 GHz. Should both ends be grounded or only one?

Because the frequency of operation of the cable is above 1 MHz, you must determine if the length of the cable is more than 5% of the frequency of operation.

$$c = \lambda f \rightarrow \lambda = \frac{c}{f} = \frac{3 \times 10^8}{1 \times 10^9} = 30 \text{ cm}$$

$$(30 \text{ cm})(5\%) = 1.5 \text{ cm}$$

$$\text{length of run} = 10 \text{ m}$$

$$1.5 \text{ cm} < 10 \text{ m} \rightarrow \text{ground each end}$$

Note that a cable run of anything more than 1.5 cm will require grounding at each end for a frequency of 1 GHz. If we drop the frequency of operation down to 1 MHz, what length of cable can we run before needing to ground both sides?

$$c = \lambda f \rightarrow \lambda = \frac{c}{f} = \frac{3 \times 10^8}{1 \times 10^6} = 300 \text{ m}$$

$$(5\%)(300 \text{ m}) = 15 \text{ m}$$

Therefore, for a cable running at 1 MHz, if the length of the run is less than 15 m, a single ground will do. As can be seen from these two calculations, as the frequency of operation of the system increases, grounding becomes more critical and a calculation such as the one above needs to be performed.

■ CROSS TALK

Cross talk is always a potential problem whenever two metallic conductors carrying different signals run along a similar path. This occurs not only in cable bundles but is a real problem on the mixed signal buses commonly implemented in a variety of complex hardware. Mixed signal means that there are analog and digital signals on the bus, or it might mean that signals of varying amplitude are on the bus. The term is used in both ways, but the first is the more traditional usage.

A detailed analysis is outside the scope of this text, but you can get a feeling for the variables involved from Figure 3.7. Essentially, each conductor is coupled to the adjacent one by a series of small capacitors spaced regularly along the length of the line. In between each of the capacitors and in series with the line is a series of small inductors. Finally, again at regular points along the line, is a capacitor to ground.

The result of all these little capacitors is to couple any excess charge onto the adjacent line. This adds to the signal on the adjacent line and appears as noise for that signal. This same effect occurs in the reverse direction, but whichever line has the greater potential swings, the more rapid signal transitions (higher frequency), or the more abrupt transitions (square waves versus sine waves) contribute more noise, or cross talk, to the other line.

It is also useful to examine what aspects of the signal affect the amount of mutual inductance. This is shown in Figure 3.7 as dotted lines connecting the self-inductance of the transmission line itself. Because inductance grows with current flow, the higher the current, the greater the relative contribution of the mutual inductance that exists between adjacent lines.

One way to reduce this is to reduce the harmonic content of the waveforms on these lines, thus eliminating their contribution to the total current. This has consequences in the transition time of the waveforms used. As will be seen in Chapter 6, the more rapid the transition of the waveform, the more high-frequency or harmonic content the waveform has. These two factors must be traded off; this is the fundamental reason for the application of trapezoidal drivers in data bus applications. Trapezoidal waveforms feature lower rise and fall times and thus have lower harmonic content.

Figure 3.7
Cross-talk model.

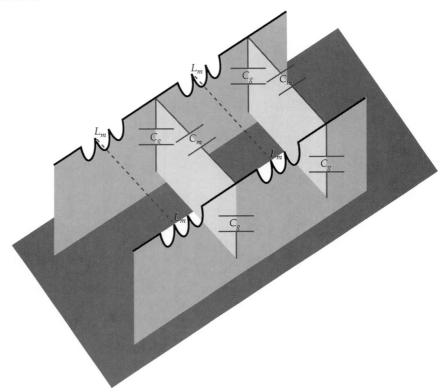

A smaller geometric size of the two lines will reduce the contribution of the mutual capacitances. This is because the capacitance of any element is determined by the surface area of the plates; therefore smaller geometries lead to smaller capacitances. You can also increase the distance between the two lines, although this is a mixed blessing and depends on the application. As you know, the capacitance of any element is reduced by the separation of the plates.

For semiconductor or PC board applications, increasing the separation means physically separating the lines. This increases the area required for the bus and is generally not a real option. For conventional wiring applications, it has the consequence of larger conduits, again, not usually a practical option.

As with all techniques, this trade-off is affected by the requirement for sufficient area to adequately conduct the current flow required. In semiconductor applications this is accomplished by reducing the horizontal dimension; in conventional wiring applications this is accomplished by reducing the cross-sectional area of the metallic conductor used for the line.

Cross talk has its own special decibel unit, the dBx. It is a bit different from the various forms of decibels that were discussed in Chapter 1 because the reference is not an absolute power level. For all the other cases defined, dBm, dBmV, and so forth, the reference was a fixed power or voltage. For the dBx, it is instead a reference from the line that is being interfered with.

$$dBx = 90 - (\text{cross talk loss in decibels}) \tag{3-12}$$

The dBx is defined by how much interference is contributed; 90 dB is assumed to be the amount of isolation that adjacent lines should have. Anything less than this reduces the signal by so much coupling loss. Example 3.8 illustrates how such a calculation is made.

■ EXAMPLE 3.8

Suppose that circuit A picks up some cross talk or a signal from circuit B, which is running adjacent to it. The magnitude of the cross talk picked up on circuit A is 70 dB lower than the power of the signal running on circuit A. The cross talk from B to A then would be 90 dB − 70 dBx, or 20 dBx. This is another example of the fact that the decibel can be added or subtracted from another related decibel value without concern.

■ CABLE CHOICES

This brings us to the question of what type of cable is best used for what frequency bands. Only the shielded twisted pair and coaxial cable will be considered. Shielded twisted pair is useful up to several hundred MHz, if special termination techniques or distortions of the transmitted waveforms are applied. Without some type of special preparation of the wavefront or termination elements, twisted pair is only good up to about 1 MHz. Coaxial cable is typically good up to about 600 MHz. Special designs can extend the useful range up to about 1 GHz. Virtually any cable can be used at any frequency if you can tolerate the attenuation that comes with increasing frequency. In fact, it is just these ideas that are being used to implement the next generation of advanced digital subscriber lines (ADSLs).

Both cable types considered here are good at low frequencies, but the cost of coaxial generally limits its use to higher-frequency applications. If the distances to travel are very short, the attenuation with frequency is not as much of a problem and will extend the useful frequency of operation of any cable. The frequency crossover points discussed above assume that the cable application is of significant length, say over 50 m.

■ COAXIAL CABLE ATTENUATION WITH FREQUENCY AND LENGTH

To illustrate just how a coaxial cable attenuates different frequencies, the representative data in Table 3.5 shows how with increasing frequency, the attenuation per unit length of a coaxial cable increases. The three types of cables listed increase in diameter and

Table 3.5
Coaxial Attenuation for 100 Ft Segments

Frequency (MHz)	RG-59 Loss (dB)	RG-6 Loss (dB)	RG-11 Loss (dB)
5	0.7	0.5	0.3
30	1.5	1.2	0.7
50	2.0	1.5	0.9
100	2.7	2.2	1.3
200	3.8	3.1	1.8
300	4.5	3.6	2.3
400	5.1	4.2	2.6
500	5.7	4.7	2.9

Table 3.6
Coaxial Cable Specifications

Type	Impedance (Ω)	Center Conductor Diameter (AWG)
RG-6	75	18
RG-11	75	14
RG-58	50	14
RG-59	75	22

hence demonstrate less loss per unit length. The losses in the table are for 100 ft lengths at room temperature.

Four common, standard size coaxial cables are summarized in Table 3.6.

■ EXAMPLE 3.9

Using Table 3.5 and equation 3-13, find the attenuation for an RG-6 cable operating at 100 MHz. The cable run is 200 ft long. A handy equation for estimating what the cable loss would be at one frequency when it is known at another is equation 3-14. The ratio of cable attenuation at two frequencies is roughly equal to the square root of the ratio of their two frequencies. This equation is best used for cables of at least $\frac{1}{2}$ in. in diameter.

$$\text{loss} = (\text{attenuation})(\text{length})$$

$$\text{loss} = (2.2)\left(\frac{200}{100}\right) = 4.4 \text{ dB} \tag{3-13}$$

$$\frac{A_{f1}}{A_{f2}} = \sqrt{\frac{f_1}{f_2}} \tag{3-14}$$

where A_{f1} = attenuation at frequency 1
A_{f2} = attenuation at frequency 2
f_1 = frequency 1
f_2 = frequency 2

Before working an example using this relationship, it is important to note that one should always use the cable attenuation with frequency data that is closest to the frequency that is to be used.

■ EXAMPLE 3.10

A certain coaxial cable has an attenuation of 2.5 dB per 100 ft at a frequency of 500 MHz. You are wondering if you can use it to hook up your new piece of equipment that has a carrier frequency of 900 MHz. It is important that the loss not be more than 3 dB for the 75 ft run that you must make. Will the cable work?

$$\frac{A_{f1}}{A_{f2}} = \sqrt{\frac{f_1}{f_2}} \rightarrow \frac{2.5 \text{ dB}}{A_{f2}} = \sqrt{\frac{500 \text{ MHz}}{900 \text{ MHz}}}$$

$$A_{f2} = 2.5 \sqrt{\frac{900}{500}} \text{ dB} = 3.4 \text{ dB}$$

The attenuation is 3.4 dB, but that is for a 100 ft run; your application only requires a 75 ft run. Can that information be used to see if it might work? Because the loss is approximately linear with distance, it is possible to divide by the ratio of the two lengths to get an answer:

$$(3.4 \text{ dB}) \left(\frac{75 \text{ ft}}{100 \text{ ft}}\right) = 2.5 \text{ dB}$$

which is only 2.5 dB for the 75 ft run that is needed, so even though the signal experiences more loss, the cable run is short enough to still meet your specification of no more than 3 dB loss. Because this is only a rough calculation, it is important to check with the manufacturer of the cable to get a specification for loss at the new frequency. This approach gives an expectation of performance, with a good expectation of success.

■ TWISTED PAIR CABLE ATTENUATION WITH FREQUENCY

Just like coaxial cable, twisted pair cables attenuation, or loss, increases with increasing frequency. Because most modern communication systems are now installed using twisted pair cable, it is instructive to compare Table 3.7 with Table 3.5. Note specifically the lower range of frequencies specified and the significantly increased loss specification.

■ STANDING WAVES

The next thing to discuss in this chapter are standing waves and reflections: what they are how they are generated, and what effect they have. First, reflections generate the standing waves. Second, standing waves are not desirable. Standing waves are measured by SWR and VSWR.

Table 3.7
Twisted Pair Cable Loss with Frequency

Frequency (MHz)	Twisted Pair Loss (dB)
1	2.0
5	3.5
10	7.0
30	10.0
50	10.5

To understand how standing waves are generated by reflections, we will explore how reflections are generated. Think about what happens when a signal is injected into a metallic conductor and then extracted at the other end. The critical issues are the characteristic impedance of the cable, the source resistance (or impedance), and the load resistance (or impedance). If all these are identical, no reflections will be generated, and no standing waves will arise. If one or more of these differ, reflections and hence standing waves occur. Note that the impedance must be constant over the entire range of frequencies—the bandwidth—that are impressed onto the cable for no reflections to occur.

To see why these reflections occur when the impedance's are different, recall that all waves when they encounter a barrier either pass through it or are reflected from it. Think about your car. As visible light reaches your windows, it passes through; as it reaches your rear view mirror, it reflects. A waveform traveling down a cable does same, depending on whether it sees windows or mirrors. The "windowness" the electromagnetic wave sees is directly related to the impedance match. If it is exact, no reflection occurs, and the wave passes through easily. If it is a mirror and total reflection occurs, the standing wave generated is the opposite of the original waveform. This is called destructive interference. See Figure 3.8.

Of course, most of the time it is somewhere in between, as shown in the third case in Figure 3.8, where a portion of the original wave is reflected back and distorts the original wave. This reflected wave is called a standing wave. The analogy is that the better the impedance match, the more "windowlike" the interface is, and vice versa. These interfaces are always at the coupling of the source to the cable and the coupling of the cable to the load. Additional interfaces form wherever the characteristic impedance of the cable varies. It now becomes clear why crimps in cable are bad; they change the impedance at the crimp and generate an interface, which generates standing waves.

Another way of looking at this is to consider a coaxial line and imagine a wave as a voltage that travels down the line. If the center conductor is shorted to the shield ground, the wave is reflected back in the way shown in Figure 3.9.

If the line is shorted to ground at the point of reflection, the voltage must be zero at that point. Therefore, during the process of reflection, the voltage of the incident wave plus the voltage of the reflected wave must always be zero. Therefore, at every instant

Figure 3.8
Standing waves and reflections.

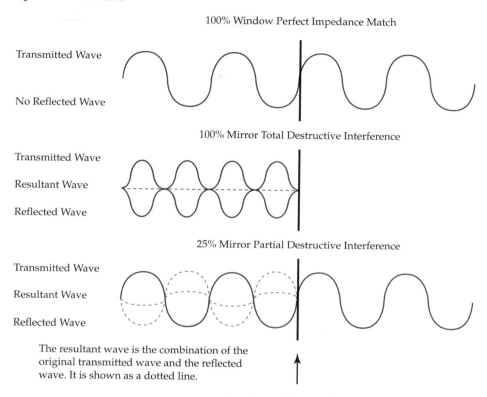

100% Window Perfect Impedance Match

Transmitted Wave

No Reflected Wave

100% Mirror Total Destructive Interference

Transmitted Wave

Resultant Wave

Reflected Wave

25% Mirror Partial Destructive Interference

Transmitted Wave

Resultant Wave

Reflected Wave

The resultant wave is the combination of the
original transmitted wave and the reflected
wave. It is shown as a dotted line.

Impedance Mismatch Location

of time during the process of reflection, the reflected wave must be the negative of the incident wave. If there is no voltage coming back toward the source, the interference is destructive and 100% effective.

If a resistor is placed between the two lines, and adjusted so that just exactly half of the voltage is reflected back, the interference is destructive and 50% effective, and so on. This is shown in the third part of Figure 3.9. If the resistance value is adjusted such that the resistor absorbs all the voltage, no energy is reflected back at all. This is an example of a perfect match.

Constructive interference is similar but exactly the opposite. If one could some-how reflect the wave back so that it adds to the voltage of the original wave, to the extent that it adds, constructive interference results. The net result is a net gain in volt-age. This is rarely the case unless it is specially provided for, and it never creates power. For our purposes, the reflections are always destructive to some extent. The ef-

Figure 3.9
Reflected wave diagram.

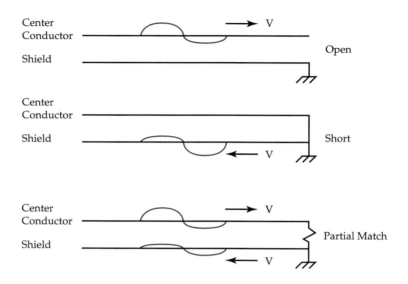

fect of standing waves is to lessen the power transfer from source to load. The extent is measured by the SWR. Again, to emphasize, reflections, when they are present, are always destructive.

The parameters SWR and VSWR describe this effect. They express the relative magnitude of the standing waves as a ratio to the desired waveforms impressed on the transmission line by the source. It can be expressed as a ratio of the net current flows produced by the two waves or the peak voltage of the two waves or by the ratio of the impedances at the interface. All are equivalent, and the standard practice of using the ratio of impedances will be used. This is shown in equation 3-15.

$$\text{SWR} = \frac{Z_{\text{larger}}}{Z_{\text{smaller}}} \tag{3-15}$$

It is important to understand that this is a shorthand way of expressing the real issue, which is power transfer. The term *VSWR* came from evaluating the peak voltage of each wave and using that definition instead of the impedance ratios. Both terms continue to be in use and mean the same thing. Additionally, another term is used to describe this ratio: *reflection coefficient*, represented by the symbol Γ. The reflection coefficient is defined by equation 3-16:

$$\text{SWR} = \frac{1 + \Gamma}{1 - \Gamma} \tag{3-16}$$

where Γ = reflection coefficient.
             For an ideal match, $\Gamma = 0$, SWR = 1.
             Worst case match, $\Gamma = 1$, SWR = ∞.
             Worst case match occurs for an open *or* short circuit.

The reflection coefficient is always expressed as a number between 0 and 1. SWR is always expressed as a number greater than 1. This means that the greater impedance will always be divided by the lower one. Ideal matching occurs at SWR = 1 and reflection coefficient = 0.

The reflection coefficient can also be expressed as a function of SWR, as can be seen from the algebra below:

$$\text{SWR} = \frac{1 + \Gamma}{1 - \Gamma} \rightarrow (1 - \Gamma)\text{SWR} = 1 + \Gamma \rightarrow \Gamma(1 + \text{SWR}) = \text{SWR} - 1$$

$$\Gamma = \frac{\text{SWR} - 1}{\text{SWR} + 1}$$

(3-17)

It is instructive to explore some limits for both variables. For a short circuit,

$$\text{SWR} = \frac{Z_{\text{source}}}{0} = \infty \; \Gamma = \frac{\infty - 1}{\infty + 1} = 1$$

For an open circuit,

$$\text{SWR} = \frac{\infty}{Z_{\text{source}}} = \infty \; \Gamma = \frac{\infty - 1}{\infty + 1} = 1$$

In a short circuit, the load is grounded, so the load impedance is 0. For any source impedance, a short circuit load implies a SWR = ∞ and $\Gamma = 1$. In an open circuit, the load is not connected and the load impedance to ground is infinity. Here again, SWR = ∞ and $\Gamma = 1$. Recall that SWR is always defined as a number greater than 1, so whichever impedance is greater is always placed in the numerator.

The value of the reflection coefficient tells directly what the voltage of the reflected wave is compared to the transmitted wave. For example, $\Gamma = 0.5$ says that the voltage of the reflected wave is exactly 50%, or one-half, of the transmitted wave voltage. Because P is proportional to voltage squared, for $\Gamma = 0.5$, the power transfer is reduced by a factor of 4, or 25%, of the power is reflected power. Check Table 3.8 and examine the algebra shown in equation 3-18:

$$P_i = \frac{V^2}{R} \qquad P_r = \frac{(V/2)^2}{R} = \frac{V^2/4}{R} = \frac{V^2}{4R}$$

(3-18)

Good design always keep the SWR less than 1.5, which implies that the reflected power is only about 4% and 96% of the power is transmitted. Virtually all designs keep it below 2, where the reflected power is about 10%, meaning that only 90% of the trans-

Table 3.8
SWR and Power Transmitted

SWR	SWR (dB)	Return Loss (dB)	Transmit Loss (dB)	Voltage Reflection Coefficient	Power Transmitted (%)	Power Reflected (%)
1.00	.0	∞	.000	.0	100.0	.0
1.05	.4	32.3	.003	.02	99.9	.1
1.10	.8	26.4	.010	.05	99.8	.2
1.15	1.2	23.1	.021	.07	99.5	.5
1.20	1.6	20.8	.036	.09	99.2	.8
1.25	1.9	19.1	.054	.11	98.8	1.2
1.30	2.3	17.7	.075	.13	98.3	1.7
1.40	2.9	15.6	.122	.17	97.2	2.8
1.50	3.5	14.0	.177	.20	96.0	4.0
1.60	4.1	12.7	.238	.23	94.7	5.3
1.70	4.6	11.7	.302	.26	93.3	6.7
1.80	5.1	10.9	.370	.29	91.8	8.2
1.90	5.6	10.2	.440	.31	90.4	9.6
2.00	6.0	9.5	.512	.33	88.9	11.1
2.50	8.0	7.4	.881	.43	81.6	18.4
3.00	9.5	6.0	1.249	.50	75.0	25.0
4.00	12.0	4.4	1.938	.60	64.0	36.0
5.00	14.0	3.5	2.553	.67	55.6	44.4
6.00	15.6	2.9	3.100	.71	49.0	51.0
10.00	30.0	1.7	4.807	.82	33.1	66.9

mitted power gets through. If the design is throwing away 10% of the generated power, it better have a good reason for doing so. Presumably, it cost money to produce that power and once money is spent producing something, it does not make good economic sense to throw a useful part of it away. The only situation where this rule is violated is when more cost is saved somewhere else in the design or system because of this trade-off.

Generally, it is desirable to keep the SWR as close to 1 as possible, with 1.2 as a realistic goal. Then only about 1% of the power is reflected back to the source. This issue is just one more variable that is traded off in the design process. Table 3.8 summarizes the effect of SWR on transmitted power in the various ways of expressing this concept.

■ **EXAMPLE 3.11**

Determine the SWR for a source impedance of 50 Ω and a load impedance of 100 Ω:

$$\text{SWR} = \frac{Z_{\text{larger}}}{Z_{\text{smaller}}} = \frac{100}{50} = 2$$

■ EXAMPLE 3.12

Determine Γ and the SWR for an incident voltage of 2 V and a reflected voltage of 0.5 V. Here, an alternate definition of the reflection coefficient is used; both are equivalent.

$$\Gamma = \frac{E_{\text{reflected}}}{E_{\text{incident}}} \qquad\qquad\qquad (3\text{-}19)$$

$$\Gamma = \frac{0.5}{2.0} = 0.25 \rightarrow \text{SWR} = \frac{1 + \Gamma}{1 - \Gamma} = \frac{1.25}{0.75} = 1.67$$

■ EXAMPLE 3.13

Calculate the SWR effect of Example 3.5 of a crimped cable.

$$\text{SWR} = \frac{Z_{\text{larger}}}{Z_{\text{smaller}}} = \frac{68.2}{46.5} = 1.47$$

As can be seen by referring to Table 3.8, this crimp resulted in almost 4% of the power being reflected back to the source.

■ WIRING STANDARDS

The EIA has standardized several types of cable for wiring in commercial buildings. This standardization was driven by the fact that often buildings are built and wired before the users define their needs for cabling. Standard EIA-568 was written to ensure support for a wide variety of applications, devices, and vendor products. This standard is a nonproprietary, flexible wiring scheme that has proved its usefulness for both new building constructions and renovations by allowing a standard, or universal, cabling system to be installed prior to occupancy. The EIA-568 standard covers six categories of unshielded twisted pair (UTP) cable types currently manufactured. All these cables feature a 100 Ω impedance.

Category 1
Category 1 cables are not strictly covered by the standard, but it does provide a placeholder so that these cables can be talked about in the same context as the rest. They typically were installed before the existence of the standard and are for the most part old copper pair telephone wiring, sometimes more than 50 years old. Cables this old are very susceptible to interference due to the insulation breakdown over time. Older cables, installed before plastics became available, were insulated with paper, cord, or rubber. These materials do not have long lives. If they are being used today, it is most likely for voice and very low-speed data communications, typically under 2400 bps. Needless to say, this cabling should not be installed today.

Category 2

Category 2 is slightly better but is still beneath the standard's minimum level of acceptance. These cables are also typically left over from copper pair telephone wiring but were more recently installed than those of category 1. They may have been installed as late as the middle 1980s. These cables meet the old standard, IBM Type 3 specification GA27-3773-1, developed to refer to cables meeting the requirements for the original IEEE 802.5 Token Ring networks operating at speeds up to 4 Mbps. Again, do not install this type of cabling today.

Category 3

Category 3 was established to accommodate the requirements of two popular networking protocols, IEEE 802.5 Token Ring UTP networks operating at speeds up to 16 Mbps and IEEE 802.3 10Base-T operating at 10 Mbps. It can be used for any voice or data transmission rate up to 16 Mbps. Four-pair cable of this type can be used in 100Base-T-type networks at data transmission rates of up to 100 Mbps, although it is recommended that Category 5 cable be installed for any new installation.

Category 4

Category 4 was established to accommodate cable characteristics that allow data transmission rates of up to 20 Mbps. Again, four-pair cable of this type can be used in 100Base-T-type networks at data transmission rates of up to 100 Mbps, although it is recommended that Category 5 cable be installed for any new installation.

Category 5

For any new installation, category 5 cable should be the cable installed. This cable is specified to operate at speeds of up to 100 Mbps. However, modern termination techniques can now allow operation at speeds exceeding 500 Mbps. Category 5 cable is an unshielded twisted pair (UTP) cable consisting of four twisted pairs for a total of eight wires. This cable is often referred to as CAT5 or CAT5 UTP cable.

The individual wires may be a single conductor or a bundle of strands. This distinction is referred to as CAT5 solid or CAT5 flex. If both are used in a single installation, the solid conductor cable is used for all backbone applications and any passages through walls and ceilings. The stranded or flex cable is used for the patch and drop cables, those cables that connect directly between the hubs and patch panels and those that connect directly to the user computers, respectively.

As stated, CAT5 cables are typically shipped with four pairs; however, only two pair, 2 and 3, are intended to be used for connectivity. The other pairs are reserved for spares. The pairs can be identified by color. The EIA has standardized the color code as follows:

Pair 1	Blue/white stripe and blue
Pair 2	Orange/white stripe and orange
Pair 3	Green/white stripe and green
Pair 4	Brown/white stripe and brown

Not all manufacturers follow this guideline. It is usually best to pick a standard and stay with it for any installation; if this is the case, make sure that the cable that is ordered follows EIA/TIA-568B wiring standard. The most common application for this wiring is 10/100 Base-T networks using RJ-45 connectors. For the specific wiring pinout, see the section describing that connector.

Enhanced Category 5

Enhanced category 5 cables are specified up to 250 Mbps. They have more critical requirements than category 5 cables. Although the specification indicates that these cables can be used up to 350 Mbps, due to signal-to-noise concerns with connectors, they are specified for safe transmission only up to 250 Mbps. All enhanced category 5 cables feature individually shielded twisted pairs, a very effective shielding technique and overkill for most applications. There are three different shielding options for this type of cable, with decreasing degrees of effectiveness: overall double foil shielding, overall foil shielding, and individual foil shields.

■ PLENUM CABLE

When discussing cable installations, installers often refer to plenum and nonplenum cables. In newer buildings the air ducts are not the traditional metal rectangles often depicted in movies. Typically the hero must find a secret way from one room to another and "discovers" the air ducts, thereby thwarting the evil villain and rescuing the fair maiden. In modern buildings the ceiling is actually used to control the airflow in the building. Such ceilings are referred to as plenum ceilings.

Because the airflow is not contained in a fire resistant rectangle, a dangerous situation can occur if a fire starts in the building. Virtually all non-plenum cables use PVC sheathing for the outside insulator. This material is very toxic if ignited. Because cables are often routed through the air ducts, whatever their construction, a hazardous condition can arise with PVC jacketed cables. If the air system in a fire emergency suddenly starts routing toxic chemicals around the building, not only do you have to be careful not to get burned, you also have to worry about breathing. As you can imagine, fire departments are very concerned about this. After all, firefighters will most likely be breathing the air in a burning building.

This situation explains why there are special plenum cables. A plenum cable is any cable that does not use PVC material for the insulating jacket. Typically, the material used for plenum cables is Teflon. Because Teflon is not toxic when burned, those cables can be used to route signals through the air ducts. Nonplenum cables are used everywhere else because plenum cables are much more expensive. A nonplenum cable is any cable that uses PVC coating as its outside jacket. Virtually all cables are available with either plenum or nonplenum coatings.

■ CABLE SYSTEM STRUCTURE

Before discussing cable system structure in a building, in the section below, we will define that several terms pertain to LAN-specific hardware components. These components are described in detail in Chapter 15.

When discussing how to lay out the cable structure inside a building, three logical areas are used:

1. Backbone cabling structure
2. Horizontal cabling structure
3. Wiring closet

The backbone cabling structure connects the wiring closets and equipment rooms. It functions as the main and intermediate cross connects between primary subnetworks or buildings in a campus environment. Today, these are typically installed with four-pair category 5 cable. The recommended maximum length between repeaters is 500 m. If a piece of equipment is to be connected directly to the backbone cable without going through a wiring closet, the recommended maximum length of the cable is 30 m.

The horizontal cabling structure connects the wiring closets and the work areas. It functions to connect the large number of users to a central point, the wiring closet. The topology of horizontal cabling should always be a star. That means that each user is connected to a wiring closet. The wiring closet acts like a central hub for each user in a particular area. These are typically installed with four-pair category 5 cable. The maximum recommended length between repeaters is 90 m.

The wiring closet is the location in each work area where all local cables that connect each user are terminated and are connected to the backbone. It is either just a wiring closet or, more typically, both a wiring closet and equipment room. These areas are shown in Figure 3.10.

Figure 3.10
Cable system structure.

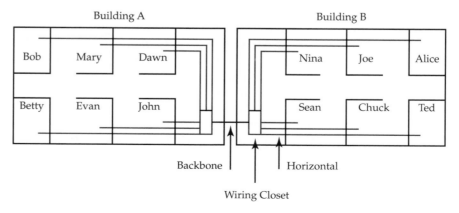

■ TROUBLESHOOTING WITH A TIME DOMAIN REFLECTOMETER

One of the basic instruments that is used to qualify and locate cable faults in a LAN environment is the TDR which is a handheld device about the same size as a sophisticated graphical calculator. Usually, a TDR is made to qualify one or more of the category, or CAT, types listed above. It is relatively inexpensive as test equipment goes and does a good job of ensuring that the physical cable system is clean, or if it is not, of identifying where the problem lies. In general, it is a good, basic troubleshooting tool.

A TDR works by connecting to the cable system at any port, and it generates a fast rise time pulse that is injected into the cable plant. This pulse travels along the cable until it finds an impedance mismatch, where some percentage of the signal is reflected back. The instrument essentially looks for impedance mismatches and reports the location of any it finds as cable faults.

These cable faults can arise from many sources, such as opens, shorts, kinks, bad terminations, knotted cable, and rodent damage. A TDR will only indicate the first fault it finds; if there are other faults farther from the injection point, they will sometimes be masked by the first fault encountered. Therefore, always recheck the cable after fixing any fault located.

To see how these devices work, examine the equations that a TDR uses to calculate the fault location. The signal travels along the cable until a portion of it is reflected back to the device. Therefore, the pulse takes the time to travel to the fault and then back again. The location of the fault is found by measuring the time it takes for the pulse to arrive back at the TDR using the following formula, which is just a version of the old reliable, distance equals rate times time.

$$D = \frac{v_p t}{2} = \frac{v_f c t}{2} \qquad \text{(3-20)}$$

where $\quad D$ = distance to fault
$\quad\quad t$ = elapsed time or propagation delay
$\quad\quad v_p$ = velocity of propagation
$\quad\quad v_f$ = velocity factor

Note that the time is divided by 2 to account for the travel to and from the fault location. The material of the conductor determines the velocity, what is called the velocity of propagation. As you know from the discussion on electromagnetic signals in Chapter 2, every material has its own characteristic velocity of propagation. Recall that the velocity in the above equation is determined by multiplying the appropriate velocity factor by the speed of light.

With any waveform traveling at a fixed velocity, there will be some elapsed time between when it enters one end of the cable and when it comes out the other. This elapsed time is called the propagation delay. As shown below, it can be determined from the velocity of propagation and the distance to the fault location.

$$D = \frac{v_f c t}{2} \rightarrow t = \frac{2D}{v_f c} = \frac{2D}{v_p} \qquad \text{(3-21)}$$

With the relationship in equations 3-20 or 3-21, it is straightforward to calculate the location of a fault caused by an impedance mismatch if you know the elapsed time and the material of the conductor in the cable. The accuracy of such a device depends strongly on how accurately you can measure the elapsed time for the pulse to travel to the fault and return. Typical accuracies for these types of devices are about 4%. This number will break down for faults located too close to where the TDR is attached to the network. Usually, if the fault is at least 20 m away, the accuracy holds up; if it is closer, the accuracy goes down dramatically and at close distances, unless special very short rise time pulses are used, under 2 ns, the meter is not at all accurate. This illustrates an important point when using this type of gear: If a reading for a fault location is indicated to be less than 20 m away unless you are using a specialized TDR with very short rise time pulses, do not trust it. Find another port to attach the TDR to that is farther away and perform the measurement again. Follow the old adage, measure twice and cut once.

One other important limitation of these devices is that if the fault is too far away from the location of the TDR, it might not find it at all. This is because at long distances, the attenuation of the cable reduces the signal strength too much to accurately determine which is the signal and which is the reflection. The best approach is to measure at several points in a large network. Use the rule of thumb that you need to measure at least once every 250 m. Check the manufacturer's data sheet on the particular device you have for exact performance specifications.

■ EXAMPLE 3.14

Use a TDR to determine the location of an impedance mismatch in a cable plant. The TDR measures an elapsed time of 1.5 μsec when it is applied. What is the distance to the fault? Assume the cable has a velocity factor of 0.85.

$$D = \frac{v_f ct}{2} = \frac{(0.85)(3 \times 10^8)(1.5 \times 10^{-6})}{2} = 191.25 \text{ m}$$

Because the value obtained for the distance to the fault is more than 20 m and less than 250 m, it should be considered a reliable value and no further readings are required. Although a numerical answer is shown above, it is doubtful that the fault location is known that precisely. A more probable estimate is that the fault is somewhere about 190 m away plus or minus a couple of meters.

■ SINGLE-ENDED AND DIFFERENTIAL SIGNALING

The distinction between two methods of sending signals from one point to another is fundamental, and virtually all communication interfaces use one or the other method. For example, the various specifications for the 232 standard and its relatives categorize each interface circuit by this distinction. Sometimes the words *balanced* and *unbalanced* are used instead of differential and single-ended to describe these two techniques. *Balanced* and *unbalanced* are probably technically more correct and avoid a confusion between the types of devices used to implement the circuits and the general term describ-

Figure 3.11
Unbalanced connection.

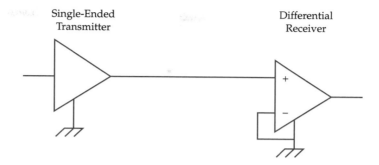

ing them. Therefore, these will be used to classify these two approaches. Because the unbalanced method is less sophisticated, it will be explored first.

■ UNBALANCED CIRCUITS

An unbalanced circuit is a circuit that uses a single line to send the information from source to destination, and the ground for the transmitter and receiver is common and shared. Most circuit connections made in the laboratory are unbalanced. See Figure 3.11.

Unbalanced circuits have the advantage of only requiring a signal line for each signal, and only one ground line is required no matter how many signals are grouped into one connector. Traditionally, these advantages have outweighed the performance disadvantage of a shared ground. This is still true today for short runs of moderate speeds, but as the length and speed requirements increase, balanced circuits become a requirement. Virtually all coaxial lines are unbalanced.

The primary disadvantage of a single, and hence shared, ground line is that because the ground wire does not follow the same physical path as the signal line, common mode noise cannot be reduced through the use of differential amplification.

■ BALANCED CIRCUITS

A balanced circuit is a circuit that uses two lines to send the information from source to destination. The first carries the signal and the second is a dedicated ground wire for that signal. The ground is isolated from other grounds and is not shared. Additionally, it is not connected to the common or system ground. It is a dedicated ground wire for the signal.

Usually, when a balanced circuit is implemented, the two lines are twisted around each other. The dedicated ground line is then used to send the same signal as the signal line but of opposite polarity, for example, Q and Q-bar of the output of a flip-flop device. This allows for much greater noise immunity; therefore signals can be sent farther and faster than in the unbalanced case. Of course, the cost is that two lines are run for each signal, and the transmit section of the circuit is a little more complex. See Figure 3.12.

Figure 3.12
Balanced connection.

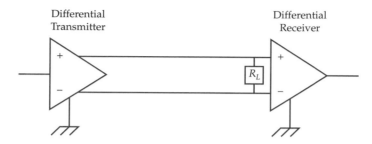

Traditionally, most interface circuits have been designated as unbalanced; the speeds and distances required did not force the use of balanced designs. However, in the last 10 years there has been an explosion in speed and distance requirements for interfaces, and therefore most interfaces used in modern communication systems are balanced. For example, RS-232 is an unbalanced interface, RS-449 is a balanced interface. RS-449 uses twisted pair wiring; RS-232 does not. A specialized transformer that is used to connect balanced configurations to unbalanced ones is discussed in the section, "Balans," later in the chapter.

■ NOISE REDUCTION THROUGH THE USE OF BALANCED CONFIGURATION

It is of interest to investigate just how much performance improvement is obtained by using balanced circuits. The primary disadvantage of a shared ground is that the signal currents running on it are a concatenation of many different noise sources. A balanced configuration where the dedicated ground follows the same path as the signal circuit means that the currents flowing on the dedicated ground are due to the noise environment of the path and only the path. Further, the noise currents on the ground will be the same as on the signal circuit. These signals are shown in Figure 3.13. The signal is shown as S, and the noise is shown as N.

Figure 3.13
Balanced configuration showing noise reduction.

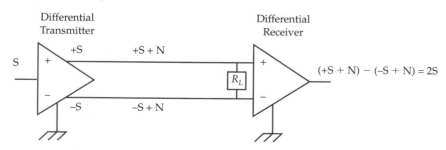

As can be seen, the signal is applied to the input of the transmitter, and during the time of transmission between source and destination, noise is added to both lines in equal amounts. At the receiver, the differential amplifier substracts the dedicated ground line from the signal line. This results in a doubling of the signal component and very effectively removes any noise contributed by the path. Very often this technique is used instead of shielding to provide effective noise reduction.

■ ATTENUATOR

This section will introduce an approach that is sometimes useful in minimizing SWR in circuits. An attenuator is a simple resistive network that places a known loss between two impedances, Z_1 and Z_2. The nice thing about the approach that will be discussed here is that the input and output impedances of the attenuator are matched to the impedances Z_1 and Z_2. This means that any reflections that would be generated are attenuated before they can propagate. Table 3.9 is useful for choosing the correct resistance values of the classic unbalanced π network that is used to match Z_1 to Z_2. See Figure 3.14.

Table 3.9 summarizes resistance values sorted by the attenuation in decibels needed to get the SWR ratio low enough to match the input to the output. Although this technique always introduces a net power loss, it is very helpful in improving the overall performance of a communications system. For example, when demodulating a signal, it is important that the input impedance of the demodulator match the characteristic impedance of the communications channel and that the output impedance of the modulator matches as well.

Table 3-9
Resistance Values

Attenuation (dB)	R_1 (Ω)	R_2 (Ω)
0.5	3.3	2200
1.0	4.7	820
2.0	10	430
3.0	18	300
4.0	22	220
5.0	30	180
6.0	36	150
7.0	43	130
8.0	51	110
9.0	62	110
10.0	68	91
12.0	91	82
20.0	240	62

Figure 3.14
The π attenuator schematic.

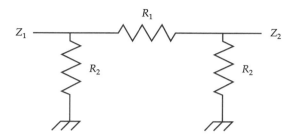

Note that the resistance values shown in Table 3.9 are not those exactly calculated. They instead represent standard resistance values, which were substituted in the table for the precisely calculated numbers. This makes the table immediately useful, if not quite so precise.

■ EXAMPLE 3.15

This example shows how to use Table 3.9 to reduce SWR at the cost of attenuating some power output to get improved matching. In this example, the SWR match is required to be no greater than 1.2. Design a resistor network to accomplish this and evaluate the power loss required:

$$Z_{in} = 100 \ \Omega, Z_{out} = 50 \ \Omega \qquad \text{SWR} = \frac{100}{50} = 2.0$$

The goal is to set the SWR = 1.2, so enough power must be attenuated to accomplish this. The required power reduction in decibels is given by the ratio of the two SWR values:

$$\text{attenuation needed} = \frac{\text{SWR}_{actual}}{\text{SWR}_{required}}$$

(3-22)

$$\text{attenuation needed} = \frac{2.0}{1.2} = 1.66 \ \text{dB}$$

Because the closest values from Table 3-9 are for a power attenuation of 2.0, choose that resistor network. To calculate the power penalty, remember that the original power loss was 0.512 dB because the SWR = 2.0 (this value can be taken directly from Table 3-4). Therefore, the net power loss with this added resistor network inserted is given by

$$2.0 - 0.512 = 1.488 \ \text{dB}$$

Note that this number agrees closely to the value calculated above by taking the ratio of the SWR values. Usually the actual value is somewhere in between these two calculations, depending on how closely the resistor values match, and so forth. Either calculation will serve as a first approximation and can be refined if more precise measurements are necessary.

MATCHING USING TRANSFORMERS

There are two primary ways to match impedances using the principle of mutual inductance, exemplified by the transformer. A transformer, because the mutual inductance of both coils that make up a transformer is always the same regardless of the individual inductance of either, has a unique ability to match impedances in a circuit. See Figure 3.15.

It is straightforward to determine the correct winding for the impedance match that is desired. Because the number of turns of wire defines the impedance of each individual coil, this is used to set the individual inductance in the correct ratio defined in equation 3-15:

$$\frac{Z_s}{Z_l} = \left(\frac{N_p}{N_s}\right)^2 \tag{3-23}$$

where Z_s = source impedance
Z_l = load impedance
N_p = number of turns for primary coil
N_s = number of turns for secondary coil

Here the general way of talking about the two coils is primary and secondary. In traditional usage either coil may have more turns. Then the type of transformer was defined as step-down if the primary coil had the most turns and step-up if the secondary had more turns. These terms have no real applicability for the transformers used to impedance match. They are used primarily to describe transformers for alternating current voltage shifts.

Figure 3.15
Mutual inductance.

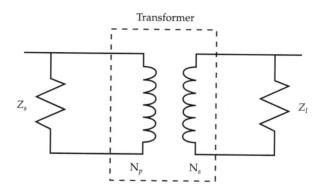

Transformer

For most frequencies of interest to communications, impedance matching transformers have only a few turns of wire on each coil. Only at audio frequencies will the number of turns on each coil reach significant numbers.

■ EXAMPLE 3.16

Find the ratio of coils needed to match a 50 Ω source to a 75 Ω load:

$$\frac{Z_s}{Z_l} = \left(\frac{N_p}{N_s}\right)^2 = \frac{50}{75} = \left(\frac{N_p}{N_s}\right)^2$$

$$\frac{N_p}{N_s} = \sqrt{0.667} \rightarrow N_p = 0.82N_s$$

Therefore, the ratio of turns is 82%. Stated in another way, for every 82 turns of primary winding, 100 turns must be applied to the secondary. Usually, the core type has little effect on the performance of matching transformers at frequencies above 1 MHz. Theoretically, iron coil transformers are said to perform better due to the better mutual inductance tracking. On the other hand, air core impedance matching transformers are widely used in high frequency design and perform well.

■ BALUNS

Baluns are specialized transformers used to impedance match a balanced load to an unbalanced source or vice versa. The name *balun* comes from concatenating the terms *balanced* and *un*balanced. This application requires specialized connections for the individual coils that make up the transformer, or in this case, the balun.

A balun can be manufactured for any ratio of impedance, but the vast majority of the connectorized devices are for use with Token Ring LAN systems. In this application the balun is used to convert the BNC coaxial connector to a twisted pair connector, such as a telephone-type plug. In fact, it is not the Token Ring LAN that drives this but the types of devices that it was originally designed to interconnect. Those devices were IBM 3270-type terminals, probably the most widely placed terminal, and required a coaxial connection. The Token Ring standard actually specified a balun for use with 3270-type terminals to connect to the dual twisted pair LAN media. These are widely sold and for most constitute the definition of a balun.

As mentioned above, the connection of the individual coils is a little different in a balun. This is shown in Figure 3.16. The configuration shown is for converting a balanced source to an unbalanced load. Balans always have the same number of primary and secondary windings. Because of the way they are manufactured, a balun also features very wide bandwidths. This feature can be a critical advantage because high data rate communication systems are often wide bandwidth.

A balun is typically manufactured on a toroid, which is a specialized piece of powdered iron that is shaped like a donut. The primary and secondary windings are both wound on this donut, typically on opposite sides and in opposite phasing. In Figure

Figure 3.16
Balun wiring.

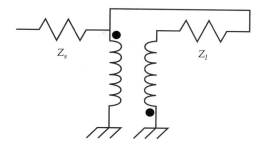

3.16, the unbalanced load is assumed to have the higher impedance. The dots represent the phasing of the windings.

CONNECTORS

All connectors are divided into two groups, plugs, or male, and jacks, or female. As simple as this seems, this naming terminology is only followed occasionally. Perhaps because it is so simple, some people never bother following the rule. This is more common than one might think. For example, most people refer to the RJ-14 plug, perhaps the most common connector in the world, as either a plug or jack, seemingly at whim. In this section the rule mentioned above will be strictly followed for clarity. Once you get into the workplace, you can be as casual as you want.

COAXIAL CONNECTORS

F-Connector
The F-connector is the cheapest coaxial connector available. See Figure 3.17. This is the connector that you see on the back of your television and VCR. It is the connector that, if you have cable TV, finishes the end of the cable coming into your home. Although available in a form with a dedicated center pin, most connectors in the field are crimped-on cable plugs with the center connector formed of the solid wire center conductor of the coaxial cable. The shield of the coaxial cable is not mechanically attached to the cable plug in any permanent way; it is just crimped to the outside of the cable plug. The F-connector uses a threaded mechanical attachment to couple the plug to the mating jack. It is usable at frequencies up to the low UHF range, about 500 MHz.

RCA Plug and Jack
Another very inexpensive connector is the old standby, the RCA plug and jack. See Figure 3.18. This connector can be found on the back of any audio equipment you might have. It is commonly used to connect the phonograph or CD audio channels from the

Figure 3.17
F-connector plug and jack.

phone/CD unit to the amplifier. This connector has been in use for at least 50 years on a wide variety of equipment. It is invariably only offered in a molded form. This means that the connector is permanently attached to the cable and is then "dipped" in a moldable material to form the physical connection between the wire and connector.

The plug uses a dedicated center pin and a nice shield arrangement that mates with the female jack. The shield is a sort of slotted cylinder that slides over the solid conducting outer ring of the mating jack. It is usable up to the low VHF range, about 100 MHz.

BNC Connector

The BNC connector is probably the most popular connector that is used in laboratory equipment of all kinds including oscilloscopes, signal generators, spectrum analyzers, frequency counters, frequency synthesizers, and so forth. See Figure 3.19. The BNC connector is fairly inexpensive and quite good. Most BNC connectors have the connections to the coaxial cable soldered on, which gives a better impedance match than does a crimp. The BNC connector features a dedicated center pin that is attached to the center conductor of the coaxial cable.

The physical attachment of the BNC plug to the jack is done with a bayonet-type lock. That is, the plug is inserted into the jack and then rotated and locked onto a small pin located on the outside of the mating jack's outer shield solid conducting ring. BNC connectors are supposed to always be user accessible, never molded, which is usually true. This connector pair is usable up to the mid-UHF range, about 1 GHz.

Figure 3.18
RCA plug and jack.

Figure 3.19
BNC plug and jack.

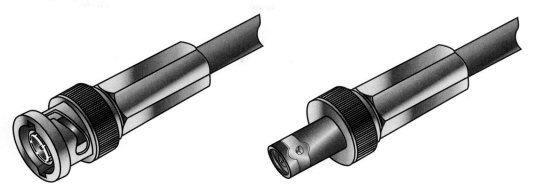

SMA Connector

The SMA connector is a fairly expensive connector that is very small. See Figure 3.20. It is used in a variety of applications where either the cable diameter is too small for BNC connectors or where space is at a premium and performance is important. The diameter of an SMA connector is about half that of the BNC connector. It is not unusual to find SMA and BNC connectors used interchangeably. Like most BNC connectors, SMA connectors are never molded onto a coaxial cable; they are always soldered. They use a dedicated center pin attached to the center conductor of the coaxial cable. The SMA connector uses a threaded physical attachment to connect the plug to the mating jack. SMA connectors can be used throughout the UHF range up to about 3 GHz.

The SMA connector has a specific torque specification that must be followed for optimum attachment. There is a special torque wrench available for tightening SMA connections. If you use SMA connectors at all frequently, acquire one of these; it will pay for itself very quickly by eliminating damaged connectors.

The BNC, RCA, and SMA connectors are widely used and their application areas overlap, so there are a wide variety of mating connectors designed to convert from one connector type to another or to flip the gender of the connector, etc. Nine of the more

Figure 3.20
SMA plug and jack.

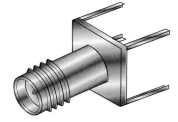

popular ones are shown in Figure 3.21, and they are listed in Table 3.10. In Figure 3.21, they are shown from left to right, top to bottom. Any female-to-female connector is also referred to as a "barrel connector" due to the cylindrical, or barrel, shape; look at connector converter numbers 3 and 8. There doesn't seem to be a commonly used name for

Figure 3.21
Nine connector converter types.

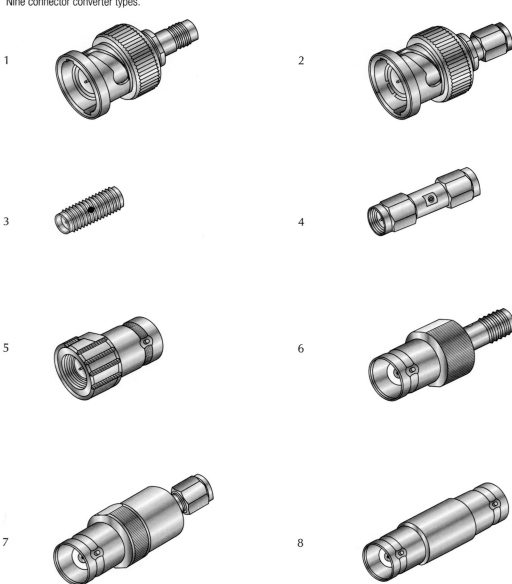

1

2

3

4

5

6

7

8

Table 3.10
Connector Converters

Connector Converter	To/From	From/To
1	Female SMA	Male BNC
2	Male SMA	Male BNC
3	Female SMA	Female SMA
4	Male SMA	Male SMA
5	Male SMA	Female BNC
6	Female SMA	Female BNC
7	Male SMA	Female BNC
8	Female BNC	Female BNC
9	Male RCA	Female BNC

a male-to-male connector such numbers 2 and 4. Finally, note the two styles of male SMA to female BNC, numbers 5 and 7.

N-Connector

The last coaxial cable connector considered here is the N-connector. The N-connector is the most expensive connector in this group. It is physically larger than any of the other connectors, about twice the diameter of a BNC connector. This connector is used on expensive laboratory equipment designed to operate in the UHF and lower SHF frequency bands. Because it is the largest connector, sometimes it is used at lower frequencies when the coaxial cable is of large diameter. The N-connector is always soldered and uses a dedicated center pin and a sophisticated ground connection in which the shield extends beyond the center pin, offering superior shielding. The physical mating between plug and jack is a screw thread. Unlike the other screw thread connectors, this is not designed to be torqued down with a tool, such as a wrench. It is a delicate connection for high-performance applications.

There are many other types of coaxial connectors available that were not considered here; some that may be of interest include the so-called UHF connector, SMB, SMC, T-connectors, and so forth.

Amphenol Connector

Amphenol is a company that manufactures a lot of connectors. Just like tissues are often called Kleenex and a copying machine is often called a Xerox, a certain connector is called an Amphenol connector. See Figure 3.22. The Amphenol connector is a 50 pin connector used for connecting to many communications devices. The 50 pin connector is ideal for carrying 24 pairs of wires. Twenty-four is a nice number because it is also the number of TDM DS-0 channels in a DS-1 or T-1 line. The Amphenol connector is widely adapted as a de facto standard in the telecommunications field.

It is an oblong-shaped connector that bears a slight resemblance to the old Centronics printer connector. Of course, just as tissues are available from other manufactur-

Figure 3.22
Amphenol connector.

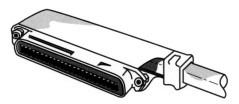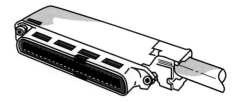

ers than Kleenex, the so-called Amphenol connector is available from other sources as well. It is still referred to as an Amphenol connector. It has become such a standard that the FCC decided to standardize it and give it an official RJ number: RJ-21X. Everyone still calls it an Amphenol connector; ask for a RJ-21X and many in the field will look at you in a puzzled fashion, but if you call it an Amphenol connector, most will know immediately what you mean.

■ TELEPHONE-STYLE CONNECTORS

The FCC has standardized a number of connectors for use in the telecommunications field. Each one is named the same way. There is a RJ prefix and then some combination of numbers and letters. The RJ prefix stands for Registered Jack. This naming probably contributes to the fuzziness of talking about these as jack and plug. Again, the standard terminology is that the male unit is a jack and the female unit is the plug.

The names that will be used in this section are the commonly used names. Actually, there are only three basic types, four, six, and eight pin. The six and eight pin types are also available in a keyed form.

RJ-11

The RJ-11 is the modular plug that is used to connect your telephone to the wall socket. It is a six pin connector that is typically only wired with four lines. The wires that are used in this connector are color coded for function. They are composed of two pairs of wires, red and green and black and white. The red and green pair carry the communications over the connector. The red and green pair are wired to the center pair of the six wire connector. The connector is designed to make a single connection only. This pair of wires is where the need is to be sure the connection is good when debugging potentially bad connections. These are the wires that were traditionally called tip and ring when the operators still connected calls by hand.

The black and white pair was traditionally used to carry low-voltage power for office phone installations. Today, often these will not be wired and the six wire connector will have only two lines wired.

RJ-11s are used for both voice and data communications. That means that they will be used for three widely installed systems, for standard telephone connections, as jacks into modern plugs, as on a card in your PC, and as jacks into LAN plugs to connect the Ethernet transceiver LAN card in your PC to the LAN.

RJ-14

The RJ-14 connector looks exactly like the RJ-11 except for how it is wired. It also is a six pin connector. Where the RJ-11 was designed for a single connection, the RJ-14 is designed for two connections. This means that it will require four wires, if wired for two connections. The center pair of lines in the connector is wired with red and green wires, just like the RJ-11. This pair carries one connection. The outer pair, pins 1 and 6, are wired with black and yellow wires and carry the second connection. Pins 2 and 5 are left unconnected.

Because the RJ-14 connector is a superset of the RJ-11 as typically wired, RJ-14s can be used to substitute for RJ-11s. You just do not use the outside pair, or second connection. Although this is possible in an emergency, it is not recommended due to the increased cost that results from running four wires when only two are needed.

RJ-22

The RJ-22 is the miniaturized version of the RJ-11 connector. The connector uses four pins, which are always wired. This connector can be seen in the cables that connect the telephone handset to the telephone base. These connectors are not used elsewhere or ever wired differently. The only exception to that rule is where the connection is not designed to be user accessible and the jack and plug combination was selected for cost or miniaturization reasons.

RJ-45

The RJ-45 connector has eight pins. This connector is widely used for two primary purposes. The first is for standard low-speed data applications such as connecting a DTE device to a DCE device. When used for this purpose, it is generally wired with a flat greenish cable where the wires in the cable are laid out in parallel fashion, like a ribbon cable. Such a wiring arrangement limits the maximum data rate that such a cable can effectively pass. A good rule of thumb is to not use such lines for data rates over 64 kbps or DS-0 rates.

The second use of this connector is for connection to a LAN system. The very popular networking standard 10/100BaseT is widely adapted and uses this connector. It is usually easy to identify when the cable is designated for LAN applications. Instead of a flat cable with a greenish coating on the wire, it is circular in shape and arbitrary in color. When used for LAN applications, the wiring is typically CAT5 and the pin assignments are as follows:

Pin 1   Orange/white striped

Pin 2   Orange

Pin 3   Green/white striped

Pin 4   Blue

Pin 5   Blue/white striped

Pin 6   Green

Pin 7   Brown/white striped

Pin 8   Brown

Remember that only pairs 2 and 3, pins 1 and 2, 3 and 6, respectively, are used for data. Figure 3.23 shows these common RJ connectors, illustrating the relative size of each.

RJ-48

The last RJ connector pair that will be discussed here is the RJ-48 connector that is used to connect DS-1 or T-1 circuits. This is an eight pin connector that is wired with four

Figure 3.23
RJ-11/14, RJ-22, and RJ-45 connector.

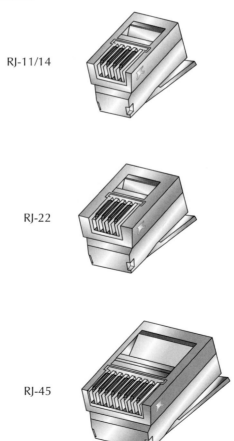

RJ-11/14

RJ-22

RJ-45

lines, one pair each for transmit and receive. Finding a RJ-48 connector is one good way to locate where the T-1 circuits come into your facility. You may also want to track back from the private branch exchange (PBX) in your facility to find the punch down location from where the T-1 line is brought into the building. The RJ-48 is not shown.

Just like the case with the coaxial connectors, there are several RJ-classifications not considered here. At last check there were at least 25 different RJ connectors standardized. The ones discussed above are the most commonly encountered; refer to other sources for a comprehensive list.

■ BASIC RJ CABLE TROUBLESHOOTING

There is one important item that can lead to confusion. Cables using RJ connectors are wired in two separate ways. By far the most common is the straight-through version. This means that pin 1 is wired to pin 1, pin 2 to pin 2, and so forth, on each end of the cable. This is the type of cable you will want to use in any data applications.

There are also cables available with the so-called reversed or crossover connection. These cables are wired such that pin 1 is wired to pin 6, pin 2 to pin 5, and so on. These cables are intended for use with certain proprietary voice systems. Because the cables look virtually identical, it is important to check with the manufacturer's recommendations to determine which type of cable was shipped with the equipment.

There is another way to determine which type of cable you are working with. Because the wires used to connect to the connector are always color coded, look at the color wires connecting pin 1 on one end of the cable and compare it to the color wire used on the other end. If they are the same color, it is wired as a straight-through cable. If not, it is wired as a reversed cable. This tip could save you some time.

PROBLEMS

1. For a copper wire, find the skin depth for the following frequencies:
   (a) 500 Hz   (b) 5 kHz
   (c) 500 kHz   (d) 50 MHz

2. Find the characteristic impedance for a coaxial line with an outside diameter of 5 mm, a center conductor diameter of 1.25 mm, and a jacket thickness of 0.5 mm.

3. Find the characteristic impedance for a parallel cable with a separation of 1 cm and wire radius of 0.2 cm.

4. Find the fill and shield coverage of a coaxial cable with a shield radius of 0.2 cm, a strand radius of 0.04 cm, a weave angle of 20°, and 10 bands of five strands each making up the shield.

5. For an RG-59 coaxial cable, determine the loss per 100 ft for a frequency of 200 MHz.

6. For an RG-11 coaxial cable, find the loss at 700 MHz for a run 500 ft long.

7. Which connector offers better shielding effectiveness, one that has the shield extending beyond the center pin or one for which the center pin extends beyond the shield?

8. Find the SWR and Γ for a 50 Ω line terminated into a 60 Ω load.

9. Using a TDR, you are to locate the fault in the cable. The TDR measures an elapsed time of 2.0 μsec when you apply it. The distance display is burned out. What is the distance to the fault? Assume the cable has a velocity factor of 0.90.

10. Using a *PI* attenuater as shown in the text, determine the values of R_1 and R_2 to set the SWR to 1.15 for source impedance of 25 Ω and load impedance of 60 Ω.

11. Design a *PI* attenuater to reduce power by a factor of 10. (From Table 1.1 a power ratio of 10 corresponds to an attenuation of 10 dB.)

12. For the same impedance values as in problem 10, use a matching transformer. Set the number of primary windings to 100. How many windings does the secondary have?

4

Optical Media

In this chapter, optical media will be introduced. After describing the optical spectrum, the advantages and disadvantages of optical versus metallic media will be summarized. Following that, four key physical ideas that are needed to understand how fiber optic systems work will be described. These are index of refraction, numerical aperture, total internal reflection, and dispersion. How bandwidth and distance are traded off and how optical cables are specified will be included. Additionally, how fiber cables are constructed and how the material used affects their performance will be explored. Next, light sources and detectors will be discussed, and there will be a brief introduction to two applications, the synchronous optical network (SONET) and infrared remote controls. The chapter will close with a brief discussion on troubleshooting optical fibers.

When working with fiber optic systems, there is an important safety warning that needs to be emphasized. A fiber optic cable can transmit a large amount of optical radiation, or light. This light is concentrated and is in a narrow frequency range. It is very possible to permanently damage your eyes by looking directly into an active fiber optic cable. It is an easy way to tell if the cable is active or has a signal propagating down it, but use an optical power meter to make this test, and not your nonreplaceable eyes.

■ SPECTRUM

The frequency band that is used for optical media is identified in Chapter 2 as above 300 GHz. In this region, instead of frequency being used to commonly discuss the band, wavelength is used because wavelength plays such an important role in how a light wave propagates down a fiber optical cable. Figure 4.1 illustrates the optical portion of the electromagnetic spectrum with a focus on wavelength rather than frequency. In this figure, the wavelength is given in a new unit, the angstrom (Å). One angstrom is a very small quantity. To give you some feel for just how small an angstrom is, in a solid, atoms are spaced about 10 Å apart. A better way to understand how small an angstrom is to imagine the spacing between your pants and the seat of your chair. Due to atomic forces there is a small space between these two solids. This space is a few Å in size.

Note that Figure 4.1 shows increasing frequency from left to right. Usually, when discussing the optical portion of the electromagnetic spectrum, a spectral diagram is drawn with the wavelength increasing from right to left. This is because, when discussing optical media, the term *wavelength* rather than frequency is usually preferred. However, because the spectral diagram in Chapter 2 of the electromagnetic spectrum showed increasing frequency from left to right, this one is done the same way for clarity. Note the frequencies illustrated in the figure. This range of frequencies is known as the terahertz bands. The terahertz region is defined by 10 raised to the power of 12, or tera, meaning 12. One terahertz is abbreviated as 1 THz.

Because the frequency range of optical communications is above 30 MHz, one would expect that transmission would be by the LOS mode, and it is. Waves in the optical spectrum travel in straight lines. Also, just like the rest of the electromagnetic spectra, optical waves slow down when not in free space, the decrease in speed depending on the material through which they are propagating.

Everyone is familiar with how a mirror reflects light, so it will not be explored further here. There is a related effect of light called refraction. Refraction is the perceived bending of light as it passes through different media with different velocities of propagation. If you have ever tried to catch a fish with your hand or reached for a pretty rock in the water and discovered that the apparent position of the object was different than it appeared, you understand refraction as well.

Optical waves propagate down fiber optic cables using these two principles. The light ray refracts its way along the optical path in the fiber cable. Essentially the wave bounces along the cable, staying in the desired location by proper choices of material with differing velocities of propagation. This will be discussed further when the construction of fiber cables is explored below. The next section summarizes the advantages and disadvantages of using optical media as compared to metallic media.

Figure 4.1
Optical portion of electromagnetic spectrum.

$1\text{ Å} = 10^{-10}\text{ meters}$

Frequency	0.3-30 THz	30-300 THz	300-3000 THz
	Infrared	Visible	Ultraviolet
Angstroms	10 M–100 k	100 k–10 k	10 k–1 k

■ ADVANTAGES OF OPTICAL MEDIA

There are several reasons why fiber is replacing metallic conductors; six important ones are listed below:

1. Greater bandwidth.   Bandwidth, as explained in Chapter 2, is often limited by the choice of the carrier wave frequency. Recall the discussion on percentage bandwidth. The higher the carrier frequency, the wider bandwidth signal that can be accommodated. Because the typical optical frequency used in fiber channels is on the order of 100 THz, very much wider bandwidth signals can be accommodated than is the case with metallic conductors.

2. Size and weight.   Glass or plastic fibers are much lighter per unit length than copper wire, especially coaxial cable. A spool of coaxial cable 500 ft long is too heavy to lift. Most of the weight of a spool of fiber cable 500 ft long is due to the spool, not the fiber cable itself. Additionally, a single fiber cable can often be used to send the same information that previously required many individual metallic cables. Probably the best example of this is the swapping out of large bundles of copper telephone pairs with a single fiber cable.

3. Attenuation characteristics.   Attenuation or signal loss in fiber optic cable is much less than it is in equivalent metallic coaxial cable. This means that for long-distance applications, fiber will require fewer repeaters than an equivalent metallic run. Also, in any metallic cable the attenuation increases with frequency. This can be a real problem in wideband transmissions and is a constant concern of cable TV engineers. Because the loss is less per unit distance and is flat across any reasonable frequency bandwidth, fiber emerges as a clear winner for wide bandwidth long-distance applications.

4. Electromagnetic interference immunity.   Because fiber optic cable is constructed of a dielectric material (dielectric just means nonconducting as compared to a metallic substance), it is naturally free of interference from electromagnetic fields of any kind. As a result, fiber optic cable is naturally immune to most noise sources generated by machinery, power generation, and so forth. Additionally, because fiber does not conduct, it is not vulnerable to lighting. This makes it ideal for stringing between buildings on a campus to connect various LAN systems together. Finally, fiber has applications in flammable or explosive environmental applications where the slightest spark could cause a catastrophe. Because fiber does not conduct electricity, there is no danger of a spark or short.

5. More secure.   Any metallic conductor carrying a signal will radiate an electromagnetic field. Even expensive shielding approaches cannot eliminate stray electromagnetic radiation completely. If one can measure the way the field around a conductor is changing, it is possible to infer the nature of the signal. It is also true that any metallic conductor is susceptible to covert monitoring by just inserting a tap at a convenient location. Because fiber cable is a dielectric, it radiates no electromagnetic field to monitor covertly. Also because it is a di-

electric and conducts no current, there is no easy way to tap the line without interrupting it.

6. Lower total cost.   Although it is true that viewed strictly from a per foot cost, fiber is more expensive than some metallic conductors, it must be realized that the cable cost is only a small component in the overall cost of a connection. Typically, installation cost far outweighs any cost contribution of the cable itself. It is also true that from a bandwidth perspective, fiber can grow as your bandwidth requirements grow, saving a potential second installation. For long runs, fewer repeaters are required as well. For this economic reason alone, it makes more sense today to install fiber rather than metallic conductors for most communications applications.

■ DISADVANTAGES OF OPTICAL MEDIA

There are not many disadvantages to list here, and the ones that are listed are a bit of a reach. However, balance in all things is a nice philosophy.

1. Bending loss.   Because signals on fiber optic cables propagate by "bouncing" along, if the diameter of the cable is changed, the bouncing changes. Violating the bend radius recommendations of the manufacturer can introduce unwanted modulation into the fiber and distort the transmission. Also by regularly flexing and relaxing a fiber cable it is possible to impress a signal onto it that will interfere with the desired signal transmission. It is not a good idea, then, to use fiber for in an application where the cable is likely to be susceptible to this mechanical modulation distortion.

2. Safety.   This is really just the flip side of the fourth disadvantage of metallic conductors. When there is a current flowing in a wire, there is the potential for electrical shock, although in communications the current flow is usually not at dangerous levels. There is no danger of electrical shock from a fiber cable because there is no current flow. There is however, an optical flow of photons. As recommended earlier, do not look directly into the end of a fiber cable. The light is concentrated and can damage your vision. Additionally, because light is not generally perceived as dangerous, many more people are aware of and cautious about electrical shock; very few worry about optical damage from light. Because it is not perceived as a danger, it has the potential to be more of one.

3. Hidden faults.   Because fiber cable is made up of a center glass or plastic fiber that is covered by an optically opaque outside cover, it is possible for the center fiber to break and the outside cover to stay intact. This can make discovering the fault location very difficult because from the outside the cable looks fine. There are optical TDRs to address this problem, but it remains a disadvantage over metallic cable, which when it breaks, usually breaks in a visually accessible way.

4. Electron-to-photon conversion and back.   The last disadvantage of fiber is that today the signals are in electrical form at each end of the communications link. This means that an electron-to-photon converter and photon-to-electron con-

verter are required at each end of the link for a simplex connection. This is an additional cost that needs to be taken into account as part of the overall cost of the installation.

Many of the fundamental characteristics of fiber optic cables are due to how they are constructed. To explore this in some detail it is necessary to introduce four basic concepts of the field of optics: index of refraction, numerical aperture, total internal reflection, and dispersion.

■ INDEX OF REFRACTION

The index of refraction of a material is an expression of one of the two most fundamental concepts of geometrical optics. These two concepts are the laws of refraction and reflection. These two laws are as fundamental to geometric optics as Newton's laws are to macroscopic motion. Because it is almost impossible to talk about one without mentioning the other, both will be introduced in this section.

First, when a wave strikes any surface, there are two components, the part that goes through it and the part that does not. The part that goes through the surface is called the transmitted wave; in optics it is called the refracted wave. The part that does not go through is called the reflected wave. In the mathematics below, the subscript t is used for the refracted (transmitted) wave, making clear the distinction between it and the reflected wave using the subscript r.

The first principle of geometric optics simply states that when a ray of light, called the incident wave, strikes any barrier or boundary between two transparent surfaces with different velocities of propagation, it splits into two parts, a reflected ray and a refracted ray. Further, it states that all three parts, the incident, reflected, and refracted or transmitted wave, lie in the same plane.

The velocity of propagation is dependent on the material and is discussed either as a velocity of propagation or the dielectric constant. This is exactly the same effect that was explored in Chapter 3. It shows how the dielectric constant changes the perceived speed of any electromagnetic wave in a material. To relate the two concepts examine the following equation:

$$v_p = cv_f = \frac{c}{\sqrt{\varepsilon_r}} = \frac{c}{n} \rightarrow n = \sqrt{\varepsilon_r} \qquad \textbf{(4–1)}$$

As can be seen, the index of refraction is equal to the square root of the dielectric constant.

The second basic principle of geometric optics states that the ratio of the sine of the angles that the reflected and transmitted waves take always equals a constant. For our purposes, these two principles can be combined and stated mathematically as

$$\theta_i = \theta_r \tag{4-2}$$

$$n_i \sin(\theta_i) = n_t \sin(\theta_t) \tag{4-3}$$

where $\quad \theta_i$ = angle of incidence
θ_r = angle of reflection
θ_t = angle of refraction (transmission)
n_i = index of refraction (material 1)
n_t = index of refraction (material 2)

In texts on optics, you will find these relationships stated as the laws of refraction and reflection. The angles are described in Figure 4.2 and the n values are the index of refraction of the two materials. A key requirement for fiber construction is that one of these indexes of refraction, the core must be larger than the cladding.

Numerical Aperture
The numerical aperture (NA) is described by equation 4-4:

$$NA = n \sin(\theta) \tag{4-4}$$

Fundamentally, the NA of a system defines the light-gathering power of the system. For those familiar with photography, the f-stop number on the lens is derived from this principle. It is often referred to as the "speed" of the lens. This use of the term *speed* is an attempt to capture the idea that the more light-gathering power a lens has, the less time is needed to gather enough light for a proper exposure. Some representative indexes of refraction for common materials are given in Table 4.1.

Figure 4.2
Incident, reflected, and refracted waves.

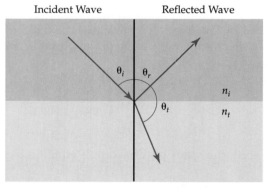

Table 4.1
Index of Refraction

Material	Index of Refraction
Vacuum (free space) and/or air	1.0
Water	1.33
Glass and/or glass fiber	1.5–1.9
Diamond	2.4
Silicon	3.4

■ EXAMPLE 4.1

A light wave strikes the surface of a glass with an index of refraction of 1.5 at an angle of 25°. Find the angle of angle of reflection, refraction (transmission), and the NA:

$$\theta_i = 25$$

From equation 4−2,

$$\theta_i = \theta_r = 25$$

Because $n_i \sin(\theta_i) = n_t \sin(\theta_t)$,

$$1 \sin(25) = 1.5 \sin(\theta_t) \rightarrow \theta_t = \sin^{-1}\left(\frac{1}{1.5} \sin(25)\right) = 16.4$$

$$\text{NA} = n \sin(\theta) = 1.5 \sin(16.4) = 0.42$$

Another way of looking at the refractive index is to view it as the ratio of velocity of light in free space to its velocity in the material. This approach is similar to the earlier discussion about how the velocity of propagation was related to the dielectric constant and was determined by the chemistry of the material. This concept is exactly the same as in the electrical case except the concept of refractive index is introduced because rays of light are the subject.

■ TOTAL INTERNAL REFLECTION

Total internal reflection is a special case of reflection, where the angle is over some critical value. For this special case, there is no refracted or transmitted wave. This means that *all* the wave's energy is reflected. Depending on the index of refraction of the two materials that form the boundary, there is a critical angle where the angle of refraction or transmission is exactly equal to 90°. When the rays strike the boundary at any angle

Table 4.2
Critical Angles

Ratio of Index of Refraction	Critical Angle (°)
1.3	50.3
1.4	45.6
1.45	43.6
1.5	41.8
1.6	38.7

greater than the critical angle, total internal reflection happens. This is the principle that fiber optic cables use to bounce the light along the core.

Stated differently, the critical angle is the special angle of the incident ray for which the refracted or transmitted angle is exactly equal to 90°. Each pair of materials has its own critical angle. It is found by applying the following equation:

$$\sin(\theta_c) = \frac{n_i}{n_t} \qquad \textbf{(4–5)}$$

where θ_c = critical angle. The critical angles for a few representative ratios of index of refraction are given in Table 4.2.

■ EXAMPLE 4.2

Consider a glass fiber such as shown in the Figure 4.3 (in the section on fiber construction). The two dielectrics that are of concern for a light ray entering the fiber are that of the air surrounding it and the glass material of the core. Assume the glass core features an index of refraction of 1.5. Find the critical angle:

$$\sin(\theta_c) = \frac{n_i}{n_t} = \frac{1.5}{1} \rightarrow \theta_c = \sin^{-1}\left(\frac{1}{1.5}\right) = 41.8$$

Note that this agrees with the value listed in Table 4.2.

■ DISPERSION

Optical dispersion is a complex topic that describes the changes that occur in a dielectric when an electromagnetic field is applied to the optical conductor. Fundamentally, one observes a perceived slowing down of the speed of light. This is similar to what was discussed in Chapter 3 and described by velocity of propagation. We will see that this has two primary effects that are of concern:

1. There will be a wavelength (frequency) dependence of the index of refraction.

2. Dispersion will limit the maximum frequency of modulation, or data rate, in some fiber types (multimode only).

Every material used to make fiber has some characteristic frequency. If you can see through a material such as plastic or glass, it is transparent. If it is transparent, the characteristic frequency is outside the optical spectrum. If you could "see" at a different wavelength, the same material might not be transparent. For example, if you could, like in science fiction stories, see in the ultraviolet spectrum, glass would not be transparent, but opaque. You can make an analogy with resonance; at the characteristic frequency, the material resonates and if you could "see" at that frequency, the resonance energy of the material "blinds" you. This is described as absorption and renders the material effectively opaque.

As you approach the characteristic frequency of a material, it becomes more optically dense. The optical density is defined by the index of refraction. The larger the index of refraction for the wavelength used in the communication system, the more attenuation will result. Refer to Table 4.1, clearly silicon is more optically dense than glass, and its index of refraction is also larger. Just as in the discussion on numerical aperture, the chemistry of the material, dielectric constant effects the propagation of light, or any electromagnetic energy.

For practical purposes, the materials chosen for construction of the fiber cable take the index of refraction into consideration and as a result, dispersion is not usually a concern. Glass, for example, has a constant index of refraction for wavelengths greater than about 800 nm. Because the shortest wavelength typically used in fiber systems is 860 nm, this variation of index of refraction, and hence attenuation, does not concern us. Table 4.3 (in the section on core construction) gives the three primary wavelengths used in fiber systems.

The second effect, which limits the data rate that the fiber cable can transport, occurs only in those cables that are multimode in construction. This will be discussed in more detail when multimode is described later in the chapter.

■ FIBER CONSTRUCTION

Two things, the core and cladding, characterize every fiber cable. There are other distinctions that will be explored, but every fiber cable's optical performance is characterized by the physical construction and chemical structure of the optical core and cladding.

The optical core, or just core, is the light transmission path. It is located in the center of most fiber cables. The most important thing is that the material that the core is made out of has a higher refractive index than the cladding. This ensures that there is some critical angle so that total internal reflection occurs. Again, fiber optic cables depend on total internal reflection to work the way they do.

The cladding is a material that has a low index of refraction and surrounds the optical core, it does two nice things. First, it provides optical insulation for the core, and second, it provides a level of physical protection for the core. Figure 4.3 illustrates how

Figure 4.3
Fiber construction.

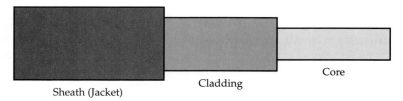

Sheath (Jacket)   Cladding   Core

these are put together. This figure illustrates the most basic fiber cable design. This type of cable is referred to as a tight buffer cable to distinguish it from loose buffer cables. The distinction between these two types of cable is that in the tight buffer situation, the core/cladding is tightly held or secured by the sheath. In loose buffer cables the core/cladding element is free to "float" inside the sheath.

Since in loose Butler Cables the core/cladding element floats inside the sheath, often, there is a water-blocking substance, usually a gel of some type, in which the core/cladding element floats. This type of cable is designed for additional ruggedness in long-distance, harsh environmental conditions. Due to the floating nature of the core/cladding element, external stress on the cable during installation or service is borne by the sheath, not the core/cladding element. This gives this type of cable a much better crush resistance. The water-blocking gel used acts to protect the fibers from any water penetration. These cables are almost always made of glass core/cladding and feature low attenuation because they are designed for long-distance runs, especially those runs that are outdoors.

Most actual cables have additional strengthening elements such as additional sheaths for strength or resistance to special environments, or several core/cladding elements bundled into one sheath. There are fiber optic cables constructed like ribbon cable with several core/cladding elements arranged in parallel fashion and many others.

Figure 4.4
Duplex fiber construction.

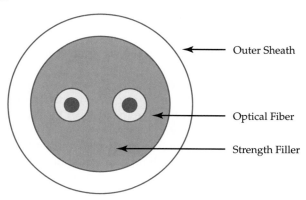

Outer Sheath

Optical Fiber

Strength Filler

Figure 4.5
Propagation in a optical fiber.

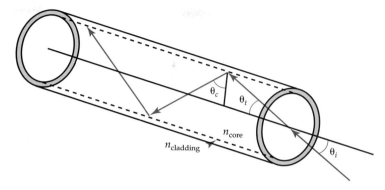

Virtually all indoor optical fiber applications use a tight buffer arrangement with two fibers bundled into one outer sheath. This is called a duplex arrangement after the function of each fiber (e.g., one fiber for transmission and one for reception). Ethernet, Token Ring, and optical cables used in voice telephone applications have this type of construction. Figure 4.4 illustrates this arrangement. The diagram is on end rather than on its side to give you an alternate perspective of the physical arrangement of the fiber(s) placed inside the strength filler. The two concentric small circles set inside the strength filler represent the fiber itself surrounded by the cladding for that individual fiber.

The core/cladding construction is the critical component of a fiber optic cable. Although this is shown as two separate materials in Figure 4.4, often it is made of the same material and adjusted chemically to yield the different refractive index. This means that the difference may not be visible to the naked eye.

The sheath material can be made of different materials; the most common is the same material used for metallic cables, PVC. Because fiber optic cables tend to be more fragile than their metallic cousins are, often somewhat exotic materials are used to add additional strength to the cable. Most readers are probably familiar with one of these materials, Kelvar, which is the same material used to make bulletproof vests.

Figure 4.5 illustrates how the light ray is reflected and propagates down the cable. It also shows the critical angle. Note the index of refraction for the core and cladding are also shown.

■ OPTICAL FIBER SPECIFICATIONS

Core Construction

Two main types of cores are in use. The two types use different materials, glass and plastic, to make the fiber cables. Both materials are capable of being constructed in two different ways: step index and graded index. The step index type has two further divisions, single-mode and multimode. All graded index fibers are multimode. That means that

Figure 4.6
Optical cable propagation modes.

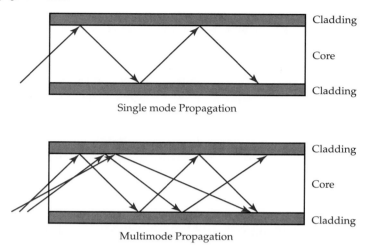

there are three types of fibers in use, each made with either a glass or plastic core/cladding construction. Each of these three types will be examined in the following sections. Table 4.3 illustrates this grouping of fibers by construction material.

Figure 4.6 illustrates the two types of fiber cable propagation, single- and multimode.

Glass Fibers
Single-Mode Step Index.   Single-mode step index produces the highest performance fiber. All glass core fibers feature lower loss than their plastic cousins and the single-mode propagation means that all the rays of light entering the fiber travel the same path, or mode (e.g., *single mode*). Step index just means that the entire core has the same index of refraction (e.g., the index of refraction of the fiber cable abruptly shifts, or steps, at the core/cladding boundary; the core itself has no variation in index of refraction).

The high performance of this type of cable is due to the two facts listed above. All the light rays travel the same path, so they enter and exit in the same order they were impressed. This means that they are coherent, or in phase with each other. Another factor in rating this as the highest performing fiber is its small size.

Table 4.3
Fiber Types

Glass	Plastic
Single-mode step index	Single-mode step index
Multimode step index	Multimode step index
Multimode graded index	Multimode graded index

Because all the rays travel the same path, the diameter of the core is the smallest of any of the three types of fiber. Also, because all the rays travel the same path, single-mode fibers always have the highest bandwidth. The coherent nature of the light rays as they travel down the fiber is an important feature, and so these fibers are often used with laser light sources; lasers are coherent output devices (this will be discussed later). The only problem with this fiber type is the cost. It has the highest cost of any of the three types of fibers. For short runs, plastic single-mode step index fibers are a good compromise between cost and performance.

Multimode Step Index. Multimode step index fiber has a good performance and is inexpensive to manufacture. Again, it is a glass and step index fiber, so the comments concerning those items above apply here as well. The multimode operation means that instead of a single path for the light rays, there are many. This has two consequences. First, because the rays travel different paths down the core, they may arrive at the other end out of order, increasing distortion. Second, the core has a large diameter to accommodate the different paths and hence angles that the rays take.

The first consequence, that the light ray takes many paths down the fiber instead of just one, results in the effect called dispersion. The multiple paths that the light rays take result in the individual rays arriving at the other end out of order. Longer paths take longer to travel the same distance. This spreading out in time of the light rays means that the pulses applied at the source start to overlap one another. As you might expect, once this overlap exceeds a certain limit, the pulses are not easy to tell apart and the maximum data rate is reached. This limit occurs only at very high data rates. Also remember that this effect only occurs in multimode fibers, offering an easy solution: Use single-mode fibers for those applications that require high data rates.

The second point is an advantage because the bigger the core size, the easier it is to launch the light into the fiber. Another way of stating this is that the larger the diameter of the fiber, the easier it is to align the fiber so that the light enters the fiber at the correct angles. Therefore, multimode fibers are lower performing but easier to work with than single-mode fibers.

Multimode Graded Index. Multimode graded index fiber seems to have emerged as the grand compromise that excels nowhere but in cost. It operates in multimode fashion, so it is easy to work with, but it has a graded index core. A graded index core means that the index of refraction is not constant across its diameter. This lack of control in the manufacturing process makes it cheaper to manufacture. This variation in index of refraction means that light rays entering at different points will have different critical angles. Therefore, the problems of all the light rays not exiting in the same order as they were put in is worse than with the multimode step index fiber. This is clearly a bad situation and is minimized only by precise alignment so that the impact of this variation in index of refraction is reduced.

Graded index fibers are cheaper to manufacture, but because of the graded index, alignment to launch the rays is more critical, taking away one key advantage to a multimode fiber. This fiber has little use except in very low-cost applications.

Plastic Fiber

The other material that fiber optic cables are manufactured in uses plastic as the core/cladding material. All three types of fibers considered above are also present here. Plastic is less expensive than glass and exhibits higher attenuation. However, plastic comes with its own advantages. For example, plastic fibers are more flexible than glass. Additionally, they are more resistant to damage during installation due to that flexibility. Plastic is also lighter per unit length than glass. Sometimes this is an important trait in weight-critical applications.

The biggest difficulty with plastic fiber is the high attenuation of plastic compared with glass. A plastic fiber requires a repeater more often than a glass fiber. As rule, do not use a plastic fiber for a run of over 200 ft.

Size

Fiber optic cables are specified by the relative sizes of the core and cladding diameters. Because these sizes determine what type of propagation mode the cable can support, they are a natural choice. Different countries have standardized on different sizes, but there are three primary ones used in the world today. The U.S. standard is 62.5/125 μm. The most common size that you will encounter is 62.5/125 μm. The first number is the outside diameter of the core and the second number is the outside diameter of the cladding. The actual outside diameter of the physical cable depends on the choices made for the sheath. Depending on the amount of protection, this can vary.

The other two sizes in wide use are 50/125 and 100/140 μm. Although any fiber that has a sufficiently small core diameter can be manufactured as single-mode fiber, it is not uncommon to find the same size cable offered in both multi- and single-mode versions. It is important to confirm not only the size but also the core construction to determine the right cable for an application.

Attenuation

As in metallic cables, attenuation is expressed as a logarithmic ratio of power out to power in, yielding a loss per unit distance. The equation is

$$\text{attenuation (dB)} = 10 \log\left(\frac{P_o}{P_i}\right) \qquad \text{(4–6)}$$

In fiber optic cables, the attenuation, or optical power loss, is always expressed in decibels per kilometer (dB/km) at a specific wavelength. The wavelength is important because different wavelengths have different attenuations for a given cable. As will be shown a little later, different optical sources also output different wavelengths of light. Naturally, one wants to make sure that the cable is matched to the optical source, so all cables come with a wavelength specification associated with the attenuation specification.

The attenuation of fiber cables can vary widely; the best single-mode step index glass fiber can feature attenuation as low as 1 dB/km. Very inexpensive multimode graded index plastic fiber can have an attenuation as high as 1000 dB/km. As a short-hand expression of the attenuation featured by an optical fiber, fibers with an attenuation of 10 dB/km or less are known as low-loss fibers; those with a greater attenuation are known as high-loss fibers. Virtually all low-loss fibers are single-mode step index glass fibers, whereas all large-diameter core, multimode graded index plastic fibers are high-loss fibers.

■ EXAMPLE 4.3

A certain fiber cable has attenuation rating of 8 dB/km. For a 5 km run, what will be the signal attenuation at the destination?

$$\text{loss (dB)} = (\text{attenuation})(\text{length}) \tag{4--7}$$

$$\text{loss (dB)} = (8 \text{ dB/km})(5 \text{ km}) = 40 \text{ dB}$$

Wavelength

As discussed above, optical cable attenuation is always expressed at some wavelength. Three wavelengths are used widely in the industry today, and they are all in the infrared band. That means that they are all higher in frequency than the color red and are not readily visible to the naked eye. Manufacturers design the core chemistry, using dopants in the glass or plastic, to change the index of refraction. This means that one or more of these three wavelengths have the least loss, that cable is then marketed for that wavelength. The two primary dopants used are germanium and boron oxide. The three wavelengths used are shown in Table 4.4.

■ EXAMPLE 4.4

You are asked to determine what effect the purchase of the wrong fiber will have on a project to run a fiber line connecting two buildings across San Francisco Bay. Someone ordered 25 km of cable with the special sheathing and strength members needed but specified the wrong wavelength. The end systems are designed to operate at 860 nm, and the cable is specified at 1550 nm. Swapping out the end systems for the correct wavelength operation is not an option.

You contact the manufacturer and determine that the rating on the cable ordered is 5 dB/km at 1550 nm, as compared to the 3 dB/km at 860 nm intended. You get out your calculator and first double-check that the original specification could meet the attenuation specification of 80 dB:

$$\text{loss} = (25 \text{ km})(3 \text{ dB/km}) = 75 \text{ dB}$$

Table 4.4
Fiber Wavelengths

Wavelength (nm)	Frequency (THz)	Band
860	349	Infrared
1300	231	Infrared
1550	194	Infrared

That checks, but with almost no margin; you are not confident of success when using the attenuation of the incorrect cable:

$$\text{loss} = (25 \text{ km})(5 \text{ dB/km}) = 125 \text{ dB}$$

With the above calculation, you determine that the cable will not meet the system specification for loss. The manufacturer will not let you return the cable for the correct one, however, your supplier's project engineer tells you about a new repeater unit the company is coming out with that is designed to operate in salt water and will give 50 dB of gain. It is inexpensive and very reliable. You are excited and get out your calculator and see if this will work. You plan to place the repeater in the center of the run, 12.5 km from the source:

$$\text{loss} = (12.5 \text{ km})(5 \text{ dB/km}) + 50 \text{ dB} + (12.5 \text{ km})(5 \text{ dB/km}) = 75 \text{ dB}$$

This looks like it will work, so you offer this solution to your manager, and the additional expense is quietly approved.

Bandwidth

The bandwidth of an optical cable is expressed in units of Megahertz kilometers (MHz-km). Interestingly, the bandwidth number is always the lowest frequency where the magnitude of the frequency response is decreased by 3 dB as compared to zero frequency. As you recall from Chapter 1, 3 dB represents a reduction in power by half. That means that the specification is telling you that from zero to the specified frequency, no frequency is attenuated by more than half its original power.

The kilometer part of the specification specifies how far the cable can be run at that bandwidth. For example, if the specification is 500 MHz-km, a run 1 km with a bandwidth of 500 MHz, 2 km with a bandwidth of 250 MHz, or 5 km with a bandwidth of 100 MHz would be within specification. Just like with metallic cables, bandwidth, or data rate, can always be traded off with distance.

This is the way manufacturers quantify dispersion effects in fiber cables. Instead of discussing the different aspects of dispersion, the preferred approach is to lump all dispersion effects into one number, and this specification captures the relevant information. Therefore, just like metallic media, optical fibers have some attenuation with length independent of wavelength. Also, just like metallic media, length can be traded off for data rate. Table 4.5 illustrates a typical trade-off between distance and data rate. Note the greater sensitivity of multimode fibers as compared to single-mode fibers.

Table 4.5
Distance Trade-off with Data Rate

Fiber Type	800 Mbps (km)	400 Mbps (km)	200 Mbps (km)	100 Mbps (km)
Single-mode	10	10	10	—
50 μm multimode	0.5	1	2	10
62.5 μm multimode	175	350	1500	1500

■ EXAMPLE 4.5

A certain fiber optic cable has a specification of 800 MHz-km. You want to use this cable for an application that has a run length of 10 km. What is the maximum bandwidth for this run length?

$$\frac{800 \text{ MHz-km}}{10 \text{ km}} = 80 \text{ MHz}$$

Fiber Cable Connectors

Just like metallic cables fiber optic cables need connectors to physically attach to the modulation source. All fiber connectors add loss to the fiber cable. Typical values are between 1 and 2 dB per connector. At one time there was a great debate about how to make fiber optic cable connectors that precisely aligned when joined. If the two fiber segments are not aligned correctly, the light ray will not enter the next segment correctly and the signal loss will greatly increase. This problem was solved with the idea of a ferrule, which is a device designed to hold the cable firmly in place, thus ensuring a correct alignment. Today there are many different types of fiber optic connectors, all based on the ferrule principle.

Basically, the ferrule is a female connector, or plug, that the jack, or male connector, is inserted into. Once snuggly in this cylinder, the plug is held firmly and the two connectors can be screwed together, ensuring a precise alignment along with a physical attachment. Figure 4.7 shows a typical ferrule design. In this figure, the top diagram shows an end view of the ferrule along with the position guides used to guide the fiber to the correct position. In the second part of the figure, a side view illustrates how the

Figure 4.7
Ferrule connector.

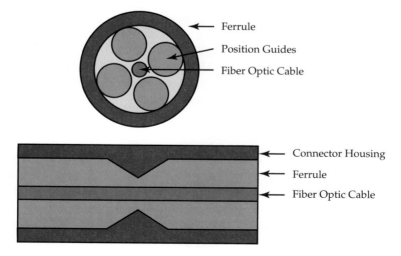

ferrule is compressed at the point of joining the two cable ends. This compression occurs at the midpoint of the illustration where the ferrule narrows down. The position guides are not shown.

Just like metallic media, a few standardized connectors are widely used for optical connections. All these use the ferrule principle. The most common in use today is the ST connector, which is a small connector that uses a bayonet type physical attachment for the jack and plug.

Another commonly seen fiber optic connector is the SC type. With these connectors the physical attachment is accomplished by a plastic plug and instead of a traditional jack, a connector housing is used. These connectors provide high performance and are very easy to use. If you have a recently manufactured automobile, the black plastic, rectangular connectors used to mate with the fuse box are similar in appearance to the SC connector. There is no standard appearance for this connector; it is available in both simplex and duplex styles.

SC connectors are almost always used in premise wiring situations. Refer to the discussion on backbone and horizontal wiring practices in Chapter 3. A similar set of recommendations exists for fiber optic installations, using the same terms. The two types of fiber recommended are 62.5/125 μm multimode for horizontal applications and 62.5/125 μm multimode or 50/125 μm single-mode for backbone applications.

Further, there is a specification where the user side of the connection is designated to use a duplex SC style connector attached to two individual simplex connectors, also of the SC type, which run to and from the wiring closet. To picture this, imagine a wall between the user side and the cabling side. On the user side of the wall is a keyed duplex connector, ensuring correct polarity in the attachment.

To see why this is done this way, consider that the user may have very little technical skill, so the wiring system needs to make sure the plug is put in the correct way. On the wiring side, the only ones who will encounter this connection are the technicians and engineers who are responsible for the installation and maintenance of the communications system. Presumably, they know what they are doing and will not make the mistake of plugging the wrong cable into the wrong housing. Additionally, the use of two simplex connections allows the individual cables to be run on different paths, increasing the flexibility of installation.

Never try to splice two fiber optic cables with your knife and some tape, as you might do with metallic cables. The requirement of precise alignment of the two optical cable ends will doom your efforts before they are begun. Special machines and tools for splicing optical cables must be used.

■ OPTICAL LIGHT SOURCES

The optical light sources that are used with optical media operate on the same three wavelengths specified above. There is an important difference in the two types of light sources used. The least expensive, using a light-emitting diode (LED) for a source, is a noncoherent source and is generally used with multimode fibers, which due to their multimode wave propagation are naturally noncoherent. The second type, laser diodes, are naturally coherent and so are used with single-mode fibers, which due to single-mode wave propagation are naturally coherent.

Coherent just means that the amplitudes of all light waves produced by the source rise and fall at the same time (e.g., they are coherent). In electrical or mechanical systems, one would say that they are synchronous; all waves rise and fall at the same time.

LED (Noncoherent)

An LED is a semiconductor device made up of a single *p-n* junction. Unlike a normal diode, an LED emits noncoherent light formed by the *p-n* junction. The light intensity is roughly proportional to the current flow through the diode. Unlike the diodes you are probably familiar with, LEDs are usually gallium arsenide (GaAs) devices. That means that instead of silicon *p-n* junction, a GaAs *p-n* junction is formed.

Although the light emitted from a LED is noncoherent, it can be designed to emit almost any wavelength range. In the last few years, blue LEDs came onto the market, and red, green, and yellow LEDs have been commonly available for years. As you can see, the requirement to output light in a specific wavelength range is no longer a problem for a LED. Manufacturers can easily make them to output at one of the three wavelengths discussed above, but in a narrow range, not at a single frequency.

There are many different types of LEDs designed for use with fiber optic cables, and they emit light with various coherencies from various directions at various powers. All are designed to provide a linear output power at a specific wavelength with increasing current flow. The more current, the brighter the output. Typical output currents for these LEDs are from about 10 to 50 nW or -15 to 30 dBm.

LEDs designed for use as light sources for fiber optics have one more distinguishing feature. They are designed to switch ON and OFF much more rapidly than the familiar visible-light LEDs. The LED you have probably worked with in the laboratory has a maximum switching rate of about 5 MHz. Diodes designed for use with fiber feature switching rates of up to about 50 MHz. For higher data rate systems, the laser diode becomes the optical source or modulator of choice.

Laser Diode (Coherent)

The lasers discussed here are those manufactured as laser diodes and designed to act as a light source to drive a fiber optic cable. They are not sophisticated laser systems designed for exotic applications, such as the "Star Wars" missile shield in space. However, it is sometimes nice to be able to make rough comparisons, so you should know that semiconductor lasers operate at much lower powers than ruby or carbon dioxide lasers. On the other hand, the injection laser diodes, (ILDs) discussed in the next paragraph, do compare well with helium-neon lasers in power output. Additionally, they are much smaller.

Laser is actually an acronym for the light amplification by stimulated emission of radiation. The most widely used light source is the injection laser diode. Just like LEDs, ILDs are manufactured with gallium arsenide (GaAs) instead of silicon (Si). Again, just like LEDs, if the GaAs is combined with phosphide (P), the output of the device is in the visible region. Our concern is with those devices that operate in the infrared region, and those are manufactured without phosphide.

It may be interesting to note that LEDs and ILDs are manufactured with GaAs instead of Si because GaAs is an example of a direct recombination semiconductor. This means that instead of electron hole recombination occurring through trapping processes, the recombination occurs directly, thus enabling the lasing process. The addition of phosphide or aluminum (Al) to the semiconductor changes the band gap voltage. As this is changed, the output wavelength of the device is changed. That's how different colors, including infrared, are actually accomplished. It is all chemistry and geometry. Different semiconductor materials can be used to generate output wavelengths, spanning the entire optical spectrum, from ultraviolet to infrared. Figure 4.8 illustrates the basic GaAs ILD construction.

ILDs behave like LEDs below a certain current flow. As the current flow is increased through the device, the operation of the device alters and starts to lase. This level of current flow, where the performance of the device changes, is known as the threshold current. ILDs feature output powers up to 10 W. The maximum power output of an LED is about 1/2 W. Because an ILD is much more powerful than an LED, for any long distance run, the choice for an optical source is an ILD. Also, as mentioned above, an ILD device features much higher switching rates then an LED device. ILDs are capable of switching rates on the order of 1 GHz.

Finally, do not forget that any laser has a naturally coherent output. The ILD considered here, when the current flow exceeds the threshold amount, also exhibits a coherent output. The coherent nature of the light makes an ILD a natural choice for any high data rate system when coupled with single-mode fiber cable. The only difficulty in using ILD devices is their high heat dissipation. If operating at high output powers, extensive measures must be taken to flow this heat away from the device location using some kind of heat sink strategy. This is important not only so that the heat does not dam-

Figure 4.8
GaAs laser.

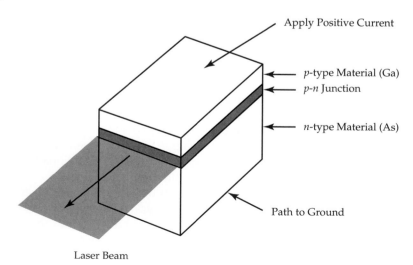

Laser Beam

age the component or other components close by but also because ILD device performance characteristics vary with temperature. This means for consistent, reliable long-term operation, a heat sink strategy is important.

■ OPTICAL DETECTORS

Just as optical sources are required to drive the fiber cable, optical detectors are used to sense the optical energy and convert it back into electrical energy. Three types of devices are used. They will be examined in increasing order of cost and performance.

Photodiode and Phototransistor

The photodiode, or as it is more commonly known, the solar cell, converts optical energy into electrical current. A photodiode is a single junction device that produces a forward voltage across the p-n junction when it is illuminated. This voltage is called the photovoltaic, or photoelectric, effect. The band gap voltage limits the voltage produced in the same way the wavelength produced by an ILD or LED is controlled by the band gap. The current produced depends on the size of the illuminated area of the p-n junction; typical values are in the milliampere range.

The phototransistor is a photodiode that has an extra junction to get some amplification of the optical energy and produce a larger current flow for low-light applications. Photodiodes and phototransistors are not widely used in communication systems because of their slow switching speeds. Photodiodes find most of their applications in power generation and phototransistors in measurement applications.

PIN Diode

A PIN diode is a device used to convert optical signals into electrical signals. The PIN diode was developed in response to the slow switching speeds of photodiodes. Because how fast carriers move often limits the speed of a semiconductor device, in the PIN diode an extra layer is inserted between the conventional p and n layers. This layer is known as the intrinsic layer and is characterized by a high resistance. This might seem counterintuitive—why a high-resistance layer to speed up carrier flow—but if you think about it, high resistance, for a given current produce higher voltage drops. A high voltage differential in the right location can act to accelerate any charged carrier flow. Faster carrier flow means faster switching.

PIN diodes are the most widely used optical detectors in those applications that call for relatively fast switching speeds and moderate sensitivity. (They are more sensitive to low-light energies than photodiodes and so need less power to produce a given output.) PIN diodes are most commonly used for systems operating at 860 nm wavelengths.

Avalanche Diode

Avalanche diodes, or avalanche photodiodes (APDs), are like phototransistors in that they combine light detection with amplification of the photo current. Thinking about an avalanche as an analogy gives the right idea of how such a device works (e.g., one snowflake starts rolling, which starts two more rolling, etc.). As a photo current starts to flow, a special chemical structure causes an avalanche effect, significantly multiplying that current flow. As a result, APDs are more sensitive than PIN diodes. They also feature a better S/N ratio because of the internal amplification. Additionally, due to the avalanche effect, APDs operate at higher switching speeds than PIN diodes. These devices are often paired with ILD optical sources, enabling operation at gigabit switching speeds.

■ EXAMPLE 4.6

This example will illustrate how to calculate a loss budget for an optical system. All communication systems use this technique to ensure that sufficient power reaches the receiver, or in this case, the detector. The approach is to first determine the transmit power and then add up all the losses or attenuations in the channel. This total loss is then subtracted from the transmit power, and the resultant number is compared with the detector sensitivity. For the system to work, the sensitivity of the detector must be less than the applied power at the receiver. System specifications are

LED transmit power	25 μW
Fiber	5 dB/km and 100MHz-km
Run length	2 km
Connector loss	1.5 dB
Detector sensitivity	100 nW
Bandwidth	20 MHz

First, find the attenuation that the LED and detector selected can accommodate. Applying equation 4−6,

$$\text{attenuation (dB)} = 10 \log \left(\frac{P_o}{P_i}\right) = 10 \log \left(\frac{P_{\text{LED}}}{P_{\text{Detector}}}\right) = 10 \log \left(\frac{25 \times 10^{-6}}{100 \times 10^{-9}}\right) = 24 \text{ dB}$$

Now the total attenuation that the system is known. This value must not exceed the transmit power. It is usually a good idea to account for a margin of safety to this number, so subtract 3 dB to yield 21 dB.

Now, adding up the losses (computing the loss budget), the following is found:

$$\left(\frac{5 \text{ dB}}{\text{km}}\right) 2 \text{ km} + (2)1.5 \text{ dB} = 13 \text{ dB}$$

Because 13 dB is less than the maximum attenuation, the loss budget is met. This computation so far does not include consideration of the dispersion effects. Recall that this effect is captured by the bandwidth−distance specification, here 100 MHz−km. If this specification is exceeded, the cable will not be appropriate for the application, independent of what the loss budget calculation predicts.

$$100 \text{ MHz-km} > (2 \text{ km})(20 \text{ MHz}) = 40 \text{ MHz-km}$$

It is seen that the loss budget is satisfied as well as any dispersion effects due to data rate.

■ FIBER APPLICATION: SONET

SONET is probably the most widely applied use of fiber optic communications systems in the telephone system. Since its development, the technical name for this system has changed; it is now known as the synchronous digital hierarchy (SDH). Most users still refer to it as SONET. The key difference in this system over earlier systems is its synchronous nature. All equipment is synchronized to a single master clock. This offers many advantages, but they will not be explored here.

The SONET hierarchy is shown in the Table 4.6. In this table, the first column is the multiplexing level. Each level is combined some integer number of times to form the next level. For example, to go from level 2 to level 3, three STS-3 signals are multiplexed together to form a level 3 multiplexed data stream.

The two listings in the second column illustrate the two names the signals on the SONET are described by. While the signal is in electrical form it is called an synchronous transport signal (STS). When it is impressed onto the optical fiber it is referred to as the optical signal (OC). This is similar to the T-carrier nomenclature. There, for example, a T-1 is the name if the signal is electrical and F-1 is the name if the signal is carried by fiber.

The third column gives the new names using the new SDH terminology, with STM standing for synchronous transport module. The SDH and STM nomenclature is much more common in Europe than in the United States. The last column gives the data rates each level of the hierarchy is designed to transport; STM-8 and above systems are now in the field, transporting telephone calls across country and around the globe.

■ INFRARED APPLICATION: REMOTE CONTROL

If you own a television, VCR, or CD player purchased recently, it almost certainly came with a remote control. These devices all work in the same manner. They use an infrared LED to transmit a series of binary-coded pulses of light, which are received by the device and decoded into commands.

Table 4.6
SONET Hierarchy

Level	SONET	SDH	Data Rate (Mbps)
1	STS-1/OC-1		51.84
2	STS-3/OC-3	STM-1	155.52
3	STS-9/OC-9	STM-3	466.56
4	STS-12/OC-12	STM-4	622.08
5	STS-18/OC-18	STM-6	933.12
6	STS-24/OC-24	STM-8	1244.16
8	STS-36/OC-36	STM-12	1866.24
9	STS-48/OC-48	STM-16	2488.32

Only the actual pulse sequences differ from one consumer appliance to another. The technique and frequencies used are always the same. For this reason, it is possible to purchase so-called master controls that will work with "any" device. This is possible because all that is necessary to convert from one type of device to another is a new code. The modulation stays the same. The more sophisticated the consumer device, the more codes that are stored in the remote control.

Infrared was chosen as the wavelength to avoid any potential damage to eyes. Because humans cannot see infrared, there is no danger of potential blindness. Another advantage to infrared wavelengths is that the walls and coverings common in a home readily reflect them. This is why you can point the remote control at the ceiling and "bounce" the signal to the TV or other appliance.

Visible optical wavelengths are often reflected. For example, the reflection of the TV from a window can allow the signal to be seen from another room. All optical waves propagate in LOS mode, but the physical and chemical properties of paint, stucco, and so forth act as "relay stations" to the infrared waves because of chemistries used for everyday objects. Human beings see in wavelengths very near infrared. Because the objects in our homes should not be transparent or absorb all light, these objects reflect some portion of light in the visible wavelength range. Color is determined by the reflected light; what is not absorbed is reflected, and we see that as the color of the object. Clearly, almost everything in the home is designed to reflect light at wavelengths near to infrared. Naturally, most things in the home also reflect infrared, and this is the reason for why the remote control signal can be bounced off the ceiling. White stucco, by the way, is an excellent reflector of infrared wavelengths.

The binary data rate of these devices is about 30 kbps. The transmitted bit rate of these devices is 16 times higher, each command bit is sent out as a group of 16 transmitted bits, clocked at about 500 kbps. This means that to receive a 1 or 0 at the consumer device, 16 pulses of light are sent. Because these are designed to be consumer friendly and are not always pointed directly at the appliance, the output of the infrared LED optical source is always set quite high. The optical detector is a PIN diode operating at an infrared band gap. With fresh batteries, LOS-only propagation, and no relays off the ceiling, typical transmission distances are about 3 m.

■ OPTO-ISOLATION

Opto-isolation is a technique to avoid damage from potential difference in the two ends of a metallic wired connection. These potential differences arise because of the potential difference in the ground potential or voltage at two sites not sharing a common ground. These potential differences give rise to current flows, called ground loop currents.

Many times when wiring circuits using metallic media between two buildings, each building has its own reference ground. The two buildings do not share any current-carrying path except the communications line. Once connected, the potential differences try to balance out and a current flows from one building to the other through the metallic line you just ran.

Only very occasionally are these potential differences large enough to actually damage the line driver or modem that is used to terminate the line at each end of the run. However, it is very common for these current flows to increase the error rate of the communications link. In fact, unexplained high error rates are usually what alerts one to this problem.

One solution would be to run fiber optic cable instead of metallic cable; however, this can be time consuming and expensive once the metallic cable is installed. A nice solution is using a component called an opto-isolator, which is just an electron-to-photon converter that prevents any current flow across it. Because photons are not charged particles, they cannot conduct any current; therefore, no current flow results from the differing ground potentials. In other words, the opto-isolator changes the voltage swings on the metallic conductor to light pulses and back again. By placing a par at each end of the metallic link, no ground loop currents can flow.

These types of devices are also very useful as lighting or surge arrestors. They will not stand up to a direct lighting strike but will prevent stray surges of up to about 2000 V. This can be an important safety issue in tropical and semitropical areas of the country that experience regular thunderstorms.

■ TROUBLESHOOTING OPTICAL FIBERS

A very useful troubleshooting instrument is an optical time domain reflectometer (OTDR). This device performs very similarly to the TDR except it measures loss rather than reflection energy. In optical systems any loss of light represents a loss in signal strength; just as in electrical systems, an impedance mismatch that generates reflections represents a loss in signal strength.

OTDRs measure the loss in light energy as expressed in decibels and, in the same way a TDR operates, measure the length of the cable by measuring the time it takes a light pulse to travel from end to end. One must determine the dielectric constant of the fiber to determine the velocity of propagation in the optical cable, just as was done in the electrical case.

OTDRs also reveal the optical attenuation along the entire optical path length of the fiber. It does this by making use of a phenomenon that results in some reflection back to the source at every point along the fiber. Therefore, the OTDR display is somewhat different from what would be seen with a TDR. The OTDR display shows a graph where attenuation is displayed against distance from the source. Reflections are illustrated by spikes in the graph. The height of the spike represents the attenuation of the optical path.

Just like TDR devices, OTDRs have limitations. It is especially important to make sure that the device that is being used is appropriate for the distance that is of interest. There are two broad classes of OTDR devices, short and long haul. Long-haul devices are designed for fiber lengths of over 10 km and have resolutions of about 10 m. Short-haul devices have resolutions of about 1 cm.

Figure 4.9
Optical power meter hookup.

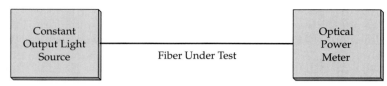

Additionally, it is often necessary to measure the loss of the optical cable. To do this, use a constant light source of known power output on one end of the optical cable and an optical power meter on the other end to measure the light loss. The resulting number is compared with the number calculated in a loss budget analysis to determine if the loss specification has been exceeded.

If so, it is usually because excessive splicing has occurred on the line. Whenever an optical cable needs to be repaired or a new tap is needed, this requires a splice in the line; these splices contribute attenuation to the line of about 1.5 dB per splice. As a fiber installation ages, additional splices are often required; a good rule of thumb is to always recheck a fiber installation every time it is spliced and verify that the loss budget has not been exceeded. Figure 4.9 illustrates how an OTDR and optical power meter are used to measure loss in a fiber.

■ SUMMARY

Optical media have wide application in many industries and can achieve performance that metallic conductors cannot. Fiber optic cable performance is determined by the construction of the core. There are two approaches to this, step index and graded index. Two classes of materials are used to construct the core/cladding: glass and plastic. All fiber optic systems used in communications applications operate at wavelengths that lie in the infrared band. Fiber optic cables operate in the infrared zone of a wavelength, and cables are specified by the bandwidth distance product at a specific wavelength.

There are two classes of optical sources, the LED and ILD, and three classes of optical detectors, the photodiode, PIN diode, and avalanche diode. Each has its own application niche. Troubleshooting optical systems always concerns the optical power transmitted and the attenuation of the cable itself.

PROBLEMS

1. Find the wavelength in angstroms for the following frequencies:
(a) 1 THz
(b) 10 THz
(c) 100 THz
(d) 1000 THz

2. A light ray hits a mirror at 30° from perpendicular. Find the angle at which it reflects.

3. A light ray traveling through air hits a dielectric with an index of refraction of 2.0 at 35° from perpendicular. Find the angle of reflection and transmission (refraction).

4. For the light ray in Problem 3, find the numerical aperture.

5. For the situation in Problem 3, find the critical angle.

6. Now change the situation in Problem 3; instead of traveling through air, the light ray is moving through water when it hits the dielectric material. Find the angle of reflection, transmission, NA, and critical angle.

7. For a fiber cable with attenuation rating of 15 dB/km, how much attenuation will be exhibited if it is used for a 100 ft run?

8. For a fiber cable with a bandwidth rating of 200 MHz-km, find the bandwidth for a 5-mile run.

9. Using the data from Example 4.6, what is the maximum-length fiber that could be used and still have the safety margin stated in the example?

5

Antennas

The subject of antennas is long and growing. Since the very early days of radio, antenna design has been an important issue; with no antenna, how could the broadcast be transmitted or received? These early antennas were either Hertz or Marconi type and almost certainly a dipole of some type, perhaps intended or just arrived at as the most straightforward way of solving a problem, namely, proving that radio worked.

A comprehensive study of antenna design is outside the scope of this book, but many excellent texts exist for detailed study. For those of you who would like a practical introduction that goes beyond what is presented here, explore the literature on amateur radio or ham radio.

This treatment will introduce some common elements of each antenna type and then move to a description of the antenna type most appropriate to each frequency band of operation, as discussed in Chapter 2. It is important to note that although most of the discussion below is only about transmitting antennas, receiving antennas work in exactly the same way. For many, it is more convenient to talk about power being transmitted from an antenna than to talk about power being received by an antenna. The chapter closes with an extended application study on FM antennas.

■ TERMS AND DEFINITIONS

The whole idea of antenna design is to get the maximum power transferred out of the transmitting antenna and pick up the maximum power from the receiving antenna. These issues drive the entire subject. The transfer of power from source to destination is always a critical issue in communication design. Because antennas radiate electromagnetic energy into free space, this energy travels in one of the three modes of propagation, GW, SW, and LOS, as described in Chapter 2.

In Chapter 2, when antennas were touched on, it was assumed that the power was radiated equally in all directions or in an isotropic manner. This assumption resulted in simple equations that relied on the geometry of a sphere to determine the power radiated and how it would dissipate with distance from the transmitting antenna.

The first broad classification of antennas is made based on how they radiate power. Many types of patterns are used, but they all fall into one of two classifications: isotropic or anisotropic. Anisotropic means different in one or more directions. Therefore, an anisotropic antenna is an antenna that does not radiate power equally in all directions. Of course, this also applies to receiving antennas; just exchange radiated power for received power in the above definitions of isotropic and anisotropic.

Virtually all real antennas are anisotropic, not isotropic, because the whole point is to get power to the receiver most efficiently; most of the time there is a particular direction in which it is more desirable to transmit power than another. A radio or TV station positioned on the coastline comes to mind, or perhaps a radio or TV station at the edge of a city rather than at city center. There are many examples, some driven by technical considerations, some by regulatory requirements. Because the terms *isotropic* and *anisotropic* are scientific and not easily remembered by most people, for the rest of this discussion the terms *unidirectional* or *directional antennas* will be used instead.

Those antennas that have no preferred direction will be called unidirectional, or all directional. Those antennas that do exhibit preferred direction(s) will be called directional antennas. Again, this later group forms most types of antennas of interest.

◼ RADIATION PATTERN

The radiation pattern of an antenna is that shape or pattern that the electromagnetic signals radiated by the antenna take. These patterns are usually plotted on graphs like those shown in Figure 5.1, called polar coordinate graphs, because they use the polar coordinate scheme, r and θ, rather than the typical rectangular coordinate scheme, x and y. The two patterns shown are for a unidirectional antenna and a very basic directional antenna design called a dipole. Here you are looking down onto the antenna from above.

As can be seen from Figure 5.1, the power radiated from the first antenna is isotropic, or unidirectional. The second is radiating power in an anisotropic, or directional pattern. In the first antenna diagram, the power radiates equally in all directions, again, unidirectional. In the second antenna diagram, although the power is the same in all horizontal directions, from the top and bottom, or vertical directions, there is no power radiated. The shading in the figure represents power radiation. Where there is no shading, there is no radiation. There is no shading in the center of the directional antenna. Since we are looking down on the antenna from above in this figure, the hole tells us that there is no power being radiated from a dipole directly above or below its long axis. Again, Figure 5.1 shows the horizontal radiation pattern of the two antennas. This perspective is the one seen by looking down at the power radiating from this antenna from above.

Figure 5.1
Radiation patterns, top view.

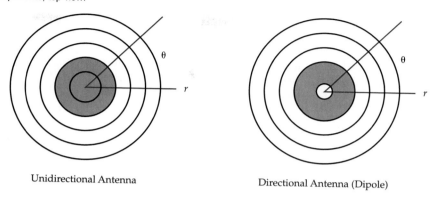

Unidirectional Antenna   Directional Antenna (Dipole)

This terminology is a little confusing. The horizontal radiation pattern is found by looking from a vertical perspective. The vertical radiation pattern is found by looking from a horizontal perspective. When you are first introduced to antennas and their terminology, this is often confusing. It should be clear that you can only view a horizontal pattern by looking at something from a vertical perspective. For example, you are now reading a pattern of letters and spaces, a horizontal pattern, from a vertical perspective.

A natural question to ask is, What does it look like in the vertical direction? From the side, the unidirectional antenna looks just the same; after all, if it is radiating equally in all directions, it must fill a spherical shape, just like blowing up a balloon. The dipole antenna radiation pattern looks like a doughnut with a very small hole from the side. The doughnut is placed in such a way that its hole is placed at the middle of the antenna. The antenna element would be placed vertically through the center of the donut. The diagram in Figure 5.2 shows the doughnut on its side, cut in half. If you like, imagine you

Figure 5.2
Radiation patterns, side view.

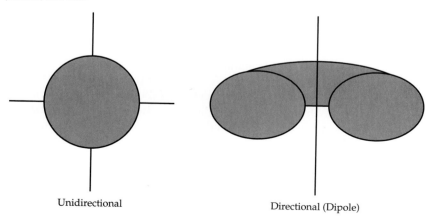

Unidirectional   Directional (Dipole)

have eaten half while trying to picture this. In fact, why not get a doughnut, cut it in half, and see if you can get it oriented correctly so the diagrams in Figures 5.1 and 5.2 make sense?

The different perspective shown in the Figures 5.1 and 5.2 should give a good idea of how power radiates from two simple antennas. In general, the patterns that result are not as regular. In most cases antennas radiate different amounts of power in different directions, as will be seen a little later in the chapter.

■ POLARIZATION

The polarization of a radiated electromagnetic signal is always considered to be in the direction of the electric field of the antenna. Antennas designed for different purposes use different polarization's, depending on the propagation mode that the electromagnetic signals that are being transmitted use to propagate through the atmosphere. There are only two polarizations to consider, vertical and horizontal.

For example, waves below 3 MHz use GW propagation and virtually all signals transmitted in that frequency range use vertically polarized waves. All AM broadcast stations use vertically polarized transmitters, and hence best results come from using vertically polarized antennas like your car antenna.

In the 3 to 30 MHz band, both vertical and horizontally polarized antennas are used, depending on transmission distance and environmental conditions. For waves above 30 MHz, where LOS propagation dominates, the signals are virtually always vertically polarized. There are two big exceptions in those bands, however: Both TV and FM broadcast radio use horizontally polarized antennas for historical reasons.

Use the same type (vertical or horizontal) of antenna to best receive a vertically or horizontally polarized transmitted signal. That is, vertical antennas best receive vertically polarized transmissions and vice versa. One caveat, however, for those transmissions below 30 MHz: The ionosphere sometimes twists ground waves or sky waves out of polarization due to reflection effects. Therefore, occasionally, better reception will result using the opposite polarized antenna than the one that might be expected to work best. Sometimes, the best results are obtained somewhere in between. As with the reflection of electromagnetic waves from the ionosphere, the type of antenna used is not a hard and fast line; it depends on the frequency, time of day, angle of impact, chemical content of the ionosphere, and so forth.

Another good question many people have is, how can you tell just by looking what the polarization of an antenna is? This question is not very easy, but if it is a simple antenna, like a wire or aerial, the direction of the wire is the polarization. If it is horizontal with respect to the surface of the planet, it is horizontally polarized, and vice versa. Very often, antenna towers are erected vertically to get height, but the actual antenna elements in those towers are oriented horizontally or vertically depending on which polarization is intended. Thus, radio and TV towers are very tall and yet transmit horizontally polarized waves. And TV antennas are horizontally polarized on top of a mast. (See Figure 5.3.) The mast gets height and the antenna elements are held horizontally. Also, the old "rabbit ears" were simple conductors that could be tilted from horizontal

Figure 5.3
TV and FM transmitter tower.

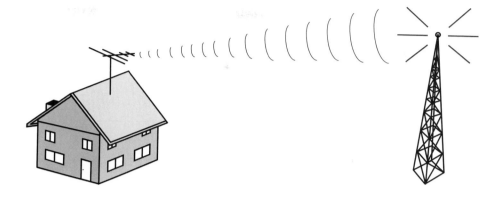

to vertical to best receive the particular station that had been tuned in. This design allowed consumers to adjust the antenna to the best polarization at that time for that station.

■ ANTENNAS AND ELECTROMAGNETIC RADIATION

Before going any further with technical descriptions of antennas and how they radiate, it is appropriate to describe how a very simple antenna really works and how simple ones are made. The basic antenna is a piece of wire with an insulator at each end, and it is suspended above the ground either horizontally or vertically. If the wire is cut to equal half of the wavelength of the signal, it is designed to radiate or receive; it acts like a simple LC oscillator. This type of analog oscillator is covered in every textbook on basic electronics; however, a brief review is presented here. The paragraphs below analyze the circuit with a classic mechanical analogy for oscillators, the flywheel analogy.

In Figure 5.4a, a simple LC circuit with a battery in series and a switch attached across the capacitor is illustrated. As the switch is closed instantaneously and then opened again, electrons flow from the battery and deposit themselves on the top plate of the capacitor, charging it negatively. Simultaneously, electrons are pulled from the bottom plate of the capacitor, giving it a positive charge.

Because the coil has inductance and inductance resists the flow of current through its electromotive force, or EMF, no significant current flow occurs in the brief instant that the switch is closed. When the switch is opened, the electrons on the top plate start to move through the inductor toward the bottom plate of the capacitor to even out the charge across the capacitor. In essence, the switch operation has started the current moving using the power from the battery to get it going.

To illustrate, examine the following sequence. In Figure 5.4a, as current flows through the inductor, it generates a magnetic field, which generates a *counter-EMF* in the

Figure 5.4
Antenna flywheel analogy.

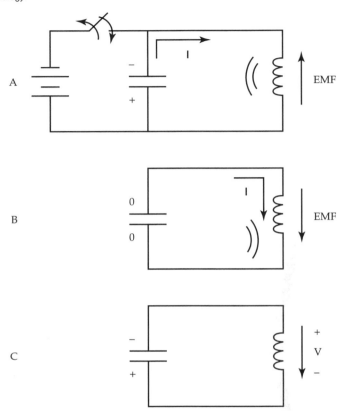

inductor that resists the flow of current and prevents the capacitor from discharging immediately. Recall your work with time constants of capacitors and inductors. The important part here is the generation of the magnetic field that expands outward from the inductor.

In Figure 5.4b, the capacitor discharges, eventually both plates of the capacitor have the same number of electrons, and the current flow slows and stops. This causes the magnetic field generated in the inductor to collapse inward, which induces a voltage in the inductor. This voltage is shown in part C. This voltage acts to give the bottom plate of the capacitor a slightly negative charge and the top plate a slightly positive one.

Now, if this is done again but if the polarity of the battery is switched before briefly closing the switch, the same thing happens except in the opposite direction. For an ideal circuit with no resistance, the charging and discharging cycle would continue and a generated alternative current (ac) voltage results. This oscillation of electrons is where the analogy to a flywheel comes in. Many traditional designs of sinusoidal oscillators use this or some variation of this effect to produce ac oscillators.

The same kind of thing is happening in simple antennas. When an antenna is cut to the proper length, one-half the wavelength, and is excited by an ac voltage at the corresponding frequency, the free electrons in the antenna will oscillate forth and back along it. Now most antennas have very low resistance; they are made of conductors, so this oscillation can continue for some time, but what really steals the energy from the system is the radiation of the electromagnetic field. This energy lost by the antenna while oscillating is what generates the electromagnetic signals that propagate the electromagnetic wave through free space.

Further, as the electrons propagate from one end of the antenna to the other, (just like the electrons propagated from one plate of the capacitor to the other), they pile up at one end or the other and create an electric field. One end is full of electrons, and the other has none. Of course, the electrons immediately move to correct this, and a little time later the other end is full of electrons and the original one is empty.

As the electrons move forth and back, they produce changing electromagnetic fields that expand and then contract just like the magnetic field produced by the inductor in the above example. Some of these fields travel so far that they are not coupled back in by the reverse action, and this lost energy is transmitted out from the antenna as an electromagnetic wave. This is the radiated power of the antenna.

■ RADIATION RESISTANCE

As was just discussed, when an antenna is excited into oscillation, the antenna radiates power. Conceptually, the antenna is acting as a voltage or current source and like any such source it has some impedance associated with it. Applying Ohm's law, the radiation resistance can be computed by knowing the power and current from the formula $R = P/I^2$. The current is measured at the center of the antenna or at the designated feedpoint. The resistance computed is the radiation resistance. Each antenna type has a different radiation resistance, depending on its geometry and the construction materials used.

Radiation resistance is important because it defines the matching impedance necessary to couple maximum power either into or out of the antenna. In any antenna application, there is a cable that connects the antenna to the transmitter or receiver. It is important to choose an impedance for that cable that matches as closely as possible the radiation resistance exhibited by the antenna.

Refer to Chapter 3 and recall that every cable has an associated characteristic impedance. This impedance should match as closely as possible the radiation resistance of the antenna for maximum power transfer between the antenna and the cable that connects it to your transmitter or receiver. Of course, the output impedance of the transmitter must also match this impedance for maximum power transfer to the load. Recall that when these impedances are not the same, standing waves result and the SWR gives a direct reading of how much power is being transferred to the antenna.

Sometimes this impedance calculated from the radiation resistance is called the input impedance of the antenna. When used this way, it is usually discussed as the input impedance of the feedpoint of the antenna. The feedpoint of the antenna is that point where the cable is attached to the antenna.

Radiation resistance can also be used to calculate the efficiency of an antenna, which is defined as the ratio of the actual power radiated or received to that of an ideal antenna. For most basic antennas the efficiency is very high because the loss in the antenna itself is very small. The loss in the antenna depends on the impedance matching. This efficiency, η, can be expressed in the following way. Note that radiation resistance can be defined for an antenna transmitting or receiving.

$$\eta = \frac{P_{tx}}{P_{\text{input}}} = \frac{P_{rx}}{P_{\text{output}}} = \frac{R_r}{R_r + R_a} \tag{5-1}$$

where η = antenna efficiency
P_{tx} = transmitted power
P_{rx} = received power
P_{input} = applied power
P_{output} = extracted power
R_r = radiation resistance
R_a = antenna resistance

As you explore different antenna types, you will often find that a particular type has an impedance associated with it. For simple dipole-type antennas, this dependence is based on the length of the antenna. For example, half-wave dipole antennas have a radiation resistance of 73 Ω, whereas quarter-wave antennas have a radiation resistance of half that, or about 36 Ω. Smaller, radiation resistances lead to less efficient antennas. This is somewhat counterintuitive, so Example 5.1 demonstrates it.

■ EXAMPLE 5.1

Determine the antenna efficiency for the two antennas mentioned above. Assume the antenna resistance of both is 1 Ω. This value is a reasonable number for an antenna made of a metallic conductor.

$$\text{half-wave dipole:} \quad \eta = \frac{R_r}{R_r + R_a} = \frac{73}{73 + 1} = 0.986 = 98.6\%$$

$$\text{quarter-wave dipole:} \quad \eta = \frac{R_r}{R_r + R_a} = \frac{36}{36 + 1} = 0.973 = 97.3\%$$

■ EFFECTIVE RADIATED POWER (GAIN)

Antennas must be classified according to how much power they radiate as a fraction of how much power is used to excite them. This is called the gain of an antenna. Of course, an antenna is a passive device, so it cannot actually supply gain to the signal, but the term is a good one for classifying antennas by how well they work. Antenna gain is typically expressed in decibels.

Precise definitions of the effective radiated power (ERP) of an antenna are complex and are always referenced to an equivalent perfect antenna that radiates isotropically. In this way, the directivity of the antenna plays a role in determining its power gain. This analysis is outside the scope of this book. For most applications except actual antenna design, it is sufficient to be able to measure the power into an antenna, measure the output power, and determine if the antenna is operating effectively at the frequencies and directions of interest.

Most antenna configurations are specified by their directive gain and radiated power. These two components can be used to determine what the ERP will be.

$$\text{ERP (dB)} = 10 \log(G_d) + 10 \log(P_r) \tag{5-2}$$

where
G_d = directive gain
P_r = radiated power

The directive gain component in equation 5-2 is a measure of how much power gain a particular antenna has compared with the equivalent perfect isotropic radiating antenna. The equations developed in Chapter 2 for power density from an antenna at any distance apply here as well, with a small change to account for the directivity of most antennas.

In Chapter 2, it was assumed that the antenna radiated unidirectionally and that the power expanded out like a balloon when inflated. The directive gain will modify this in the same way an entertainer can when he or she blows up balloons and twists them into interesting and diverse shapes.

To obtain the anisotropic gain, multiply the isotropic gain by the directive gain to find the power density at any point. Note that the directive gain changes as the direction changes, the directive gain will be different in different directions. That is why Figures 5.1 and 5.2, illustrating the radiative patterns, are important. They show graphically what the directive gain shapes are. To find the power density at any point in any direction from an antenna, apply the following formula:

$$P = \frac{P_r G_d}{4\pi r^2} \tag{5-3}$$

■ EXAMPLE 5.2

Find the ERP of an antenna with a directive gain of 6 in the direction of interest and a radiated power of 10 W. Further, at a distance of 2 km, find the power density.

$$\text{ERP (dB)} = 10 \log(P_r) + 10 \log(G_d) = 10 \log(10) + 10 \log(6) = 17.8 \text{ dB}$$

Realizing that 6 dB corresponds to a power ratio of 4:

$$P = \frac{P_v G_d}{4\pi r^2} = \frac{(10)(4)}{4\pi(2 \times 10^3)^2} = 795 \ \mu\text{W}/\text{m}^2$$

This approach can also be used to calculate the power received at one antenna from another. The idea is that if one antenna radiates so much power and another absorbs so much power, the product of the two gains must yield the ratio of power transferred. The wavelength of interest must also be accounted for because any particular antenna's performance differs dependent on the wavelength used:

$$P_{tx} = \frac{P_r G_{dtx}}{4\pi r^2} \qquad P_{rx} = \frac{P_{tx} G_{drx}\lambda^2}{4\pi r^2} \rightarrow P_{rx} = \frac{P_r G_{dtx} G_{drx}\lambda^2}{16\pi^2 d^2} \tag{5-4}$$

With this too brief explanation, a factor is added that expresses this dependence. If you like, note that to get watts as the result, the meter squared factor must be canceled out, and the insertion of the wavelength squared does this. In equation 5-4, the variable d is substituted for the sum of the distance between the two antennas.

There is another way to understand the above relationship. This approach uses the idea of the effective area of an antenna. This concept can lead to the same conclusion by defining the effective area of an antenna. This quantity is the same for all simple dipole-type antennas:

$$A_{eff} = \frac{G_d \lambda^2}{4\pi} = \text{effective area}$$

If this is inserted into equation 5-4 instead of the product of the two powers, the result is the same. Constants of proportionality can be uncomfortable to use, so the less-precise approach was used above. It is interesting that all simple antennas have this same result.

One important physical idea captured in both of the equations above is that the power received by such an antenna is directly proportional to the wavelength squared and inversely proportional to the distance squared. This idea is expressed in the proportionality relationship shown in equation 5-5:

$$P \propto \frac{\lambda^2}{d^2} \tag{5-5}$$

This fundamental result will always give you a rough idea of how effective a pair of antennas will be. The longer the wavelength or the lower the frequency, the more effective the antennas will be. (Newer communications systems utilizing higher frequencies will have to pay this penalty.) Second, the farther the distance between them, the less effective they will be. The later result is just an expression of the inverse square law.

■ **EXAMPLE 5.3**

Assume that two antennas are half-wave dipoles and each has a directive gain of 3 dB. If the transmitted power is 1 W and the two antennas are separated by a distance of 10 km, what is the received power? Assume that the antennas are aligned so that the directive gain numbers are correct and that the wavelength used is 100 MHz. Remember that 3dB corresponds to a power gain of 2.

$$P_{rx} = \frac{P_r G_{dtx} G_{drx} \lambda^2}{16\pi^2 d^2} = \frac{(1)(2)(2)(3 \times 10^8 / 100 \times 10^6)}{16\pi^2 (10 \times 10^3)^2} = 0.76 \times 10^{-9} \text{ W}$$

In practical situations, although it is nice to know the power, what really is of interest is the voltage that is applied to the input of the receiver. Most receivers specify their sensitivity as a voltage. This sensitivity specification tells how much signal the receiver needs to supply an output other than noise. Assuming that the receiver is matched to the radiation resistance of the antenna, here 73 Ω, the following sensitivity is found:

$$P = IR = \frac{V^2}{R} \rightarrow V = \sqrt{PR} = \sqrt{(0.76 \times 10^{-9})(73)} = 2.36 \times 10^{-4} = 236 \text{ uV}$$

To explore this further, check the specification sheet of your stereo receiver or radio and see how this number compares with what your receiver expects as a minimum signal strength. It should be more than enough. Note that the frequency used in this example is close to the center of the FM broadcast band.

■ BANDWIDTH AND QUALITY (Q) FACTOR

Just as any passive component, antennas can be classified by their bandwidth and Q value. Bandwidth is the familiar expression of what frequencies are passed by the device without undue attenuation. Q is almost the opposite concept; it defines how "sharp" the response curve of the device is. So, large bandwidths mean low Q values, and narrow bandwidths mean high Q values. Q is short for quality factor; here quality means how narrow the passband of the device is.

For almost all passive devices, you usually want high Q factors, but for antennas, the opposite is the case. Typically, an antenna will be used over a range of frequencies that is quite wide. For example, the antenna on your car is designed to receive frequencies from hundreds of kilohertz to over a 1000 MHz. Other examples abound. So, for antennas, Q just tends to be confusing because low Q values mean that antennas are performing over a wider range of operation. For this reason, Q is used little today when talking about antennas, and bandwidth is the preferred term.

■ GROUND LOCATION

The surface of the planet plays a big role in some antenna systems. For antenna discussions the surface of the planet is defined at the ground. Some antennas use the ground as part of its resonant circuit. When an antenna does so, it is classified as a Marconi antenna. Most low- and medium-frequency antennas are of this type and are referred to as Marconi antennas. Marconi antennas use the ground as one-half of the antenna. Figure 5.5 illustrates how this comes about. Compare this figure with Figures 5.1 and 5.2. You should be able to imagine this as a dipole antenna that is half buried in the ground. Make an analogy with the donut; it not only is sliced horizontally but vertically as well. If you further imagine an imaginary antenna extending down into the earth, you can see that the ground is forming an imaginary double of the antenna above ground. This forms the basis of understanding how a Marconi antenna works.

Figure 5.5
Marconi antenna.

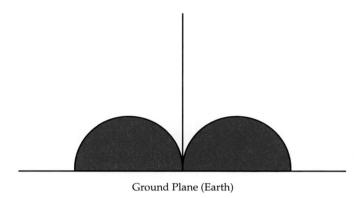

Ground Plane (Earth)

Unless the ground surface is specially prepared, the ground may not actually be "the ground." Because the height of an antenna is an important design criterion, it is important to know from where to measure its height. The actual ground may be anywhere from a few inches below the surface to many feet, depending on the characteristics of the soil at the antenna location. As a rule of thumb, dry, sandy soil fools you the most when calculating the "electrical height" of the antenna; wet, salty slush is the best. On the other hand, where would you rather put an antenna? This illustrates the importance of this consideration.

This issue can be avoided by preparing the surface prior to using the antenna. To do this, establish a good ground plane at the base of the antenna. To establish a ground plane, you must prepare the surface properly. This preparation can range from a metal sheet several times the height of the antenna in the extreme case to running 20 to 30 copper wires that radiate out from the antenna, each about half the antenna's height. If these lines, or radials as they are called, are broken, the performance of the antenna will change as its "electrical height" changes.

If an antenna is complete in and of itself, it is referred to as a Hertz antenna. A Hertz antenna does not use the ground plane to form part of the antenna. A Marconi antenna does. Both of these names have historical significance and honor two key contributors to the field of electromagnetics.

■ DETERMINING ANTENNA LENGTH

Returning to the simple half-wave dipole antenna, because the length of such an antenna is half the wavelength of the signal it is designed to radiate, or receive, low frequencies require big antennas and vice versa. For example, an antenna designed to receive the center of the AM broadcast band, 1000 kHz, needs to be 468 ft long; at lower frequencies, it must be even longer. Obviously, the antenna in your car is not hundreds of feet long. Special techniques called antenna loading are used to make shorter antennas "look" much longer. Two lengths are of concern with antennas, the physical length of the antenna and the electrical length (talked about as electrical height in the section above), which depends on the loading. In the discussion above, the planet formed part of the resonant circuit of Marconi antennas, so it formed part of the electrical length of the antenna.

Recall that the discussion above stated that those antennas designed to work in the low- and medium-frequency bands are Marconi antennas. Note that both of these bands use the GW propagation mode. This frequency range is from 30 kHz to 3 MHz, the entire broadcast AM/FM band, so many antennas are of this type; therefore, it is fortunate that antennas can be loaded or tuned to make them look much longer than their actual physical length.

The simplest way to determine the length of an antenna for use in these bands is to calculate the wavelength of the carrier signal used by the transmitter, divide it by 2, and cut a wire to that length. This will yield a half-dipole antenna that would effectively radiate and receive at that frequency. As in most engineering situations, there are other ways to accomplish this as well.

If the length of wire is too short, its effective length can be increased by adding an inductor in series with it. Because inductance increases inductive reactance, it increases the total inductive reactance of the antenna and the length of the antenna so that it is at resonance at the desired frequency (e.g., inductive reactance equals inductive capacitance). Similarly, if the antenna is too long, add a capacitor to increase its inductive capacitance and again achieve resonance.

It should make sense that an inductor, which after all is just wire coiled in a certain way to increase its inductance, would act to increase the inductance of a wire. Although the capacitor does not affect the inductance of the wire, it does increase the capacitance so that the increased inductance of the antenna due to its extra length is also compensated for and again resonance results. Because an antenna works like a resonant circuit, oscillating at a resonant frequency, it makes sense that an antenna could be tuned just as a resonant circuit can be tuned.

Clever designers of radios use a combination of these two components, each inserted in series with the antenna. When the tuning dial of the radio adjusts to a different carrier frequency, a variable inductor and/or a variable capacitor is also adjusted. This adjustment is done in such a manner that the electrical length of the antenna is adjusted to match the desired frequency without changing the actual antenna physical length. These three situations are illustrated in Figure 5.6.

These techniques can be used to make a single physical antenna, operating in these frequency ranges, work over a very wide range of frequencies. Now it is clear how your car antenna works over such a wide range of wavelengths and why it does not have to be hundreds of feet long just so you can listen to the ball game. In some specialized applications, these techniques can also be used to tune the antenna very exactly over a narrow range of frequencies to minimize radiation resistance and achieve optimum power transfer.

Figure 5.6
Tuning an antenna.

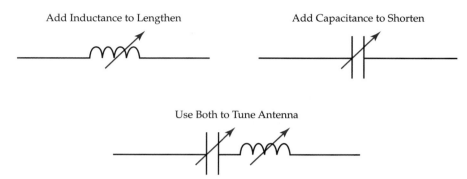

■ SOME COMMON ANTENNA TYPES

The next portion of this discussion is an examination and classification of several common antennas. A review of the fundamentals of a classic half-wave dipole will begin this section. Following that, a close relative of the half-wave or half-dipole antenna, the folded dipole will be explored.

Half-Wave Dipole

The half-wave dipole antenna is an antenna that is constructed of two conductors arranged end to end and tied to some kind of metallic conductor, for example, coaxial or twin lead wire. A traditional half-wave dipole antenna is shown in Figure 5.7. The length shown in the figure defines the wavelengths or frequencies that the antenna is designed to radiate or receive. To calculate this, set the length equal to half the wavelength as shown below. Of course, you can also relate the length to frequency by recalling that $c = \lambda f$.

$$l = \frac{\lambda}{2} = \frac{c}{2f} \tag{5-6}$$

Figure 5.7
Half-wave dipole.

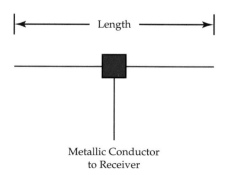

■ EXAMPLE 5.4

Find the optimum wavelength and frequency for a half-wave dipole of length 10 m:

$$10 = \frac{\lambda}{2} \rightarrow \lambda = 2l = (2)(20) = 40 \text{ m}$$

$$l = \frac{c}{2f} \rightarrow f = \frac{c}{2l} = \frac{3 \times 10^8}{(2)(20)} = 7.5 \times 10^6 \text{ Hz} = 7.5 \text{ MHz}$$

Antenna impedance, just like the metallic conductors studied in Chapter 3, is determined by the geometry of the antenna. For the half-wave dipole antenna, constructed traditionally, the impedance is always about 73 Ω.

Folded Dipole

The folded dipole antenna is a very simple antenna design based on the half-wave dipole. Essentially, it consists of two conductors connected together at each end instead of a single conductor. One of the conductors is split in the middle and conducted to the antenna leads attached to the receiver. To picture this, recall the free antenna received with your last clock radio or receiver. In all likelihood, it was a T-shaped piece of 300 Ω twin lead wire. This is a folded dipole antenna. The top of the T is the horizontal segment, and the two conductors are connected at each end. Actually, because the active element is a half-wave dipole, this type of antenna should be referred to as a folded half-wave dipole antenna, but it is not.

One of those conductors is broken in the middle and the vertical part of the T leads down to attach to the TV or radio. Because all simple folded dipole antennas have a characteristic impedance of 73 Ω, we will examine how good a match such an antenna offers. Recall that the quality of a match is determined by the ratio of the two impedances, which gives the SWR. For close impedances, a very good match results. The SWR calculation for such a system is

$$\text{SWR} = \frac{Z_{\text{larger}}}{Z_{\text{smaller}}} = \frac{300}{73} = 4.31$$

As can be seen from this calculation, the match is terrible. One would imagine that a matching transformer would be needed. However, due to the special way such a T antenna is manufactured, as shown in Figure 5.8, the actual impedance of the antenna becomes about 290 Ω. This allows a direct connection without any matching circuitry required, a real cost saving.

This type of design yields such a high impedance because of the construction techniques used. Because the two wires that make up the loop are so close together, the relative phase of the currents flowing in them are the same. This results in an impedance that is about 4 times the expected impedance of a half-wave dipole. Therefore, the impedance that results is

$$Z = 4Z = (4)(73) = 292 \text{ Ω}$$

Figure 5.8
Half-wave folded dipole.

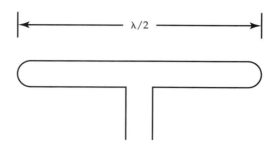

This equation can only be applied to the special situation where the two conductors that make up the antenna are very close together, which the case with the T antennas commonly shipped with clock radios and inexpensive receivers. Recalculating the SWR, a very good match now results:

$$\text{SWR} = \frac{Z_{\text{larger}}}{Z_{\text{smaller}}} = \frac{300}{292} = 1.03$$

Folded dipole antenna elements are used in many other antenna designs. For example, both the Yagi and log-periodic antennas use half-wave folded dipoles as elements. These elements will be explored further when we discuss those designs, here Figure 5.8 shows what a half-wave folded dipole looks like and how the wavelength is determined.

■ EXAMPLE 5.5

Calculate the optimum wavelength for a half-wave folded dipole such as depicted in Figure 5.8. Assume a length of 1.5 m. Find the optimum frequency:

$$l = \frac{\lambda}{2} = \frac{c}{2f} = 1.5 \rightarrow f = \frac{c}{(1.5)(2)} = \frac{3 \times 10^8}{(3)} = 1 \times 10^8 \text{ Hz} = 100 \text{ MHz}$$

Quarter-Wave Antenna

The quarter-wave antenna is commonly substituted for the half-wave antenna. It is almost always mounted vertically and receives and transmits effectively the same bands as the half-wave antenna, namely, low and medium frequency. It works by using the ground plane as at least one additional quarter wavelength of the desired frequency. Its physical length is one-quarter the wavelength it is designed to operate with. Its radiation resistance is about half of the half-wave antenna, or about 36 Ω.

This antenna is the type that is used in automobiles for AM, FM, and CB antennas. When mounted on an automobile, the metal surface of the car acts as the ground plane, sometimes extending into the surface of the road. It is interesting to note that the little metal ball on the top of the antenna is a safety device. If the tip of the antenna was not rounded off and were instead a sharp point, the electrical field concentration would be increased dramatically.

Because an antenna oscillates, or resonates, the electrical field becomes very concentrated every half cycle of the oscillation. Given atmospheric conditions that enhance static electric charge, the tip of the antenna could actually discharge a spark. This in and of itself is not a danger because there is virtually no current flow, but around gas fumes, it could be a real problem; the spark could ignite the gas and an explosion would occur. Imagine it being considered dangerous to turn on the radio when working on your car in the garage or when pulling into a gas station.

Array Antennas

Array antennas are those antennas that make use of multiple elements, usually half-wave dipoles. As implied in the previous sentence, each of the dipoles in such an antenna is called an element. For example, one might say it is a six-element array. Using an array of elements increases the sensitivity, or power gain, and directionality of the antenna as a whole. The more elements, the more power gain.

To make an analogy, if it is raining outside and you want a drink of water, you could put one cup out and wait for it to fill up. This, however, could take some time. If you instead put out several cups, the time it takes to get enough to quench your thirst will be lessened by the number of cups put out. Five cups yields one full cup of water faster than two cups. If you think of the rain as electromagnetic radiation from the transmitter and the cup as one element of an array, you have the idea.

We will study two types of arrays, the parasitic or Yagi antenna and the familiar log-periodic antenna that is almost universally used for TV reception. Each of these antennas uses a series of elements to accomplish a particular optimization for receiving electromagnetic waves.

Parasitic Array and Yagi Antennas

As discussed above, the parasitic array antenna is made up of multiple elements. One of the individual elements is a half-wave dipole, which is actively driven; the other elements of the array, also sized accordingly to half-wave dipoles, are not driven and are said to be parasitic. This is where the name parasitic antenna comes from. The other elements are parasites on the energy from the driven element. The mutual impedance coupling with the driven element excites these elements.

In a Yagi antenna, named after the discoverer of this type of array, the parasitic elements are all close to the same size. The length of the folded dipole, which forms the driven or driving element, is the wavelength at which the antenna will work best (e.g., has the maximum power gain). Usually, there is a single element "behind" the folded dipole that acts as a reflector, essentially reflecting some energy that did not couple into the dipole back toward it and increasing the gain of the antenna. The reflector element is just a bit longer than the active element.

Also, there are usually three to five parasitic director elements on the other side of the dipole that are just a bit shorter than the active element; they direct the energy into the active element. All these passive and active elements are spaced in such a way that

Figure 5.9
Yagi antenna.

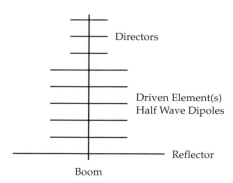

the energy is coupled into the active element in phase. Figure 5.9 illustrates this and the various elements.

Careful readers are probably wondering how much is meant by "just a bit" and why it is stated that way. The design of Yagi's and the next antenna to be discussed, the log-periodic, are not exact sciences. Most of the useful results have been determined experimentally. Therefore, rules of thumb apply.

A good rule is to make the reflector about 5% longer and the director about 5% shorter than the active element. The spacing for the position of the reflector and director(s) is governed by experimental results, and a good rule is to separate each by one-third of the length of the half-wave active element. Another way of stating this is to place them at about 0.15 the wavelength the antenna is designed to optimally receive away from the active element(s).

Figure 5.10
Yagi radiation pattern.

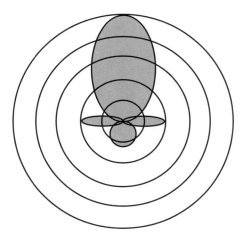

Figure 5.11
Reflector types.

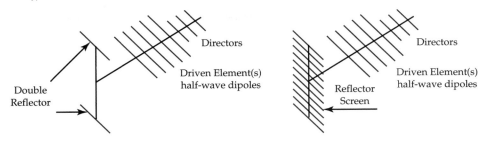

Another experimentally determined rule is to use a single reflector and several, usually three, directors. A single reflector does a good job of reflecting any energy that the active element(s) miss, but several directors increase the directivity of the antenna. Most Yagi antennas have a radiation resistance of about 280 Ω.

To illustrate that most antennas do not have such a symmetric radiation pattern, radiation pattern for a Yagi antenna is shown in Figure 5.10. Most antennas have a preferred direction in their radiation pattern, this was shown in the general equations 5-1 and 5-2. This effect is seen in Figure 5.10.

There are other ways to increase the power gain of any such array antenna, a Yagi or the one examined next, the log-periodic. You can use more than one reflector rod or even a reflector screen. These two approaches are illustrated in Figure 5.11. Examples of both these are common on rooftops.

Yagi antennas have one major advantage and one major disadvantage. The major advantage of a Yagi antenna is that it is inexpensive and simple to build. The disadvantage is that it features very narrow percentage bandwidths, which means that a Yagi antenna will only be good for a very narrow range of carrier frequencies. For example, a Yagi antenna designed to receive 100 MHz is about in the center of the FM broadcast band. Typical Yagi antennas have a percentage bandwidth of about 3%. That means that this antenna would only operate at maximum power gain only over the frequency range of 98.5 MHz to 101.5 MHz. This is a very narrow range and as a choice for a FM or TV antenna would not be appropriate unless only one or two stations were listened to or watched. The log-periodic antenna overcomes this difficulty.

■ EXAMPLE 5.6

This example will illustrate how to design the active element of a Yagi antenna. As mentioned above, the reflector element(s) it uses are longer and the director element(s) are shorter. The length of the folded dipole itself is given by the simple relationship expressed earlier in equation 5-6 and reproduced here.

$$l = \frac{\lambda}{2} = \frac{c}{2f} = \frac{3 \times 10^8}{(2)(100 \times 10^6)} = 1.5 \text{ m}$$

For a Yagi antenna designed for a frequency of 100 MHz, the length of the active element would be 1.5 m.

Log-Periodic Array

The log-periodic antenna is probably the most familiar antenna. It is the type of antenna that is almost universally used to receive the VHF TV and FM channels and so is commonly referred to as a TV antenna. As discussed above, this type of antenna is just one example of a general class of antennas that make use of the folded dipole design. An example log-periodic antenna is shown in Figure 5.12.

The log-periodic array overcomes the chief disadvantage of the Yagi antenna by using an array of driven elements that have different lengths. These lengths decrease or increase according to a simple formula that is dependent on the ratio of the two wavelengths the elements are designed to receive. Because each element "steps" down or up in wavelength, adding them all up produces a large percentage bandwidth. The idea is that if an element of an antenna performs well at one wavelength, another element of that antenna will perform well at a second wavelength if its length is modified by the ratio of the two wavelengths.

Therefore, this array of elements allows the extremely wide bandwidth associated with these antennas. Essentially, each element is an antenna itself with its own bandwidth; by placing them into an array, all the bandwidths add up to get a wider result. That explains the characteristic shape of TV antennas; each element is a half-wave dipole cut to the appropriate length. Although all log-period antennas have this same basic relationship of lengths of the dipoles, they can be seen in many different structures. Several structures or shapes of log-periodic dipoles have virtually the same performance. Some of the more illustrative ones are shown in Figure 5.13. Again these are the antennas that are common on rooftops. Look closely, examples of all three types can be seen.

Log-periodic antennas also employ directors and radiator elements just like a Yagi antenna does, and single radiators, dual radiators, and screen radiators are common on log-periodic antennas just as on Yagi antennas. Both Yagi and log-periodic antennas are widely used in a variety applications in the VHF and the lower UHF frequency band, 30

Figure 5.12
Log-periodic array.

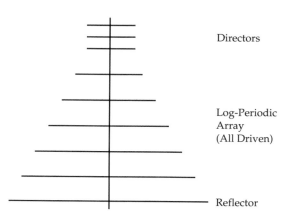

Directors

Log-Periodic
Array
(All Driven)

Reflector

Figure 5.13
Log-periodic structures.

MHz to 1 GHz. Figure 5.14 shows the important parameters involved in antenna design that relate the length, spacing, radius, and frequency of each element in the array.
The values shown in the figure are related in the following way:

$$\tau = \frac{f_n}{f_{n+1}} \rightarrow \tau = \frac{x_{n+1}}{x_n} = \frac{l_{n+1}}{l_n} = \frac{d_{n+1}}{d_n} \qquad \textbf{(5-7)}$$

Figure 5.14
Log-periodic design.

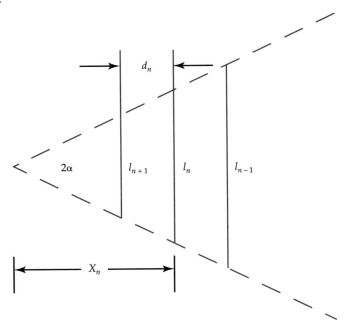

Table 5.1
τ Values

τ	d (m)	α (°)
0.98	0.19	1.5
0.96	0.18	3.2
0.92	0.17	6.3
0.88	0.16	10.6
0.84	0.15	15
0.80	0.14	19.6

It is interesting to note why the term *log-periodic* is used. Equation 5-7 shows that the frequencies are related by the factor τ. It is instructive to examine what happens when one takes the logarithm of the ratio of two frequencies:

$$f_2\tau = f_1 \rightarrow f_3 = \tau f_2 = \tau^2 f_1 \rightarrow \tau^2 = \frac{f_1}{f_3} \rightarrow \ln(\tau^2) = \ln\left(\frac{f_1}{f_3}\right) = 2\ln(\tau)$$

This relationship shows that τ is the log-period, from which the array gets its name. Frequency 1 is related to frequency 2 by τ, frequency 3 is related to frequency 1 by 2τ, and so forth. The "period" between the frequencies is given by τ. Table 5.1 gives some representative values for τ and the corresponding values for d and α. Most residential antennas compromise at $\tau = 0.85$.

Be cautious using Table 5.1; the values listed are only approximate and assume certain conditions that usually lead to optimum selection of α. To compute the precise values using specific optimization parameters, use equation 5-8.

$$\alpha = \tan^{-1}\left(\frac{1-\tau}{4d_n}\right) \tag{5-8}$$

■ EXAMPLE 5.7

In this example, design a log-periodic antenna for use in the FM broadcast band. The only information given is the frequency band of interest; 88 to 108 MHz. The first thing to do is choose a value of τ for the design. The larger the value chosen, the longer the overall antenna will be for any given frequency range. For most applications, it is desirable to have as long an antenna as possible to achieve more gain. Because more length means more elements, this is usually traded off with cost. For this example, choose a value for τ of 0.92. Now using Table 5.1, find the corresponding values for α and d.

$$\alpha = 6.3 \qquad d_n = 0.17$$

The next thing to do is to start determining the sizes of the individual active elements of the antenna. You can start this process a number of ways, for example, at the low end of the frequency band, the high end, or the middle. In this example, start with the center of the frequency band for which the antenna is designed.

To determine the number of elements for an antenna, start with a specific frequency and keep going until frequency band it is designed for is exceeded. However, it is good engineering practice to design the span somewhat wider than the design minimum. Therefore, begin by placing the center dipole at the center of the frequency band and compute the other elements. The center of the frequency band is 98 MHz. Because the dipoles are all half wavelength, the lengths, l, and the placement of the element x are calculated:

$$l_n = \frac{\lambda_n}{2} = \frac{c}{2f_n} = \frac{3 \times 10^8 \text{ m/sec}}{2(98 \text{ MHz})} = 1.53 \text{ m} \rightarrow x_3 = \frac{l_3}{2} \cot(\alpha) = \frac{1.53}{2} \cot(6.3) = 6.92 \text{ m}$$

The frequencies to be used for each dipole are given by equations 5-6 and 5-7. They depend only on τ. These and the entire set of values are shown in Table 5.2 and calculated below:

$$f_1 = \tau^2 f_3 = (0.92)^2 (98) = 82.95 \qquad l_1 = \frac{l_3}{\tau^2} = \frac{1.53}{(0.92)^2} = 1.81$$

$$f_2 = \tau f_3 = (0.92)(98) = 90.16 \qquad l_2 = \frac{l_3}{\tau} = \frac{1.53}{(0.92)} = 1.66$$

$$f_4 = \frac{f_3}{\tau} = \frac{98}{(0.92)} = 106.5 \qquad l_4 = \tau l_3 = (0.92)(1.53) = 1.41$$

$$f_5 = \frac{f_3}{\tau^2} = \frac{98}{(0.92)^2} = 115.8 \qquad l_5 = \tau^2 l_3 = (0.92)^2 (1.53) = 1.29$$

Note in Table 5.2 that elements 1 and 5 lie outside the frequency band of interest, here 88 to 108 MHz. This was done to make sure adequate coverage at each band edge was obtained. To economize, you could use only three elements. Because both of these resonant frequencies are close to the edge of the design goal, this compromise would probably not result in too much loss at those frequencies near the band edge. However, as stated earlier, good engineering practice always includes some overdesign, a practice that has worked well over time.

Now, a good question to ask is just how big the antenna is. The numbers in the last column do not say that the antenna is over 7 m long, only that the distance from the apex is over 8 m long. Because only five elements are needed, there is no need to make the antenna boom longer than what is necessary to support the five active elements plus any director and reflector elements that are added. The distance to the nth element from the apex is given in Table 5.2. By subtracting the shortest distance from the longest distance, the minimum length of the boom, here about 2.3 m, is found:

$$x_1 = x_5 = 8.16 - 5.86 = 2.3 \text{ m}$$

Table 5.2
Frequency, Distance, and Length

Element Number	Frequency (MHz)	Length (m)	Distance from Apex (m)
1	82.95	1.81	8.16
2	90.16	1.66	7.52
3	98.0	1.53	6.92
4	106.5	1.41	6.37
5	115.8	1.29	5.86

The last two things to do are to determine the diameter of the rod used to make the dipole element and the diameter of the boom used to hold the dipole elements. A good rule is to use a rod diameter of 1% of the wavelength of interest. For a center wavelength corresponding to 98 MHz, a rod diameter of 1.5 cm would be optimum. The boom diameter is usually set to twice this value, or about 3 cm in diameter.

Although Figure 5.14 implies that the rod diameter is always held constant, it is more precise to allow it to vary according to the length of the rod or frequency of the active element. For most log-periodic designs, this level of precision is not necessary, but if the goal is to wring every last ounce of performance out of your antenna design, each rod diameter can be specified. Equation 5-9 gives the correct approach. This is part of the art of the design of antennas. For many antenna designs, there is no one right answer; the science of antenna design is in many ways empirical rather than theoretical.

$$\frac{\text{length of dipole rod}}{\text{diameter of dipole rod}} = \text{constant} \approx 100 \qquad (5\text{-}9)$$

This completes the basic antenna design but still leaves unexplored how to attach the wire used to connect the radio to the antenna. This depends on what type of wire is used. If twin lead 300 Ω wire is the choice, the attachment goes one way, and if a low-impedance shielded coaxial cable is chosen, it goes another. Figure 5.15 illustrates the appropriate method in each case.

In the twin lead case, the leads are crisscrossed on the way down the elements, whereas in the coaxial case, the alternating dipoles are attached on either side of two rails. This is because the phases of the signals must be added correctly when coupled to the antenna or else they will cancel out. Essentially, every other element has its phase switched. Remember, only the driven elements are attached to the wire. Any directors or reflectors are left unattached electrically.

Figure 5.15
Wire attachment.

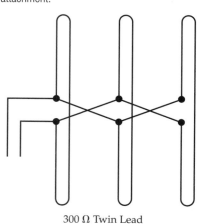

300 Ω Twin Lead

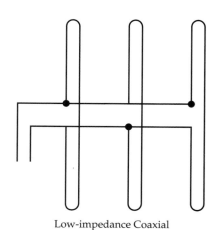

Low-impedance Coaxial

Loop Antennas

Because it has poor radiating efficiency, the loop antenna is usually used as a receiving antenna only. It is constructed of a short piece of wire, typically less than a meter in length, round or square in shape. The UHF antenna on the back of old televisions was a loop antenna. A special property of the loop antenna that makes it useful for a receiving antenna is that when it is held horizontal, it functions as a unidirectional antenna, receiving equally well from all directions. On the other hand, when held vertically, it features a very high directionality.

Remember that the orientation of the antenna determines its polarization: When horizontal, it has horizontal polarization, and when vertical, it has vertical polarization. Because all TV and FM transmitters are horizontally polarized, this antenna is a good choice for receiving these signals. The loop antenna works because as radio waves pass across the loop, they induce a voltage in it just like any receiving antenna.

The loop antenna can be used over a wide range of frequencies, from the upper high-frequency band through the UHF band. The primary limitation on the low-frequency side is the loop diameter; it just gets too big to be of practical use, and the various types of dipoles work well in those bands, limiting the loop antenna applicability.

The size of a loop antenna is always measured by the diameter of the loop. This diameter should be about 5% of the wavelength that the antenna is designed to receive. As already mentioned, the loop antenna works well over a broad range of frequencies. This means that one antenna can function well over a wide bandwidth. One example is the UHF band, where loop antennas were commonly used for television reception. The transmit band for UHF TV is over 350 MHz in bandwidth. Example 5.8 illustrates a loop antenna design using UHF television frequencies.

■ EXAMPLE 5.8

Design a loop antenna for use with the UHF TV band. The frequency range is from 470 to 800 MHz.

To begin, think about what frequency to use to set the diameter. One thought might be to use the middle of the band, as shown below:

$$470 + \frac{800 - 470}{2} = 470 + 165 = 635 \text{ MHz}$$

However, giving the matter further thought, it might be better if the low-frequency end of the range were chosen. That will ensure that even the longest wavelengths will not be too long to resonate in the loop. Therefore, using 470 MHz as our design frequency, the wavelength is found in the following way:

$$c = \lambda f \rightarrow \lambda = \frac{c}{f} = \frac{3 \times 10^8}{470 \times 10^6} = 0.64 \text{ m}$$

From the discussion above, set the diameter to 5% of the wavelength:

$$(0.64)(0.05) = 3.2 \text{ cm}$$

If you have an old TV with such an antenna, you might want to measure it and check this calculation. If you do, you will discover that the antenna in your home is much larger than this; a typical diameter is about 15 cm. The reason for this lies in how loop antennas work. The rule is that as long as the wavelength is at least 5% of the diameter, a loop antenna works well. Larger loops imply longer wavelengths and so will work for frequencies lower than the design minimum.

The larger size makes it rugged enough for consumers to work with. An antenna only 3 cm in diameter is very small and would be damaged quickly in many consumer applications. The solution was to make it a little larger for good acceptance in the marketplace.

Loop antennas are also commonly found as the antenna for AM radios. Most AM/FM radios use two antennas for reception. The telescoping metallic antenna is used for FM reception and a ferrite rod, wrapped with thick wire, functions as the AM antenna. This second antenna is usually not outside the case. The loops around the ferrite rod function as a loop antenna. The sensitivity of the antenna is increased by essentially "stacking" many loops together by winding the wire around the ferrite rod several times. The ferrite rod acts in a similar way to an iron core in a magnet; it concentrates the field lines and increases the sensitivity of the loop antenna. The three styles of loop antennas are illustrated in Figure 5.16. Note that you cannot define a radius for the second type of loop antenna shown in Figure 5.16. The solution here is to use the area defined by the square and take the square root of the area as the radius of the loop.

Finally, an interesting application area of loop antennas is direction finding. Because they feature high directionality and are small and easily constructed, they make good candidates for this application. Simply measure the power from two different locations, note the relative direction of each position of maximum power, and triangulate back to the source.

Helical Antennas

The helical antenna is used for car telephones. These short, helically wound antennas are good antennas when used in the VHF and UHF bands. The distinguishing characteristic of this type of antenna is that it radiates or receives symmetrically throughout the arc

Figure 5.16
Loop antennas.

 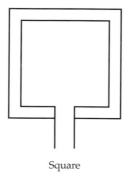 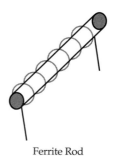

Circular   Square   Ferrite Rod

Figure 5.17
Helical radiation pattern.

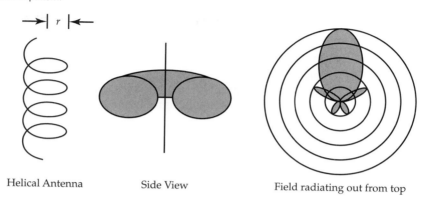

Helical Antenna   Side View   Field radiating out from top

of a circle. Therefore, it is especially good when the polarization of the transmitted wave may be altered by reflections, such as in a city environment.

It is constructed by taking a short piece of wire and loosely winding it three to six times in such a way that the number of turns times their diameter approximately equals the total length of the wire. The circumference of the turns should approximately equal the wavelength of the frequency selected.

When used as a transmitting antenna, the helix emits electromagnetic waves in two polarization's, circularly as described above and axially, that is out the end. The axial polarization is fairly broadband and directional. The radiation pattern for this type of antenna is shown in Figure 5.17. Note that the last view is the field radiating out from the top of the helix.

As already discussed, any antenna also receives the same way it radiates. Here, the helical antenna pulls signals in primarily from the vertical direction. This makes sense in designing an antenna for use in a city environment with lots of blocking buildings. The only LOS path available is often up.

■ **EXAMPLE 5.9**

Design a helical antenna for use at 1 GHz. Assume five turns of wire. First, determine the wavelength for that frequency:

$$\lambda = \frac{c}{f} = \frac{3 \times 10^8}{1 \times 10^9} = 0.3 \text{ m}$$

Next, apply the criterion that the circumference of the turns should equal the wavelength. The circumference of a circle is given by $2\pi r$, where r is the radius:

$$r = \frac{0.3 \text{ m}}{2\pi} = 4.8 \text{ cm}$$

Finally, apply the criterion that the number of turns times their diameter equals the length of wire. Because the diameter of a circle is just twice its radius and five turns of wire are necessary, the length of the wire is

$$(\text{no. of turns})(2)(\text{radius}) = (5)(2)(4.8) = 48 \text{ m}$$

Parabolic Antennas

Parabolic antennas are commonly used as satellite TV receive antennas. These are encountered in at least two sizes, each designed for a different frequency range. The larger ones are approximately 1.5 m in diameter and are designed for use in the 4 to 6 GHz range, the low end of the SHF band. The more recently introduced ones are designed to use in the 14 to 16 GHz band and are significantly smaller, approximately 40 to 50 cm in diameter. These types of antennas are designed to be used in the upper UHF band and throughout the SHF band. Certain specialized applications extend the use of these antennas down into the VHF band as well, namely, radio astronomy. The largest such antenna installation is in Arecibo, Puerto Rico, and is 305 m in diameter.

Parabolic antennas, or "dish" antennas as they are sometimes called, rely on the special shape of the parabola, hence the name parabolic, to reflect energy absorbed back to a focus that lies above the surface of the parabola. Recall that a parabola has two foci; as the electromagnetic waves reach the surface of the antenna, they are reflected back to a point somewhat above the surface and centered. This point is where the energy is gathered if the antenna is used as a receiver and is where the antenna is feed energy if used as a transmitter. In parabolic antennas, geometry rules the day; the better the surface follows the arc of a parabola, the more effective the antenna will be in gathering or transmitting power.

Another place where you may have seen parabolic antennas is on towers. Sometimes there are several drumlike shapes with what appear drum skins stretched over them. These are parabolic reflectors, sometimes called horn antennas, used to send and receive data through LOS propagation of microwaves. The shape of the horn helps direct the energy into the focus of the parabola and acts to increase the overall gain of the antenna system. The covers you have seen stretched over these antennas when mounted on towers are a plastic or fiberglass material that is transparent to electromagnetic energy at the wavelengths used. The covering has no effect on the operation of the antenna and is only there to protect the surface from imperfections and debris. Interestingly, because the shape of parabolic antenna is used to focus the electromagnetic energy and not the surface, the parabolic antenna can be made of a mesh and still operate equally well as long as the shape is preserved. It is the requirement for rigidity in shape that often drives these antennas to be made out of a solid material, although designs with rigid meshes are in use. The rule for choosing any mesh is that it is as good as a solid if the hole size in the mesh is less than a quarter of the wavelength of the electromagnetic energy. A typical parabolic antenna and a representative radiation or reception pattern is shown in Figure 5.18.

The gain of a parabolic antenna is given by the ratio of the diameter of the parabola defining the antenna and the wavelength of the signal. As the antenna gets larger, for a

Figure 5.18
Parabolic antenna radiation pattern.

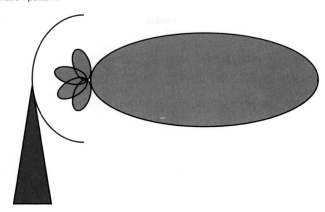

given wavelength, more gain results. Because the parabolic antenna has this relationship, the directive gain is given by the following formula:

$$G_d = 6\left(\frac{D}{\lambda}\right)^2 \qquad\qquad \textbf{(5-10)}$$

The constant 6 in equation 5-10 is a proportionality factor used to unify the units commonly encountered.

■ **EXAMPLE 5.10**

Determine the gain for a parabolic antenna that has a 3 m diameter and is designed to receive wavelengths of 10 cm. Make sure that both D and λ are in the same units, (here meters).

$$G_d = 6\left(\frac{D}{\lambda}\right)^2 = 6\left(\frac{3}{0.10}\right)^2 = 5400 \rightarrow G_d \,(\text{dB}) = 10 \log(5400) = 37.3 \text{ dB}$$

■ **APPLICATION STUDY: FM ANTENNAS**

In this section, the issues around selecting a FM antenna for best radio reception will be explored in some detail. Careful readers will realize that because FM and broadcast TV occupy the same frequency band, much of what is discussed here, also applies directly to designing an antenna system for best TV reception. It is also true that because both systems occupy the same frequency band, special techniques must be used to filter out the interference caused by TV signals when one is interested in high-quality FM reception.

The first thing to recognize is that the dipole antenna that is shipped with most radios is only designed for high signal strength regions. This is the half-wave folded dipole discussed earlier. It is hardly an optimum solution, and this discussion will focus on outdoor antennas. There are two broad classes of outdoor antennas that are suitable for FM reception, unidirectional and directional.

As you know, unidirectional antennas are those antennas that pick up signals equally well in all directions. For FM applications there are really only two types available, as shown in Figure 5.19. Both are folded dipoles. The first is a single folded dipole bent into an S shape and mounted with the plane of the curve horizontal. The second is a pair of folded dipoles mounted one above the other and arranged at right angles with each other. This is also mounted with the dipoles in the horizontal plane.

The S shape converts the radiation pattern into an approximate circle and the radiation pattern of the second type looks something like a rounded square. Both are in the horizontal plane. In the second situation, another pair of folded dipoles can be added to increase the gain of that configuration by 3 dB or so. This is accomplished by adding additional dipoles in the same way discussed earlier. This type of array antenna does not work well with the S-shape design because of the difference in the radiation patterns. Refer to an antenna design manual for more information.

Both of these antenna choices use 300 Ω twin lead cabling and provide a good S/N ratio without any need for an antenna rotor because they are unidirectional. Additionally, they are inexpensive, small, and lightweight, all advantages in many applications. Their primary drawbacks are that they offer no multipath rejection and have relatively small gains.

Multipath is the term used to describe the multiple paths that electromagnetic waves take through the atmosphere. An arbitrary amount of destructive interference in each wavelength results from the different path lengths and hence different phase relationships of the electromagnetic waves at the receiving antenna. A measure of this effect is called multipath error, or fading, and corresponds to the relative signal loss as compared to the ideal situation of no destructive interference. This ideal condition only results when there are no obstructions in the path between the transmitting and receiving antennas. The overall concept of multipath fading is very similar to the power loss that occurs when the impedance match is not perfect in a metallic conductor. We measured that by SWR; here we use multipath error or fading. The idea is that unguided channels can have multipath and guided channels can have SWR.

Figure 5.19
Unidirectional folded dipoles.

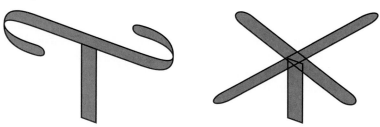

Any unguided communications channel, like the atmosphere of the earth, offers many paths for the radio energy to take from the transmitting antenna of the FM broadcast station to the receiving antenna. Therefore, the relative path lengths differ from moment to moment. This causes constructive or destructive interference, just like the waves in a cable can.

Again, both effects mean that the signals can, to some degree, cancel each other out. This is especially a problem near sunrise and sunset when the temperature of the atmosphere is undergoing rapid change due to the perceived movement of the sun and the signal strength is varying due to this effect, called multipath. The signal strength will vary up and down from moment to moment. For a radio station signal, the signal strength coupled to the radio should be as constant as possible so that any variations in volume are due to the music score, not the variation of signal strength due to multipath fading.

The other main category of outside FM antennas is directional antennas, often referred to as high-gain directional antennas. High-gain antennas are used not only in weak signal strength areas but also in high-signal strength areas because high gain also implies high directionality. As defined earlier, a directional antenna is an antenna that provides much more gain for signals in one direction than another. A highly directional antenna is the best defense against multipath distortion as well as some other forms of interference; because of its high directionality, it only picks up signals in one direction. Presumably multipath interference is coming from many directions, due to the different path lengths and hence directions, and will be naturally damped by the antenna directionality.

This directionality usually requires an antenna rotor to be used with this type of antenna. The idea is to rotate the antenna in the direction of the transmitter of the station you want to listen to. This will provide more gain for that station while reducing the interference from any other electromagnetic wave source, usually another station, not in that same direction. Of course, if two stations that are close in carrier frequency are in the same direction from your antenna, the interference will not be reduced and may be increased due to the increased gain.

The most common type of high-gain directional antenna is the Yagi antenna. The number of elements varies, from 3 to perhaps 10. The more elements, the higher the directionality and the higher the gain at certain frequencies. This frequency band is sometimes referred to as the "catch" of the antenna. Yagi antennas are not a good choice if the stations you want to listen to are spread over the entire FM band because as the number of elements increases, the catch of the antenna gets very narrow, too narrow to span the entire FM band, 88 to 108 MHz.

However, Yagi antennas are inexpensive, light, and always perform better than any unidirectional antennas and so find wide use in many applications. A five-element Yagi will yield reasonably good performance over most of the FM band and is much less expensive than the other type of directional antenna explored, the log-periodic antenna. A typical five-element Yagi antenna is shown in Fig. 5.20.

The best directional antennas are those built to the log-periodic formula. These antennas feature high directivity, very good gain, and impedance flatness across the FM band. For good performance across the entire FM band, select a log-periodic antenna.

Figure 5.20
Five-element Yagi.

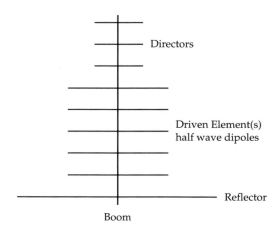

These antennas are most commonly used as TV antennas because of the flatness of the gain across the band and because the TV broadcast band is wider than the FM band. Figure 5.21 illustrates a typical log-periodic antenna.

Like Yagi antennas, log-periodic ones get better gain and directionality with more elements. The more elements, the larger the antenna, the heavier the antenna, and the more costly. A large log-periodic antenna almost requires an antenna rotor because of the high directionality. The only case where this is not true is when all the stations you want to listen to are in the same general direction. Note that the higher the directionality, the greater the requirement for an antenna rotor. When all these costs are added up, a log-periodic antenna can cost several times what a Yagi one would.

Figure 5.21
Log-periodic antenna.

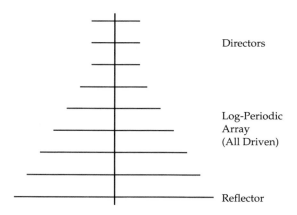

Because the same frequency band is used for FM and broadcast TV, why not use the same antenna? There is no problem with this as long as you realize that several factors must be taken into account. Some antennas that are intended to be used as TV antennas actually block the FM band. This is done to reduce interference for the TV signals. Some are designed so that both TV and FM frequencies are received, and some are designed so that the antenna will not work at all at FM frequencies. As you might expect, it pays to ask these questions before buying an antenna intended to be used for both.

Where the antenna is designed to receive both FM and TV signals, a band separator must be used to direct the TV signals to the TV and the FM signals to the radio. This is a little device, commonly available at consumer electronic supply stores, that has one input and two or three outputs. The input is connected to the antenna feed near your TV or radio. In two-output devices, one output is labeled TV and the other is labeled FM. In three-output devices, one output is labeled VHF TV, one output is labeled UHF TV, and one output is labeled FM. Connect the appropriate output to the appropriate device. These devices work by filtering out the appropriate frequency band for each type of signal.

The problem with this approach is that these band separators cannot do a good job because of how close the three bands are to each other. For example, VHF channel 6 is right next to 88 MHz, the lower end of the FM band. No reasonably priced filter can roll off fast enough to isolate the unwanted signals and maintain impedance flatness. So, if you try this approach, be aware that TV and FM channels near the band boundaries will not be received as well as those stations in the center of the bands.

The best approach is to use a switch. Essentially, you switch the entire antenna feed from one device to another. This means that you can listen to the radio or watch TV, but not both at the same time (unless you go with cable TV and only use the antenna for FM). There are switches available that will do this at reasonable costs. Today, they are sold as cable TV accessories, designed to connect two TVs to a signal cable feed. If the FM signal interferes with the TV viewing, you can insert a filter to block the FM signal and vice versa.

Next is the question of where to mount the antenna. The best advice is to mount it as high as possible and as far away from any obstructions as possible. Remember the formula we used to find out how far away a station could be heard? It depended on the height of both the transmit and receive antennas. Mounting the antenna away from obstructions such as buildings, water towers, and the like, ensures that there is a clear LOS to the transmitting antenna from your site.

For unidirectional, Yagi, and small log-periodic antennas, the mast should be about 3 m high. Use a 7 m mast for large log-periodics. If the mast is more than 3 m in height, you will need to place guy wires to secure the antenna. If two antennas are used, one for TV and one for FM, make sure the masts are not close together. Because both these signals are close in frequency, the two antennas will interfere with each other and increase multipath distortion. Never mount an FM antenna on the same mast as a TV antenna; you will never get enough separation for either to work correctly.

If your site is next to a highway or heavily traveled road, mount the antenna on the side of the house that is away from the road. Otherwise, the interference from the engines and electrical systems will prevent you from receiving weak signals. Never mount the antenna near power lines, unless you wish to gamble on a quick death; each year people are electrocuted when mounting antennas in this way.

The next major subject when optimizing an antenna is the line used to connect the antenna to your receiver or TV. There are two choices, 300 Ω twin lead or coaxial. Coaxial cable is always the better choice because it has shielding to drain away any noise currents induced by external noise sources. Additionally, coaxial cable can be run almost anywhere because of the shielding. The 300 Ω twin lead cables need to be run away from any metal conductor and not run parallel to any other wire, metal pipes, gutters, and so forth. For good performance, the cable must be at least 15 cm away from any metal object and about 3 cm away from any surface, metallic or not.

Additionally, the loss per unit length of a twin lead line goes up a lot when the line gets old or wet. If it is not installed properly as mentioned in the above paragraph, the loss also goes up. This means that a lot of the signal strength that you are gaining with a good antenna is being lost in the wire between the antenna and your radio. Coaxial cable retains its performance as it ages and getting wet does not effect it because the fields are confined inside the shield. To get some idea of how much poorer twin lead is when wet, consider that for a 30 m run, the loss for a 300 Ω twin lead cable goes from about 1.5 dB to about 7.5 dB.

An RG-59 coaxial cable features a little higher loss per unit distance when dry and new, but it does not degrade like a twin lead cable would. A typical RG-59 cable features about a 2.5 dB loss per 30 m, wet or dry. The best coaxial cable to use is the type with a foam dielectric and a copper braid shield. Stay away from the foil shield type; they are a little cheaper but do not perform as well. For the typical installation, the difference in cost is less than the cost of gasoline to the store.

For even better performance, you might use a dual shield coaxial cable, which features an aluminum foil shield surrounded by a copper braid shield. This type of cable may be difficult to find and will be more expensive and more rigid than a single shield cable, but it features excellent performance. Only in very critical applications will the difference be noticeable. Although F-connectors are easy to install by crimping, if possible purchase a fixed-length cable with true connectorized F-connectors and a dedicated center pin for best performance.

If loss is a big concern—for example, with very low signal levels or a very long run from the antenna to the receiver—you might want to consider using a thicker coaxial cable featuring lower loss, such as RG-6. The savings is only about 0.5 dB per 30 m run, so again, unless the situation is critical you probably will not notice the difference between RG-6 and RG-59.

The best solution in extreme situations is to use a twin lead coaxial cable. In these cables, the two conductors separated by the foam dielectric, so the loss from moisture, pollutants, and so forth is minimized. Make sure the twin lead is tubular, not flat. Tubular twin lead cables perform much better than flat type twin lead coaxial. (Flat-type twin lead coaxial is not the same as the 300 Ω twin lead discussed earlier.) The downside to this type of cable is the cost; twin lead tubular coaxial cable of good quality is expensive.

The next issue is how to attach the line from the antenna to the radio. Today, most high-performance receivers feature an F-connector for an antenna mount, but many radios only feature the two screw mounts designed for attaching 300 Ω twin lead. In this case, because you want to use coaxial cable to run from the antenna to your radio, you need to convert both the impedance and the connector style. A transformer configured in a special way (a balun) accomplishes this. (See Chapter 3 for more on this.) Essentially, the balun performs the balanced-to-unbalanced conversion and the impedance transformation from 75 to 300 Ω all in one small, passive device. Baluns are inexpensive and widely available at consumer electronic supply stores. Most good baluns feature a loss of about 0.5 dB and a VSWR of about 1.2.

Because most antennas designed for use with FM assume a 300 Ω balanced line (300 Ω twin lead), if you choose to use coaxial cable, you will probably need to place a balun that is designed for outdoor use where the antenna couples to the cable as well. Trying to use the inexpensive device that is designed for indoor use will not work very well because it will not be waterproof. Additionally, a balun that is designed to be used on an antenna will be configured differently from one designed to be used inside. The leads on an antenna are usually much further apart than the screw connectors on the back of a radio. Plan on leads that are at least 10 to 12 cm long if the balun is intended to be used outside on the antenna and make sure the balun is waterproof.

Now you know how to get the maximum signal strength into the radio; sometimes, however, if your site is too close to a station, too much energy is coupled into the radio. This results in an overload condition. Look at the receiver specifications for the number quoted for sensitivity. This specification will be quite low for a high-quality receiver, perhaps on the order of a few microvolts. If you are in a metropolitan area, chances are that all stations are outputting sufficient power to exceed this specification. This means that by the time the signal reaches the input to the radio, it overloads the input stage and cross-modulation interference causes distortion.

One strategy to overcome this issue is to just buy a receiver that features both low sensitivity and low cross-modulation susceptibility. However, such a unit will be difficult to locate because the same design techniques that are used to obtain one work against obtaining the other. There are two solutions. The first is to put an attenuater in line with the antenna when tuning to a powerful station. These are widely available in connectorized form at consumer electronic supply stores. They normally come in several attenuation ratings; try 6 dB and if the signal strength is still too powerful, try a 10 or even 20 dB unit. Of course, once you tune your receiver away from the powerful station to a weak one, you need to remove the attenuater to get the maximum power into the receiver.

Another related problem is when two stations are in the same direction and one is much more powerful than the other. If the stations are close in carrier frequency, the more powerful one will drown out the weaker one. Remember that you have a highly directional antenna. If the two stations are not very close together in frequency, say at least 5 MHz apart, a notch filter can be used to filter out the stronger station. Notch filters provide about 20 dB attenuation at the notch frequency. Purchase a unit with a notch frequency that is the same as the carrier frequency of the stronger station.

Another solution is to very carefully adjust the rotor on the antenna so that the highly directional antenna is used to effectively attenuate the stronger station. This solution, of course, depends on how directional the antenna is and how large an angle difference there is when pointing toward one station or the other.

Don't forget to provide lightning protection. This must be provided for any antenna installation and involves making a lighting rod. One good way is to take a 1 m metal rod and drive it into the earth. Connect the stake to the antenna using thick wire, for example, AWG 8 aluminum wire. If you use too thin a wire, the surge current will blow it like a fuse and the current will run into the receiver, usually destroying it.

If you are using 300 Ω twin lead from your antenna, you also must consider lightning arrestors to conduct the surge to ground. If you are using coaxial cable of any type, make sure the shield is well attached to ground.

If you have to go to extremes to avoid multipath or other types of interference, it is possible to stack antennas. This is accomplished by purchasing two antennas of the same type and mounting them on top of each other or beside each other, depending on the situation. Antennas used this way essentially double the sensitivity and directionality of a single antenna.

Vertical stacking improves the sensitivity of the antenna system dramatically. If the reception is too weak, vertical stacking may help. The farther apart the two antennas are, the narrower the directionality is. This is usually limited by the tower height local ordinances will allow because the lower antenna must not be closer than about 2 to 3 m from the top of the roof.

If two stations are close to the same direction and you want to be able to separate them, use horizontal stacking. This is putting the antennas side by side. Antenna systems constructed in this way will be very good at rejecting undesired signals that are almost in the same direction as the desired station. Additionally, you get about double the gain from this arrangement over a single antenna. Like any stacking approach, each antenna adds 3 dB of gain.

Stacking is an extreme solution for extreme problems. The cost at least doubles and usually a special tower or mast is required, which can add dramatically to the overall cost of the antenna system. Additionally, there are several installation details that are required in such an installation so that the stacked system will give the performance improvement desired. These are outside the scope of this application study. Suffice it to say that most are concerned with the mechanical aspects of the electrical hookup of the two antennas, and the relative phase of the signal coupled into the cable leading to the radio is also critical.

Finally, check the local ordinances; many communities now have strict laws regulating the size and height and even type of antennas that they allow. It is usually best to find out if the local law allows a certain antenna or mast height before installing one.

■ SUMMARY

This chapter has introduced the basic concepts and designs of antennas in wide use today for communications. There are many antenna design issues that have not been touched on here, just as there are specialized antenna designs for avionics, radar, surveillance, and so forth. In some cases, these antennas are similar, and are special examples, or hybrids, of the basic designs presented here. Modern antenna design uses active arrays of elements to change the antenna characteristics in real time through electronics. These are used mostly in the radar and avionics fields. The purpose of this chapter was not to teach you how to design every type of antenna in detail but to acquaint you to the common types encountered in your career in communications and provide a basis for further learning.

PROBLEMS

1. Find the antenna efficiency for a half-wave dipole. Assume that the antenna resistance is 1 Ω.

2. Find the antenna efficiency for a quarter-wave dipole. Assume that the antenna resistance is 1 Ω.

3. Find the ERP of an antenna with a directive gain of 10 in the direction of interest and a radiated power of 1 W. Assume a half-wave dipole antenna. (You need this information for Problem 5.)

4. For the situation in Problem 3, find the power density emitted by the transmitting antenna.

5. For the situation in Problem 3, find the voltage coupled to the receiver if the receiving antenna has a directive gain of 3 and is 10 km from the transmitting antenna. Assume that the antennas are aligned so that the directive gain numbers are correct and that the wavelength used is 50 MHz.

6. Briefly describe the difference between a Hertz and Marconi antenna.

7. How large would a half-wave dipole antenna be if the desired resonance frequency is 100 MHz?

8. How large would a quarter-wave dipole antenna be if the desired resonance frequency is 1 MHz?

9. How large would a half-wave folded dipole antenna be if the desired resonance frequency is 10 MHz?

10. What is the rule of thumb for sizing director elements of an antenna?

11. What is the primary application of loop antennas?

12. Assuming five turns of wire, design a helical antenna for resonance at 2 GHz. Specifically, what is the total length of the wire used? Follow the rules in the text.

13. What is the gain for a parabolic antenna that is 6 m in diameter and is designed to receive wavelengths of 10 cm? Compare the results with Example 5.10 in the text.

Signal and Fourier Analysis

In this chapter, signals and their mathematical analysis will be explored. The great advantage of the approach used in this chapter is that no integral or complex exponential mathematics are required to understand the results. Some of the topics that will be discussed include a review of sinusoidal waves and their properties, two domains of viewing waveforms, three effects of wave shapes on their spectra, and much more. The Fourier series for four common waveforms, sinusoidal, square wave, and triangle wave, will be presented, and rules about how to write the series for each of them will be established. The topics of harmonic distortion and band limiting will be discussed. The effect of rise time on bandwidth will also be explored.

Following this, an introduction to the area of pulse shapes and line codes, including Manchester encoding, will be presented. All communications systems use some type of line code. The chapter concludes with two appendices, the first with more mathematical detail on the development of the Fourier series and the second on sampling theory and the fast Fourier transform (FFT).

■ TIME AND FREQUENCY DOMAIN

Throughout this book, especially in the chapters immediately following this one, signals will be shown in two different ways, in the time and frequency domains. It is important to realize that how one looks at or shows a signal makes no difference to the signal it-self. In other words, how the signal is viewed does not change it.

> Time domain: This is the familiar way of viewing a signal. A standard oscilloscope displays signals in the time domain. The time domain is always represented with the amplitude shown vertically and time shown horizontally. In the chapters that follow, this view will be labeled the oscilloscope view.

> Frequency domain: This way of viewing a signal is probably not as familiar. In-struments that display signals in this way are called spectrum analyzers. Some-times a digital oscilloscope with FFT hardware will also have the capability of dis-playing signals in the frequency domain. The frequency domain is always represented with the amplitude shown vertically, just like the time domain, but frequency, not time is shown horizontally. In the chapters that follow, this view will be labeled the spectrum analyzer view.

When a line of certain amplitude is shown on a frequency domain display, it is telling you that there is a sinusoidal wave at that frequency with the amplitude shown. Figure 6.1 shows both the time and frequency domain representations of a signal and il-lustrates a 1 kHz sine wave. Both displays show the same waveform; the displays are showing the same information, but are displaying it differently.

In the time domain display, a 1 kHz waveform is shown with amplitude of 1 V. Note that the time for one period to complete is 1 msec and that in the first of the dia-grams this is shown on the horizontal axis: $1/1$ msec $= 1$ kHz. In the second of the dia-grams, only a single line at frequency 1 kHz is displayed.

The amplitude in the second diagram is not shown in volts. On spectrum analyzers and FFT displays, amplitude is usually shown in dBm's. Recall from Chapter 1 that a dBm is an expression of power relative to a reference power of 1 mW. To relate 1 V of amplitude to dBm, assume some load resistance. Most instruments of this type reference a 50 Ω impedance. To find 1 V measured with a load of 50 Ω expressed as dBms, per-form the following calculation:

$$10 \log \frac{P(\text{watts})}{10^{-3}} = 10 \log \frac{V^2/R}{10^{-3}} = 10 \log \frac{1^2/50}{10^{-3}} = 13 \text{ dBm}$$

Figure 6.1
Time and frequency display.

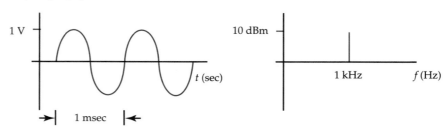

Time Domain (Oscilloscope)   Frequency Domain (Spectrum Analyzer)

Note that the above answer does not match that shown in Figure 6.1. This is because the above equation assumed that the voltage measurement was in rms volts. If, as is usually the case, one measured the voltage on an oscilloscope as a peak value, the rms value must be converted to and used in the above equation. Performing the same calculation with a peak value, it is found

$$10 \log \frac{(V/\sqrt{2})^2/R}{10^{-3}} = 10 \log \frac{(1/\sqrt{2})^2/50}{10^{-3}} = 10 \log \frac{0.01}{10^{-3}} = 10.0 \text{ dBm}$$

This now agrees with that amplitude shown in Figure 6.1. You may want to look at Table 1.1, which provided a translation for this type of calculation. Therefore, the amplitudes are the same, but they are displayed differently. The frequency domain displays usually represent amplitude in dBm. The single line shown on the horizontal axis is 1 kHz. Both displays show a single frequency of the same amplitude.

To explore further, examine what a 1 kHz square wave would look like. (See Figure 6.2) Here, the situation is not so clear. The first of the diagrams shows a square wave with a period of 1 msec and amplitude of 1 V. This is clearly a single square wave of frequency 1 kHz. In the second diagram, a more complex representation is seen than for the first example. There seem to be many lines. This is the actual situation; soon you will be able to analyze and understand it with Fourier analysis.

Fourier analysis says that any real-world, repetitive signal can be represented as a group of sine and cosine waves added up. The lines seen in the frequency domain representation are the amplitudes and frequencies of the sines and cosines that make up a square wave. This diagram will be examined in more detail later, but for now, just notice two things. First, the frequencies are odd integer multiples from the first line shown, and second, the amplitudes drop off as the frequencies get larger. Equations will be developed that allow calculation of the harmonic amplitudes.

There are some special names associated with the lines in the frequency domain graph. The first line, which is at the same frequency as the square wave, is called the fundamental or sometimes the first harmonic. The second line is called the third harmonic, the third, the fifth harmonic, and so on. Note that the 1 kHz sine wave has no harmonics, whereas the 1 kHz square wave has many harmonics. Again, this means that a

Figure 6.2
Square wave time and frequency representations.

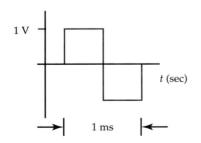

square wave is made up of sinusoids of those frequencies and amplitudes. If you could hook up a group of signal generators and set the amplitudes and frequencies as shown on the graph, then display them on an oscilloscope, you would see a square wave like that shown. These harmonics are expressed mathematically as a Fourier series.

Fourier series are at the heart of much engineering and scientific analysis. Fourier analysis of a waveform, which is using a Fourier series approach to analyzing a waveform, breaks up the waveform into a DC constant and a group of sine and cosine waves. Furthermore, these groups of sine and cosine waves are all related to each other; they are said to be harmonically related. Harmonically related waves are those waves that have frequencies that are integer multiples of each other. For example, a 1 kHz sine wave would be harmonically related to 2 kHz, 5 kHz, 10 kHz, 17 kHz, and so forth. To further illustrate what this means, the next section will review some fundamentals of sine and cosine waves.

■ EVEN AND ODD FUNCTIONS

In the Figure 6.3, the first two parts show a sine wave and a cosine wave of the same frequency. The sine wave is shifted by $\pi/2$ from the cosine wave. This illustrates an important fact about these two functions. Notice that if a line is placed along the y axis at $x = 0$, the cosine function appears identical on both sides of the line, whereas for the sine function one side is the negative image of the other. Therefore, we have that $\cos(-x) = \cos(x)$ and $\sin(-x) = \sin(x)$.

This basic property has led to a naming convention for functions that exhibit one of these properties. The cosine wave is an even function, and the sine wave is an odd func-

Figure 6.3
Even and odd functions.

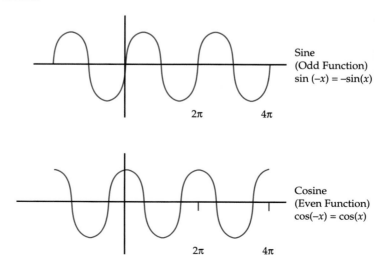

Sine
(Odd Function)
$\sin(-x) = -\sin(x)$

2π 4π

Cosine
(Even Function)
$\cos(-x) = \cos(x)$

2π 4π

tion. As will be seen later, sinusoids are not the only waveform to have this evenness or oddness. The concept will be extended to include any regular waveform that satisfies the definition stated above.

You should also note that radians, not degrees, are used to mark out, radians not the angle. Recall that 2π radians equals $360°$. As briefly mentioned in Chapter 1, frequency will be expressed both as cycles per second and angular frequency, counted in radians per second. These two units represent the same thing and can be easily converted from the other unit if so desired. For example, if a wave completes 100 cycles in a second, it completes $1/2\pi$ times that number of radians in a second. We would say its cycle time or period is 0.01 sec, its frequency is 100 Hz, and its angular frequency is 15.9 rad/sec.

Figure 6.4 shows three sine waves of different frequencies. The second is twice the first, and the third is four times the first. These waves are said to be harmonically related; the second is the second harmonic of the first, and the third is the fourth harmonic of the first. Sometimes the first is called the first harmonic, but usually it is referred to as the fundamental, or the fundamental wave.

A little more of the power of this approach can now be seen. Using Fourier series, any real-world waveform can be broken up into a DC value and a group of harmonically

Figure 6.4
Harmonics.

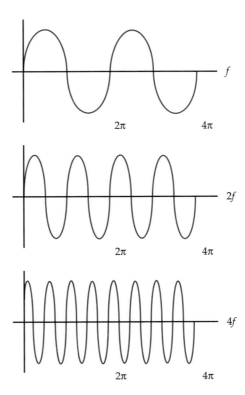

related sine and cosine waves. This means that all of the sine and cosine waves that make up the signal are multiples of *one* frequency or angular velocity. This frequency is called the fundamental frequency and the others are its harmonics.

To explore this idea further, examine the mathematical representation of a sine wave in more detail. A sine wave is usually represented as an expression like that in equation 6-1:

$$y(t) = A \sin(wt) \tag{6-1}$$

From the discussion above, all harmonically related waves have angular frequencies of the form:

$$w = nw \qquad n = 1, 2, 3, \ldots$$

The above equation is another way of saying that the frequencies are all related to one another. The only other unknown in that equation is the amplitude, A. Can all harmonically related waves have the same amplitude? Surely, they must be of different amplitudes if they represent any real-world waveform, but how does one find the amplitudes? Fourier analysis gives you those amplitudes. The mathematical basis for the equations that follow are found in Appendix, A. Fourier analysis tells you that a DC constant and a group of related sine and cosine waves could represent any real-world waveform. This relation is such that they are all harmonically related to each other. This is represented mathematically as follows:

$$\begin{aligned}
\text{Fourier series} = \text{FS} = K &+ A_1\cos(wt) + B_1\sin(wt) \\
&+ A_2\cos(2wt) + B_2\sin(2wt) \\
&+ A_3\cos(3wt) + B_3\sin(3wt) \\
&+ \cdots
\end{aligned} \tag{6-2}$$

The above equation just takes all possible harmonically related sine and cosine waves and adds them to a constant K. It would be said that for any function $y(t)$, some group of the terms on the right-hand side of the equation above will represent that wave and when added all up, is identical. Again, further exploration of the mathematical basis of the results that follow are found in the appendix.

■ GENERAL FORM OF FOURIER SERIES

With that theory behind us, we can now turn our attention to a general form for all the Fourier series expansions that we will perform in this chapter. The treatment will be limited to any function that can be considered odd or even. Arbitrary phase shifts are not explored for clarity and mathematical brevity. All of the series will take on one of the two following forms. For the next several sections, only the first listed and identified for odd functions will be used. Later, after exploration of the triangle wave, how the series changes when the waveform is shifted on the horizontal axis enough so that it becomes an even function will also be shown. In that situation use the second equation presented below.

OddFunctions:

$$FourierSeries = FS = DC_{bias} + \sum_{n=1}^{N} E_n \sin(w_n t) \qquad n=1,2,3, \ldots N \qquad \textbf{(6-3)}$$

EvenFunctions:

$$FourierSeries = FS = DC_{bias} + \sum_{n=1}^{N} E_n \cos(w_n t) \qquad n=1,2,3, \ldots N \qquad \textbf{(6-4)}$$

Each wave shape that will be explored below will have a different form for the amplitude term, $\sum_{n=1}^{N}$. Additionally, it will be seen that the form of the $\sum_{n=1}^{N}$ term changes for all even functions except for pure sinusoids. The term DC_{bias} is just the DC offset.

■ PURE SINUSOIDAL WAVE

A pure sinusoidal wave consists of only a single frequency. This means that its Fourier series is represented only by a constant, representing a DC_{bias}, (remember K), and a single sine function at the sinusoids fundamental frequency. No harmonics are needed. The multiplier gives the amplitude of the sinusoid. That multiplier represents the peak voltage of the waveform. Equation 6-3 reduces to the following:

$$FS = DC_{bias} + E \sin(wt) \qquad \textbf{(6-5)}$$

■ SQUARE WAVE (50% DUTY CYCLE)

A square wave is defined by its duty cycle. If it is 50%, then it is a square wave. Only those waveforms with a 50% duty cycle can be analyzed with the results presented in this section. The special property of a square wave when doing Fourier analysis lies in the fact that all even harmonics are zero. This means that a square waves Fourier series is represented by a constant, representing a DC_{bias}, a fundamental sine function at the square waves fundamental frequency, and all odd higher harmonics. The amplitude of the fundamental and all higher odd harmonics are given by Equation 6-6.

$$E_n = \frac{4E}{n\pi}$$

E_n = Peak voltage of nth Harmonic $\qquad \textbf{(6-6)}$

E = Peak voltage of Square Wave

Equation 6-3 now reduces to the following for an odd function square wave.

$$FS = DC_{bias} + \sum_{1}^{N} E_n \sin(w_n t) \qquad n = 1,3,5,7, \ldots N \qquad \textbf{(6-7)}$$

■ DC BIAS

The DC$_{bias}$ of any waveform can be found by taking the peak voltage extremes of the waveform, adding them together and dividing by two. This is illustrated in Figure 6.5 and the calculations for the waveforms shown follow the figure.

Figure 6.5
DC$_{bias}$ Calculations

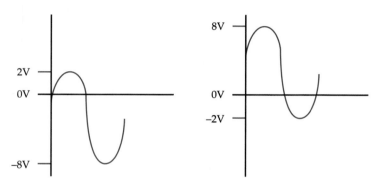

As can be seen in Figure 6.5, each of these waveforms has the same peak-to-peak and peak amplitudes. The peak-to-peak voltage is found by subtracting the lower peak voltage from the upper one and the peak amplitude by dividing the peak-to-peak result by two.

$$V_{p-p} = 2 - (-8) = 10V \qquad V_{p-p} = 8 - (-2) = 10V$$
$$V_p = \frac{2 - (-8)}{2} = 5V \qquad V_p = \frac{8 - (-2)}{2} = 5V$$

Applying the procedure outlined above to find the DC bias:

$$DC_{bias} = \frac{2 + (-8)}{2} = -3V \qquad DC_{bias} = \frac{8 + (-2)}{2} = +3V$$

A diagram illustrating the two waveform types considered so far are shown below in Figure 6.6. Note that the E used in equations is the peak voltage of the waveform. This is illustrated in Figure 6.6.

Figure 6.6
Summary.

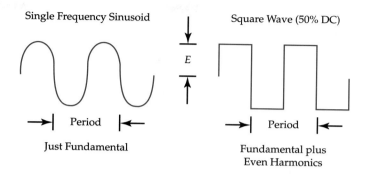

Single Frequency Sinusoid

E

Square Wave (50% DC)

Period

Period

Just Fundamental

Fundamental plus
Even Harmonics

EXAMPLE 6.1

Fill in the Table 6.1 below for each of the waveforms described in Figure 6.7, and then write the Fourier series up to the 5th harmonic.

The waveforms are shown below in Figure 6.7. Note that for clarity both waveforms have the same period. Also note that both the waveforms are odd functions.

For the sine wave shown first, there is a DC bias of 2 volts and the peak amplitude is 8 volts. The frequency is read directly from inverting the period and there are no harmonics associated with a single frequency. All the series expansions here will have their frequencies converted to radians. The Fourier Series is given by:

$$FS = 2 + 8 \sin(2\pi 1 \times 10^3 t)$$

For the square wave, there is a DC bias of −2 volts and the peak amplitude is 6 volts. The frequency is read directly from inverting the period, and there are only odd harmonics present. The first few amplitudes are found as shown below:

Table 6.1
Data for Example 6.1

Value	Sinusoid	Square Wave
DC bias	2 V	−2 V
Peak amplitude	8 V	6 V
Fundamental frequency and amplitude	1 kHz, 8 V	1 kHz, 7.64 V
Second harmonic frequency and amplitude	None	None
Third harmonic frequency and amplitude	None	3 kHz, 2.54 V
Fourth harmonic frequency and amplitude	None	None
Fifth harmonic frequency and amplitude	None	5 kHz, 1.52 V

Figure 6.7
Two odd-function waveforms.

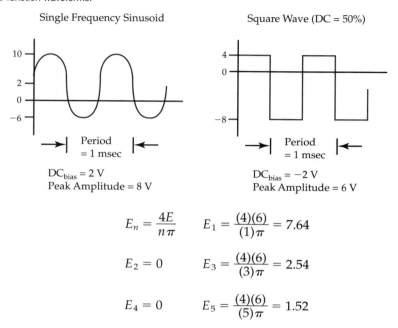

The Fourier series to the fifth-order term is given by:

$$FS = -2 + 7.64 \sin(2\pi 1 \times 10^3 t) + 2.54 \sin(2\pi 3 \times 10^3 t) + 1.52 \sin(2\pi 5 \times 10^3 t)$$

Let's explore a little more deeply and see what can be learned about how the Fourier series terms will change as the waveform is changed. To illustrate these changes one element of the waveform will be altered and its impact on the Fourier series will be shown. The first change made is to double the frequency of the three waveforms shown in Figure 6.7.

The first of the two waveforms, a pure sinusoid, does not feature any harmonics; only the fundamental wave term is included in the series along with the DC_{bias} term. Doubling the frequency will not change the DC_{bias}, only the frequency of the fundamental term. This is just what you should expect. This may seem very simple, but it is always nice to start with a simple problem before complicating it.

The next waveform, the 50% duty cycle square wave, includes not only the DC_{bias} term and fundamental term, but also all the odd harmonics. Here again, the DC_{bias} term does not change, and the fundamental term just doubles in frequency; of course, the odd harmonics also just double in frequency. There is no change in the amplitude of any of the terms. Again, the result is just what would be expected: a doubling of frequency does not change the amplitudes and the frequencies just double.

These two examples illustrate an important point in Fourier analysis, namely that *the amplitudes of the harmonics are not affected by the frequency of the waveform to be expanded.*

In other words, the amplitudes of the Fourier series terms are independent of the frequency of the original waveform. Table 6.2, shown below, gives the same data as Table 6.1, with the exception that the waveforms are all oscillating at 2 kHz instead of 1 kHz. Compare the two tables and note that the only differences are in the frequencies of the fundamental and harmonic components.

Table 6.2
Double Frequency Harmonic Values

Value	Sinusoid	Square Wave
DC bias	2 V	−2 V
Peak amplitude	8 V	6 V
Fundamental frequency and amplitude	2 kHz, 8 V	2 kHz, 7.64 V
Second harmonic frequency and amplitude	None	None
Third harmonic frequency and amplitude	None	6 kHz, 2.54 V
Fourth harmonic frequency and amplitude	None	None
Fifth harmonic frequency and amplitude	None	10 kHz, 1.52 V

■ SIN(x) OVER x

Square waves, defined by a 50% duty cycle and arbitrary duty cycle pulsed waveforms, have regular nulls in their spectrum. This is due to the Fourier series having a zero amplitude at certain locations. For square waves, which exhibit a 50% duty cycle, this occurs at every other harmonic. Therefore, the spectrum would be zero at times defined by the period divided by 2. The general form for finding any null is given by the following relationship

$$sin(n\pi DC) = 0$$

$$Where\ DC = DutyCycle$$

Since the duty cycle of a square wave is 50%, for $n = 2, 4, 6 \ldots$, the value of this function will be zero, since the $sin(n\pi) = 0$ for all integer n. For duty cycles other than 50%, just insert the appropriate value into the above relationship and the nulls can be found. For example, a 25% duty cycle waveform would have zero amplitude harmonic content for $n = 4, 8, 12 \ldots$, a 20% duty cycle waveform would have zero amplitude harmonic content for $n = 5, 10, 15 \ldots$, and so on.

Additionally, the harmonic amplitudes follow the shape of a sine wave, so when the sine wave would cross the axis, the associated harmonic will have an amplitude of zero. This is known as the sin$x$ over x response. All pulsed waveforms of any duty cycle exhibit it.

Virtually all data streams that one might use in the real world are not perfect square waves, since the data pattern is not so regular as 0 1 0 1, etc. In all real systems, the data frequency response looks like a damped sine wave with any negative values flipped up like some kind of full wave rectifier. See Figure 6.8, shown below.

Figure 6.8
Sin *x* over *x* response.

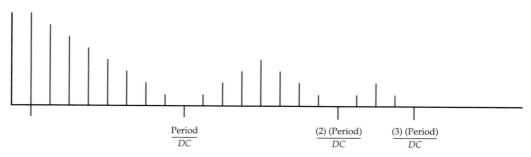

$$\frac{Period}{DC} \qquad \frac{(2)\ (Period)}{DC} \qquad \frac{(3)\ (Period)}{DC}$$

■ TRIANGLE WAVE

There is one more type of waveform that is useful to analyze to drive home the point that the shape of the wave has no bearing on the locations of the harmonics, only the amplitude of the harmonics. The waveform that will be analyzed is the triangle waveform. You may wonder why we would want to analyze such a waveform or why it is almost always included in the outputs of frequency generators. The reason will become clear as the results of this analysis are presented.

First, this type of waveform is often used in electronic circuits to provide a signal that conveys frequency information. Note that the shape of the waveform has no impact on its period or frequency. The only thing that determines this is the number of zero crossings per unit of time. A sine wave, square wave, pulsed wave, or triangle wave that crosses the zero axis once every millisecond has the same frequency, or period: 1 kHz.

Therefore, a triangle wave and a square wave can convey the same information. Square waves are easy to produce when the circuit is all digital, but many communications circuitry is fundamentally analog, even if implemented digitally; two examples are voltage-controlled oscillators and phase-locked loops. It will be often found that these types of circuit components provide a triangle wave output as triggering signals rather than a square wave.

A related reason for using triangle waves rather than square waves to provide timing or triggering information is that a triangle wave fundamentally requires less power to produce than a square wave. Because power is found by squaring the voltage and dividing by the load resistance, if the voltages of the Fourier series terms are smaller than in the square wave situation, the waveform uses less power. Using less power is always a desirable thing in system design. To illustrate, we now analyze a triangle wave using Fourier analysis. See Figure 6.9. As before, the derivation of the form of the terms will be left to further study; only the results will be presented and analyzed.

The DC_{bias} for this wave is obviously zero, additionally, because the period is 1 msec the fundamental frequency will be 1 kHz. The harmonics will then lie at multiples of 1 kHz. In an analogy to the square wave, because the duty cycle of this triangle wave is 50%, the result will be like that found with the square wave, only the odd harmonics will yield a nonzero result. The amplitudes are given by equation 6-8. The duty cycle component is shown for completeness.

Figure 6.9
Triangle wave.

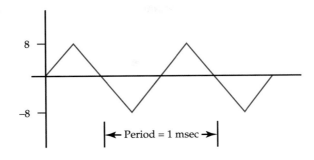

$$E_n = \frac{8E}{(n\pi)^2} \sin\left(\frac{n\pi}{2}\right) \tag{6-8}$$

This yields the amplitudes for the first several harmonics as shown below:

$$E_1 = \frac{(8)(8)}{(1\pi)^2} \sin\left(\frac{1\pi}{2}\right) = 10.18 \qquad E_2 = \frac{(8)(8)}{(2\pi)^2} \sin\left(\frac{2\pi}{2}\right) = 0.00$$

$$E_3 = \frac{(8)(8)}{(3\pi)^2} \sin\left(\frac{3\pi}{2}\right) = -0.72 \qquad E_4 = \frac{(8)(8)}{(4\pi)^2} \sin\left(\frac{4\pi}{2}\right) = 0.00$$

As can be seen, the form of the amplitudes differs slightly from the form for the pulsed wave. If you compare them, it can be seen that instead of having $n\pi$ in the denominator, $(n\pi)^2$ is present. This means that each term will be of less amplitude than in the square wave case if all other factors are equal. Therefore, the peak voltage of each of the harmonics is reduced from that in the pulsed or square wave case. Note that this effect gets more pronounced as the harmonic order increases (e.g., $1/(7\pi)$ is a lot bigger than $1/(7\pi)^2$. The Fourier series expression for this wave form is

$$\text{FS} = 0 + 10.18 \sin\left(2\pi\, 1 \times 10^3 t\right) - 0.72 \sin\left(2\pi\, 3 \times 10^3 t\right) + \ldots$$

Therefore, the result is that the triangle wave harmonic energy falls off a lot faster than the square or pulsed wave does. This should make sense to you because the shape of a triangle wave is a lot closer to a sine wave than a square wave. Pure sine waves have no energy in the harmonics, triangle waves harmonic energy falls off as the square of the order of the harmonic, and harmonic energy of square or pulsed waves falls off as the order of the harmonic.

■ EVEN FUNCTIONS

The next important thing discussed here is how the Fourier series would change if the waveforms was shifted on the x axis to obtain an even function. In this section, how to handle even functions as well as the odd functions considered above will be shown. To get an intuitive grasp of this, think about what a shift on the x axis really is: It is just a phase shift. So, in the same way that a phase shift distinguishes the sine wave from the cosine wave, the only change in shifting any waveform is a change in the phase of the frequencies. The amplitudes and frequency location will stay the same. Recall the original discussion of even and odd functions and the examples of sine and cosine waves. The result for even-function sinusoidal waves, known as cosine waves, is shown in equation 6-9:

$$\text{Cosine wave, even function:}\quad FS = DC_{\text{bias}} + E\cos(wt) \tag{6-9}$$

This situation will change when square waves are shifted to an even function. The amplitude term of the Fourier series of the square wave is modified. It now contains a sine term. In this case, the sine term just has the effect of changing the sign of every other term. This means that the fundamental, fifth, ninth, and so on, harmonics will be positive. The third, seventh, eleventh and so on will be negative. The equation is shown below:

$$\text{Square wave, even function:}\quad FS = DC_{\text{bias}} + \sum_{n=1}^{N} \frac{4E}{n\pi}\sin\left(\frac{n\pi}{2}\right)\cos(w_n t) \tag{6-10}$$

Evaluating the series for the first few terms, it can be seen that the effect of the sine term is as stated above:

$$FS = DC_{\text{bias}} + \frac{4E}{\pi}\cos(w_1 t) - \frac{4E}{3\pi}\cos(w_3 t) + \frac{4E}{5\pi}\cos(w_5 t) - \frac{4E}{7\pi}\cos(w_7 t)$$

The Fourier series for the even-function triangle wave is very similar to the previous two cases, and the change is again twofold. The amplitude term gets a sine term that just alternates sign, and the harmonic term is changed to a cosine. The equation is shown below:

$$\text{Triangle wave, even function:}\quad FS = DC + \sum_{n=1}^{N} \frac{8E}{(n\pi)^2}\sin\left(\frac{n\pi}{2}\right)\cos(w_n t) \tag{6-11}$$

The Fourier series for an even-function pulsed wave takes on a more complex form and is omitted. To make these results concrete, the Fourier series will be expanded for the two even-function waveforms shown in Figure 6.10. Note that both waveforms are of the same amplitude and period. The equations giving the Fourier series are shown below:

$$\text{Square wave:}\quad FS = 0 + \frac{(4)(6)}{\pi}\sin\left(\frac{\pi}{2}\right)\cos(2\pi 1 \times 10^3 t)$$

$$+ \frac{(4)(6)}{3\pi}\sin\left(\frac{3\pi}{2}\right)\cos(2\pi 3 \times 10^3 t) + \cdots$$

$$= \frac{24}{\pi}(+1)\cos(2\pi 1 \times 10^3 t) + \frac{24}{3\pi}(-1)\cos(2\pi 3 \times 10^3 t) + \cdots$$

Figure 6.10
Two even waveforms.

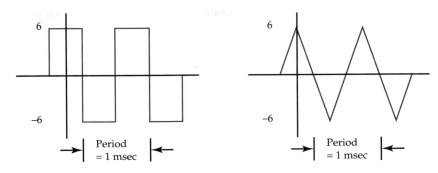

Triangle wave: $\text{FS} = 0 + \dfrac{(8)(6)}{(\pi)^2} \sin\left(\dfrac{\pi}{2}\right) \cos(2\pi 1 \times 10^3\, t)$

$$+ \dfrac{(8)(6)}{(3\pi)^2} \sin\left(\dfrac{3\pi}{2}\right) \cos(2\pi 3 \times 10^3\, t) + \cdots$$

$$= \dfrac{48}{\pi^2}\,(+1)\cos(2\pi 1 \times 10^3\, t) + \dfrac{48}{9\pi^2}\,(-1)\cos(2\pi 3 \times 10^3\, t) + \cdots$$

The results for odd and even waveforms are summarized below. For sinusoidal waves, they are:

Amplitude term: No change for odd or even function.

Harmonic term: Odd function uses sine; even function uses cosine.

For square waves,

Amplitude term: Even functions adds sine term that alternates sign.

Harmonic term: Odd function uses sine; even function uses cosine.

For triangle waves,

Amplitude term: No changes for odd or even function.

Harmonic term: Odd function uses sine; even function uses cosine.

■ POWER IN A WAVEFORM

The power in a waveform depends on its shape. As has been seen, different-shaped waves have different Fourier series. Because the Fourier series defines the amplitudes or voltages of each frequency component of any waveform, the power in a waveform can be found by applying Ohm's Law. To illustrate this, an example of each of the three basic waveforms will be taken and the power will be calculated for each. It should be clear that there is no need to do both an odd- and even-function analysis; the power in a 1 V sine wave is exactly the same as the power in a 1 V cosine wave. The only difference is in the relative phase of the two functions.

For each of the following three examples, assume a 1 V peak waveform, a load resistance of 50 Ω, and a 1 kHz frequency. The odd-function formulas will be used, but this is just an arbitrary choice. This will allow a direct comparison of the power in each waveform. Only the terms up to the fifth harmonic will be included.

$$\text{Sinusoid wave:} \quad FS = 1 \sin(2\pi 1 \times 10^3 \, t)$$

$$\text{Square wave:} \quad FS = \frac{4}{\pi} \sin(2\pi 1 \times 10^3 \, t) + \frac{4}{3\pi} \sin(2\pi 3 \times 10^3 \, t)$$
$$+ \frac{4}{5\pi} \sin(2\pi 5 \times 10^3 \, t)$$

$$\text{Triangle wave:} \quad FS = \frac{8}{\pi^2} \sin(2\pi 1 \times 10^3 \, t) - \frac{8}{(3\pi)^2} \sin(2\pi 3 \times 10^3 \, t)$$
$$+ \frac{8}{(5\pi)^2} \sin(2\pi 5 \times 10^3 \, t)$$

This is the information needed to plot the results on a frequency plot with the amplitudes shown as powers expressed in dBm's. Remember, negative values do not express negative powers, just smaller powers, here less than 1 mW because the units are dBm. The powers calculated are shown in Table 6.3 and Figure 6.11. They are calculated using equation 6-16, where it is recalled that the voltages calculated in the Fourier series are peak values and we must have rms values for computing powers.

$$\text{dBm} = 10 \log \left(\frac{P}{10^{-3}}\right) = 10 \log \left(\frac{E^2/R}{10^{-3}}\right) = 10 \log \left[\frac{(E/\sqrt{2})^2}{R(10^{-3})}\right] \tag{6-12}$$

Looking at Figure 6.11, the interesting result is that the triangle wave has the least power and the square wave, the most. This illustrates the earlier point made about how a triangle wave uses much less power than a square wave or a sinusoid. If one were to examine a pulsed wave, for a small enough duty cycle, the power requirements could be minimized but would not approach the triangle wave for realistic duty cycles.

To calculate a single number in watts for the average power in each wave, square the amplitude value of each term of the Fourier series and divide it by the load impedance as follows:

$$\text{Sinusoid:} \quad P = \left(\frac{0.71^2}{50}\right) = 10 \text{ mW}$$

$$\text{Square:} \quad P = \left(\frac{0.90^2}{50} + \frac{0.30^2}{50} + \frac{0.18^2}{50}\right) = 19 \text{ mW}$$

$$\text{Triangle:} \quad P = \left(\frac{0.57^2}{50} + \frac{0.06^2}{50} + \frac{0.02^2}{50}\right) = 7 \text{ mW}$$

Table 6.3
Harmonic Voltage and Power for Three Waves

Harmonic	Sinusoid	Square	Triangle
Fundamental	10 dBm	12.1 dBm	8.2 dBm
Third	0	2.5 dBm	1.0 dBm
Fifth	0	−1.9 dBm	−3.7 dBm

More completely, to compute the average power, one must also consider the period of the function. Here that period has been set to 1 msec. Note that after this consideration, the units of average power are in joules (J). A joule is defined as a watt-second. Its use makes sense because we are computing average power over some period of the waveform.

$$\text{Sinusoid:} \quad P = \left(\frac{0.71^2}{50}\right) 1 \times 10^{-3} = 10 \ \mu\text{J}$$

$$\text{Square:} \quad P = \left(\frac{0.90^2}{50} + \frac{0.30^2}{50} + \frac{0.18^2}{50}\right) 1 \times 10^{-3} = 19 \ \mu\text{J}$$

$$\text{Triangle:} \quad P = \left(\frac{0.57^2}{50} + \frac{0.06^2}{50} + \frac{0.02^2}{50}\right) 1 \times 10^{-3} = 7 \ \mu\text{J}$$

Finally, it should be noted that often the power components are plotted as a power spectra that is symmetric about the zero frequency axis. The average power is then calculated by integrating the area under the curve over some bandwidth. This calculation is outside the scope of this chapter; however, it is important to note that this is how a power meter operates.

As a practical matter, it is critical when making power meter measurements to always specify the bandwidth in which you are measuring. Different bandwidth measurements of the same spectra can yield quite different results. A good rule to ensure

Figure 6.11
Frequency spectra for three waves.

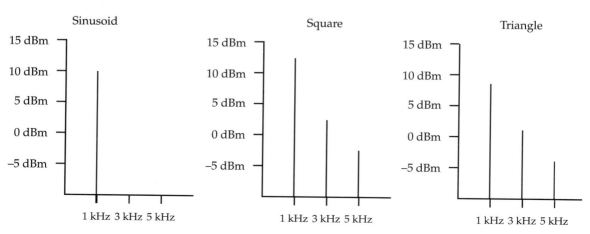

capturing the power in all significant harmonics is to set the bandwidth of the measurement to the third null of a pulse waveform or the sixth harmonic of a square wave.

■ BAND-LIMITING

In this section, Fourier analysis will be used to examine a square wave and illustrate an important relationship between a signal's harmonic content and bandwidth. Band-limiting is caused when a waveform is filtered, typically low-pass filtered. Band-limiting is widely applied in communication design to limit the bandwidth and hence power spectrum of a modulated signal. Sometimes this is done intentionally, sometimes not. When it is not intentional, distortion results in the waveform.

Figure 6.12 illustrates the effect of not including all the harmonics of a square wave's fundamental frequency or period. The first pair of signals are the 500 Hz sine wave and the band-limited version of that resulting from an ideal filter placed at 1 kHz. As can be seen, the signals appear identical. This is exactly the case; if only the fundamental wave is passed, only the pure sinusoid is seen.

In each of the following diagrams, the next harmonic shown is passed and the resultant signal is placed next to it. As can be seen, the more harmonics that are passed, the more the resultant signal appears to resemble a square wave.

Because the Fourier series must represent the original band-limited wave exactly, if the original wave is band-limited, the Fourier series cannot have any harmonics higher than the original band-limited signal. Fourier analysis says that the resultant DC component and harmonic terms are the same as the original wave. If the original has no frequencies higher than x, none of the harmonics at frequencies greater than x can be needed because they are not in the original wave. Table 6.4 summarizes the harmonics that would pass each band-limiting filter.

The Fourier series for the original waveform is shown below. It is a 500 Hz, 50% duty cycle, odd-function square wave with amplitude peak 1V.

$$\text{FS} = 0 + \frac{4E}{\pi} \sin(2\pi500t) + \frac{4E}{3\pi} \sin(2\pi1500t) + \frac{4E}{5\pi} \sin(2\pi2500t) + \cdots$$

There is another way of looking at this. Say you wanted to copy something and the original had no blue color in it. When you complete your copy, it also has no blue color. The same idea holds for the copy of the original waveform that is made by Fourier analysis.

Table 6.4
Effects of Band-Limiting

Filter (kHz)	First	Third	Fifth	Seventh	Ninth
1	X				
2	X	X			
3	X	X	X		
4	X	X	X	X	
5	X	X	X	X	X

Figure 6.12
Waveform shape changes due to band limiting

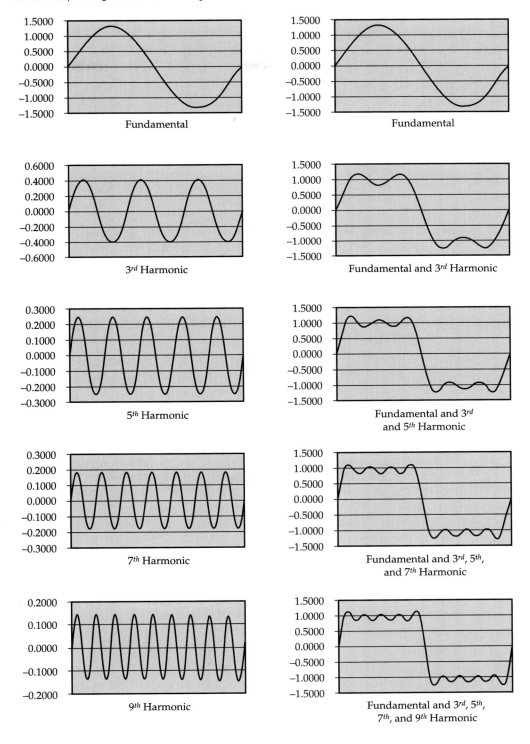

Therefore, band-limiting changes the frequency content of the waveform. Because the frequency content changes, the shape must change. Using the copy analogy, if the original is copied, and this time there is blue color in the original, if the blue color is not copied, the copy will not look like the original. Here, its color content has changed; in looking at waveforms, the shape changes if some frequency components are left out.

This illustrates an important point that should be clear by now. Virtually all waveforms that you will encounter, except pure sinusoids, are made up of many different frequencies. As illustrated in Figure 6.12, when the bandwidth of a signal is restricted, or band-limited, the shape changes as some of the frequency content is eliminated. This results in an effect called harmonic distortion. Harmonic distortion will be explored further after examining the relationship between rise time and bandwidth.

■ RISE TIME AND BANDWIDTH

Another relationship that is important to understand is the relationship between rise time and the bandwidth a signal uses. As was seen in the previous section, as harmonics are added to a sinusoidal wave, a gradual transition to a square wave results. Because higher harmonics are higher in frequency, it should be clear that as one approaches the perfect square wave, the bandwidth required to pass that signal also grows.

Reexamine Figure 6.12 closely; there is one observable result that occurs as harmonics are added: The rise time of the pulse decreases. Faster rise and fall times increase the number of harmonics that must be included. The more harmonics needed, the wider the bandwidth required to pass the signal.

From this observation, it is possible to determine the bandwidth required to pass a particular signal by measuring the rise time and calculating the number of harmonics required to achieve it. Although possible, this approach is time consuming. As a result, an engineering rule of thumb has evolved. If one measures rise time as the time it takes to transition from 10 to 90% of the peak value of the waveform, equation 6-13 can be used to estimate the bandwidth required to pass a particular waveshape. This equation assumes that the rise and fall times are the same. If they are different, always use the shorter time.

$$\text{Minimum bandwidth (Hz)} = \frac{0.35}{\text{rise time (sec)}} = \frac{0.35}{t_r} \qquad \textbf{(6-13)}$$

■ EXAMPLE 6.2

A square or pulsed waveform has a rise and fall time that has been measured to be 1 μsec. What bandwidth is required to pass this signal without any band-limiting effect?

$$BW = \frac{0.35}{1 \times 10^{-6}} = 350 \text{ kHz}$$

Once this value and the fundamental frequency of the waveform are known, the number of harmonics that will be included can be calculated.

■ EXAMPLE 6.3

In Example 6.2, the fundamental frequency of the waveform was 10 kHz. What is the highest-order harmonic that would be passed in the bandwidth calculated?

$$\text{Highest harmonic passed} = \frac{\text{BW}}{\text{fundamental frequency}} = \frac{350 \text{ kHz}}{10 \text{ kHz}} = 35$$

■ HARMONIC DISTORTION

As you might expect, one of the essential figures of merit of a communications systems is a measure of how "good" it is. Both technical and economic factors determine this. However, there is one thing that is always important and two others that let you characterize how much of the information that was sent was received correctly by the receiver.

The one thing that is always important is how much power is being transmitted. Any communications system must get sufficient power to the destination for the receiver to operate. All communications systems must meet this basic requirement. To illustrate this, think about your favorite radio station. Once you move too far away from it, the signal grows too weak for your radio to receive. However much you might want to listen to it, without sufficient power getting to your radio, you cannot do so.

In the previous section, power calculations for some specific signal shapes were carried out. Later, simple equations will be developed that will allow calculation of the average power for several different kinds of transmitters or modulators. Because these equations will be different for each modulation technique, their development will be left to the individual chapter where the associated modulation technique is discussed. However, they all depend on the power in the carrier wave to some extent.

How much of the information, voice, video, data, and so forth is reproduced correctly at the receiver is measured differently depending on if the information analog or digital. For analog data sources, the total harmonic distortion (THD) is used to characterize the quality or linearity of the receiver. Harmonic distortion is defined as the generation of harmonics of the desired signal due to amplitude distortion. For example, if the intent was to send a pure sinusoid and instead of only the fundamental, but also several harmonics were received, this would be an example of harmonic distortion. Harmonic distortion often results from amplitude distortion and is the figure of merit for communication receivers with analog data sources. These include AM and FM broadcast radio, TV, cellular radio, and so forth.

Recall that harmonic distortion was defined as the *generation* of harmonics due to amplitude distortion. What was just examined in the last section was harmonic distortion generated due to the *loss* of harmonics. As was discussed there, this effect is generally known as harmonic distortion due to band-limiting and is discussed as band-limiting effects. However, as can be clearly seen, anytime one either *adds or subtracts* harmonics of the fundamental frequency, the wave shape of the signal is changed.

Harmonic distortion traditionally is only described as the addition of harmonics. It most typically arises from passing sinusoidal signals through imperfect amplifiers. Virtually all amplifiers encountered in the real world are imperfect to some degree. When this imperfection manifests itself by adding harmonics to the fundamental frequency, it is measured by the THD. The THD is found mathematically by taking the ratio of the power in the fundamental frequency and the power in *all* higher harmonics present. Because powers are used, remember to use rms voltage values. This is illustrated in Example 6.4.

◼ EXAMPLE 6.4

A certain signal generator is designed to supply a 10 dBm, 1 kHz sinusoidal wave with no harmonic contributions. When the output is measured, you find the fundamental frequency amplified just as stated, but you also find a total power contribution of 3 dBm for all higher harmonics. Find the THD. Take the ratio of the powers to find THD.

$$\%\text{THD} = \left(\frac{\text{Power of all higher harmonics}}{\text{Power of fundamental frequency}} \right) 100 \qquad \textbf{(6-14)}$$

$$\%\text{THD} = \frac{3 \text{ dBm}}{10 \text{ dBm}} = 30\%$$

Often the values you measure are not available in such a readily usable form. What form would equation 6-14 take if the peak voltages of the harmonics were measured instead? The first thing to recognize is that rms value of the voltage will be required. The next example will illustrate the correct procedure.

◼ EXAMPLE 6.5

A certain amplifier outputs a 10 V peak signal at the fundamental frequency. You also measure a 1 V peak signal at the third harmonic and a 0.25 V peak signal at the fifth harmonic. No other harmonics have any measurable voltage. Find the THD.

First, convert from peak to RMS values for the measured voltages. Although this is not strictly necessary because harmonic distortion is a ratio of voltages and the scaling factors will cancel, it is a good practice to stay with when dealing with powers.

$$10 \text{ V peak to peak} = \frac{10}{\sqrt{2}} = 7.07 \text{ V}$$

$$1 \text{ V peak to peak} = \frac{1}{\sqrt{2}} = 0.707 \text{ V}$$

$$0.25 \text{ V peak to peak} = \frac{0.25}{\sqrt{2}} = 0.168 \text{ V}$$

Equation 6-14 is modified as follows:

$$\%\text{THD} = \left(\frac{\text{Quadratic Sum of all higher harmonic voltages (RMS)}}{\text{Fundamental voltage (RMS)}}\right)(100) \quad \textbf{(6-15)}$$

$$\%\text{THD} = \frac{\sqrt{0.707^2 + 0.168^2}}{7.07}(100) = 7.47\%$$

■ EXAMPLE 6.6

It is also possible to calculate the THD through the use of amplitudes found in a Fourier series expansion such as that of the square wave shown in Figure 6.13.

This is a 5 V peak, 50% duty cycle pulse of frequency 1 kHz. The harmonic amplitudes are found to be:

$$E_n = \frac{4E}{n\pi}\sin(n\pi DC) \qquad\qquad E_1 = \frac{(4)(5)}{\pi} = 6.37$$

$$E_2 = 0 \qquad\qquad E_3 = \frac{(4)(5)}{3\pi} = 1.91$$

$$E_4 = 0 \qquad\qquad E_5 = \frac{(4)(5)}{5\pi} = -1.27$$

$$E_6 = 0 \qquad\qquad E_7 = \frac{(4)(5)}{7\pi} = -0.91$$

Then applying equation 6-15, the THD up to the 7th harmonic is found:

$$\%\text{THD} = \left(\frac{\sqrt{1.91^2 + 1.27^2 + 0.9^2}}{6.37}\right)(100)$$

$$= \frac{\sqrt{6.09}}{6.37}(100) = 38.7\%$$

Figure 6.13
Example 6.6

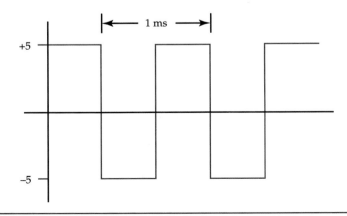

As can be seen from these three examples, the harmonic distortion in any system is determined by the power in the higher harmonics as compared to the power in the fundamental wave. This leads to two consequences in comunication system design.

Most systems combine analog and digital components, and the digital components often use square waves. If any harmonic power leaks into the analog portion of the circuitry, the effect is to degrade the performance of that portion due to the increased harmonic distortion. This component of harmonic distortion is not due to harmonics produced by the analog portion itself but rather to its physical proximity to the digital portion. This explains why the analog portion of a system is often isolated on a separate PC board with its own ground return.

The second consequence is the use of triangle waves for timing information whenever possible. A triangle wave has the lowest amount of power in its harmonics of any of the waves we have studied. Because timing information is only dependent on the rate of zero crossings, and the wave shape does not influence this, triangle waves are a good choice when concerned about minimizing harmonic contributions to the analog circuitry.

These ideas about how power is influenced by the shape of the wave leads us into the last two topics for this chapter, pulse shapes and line codes.

■ PULSE SHAPES

Different pulse shapes have different frequency components. Although many different kinds of pulse shapes are possible, only those that arise from an alteration of the duty cycle will be considered to illustrate the concept. The central idea in this section is that the shape of the spectrum, defined by its frequency locations and amplitudes at those locations, depends only on the duty cycle of the pulse. Specifically, it does not depend on the repetition rate or frequency.

To start the discussion on this subject, recall earlier in the chapter where the frequency of the two waveforms—sinusoid and square—were doubled. The only thing that changed in the spectral components was their location. Each doubled in frequency. The amplitude of each harmonic stayed the same. The conclusion from that example is that what changed is called the "spread" of the line spectrum, and not its shape. The spread of a spectrum is a way of referring to how wide in frequency it is. The wider the frequency, the greater the spread. Wide frequency bands are usually undesirable because they consume more bandwidth.

Reexamine Figure 6.8 and note that the sin x over x response, or the shape, depended on the duty cycle of the pulse. The shape was the same, but the spread of the spectrum would increase with decreasing duty cycle.

Again it is seen that the shape of the spectrum depends only on the duty cycle of the pulse. To give you a better feel for how these would change, three waveforms are shown in Figure 6.14 that illustrate how the spread of the spectrum changes with duty cycle. The frequency spread of the spectrum is inversely proportional to the duty cycle. This is expressed by the relationship shown below:

$$\text{frequency spread} \propto \frac{1}{\text{duty cycle}} \qquad \textbf{(6-16)}$$

Looking closely at Figure 6.14, it can be seen that all are of the shape of a sin x over x response, with the spread of the spectrum altered by the duty cycle. In each of the diagrams, the period or frequency of the pulse is kept constant. Therefore, it can now be seen that there is a relationship between the duty cycle of a pulsed waveform, its frequency spread, and the amplitude range of its harmonics. These are illustrated in Figure 6.14 and are summarized below. They are stated in terms of duty cycle, because this is usually an easily observed characteristic of a waveform.

As duty cycle increases,
Frequency spread of harmonics decreases, and the amplitude range increases.

As duty cycle decreases,
Frequency spread of harmonics increases, and amplitude range decreases.

Figure 6.14
Duty cycle and spectrum spread.

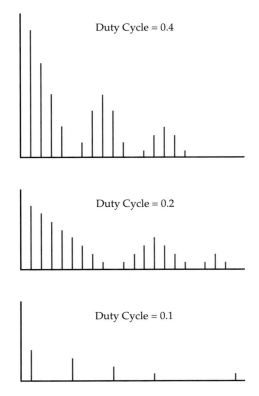

■ EXAMPLE 6.7

Determine the change in bandwidth for two pulse trains of frequency 1 kHz. The first has a duty cycle of 40%, and the second has a duty cycle of 20%. Keep up to the third frequency null in both cases.

First, determine the location of the frequency nulls. This is given by inverting the frequency of the pulse train.

$$\text{period} = \frac{1}{\text{frequency}} = \frac{1}{1 \text{ kHz}} = 1 \text{ msec}$$

Because the spectrum out to the third null will be included, that will be all harmonics out to 3 times the period divided by the duty cycle. Refer to Figure 6.8 to see this.

$$40\% \text{ DC: } \frac{1}{\text{frequency spread}} = \frac{1}{3 \text{ period/duty cycle}} = \frac{1}{[(3)(3 \times 10^3)/0.40]}$$

$$= \frac{1}{0.0075} = 133 \text{ Hz}$$

$$20\% \text{ DC: } \frac{1}{\text{frequency spread}} = \frac{1}{3 \text{ period/duty cycle}} = \frac{1}{[(3)(3 \times 10^{-3})/0.20]}$$

$$= \frac{1}{0.045} = 22 \text{ Hz}$$

As can be seen from this calculation, a halving of duty cycle results in a doubling of each sin x over x component of the spectrum. Because the first three nulls are kept, a 6 times increase for the frequency spectrum results. Decreasing the duty of a pulse greatly increases the bandwidth of the frequency spectrum.

■ LINE CODES

We will first consider the difference in power for the two basic line codes known as unipolar-NRZ (U-NRZ) and polar-NRZ (P-NRZ). NRZ stands for non-return-to-zero. These two line codes are illustrated in Figure 6.15. Both of these signals are ones with which you are already familiar. The first, U-NRZ, is the type of signal that is commonly generated from a standard TTL or CMOS part with a single 5 V power supply. P-NRZ signals are generated by those integrated circuits (ICs) you may have worked with that use a dual voltage power supply and the signal swings from the negative supply to the positive supply.

Because the peak voltage of each sequence is the same, a direct comparison of the power can be made for each basic line code. The power in each wave is given by the square of the peak voltage of each pulse in a single period divided by the resistance. For the first case, there is a single pulse of voltage $2V$. For the second case, there are two pulses of voltage V. This yields

Figure 6.15
Two NRZ line codes.

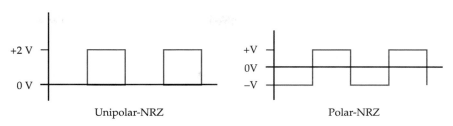

Unipolar-NRZ   Polar-NRZ

$$\text{U-NRZ:} \quad P = \frac{(2V)^2}{2R} = \frac{2V^2}{R} \tag{6-17}$$

$$\text{P-NRZ:} \quad P = 2\frac{V^2}{2R} = \frac{V^2}{R} \tag{6-18}$$

where the factor of 2 in the denominator accounts for the conversion from peak voltage to rms voltage. There is twice the power in a unipolar signal as in a polar signal. This can have a profound effect on the power in a communications system.

Although U-NRZ line codes are very common, using P-NRZ line codes can have better performance in a digital communication system. The mathematical reasoning for this is complex, but the outlines of it have been presented above. It can be stated simply by recognizing that because the P-NRZ code is symmetric about 0 V, there is a reduced DC component as compared to U-NRZ coding. This DC component "steals" energy from frequency components that the receiver could use to distinguish a 1 from a 0. This can be seen by finding the Fourier series expansion for the two pulse shapes above, assuming a frequency of 1 kHz.

$$\text{U-NRZ:} \quad \text{FS} = V + \frac{4V}{\pi}\sin(2\pi 1 \times 10^3 t) + \frac{4V}{3\pi}\sin(2\pi 3 \times 10^3 t) + \cdots$$

$$\text{P-NRZ:} \quad \text{FS} = 0 + \frac{4V}{\pi}\sin(2\pi 1 \times 10^3 t) + \frac{4V}{3\pi}\sin(2\pi 3 \times 10^3) + \cdots$$

As can be seen, the only real difference in the two expansions is the DC bias term. Therefore, for a given amount of energy used, the more that is put into DC, the less that is available for frequency components. DC tells you nothing about whether a signal is a 1 or a 0. All this information is contained in the frequency components of the waveform. Consequently, better error rate performance is obtained when using P-NRZ codes.

There are many types of line codes used by different communication systems for specific purposes. In Chapter 16 a special type of line code known as a rate reduction code will be explored. When the framing in the telephone system is discussed, the two types of line codes used there, AMI and B8ZS, will be defined. This section will close with a description of an encoding technique used widely in LANs and other applications. It is a very popular line code, called Manchester encoding.

Manchester encoding is used to ensure that a bit transition occurs in every bit cell. Manchester encoding just is another type of line code. It is very useful in environments where clock recovery from the data stream is important. Figure 6.16 shows how Manchester encoding works. Note that at every bit interval, independent of the data rate, there is a transition at the data clocking rate. This transition supplies the energy at the data clocking rate that the modem uses to extract this frequency. More generally, any line code that exhibits this characteristic is referred to as a self-clocking code.

Looking closely at Figure 6.15, it can be clearly seen that each bit interval has a transition, even when the data does not change from the previous bit interval. It is also interesting that Manchester encoding does not modify the data pattern in the case where it is alternating 1s and 0s. This is important in many LAN applications.

Figure 6.16
Manchester encoding.

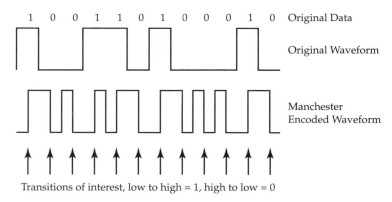

Transitions of interest, low to high = 1, high to low = 0

■ SUMMARY

In this chapter the Fourier series expansion for a number of common waveforms was introduced. Additionally, many important results that show the importance of Fourier Analysis in system design were noted. A few important points summarize this discussion:

1. The formulas for the amplitude of the harmonics are different for each waveform shape explored, sinusoid, square, and triangle.
2. The formulas for the amplitude of the harmonics are independent of frequency and evenness or oddness for any waveform shape.
3. For 50% duty cycle waves where only every other harmonic must be considered, an even function uses the even harmonic cosine terms only. For an odd function, the odd harmonic sine terms are all that are needed.

PROBLEMS

1. Write the Fourier series for all terms up to and including the fifth harmonic for each of the following waveforms:
   (a) 2 V peak amplitude, 10 kHz cosine wave, no DC offset (even function)
   (b) 2 V peak amplitude, 20 kHz sine wave, +5 V DC offset (odd function)
   (c) 5 V peak amplitude, 1 kHz square wave, −3 V DC offset, odd function
   (d) 8 V peak amplitude, 2 kHz square wave, +3 V DC offset, even function
   (e) 3 V peak amplitude, 1 kHz triangle wave, 0 V DC offset, odd function
   (f) 5 V peak amplitude, 2 kHz triangle wave, +2 V DC offset, even function

2. For each of the waveforms in Problem 1, draw the frequency domain spectrum, showing amplitudes and frequencies of each harmonic that is nonzero.

3. For each of the waveforms in Problem 1, pass the waveform through the low-pass filter listed here. Assuming an ideal filter, indicate which Fourier series terms would appear on the output of the filter. Only include up to the fifth harmonic.
   (a) 50 kHz
   (b) 10 kHz
   (c) 5 kHz
   (d) 2 kHz

4. For each of the waveforms in Problem 1, find the lowest cutoff frequency filter that will result in a single frequency sinusoid at the output of the low-pass filter.

5. For each of the waveforms in Problem 1, pass the waveform through the respective band-pass filter listed here. Assume the first frequency is the lowest frequency passed, and the second frequency, the highest. Identify which Fourier series terms would appear on the output of the filter. Only include up to the fifth harmonic.

(a) 5 kHz, 25 kHz
(b) 25 kHz, 50 kHz
(c) 2 kHz, 8 kHz
(d) 1 kHz, 5 kHz

6. Find the %THD for a waveform with a fundamental rms voltage of 10 V and a total rms voltage for all higher harmonics of 2 V.

7. Find the 8THD for a triangle wave with a pulse voltage of 5V. Increase all terms to the 9th harmonic.

8. Find the Manchester encoding for the 16-bit sequences:
   (a) 1100101000110001
   (b) 1010101011000011

9. For a square wave with the rise times shown below, calculate the bandwidth necessary to pass the signal.
   (a) 10 msec
   (b) 1 msec
   (c) 10 μsec
   (d) 10 nsec

10. A certain communications systems has a bandwidth as listed below. What is the fastest rise time signal that could be passed without band-limiting effects?
    (a) 4 kHz
    (b) 100 kHz
    (c) 1 MHz
    (d) 100 MHz

11. For each of the rise times listed in Problem 9, find the highest-order harmonic that would be passed for a square wave with a fundamental frequency of 100 kHz.

12. For each of the bandwidths listed in Problem 10, find the highest-order harmonic that would be passed for a square wave with a fundamental frequency of 10 kHz.

Amplitude Modulation

Amplitude modulation (AM) used in the form of on-off keying is one of the oldest forms of modulation. Today it is used not only for telegraph-type transmissions but also for voice transmissions, AM broadcast radio. Before starting the analysis of amplitude modulation, examine Figure 7.1. For right now, don't worry if some of the terminology is not clear.

Three signals are shown in Figure 7.1. The first is the carrier wave, which is the wave that the information is "carried on," hence the name carrier frequency. The second

Figure 7.1
AM signals.

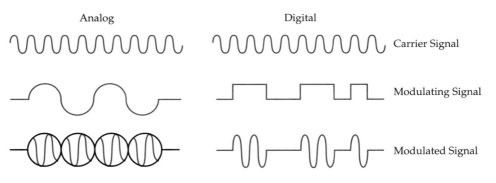

signal is the modulating signal; this modifies or adjusts the carrier wave to represent the information to be transmitted. The modulating signal is typically a baseband signal. Some examples include voice and music as in AM radio and binary data streams when sending data, just like the old telegraph system. The telegraph system worked by the operator keying dots or dashes, representing 1s and 0s by turning on and off a carrier signal. The final waveform is the resultant modulated signal. Note the terminology; the carrier frequency is modulat*ed* by the modulat*ing* signal that results in the modulat*ed* signal.

■ DOUBLE SIDEBAND, SUPPRESSED CARRIER (DSB-SC) AMPLITUDE MODULATION

The amplitude modulation process can be represented by equation 7-1:

$$m(t) = a(t)\cos(w_c t) \tag{7-1}$$

where $m(t)$ = modulated signal
$a(t)$ = modulating signal
$w_c = 2\pi f_c$, where f_c = carrier frequency

Note that this is just a cosine wave modulated by an information signal given by $a(t)$. As stated above, $m(t)$ is the modulated signal that results from a cosine wave being multiplied (or modulated) by a modulating baseband signal that contains the information to be transmitted, or $a(t)$.

The period of the waveform is expressed in radians per second so that it can be read directly from the argument of the cosine function. To see this, ask yourself which form below most clearly shows that the cosine wave is completing 100 full cycles?

$$\cos(100t) \qquad \cos(628.3t) \tag{7-2}$$

Obviously, both methods of expression are equivalent, but the first more readily yields the information. In this chapter and the next, radians will be used almost exclusively; convert than if you wish by recalling that $2\pi f = w$.

To being the exploration of equation 7.1, which will form the basis of much of this and the next chapter, examine $a(t)$ more closely:

$$a(t) = E_m \cos(w_m t) \tag{7-3}$$

where E_m = peak voltage of modulating signal
w_m = frequency of modulating signal, measured in radians per second

Now $a(t)$ is the modulating signal. That means that it is multiplying the carrier frequency, represented as the cosine function. The modulating signal is the signal that contains all the information that is to be sent. For example, in AM broadcast radio, the modulating signal is the announcer's voice or the program material to which you are listening. This can be anything, music, sports, commentary, advertisement, and so forth. As you will recall from Fourier analysis, we can represent any waveform with a series of sinusoids. Equation 7-3, does exactly that, but it represents the information signal with just one cosine wave oscillating at the modulating signal frequency w_m. By inserting this expression for $a(t)$ into equation 7-1, $m(t)$ becomes

$$m(t) = E_m \cos(w_m t)\cos(w_c t) \tag{7-4}$$

By a very useful mathematical relationship, one can always write the product of two cosine waves as the addition of half the amplitude of their sum and difference. This is done in equation 7-5:

$$m(t) = \frac{E_m}{2}\left[\cos(w_c + w_m)t + \cos(w_c - w_m)t\right] \tag{7-5}$$

This important result needs to be examined closely for what it will tell about AM. The first thing that is interesting to note is that both the original modulating signal, at the modulating frequency, and the carrier frequency are not present in the modulated signal. Note that there is no sinusoid oscillating at w_m. Instead, the carrier frequency has split into two pieces, each of half amplitude and each shifted in frequency by the modulating frequency. Therefore, when you modulate, or multiply, one frequency by another, AM, the result is that both of the original frequencies disappear and two new frequencies result.

These new frequencies are closely related to the two original ones, and the modulating frequency shifts the carrier frequency in both a positive and negative direction. Examine Figure 7.2, which illustrates this phenomenon. The figure shows the frequencies in frequency space, or as they would be viewed with a spectrum analyzer or FFT plug-in to a digital oscilloscope. It is very useful to be able to analyze modulation practices with this type of graph. It uses frequency rather than time as the horizontal axis. The farther to the right the signal is, the higher in frequency it is.

This results in two observations. First, because there are two pieces, in communications, they are called sidebands; this type of AM is called double sideband (DSB) modulation. Second, because the carrier frequency is absent from the modulated signal, this

Figure 7.2
DSB spectrum analyzer view.

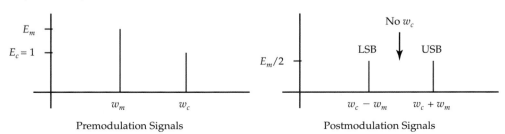

Premodulation Signals   Postmodulation Signals

Figure 7.3
DSB-SC AM with multiple frequencies, spectrum analyzer view.

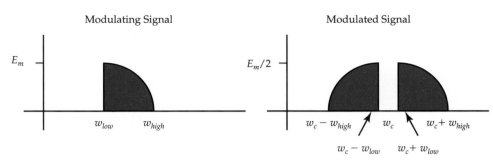

type of AM is called suppressed carrier (SC) modulation, meaning that because the carrier frequency is not present, it is suppressed. These two naming conventions are then combined, and the shorthand designation that results for this type of modulation is double sideband, suppressed carrier amplitude modulation (DSB-SC AM).

Often the last AM is not written; DSB-SC implies AM. The two pieces, or sidebands, also have special names: the upper sideband, USB, and the lower sideband, LSB. The term *sideband* is used because they are be*side* the original location of the carrier signal in frequency space. Sideband is defined carefully in Figure 7.4.

In addition, it is interesting to note what happened to the amplitudes. In the first part of Figure 7.2, the carrier frequency is assumed to have amplitude of 1 and the modulating frequency is assumed to have the amplitude E_m. When these two frequencies are multiplied, or modulated, the amplitudes of the two resulting signals are the same and are half of the product of the two individual amplitudes, or $E_m/2$.

Next, note that the carrier frequency is shown as a higher frequency than the modulating frequency. This is always the case. Usually, it is much higher, typically a factor of at least 100, but here it is shown as a much smaller multiple to clearly indicate what is happening with the two frequencies. This is just a result of a diagram designed to make a specific point, and it will be used throughout this chapter and the next. Just be aware that the carrier frequency is, in most real systems, much higher than the modulating signal. For example, in broadcast AM, the carrier frequency is about 1000 kHz, and the maximum frequency modulating signal is about 5 kHz.

Now, most of the time the modulating signal will not be just a single frequency. Not many would want to listen to an AM broadcast radio station that just transmitted a single tone or frequency. So it is important to examine how the picture would change if the modulating signal was composed of a group of different frequencies rather than just one. The frequencies that would be used would be in some bandwidth, there would be a lowest frequency and a highest frequency. Figure 7.3 shows what would result. The filled curve shown illustrates all the frequencies that would exist between the lowest and the highest frequency of the modulating signal.

Looking carefully at Figure 7.3, you would expect from our analysis of a single-frequency modulat*ing* signal that two *groups* of frequencies would result. There would be one above the carrier frequency and one below, resulting in what is called the modulat*ed* signal. Also, note that the spectrum does not extend right up to the carrier frequency. It stops a little short of it on both sides. This is because in this diagram, the assumption is that the lowest frequency in the modulating signal is not DC, but some slightly higher frequency. This results in the exaggerated "dip" shown in the spectrum in Figure 7.3. Additionally, note that because this is DSB-SC, there is no carrier present at w_c.

In the rest of the diagrams in this text, the modulating signal will be assumed to extend down to 0 Hz. This means that the group of frequencies that is modulating the carrier extends down to 0 Hz, or DC. Signals that have this characteristic are called baseband signals, (see Chapter 1). This makes the little dip around the center of Figure 7.3 disappear. In the rest of the spectral diagrams in the chapter, it will be assumed that the modulating signal is always baseband.

Another characteristic that you may be wondering about is why the shapes are shown as curved. This is because in most applications, the highest frequencies in the modulating signal occur less frequently, so there is less energy at those frequencies. If all frequencies were equally probable, the shape would be rectangular. That explains why there is more energy at low frequencies that at high ones. The spectrum is shown as smooth because most practical systems also apply something called scrambling to smooth the spectrum. If this were not done, the spectral shape would be very ragged with peaks for several common data patterns.

Finally, the diagrams that follow will do away with the high- and low-frequency markers and assume that as stated above, the low-frequency mark will be DC and the high-frequency mark will be labeled w_m, which is the maximum modulating frequency.

Sidebands

The sidebands are shown clearly in Figure 7.3 but are not labeled, as they are in Figure 7.4. This result of the sideband generation is characteristic of all DSB types of amplitude modulation. Not only will DSB-SC signals have this result, but so will the DSB-LC signals that will be discussed in the next section.

It is important to note what the bandwidth of the DSB signal is. Because there are two sidebands and each is exactly the bandwidth of the original modulating signal, as shown in Figure 7.4, the resultant bandwidth is twice the original modulating signal's bandwidth. This is expressed in equation 7-6, where if the first form is used, the modulating frequency and bandwidth is expressed in rad/sec, but if the second form is used, these same quantities are expressed in Hz.

$$\text{BW} = 2w_m \qquad \text{or} \qquad \text{BW} = 2f_m \qquad\qquad \textbf{(7-6)}$$

Additionally, the sidebands are always symmetric about the carrier frequency:

$$w_{\text{usb}} = w_c + w_m \qquad \text{or} \qquad f_{\text{usb}} = f_c + f_m \qquad\qquad \textbf{(7-7)}$$

$$w_{\text{lsb}} = w_c - w_m \qquad \text{or} \qquad f_{\text{lsb}} = f_c - f_m \qquad\qquad \textbf{(7-8)}$$

The last thing that is important to note about the sidebands is that they have exactly the same peak voltage given by $E_m/2$. Because they have the same peak voltage, the av-

Figure 7.4
DSB-SC showing sidebands and spectrum analyzer view.

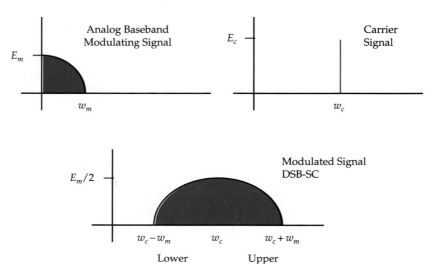

Figure 7.5
DSB-SC oscilloscope view.

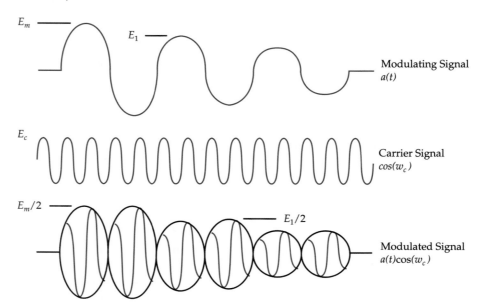

erage powers will be the same as well. Power can be found by just squaring the rms voltage and dividing by the load resistance, as will be done when power calculations are developed for DSB-LC modulation. Figure 7.5 shows how the DSB-SC signals would look on an oscilloscope. Pay special attention to the timing and voltage relationships between the modulating and modulated signal. Note especially that the shape of the modulating signal defines the shape of the modulated signals envelope. If the first changes, so does the second.

DSB-SC Average Power

To determine the power, it is helpful to recall that the power in any electronic system is given by the voltage times the current, or

$$P = EI \tag{7-9}$$

By Ohm's Law, it can be written

$$P = E * \frac{E}{R} = \frac{E^2}{R} \tag{7-10}$$

where R is the load resistance. In Figure 7.4 and 7.5, the peak voltage of the modulated signal is half the peak voltage of the modulating signal. It is also important to remember to use rms voltages for computing power and that there are two sidebands. Combining these observations, the expression for the average power of a DSB-SC modulated signal is

$$P = \frac{(E_m/2\sqrt{2})^2}{R} = \frac{E_m{}^2}{4R} \tag{7-11}$$

■ EXAMPLE 7.1

This example will show sample calculations for a particular DSB-SC modulator with a carrier frequency of 1000 rad/sec, a load resistance of 50 Ω, and a modulating signal $a(t)$ given by the following expression:

$$a(t) = 10 \cos(20t)$$

Find the following:

1. The peak voltage, E_m
2. The carrier frequency, w_c
3. The modulation frequency, w_m
4. The DSB-SC bandwidth
5. The USB bandwidth and frequencies
6. The LSB bandwidth and frequencies
7. The average power P

Because the carrier signal amplitude is assumed to be unity, the peak voltage is just the peak voltage of the modulating signal $a(t)$, or 10 V. The carrier frequency is 1000 rad/sec. The modulation frequency is 20 rad/sec. The DSB-SC bandwidth is twice w_m, or 40 rad. The USB and LSB are each 20 rad in width. The LSB starts at 980 rad and extends to 1000 rad. The USB starts at 1000 rad and extends to 1020 rad. The average power is given by equation 7.11 and is 0.50 W:

$$P = \frac{E^2{}_m}{4R} = \frac{10^2}{4(50)} = 0.50 \text{ W}$$

■ DOUBLE SIDEBAND, LARGE CARRIER (DSB-LC) AMPLITUDE MODULATION

If the carrier is not present in the modulated signal, then the receiver must incorporate some method for locating it in order to tune the radio to the desired channel. Because in DSB-SC the carrier frequency is always suppressed, DSB-SC sounds like a bad choice for an inexpensive receiver. Any extra circuitry required to locate and track the carrier must increase the cost of the receiver. Inexpensive receivers or radios are a big reason why AM broadcast radio became so popular.

To explore this, set your "way-back" machine to the early portion of this century and imagine that you are doing a design study to recommend the type of AM radio system to be used in the United States. Now as you are thinking about this, you realize that to gain wide acceptance in the marketplace, the radios will need to be inexpensive and reliable. There will be only one transmitter for a large number of receivers. So it makes sense to put as much complexity, or cost, in the transmitter as you can where it trades off complexity in the receiver. This type of AM system is known as DSB-LC, LC standing for large carrier. It is commonly known as just AM radio, or broadcast AM.

There is a little confession to be made: AM broadcast radio is of the DSB-LC type, and not the DSB-SC type discussed above. Apologies for using it as an example there, but on balance, it cleared up more than it obscured. Before getting into the mathematics of DSB-LC, it may be interesting to summarize the four licensed classes of broadcast AM radio that are encountered in the United States.

There are four classes of stations licensed to operate in the United States. The first and by far the most powerful are the class 1 stations. These are nicknamed the clear channel stations, and most major cities, as measured in 1940, have one. They are licensed to make sure that there is a clear frequency channel as far as their powerful transmitter can reach. No other licensed radio station broadcasts on that carrier frequency. Due to propagation effects, it is the only station licensed in the United States on that frequency. The idea was to make sure as many people as possible had access to a network of powerful stations for information, official announcements, and news.

Class 1 stations all operate at a transmitted power of 50,000 W. One example is WJR in Detroit; in Chicago, the station is WGN. Often they have three-letter call names. Typically, they broadcast the baseball games in summer and the football games in winter because they reach very large audiences. Because they are clear channel and have very powerful transmitters, often at night, due to SW propagation effects, these stations can often be heard at great distances. There is a subclass of stations called class 2, which although not clear channel, operate at some power between 5000 and 50,000 W. These typically are in geographical and frequency position situations where if they transmitted at full 50,000 W power levels, they would interfere with previously designated class 1 stations.

Another class of stations is called class 3. These stations operate at a transmit power of up to 5000 W. They can cover a reasonably sized area, perhaps several counties or a large metropolitan area.

Finally, there are the class 4 stations, licensed to maximum transmit power levels of 1000 W. These are intended to be low enough in power that virtually any city or county in the states could reasonably expect to find a frequency slot to operate in that would not interfere with a previously licensed station.

Mathematically, DSB-LC is obtained by just adding a term to equation 7-1, which was used to describe DSB-SC. The term to add is a fixed amplitude, E_c, for the carrier wave. The symbol E_c was chosen as a reminder that it is representing the carrier voltage. With this change, $m(t)$, becomes

$$m(t) = [a(t) + E_c](\cos(w_c t) = a(t)\cos(w_c t) + E_c\cos(w_c t) \qquad \textbf{(7-12)}$$

It is important to note that the only difference between DSB-SC and DSB-LC is that a DC voltage is added to the modulation signal. This addition of E_c changes DSB-SC to DSB-LC. That is the only difference between the two AM modulation schemes. It is possible to think of this as a DC offset to the information or modulating signal, which results in just a cosine wave modulated by a signal given by $[a(t) + E_c]$. Its form is very similar to equation 7-1, and as a result, the spectrums are very similar as well. The spectrum diagrams are shown in Figure 7.6, and what a DSB-LC signal would look like on an oscilloscope is shown in Figure 7.7.

Figure 7.6
DSB-LC spectrum analyzer view.

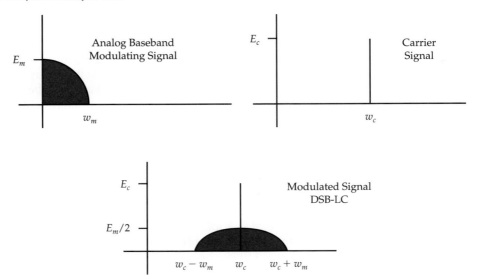

Figure 7.7
DSB-LC oscilloscope view.

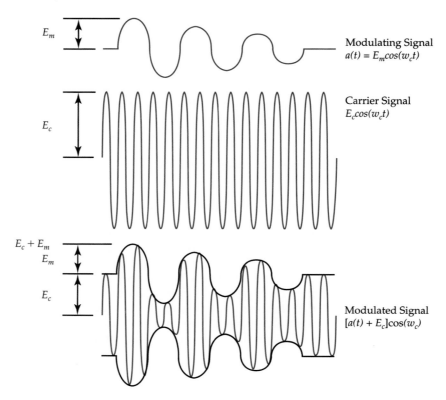

The most obvious difference in the two spectrums, DSB-SC and DSB-LC, is that now at the carrier frequency there is a component. This is shown by the "spike" in the center of the spectrum, right at the carrier frequency. The presence of this spike indicates that there is a lot of energy at the carrier frequency to use in the receiver. It also says that the energy is there no matter what the modulating signal $a(t)$ may be. Examining equation 7-12 carefully, it is possible to see that even if $a(t) = 0$, there will still be a component of $m(t) = E_c\cos(w_c t)$.

This energy comes directly from the amplitude E_c multiplying or being modulated by the carrier frequency. This results in the modulated signal, or the modulated signal envelope. The reason for calling in an envelope will become clear after looking at Figure 7.7. The envelope shape is defined by the modulating signal and the envelope is "filled" by the carrier signal. Effectively, the carrier is modulated by the modulating signal and that modulation defines the envelope of the carrier.

There is another term that is applied to DSB-LC with which you need to be familiar: repetition rate. The repetition rate of the modulated signal envelope is how often it opens and closes. In Figure 7.7, it can be seen that the modulated signal envelope opens and closes at the same frequency as the modulating signal. This is an important result.

Pay close attention to the timing relationships shown in Figure 7.7, between the modulating signal and the modulated signal. Further, the peak voltage for the modulated waveform is just the sum of the modulating signal and carrier signal voltages.

Now, remember that the goal of all this is to give the receiver some carrier energy so the demodulation process becomes simpler and less costly. Therefore, it is important to look at the modulating term $[a(t) + E_c]$ and what happens to the resultant modulated signal when $a(t)$ and/or E_c are varied. Specifically, examine the relative amplitudes of $a(t)$ and E_c.

If E_c is large enough, the envelope or magnitude of the modulated waveform will be dominated by $a(t)$ and will be proportional to $a(t)$. This sounds like what is needed to make the system work. To see this, think of what will happen when $a(t)$ is its smallest value. If E_c is not big enough to still provide some energy at that time into the receiver, the signal will essentially "go away." Remember that the cosine function magnitude varies from 0 to 1: if E_c is too small and $a(t)$ gets small, we have a small number multiplying a number between 0 and 1. This can result in very small amplitude. Verify this yourself by reexamining equation 7-12.

E_c must be above some minimum value for this approach to work; E_c must be greater than or equal to the smallest value that $a(t)$ can obtain. Expressed mathematically, this becomes

$$E_c \geq \min[a(t)] \tag{7-13}$$

If this rule is obeyed, it is possible to demodulate the AM waveform with a simple diode. This is called envelope detection and will be discussed in more detail in Chapter 8, when demodulation circuits are examined.

Modulation Index

All linear modulation schemes can be measured by something called the modulation index, which is a way of talking about the percentage modulation of a DSB-LC or broadcast AM transmission. Figure 7.8 illustrates how the modulation index changes the DSB-LC envelope. To define modulation index, describe a dimensionless number m, which is defined as the ratio of the sideband energy to the carrier energy. (Don't mistake this m for $m(t)$; they are unrelated. m is a dimensionless number, and $m(t)$ is a function of time.)

$$m = \text{modulation index} = \frac{\text{peak modulating voltage}}{\text{peak carrier voltage}} = \frac{E_m}{E_c} \tag{7-14}$$

Alternatively, one can express this as a percentage. As is shown in equation 7-15, multiply m by 100% to obtain the number in percentage form. This is referred to as percentage modulation. Both forms are used to discuss modulation. The most relevant for the discussion at hand will be used.

$$\text{percentage modulation} = m * 100\% \tag{7-15}$$

For proper operation, the modulation index m should always be greater than 0 and less than or equal to 1. If $m = 0$, the resultant modulating waveform is just a constant envelope of amplitude E_c, the amplitude of the carrier frequency. There is no modulation of the carrier wave. If m becomes greater than 1, the resultant modulated

Figure 7.8
DSB-LC, modulation index, oscilloscope view.

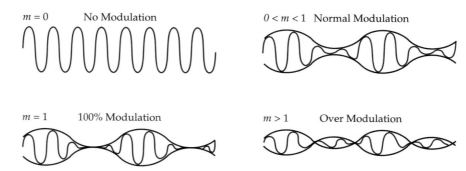

waveform is called overmodulated. Note that overmodulation results in percentage modulation numbers greater than 100%, making the term *overmodulated* quite clear. Figure 7.8 illustrates what the DSB-LC modulated signal looks like on an oscilloscope for various values of the modulation index. Note in Figure 7.8 what happens when *m* becomes greater than 1: The signal overmodulates and essentially "slides up" and "slides down" the two edges of the envelope. Quite obviously, the signal is distorting.

DSB-LC Average Power

Recall that for any communication system the idea is to get sufficient power from the source to the destination so that the modulating signal is transported. Therefore, it is a good idea to be able to compute the power in any transmitted signal. To get started, look back at Figure 7.6. It shows clearly that there are three components to any DSB-LC waveform, the upper and lower sidebands and the carrier frequency. If the powers in all three of these are added up, the total average power in the modulated signal will result, as shown in equation 7-16:

$$P = P_c + P_{usb} + P_{lsb} \tag{7-16}$$

To determine the power, it is helpful to recall that the power in any electronic system is given by the voltage times the current, or

$$P = EI \tag{7-17}$$

By Ohm's Law, because R is the load resistance,

$$P = E * \frac{E}{R} = \frac{E^2}{R} \tag{7-18}$$

Substituting in this expression for the power, equation 7-16 becomes

$$P = \frac{E_c^2}{R} + \frac{E_{usb}^2}{R} + \frac{E_{lsb}^2}{R} = \frac{E_c^2}{R} + \frac{2E_{sb}^2}{R} \tag{7-19}$$

where it was recognized that the sideband powers are equal. Now noting that the peak voltage of each sideband is $E_m/2$,

$$E_m = 2E_{usb} = 2E_{lsb} \tag{7-20}$$

It is straightforward to substitute this back into equation 7-19 to obtain an expression for the power in a DSB-LC waveform, depending only on the peak voltages of its components. This is shown in equation 7-21:

$$P = \frac{E_c^2}{R} + \frac{2(E_m/2)^2}{R} = \frac{E_c^2}{R} + \frac{E_m^2}{2R} \tag{7-21}$$

It is also true that it is possible to relate the modulating signal voltage with the carrier voltage through the relationship defining the modulation index from equation 7-14. Substituting that relationship into 7-21 results in

$$P = \frac{E_c^2}{R} + \frac{(mE_c)^2}{2R} = \frac{E_c^2}{R}\left(1 + \frac{m^2}{2}\right) \tag{7-22}$$

Above, a nice relationship for the average power in a DSB-LC modulated signal was developed. However, peak voltages were used to compute a power. As is well known, to compute the power in any system, rms values must be used, not peak values. Therefore, to compute power values the peak voltages are divided by the square root of 2, or by about 1.414. Considering this, equation 7-22 becomes

$$P = P_c + 2P_{sb} = \frac{(E_c/\sqrt{2})^2}{R}\left(1 + \frac{m^2}{2}\right) = \frac{E_c^2}{2R}\left(1 + \frac{m^2}{2}\right) \tag{7-23}$$

Equation 7-23 is a nice, useful, relationship; it gives a formula for the total power in the modulated waveform in terms of the peak carrier voltage and the modulation index. Both are easily measured values when looking at the signal on an oscilloscope. It is also possible to write equation 7-23 in terms of the modulation voltage by recalling equation 7-14:

$$P = \frac{(mE_m)^2}{2R}\left(1 + \frac{m^2}{2}\right) = \frac{E_m^2}{2R}\left(\frac{1}{2} + \frac{1}{m^2}\right) \tag{7-24}$$

For the special case of zero percentage modulation,

$$E_m = E_c \qquad m = 0 \tag{7-25}$$

This should be the same as the power for an unmodulated carrier, and substituting the conditions of equation 7-25 into equation 7-23 results in

$$P = P_c = \frac{E_c^2}{2R}\left(1 + \frac{0}{2}\right) = \frac{E_c^2}{2R} \tag{7-26}$$

It is straightforward to develop the equations for current; recall Ohm's Law and substitute for carrier voltage in terms of I and R:

$$E_c = I_c R$$

where R is the load resistance. Rearranging,

$$I_c = \frac{E_c}{R}$$

and for a modulated waveform,

$$I = I_c \sqrt{\left(1 + \frac{m^2}{2}\right)} \qquad \textbf{(7-27)}$$

Now that the equations have been developed for power, it is interesting to see how they form directly from the equation used to define AM modulation with a carrier, DSB-LC. Equation 7-12 is reproduced below:

$$m(t) = [a(t) + E_c] \cos(w_c t) = a(t) \cos(w_c t) + E_c \cos(w_c t) \qquad \textbf{(7-12)}$$

Now substitute for $a(t)$ a cosine wave with peak voltages represented as before. This should give an equation for the peak voltage of each component of the modulated signal envelope:

$$m(t) = [E_c + E_m \cos(w_m t)] \cos(w_c t) \qquad \textbf{(7-28)}$$

Substituting in expression 7-14 and relating the modulation index to the peak voltages of the carrier and modulating signal,

$$m(t) = [E_c + mE_c \cos(w_m t)] \cos(w_c t) = [1 + m \cos(w_m t)]E_c \cos(w_c t) \qquad \textbf{(7-29)}$$

where the first bracketed term is a constant plus the modulating signal, and the second term is just the unmodulated carrier frequency. The constant multiplier, 1, is responsible for the generation of the carrier, whereas the modulating signal is responsible for generating the sidebands. Rearranging equation 7-29, gives

$$m(t) = E_c \cos(w_c t) + mE_c \cos(w_c t)\cos(w_m t) \qquad \textbf{(7-30)}$$

Now, substituting for the product of the cosines, it is found that

$$m(t) = E_c \cos(w_c t) + \frac{mE_c}{2} [\cos(w_c + w_m)t + \cos(w_c - w_m)t] \qquad \textbf{(7-31)}$$

This is just where we started in our relationship above, with equation 7-16, except that the expression here is in peak voltages. Remember the assertion that the power in the total modulated signal was just the sum of all the powers present? If the peak voltages add up in that way, the powers must too. Note that in equation 7-31, the first term is the carrier signal and the second and third terms are the sidebands. Note that the modulation process does not effect the amplitude of the carrier. Additionally, note that the amplitude of the sidebands is the same as derived above. Finally, note that for 100%

modulation, $m = 1$, the sideband's amplitude is just half of the carrier frequencies amplitude.

■ **EXAMPLE 7.2**

This example will show sample calculations for a particular broadcast AM radio station with a carrier frequency of

$$40 \cos(1000t)$$

a load resistance of 50 Ω, and a modulating signal $a(t)$:

$$a(t) = 10 \cos(20t)$$

Find the following:

1. $m(t)$
2. The peak carrier voltage, E_c
3. The carrier frequency, ω_c
4. The peak voltage, E_m
5. The modulation frequency, ω_m
6. The LSB bandwidth and frequencies
7. The USB bandwidth and frequencies
8. The DSB-LC bandwidth
9. The modulation index
10. The average power, P

$$m(t) = [E_m\cos(w_mt) + E_c]\cos(w_ct) = [10 \cos(20t) + 40]\cos(1000t)$$

The peak carrier voltage $E_c = 40$ V. The carrier frequency is 1000 rad/sec. The peak modulation voltage $E_m = 10$ V. The modulation frequency is 20 rad/sec. The LSB bandwidth is 20 rad, starts at 980 rad, and extends to 1000 rad. The USB bandwidth is 20 rad, starts at 1000 rad, and extends to 1020 rad. The DSB-LC bandwidth is 40 rad. The modulation index is given by equation 7-14 and is 0.25 for a percent modulation of 25%:

$$m = \frac{E_m}{E_c} = \frac{10}{40} = 0.25$$

$$P = \frac{E_c^2}{2R}\left(1 + \frac{m^2}{2}\right) = \frac{40^2}{2(50)}\left(1 + \frac{0.25^2}{2}\right) = 16.5 \text{ W}$$

$$P = \frac{E_m^2}{2R}\left(\frac{1}{2} + \frac{1}{m^2}\right) = \frac{10^2}{2(50)}\left(\frac{1}{2} + \frac{1}{0.25^2}\right) = 16.5 \text{ W}$$

The average power is given by either equation 7-23 or 7-24 and is 16.5 W.

Now, investigate a little further and find the power of the carrier wave alone and determine how much of the total power in the DSB-LC signal is contained in the carrier. The power of the carrier is given by equation 7-26 and is 16 W:

$$P_c = \frac{E_c^2}{2R} = \frac{40^2}{2(50)} = 16 \text{ W}$$

The total power was 16.5 W, so 97% of the total power is supplied by the presence of the carrier frequency. That means that only about 3% of the power is contained in the sidebands of the modulated signal. Because the sidebands is where all the information is contained, it is interesting to note that only 3% of the total power is being used to convey the informational part of the signal.

The answer to whether a system makes good economic use of the carrier power is revealed by examining the value of the modulation index. Because it is only 0.25, it is not making good use of all the money spent to buy a big transmitter. As seen above, only about 3% of the power is contained in the sidebands. Optimum theoretical use would be a modulation index of as close to 1.0 as possible. For that to happen, the modulating signal would need to be changed to something like

$$a(t) = 39 \cos(20t)$$

Now the modulation index soars to 0.975, or a percentage modulation of 97.5%. The power now contained in the sidebands also soars, as shown below:

$$P_c = \frac{E_c^2}{2R} = \frac{40^2}{2(50)} = 16 \text{ W} \qquad m = \frac{E_m}{E_c} = \frac{39}{40} = 0.975$$

$$P = P_c\left(1 + \frac{m^2}{2}\right) = 16\left(1 + \frac{0.975^2}{2}\right) = 16(1.475) = 23.6 \text{ W}$$

$$P_{usb} = P_{lsb} = \frac{P - P_c}{2} = \frac{23.6 - 16}{2} = 3.86 \text{ W}$$

$$\%P_{sb} = \frac{P - P_c}{P} = \frac{23.6 - 16}{23.6} = 32 \%$$

It should be clear that as the modulation index is increased, the amount of power in the sidebands also increases. Next, does the original example satisfy the condition for an effective broadcast station? In other words, does it satisfy equation 7-13, which must hold for any effective DSB-LC AM transmitter? Examining equation 7-13, it is determined that the smallest value that $a(t)$ can obtain must be less than the peak carrier voltage. The smallest value that $a(t)$ can obtain is -10 V as it swings from $+10$ to -10. Because 10 V is smaller than 40 V, the peak carrier voltage, the answer is yes.

Additionally, note that the new $a(t)$ values also satisfy equation 7-13, but barely. This points out that the economic requirement of maximizing modulation index coincides with the limiting equality of equation 7-13. This is not happenstance. To see how these relate, consider the next section.

DSB-LC Transmission Efficiency

It would be nice to be able to have a single quantity that could be used to define the transmission efficiency of any DSB-LC transmitter. As seen in the above example, a lot of power is placed in the carrier, and this depends on the value of the modulation coefficient m. A formula will be developed below that will give this efficiency rating. To begin, recall where we started in the last section with equation 7-16:

$$P = P_c + P_{usb} + P_{lsb} \qquad \text{(7-16)}$$

Because the sidebands have equal power,

$$P = P_c + 2P_{sb} \qquad \text{(7-32)}$$

Now define transmission efficiency α:

$$\alpha = \frac{\text{power in sidebands}}{\text{total average power}} = \frac{2P_{sb}}{P} \qquad \text{(7-33)}$$

Although this is nice, it would be better to have a relationship in terms of peak voltages and modulation index. Earlier, relationships were developed that related the power in a sideband and total average power to these quantities. Substituting, it is found that

$$\alpha = \frac{2P_{sb}}{P} = \frac{2(m^2 E_c^2 / 8R)}{(E_c^2 / 2R)(1 + m^2/2)} = \frac{(E_c^2/2R)(2m^2/4)}{(E_c^2/2R)(1 + m^2/2)} = \frac{m^2}{2 + m^2} \qquad \text{(7-34)}$$

where α is the transmission efficiency of DSB-LC transmitter. Another approach to deriving the transmission efficiency is found in Appendix C.

This result has some important implications and will reveal something interesting about DSB-LC broadcast transmitters. By now it should be well understood that maximum DSB-LC efficiency is obtained at $m = 1$. For a 100% percentage modulation, it is found that $\alpha = 33\%$. This means that the maximum transmission efficiency only results in one-third of the power being used to transmit the information. The remaining 66% of the power is "wasted" in sending the carrier. Of course, this waste is necessary for inexpensive demodulation, so it is not wasted so much as traded off for inexpensive radio receiver designs.

A comparison of the two defining equations for the power in both forms of AM studied is of interest:

$$\text{DSB-SC:} \quad P = \frac{E_m^2}{4R} \qquad \text{DSB-LC:} \quad P = \frac{E_m^2}{2R}\left(\frac{1}{2} + \frac{1}{m^2}\right)$$

As can be seen, the only difference is in the modulation index term. If this is set to the two limiting cases of interest, $m = 0$ and $m = 1$ and the equivalent expression using the carrier voltage is evaluated, the point made above that the carrier always consumes at least 66% of the power should be clear. Even for maximum modulation index, $m = 1$, the power in a DSB-LC modulated waveform is only 1.5 times as large as the power in the unmodulated carrier. Clearly, the maximum power is contained in the sidebands for $m = 1$, and this still results in two-thirds of the power residing in the carrier (invert 1.5 = 0.666):

$$\text{DSB-LC, } m = 0: P = \frac{E_c^2}{2R}\left(1 + \frac{0^2}{2}\right) = \frac{E_c^2}{2R}$$

$$\text{DSB-LC, } m = 1: P = \frac{E_c^2}{2R}\left(1 + \frac{1^2}{2}\right) = \frac{E_c^2}{2R}(1.5)$$

■ EXAMPLE 7.3

Suppose you are employed in an AM broadcast radio station that has an average carrier output power of 10 kW. The modulation index is 0.80. Find the total average power output, the peak amplitude of the output for a load resistance of 100 Ω, and the transmission efficiency.

$$P = \frac{E_c^2}{2R}\left(1 + \frac{m^2}{2}\right) = P_c\left(1 + \frac{m^2}{2}\right) = P_c\left(1 + \frac{0.64}{2}\right) = (10^4)(1.32) = 13{,}200 \text{ W}$$

$$P_c = \frac{E_c}{2R} \rightarrow E_c = \sqrt{2RP_c} = \sqrt{2(100)(10^4)} = 1414 \text{ V}$$

$$\alpha = \frac{m^2}{2 + m^2} = \frac{0.64}{2.64} = 24.2\%$$

Relating Oscilloscope Readings of the Modulated Waveform to E_m and E_c

It is important to get a good idea of what the various waveforms look like on a common instrument, the oscilloscope, and how they relate to the peak voltage values measured there. To get started take a close look at the waveforms that a DSB-LC amplitude modulator generates in Figure 7.9. Examining Figure 7.9, observe two things. First, the frequency and shape of the modulating signal's envelope the same as the modulated signal. Although this point has been made earlier, it is an important one and is emphasized here again. Second, V_{max} and V_{min} are the peak voltages of the modulated signal's envelope. The equations shown below are useful because it is much easier to measure V_{max} and V_{min} on an oscilloscope than it is to measure E_m or E_c once the modulation has oc-

Figure 7.9
DSB-LC oscilloscope view.

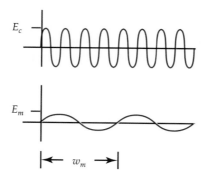
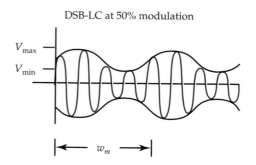

Figure 7.10
DSB-LC modulated waveform, oscilloscope view.

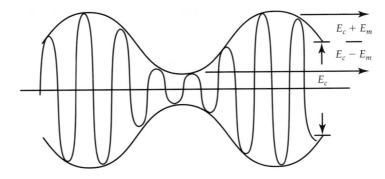

curred. Several other relationships can be generated from this observation and are shown below:

$$V_{max} = E_c + E_m \tag{7-35}$$

$$V_{min} = E_c - E_m \tag{7-36}$$

$$E_{usb} = E_{lsb} = E_{sb} = \frac{E_m}{2} = 1/4\,(V_{max} - V_{min}) \tag{7-37}$$

$$V_{max} = \frac{E_m}{m} + E_m = E_m\left(1 + \frac{1}{m}\right) = E_c + mE_c = E_c\,(1 + m) \tag{7-38}$$

$$E_m = 1/2\,(V_{max} - V_{min}) \tag{7-39}$$

$$E_c = 1/2\,(V_{max} + V_{min}) \tag{7-40}$$

Additionally, it seems reasonable that the peak voltage, at any moment of time, of any DSB modulated signal is just the addition of the peak carrier signal amplitude plus or minus the peak modulating signal amplitude. Figure 7.10 summarizes this statement, which is also captured by the equations above.

Figure 7.11 shows how the various voltages of the signals relate to each other. Figure 7.11 shows the voltages for two special cases. Case 1 is where the percentage modulation is 0%, or the modulation index $m = 0$. Case 2 is where the percent modulation is 100%, or a modulation index $m = 1$.

In examining these two diagrams in Figure 7.11, for case 1, where the percentage modulation is 0%, it is seen that the modulated signal is just the carrier signal. Further, at any moment in time, the voltage is equal to the voltage of the carrier wave. This should make sense, because in any form of amplitude modulation, it is the amplitude of the modulating carrier signal that shapes the amplitude of the modulated signal. Again, this is often called the modulation envelope. Because there is no modulating signal, $m = 0$, the result is just the carrier.

Figure 7.11
DSB-LC modulated waveforms, oscilloscope view.

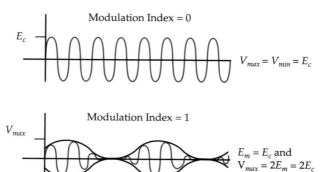

In case 2, the maximum voltage occurs when the peak voltage of the modulating signal reaches a maximum. This voltage, for the special case of 100% percentage modulation, is equal to twice the modulation voltage *or* twice the carrier voltage. Again, only for this special case, the minimum voltage of the modulated signal is defined as 0 V.

■ EXAMPLE 7.4

You are in the laboratory and are examining a DSB-LC waveform on the oscilloscope. You decide to try out the equations listed above to see if you can determine the modulating voltage, carrier voltage, modulation index, and modulation frequency from the readings you take off the display shown in Figure 7.12.
From the figure, read the following values:

$$V_{\max} = 12 \text{ V} \qquad V_{\min} = 6 \text{ V}$$

Figure 7.12
DSB-LC waveform, oscilloscope view.

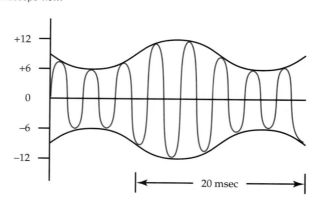

$$f_m = \frac{1}{20 \times 0^{-3}} = 50 \text{ Hz}$$

Now applying the formulas above,

$$E_m = 1/2 \,(V_{\max} - V_{\min}) = 1/2 \,(12 - 6) = 3$$

$$E_c = 1/2 \,(V_{\max} + V_{\min}) = 1/2 \,(12 + 6) = 9$$

$$m = \frac{E_m}{E_c} = \frac{3}{9} = 0.33$$

You also realize that it is possible to compute the power if you know the load resistance. Assuming a value of 100 Ω, apply the appropriate formula as shown below:

$$P = \frac{E_m^2}{2R}\left(1/2 + \frac{1}{m^2}\right) = \frac{3^2}{2(100)}\left(1/2 + \frac{1}{0.33^2}\right) = 435 \text{ nW}$$

■ EXAMPLE 7.5

These four thought experiments on modulation index apply to all types of amplitude modulation, including both forms of single sideband (SSB) discussed next. They seem simple, but make sure they are self-evident to you. Refer to equation 7-14.

If the voltage of a modulating signal is doubled, what happens to the modulation index? It doubles.

If the voltage of the carrier signal is doubled, what happens to the modulation index? It halves.

If the frequency of a modulating signal is doubled, what happens to the modulation index? Nothing.

If the frequency of the carrier signal is doubled, what happens to the modulation index? Nothing.

■ EXAMPLE 7.6

Here are two more thought experiments, this time just for large carrier systems, DSB-LC and SSB-LC. Both have to do with power. Again, they seem simple, but make sure they are self-evident to you. Refer to equations 7-23 and 7-24.

If the voltage of the modulating signal is doubled, what happens to the average power? It goes up by 4.

If the voltage of the carrier signal is doubled, what happens to the average power? It goes up by 4.

■ EXAMPLE 7.7

Now we have five more thought experiments, this time for all forms of AM, including SSB systems, studied next. There is no reminder about seeming simplicity this time. These have to do with bandwidth. Refer to Figure 7.4.

If the frequency of the modulating signal is doubled, what happens to the bandwidth? It doubles.

If the frequency of the carrier signal is doubled, what happens to the bandwidth? Nothing.

If the voltage of the modulating signal is doubled, what happens to the bandwidth. Nothing.

If the voltage of the carrier signal is doubled, what happens to bandwidth. Nothing.

If the modulation index is doubled, what happens to bandwidth. Nothing.

■ EXAMPLE 7.8

These are the last thought experiments for this chapter, they concern transmission efficiency, or α. Refer to equation 7-34.

If the frequency of the modulating signal is doubled, what happens to α? Nothing.

If the frequency of the carrier signal is doubled, what happens to α? Nothing.

If the voltage of the modulating signal is doubled, what happens to α? It gets larger.

If the voltage of the carrier signal is doubled, what happens to α? It gets smaller.

If the modulation index is doubled, what happens to α? It gets larger.

■ SINGLE SIDEBAND (SSB) MODULATION

There is a related type of modulation, which is similar to both types of DSB studied already. It is called single sideband (SSB) modulation. The SSB signal is just the upper or lower sideband only of the DSB signal. SSB can be generated either with a suppressed carrier, SSB-SC, or with carrier energy present, SSB-LC. As seen in the discussion on DSB, both sidebands are generated in the modulation process. To obtain SSB, one of sidebands is then filtered out. Figure 7.13 illustrates the frequency domain generation process to produce SSB. What is illustrated is the form of SSB known as SSB-LC. As can

Figure 7.13
Generation of SSB-LC from DSB-LC source, spectrum analyzer view.

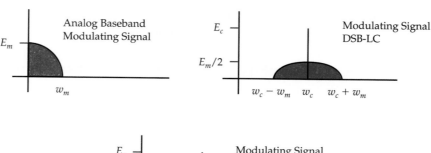

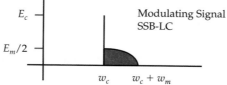

be seen, it is very similar to DSB with only one sideband. Again, just like DSB, there are two forms, SSB-SC and SSB-LC. The only difference is the presence of the carrier energy.

This has one major advantage over DSB: The bandwidth is not doubled. DSB generates two identical versions of the modulating signal displaced in frequency from each other. Refer to Figure 7.4 to confirm this. It was briefly pointed out it in that section, but you should now verify for yourself that this is exactly what is happening.

Not doubling the bandwidth of the modulating signal to transmit it is a big advantage for SSB modulation. As discussed many times, bandwidth is valuable. Only using half as much to send the same information as compared with DSB is a significant figure of merit. On the other hand, as can be seen from the following reasoning, the power of the SSB modulated signal is less than what would be obtained using DSB modulation.

Referring to Figure 7.13, it should make sense that if only half the DSB envelope is present; that component of power that was attributed to the sideband that is missing will not be present. Remember how the power was added up in a DSB-LC modulated waveform? The approach was to just add the power in each component, the carrier, the USB and the LSB. Equation 7-16 is reproduced below for your reference.

$$P_{\text{DSB-LC}} = P_c + P_{\text{usb}} + P_{\text{lsb}} \qquad \textbf{(7-16)}$$

Therefore, by removing one sideband, here the LSB, the following expression for the power in a SSB-LC modulated wave is found. For your reference, the expression for a SSB-SC wave is also shown. As can be seen, it is the same except for the contribution of the carrier power. Again, it is just like the DSB case.

$$P_{\text{SSB-LC}} = P_c + P_{\text{usb}} \qquad \textbf{(7-41)}$$

$$P_{\text{SSB-SC}} = P_{\text{usb}} \qquad \textbf{(7-42)}$$

From this reasoning the equations for the power in each type of modulated signal can be written by just removing that component that added the power for the LSB:

$$P_c = \frac{E_c^2}{2R} \qquad P_{\text{usb}} = P_{\text{lsb}} = \frac{E_c^2 m^2}{8R} \rightarrow P_{\text{SSB-LC}} = \frac{E_c^2}{2R} + \frac{E_c^2 m^2}{8R} = \frac{E_c^2}{2R}\left(1 + \frac{m^2}{4}\right) \qquad \textbf{(7-43)}$$

This can be rearranged to give an expression with the modulating voltage instead of the carrier voltage in just the same way as was done for the DSB case, only the result will be

$$P_{\text{SSB-LC}} = \frac{E_m^2}{2R}\left(1/4 + \frac{1}{m^2}\right) \qquad \textbf{(7-44)}$$

Finally, by just considering only the single sideband, it is possible to find an expression for the SSB-SC case as well:

$$P_{\text{SSB-SC}} = P_{\text{usb}} = \frac{E_c^2 m^2}{8R} = \frac{E_m^2}{8R} \qquad \textbf{(7-45)}$$

Note that this is exactly half of what was obtained in equation 7-11 for the DSB-SC situation. Figure 7.14 illustrates just how the SSB-LC signal would look like on an oscilloscope.

Figure 7.14
SSB-LC oscilloscope view.

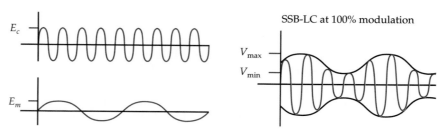

Now, from the mathematical analysis presented above, the power in a SSB-LC signal is reduced from that in the DSB-LC situation. As can be seen in Figure 7.14, the form of the SSB signal remains quite similar to that obtained in the DSB case. However, by looking closely, one can see that the voltage swings are different. This is because one sideband is missing, so that component is not present. Just like when viewing in the frequency domain, this must have an impact on the signal in the time domain.

Just like the DSB case, the V_{max} and V_{min} numbers are determined by the addition and subtraction of the sideband voltage from the carrier voltage. Only here there is just one sideband, in this case the upper sideband, so the equations change a little bit. This is shown below. Note how the only real differences are that the value of E_m is now only the upper sideband voltage. This is shown in Figure 7.13.

Essentially, the only difference is the difference in voltage swing of the carrier inside the envelope. Because the envelope is defined by the modulation voltage, and it is now only half as large (only includes one sideband), the result is less potential modulation. The modulation index describes this. One way of looking at SSB-LC is to realize it is the same as DSB-LC except the maximum modulation index is 0.50, or 50% percent modulation. This is why the envelope does not close down as it did in the DSB-LC case for 100% percent modulation. The equations below relate the peak voltages of the SSB modulated waveform to the peak voltages of the modulating and carrier signal, as well as their ratio, the modulation index:

$$V_{max} = E_c + E_{sb} = E_c + \frac{E_m}{2} \tag{7-46}$$

$$V_{min} = E_c - E_{sb} = E_c - \frac{E_m}{2} \tag{7-47}$$

$$E_{sb} = \frac{E_m}{2} = 1/4 \, (V_{max} - V_{min}) \tag{7-48}$$

$$V_{max} = \frac{E_m}{m} + \frac{E_m}{2} = E_m \left(\frac{1}{m} + \frac{1}{2} \right) = E_c \left(1 + \frac{m}{2} \right) \tag{7-49}$$

$$V_{min} = \frac{E_m}{m} - \frac{E_m}{2} = E_m \left(\frac{1}{m} - \frac{1}{2} \right) = E_c \left(1 - \frac{m}{2} \right) \tag{7-50}$$

■ VESTIGIAL SIDEBAND (VSB) MODULATION

Another form of amplitude modulation that is related to SSB is vestigial sideband (VSB) modulation. This works by combining some "vestige," or small part, of one of the sidebands together with the entire other one. One way of thinking about VSB is that it is an in-between form of modulation, between DSB and SSB. DSB transmits the both entire sidebands, SSB transmits only one entire sideband, and VSB transmits one entire sideband and some vestige of the other. As you can imagine, the bandwidth used by VSB also lies between that calculated for DSB and SSB.

Therefore, there are situations where VSB is desirable. These situations are where the input signal is very wide and there is a need to conserve frequency or spectrum space. Again, VSB can be viewed as a compromise between DSB and SSB, its transmission contains all of one sideband, and a portion of the other. Because a portion of one sideband is not transmitted, a portion of frequency space is not needed. The bandwidth of a VSB signal is between 1 and 2 times the original modulating signal bandwidth, depending on how much of the vestige sideband is transmitted. VSB is usually chosen when bandwidth conservation is critical and SSB is not considered appropriate because it is too expensive to implement.

VSB modulation is the only modulation technique that will be discussed that does not have a symmetric spectrum about the carrier frequency. Because in the application examined VSB transmits with a large carrier, envelope detection can be used; other applications might not transmit the carrier, and then the techniques used with DSB-SC demodulation are required. Again, demodulation will be covered in the next chapter.

The VSB application that will be briefly described is traditional broadcast TV. In the United States, TV transmissions require 525 lines of video sent 30 times a second. The idea is to send many frames per second to eliminate the flicker that would result from a lower number of frames per second. Due to how the lines making up each frame are combined, using interlacing, this rate eliminates any possibility of flicker. Interlacing the lines making up the frame is accomplished by sending all the odd-numbered lines first, and then once all these have been drawn on the screen, the even-numbered lines are drawn.

It is instructive to briefly explore the ideas behind each of the above assertions about how TV works. The frame rate, here 30 frames per second, and how the lines are drawn on the screen, the interlacing, combine to eliminate the flicker one would normally expect from a sequence of still pictures being presented as motion. A rate of 30 frames/sec would not have much flicker discernable to the human eye. However, the frame rate can be essentially doubled by sending only half of each image at a time by combining the frame rate with interlacing. Essentially, because two separate frames must be combined to make one, the perceived frame rate is 60 frames/sec. This rate is a little higher than is actually necessary to eliminate flicker but was chosen so that it would synchronize with the power line frequency of 60 Hz.

Therefore, the combination of frame rate and interlacing combine to decrease flicker for TV. Interlacing is a separate subject that will be discussed next. You may be wondering just how this works. How is only one-half the frame sent at one time and just how are they combined into a single frame? Interlacing is accomplished by sending all the odd-

Figure 7.15
TV interlacing.

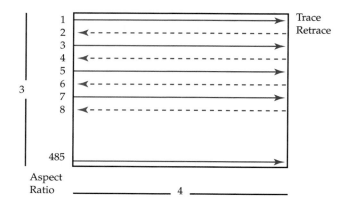

number lines on the screen first and then sending all the even-number lines. These two half-frames are combined into a single complete frame. To see how this works, one must understand that the TV picture tube is designed in a very similar way to the oscilloscope. There is an electron beam that sweeps across the screen at a fixed rate. This is just like the time base control on an oscilloscope. What that rate is will be calculated a little later.

This beam sweeps across the TV tube in the manner shown in Figure 7.15. As can be seen from the figure, the beam traces line 1 and then returns along the path of line 2, without leaving any trace of its passage. Then it traces line 3 and returns along the path of line 4, again without leaving any trace of its passage. Usually *trace* is the term used when writing to the screen and *retrace* is used when not writing to the screen. For the first half-frame, the odd-number lines are traces and the even number lines are retraces. For the second half-frame, the situation is reversed. Once both have been written, a single frame is presented for viewing.

To calculate the trace time, it is necessary to know an additional fact or two. Although the TV image is composed of 525 trace lines, only about 485 are used to display the image. The extra 40 or so lines are used to synchronize the television set so that the picture always starts at the top of the screen. The lines that are not intended to be displayed are "sent" to the screen during the time it takes the electron beam to move from the lower right-hand corner after tracing the last even trace line to the upper left-hand corner, ready to trace the first odd-line trace of the next image. During this time, the synchronization occurs.

The next item that must be understood to compute the bandwidth or rate of scanning is that all TV transmissions are sent at a specific aspect ratio. The aspect ratio is a way of talking about the relative sizes of the horizontal and vertical dimensions of the image. For broadcast TV, this aspect ratio is 4:3. That means that the picture on the screen is four units wide by three units tall. This means that to obtain equal resolution in both the horizontal and vertical directions, the line rate must be multiplied by this aspect ratio.

Therefore, there are four factors that will determine the bandwidth or electron beam rate required: the number of lines transmitted, 525; the fact that only 485 are displayed and that these take two half-frames to display; the aspect ratio, 4/3; and the perceived frame rate, 30. The calculation is shown below:

$$\text{BW} = (N_l)(\text{AR})(\text{BW}_l)(N_f) = (525)\left(\frac{4}{3}\right)\left(\frac{485}{2}\right)(30) = 5.09 \text{ MHz} \qquad \textbf{(7-51)}$$

where N_l = number of lines transmitted = 525
         AR = aspect ratio of screen = 4/3
         BW_l = line bandwidth = 485/2
         N_l = number of frames per second

This would indicate that a bandwidth of a little over 5 MHz would be needed. It was determined experimentally that an acceptable video image could be obtained using only about 4 MHz. Essentially, part of the spectrum is thrown away (the high frequency part). This results in a minimum video bandwidth of 4 MHz.

If a DSB technique were to be used to transmit this 4 MHz modulating signal, it would require 8 MHz of bandwidth for just the video signal. However, most people like to listen to the TV as well as watch it, so some additional spectral space must be allocated for the audio portion. Also, because it is important to manufacture televisions relatively inexpensively, one must consider the cost of the channel filter that will be used to tune the TV to different stations. Adding all these considerations up results in a bandwidth that is much too wide to be considered.

The result is that instead of at least 8 MHz of bandwidth being required for each broadcast TV station, only about 5 MHz is. This is arrived at by transmitting one sideband of 4 MHz and a vestige of the other, here the LSB, of about 1 MHz. Allowing for guardbanding, in the United States TV stations are placed 6 MHz apart. Guardbanding is the separation of two adjacent signals by some amount of frequency space. This frequency gap, where no signal is transmitted, allows the receiver to discern the two signals. If the two signals were precisely adjacent, when the receiver was tuned to either one, a portion of the other would also be received. This would appear to be distortion on the desired signal. Note in Figure 7.16 that the signal is *not* symmetric about the video carrier. This is the result of VSB modulation. Such a nonsymmetrical spectrum it is usually a good indicator that the modulation is VSB.

To close the discussion on VSB, note that the filtering required for VSB modulation is complex and has special requirements due to the special requirement of rolling off smoothly and quickly on the lower, or vestige sideband. This study is beyond the scope of this book. Also, note that VSB waveforms can be demodulated with either simple envelope detection, as is the case for DSB-LC transmissions when sufficient carrier energy is present in the transmitted signal. This is the case for broadcast TV, as shown by the very large video carrier energy. When this is not the case, the techniques used for DSB-SC demodulation must be employed.

There are a lot of interesting things about conventional TV that are also indicative of other issues explored in the text. For example, the frequency that VHF TV transmits in is the VHF band. This band uses LOS propagation. Hence, your TV antenna must be

Figure 7.16
VSB modulation, broadcast TV, spectrum analyzer view.

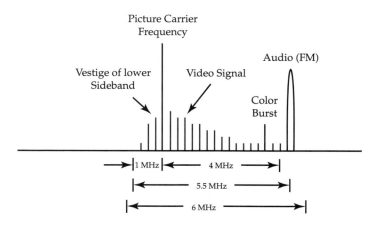

able to "see" the transmit antenna of the TV station. This usually limits the range to about 40 miles, just like FM.

Finally, observe that the audio signal for your TV is not sent as part of the video signal. This was mentioned earlier. Note that it is a separate audio FM channel, located at the far right of the channel spectrum. This is done in almost exactly the same way as broadcast FM radio and is demodulated exactly like a FM receiver. The only difference is that for the audio signal application in television broadcasting, no pilot tone is transmitted and there is no secondary revenue channel. This results in a bandwidth of about 25 kHz for the baseband audio signal and means that the carrier swing is 25 kHz and the frequency deviation is 50 kHz. See Figure 9.2 for what these are. Demodulation techniques for FM will be explored in Chapter 9.

■ SIGNAL-TO-NOISE (S/N) COMPARISON

DSB-SC S/N

From Chapter 1, we have the expression for calculating signal-to-noise ratio, reproduced here:

$$\frac{S}{N} = 10 \log\left(\frac{S}{N}\right)$$

One of the things that it is nice to compare is the relative performance of each type of amplitude modulation examined in this chapter. The above relationship defines signal-to-noise ratio for any modulation scheme. By modifying it to reflect the relative value of the signal, we can find a specific expression for each of the various flavors of amplitude modulation considered. For DSB-SC, this results in the following expression:

$$\frac{S}{N} = 10 \log\left(\frac{E_m}{N}\right)$$ (7-52)

DSB-LC S/N

The signal-to-noise comparison will be made only for the case of 100% modulation. In the 100% case, the signal envelope of the DSB-LC signal is twice the amplitude of an equivalent DSB-SC signal. This means that the signal-to-noise ratio for a DSB-LC signal is half that of the SC signal. Therefore, with equivalent transmit powers, the DSB-SC approach will yield twice the signal-to-noise performance of a 100% modulated DSB-LC signal. That is expressed below by the addition of 3 dB to the S/N value found for the DSB-SC situation:

$$\frac{S}{N} = 10 \log\left(\frac{S}{N}\right) = 10 \log\left(\frac{2E_m}{N}\right) = 10 \log(2) + 10 \log\left(\frac{E_m}{N}\right)$$

$$\frac{S}{N} = 3 \text{ dB} + 10 \log\left(\frac{E_m}{N}\right)$$ (7-53)

SSB S/N

Just as there are two forms of SSB modulation, there are two situations for the signal-to-noise calculations. In the SSB-SC case, the signal strength is twice what it was in the DSB case because only one side of the band is being transmitted. Therefore, the signal-to-noise performance of an SSB-SC will be twice that of a DSB-SC signal.

In the SSB-LC case, the situation is not as clear. We have the carrier component and one of the sidebands. The performance should be somewhat better than the DSB case, because of the savings of transmitting the extra sideband, but this factor depends on the modulation coefficient m. The performance of SSB-LC is always better; how much better, depends on the value of m. This is seen in the equations presented below:

$$\frac{S}{N} = 10 \log\left(\frac{S}{N}\right) = 10 \log\left(\frac{E_m/2}{N}\right) = 10 \log\left(\frac{E_m}{2N}\right) = 10 \log(1/2) + 10 \log\left(\frac{E_m}{N}\right)$$

$$\frac{S}{N} = -3 \text{ dB} + 10 \log\left(\frac{E_m}{N}\right) \text{ SSB-SC S/N}$$ (7-54)

As can be seen from the above equations, SSB-SC will, for equivalent transmit powers, exhibit half the performance that DSB-SC will. Although SSB-LC will exhibit equivalent performance for equivalent transmit powers, this result comes about because although both SSB forms of modulation feature a peak signal voltage of half the DSB-LC, each also has only one sideband, halving the total signal strength:

$$\frac{S}{N} = 10 \log\left(\frac{S}{N}\right) = 10 \log\left(\frac{E_m}{N}\right) \text{ SSB-LC S/N}$$ (7-55)

◼ SUMMARY

This chapter explored the first of three types of analog modulation, amplitude modulation. As in any wave, there are three things that one can change, amplitude, frequency, and phase. In this chapter, it was found that the amplitude of the carrier signal can be used to carry information about the amplitude and frequency of the modulating signal. The following two points are key:

Figure 7.17
Comparison of AM modulated waveforms.

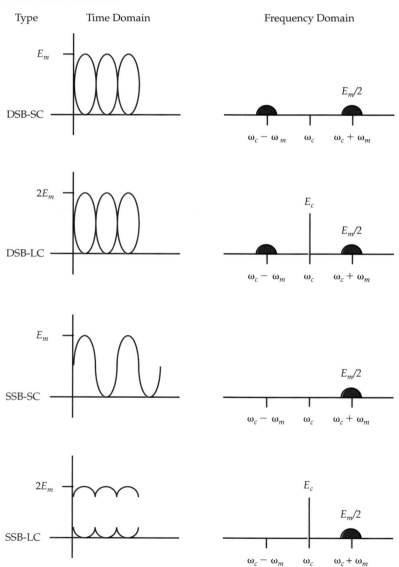

The amplitude of the modulating signal is represented by the relative amount of opening and closing of the carrier envelope. The carrier amplitude matches the amplitude variation of the modulating signal.

The frequency of the modulating signal is represented by how often the envelope opens and closes. This is sometimes called repetition rate: the higher the frequency of the modulating signal, the greater the repetition rate of the modulated envelope.

The modulation index tells us something about how efficient the modulation is in power through the definition of the transmission efficiency. The amplitude of the carrier signal is directly related to the power of the waveform and, for the suppressed carrier case, is the only real variable.

SSB modulation is very similar to DSB modulation except that it uses half the bandwidth because only one sideband is transmitted. An application of VSB modulation, broadcast NTSC video (TV), was described.

Figure 7.17 shows what the signals will look like for each of the modulation types discussed. Spend a few minutes comparing the signals shown. Table 7.1 shows the relative performance of the modulation techniques discussed in this chapter. The values listed are theoretical; practical implementations will always be a little different, but as a tool to compare relative performance, the table should serve. In each case the amplitude of the baseband modulating signal is the same and represented by E_m. Compare this with Figure 7.17.

It is also possible to express the average power for the large carrier modulation techniques as a function of the carrier voltage; these formulas are reproduced below as well:

$$\text{DSB-LC} \quad P = \frac{E_c^2}{2R}\left(1 + \frac{m^2}{2}\right) \qquad \text{SSB-LC:} \quad P = \frac{E_c^2}{2R}\left(1 + \frac{m^2}{4}\right)$$

These expressions are equivalent to the ones listed in Table 7.1. They are arrived at by

Table 7.1
Average Power Comparison Using E_m

Modulation	Peak Voltage	Average Power	Baseband BW	Modulated BW
DSB-SC	E_m	$\dfrac{E_m^2}{4R}$	ω_m	$2\omega_m$
DSB-LC, $m = 1$	$2E_m$	$\dfrac{3E_m^2}{4R}$	ω_m	$2\omega_m$
DSB-LC, m arb.	$E_m\left(1 + \dfrac{1}{m}\right)$	$\dfrac{E_m^2}{2R}\left(\dfrac{1}{2} + \dfrac{1}{m^2}\right)$	ω_m	$2\omega_m$
SSB-SC	E_m	$\dfrac{E_m^2}{8R}$	ω_m	ω_m
SSB-LC, $m = 1$	$2E_m$	$\dfrac{5E_m^2}{8}$	ω_m	ω_m
SSB-LC, m arb.	$E_m\left(1 + \dfrac{1}{m}\right)$	$\dfrac{E_m^2}{2R}\left(\dfrac{1}{2} + \dfrac{1}{m^2}\right)$	ω_m	ω_m

applying the important relationship between the carrier and modulation signals peak voltage, the modulation index:

$$m = \frac{E_m}{E_c}$$

PROBLEMS

1. Find the bandwidth of a DSB-SC modulated signal if the bandwidth of the input modulating signal is
   (a) 10 kHz   (b) 100 kHz
   (c) 1 MHz   (d) 10 MHz

2. Find the lower and upper sidebands for a carrier frequency of 1 MHz and a modulating frequency of
   (a) 10 kHz   (b) 100 kHz
   (c) 1 MHz   (d) 10 MHz (be careful)

3. For a DSB-SC modulator, with a load resistance of 100 Ω, find the total average power for peak modulating voltages of
   (a) 1 V   (b) 100 V
   (c) 1 mV   (d) 1 μV

4. For a DSB-SC modulator with a carrier frequency of 1M rad/sec, a load resistance of 75 Ω, and a modulating signal $a(t) = 50 \cos(20t)$, find the following:
   (a) Peak voltage of modulating signal
   (b) The carrier angular frequency
   (c) The modulation angular frequency
   (d) The DSB-SC bandwidth
   (e) The USB bandwidth and angular frequencies
   (f) The LSB bandwidth and angular frequencies
   (g) The total average power

5. Find the modulation index and percent modulation for the following pairs DSB-LC of peak modulating and carrier voltages:
   (a) 10V, 10V   (b) 10V, 20V
   (c) 20V, 10V   (d) 20V, 20V

6. Find the total average power in a 100% modulated DSB-LC system with a load resistance of 50 Ω and an unmodulated carrier of peak voltage of:
   (a) 10 V   (b) 100 V
   (c) 1 mV   (d) 1 μV

7. Find the following for a DSB-LC system—for a carrier frequency of 100 k rad/sec, a peak carrier voltage of 20 V, a load resistance of 100 Ω, and a modulating signal of amplitude 5 V at a frequency of 20 k rad/sec.
   (a) $m(t)$
   (b) Peak carrier voltage
   (c) Carrier angular frequency
   (d) Peak modulation voltage
   (e) Modulation angular frequency
   (f) The LSB bandwidth and angular frequencies
   (g) The USB bandwidth and angular frequencies
   (h) The DSB-LC bandwidth
   (i) The modulation index
   (j) The average power

8. For Problem 7, determine the transmission efficiency.

9. Why is the transmission efficiency of a DSB-SC transmitter always 100%?

10. What is the maximum transmission efficiency of a DSB-LC transmitter and why?

11. What benefit does broadcast AM radio get from the transmission efficiencies used?

12. For a DSB-LC modulator, with $m = 1.0$, find the peak carrier and peak modulating signal voltages for a modulated waveform with $V_{max} = 10$ V. For a modulation index of zero, what is the peak carrier voltage for the same system?

13. For an SSB-SC modulator, find the average power for a peak modulation voltage of 10 V and a load resistance of 50 Ω.

14. For an SSB-LC modulator, find the average power for a peak carrier voltage of 20 V, a load resistance of 50 Ω, and a modulation index of 0.75.

8

Amplitude Modulation and Demodulation

With the modulation theory from Chapter 7 behind us, it is time to begin an examination of the methods for modulation and demodulation of an AM signal. The basic idea of all types of amplitude modulators is to mix a baseband data source with a carrier frequency. Varying of the peak voltage of the carrier envelope produces the resultant modulated signal by the modulating signal, the baseband data source. This data source can be analog or digital, and it can be smoothly varying or abruptly turning ON and OFF like a digital data stream. The type of data makes no difference in the basic design of the modulator, but it does have an effect on the shape of the time domain envelope and, hence, the frequency domain spectral characteristics.

A very basic AM modulator is shown in Fig. 8.1. This circuit will produce a DSB-SC type of modulated signal. The circle with an X in it is the device that actually accomplished the frequency translation. It is called a frequency converter, frequency mixer, or most typically, mixer. It works by translating the frequency spectrum of any baseband data source by $\pm w_c$ but leaves the spectral shape unaltered.

Remember that in DSB-SC modulation there is no separate carrier present in the modulated signal. In addition, recall that the most important application of this type of circuit is not to produce AM signals for some transmitter. Rather, it is used for frequency translation of an arbitrary baseband data source in a variety of applications. This is called by a number of additional names, including frequency conversion, frequency mixing, and more historically, heterodyning. It can also work to translate data sources

Figure 8.1
DSB-SC amplitude modulator.

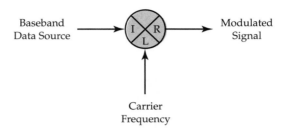

that are not baseband in nature, with the provision that the center frequency of the data source is not too close to the carrier frequency.

Before getting into a brief examination of modulator circuits useful for AM modulation, two basic components will be introduced. These are the passive mixer and the summer and splitter. Both are very useful for describing how modulators and demodulators work.

■ PASSIVE MIXERS

To understand how this fundamental component works, an schematic diagram of a passive mixer is shown in Figure 8.2, and its operation will be briefly discussed. A passive mixer combines two signals and produces an output on the third port. Mixers have special names for each of these inputs, the local oscillator (LO) port, the intermediate frequency (IF) port, and the radio frequency (RF) port, respectively. These names come from RF design applications, typically from frequency translation.

As can be seen in the figure the isolation of the three ports just mentioned is accomplished by the use of center-tapped transformers. The carrier frequency applied to the LO port must be of sufficient amplitude to control the ON-OFF cycle of the diodes. Once each cycle of the carrier signal applied to the LO port, one pair of the diodes is turned ON and one pair is open. At each alternating half-cycle this acts to couple the two center-tapped transformers together in opposite phase. In Figure 8.2, on one half-cycle the two tops of the transformers are connected, and on the other half-cycle the top of one is connected to the bottom of the other.

If the diodes used in the device are silicon, it is possible to calculate what the peak voltage of the signal applied to the LO port needs to be. Assume that this signal is being generated from a signal generator, and hence the output is calibrated in dBm and terminated into 50 Ω:

$$10 \log \frac{(V/\sqrt{2})^2/R}{10^{-3}} = 10 \log \frac{(0.7/\sqrt{2})^2/50}{10^{-3}} = 10 \log \frac{0.0049}{10^{-3}} = 7 \text{ dBm}$$

Turning the diode ON and OFF is accomplished by two things. First, sufficient volt-

Figure 8.2
Passive mixer.

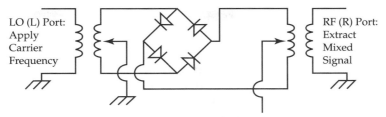

LO (L) Port:
Apply
Carrier
Frequency

RF (R) Port:
Extract
Mixed
Signal

IF (I) Port: Apply Signal Input

age must be applied at the LO port. Second, the currents flowing in the IF port must be small compared to the current flowing in the LO port. The current flow in these circuits will depend on the voltage applied to the port; the more voltage, the more current up to some point. Current flow varies in direction and path depending on the relative polarity of the diode ring induced by the voltage swings at the LO port. This induces current flow and, hence, voltage swings on the output RF port.

Probably the easiest way to think of a mixer is to imagine it as a multiplication device. Essentially one can imagine a mixer multiplying the two input signals to produce an output signal. This can be seen in equation 8-1. The resultant signal is just the product of the two signals applied to the LO and IF ports.

To do the multiplication, the device must be able to mix frequencies. This is because when you multiply two sinusoids, the result is a mix of the two inputs. This is seen in the equations below. To examine this we will use the same identity that was used earlier for the product of two sinusoids.

$$\cos(a)\cos(b) = 1/2[\cos(a - b) + \cos(a - b)] \qquad \textbf{(8-1)}$$

Therefore, the two signals that are applied to the IF and LO ports will result in an output at the RF port that will be given by the product of those two applied signals:

$$\text{LO port: } \cos(w_{LO}t) \qquad \text{IF port: } \cos(w_{IF}t)$$

$$\text{RF port: } \cos(w_{LO}t)\cos(w_{IF}t) = 1/2[\cos(w_{LO} - w_{IF})t + \cos(w_{LO} + w_{IF})t]$$

As can be seen from the above equations, the output of the mixer is two signals translated in frequency, exactly like the output of a DSB-SC modulator. These two resultant signals are called the sum difference signals, respectively. These are the same signals that are shown in equation 7-5, which was used to define DSB-SC modulation in the last chapter. Therefore, the result of mixing two signals is two replicas of the signals translated in frequency and halved in amplitude. Again, we see the same result as in DSB-SC modulation. If one only wants to determine the frequencies present on each port, apply the following equations. Use the first set for hertz and the second set for angular frequency:

$$f_{\text{sum}} = f_{\text{LO}} + f_{\text{IF}} \quad \text{or} \quad w_{\text{sum}} = w_{\text{LO}} + w_{\text{IF}} \tag{8-2}$$

$$f_{\text{diff}} = f_{\text{LO}} - f_{\text{IF}} \quad \text{or} \quad w_{\text{diff}} = w_{\text{LO}} - w_{\text{IF}} \tag{8-3}$$

$$f_{\text{RF}} = f_{\text{sum}} + f_{\text{diff}} \quad \text{or} \quad w_{\text{RF}} = w_{\text{sum}} + w_{\text{diff}} \tag{8-4}$$

In most applications the signal applied to the LO port is a single frequency, usually the carrier frequency. This means that what results from the mixing process are two replicas of the signal applied to the IF port, shifted by the LO frequency.

This type of circuit is widely used in passive mixers. If the transformer windings are accurate and balanced and the diodes are matched, very good performance can be obtained. Because it is a passive circuit, there is some conversion loss. This typically is 7 dB from the IF port to the RF port. Although 6 dB would be the theoretical minimum, there is usually about a 1 dB additional loss due to nonideal components. If the voltage swings of the LO port carrier frequency are not sufficient, this conversion loss can grow dramatically. Additionally, although the LO and RF ports are isolated from each other, some inductive coupling occurs. It is typical to see the LO signal on the RF port damped by anywhere from 30 to 50 dB, depending on the construction of the mixer.

Not discussed here, but implied from the above paragraph, is the class of mixers known as active mixers. These are usually constructed of a few transistors and a number of discreet components. These offer the advantage of no conversion loss when using a mixer for frequency translation, and they usually provide 10 to 20 dB of conversion gain. This can both a blessing and a curse; the blessing is due to the lack of loss and hence the avoidance of adding gain. The curse is that it is common for such a mixer to be a significant source of noise, and an active mixer, like any amplifier, can add noise, especially intermodulation noise to the output.

■ EXAMPLE 8.1

If a 1 MHz signal at 5 V peak is applied to the LO port of a mixer and a 10 kHz signal at 1 V peak is applied to the IF port of a mixer, what is the mathematical expression for the signal seen at the RF port?

Figure 8.3
Frequency mixing, spectrum analyzer view.

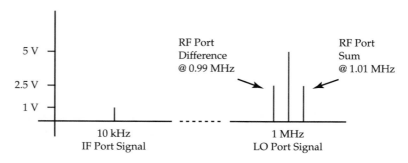

$$\text{LO port: } 5\cos(1 \times 10^6 t) \qquad \text{IF port: } 1\cos(10 \times 10^6 t)$$

RF port: $5\cos(1 \times 10^6 t)1\cos(10 \times 10^6 t)$

$$= 5/2 \,\{\cos[(1 \times 10^6 - 10 \times 10^3)t] + \cos[(1 \times 10^6 + 10 \times 10^3)t\}$$

The result is two signals, each at half the amplitude of the product of the two individual signal amplitudes located at 1 MHz + 10 kHz and at 1 MHz − 10 kHz. Figure 8.3 illustrates the three signals.

■ SUMMER AND SPLITTER

A summer is a passive device that sums two signals and yields the vector result of those two signals at the output. A splitter is just the opposite; when a signal is applied to its input, it splits the signal into two replicas of the original signal, each at half the amplitude of the input signal. Half the amplitude is exactly 3 dB attenuation. In actual devices, a little more attenuation is experienced because there is some conversion loss because real devices are not perfect. The implementations always have a little extra loss over the theoretical loss.

To illustrate how these devices are constructed, see Figure 8.4. As can be seen, these devices work very simply. They are essentially just a center-tapped inductor, actually implemented as a transformer, with a some internal resistance to increase the isolation between ports A and B. This inductor winding is such that from the center tap to port A or port B, the number of turns is equal.

When used as a summer, two input signals are applied to ports A and B. The signal applied to port A will cause a current to flow through the inductor path A to B. This signal will undergo a 180° phase shift by the time it arrives at port B. The signal applied to port A will also flow through the internal resistor, and this signal will not undergo any phase shift on this path by the time it reaches port B. The same situation, although reversed, will apply to any signal that is applied to port B.

This is a situation where two replicas of the signal applied to either port, A or B, arrives at the opposite port, B or A, each 180° out of phase with the other. If the internal resistor shown in Figure 8.4 is equal to the impedance of the inductor, the signals when reaching the opposite port add 180° out of phase. This is 100% destructive interference,

Figure 8.4
Summer and splitter circuit diagram.

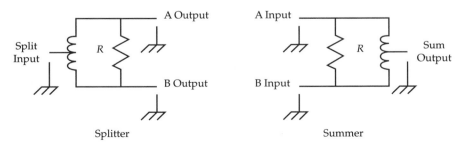

with equal amplitude, and no signal is seen. That means that any signal applied to port A is not seen at port B and vice versa. This result is specified as the isolation between ports A and B. Typical values for such isolation are $20 - 40$ dB. That means that only 1 part in 100 to 1 part in 10,000 can be seen at the opposite port.

The signals are summed at port S exactly equally as the circuit path, and hence the impedance from either port A or port B is the same to port S. It should be also clear that any signal applied to port S will be split evenly at ports A and B when this device is wired as a splitter. In this case, each signal will attenuate equally; this is shown in the examples below. In summary, a power summer and/or splitter is a passive device that offers a way to combine or split signals equally. This device is used widely in all kinds of communication systems because it offers a handy way to sum or split signals.

■ **EXAMPLE 8.2**

What signal would one expect to see at the S port if a 10 V peak signal at 10 kHz is applied to port A and a 5 V peak signal at 5 kHz is applied to port B? Both signals have the same phase.

Because a summer just adds the two signals, we can do the same. It is very straightforward because the signals have the same phase.

$$S \text{ port} = 1/2 \, [A \text{ port} + B \text{ port}] \tag{8-5}$$
$$S \text{ port} = 1/2[10 \cos(10 \times 10^3 t) + 5 \cos(5 \times 10^3 t)]$$
$$S \text{ port} = 5 \cos(10 \times 10^3 t) + 2.5 \cos(5 \times 10^3 t)$$

The result is the two signals, each reduced by half amplitude due to the summer loss of 3 dB.

■ **EXAMPLE 8.3**

What signal would be seen at the S port if a 10 V peak signal at 10 kHz is applied to port A and a 5 V signal at 5 kHz is applied at port B? The signal applied to port B is 90° out of phase with the signal at port A.

This is a little tricky because the phase difference between the two signals must be taken into account. To do so, add a phase term to the argument of the sinusoid:

$$S \text{ port} = 1/2 \, [A \text{ port} + B \text{ port}]$$
$$S \text{ port} = 1/2 \, [10 \cos(10 \times 10^3 t + 0) + 5 \cos(5 \times 10^3 t + 90°)]$$
$$S \text{ port} = 1/2 \, [10 \cos(10 \times 10^3 t) + 5 \cos(5 \times 10^3 t)\cos 90° - 5 \sin(10 \times 10^3 t)\sin 90°]$$
$$S \text{ port} = 5 \cos(2\pi 10 \times 10^3 t) - 2.5 \sin(2\pi 10 \times 10^3 t)$$

Note that here because the signals are not in phase to begin with, instead of the positive sum of both signals, one obtains the difference. We still see two distinct signals at their respective frequencies, but if displayed on an oscilloscope, one would see a different signal than in the first case due to the opposite sign on the second term. Note that the phase difference in the second term would not be noticeable. The reasons for this will be discussed in the next chapter.

■ EXAMPLE 8.4

This example illustrates how a splitter works. A 10 V peak, 1 kHz signal is applied at port S as shown below. The resultant signal at ports A and B is reduced by 3 dB, or half power.

$$A \text{ port} = B \text{ port} = 1/2 \text{ (S port)} \tag{8-6}$$

$$A \text{ port} = 1/2 \, [10 \cos(1 \times 10^3 t)] = 5 \cos(1 \times 10^3 t)$$

■ AMPLITUDE MODULATOR CIRCUITS

Interestingly, an *amplitude* modulator requires *frequency* mixing to work. There are a variety of methods for generating these types of signals. Most use specific devices that accomplish the frequency mixing necessary for a modulator to work. All these do so in one of two ways; either they are nonlinear in nature, for example, a diode or transistor, or they are time varying, for example, they switch. As was seen in the previous section, diodes can be used as switches. This fact is explored further in Figure 8.5.

The circuit presented is a balanced ring modulator that uses a diode ring to provide the switching necessary. Note that the configuration is the same as the mixer shown in Figure 8.2 and that it is the same circuit as shown in Figure 8.1. This is one of the chief reasons for its popularity; it is widely applicable and reliable. An extra bonus is that the signal can many times be used directly at the output without any extra filtering.

The next type of modulator that will be shown is in wide use for transmitting DSB-LC signals. Recall equation 7-12, describing the operation of this type of circuit:

$$m(t) = [a(t) + E_c] \cos(w_c t) = a(t) \cos(w_c t) + E_c \cos(w_c t) \tag{7-12}$$

The DSB-LC modulator shown is composed of a time-varying modulation signal $a(t)$ plus a constant multiplied by a fixed amplitude carrier signal. This suggests one way to generate this signal, which is shown in Figure 8.6.

In this figure, observe that a DSB-LC signal is just a DSB-SC plus a carrier. Therefore, the same circuit is used as earlier to generate the DSB-SC signal. All that was done

Figure 8.5
DSB-SC balanced ring modulator.

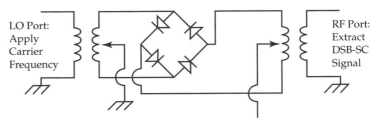

LO Port:
Apply
Carrier
Frequency

RF Port:
Extract
DSB-SC
Signal

IF Port: Apply Modulating Signal

Figure 8.6
Basic amplitude modulator design.

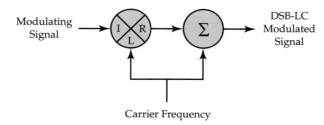

was to add a carrier component through a splitter/combiner used a summer. Review equation 7-12; note how it is just two terms added together, exactly what is implemented in Figure 8.6. Now you see why mixers are so useful when explaining how these circuits work.

A more practical circuit used in many commercial applications to implement an AM modulator is shown in Figure 8.7. The idea is similar, but the implementation is slightly different. Here, one adds to the input signal a carrier frequency at the desired amplitude. This combined signal is then switched at the carrier frequency. Finally, pass the resultant wave through a bandpass filter to select the desired frequency components and a DSB-LC signal is obtained.

Although it will not be demonstrated, the switching action simulates the multiplication (mixing) of the input signal, with a square wave switching waveform at frequency w_c. Because this approach will produce many replicas of the desired waveform at odd harmonics, the bandpass filter is used to select the correct one for the application at hand. Clearly, many different types of devices could be substituted for a switch. Diodes and transistors can make good switches. If a diode is used, this circuit is sometimes referred to as a rectifier-type modulator. AM commercial broadcast stations often use this approach.

Figure 8.7
Practical AM modulator.

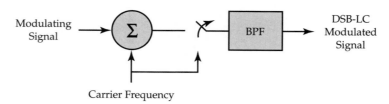

■ SSB MODULATORS

The next modulators that will be shown are those used to create SSB signals. Two types are shown in Figure 8.8. Both types produce SSB-SC signals.

In the top part of Figure 8.8, the most straightforward implementation of a method to generate SSB signals is shown. This implementation takes advantage of the fact that when a DSB-SC signal is generated, both sidebands are generated. In fact, that is one way of defining such a modulator. A SSB signal could be generated, in theory, from the DSB-SC signal just by filtering out one of the sidebands. This is what is shown in the first part of Figure 8.8, and is often used in amature radio applications.

Although this seems straightforward, it suffers from one major drawback in the real world. Depending on the bandwidth of the input signal and the frequency of the carrier signal, the filtering requirements can become impossible. Real filters take some frequency space to roll off, and in many commercially important cases, including the audio band, this implementation does not allow for that frequency separation.

Taking into account that most commercial implementations of SSB modulators are designed to work with audio band frequencies, a way to overcome the problem with the above approach must be found. Somehow, the input audio signal needs to be moved so that the filtering requirements are relaxed. This more realistic implementation is shown in the bottom portion of Figure 8.8. In this method, two frequencies are used to first "mix up" the baseband input signal to frequency one. Then there is a filter for the desired sideband, a "mix up" to the desired carrier frequency, and finally a bandpass filter for just the desired sideband.

In this implementation because of the frequency separation between the carrier frequency and f_1, the first bandpass filter design or sideband filter is made much simpler. The second bandpass filter is just a channel filter that is very similar to that used as the last stage in the first example of a SSB modulator. This method is widely used.

There is a third type of SSB modulator; it uses the phasing method. It depends on a phase shift component that will provide a $\pm 90°$ phase shift over the entire input signal

Figure 8.8
SSB modulators.

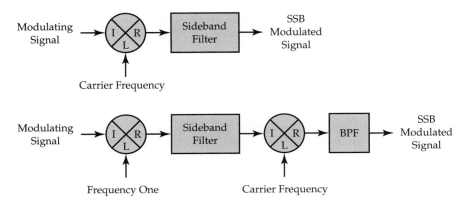

Figure 8.9
Single-frequency amplifier chain.

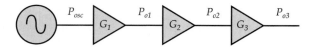

bandwidth. This component is very expensive and difficult to manufacture. Most phase shift components do so over a very narrow range of frequencies, a few percentages of the center frequency. Because most SSB modulators that are of commercial interest work in the audio band, this requirement for wideband phase shifters becomes onerous. Therefore, this method will not be explored further here.

You should be aware that there are many ways to implement modulators in circuitry. What this very brief discussion has stressed is what these various technical approaches must accomplish. Modulators can be implemented using transistors, op-amps, diodes, transformers, and so forth. The choices are only limited by imagination and understanding.

Additionally, the amplifier chain analysis shown in Figure 8.9 would not be suitable for most SSB-type transmissions (most especially those used in military applications). To perform that design it will be assumed that the signal source is very narrow in bandwidth. SSB transmitters are often required to operate over a very wide band. This means that the simple single-frequency analysis technique shown in Figure 8.5 would not be suitable for such a transmitter. Such wideband transmitters almost always use mixing and frequency doubling techniques to satisfy the wide bandwidth requirements. However, for those applications where the SSB signal is well confined, the single-amplifier chain approach will work.

■ TRANSMITTERS

Now that a way to construct an AM modulator has been shown, it is interesting to ask how this signal is amplified to generate the large power outputs typically encountered in broadcast AM radio and other applications. One way is to use an amplifier chain. There are ways to enhance the design approach discussed below, utilizing power splitters and combiners and frequency multiplication. This discussion will not extend into such areas; the only focus is on the basic amplifier chain. The approaches used to determine the design of such systems do not differ greatly from that presented here. Figure 8.9 illustrates the basic amplifier chain approach that is used to obtain the high power outputs commonly encountered.

The purpose of this section is to guide you through a design of an amplifier chain that will accomplish the power increase that is required by a system. It will be assumed that three amplifier stages are sufficient. This is a good assumption for most high-power applications.

Begin by simulating the broadcast source with an oscillator running at the carrier frequency of the station. This approximation uses a single frequency or, as it is sometimes known, a continuous wave (CW) source. This is a good one to begin with. Subsequent to completing this portion of the design cycle, it is often necessary to refine the design with a source that better approximates the information content contained in the modulating signal. For this example, this will not be necessary.

The total power gain from the amplifier chain is given by equation 8-7. It expresses the logarithmic ratio of the desired output power of the transmitter to the output power of the oscillator.

$$\text{power gain} = 10 \log \left(\frac{P_{o3}}{P_{osc}} \right) \tag{8-7}$$

Different types of amplifiers are used for different stages; it should make sense to you that different designs might be more appropriate for different output levels. For example, take the familiar stereo system. A different design is needed for a system designed to fill the ball park or stadium than for that designed for use in your automobile or for private listening with headphones.

Although it is outside the scope of this text to explore the different amplifier classes, lower output power amplifiers are designed differently from high output power ones. A good rule of thumb is to use class A amplifiers for outputs of less than 1/2 watt, and class C amplifiers for outputs over 1/2 watt. Class A amplifiers are used in the first stage because they offer high gain with low distortion contributions. Both of these characteristics are critical for a first-stage amplifier.

Class C amplifiers do not offer the same level of distortion performance as class A, but they do offer much higher efficiencies, an important issue at the higher power levels. Because the first stage does not contribute much in the overall power consumption, the efficiency is not as critical. Class C amplifiers are often used for the second two stages. The only characteristic that will be of concern is the relative efficiencies of the two classes of amplifiers. Example 8.5 illustrates the design process.

■ EXAMPLE 8.5

You are assigned to design the amplifier chain for a low-power AM radio station. The output power for the transmitter is specified to be 50 W. Your job is to design the chain that takes the output signal of 20 mW and applies sufficient gain to meet the 50 W output specification. Also, determine the power supply requirements of the design.

$$P_{osc} = 20 \text{ mW} \qquad P_{o3} = 50 \text{ W} \rightarrow \text{power gain} = 10 \log \left(\frac{50}{0.020} \right) = 34 \text{ dB}$$

This indicates that the total power gain required is 34 dB. The next question is how to proportion the gain out among the three stages. Because class A amplifiers are good up to about 1/2 W output, set that as the output of the first stage:

$$\text{stage one power gain} = G_1 = 10 \log \left(\frac{0.50}{0.020} \right) = 14 \text{ dB}$$

Now observe that an additional 20 dB of gain from the second two stages of the chain will be required. Split that between the two stages and see how that comes out. Usually it is a good idea to have similar amplifiers all amplifying about the same logarithmic amount. The equations below calculate the power outputs for a 10 dB gain for each of the second two stages:

$$\text{stage two power gain} = G_2 = 10 \text{ dB} = 10 \log \left(\frac{P_{o2}}{0.50} \right) \rightarrow P_{o2} = (0.5)(10^1) = 5W$$

$$\text{stage three power gain} = G_3 = 10 \text{ dB} = 10 \log \left(\frac{P_{o3}}{5} \right) \rightarrow P_{o3} = (5)(10^1) = 50W$$

The input and output powers for each stage are determined. Next, calculate the total power output for each stage and using the efficiencies of each amplifier class, compute the power consumption. This will indicate how big a power supply will be needed. For this example, a class A amplifier has an efficiency of 30%, and a class C amplifier an efficiency of 50%. Table 8.1 can now be constructed.

The total power consumed by the amplifier chain and oscillator is found by adding up the difference of output power minus input power for each stage and then dividing by the efficiency of that stage:

$$\text{power} = \frac{P_n - P_{n-1}}{\text{efficiency of stage n}} \tag{8-8}$$

$$\text{stage one: } \frac{0.5 - 0.020}{0.30} = 1.6 \text{ W}$$

$$\text{stage two: } \frac{5.0 - 0.5}{0.50} = 9 \text{ W}$$

$$\text{stage three: } \frac{50.0 - 5.0}{0.50} = 90 \text{ W} \rightarrow \text{total power} = 1.6 + 9 + 90 = 100.6 \text{ W}$$

With the total power calculated, it is a simple matter to determine the power supply requirements once the voltage is known. This example will assume a 12 V power supply, typical for solid state RF amplifiers.

$$P = EI \rightarrow I = \frac{P}{E} = \frac{100.6}{12} = 8.38 \text{ A} \approx 8.5 \text{ W}$$

The minimum power supply requirement is for a 8.5 A supply at 12 V. Being a conservative fellow, you decide to increase it by about 50%, a good safety margin. This specifies a power supply of 12 A at 12 V. When the

Table 8.1
Example 8.05

Stage	Class	Efficiency (%)	Power In	Gain	Power Out
Oscillator	N/A	N/A	N/A	N/A	20 mW
One	A	30	20 mW	14 dB	0.5 W
Two	C	50	0.5 W	10 dB	5 W
Three	C	50	5 W	10 dB	50 W

disk jockey decides to "pin the needle," the power supply will be able to handle the peak load without adding excess distortion.

Now you might think you are done, but you still need to decide what kind of heat sink to use.

■ HEAT SINK DESIGN

Heat sinks are an often overlooked area of system design. Yet, without them, many of today's most impressive technical achievements would not work in the way expected. Probably the best example of this is the current generation of PCs. These devices feature very fast clock times, and as a result the digital circuitry, especially the microprocessor, dissipates a lot of heat. Without heat sink design, a big fan would be needed, and big fans are loud. This is not the right solution for an office environment.

In the example of the radio station, the noise the addition of a fan would add would probably make no difference, but this section will proceed to demonstrate the design of a heat sink. Earlier when ILDs were discussed, it was pointed out that these devices dissipate a lot of heat and need to be provided with some kind of heat sink to work reliably. If you prefer, imagine that that is the application for which this section is intended.

Heat sink design is quite similar to electrical design. The correspondence to make is that current power is rather like heat flow, and voltages are rather like temperatures. Therefore, just as each element in a circuit has a voltage drop due to its resistance, each element in a heat sink has a temperature drop due to its thermal resistance. If this seems incredible to you, think about the pans used to cook meals. Most are made of metal, and as you know, metal is a good conductor of electricity. Because the job of most pans is to transfer heat from the stovetop to the food, metal must be a good conductor of heat as well. Most natural materials that conduct electricity well also act as good conductors of heat (e.g., their thermal resistance is low, just as their electrical resistance is low).

Most heat sinks are made of extruded aluminum fashioned into some kind of finned arrangement that features a high surface area to volume ratio. This type of arrangement is used throughout nature for efficient heat radiation. A cactus has lots of thin needles to radiate heat and a polar bear, with padded everything, has no exposed thin ears, toes, and so forth, and is quite good at conserving heat. For a rough estimate of any object's heat conservation capability, just take the ratio of surface area to volume. The higher this is, the better the object is at radiating away excess heat.

Heat sinks are classified by their temperature radiation per watt of electrical energy. There are two primary elements of any heat sink design, the thermal resistance of the mounting location to the case of the amplifier and the radiative and conductive thermal resistance of the heat sink design itself. The first is usually between 3 and 5° C/W and the second depends on the physical design of the heat sink. This is usually the number you need to know to specify a heat sink.

Take the first thermal resistance to be 4° C/W. The total power to be dissipated for the stage three amplifier is 90 W. The maximum temperature that the mounting material can handle is 90° C and the air surrounding the amplifier must reach no more than 40° C. Use the circuit diagram in Figure 8.10 to visualize the system.

Figure 8.10
Heat sink model.

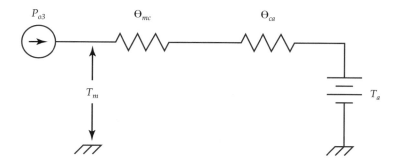

Θ_{ma} = Thermal Resistance from mounting location to air

Θ_{mc} = Thermal Resistance from mounting location to case

Θ_{ca} = Thermal Resistance from case to air

T_m = Maximum mounting location temperature = 90° C

T_a = Maximum air temperature = 40° C

$$\Theta_{ma} = \Theta_{mc} + \Theta_{ca}$$

$$\frac{T_m - T_a}{P_{o3}} = \frac{T_m - T_c}{P_{o3}} + \frac{T_c - T_a}{P_{o3}}$$

$$\frac{90° - 40° \text{ C}}{90W} = 4° \text{ C}/W + \frac{T_c - T_a}{90W} \rightarrow T_c - T_a = -310° \text{ C}$$

Heat Sink Specification = $-310°$ C/W

Once this calculation is completed, go to a heat sink manufacturter and look for a size and configuration that meets the need. For this example, the heat sink must exhibit at least a $-310°$ C/W thermal resistance. This is a large heat sink due to the large power consumption of the third stage amplifier. Typical values for a microprocessor application such as in your PC would be about $-20°$ C/W thermal resistance.

◼ DEMODULATION

Because the first subject we discussed in the modulator section was DSB-SC modulation, the first demodulators that will be shown are used for this type of modulation. A demodulator, in essence, remodulates the received signal back, ideally, to its original input signal form. Virtually all DSB-SC demodulators work on the principle of synchronous detection. In essence, they just multiply the received signal by the carrier frequency and low-pass filter the result. Therefore, the same circuits can be used for demodulation that were used for modulation, with only two minor variations.

First, in the modulator a bandpass filter was used to band-limit the transmit spectrum to some frequency band centered on the carrier frequency. In the demodulator, because the input data was baseband, use a low-pass filter after "mixing down" the received signal.

Second, because a synchronous detection process is indicated, some circuitry must be added to synchronize the two waveforms that are mixed down. If the carrier frequency generator in the demodulator is not in phase with the carrier component in the received modulated signal, the results desired will not be achieved.

To get a feeling for why this is true, think about how a mixer works. Its operation was described as a multiplier. If the carrier that is applied to the LO port is not in phase with the carrier component of the received modulated signal, when the two are multiplied, the recovered modulating signal will not match the modulating signal. What one can think of as sign distortion will be introduced. This is illustrated in Figure 8.11. When examining this figure, remember that the envelope is defined by the peaks of the carrier, so when demodulating, the only two signals that are multiplied are the modulated carrier and the local carrier frequency generator.

Note that in the second case where the local carrier frequency is 180° out of phase the inverse of the modulating signal is obtained. In the first case an exact duplicate of the modulating signal results. Other phase errors lie in between; obviously, synchronization is important for accurate demodulation (recovery of the original modulating signal). This synchronization can be accomplished in several ways, but the most general solution is to use a phase-locked loop (PLL). To describe a PLL, one must first describe a voltage controlled oscillator (VCO). This is done in the next section.

Figure 8.11
Demodulation synchronization.

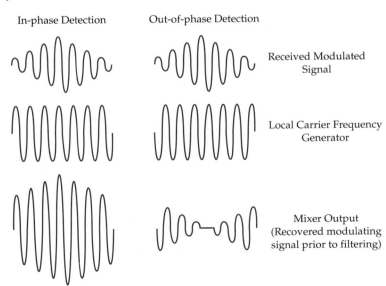

In-phase Detection

Out-of-phase Detection

Received Modulated
Signal

Local Carrier Frequency
Generator

Mixer Output
(Recovered modulating
signal prior to filtering)

Figure 8.12
VCO operation.

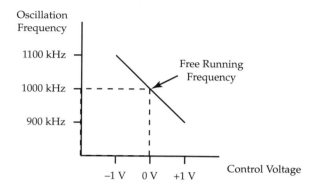

VOLTAGE CONTROLLED OSCILLATOR

A VCO is just an oscillator that changes its output frequency with input voltage or current. That is, as the voltage applied to a VCO increases, the frequency decreases. Probably the best way to think of a VCO is as a voltage-to-frequency converter. Because as the voltage applied to a VCO increases, the frequency decreases, so the frequency produced is inversely proportional to the applied voltage. Most VCOs have this inverse relationship with applied voltage. The reason for this will become clear when examining how a PLL works.

Every VCO has a single frequency at which it will oscillate with no applied voltage. This frequency is called the free running frequency of the VCO. An imaginary VCO might output 1 MHz with 0 V applied. Change the applied voltage to +1 V and the output frequency changes to 900 kHz. Change the applied voltage to −1 V and the output frequency changes to 1100 kHz. Figure 8.12 illustrates how the output frequency of this VCO varies with an applied control voltage.

PHASE-LOCKED LOOP

The next type of component is a PLL, which is a fundamental component used in many demodulator designs. Probably the best way to think of a PLL is as a frequency-to-voltage converter. As will be discussed, as the frequency applied to a PLL increases, the voltage decreases; the voltage produced is inversely proportional to the applied frequency. The two primary uses in communication systems are to track a slowly varying frequency and to perform demodulation of FM and most FSK signals. Many times the purpose of a PLL is to synchronize two sinusoids to each other. A PLL does this by generating an output voltage that is a function of the phase difference of the two input signals. To discuss such devices, a couple of new terms need to be defined.

Input frequency.   The first sinusoid referred to above. It is that frequency that is applied to the input of the PLL.

Free running frequency.   The second sinusoid referred to above. It is that frequency at which the VCO will oscillate when no voltage is applied to its control port. In PLL terminology this is the frequency at which the PLL will oscillate when it is said to be out of lock. The free running frequency is the center frequency of the PLL lock range.

Lock range.   That range of frequencies that the PLL will track. It is found by slowly varying the input frequency until the phase error between the input frequency and the free running frequency exceeds, in either direction, a maximum of 90°. Typical devices work over a range of ±80°.

Loop filter.   This is a low-pass filter that is used to convert the frequency of a sinusoid into a dc voltage that is used to drive the VCO. Any low-pass filter can transform a frequency into a dc voltage; essentially it smoothes out the peak amplitudes of the input frequency and outputs a voltage that tracks the peak amplitudes of each cycle of the waveform. This voltage is not actually dc, unless the amplitude of the input waveform remains unchanging; it really is a slowly varying ac signal. After this discussion on PLL, how a low-pass filter can be used to demodulate a DSB-LC waveform directly will be explored.

A typical block diagram of a PLL is illustrated in Figure 8.13.

As can be seen from Figure 8.13, there are four basic components that make up a PLL. An input frequency is applied to the mixer IF input port. This is typically a modulated signal. A VCO is chosen so that when its free running frequency is divided by N, it approximates the input frequency. This frequency is then applied to the mixer LO port. It is the center frequency of the PLL lock range. The mixer will output both the frequency sum and difference between the two frequencies applied. For PLL operation only the difference frequency is of interest. The loop filter eliminates the sum frequency.

Figure 8.13
PLL block diagram.

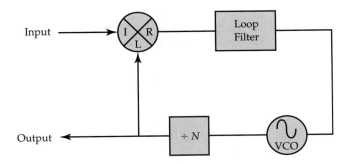

This frequency difference is obtained by the mixer multiplying the two signals presented at the LO and IF ports. Refer to the earlier discussion of how a mixer works. When the two frequencies are similar, as is usually the case in communications applications, the difference frequency will be small. This low-frequency output is a measure of the phase difference of the two input frequencies. For this reason, the mixer is often identified as a phase detector. This is because frequency is the first derivative of phase. This fact tells you something about why these devices are called phase-locked loops.

Anyway, a small frequency difference on the RF port of the mixer corresponds to a small difference in frequency between the two signals, and a larger frequency corresponds to a larger difference. Because low-pass filters can convert frequency to a dc value, we have a dc voltage on the output of the loop filter that corresponds to the difference in frequency. This dc voltage, often called an error voltage, drives the VCO in the opposite direction of the frequency difference, reducing it in an amount corresponding to the magnitude of the error voltage. As a result, the frequency output by the VCO moves in the same direction as the input signal frequency. Viewed as a control application, it is trying to minimize the error voltage.

The lock range of a PLL is determined by the bandwidth of the loop filter. The smaller the bandwidth, the slower the loop obtains lock and the narrower the range of frequencies the PLL can track. Usually one can estimate the lock range of a PLL by knowing the bandwidth of the loop filter. This brief analysis should give you a working knowledge of what to expect PLLs to do in a circuit when applied to communications. Example 8.6 will illustrate a basic step in PLL design.

■ EXAMPLE 8.6

Determine the divider ratio for a simple PLL. The design goal is to have the PLL lock to a 10 kHz input signal. The VCO has a free running frequency of 1 MHz. Find the divider ratio needed:

$$N = \frac{\text{free running frequency}}{\text{input frequency}} = \frac{1 \text{ MHz}}{10 \text{ kHz}} = 100$$

■ DSB-SC DEMODULATOR

This section now returns to an analysis of how demodulators work, starting first with the DSB-SC type, because we first discussed that type of modulator. A typical demodulator design using a PLL is shown in Figure 8.14. Following the signal path through the diagram, the modulated signal is first passed through a summer splitter hooked up through a splitter. The modulated signal is then applied to both the IF port of a mixer and the control input to the PLL. The PLL generates a single-frequency output that is very close to the carrier frequency, and that output is then applied to the LO port of the mixer. Finally, the mixing action yields a baseband signal that is the recovered modulating signal and some harmonics. The harmonics are filtered out by the low-pass filter.

Other ways exist. Of course, if the transmitter and receiver are colocated, just run a connection from the carrier oscillator in the modulator to the demodulator and dispense

Figure 8.14
Synchronous detection of DSB-SC modulator.

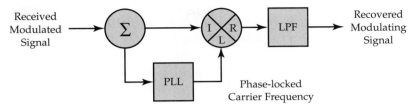

with the carrier recovery circuitry implemented by the PLL. Only very infrequently is this the case.

A very widespread method used to recover the carrier is in use is in commercial FM broadcast stations. This is the pilot tone approach. Stereo FM broadcast stations actually transmit several signals separated in frequency. The bandwidth used is 75 kHz. The central idea to understand is the how the use of the pilot tone allows synchronous demodulation without requiring a lot of extra circuitry, the PLL, in the receiver.

■ PILOT TONE DEMODULATION

It is usually very interesting to realize that FM broadcast radio is an example of DSB-SC being used to generate the signals necessary for stereo FM radio. The older FM monaural transmissions did not need this technique. The spectrum shown in Figure 8.15 is what each station generates prior to frequency modulating it for transmission. Note that

Figure 8.15
FM spectrum.

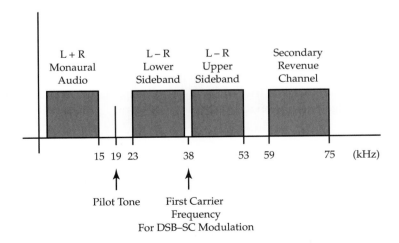

each station uses 75 kHz of bandwidth for its transmission. This of course, is shifted to an appropriate carrier frequency in the FM broadcast band prior to transmission.

The reasons are historical. If you think about it, back in the early days of stereo broadcasting, most receivers were monaural. Therefore, when the shift came to stereo radio, there was a need to accommodate both the old monaural radios and the new stereo radios with a single transmission format. Also, there has to be two separate transmissions for each channel, left (L) and right (R) to get the stereo effect. To accomplish the move to stereo broadcasting the broadcasters had to transmit three separate signals, the old mono band, the left channel, and the right channel.

These three signals are as follows:

1. L + R; frequency modulated monaural signal
2. L − R; DSB-SC lower sideband signal
3. L − R; DSB-SC upper sideband signal

The first signal is the same FM signal that was transmitted before stereo FM was available and kept the current generation of monaural radios operating. The next two signals allow the operation of the stereo radios by providing two separate signals for each stereo channel. The use of L − R for the two channels allowed the radio to just add or subtract the sideband signal to the monaural signal to obtain the left or right stereo channel, respectively.

Because there is no carrier present in a DSB-SC modulation, there was a need to implement some kind of phase lock with the transmitted carrier in each radio.

The approach used was to transmit a pilot tone that was the same phase as the carrier frequency and could be used to synchronize the demodulator. The first carrier frequency used for stereo FM broadcast radio is 38 kHz. This frequency is not the final carrier frequency to which one tunes a radio. Rather, it is the carrier frequency that is used to perform the DSB-SC modulation. This choice of 38 kHz as the DSB-SC carrier frequency led to the selection of 19 kHz as the pilot tone. Because it is exactly half of the carrier frequency, when it is picked out of the signal by a narrow bandpass filter and then frequency doubled, the phase relationship is exact.

Figure 8.15 shows a frequency spectrum picture of the FM stereo broadcast spectrum for any station. The band of frequencies between 59 and 75 kHz is used for monitoring remote industrial sites, to provide remote communication, to provide weather monitoring, and so forth. It always has some economic use that each station negotiates with users of that spectrum. In some cases, especially rural stations, this can be a significant source of additional revenue for a station.

■ DSB-LC DEMODULATION

This section describes systems used to demodulate DSB-LC transmitters. The first of the two types of circuitry used lends itself to some simple calculations that will allow a somewhat detailed illustration of the design of such a system. To review, DSB-LC modulators are used for commercial AM broadcasting. There are two main types of demodulators that are used to demodulate these transmissions: diode detector (envelope) and dual conversion (heterodyne). Of course, a synchronous detector, such as the PLL approach described earlier, can also be used. However, they are more expensive than the diode approach and are not needed because a carrier exists in the transmission naturally; therefore they are not used.

■ ENVELOPE DEMODULATION

The envelope detector is by far the most straightforward and popular approach to demodulating DSB-LC transmissions. Because it is cheap and effective, it is used widely. It works by detecting the envelope of the modulated waveform directly. See Figure 8.16. However, *envelope detection is only possible when the carrier frequency is much larger than the highest frequency in the input signal.* Fortunately, for most commercial applications this is true. The basic circuit consists of a single diode, resistor, and capacitor. The trick to designing one correctly is setting the charging and discharging times appropriately.

Before examining how to choose the resistor and capacitor values correctly, the circuit operation will be described. As the input signal goes positive, the diode conducts and the capacitor charges to the peak value of the modulated DSB-LC waveform. As the signal falls, the diode turns OFF and the capacitor discharges through the resistor. This cycle repeats as the signal returns positive. The net result is that the voltage across the capacitor builds up to the peak of each carrier cycle and, hence, represents a good approximation to the transmitted envelope. It is important for circuit operation that the amplitude of the signal to be demodulated be sufficient that some current flows for each cycle of the carrier frequency.

Equations to find the exact amplitude needed are shown below, but if the voltage swing is not at least somewhat greater than a diode drop, no current will flow. It is also interesting to note that the higher the carrier frequency, the more closely the envelope detector can track the modulation envelope. This is the reason that the carrier frequency must be large compared to any frequency in the input signal and, for any given carrier frequency, also places an upper limit on the values of resistance and capitance that are chosen.

Figure 8.16
Envelope detector.

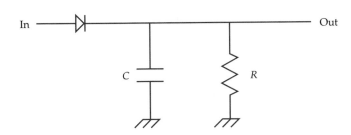

Because a diode drop will occur, the peak voltage of the envelope must be at least 0.7 V for a silicon diode to work. The peak recovered signal amplitude can be found by subtracting the diode drop from the peak voltage. Therefore, from the last chapter,

$$V_{max} = E_m \left(1 + \frac{1}{m}\right) = E_c(1 + m) \qquad \text{and} \qquad V_{peak\ output} = V_{max} - 0.7\ V$$

■ EXAMPLE 8.7

For a DSB-LC modulated signal with $m = 0.8$ and the peak carrier voltage equal to 2 V, find the peak voltage of the modulated envelope and the peak output of the envelope detector:

$$V_{max} = E_c(1 + m) = 2(1 + 0.8) = 3.6\ V$$

$$V_{peak\ output} = V_{max} - 0.7 = 3.6 - 0.7 = 2.9\ V$$

The value found above is a maximum value for the peak output. Some voltage drop will occur across the resistor, depending, of course, on the current flow.

Ripple Distortion

Now the idea is to choose the resistance and capitance (RC) value so that the output follows the peak of the input signal envelope. If the discharge time is too slow, or RC is too big, some of the fast-changing directions of the envelope may be missed. If the discharge time is too fast, or RC is too small, high-frequency distortion is introduced into the output due to the fast switching. This distortion is referred to as ripple distortion.

Therefore, the result desired is fast enough to track quick changes and slow enough to not introduce high frequency distortion. Ideally, the voltage on the output should track the input envelope smoothly. If you must err, err in the direction of making the time constant fast. You may introduce some distortion but will be sure of tracking fast changes in the envelope. Other than the effect due to the time constant, the ripple depends on the threshold voltage of the diode and the frequency of the carrier signal. By choosing a low-threshold germanium diode, this ripple can be minimized. By choosing a higher carrier frequency, the ripple can also be made smaller.

The three cases of choices of the RC value are shown in Figure 8.17. The first case is for an RC that is too large. Here the envelope does not track all the changes in the envelope. In the second case, the RC is too small. One sees excessive ripple in the envelope as the envelope follows the carrier too closely for too long. In the third case, the RC is chosen correctly. One sees that the ripple is small and all changes in the envelope are tracked.

Finally, in most implementations, a low-pass filter is used after the demodulation to filter out any high-frequency ripple components in the output, and a coupling capacitor is used to remove any dc component. Because these systems are used primarily with audio band input signals, the input frequency spectrum does not extend down to dc. As a result the coupling capacitor is used to remove any residual dc does not present a problem.

Figure 8.17
RC choices for envelope detection showing effect on ripple distortion.

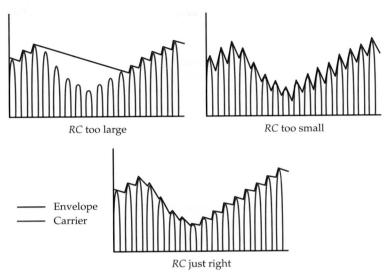

EXAMPLE 8.8

Determine the values of *C* and *R* for a voice-band modulating signal using the envelope detector.

The fact that the input signal is in the voice band can be used to set an upper limit for the discharge rate. Observe that it is necessary to make sure that the discharge rate is never exceeded by the rate of change in the envelope. Because the audio band is defined to be 300 to 3400 Hz, the fastest rate of change in the input signal is 3400 Hz. This yields a discharge time of 294 μsec as shown below:

$$f_{\max} = 3400 \rightarrow t = \frac{1}{f_{\max}} = \frac{1}{3400} = 294 \times 10^{-6} = \text{discharge time}$$

Following the 5 times constant rule, set 5τ equal to the discharge time, or 294 μsec. This makes sure the capacitor is completely discharged in the time allowed. Then the product $RC = 58.8$ μsec. For a capacitor value of 1 μF, choose a maximum resistor value of 58.8 Ω; this is shown below:

$$5\tau = 294 \times 10^{-6} \rightarrow \tau = 58.8 \times 10^{-6} = RC \rightarrow R = \frac{58.8 \times 10^{-6}}{1.0 \times 10^{-6}} = 58.8 \; \Omega$$

This may lead to a too fast discharge time, but it will ensure that the circuit can track any variation in the transmitted envelope, and it is a simple matter to alter the *RC* product until distortion is minimized. The next section will explore further how to choose the resistor and capacitor values in such a way that the ripple distortion is minimized.

Choosing the Resistor and Capacitor

From Chapter 7, the expression for the peak voltage value of the DSB-LC waveform, or envelope, is

$$m(t) = [1 + m\cos(w_m t)]E_c\cos(w_c t) \tag{7-29}$$

Because the peak value is determined by the modulating frequency and not the carrier frequency, that part of the expression can be dropped, and no information on the shape of the envelope will be lost. The amplitude term is retained because it defines the amplitude swings that the diode will need to experience to allow this method to work. Again, the frequency of the swings can reduce the ripple in the demodulated signal but can have no effect on the shape of the modulated envelope. Then equation 7-29 becomes

$$E_{\text{envelope}} = E_c[1 + m\cos(w_m t)] \tag{8-9}$$

Because the envelope detector works by tracking the slope of the envelope, differentiate expression 8-9, and find the slope:

$$\text{slope}_{\text{envelope}} = \frac{d}{dt}\{E_c[1 + m\cos(w_m t)]\} \tag{8-10}$$

$$\text{slope}_{\text{envelope}} = w_m E_c m\sin(w_m t) \tag{8-11}$$

where the derivative of a constant is zero and the sign change has been dropped because it has no physical meaning. Now, recall that the RC discharge follows the relationship

$$E(t) = Ee^{(t-\tau)/RC} \tag{8-12}$$

Substituting in for E the expression 8-9,

$$E(t) = E_c[1 + m\cos(w_m t)]e^{(t-\tau)/RC} \tag{8-13}$$

Taking the first derivative to find the slope,

$$\text{slope}_{RC} = \frac{E_c}{RC}[1 + m\cos(w_m t)]e^{(t-\tau)/RC} \tag{8-14}$$

Now evaluating this at time $t = \tau$ gives an expression for the slope of the RC discharge cycle at time τ.

$$\text{slope}_{RC} = \frac{E_c}{RC}[1 + m\cos(w_m\tau)] \tag{8-15}$$

This gives a relationship that tells the slope of the RC discharge cycle at one moment in time, represented by τ. Earlier in equation 8-11, a relationship was found that gave the slope of the DSB-LC envelope. By setting the two equal, it is possible to obtain an expression that will give the maximum value of RC that would be used:

$$\text{slope}_{\text{envelope}} = \text{slope}_{RC} = w_m E_c\sin(w_m\tau) = \frac{E_c}{RC}[1 + m\cos(w_m\tau)] \tag{8-16}$$

$$RC \le \frac{1}{w_m} \frac{1 + m \cos(w_m \tau)}{m \sin(w_m \tau)} \tag{8-17}$$

where the less than symbol has be substituted because the maximum value of RC is desired. Now this function is not really ideal. It would be best to get rid of the τ in the expression so that the expression is independent of time. This can be found by further differentiation, to evaluate the value of τ for which equation 8-17 achieves a minimum. Once this is found, it can be substituted back into equation 8-17. This removes the variable τ from the expression and the following result for the maximum value of RC that could be used for a given modulation frequency and modulation index results:

$$RC \le \frac{1}{mw_m} \tag{8-18}$$

This differentiation is found in Appendix D. To illustrate how to apply this equation, Example 8.9 is provided.

■ EXAMPLE 8.9

Find the maximum value of R for a modulation frequency of 1 kHz, a modulation index of 0.80, and a capacitance value of 1 μF. Remember to convert the frequency to radians per second.

$$RC \le \frac{1}{mw_m} \rightarrow R \le \frac{1}{m2\pi f_m C} = \frac{1}{2\pi(1 \times 10^{-6})(0.80)(1 \times 10^3)} = 199 \ \Omega$$

Another way of looking at equation 8-18 is to use it to find the maximum modulation frequency a given diode detector can demodulate. To do this, rearrange the equation, resulting in the following relationship:

$$w_m(\max) = \frac{1}{mRC} \tag{8-19}$$

For any given value of the modulation index, this relationship gives the maximum modulation frequency that can be demodulated with this type of detector without excessive attenuation. Note that for 100% modulation, $m = 1$, and equation 8-19 reduces to

$$w_m(\max) = \frac{1}{RC} \tag{8-20}$$

■ EXAMPLE 8.10

How does the value of the RC time constant vary with the modulation index? Does it depend on anything else? Can you establish a rule of thumb for how these two interact? To answer these questions plug in some numbers into equation 8-18 and see what happens. The entries Table 8.2 are the values for the RC product predicted by equation 8-18.

As can be seen, as the modulation index rises, the value of the RC product falls. That means for larger modulation indexes, smaller resistors and capacitors are needed in the envelope detector design. It also is ap-

Table 8-2
Example Values from Equation 8–18

Modulation Index	Fm = 1 kHz	Fm = 10 kHz	Fm = 100 kHz
$m = 0.2$	7.96×10^{-4}	7.96×10^{-5}	7.96×10^{-6}
$m = 0.4$	3.98×10^{-4}	3.98×10^{-5}	3.98×10^{-6}
$m = 0.6$	2.65×10^{-4}	2.65×10^{-5}	2.65×10^{-6}
$m = 0.8$	1.99×10^{-4}	1.99×10^{-5}	1.99×10^{-6}
$m = 0.8$	7.96×10^{-4}	7.96×10^{-6}	7.96×10^{-8}

parent that as the modulation frequency rises, the RC product falls. So, as the modulation frequency rises, smaller resistors and capacitors are needed in the design as well. Recall that the RC product gives you the time constant. Further, as both the modulation index and modulation frequency rise, the time constant must fall to track the higher frequency of the envelope.

Rectifier Distortion

Up to this point, only one type of limitation on the envelope detector has been considered, namely, the ripple distortion. Equations have been developed to minimize this effect. However, there is another source of distortion present in such a demodulator, the rectifier distortion. Rectifier distortion is the result of the diode not conducting throughout the entire period of the modulating signal frequency.

Recall that for 100% modulation the envelope closes down completely. When this happens, there is no carrier voltage present and the diode does not conduct. Review Example 8.7. It should be clear that for an accurate recovered modulating signal recovery, the diode must be conducting throughout the entire period of the modulating signal. This is illustrated in Figure 8.18.

The dotted line represents the recovered modulating signal for reasonable values of RC. As can be seen, the modulation index must not exceed some certain value for accurate recovery of the modulating signal. This value can be found through the following approach. Recall from the previous chapter,

$$V_{\max} = E_m \left(1 + \frac{1}{m}\right) \qquad \text{and} \qquad V_{\min} = V_{\max} - 2E_m$$

Setting $V_{\min} = 0.7$ V to ensure that the diode is always conducting,

$$0.7 = V_{\min} = V_{\max} - 2E_m = E_m \left(1 + \frac{1}{m}\right) - 2E_m = \frac{E_m}{m} - E_m$$

Rearranging,

$$m \leq \frac{E_m}{E_m + 0.7} \qquad \text{for no rectifier distortion}$$

Figure 8.18
Rectifier distortion.

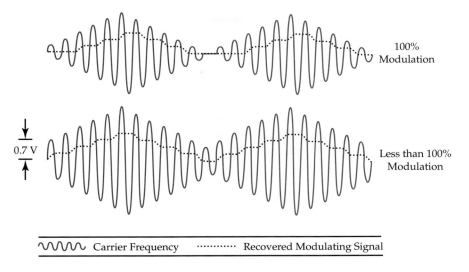

0.7 V

100% Modulation

Less than 100% Modulation

〜〜〜 Carrier Frequency   ·········· Recovered Modulating Signal

As can be seen from Table 8.3, the maximum value of m increases for increasing modulating voltages; however, low peak modulating voltages limit the maximum modulation index achievable when the restriction of no rectifier distortion is engaged. Because the value of the modulation index leads directly to the modulation efficiency, this is an important consideration. It is also possible to relate the modulation index to the peak carrier voltage; this will be left to the interested reader.

■ SUPERHETERODYNE DEMODULATOR (DUAL CONVERSION)

The second type of demodulator discussed is the superheterodyne approach. *Heterodyne* just means to shift frequency, typically by the sum or difference of two frequencies. The so-called heterodyne whistle is the steady tone heard in the output of an AM receiver

Table 8-3
Modulation Index Values for No Rectifier Distortion

Peak Modulating Voltage	Modulation Index
1	0.59
2	0.74
5	0.88
10	0.93
20	0.97

due to the beating of two frequencies that have a small frequency difference. The use of this frequency shift property in demodulation should not be surprising because it is already known that AM modulation results in a shift of frequency. This type of demodulator was first implemented about 1920 and was widely used in better-class radio receivers for many years. It, or one of its variations, is still used today in many applications where quality of reception of the AM signal is important.

The origin of the prefix *super* with the word *heterodyne* seems to come from the word *supersonic,* meaning faster than the speed of sound, a big deal in 1920. Perhaps because the superheterodyne receiver uses two frequencies, one larger than the other, it is in some sense that one of these frequencies is "faster" than the speed of the other. Hence, the name superheterodyne. Because heterodyning was known and used in regenerative or autodyning (self-heterodyning) detectors, the inventor may have desired a term that would distinguish it from those approaches.

The chief advantages of the superheterodyne approach are

1. Better sensitivity via a larger gain
2. Constant selectivity across a wide band of carrier frequencies

These two advantages were significant compared to the conventional methods used at that time, mainly the tuned radio frequency (TRF) approach, in which no IF stage was used. See Figure 8.19. As can be seen from the diagram, the superheterodyne (SH) approach is a direct evolution from the TRF approach. It adds an intermediate stage where the real advantage of the SH approach becomes evident; the IF filter and amplifier com-

Figure 8.19
TRF and superheterodyne receivers.

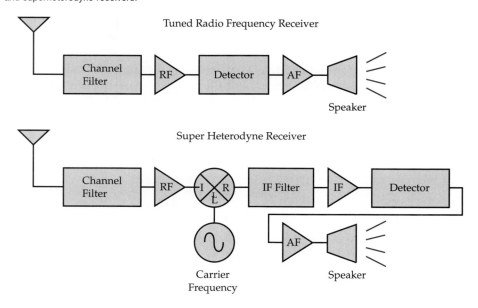

bination do not need to tune when there is a change in channel selection. This results in a much more stable design, with more gain, a big advantage.

Additionally, because the IF section does not need to be tunable, amplification is constant independent of the channel selected. Because most of the gain in such a receiver occurs in the IF amplifier stages, not having to operate these over a wide frequency range results in much better and simpler designs. In the older TRF approach, the RF amplifier and filter needed to tune to receive different channels and so could not be optimized for performance in a specific frequency band. So, again, the primary advantage of the SH over the TRF approach is that amplification and filtering are performed at a fixed frequency independent of the channel selection.

The SH approach uses frequency translation as its basic advantage. Two translations are generally used, although more could be implemented for special situations. First, the RF carrier signal is "mixed down" to an IF. This frequency is chosen so that the IF is equal to the difference between the received carrier frequency and the LO frequency. This means that one tuning element can be used to both select the channel and pull the LO, a significant cost and complexity advantage. This is called *gang tuning* and was traditionally done using mechanically adjusted variable capacitors. Today, a varactor diode or VCO is commonly used to accomplish this, and a knob or digital pushbutton controls a voltage rather than mechanical action accomplishes the tuning.

Most commercial AM broadcast receivers use the SH approach, and most use an IF of 455 kHz. Commercial FM and television receivers also use these type of receivers with the IF set at 10.7 and 44.1 MHz, respectively. Knowing these frequencies can lead to an important cost reduction in systems you build that use the SH principle. Because many, many of these local oscillators must be manufactured at these frequencies, crystal oscillators are very inexpensive. Many times the LO frequency can be specified by the designer without affecting the external performance of the system, and lower-cost systems sell more than higher-cost systems that perform the same from a user perspective.

The almost last thing to say about this approach and the discussion above is that the terms *RF* and *IF* have nothing to do with absolute frequencies. RF does not mean a certain frequency band, no more than IF does. They are relative terms, and the only meaning that can be obtained is when both are used discussing the same system: The RF is higher than the IF. However, when discussing some other system, it may be that in the system A the RF is lower than IF in system or vice versa, but in *both* systems the RF is higher than the IF of that system.

Finally, there is another evolutionary step in SH design that is sometimes taken where image frequency interference is a problem. Image frequencies are those other RFs that, if passed into the receiver, will mix with the LO to produce a cross-product frequency that is identical to, or the image of, the IF, hence, the term *image frequency*. This effect can be eliminated by changing the input channel filter or by changing the IF choice and hence changing the LO frequency.

What is done is that two LOs are used, resulting in two IF stages. The first LO is chosen so that the IF is as far away as possible from the desired RF signal. This allows filtering to get rid of the unwanted signal. The second LO is chosen so that the IF is relatively low because it is cheaper to amplify at lower frequencies than it is at high frequencies. This evolution from a standard SH approach is called the double conversion approach (DCA). Instead of using one IF stage, it uses two, selecting the LO frequencies such that the interference is minimized at the output.

■ CRYSTAL DETECTOR

An interesting historical note is the old crystal detector scheme using a "cat's whisker." This was a thin pointed wire pressed against the surface of a special type of crystal known as a rectifier crystal. This was an early version of the diode envelope detector, and it worked on the same principles. The crystal detector was the first junction rectifier. You can still find hobbyist kits that use this approach to demodulate an AM broadcast signal.

It has the disadvantage that it provides no amplification to the received signal. Today's implementations generally use a low-threshold voltage diode such as a germanium diode instead of a metallic crystal detector as shown in Figure 8.20. It is very inexpensive to implement, requiring only a coupling transformer to the antenna, a variable capacitor for tuning the station, the diode already mentioned, and a capacitor to filter out the carrier frequency. By adding a simple transistor amplifier just before the load, shown as an amplitude frequency amplifier in the Figure 8.20, you can implement a very inexpensive AM broadcast radio. This is a historical design; tuned capacitors are bulky and not in wide use today. If you can find one, or a capacitor substitution box, it might be interesting to construct the circuit in Figure 8.20.

■ AUTOMATIC GAIN CONTROL (AGC)

A component of most AM and television receivers is the AGC circuit. This device acts to compensate for small variations in the received signal strength. This is required because of the fairly wide variation in signal voltages received at the receiver from the antenna. Wherever you are located, some broadcast stations are closer to your house than others.

Figure 8.20
Simple radio.

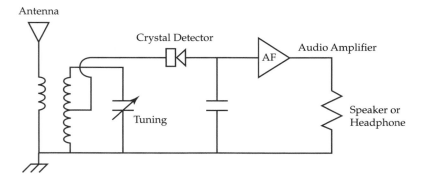

Additionally, some transmit with more power than others. As you tune your receiver or radio to different channels, the signal strength varies significantly; an AGC circuit can compensate for those variations if they are not too large.

If an AGC circuit was not present, the receiver could only be adjusted to work with minimum distortion for a very narrow range of input signal strength. As you moved closer to a transmitter and exceeded this level, overloading would occur and distortion would result. If you moved too far away, the signal strength would fall below this level, and the receiver would not pick up the station. This circuit allows a wider variation in received signal strengths; for example, it allows your AM car radio to work well for a large number of stations, all of which send out signals that reach your car antenna at different voltages.

In summary an AGC circuit automatically increases the gain for weak signals and decreases the gain for strong signals. We will examine one straightforward way that an AGC circuit can work. It should be pointed out that there are several different ways of applying AGC circuits, but only this method will be explored here. It is known as simple AGC, delayed AGC, or sometimes negative AGC. The demodulator that is applied to is the envelope detector used for broadcast AM radio. The circuit is shown in Figure 8.21.

Note that the addition of a single resistor and capacitor to the envelope detector shown in Figure 8.22 generates the AGC voltage that will be used to control the amplification of the received AM signal. There are many ways such a variable gain amplifier could be used to control the amplification of the received signal; these will not be explored here. Functionally, they usually work as illustrated in Figure 8.22.

This single resistor and capacitor effectively act as a simple *RC* low-pass filter. As was shown when the envelope detector was examined, the output voltage after the diode is a voltage that follows the shape of the modulating signal or, equivalently, the shape of the modulated envelope. As explained in that section, there is a ripple on top of the detected signal that is proportional to the fall time of the *RC* pair used to set the time constant. The low-pass filter filters this out and provides a clean signal that accurately follows the shape of the envelope.

Because the absolute magnitude of the envelope will vary directly with the received signal strength, the signal needed to control the amplification of the received AM signal is found. In Figure 8.22, the AGC voltage is tied to an amplifier that uses a voltage to set

Figure 8.21
Simple AGC.

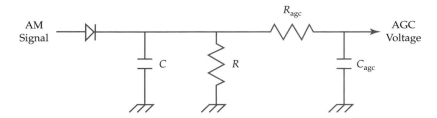

Figure 8.22
AGC in action.

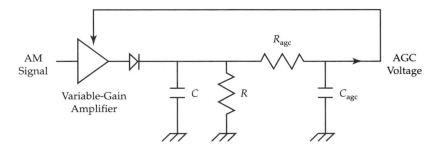

its gain. To conclude this section, Example 8.11 will show a simple design for the resistor and capacitor used in an inexpensive AM radio receiver.

■ EXAMPLE 8.11

This is really a design example for a low-pass filter (LPF) that is intended to pass the audio information or signal and block the carrier ripple introduced by the envelope demodulation technique. The audio signal has a maximum frequency component at 20 kHz. Additionally, the carrier signal must always be higher than the lowest licensed AM broadcast frequency, or 540 kHz. With these two observations the parameters for the design are set:

$$\text{voltage gain} = \frac{1}{1 + jwRC} = \frac{1}{1 + jw\tau} \tag{8-21}$$

where $\tau = RC$, or the time constant. Now the maximum gain occurs when this equation is a maximum; this happens at DC, or when $\omega = 0$. This confirms that this is a LPF because the point of maximum gain is located at dc. To find the amplitude for any ω, find the magnitude of the expression above. This is given by

$$A(w) = \frac{1}{\sqrt{1 + (w\tau)^2}} \tag{8-22}$$

The goal is to find that τ for which very little attenuation occurs for frequency values below 20 kHz and sufficient attenuation occurs for frequency values above 540 kHz. The easiest way to find this is to notice that the half-power point occurs when $\omega = 1/\tau$. The half-power point occurs when the rms voltage is reduced by half. This occurs when the magnitude or peak voltage is reduced by the factor shown below:

$$A(w) = \frac{1}{\sqrt{1 + (w/w)^2}} = \frac{1}{\sqrt{1 + 1^2}} = \frac{1}{\sqrt{2}} \tag{8-23}$$

Therefore, a RC value that lies between the highest frequency that we want to pass, 20 kHz, and below the lowest frequency we want to block, 540 kHz, is desired. A typical choice for the R and C values might be $R =$

Figure 8.23
Amplitude plot of LPF.

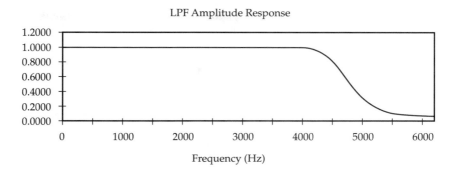

1 kΩ and $C = 0.10$ μF. These choices for R and C yield a $\tau = 0.1$ msec. An amplitude response plot of the LPF is shown in Figure 8.23.

As can be seen from inspection of Figure 8.23, the amplitude response falls off rapidly above about 30 kHz. Note that the bottom axis is in a log sequence. If you do a laboratory experiment using the envelope detector to demodulate an DSB-LC AM signal, try applying the filter design shown in this figure. Examine how the ripple on the recovered signal is reduced, and remember to adjust the design for the carrier frequency you are using. You might also try designing filters that have a better attenuation characteristic. For example, try using a three-pole filter instead of the simple one-pole design shown above.

■ SUMMARY

In this chapter, three types of AM modulation and demodulation, DSB-SC, DSB-LC, and SSB systems have been discussed. For a given amount of information to transmit, SC systems require less power than LC systems. In compensation, SC receivers are more complicated than LC systems, so if an inexpensive receiver is important, LC modulation is the better choice as long as you recognize that more transmit power will be required. Interestingly, high-power transmitters are easier to build in LC systems due to the presence of the carrier frequency. In SC systems, this must be filtered out, adding cost and complexity.

A comparison of DSB and SSB systems reveals that the transmitter requirements are essentially identical, except that SSB transmitters need to filter out the unwanted sideband. However, many times this is actually an advantage because the bandwidth for an SSB modulator is half that of a DSB modulator. Each type of modulator and demodulator discussed here has its own advantages and disadvantages; there is no one right solution for all applications.

The mixer, summer and splitter, VCO, and PLL were introduced and their operation briefly explored. A detailed treatment was given to the simple envelope demodulator and unique equations were developed to design one.

PROBLEMS

1. Find the sum and difference frequencies for a mixer when a 100 kHz signal is applied to the LO port and a 10 kHz signal is applied to the IF port. What frequencies will be seen on the RF port?

2. Find the mathematical expression for the RF port of a mixer if the LO port has a 10 V peak, 10 kHz sinusoid applied to it, and the IF port has a 2 V peak, 1 kHz sinusoid applied to it.

3. If two 10 kHz signals at 5 V peak are applied to ports A and B of a summer and splitter, what is the signal seen at port S? The device is used as a summer.

4. If a single 10 kHz signal at 5 V peak is applied to port S of a summer and splitter, what is the signal seen at ports A and B? The device is used as a splitter.

5. Design an amplifier chain to take an input power of 10 mW and raises it to 60 W. Use three amplifiers and specify the class of amplifier used and the power gain at each stage. Use the efficiency numbers as in Example 8.5.

6. Find the total power consumed and specify the minimum current needed for a 12 V power supply. Additionally, follow the conservative approach used in the text and suggest a more appropriate design.

7. Find the value of τ and R for an envelope detector used to demodulate a DSB-LC modulated signal. The modulating signal spans the range 20 to 20,000 Hz. Use a 10 μF capacitor.

8. Find the maximum value of R for the problem above, assuming a modulation index of 0.90.

9. Determine the maximum modulation frequency that a diode detector could demodulate for a modulation index of 0.90 and a RC value of 1.0.

9

Angle Modulation and Demodulation

This chapter will explore the form of modulation and demodulation known as angle modulation. Angle modulation is a type of modulation where the angle of the carrier signal is modulated. This form of modulation can be described with the same equation that was used to describe amplitude modulation, but with an extra term. This new equation will then be able to define all three types of analog modulation that will be explored, amplitude, frequency, and phase. The latter two are often grouped together and called angle modulation. These two properties, phase and frequency of an analog signal, are related to each other, and this both confuses and simplifies understanding. This relation is explored in Appendix E.

■ AMPLITUDE AND FREQUENCY MODULATION COMPARISON

Although this chapter will present frequency and phase modulation as one unified form of modulation, it is helpful to get some intuitive grasp of the difference between AM, the most familiar form of angle modulation, and FM quickly. Both of these modulation techniques are encountered everyday when tuning a radio. Therefore, at the risk of breaking frequency and phase modulation apart, the following section appears. After this section concludes, a unified treatment will be presented.

As you recall, with amplitude modulation the envelope responds to the changes in amplitude and frequency of the modulating signal. To review, the amplitude of the

Figure 9.1
AM and FM comparison, oscillocope view.

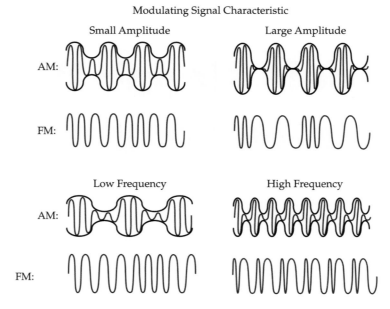

modulating signal changes the amount the envelope opens or closes. The frequency of the modulating signal changes the repetition rate of the envelope, or the number of opening and closings per unit time. Both factors directly relate to their effects. The larger the amplitude, the larger the opening and closing; the higher the frequency, the more often the opening and closing or repetition rate was.

Frequency modulation works somewhat differently. Here instead of the amplitude of the modulation envelope changing, the "frequency width" changes. As the amplitude of the modulating signal increases, the more frequency shift that occurs. As the frequency of the modulating signal increases, the more rapidly that frequency shift set by the amplitude will occur.

In a certain sense AM works kind of like a pogo stick: The larger the amplitude, the higher you jumped, and the higher the frequency, the more often you jumped. One can make a similar analogy to FM as a spring. The larger the amplitude, the more the spring is stretched, and the higher the frequency, the more often the spring is stretched.

Figure 9.1 shows the modulated signals for eight conditions. Please study it well; it should give an intuitive understanding of how these two modulation techniques compare.

■ ANGLE MODULATION

To begin, examine equation 9-1, which will be used to explore angle modulation:

$$m(t) = E_c \cos(w_c t + \phi(t)) \tag{9-1}$$

Recalling the equation that was used to define amplitude modulation (equation 7-3), we can make a comparison between these two equations:

$$m(t) = E_m \cos(w_m t) \, E_c \cos(w_c t) \qquad \textbf{(7-3)}$$

As you can observe from comparing the two equations, in the amplitude modulation case the modulating signal *multiplies* the carrier. As the modulation function varies in magnitude, the amplitude of the carrier will change. In the angle modulation case, the modulating signal, $\phi(t)$, is part of the *argument* of the carrier and as such can only change the relative frequency or phase of the carrier, not the amplitude. This change, referred to as the frequency deviation, is introduced in the next section.

■ FREQUENCY DEVIATION, PART 1

Deviation is a term that expresses *the change in phase or frequency of the carrier signal due to the amplitude of the modulating signal.* This will always be discussed as frequency deviation; if you are unsure that frequency and phase deviation amount to the same thing, please refer to Appendix E.

The definitions of frequency deviation are very similar for phase modulation (PM) and frequency modulation (FM). These are shown below:

$$\text{PM frequency deviation: FD} = K_1 E_m \qquad \textbf{(9-2)}$$

$$\text{FM frequency deviation: FD} = K_2 E_m \qquad \textbf{(9-3)}$$

Note that these are very similar definitions; both depend directly on the amplitude or voltage of the modulating signal and differ only in the definition of the constant term K_1 and K_2, which allow one to account for different implementations. Some FM systems will have a large gain and will have large K_2 values; some PM systems might feature small gains and will have small K_1 terms. These constant terms just multiply or add gain to whatever frequency deviation the modulator might produce.

The other main difference in the two definitions is that the FM deviation is defined by the derivative of $\phi(t)$. The reason for this lies in the equivalence of PM and FM systems; refer to Appendix E for a discussion. For now, it will not affect the equations and problems performed, but it does reveal an important part of angle modulation.

■ DEVIATION SENSITIVITY

These gains have special names in communications; they are referred to as deviation sensitivities. They are a measure of the sensitivity of the modulator. The more sensitive, the larger the gain and hence the larger frequency deviation:

$$\text{PM deviation sensitivity: } K_1 \qquad \textbf{(9-4)}$$

$$\text{FM deviation sensitivity: } K_2 \qquad \textbf{(9-5)}$$

The idea of a gain that does not imply increasing the voltage of a signal is confusing to some the first time it is encountered in the study of electrical systems. However, in daily life the word *gain* is used in all kinds of ways that imply not more voltage but increase in some specific thing. For example, when you gain weight, it is not meant that you get taller, but rather wider.

Using gain to discuss deviation sensitivity is very similar. The greater the gain (deviation sensitivity), the greater the spread of frequency that is caused by some change in amplitude of the modulating signal. This means that a large deviation sensitivity modulator will, for the same modulating signal, result in a greater modulated signal bandwidth. This should be made clear by the following example.

■ EXAMPLE 9.1

Two FM modulators that have a peak modulating signal voltage of 10 V have different deviation sensitivities. Modulator 1 has $K_2 = 10$, whereas modulator 2 has $K_2 = 50$. What are the frequency deviations for the two modulators?

$$\text{Modulator 1: } K_2 E_m = FD = 100$$

$$\text{Modulator 2: } K_2 E_m = FD = 500$$

Although all the information is not yet available to actually calculate a number for the two bandwidths, it should be clear that the second modulator will have a bandwidth 5 times greater than the first. This is exactly the ratio of the two deviation sensitivities.

■ MODULATING SIGNAL

To take the next step in the study of angle modulation, $\phi(t)$ must be defined; it is the modulating signal. For this chapter, PM and FM will only be explored when the modulation is a simple sinusoid. This is the same approach taken when amplitude modulation was studied in the previous chapters. This is called tone modulation. With this assumption, rewrite equation 9-1 in the following way:

$$m(t) = E_c \cos[w_c t + m \cos(w_m t)] \tag{9-6}$$

where E_c = the peak voltage of the carrier wave
w_c = the carrier frequency
m = the modulation index
w_m = the modulation frequency = $2\pi f_m$

This equation will be used throughout this chapter to solve problems and illustrate how PM and FM work. Notice that a familiar term, m, appeared in the above equation; it is the modulation index. You certainly recall amplitude modulation also defined the modulation index. The same is done for angle modulation; however, just as with the frequency deviation, there is a difference in the definition for PM and FM. The three definitions are presented below:

Modulation index for the AM case is defined as the peak amplitude shift experienced by the carrier.

Modulation index for the PM case is defined as the peak phase shift experienced by the carrier.

Modulation index for the FM case is defined as the peak frequency shift experienced by the carrier.

Mathematically, the latter two definitions are expressed as follows:

$$\text{PM modulation index: } m = K_1 E_m = FD \tag{9-7}$$

$$\text{FM modulation index: } m = \frac{K_2 E_m}{w_m} = \frac{FD}{w_m} = \frac{FD}{2\pi f_m} \tag{9-8}$$

Examining equation 9-6, one can see the same variables that were used in the study of AM modulation. The central difference now is that instead of multiplying the cosine of the carrier frequency, the modulation index and modulation frequency are part of the *argument* of the cosine. This means that instead of increasing or decreasing the amplitude of the carrier wave, as was seen in AM, these variables m and w_m will change the frequency of the carrier wave.

■ FREQUENCY DEVIATION, PART 2

The constants K_1 and K_2 account for the fact that the performance of all modulators are not the same. K_1 and K_2 are proportionality constants that represent the gain of the modulator in an actual implementation. Various implementation techniques yield various gains in the modulator stage. To account for this, K_1 and K_2 constants fit the theory into any implementation that is measured. K_1 and K_2 are defined as the deviation sensitivity of the modulator.

FD is the term used to describe the change in the carrier signal due to the modulating signal. Because phase and frequency are related to each other, frequency deviation can be used to talk about both:

Frequency deviation: The change in the frequency of the carrier signal due to the modulation signal.

Just like in amplitude modulation, the act of modulation changes the carrier signal due to the modulating signal. In communications one would say the modulation causes a deviation in the carrier signal. In amplitude modulation, that change was a change in the amplitude of the carrier envelope. Here, the change will be inside a constant amplitude envelope. The change inside the envelope will be the shift of phase or frequency of the carrier wave. This change is produced by the amplitude of the modulating signal.

To explore further what FD means, we will use the definition of modulation index for FM.

$$m = \frac{\text{frequency deviation}}{w_m} = \frac{FD}{w_m} = \frac{K_2 E_m}{w_m} = \frac{K_2 E_m}{2\pi f_m} \tag{9-9}$$

where K_2 is the same constant used earlier. The frequency deviation of the carrier wave is produced by variation in E_m, the amplitude of the modulating signal. The frequency deviation is just the magnitude of the modulating signal, or E_m again scaled by the gain of the modulator.

Therefore, frequency deviation is equal to the magnitude of the modulating signal times the deviation sensitivity. This is also equal to the change in frequency caused by the modulating signal. This change in frequency is known as the carrier swing (CS). Note that, as equation 9-10 shows, the frequency deviation is twice the carrier swing. This is because the carrier swing is always defined as half the total frequency deviation, or the amount the carrier changes from the center frequency.

$$m = \frac{FD}{w_m} = \frac{K_2 E_m}{w_m} = \frac{\Delta w}{w_m} = \frac{2CS}{w_m} = \frac{2CS}{2\pi f_m} \qquad \text{(9-10)}$$

The carrier swing approach to defining frequency deviation relies on the concept of a rest frequency. The rest frequency is defined as the carrier frequency location that would be occupied by a FM modulator with no modulating signal applied. This frequency location would then "swing" to each side by a maximum amount defined by the carrier swing. This concept arises from one common way of implementing FM modulators, namely, using a VCO and applying a modulating signal that pulls, or swings, the center frequency one way or the other. The rest frequency is the free running frequency of the VCO.

Using this idea, it is possible to construct a graph that is helpful in understanding how FM works. In Figure 9.2, the carrier is shown as a vertical line as on a spectrum analyzer. The modulating signal is shown below, and the variance in frequency, the frequency deviation, is shown by the dotted lines. The modulating signal causes the carrier to deviate an amount depending on the amplitude of the modulating signal. The time

Figure 9.2
FM carrier swing.

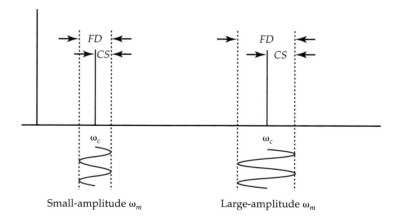

Small-amplitude ω_m Large-amplitude ω_m

variation or rate the carrier deviates is difficult to illustrate, but you should be able to imagine that as the frequency of the modulating signal increases, the rate the carrier frequency deviates will increase, but not the amount.

It is now possible to write the final equations for PM and FM modulated signals including all the factors. Equations 9-11 and 9-12 assume a sinusoidal modulating signal, and this will always be the case. Use equations 9-11 and 9-12 for all problems at the end of the chapter. Note that they are very similar in form to equation 9-6.

$$\phi(t) = m \cos[w_c t + \phi(t)]$$

$$\text{PM: } m(t) = E_c \cos[w_c t + m \cos(w_m t)] \qquad m = K_1 E_m = FD \qquad \textbf{(9-11)}$$

$$\text{FM: } m(t) = E_c \cos[w_c t - m \sin(w_m t)] \qquad m = \frac{K_2 E_m}{w_m} = \frac{FD}{w_m} \qquad \textbf{(9-12)}$$

In Figure 9.3 there are two graphs that can tell you a lot about how PM and FM work. Study them carefully and make sure that they make sense to you. Both of these graphs plot frequency deviation on the vertical axis as a function of E_m and w_m respectively.

Remember that the modulation index is defined by the frequency deviation. This means that as the frequency deviation grows, so does the modulation index. The first graph shows how both of these quantities change depending on the peak voltage of the modulating signal, and the second shows how they changes depending on the value of the modulating frequency. Note that the magnitude or amount of frequency deviation is independent of the frequency of the modulating signal. In other words, the amount of frequency deviation in an FM system has no dependency on the frequency of the modulating signal. As will be seen later, the frequency of the modulating signal effects the rate the carrier frequency deviates.

It is sometimes helpful to see the mathematical relationships that are illustrated in Figure 9.3:

Figure 9.3
Deviation graphs.

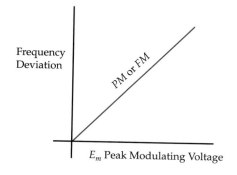
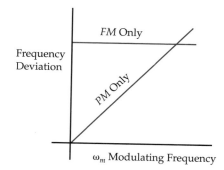

$$\text{FM or PM: FD} \propto E_m \qquad \text{PM: FD} \propto w_m$$

Again, note that the relationship between frequency deviation and modulating frequency for FM is a constant one. Stated another way, that means that no change in frequency deviation occurs as the modulating frequency changes. It will be seen later that this gives rise to additional complexity in FM, requiring the modulating signal to be pre-emphasized.

■ EXAMPLE 9.2

Here are two thought experiments on the effect of changing the amplitude and frequency of the modulating wave, this time in a *PM* modulator. Keep Figure 9.3 in mind.

If the frequency of the modulating wave doubles, what happens to the frequency deviation? It doubles.

If the amplitude of the modulating wave doubles, what happens to the frequency deviation? It doubles.

■ EXAMPLE 9.3

To drive home the differing effects of amplitude and frequency of the modulating wave on the frequency deviation of an *FM* modulator, work through the following thought experiments. Keep equation 9-8 in mind.

If the amplitude of the modulating wave doubles, what happens to the frequency deviation? It doubles.

If the frequency of the modulating wave doubles, what happens to the frequency deviation? Nothing happens.

Having reminded yourself of these facts, look again at Figure 9.3 and make sure the graph says the same thing to you as equations 9-7 and 9-8. Remember, the deviation sensitivities K_1 and K_2 are just constants, so they will just scale the results, not alter their relationships. If it helps, just set them to unity and concentrate on the functional relationships to E_m and w_m. (Just don't forget that they are there for the problems in the back of the chapter.)

Next, two examples will be worked to illustrate how to use the equations developed above. As always the PM example will be worked first; those of you who have referred to Appendix E know why. If you have not yet looked at it, please take some time and read through it after finishing with these two examples.

■ EXAMPLE 9.4

Find the modulation index and amplitude of the modulating signal for the PM modulated wave defined by the equation below. For the PM modulator, $K_1 = 3$.

$$m(t) = 20 \cos(100t + 2 \cos(5t))$$

$$m = K_1 E_m = 2 \rightarrow E_m = \frac{m}{K_1} = \frac{2}{3} = 0.667$$

■ EXAMPLE 9.5

Find the modulation index, amplitude of the modulating signal, frequency deviation, and carrier swing for a FM modulated wave defined by the equation below. For this FM modulator, $K_2 = 3$.

$$m(t) = 20 \cos(100t - 2 \sin(5t))$$

$$m = \frac{K_2 E_m}{w_m} = 2 = \frac{(3)E_m}{5} \rightarrow E_m = \frac{m w_m}{K_2} = \frac{(2)(5)}{3} = 3.33$$

$$FD = K_2 E_m = (3)(3.33) = 10 \rightarrow CS = \frac{FD}{2} = \frac{10}{5} = 2$$

■ BANDWIDTH OF ANGLE MODULATED SIGNALS

Recall that examination of the bandwidth of amplitude modulated signals showed that the bandwidth depended only on the magnitude of the modulating frequency W_m. In angle modulated systems, this simple relationship no longer holds. Instead, the bandwidth depends on both the modulating frequency and the modulation index.

The analytical reasons for the following discussion are outside the scope of this text. However, examining equation 9-11, reproduced below, will illustrate the fundamental concepts. This is the equation defining PM modulation. Due to the equivalence of the two forms of angle modulation, most results from analyzing this equation will also apply to FM.

$$m(t) = E_c \cos[w_c t + m \cos(w_m t)] \qquad \textbf{(9-11)}$$

This equation shows that the amplitude of the harmonics will depend on the modulation index. The harmonics come from "mixing" w_c with $m \cos(w_m t)$, and because the amplitude of the carrier wave E_c remains constant, only m determines the amplitude of the harmonics. Although it will not be demonstrated, the amplitude for each harmonic is found by referencing the integer order Bessel function of the first kind for the value of the modulation index.

Fundamentally, any angle modulated wave produces harmonics through the process of modulation. Recall from chapter 6 that harmonics are frequency multiples of the fundamental frequency. Any angle modulated wave produces all possible harmonics. Happily, not all harmonics must be considered, or the bandwidth of all angle modulated waveform would be infinite. The harmonics fall off fairly quickly in power, and this fact lets you ignore many of the higher harmonics. If the nth harmonic contributes less than 1% of the power of the unmodulated carrier, it is safe to ignore it.

Now the next thing is to determine how you can find the amplitude of the harmonics so that you can tell if it needs to be considered. This is accomplished by making use of a special mathematical function called the integer order Bessel function of the first kind.

There are all kinds of Bessel functions, so for those of you interested, the sentence above told you the precise type of Bessel function. The values of this function are shown in Table 9.1. For the rest of the discussion, these will just be referred to as Bessel functions. The order of the Bessel function is the subscript (e.g., J_0 would be the order 0 and would be associated with the fundamental carrier term; J_1 would be the order 1 and would be associated with the first set of sidebands or harmonics called the second harmonic).

Note that this 1% rule is about the same value that is used for the rule of thumb on charging and discharging times. Recall the five time constant rule; after five time constants, the charging is more that 99% complete or, if discharging, has discharged 99% of the voltage. So as an engineering approximation, the 1% rule is a good one and is used in many fields. The rule can be expressed mathematically as

$$| J_n(m) | \geq 0.01 \tag{9-13}$$

This is the reason why the values in Table 9.1 below are not carried out past that point.

Table 9.1
Bessel Table

m	J_0	J_1	J_2	J_3	J_4	J_5	J_6	J_7	J_8	J_9	J_{10}
0.0	1.00										
0.2	0.99	.010									
0.4	0.96	0.20	0.02								
0.6	0.91	0.29	0.04								
0.8	0.85	0.37	0.08	0.01							
1.0	0.77	0.44	0.11	0.02							
1.2	0.67	0.50	0.16	0.03	0.01						
1.4	0.57	0.54	0.21	0.05	0.01						
1.6	0.46	0.57	0.26	0.07	0.01						
1.8	0.34	0.58	0.31	0.10	0.02						
2.0	0.22	0.58	0.35	0.13	0.03	0.01					
2.2	0.11	0.56	0.40	0.16	0.05	0.01					
2.4	0.00	0.52	0.43	0.20	0.06	0.02					
2.6	−0.10	0.47	0.46	0.24	0.08	0.02	0.01				
2.8	−0.19	0.41	0.48	0.27	0.11	0.03	0.01				
3.0	−0.26	0.34	0.49	0.31	0.13	0.04	0.01				
3.2	−0.32	0.26	0.48	0.34	0.16	0.06	0.02				
3.4	−0.36	0.26	0.48	0.34	0.16	0.06	0.02				
3.6	−0.39	0.10	0.44	0.40	0.22	0.09	0.03	0.01			
3.8	−0.40	0.01	0.41	0.42	0.25	0.11	0.04	0.01			
4.0	−0.40	−0.07	0.36	0.43	0.28	0.13	0.05	0.02			
4.2	−0.38	−0.14	0.31	0.43	0.31	0.16	0.06	0.02	0.01		
4.4	−0.34	−0.20	0.25	0.43	0.34	0.18	0.08	0.03	0.01		
4.6	−0.30	−0.26	0.18	0.42	0.36	0.21	0.09	0.03	0.01		
4.8	−0.24	−0.30	0.12	0.40	0.38	0.23	0.11	0.04	0.01		
5.0	−0.18	−0.33	0.05	0.36	0.39	0.26	0.13	0.05	0.02	0.01	
6.0	0.15	−0.28	−0.24	0.11	0.36	0.36	0.25	0.13	0.06	0.02	0.01
7.0	0.30	0.00	−0.30	−0.17	0.16	0.35	0.34	0.23	0.13	0.06	0.02
8.0	0.17	0.23	−0.11	−0.29	−0.11	0.19	0.34	.032	0.22	0.13	0.06
9.0	−0.09	0.25	0.14	−0.18	−0.27	−0.06	0.20	0.33	0.31	0.21	0.12
10.0	−0.25	0.04	0.25	0.06	−0.22	−0.23	−0.01	0.22	0.32	0.29	0.21

It is also the reason why once the values reach 0.01, they are omitted in the table. For an analytical rule to determine the bandwidth using the Bessel table, apply the following formula:

$$BW = 2nf_m \text{ Hz} \quad \text{or} \quad BW = 2nw_m \text{ rad/sec} \qquad \text{(9-14)}$$

where n = number of sidebands (read from Table 9.1).

The next two examples illustrate how to apply this formula.

■ **EXAMPLE 9.6**

For an FM modulator with a modulating frequency of 100 rad/sec, and a modulation index of 2.4, find the bandwidth required.

The first thing to note is the modulation index; this will tell us what row in the table is to be read. Find 2.4, and read across to the last entry in Table 9.1. The value read is 0.02 for J_5. The subscript, here 5, indicates that there are five pairs of sidebands in addition to the fundamental component. The bandwidth is then found by the applying equation 9-14:

$$BW = 2(5)(100) = 1000 \text{ rad}$$

It is also very interesting to note that by proper choice of the modulation index, one can turn this around. It is possible to set any harmonic, including the carrier, to any value wished, just by looking at the Bessel function plots and tables. The next example illustrates this.

■ **EXAMPLE 9.7**

Find the value for the modulation index that will set the amplitude of the carrier term to zero, essentially suppressing the carrier term. To solve this, look for values of m where the Bessel function of the term desired equals zero. In this case find values of m where $J_0(m) = 0$. This function is zero for $m = 2.4$. It also will be zero for a modulation index of about 5.5 and 8.6.

Therefore, any choice of modulation index where the appropriate Bessel function is zero will yield a modulated waveform with no component at that harmonic. These values of modulation index have a special name in communications; they are called carrier nulls and are often used to calibrate transmitters. Table 9.1 gives the values of the various orders of Bessel functions as a function of m. The bandwidth of any angle modulated wave is found by noting the value of the modulation index and using the Bessel table.

To summarize, for both PM and FM, the Bessel table is used to determine how many sidebands are necessary to give a good reception of the signal. Further, the table can be used to set the amplitudes of the fundamental carrier waveform and the sidebands by using the modulation index. For FM the modulation index is a dimensionless number and represents the frequency deviation divided by the modulation frequency. With PM the modulation index is in radians and represents the phase deviation.

An important observation for understanding angle modulation is that, as Table 9.1 shows, as the modulation index grows, the number of sidebands grows. This emphasizes that fact that the bandwidth of an angle modulated waveform depends critically on the modulation index.

Always use the Bessel function table to determine the bandwidth required. If the Bessel function order is nonzero for the modulation index, that sideband must be included. It is important to know that better fidelity is not always the goal; many times the goal is intelligibility at minimum cost. This will often result in dropping sidebands that the Bessel function table would imply must be kept.

It is also important to understand that although this chapter considers analog modulation, which implies audio frequencies and the whole notion of fidelity, in many applications the modulating waveform will be digital in nature. Here fidelity has no meaning at all, and all that is important is the error rate of the received waveform. This is not always helped by adding bandwidth and getting more sidebands because you also capture more noise due to the wider bandwidth passing into the receiver. These ideas will be studied further in Chapter 13.

■ NARROWBAND AND WIDEBAND SYSTEMS

The relative magnitude of the modulation index for any angle modulation system has been used to define terms with which you should be familiar. For PM or FM transmissions, if the modulation index is less than or equal to 0.6, that type of modulation is known as narrowband FM (NBFM) or narrowband PM (NBPM).

These classifications arise from a historical rule of thumb that said that systems are classified as narrowband only if they use two or fewer sets of sidebands. Looking back at Table 9.1 it will be clear why the modulation index is limited to values less than 0.6 for this to hold. Most of the power in these situations are carried by the first set of sidebands. For narrowband systems, the bandwidth of an angle modulated signal is no more than 4 times the result for DSB AM systems. As is clear, even narrowband angle modulated signals require wider bandwidths than DSB AM modulated signals.

Systems where the modulation index is greater than or equal to 10 are sometimes called wideband, or WBFM and WBPM. Systems that exhibit a modulation index in between are not generally assigned any special name. Typically, if the implementation satisfies the bandwidth criteria for narrowband designation it is called narrowband; otherwise no special designation is used.

Virtually all commercially important systems today are narrowband systems, or close to it. The reason is not only a technical one; in fact it is possible to make a good argument that wideband systems perform better in many situations than narrowband systems. The next examples should make this clear.

EXAMPLE 9.8

Compare two FM systems with different modulation indexes. Both systems feature a modulation frequency of 100 rad/sec. System 1 has a modulation index of 0.4, a narrowband system. System 2 has a modulation index of 10, a wideband system.

The bandwidths required are shown below:

$$BW_1 = 2(2)(100) = 400 \text{ rad} \qquad BW_2 = (2)(10)(100) = 2000 \text{ rad}$$

Clearly, the first system uses significantly less bandwidth than the second; this is why narrowband systems are preferred. Less bandwidth is used for the same modulation frequency, a commercially important situation because bandwidth is a limited resource. On the other hand, the second system takes advantage of the fact that the total bandwidth is much wider, so for environments where the communications channel is bad, it is not usually bad over the entire bandwidth. Some frequency components of the signal arriving at the receiver will be received where others would not be. In a narrowband system the entire bandwidth might lie in the "bad" part of the channel, and so none of the signal would be received. In some specialized situations this also can be commercially important.

To make sure you understand what is meant when communication systems are defined as narrowband or wideband as compared with narrow bandwidth or wide bandwidth, examine the following example. It emphasizes that although modulation index can be used to classify the system, it is the only reliable measure of the bandwidth required by the system.

■ EXAMPLE 9.9

Probably the two most common FM systems are two-way radio systems like those used in emergency vehicles or taxicabs and broadcast FM radio. The first systems are designed to transmit a bandwidth of about 3 kHz (voice only) in a bandwidth of about 30 kHz. The second is designed to transmit a bandwidth of 15 kHz in a bandwidth of 200 kHz of which only 150 kHz is actually used for transmission; the rest functions as a guard-band to the adjacent stations.

For the two-way radios the number of sidebands required is given by the following equation:

$$BW = 2nf_m \text{ Hz}$$

$$30 \text{ kHz} = 2n(3 \text{ kHz}) \rightarrow n = \frac{30 \text{ kHz}}{(2)(3 \text{ kHz})} = 5$$

Knowing that there must be 5 sets of harmonics, use Table 9.1 to determine the modulation index, which must lie somewhere between 2.0 and 2.4.

In the second case, broadcast FM radio, the number of sidebands is also five:

$$BW = 2nf_m \text{ Hz}$$

$$150 \text{ kHz} = 2n(15 \text{ kHz}) \rightarrow n = \frac{150 \text{ kHz}}{(2)(15 \text{ kHz})} = 5$$

Again, referring to Table 9.1, the modulation index must lie somewhere between 2.0 and 2.4.

To summarize, the bandwidth of the two systems differ by a ratio of 150/30, or 5. Note that the modulation index for the two cases are identical. Modulation index is one way to estimate the bandwidth of angle modulated systems, but to classify the bandwidth of angle modulated systems exclusively by the modulation index is flawed. The only situation where this approach works is where the bandwidth of the modulating signal is constant in the systems being compared.

■ LARGE MODULATION INDEXES

What does a large modulation index really offer? Large modulation index FM modulators always require more bandwidth for a given information rate. This does yield better noise and interference properties but at a high cost, especially for wireless systems. Essentially, you have wasted bandwidth. Consider Example 9.8. System 1 uses 400 radians of bandwidth to send an information bandwidth of 100 Hz. System 2 uses 2000 radians of bandwidth to send the same amount of information.

The better noise and interference properties of large modulation index systems can be seen by thinking about how one tells two things apart. This is always done based on some measurable quantity that is different for the two items. For example, it is easy to tell black from white but not so easy to tell light gray from medium gray.

Extending this analogy to communications systems, imagine a binary modulation signal. This would produce two distinct signaling frequencies in the modulated waveform. The larger the modulation index, the larger the difference between these two signaling frequencies. The larger the difference, the easier to tell them apart, even in a noisy and interference-filled environment. This is the same thing as telling apart two colors: The greater the difference in the colors, the easier it is to tell them apart, even in dim light.

For wideband systems there is a relationship, known as the Carson rule, that states that the bandwidth of a wideband angle modulated waveform is given by the expression

$$BW = 2(f_m + FD) \text{ Hz} \tag{9-15}$$

Either the Carson rule or the Bessel table can be used to estimate the bandwidth required for a wideband angle modulated signal, but in this text all problems will use the Bessel table unless specifically stated otherwise.

■ VOLTAGE, CURRENT, AND POWER

The next subject to examine is the voltage, current, and power expressions for angle modulated signals. As always, power equals voltage times current or voltage squared divided by resistance. The latter expression will be used. Begin by examining the power in the carrier signal; it is defined for PM and FM just as it was for AM:

$$P_c = \frac{E_c^{\,2}}{2R}$$

(9-16)

where E_c is the peak carrier voltage (unmodulated), R is the load resistance, and the 2 in the denominator comes from the conversion to rms voltage from peak voltage, just as in the AM case. It should make sense that the power of an unmodulated carrier wave has no dependency on modulation effects, index, and so forth. It will be interesting to determine what effect, if any, these things will have on the total power of the angle modulated waveform.

The derivation of the result expressed in equation 9-17 appears in Appendix E. The result is that the average power in the modulated waveform is exactly equal to the power in the unmodulated carrier. Therefore, the average power of the waveform is just equal to the average power of the unmodulated carrier waveform. Unlike the general situation in AM, the power of the carrier signal is found to be *the same as the average power of the modulated signal*. This result is shown below:

$$P = P_c = \frac{E_c^2}{2R}$$

(9-17)

This answer results because in pure angle modulation there is no amplitude modulation of the carrier wave. This is usually a good assumption when evaluating analog PM and FM systems.

Again, in pure angle modulation, because there is no amplitude modulation of the carrier envelope, the average power of the unmodulated carrier wave is exactly equal to the total power. This should make a kind of sense. Because the only thing that is changing is the angle of the carrier wave, its average power should stay the same. Referring to equation 9-17, the only thing that matters to compute the power is the voltage of the carrier wave and the load resistance. Neither are changed by altering the angle or phase of the carrier wave.

Before turning to an examination of the power of the sidebands, a short comparison of the power results may be instructive. Again, note that the average power in an angle modulated wave is a constant, *independent* of the modulation index. Compare this to the power in the DSB-LC AM case where average power was *proportional* to the modulation index.

Therefore, no matter what level of modulation is performed on an angle modulated wave, whether PM or FM, the power remains constant, as long as there is no amplitude modulation. This result, and some of its implications, are key factors that determine what modulation scheme to use for a particular application.

It is also possible to obtain the total average power by adding up the average power of all the harmonics that are produced by the modulation process. Each harmonic has a peak voltage value; this is squared and divided by twice the load resistance. Then these are summed with the value for the average power of the modulated carrier. Remember that each harmonic builds two sidebands at $w_c \pm w_m$. This is shown in Example 9.10.

EXAMPLE 9.10

This example will show how the two ways to compute total average power in an angle modulated signal are equivalent. To illustrate, take a FM modulator with a modulation index of 1.6, and a carrier frequency of 1000 rad/sec at 10 V operating into a load of 50 Ω. The modulation frequency is 50 rad/sec:

$$P_c = P = \frac{E_c^2}{2R} = \frac{10^2}{2(50)} = 1.0 \text{ W}$$

Now do the same calculation by using the Bessel table and adding up all the components.

First, calculate the voltages of each of the components of the angle modulated signal. First calculate the voltages of each component of the angle modulated signal. The Bessel function values are taken from Table 6.9.

J_0 = fundamental modulated carrier voltage = (0.46)(10)   = 4.6 V

J_1 = first modulated harmonic   = (0.57)(10)   = 5.7 V

J_2 = second modulated harmonic   = (0.26)(10)   = 2.6 V

J_3 = third modulated harmonic   = (0.07)(10)   = 0.7 V

J_4 = fourth modulated harmonic   = (0.01)(10)   = 0.1 V

Taking these voltages and inserting them into the formula for computing power, equation 9-16, and remembering that for each of the harmonics there are two of them:

$$P = \frac{(4.6)^2}{2(50)} + \frac{2(5.7)^2}{2(50)} + \frac{2(2.6)^2}{2(50)} + \frac{2(0.7)^2}{2(50)} + \frac{2(0.1)^2}{2(50)}$$

$$= 0.2116 + 0.6498 + 0.1352 + 0.0098 + 0.0002 = 1.0066 \text{ W}$$

After accounting for rounding errors from the Bessel table, this matches the calculation of the power performed first. The spectrum is shown in Figure 9.4.

Again, it is important to understand that in any angle modulated system, if there is no amplitude modulation added, the total power of the modulated signal is exactly the same as the power in the unmodulated carrier wave. This is always true in pure angle modulated systems. Once the voltage for each harmonic is known, it is straightforward to determine the shape of the spectrum.

As can be seen from Figure 9.4, the spectrum components follow exactly the values shown in the Bessel table scaled by the peak modulating voltage. Note that the center frequency is the carrier frequency, and the spacing of the harmonics is the modulation frequency.

To give an intuitive feel for how the modulation index changes what the frequency spectra of FM modulators would look like, a few graphs are presented in Figure 9.5.

Figure 9.4
Example 9-10, spectrum analyzer view.

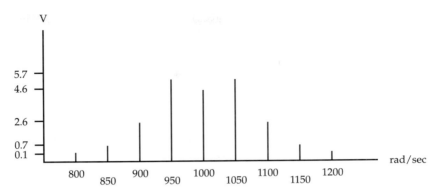

These are of the type seen on a spectrum analyzer or FFT plug-in. The values of the harmonics were taken directly from the Bessel table. The spacing between each harmonic is the modulating signal frequency. As can be seen, as the modulation index grows the bandwidth grows due to the requirement that more harmonics must be included. However, it is also important to note that the relative amplitudes of the harmonics changes as the modulation index grows. Finally, note that the frequency location of any harmonic is independent of the modulation index.

Figure 9.5
Spectral shapes for values of modulation index, spectrum analyzer view.

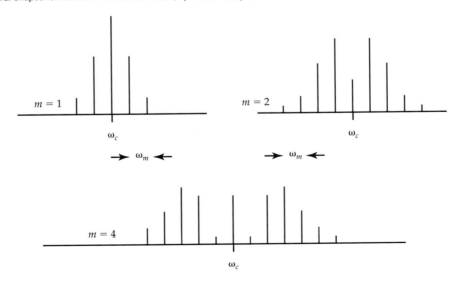

■ PERCENTAGE MODULATION

Percentage modulation is not quite as obvious as it was in the case of AM modulation. For both PM and FM it is defined in terms of the frequency shift experienced in the modulated waveform divided by the maximum frequency shift possible. Remember that the carrier frequency experiences change in both angle modulation "flavors," PM and FM. This quantity, the maximum frequency shift, although a physical result, is usually set by a regulatory decision. The appropriate governing body of the government typically defines it when it licenses a type of transmission for commercial use. For communications issues in the United States, this body is the Federal Communications Commission (FCC), which has jurisdiction over a wide range of communications issues.

EXAMPLE 9.11

If the FCC licensed a new FM service, it might define the maximum frequency shift or deviation as 50 kHz. If a particular implementation produces a signal that has a deviation of 40 kHz, the percentage modulation would be:

$$\% \text{ modulation} = \frac{\Delta f_{\text{actual}}}{\Delta f_{\text{max}}} \times 100\% \qquad (9\text{-}18)$$

$$\% \text{ modulation} = \frac{40}{50} \times 100\% = 0.8 \times 100\% = 80\%$$

Note that percentage modulation can be described equally well for either frequency or phase modulation.

Once again, and especially for those who have read Appendix E,

$$\text{frequency} = \frac{d}{dt}\,(\text{phase}) \qquad (9\text{-}19)$$

The terms *phase modulation* and *frequency modulation* only tell which parameter, phase of the carrier wave, or frequency of the carrier wave, respectively, is made proportional to the modulation signal.

These represent *two cases of the same type* of analog modulation. This commonality is due to the relationship above; frequency is equal to the first derivative of phase. The terms *FM* and *PM* apparently continue to be used because the abbreviations PM and FM are unique. On the other hand, the common abbreviations for amplitude modulation and angle modulation are both AM and therefore not unique.

■ MODULATORS

Now let's examine what modulator might look like for each of the narrowband cases. See Figure 9.6. The figure also includes a balanced modulator for the AM case to com-

Figure 9.6
Three modulators.

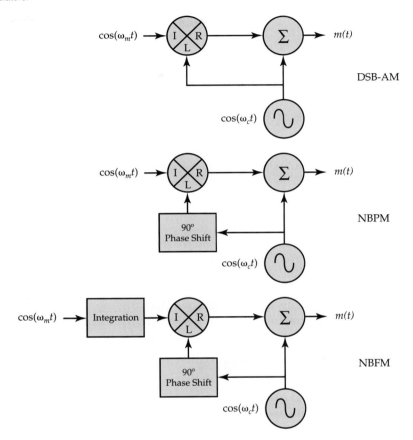

pare it to the NBPM and NBFM implementations. As is seen, they are very similar, and this should not be so surprising; after all a single equation describes all three.

The only thing that might not be familiar in Figure 9.6 at this point is the block with the integration text. What was desired here was to stress similarity; therefore each needed to have the same data source in each design. Because frequency is the derivative of phase, the integration block is used to get the antiderivative or integral of the modulating function for the NBFM modulator design. Then it is possible to use the same circuit for NBPM and NBFM.

■ DIRECT FM AND PM MODULATION

Although the Figure 9.6 shows how an angle modulated signal might be generated from theory, it does not illustrate practical designs. Direct FM or PM modulation is where the

Figure 9.7
Direct generation of FM.

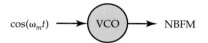

$$\cos(\omega_m t) \longrightarrow \boxed{VCO} \longrightarrow NBFM$$

carrier signal is directly modulated by the modulating signal. This means that the frequency deviation is directly proportional to the magnitude of the modulating signal.

Direct NBFM is commonly implemented today using a VCO. Recall the discussion of this device in the last chapter. Briefly, a VCO allows you to directly control the frequency of oscillation by a voltage. Fundamentally, the amplitude of the modulating signal directly controls the carrier frequency. The VCO's free running frequency is set to the middle of the frequency spread. See Figure 9.7.

A PM direct modulator could be generated from Figure 9.7 by simply differentiating the modulating signal prior to applying it to the VCO. Again, for a review of how a VCO works, refer to Chapter 8.

This circuit works because the frequency of the VCO is directly dependent on the amplitude of the modulating signal. As the voltage of the modulating signal increases, the frequency output of the VCO decreases and vice versa. It is also possible to generate WBFM signals from the above diagram as well, but the pull range specification of the VCO limits the wideband application. More traditionally, WBFM signals are generated from a NBFM signal using one of the two indirect methods discussed below.

■ INDIRECT FM MODULATION

Indirect FM is where the carrier signal is indirectly modulated by the modulating signal. Indirect FM can be used to generate NBFM or WBFM signals. Figure 9.8, shows an example of the technique. This indirect modulation is typically accomplished with frequency multiplication. In the multiplication approach, all spectral components are multiplied by themselves. Note that in this case, all possible components of frequency occur.

The multiplier box used in the multiplication approach is implemented in a number of ways. Typically, it is some nonlinear device that follows a power law output

Figure 9.8
Indirect generation of WBFM.

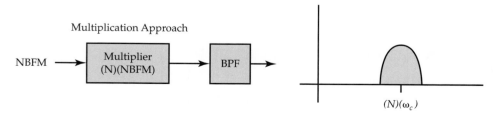

curve, like a diode or a varactor. Because this is almost the same as the simple AM transmitter using a varactor, it will not be discussed further here. Sometimes special devices are constructed to get a specific modulation index or several multipliers are cascaded to achieve very high values of multiplication and, hence, the modulation index. With these two techniques, values of up to 1000 can be readily implemented with good quality results.

You should note that indirect FM actually produces PM. Because any FM demodulator that works will also demodulate a PM signal, this fact is usually ignored, which is why there is no separate discussion on indirect PM modulation.

■ BROADCAST FM RADIO

In the chapter on AM demodulation, the FM broadcast radio was used as an example of one type of demodulation, pilot tone demodulation. Because this is the appropriate chapter to explore FM radio more completely, the diagram used there will be reproduced (see Figure 9.9), and a block diagram approach to how the signals are actually generated will be given (see Figure 9.10).

Broadcast FM stereo is a good example of the conversion approach to generate a FM signal. This is an indirect method, and the same one is used to produce the FM audio signal for TV broadcasting. Although FM is not truly classified as WBFM, wideband techniques are quite applicable. Note the presence of a mixer and secondary carrier signal (38 kHz) in Figure 9.10. Compare these to the conversion approach shown in Figure 9.8.

Figure 9.9
Baseband signal used for broadcast FM radio, spectrum analyzer view.

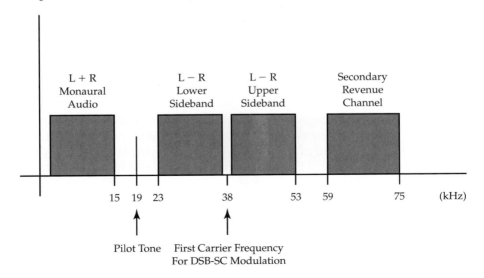

Figure 9.10
Block diagram, FM radio generation.

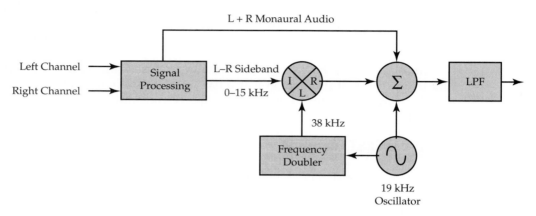

You should be able to make the analogy between the mixer in Figure 9.10 and the multiplier in Figure 9.8. Recall that a mixer essentially produces the product of the two inputs at its output. In Figure 9.10, the modulating signal is baseband, so the filtering is low pass. In Figure 9.8, the modulating signal is not baseband, but already frequency modulated around some carrier, so the filtering is bandpass. To illustrate the point clearly, certain filtering components have been left out, and the generation and summing of the secondary revenue channel has also been omitted. Additionally, other methods could be used, employing additional signal processing and delay networks.

It is interesting to examine just how the signal at the output of the LPF looks like. This is the baseband signal that is applied to the FM modulator for transmission. The signal plots in Figure 9.11 show what this signal looks like for two sinusoids applied to the left and right channel. The two signals are the same frequency, but the right channel is half the amplitude of the left channel. Additionally, the 19 kHz pilot tone is omitted for clarity.

In Figure 9.11a, the two tones applied to the left and right channels are shown. In Figure 9.11b, the output of the mixer is shown. Note how the envelope of the signal resembles a DSB-SC signal. This should not come as a surprise because that is exactly what it is. (Review the discussion in the last chapter for more detail.) The abrupt switching noticeable is the result of the 38 kHz LO signal switching the diodes in the mixer. Therefore, the frequency of the switch points is exactly 38 kHz.

Figure 9.11c shows the baseband FM signal after filtering. This has eliminated the high-frequency components that you might expect to see here from an examination of the Figure 9.11b. Again, this diagram does not show the pilot tone to clearly illustrate what the stereo FM signal looks like. This is the sum of the mixer output and the monaural L + R signal. The baseband FM stereo signal is seen to be the monaural L + R signal with the DSB-SC envelope riding on top of it.

Figure 9.11
Baseband FM generation.

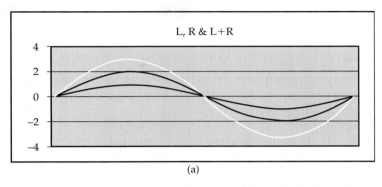

(a)

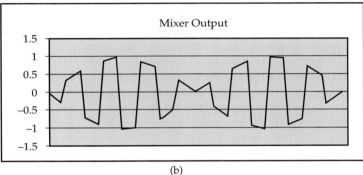

(b)

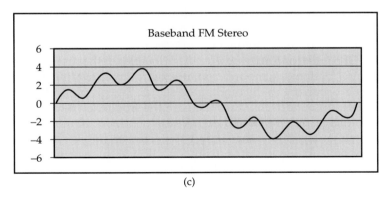

(c)

■ PERFORMANCE CONSIDERATIONS FOR ANGLE MODULATION

There are very different results for how background noise signal level affects the two different forms of angle modulation, FM and PM. Because this has a direct impact on how broadcast FM signals are conditioned before modulation, it is discussed here. These two different results are summarized below:

FM transmissions suffer from decreased signal-to-noise ratios as the modulation frequency increases.

PM transmissions have a constant signal-to-noise ratio independent of modulation frequency.

PM transmissions have a big advantage over FM transmissions. The result of this effect of decreasing signal-to-noise ratio as the modulation frequency increases is to cause all FM transmitters and receivers to require additional circuitry to compensate for this effect. This circuitry is discussed in the next section and is called an emphasis circuit because it boosts the emphasis or power of high frequencies in the transmission.

To see how this effect of decreasing signal-to-noise ratio with increasing modulation frequency for FM comes about, recall the following observations that were illustrated in Figure 9.3. In the second of these two graphs, it is shown that as the modulation frequency increases, the frequency deviation increases for PM but is held constant for FM. This means that FM frequency deviation has *no* dependency on the modulation frequency. Therefore, for increasing modulation frequency the frequency deviation does not increase for FM, whereas for PM it does.

Another way of looking at this same idea is to look at how the modulation index is defined. For FM the modulation index was divided by the modulation frequency, so as the modulation frequency increased, the modulation index decreased. For PM, there was no dependence on modulation frequency. These relationships are reproduced below for your reference:

$$\text{PM: } m = K_1 E_m \qquad \text{FM: } m = \frac{K_2 E_m}{w_m}$$

If one accepts that modulation index is a good measure of how easy it is to demodulate any modulated signal, it is easy to see why the performance of FM decreases with increasing modulation frequency.

Of course, one must accept this principle for the reasoning above to be valid. For angle modulation, the modulation index is a direct reading of how much frequency deviation is occurring in the modulated signal. The graphs in Figure 9.3 show that although both modulation techniques increase the frequency deviation with increased modulation voltage, only FM does not increase it for increasing modulation frequency. Another way of saying this is that only FM decreases the *percentage* frequency deviation and hence modulation index as the modulation frequency increases.

But how does a demodulator work? For angle modulation, the only thing that is being modulated is the frequency or phase of the carrier signal. Therefore, the only thing that can be used to demodulate the information in the modulated signal is the frequency deviation of the carrier signal.

In conclusion, because FM does not increase the frequency deviation as modulation frequency increases, as the modulation frequency increases, the signal that is used to energize the demodulator (the frequency deviation at any particular modulation frequency) does not increase proportionally. That tells us that the signal-to-noise ratio decreases with increasing modulation frequency for FM. PM does not suffer from this effect, and it is an inherent advantage of PM over FM.

■ PREEMPHASIS AND DEEMPHASIS

The effect of decreasing signal to noise as the modulating signal bandwidth grows exhibited by FM requires addressing in the modulator and demodulator of a FM communication system. As alluded to above, this is called preemphasis in the transmitter and deemphasis in the demodulator. Effectively what is done is that as the frequency of the modulating signal increases above some specific frequency, additional gain is applied. Because the object of a communication system is to accurately reproduce the modulating signal at the destination, the demodulator must subtract this gain in exactly a symmetrical way.

This additional gain is applied to the modulating signal before it is passed to the modulator and is subtracted out after it is demodulated. The block diagram in Figure 9.12 illustrates where this occurs.

The additional gain in the signal with increasing modulation frequency effectively balances out any decrease in signal to noise as modulation frequency increases. It does this because the signal grows in strength as the noise stays constant. This increasing signal strength just exactly balances out the decreasing frequency deviation caused by the act of FM modulation.

As you might expect, there has to be a standard for how much preemphasis is used so that when radios are designed, each station is deemphasized the same amount. In the United States the standard that is used starts at 500 Hz and extends up to 15 kHz. Over this frequency range a total of 17 dB of gain is applied. The standard curve follows a low-pass-type response curve for the deemphasis curve. As discussed above, the preemphasis curve is the inverse response.

Like any filter response, the 3 dB point can be determined by the time constant of the filter. The U.S. standard specifies the time constant to be 75 μsec. Therefore, one can predict the 3 dB point of the filter by the following calculation:

$$w = \frac{1}{\tau} = \frac{1}{RC} \to f_{3\,dB} = \frac{1}{2\pi\tau} = \frac{1}{2\pi 75 \times 10^{-6}} = 2122 \text{ Hz}$$

Therefore, at 2122 Hz, there would be 3 dB of gain applied to the modulating signal prior to being applied to the modulator, and similarly, there would be 3 dB of attenuation applied to the recovered modulating signal after demodulation.

Figure 9.12
FM Preemphasis and deemphasis shown.

■ DEMODULATORS

This chapter now turns to a discussion on angle modulation demodulators and receivers. The entire field is dominated by FM receivers, and that trend is followed here. The reason, as stated earlier, is that any FM demodulator that works will also be able to demodulate PM signals, for the reasons outlined in Appendix E. Therefore, this discussion will be limited to FM demodulation systems. The basic block diagram of a FM receiver is shown in Figure 9.13.

First, the limiter, why it is there, and how it works will be described. A discussion of discriminator types and their relative advantages and disadvantages will follow. This section discusses what is usually the heart of the demodulation process. The other components of the receiver are straightforward and very similar to those encountered in AM receivers. The channel filter, or BPF, RF amplifier, frequency converter or mixer, IF amplifier, and AF amplifier are all common to the AM case.

In FM receivers, the limiter and discriminator combine to form the central signal processing required to demodulate the FM signal. The basic idea of a limiter is to clip (e.g. limit) the input signal; another way of expressing this is to say the limiter produces a constant output voltage over a range of input voltages. This is important for two reasons that concern the design of discriminators. First, information about the modulation is contained in the zero crossings of the waveform. This forms the basis of the direct approach to implement a discriminator as described below.

When the limiter is adjusted so that the only information obtained from its output are the zero crossing locations, it is said to be hard limited. Only discrimination techniques similar to the zero crossing discriminator use hard limiting. One then just counts the zero crossings to determine the frequency.

Other approaches to discrimination still need the limiter, but with them it functions in a different way for different results. In these approaches, the limiter is used only to limit the amplitude of the carrier to a constant value; this is the second reason limiters are important to the design of discriminators. When used in this way, limiters are referred to as soft limiters.

The basic problem is that discriminators are susceptible to amplitude variations; by limiting these effects, using some form of limiting, the frequency deviation alone produces results. As is explained in the following paragraphs, the direct discriminator dis-

Figure 9.13
FM receiver.

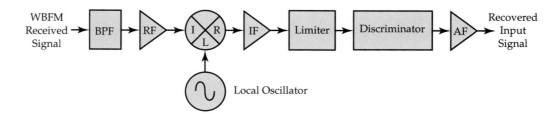

cussed relies on some method of converting FM deviation to AM. If there is already AM modulation produced by variations in the carrier energy, these will pass through and distort the signal. Figure 9.14 illustrates the operation of both hard and soft limiters.

The basic idea of any demodulation system is to provide an output signal that matches the modulation impressed on the input signal. For FM, this means that the output signal voltage should vary linearly with the instantaneous frequency of the modulated waveform. The general term for a circuit that responds in this way is *frequency discriminator.* Another way of saying this is that it is a device that converts a property of the signal, here frequency, but also phase, into an amplitude variation, here voltage. You are already familiar with one type of device that accomplishes this frequency-to-voltage conversion, the PLL. PLL's are an example of indirect frequency discrimination and will be discussed in the section immediately following the next one.

Direct Discrimination

Some frequency discriminator type receivers are also called direct FM receivers or demodulators. One of the oldest and simplest methods of direct demodulation is to use a slope detector, which uses a high pass filter (HPF) and diode to convert frequency variations into voltage variations. This is an example of direct FM detection. The detector circuit is tuned such that the lower end of the diode curve corresponds to the center frequency of the FM transmission. The general term for this type of direct discrimination is slope detector. In the frequency to voltage conversion, you make use of the slope of the transfer portion of the high-pass filter response, hence the word *slope.*

This tuning is typically done using a HPF just prior to the detector circuit. As can be seen in Figure 9.15, it is useful only in NBFM receivers because if the FM transmitted signal's deviation is greater than the linear slope of the response curve, distortion results. In other words, if the bandwidth of the FM transmission is wider than the linear portion of the HPF response curve, you do not get a good representation of voltage for frequency variation and, hence, get distortion.

This circuit works by using the HPF to generate amplitude variations as the frequency of the FM signal varies. This variation is accomplished by the transfer characteristic of the HPF. For high deviations, the output of the HPF is low in amplitude, and

Figure 9.14
Limiters.

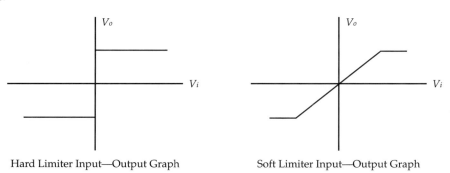

Hard Limiter Input—Output Graph   Soft Limiter Input—Output Graph

Figure 9.15
Slope detector.

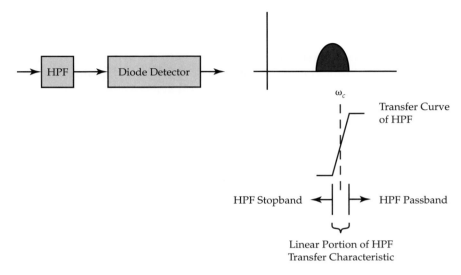

for large variations, it is high. This swing is then rectified by the diode and a varying dc voltage results that corresponds to (discriminates) the frequency deviations of the input signal.

Apart from the limitation to NBFM signals, another obvious problem with this type of design is the necessity of tuning the HPF for reception. If the FM signals that are to be received are at different carrier frequencies, a tuned filter is a requirement using this approach. A tuned filter is always expensive and to be avoided if possible. On the other hand, for many data applications, there is only one carrier frequency used, and this approach becomes very useful.

There are several types of slope detectors that have been developed over the years, including the Foster-Seeley or phase-shift detector, ratio detectors, differential peak detectors, coincidence or quadrature detectors, and so forth. These basic types all have similar advantages and disadvantages; mostly they apply additional circuitry to try to overcome the limitation to NBFM, but they still suffer from the potential need for a tuned filter front end.

Another good example of a direct FM detector is the zero crossing or pulse averaging discriminator. This circuit is composed of three main sections, a zero crossing detector, a monostable multivibrator (known more commonly as a one-shot), and a low-pass filter. More advanced versions take advantage of the dual outputs offered by most one-shots and add a second low-pass filter and utilize a fourth section, a differential amplifier. The two basic designs are shown in Figure 9.16.

Both of these circuits work in the same way. The input FM signal is applied to the zero crossing detector, which triggers the one-shot at each transition of the FM signal. This occurs each time the circuit senses a positive zero crossing of the input signal. Be-

Figure 9.16
Zero cross detectors.

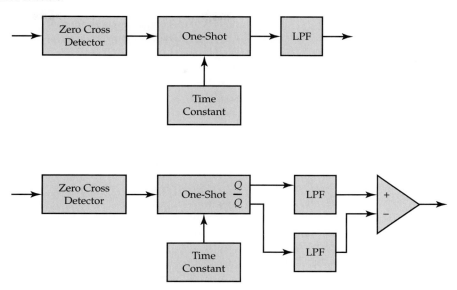

cause the circuit is responding to the positive zero crossings, it senses the leading edge of the FM signal. When triggered, the one-shot produces a DC level on its output or on both outputs in the second case.

The dc level is held for one-half cycle of the input FM signal. This time period is set by selection of the proper time constant for the one-shot. In the first case, the pulse train thus produced is applied to the input of a LPF, which averages the pulses to produce a dc voltage that represents the modulating signal. In the second case, the differential amplifier varies its dc output voltage, moving more positive the more frequently the pulses occur and dropping as the frequency of occurrence drops, again producing a voltage that represents the original modulating signal.

This circuit approach can be much more accurate than the other direct discriminator approach discussed. Its advantages of no tuning circuit and a fundamentally digital approach, allowing easy integration, are making it one of the most common approaches used today. An entirely different approach can be implemented using a PLL. This approach differs from the preceding ones discussed because it is an indirect approach to discrimination.

Indirect Discrimination

Using a PLL approach to indirect discrimination works by detecting phase shift or frequency difference and pulls a VCO to track the input frequency. (Remember frequency is the derivative of phase; if there is a phase difference, there must be a frequency difference as well.) This tracking of the input frequency accurately matches the modulation applied, and a demodulator results. There are lots of interesting things about how a PLL

Figure 9.17
Phase discriminator (PLL).

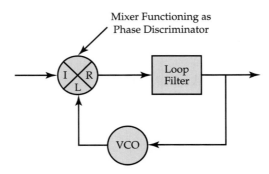

works and what specifications it has. Refer to Chapter 8 where the PLL was introduced. A block diagram of the FM demodulation approach using one is shown in Figure 9.17.

It is interesting to note that modulators and demodulators are designed to perform inverse operations. This can be readily seen by thinking about how one generates an angle modulated signal, the simple approaches outlined earlier involved using a VCO, and pulling the VCO with a voltage to produce the frequency differences. The PLL approach to indirect discrimination essentially inverts this idea, using the frequency differences or deviation present in the modulated signal to generate a voltage that tracks the modulation voltage swings that were present in the modulating signal.

This ends the discussion of how angle modulation receivers are designed to work with audio or analog inputs signals. In the discussion on digital angle modulation and demodulation, the differences in design will be illustrated and there will be more focus on PM applications.

The next two sections examine two applications of analog narrowband FM, cordless telephones, and cellular radio systems. These are excellent examples of the widespread adoption of angle modulation systems in the marketplace of today.

■ CORDLESS TELEPHONE

First, cordless telephones are not the same as cellular telephones or cellular radio. There are two types of cordless telephones in use in the United States today. They first appeared about 1985 when frequency spectrum was allocated by the FCC for this use. The frequencies were in the range of 43 to 49 MHz. There were 25 duplex channels allocated, one frequency bandwidth for transmission from the base unit to the hand held unit, and one pair for the reverse channel. The bandwidth of each of these channels is 30 kHz. Interestingly, this is the same bandwidth used for the cellular telephone voice channels, also implemented as a pair of simplex channels, each 30 kHz in bandwidth.

The second type of cordless telephone operates in just the same way as the first, but with a different frequency allocation. Recently, the FCC has also allocated bandwidth in the 900 MHz range for cordless telephones. The frequency band lies just above the frequency band used by cellular radio. The frequencies authorized are from 902 to 928 MHz. Sometimes this will be referred to as the industrial, scientific, and medical band (ISM); actually this portion of that band is just the industrial part. Refer to Chapter 2 for the frequency specifications. Again, these systems use a pair of simplex channels each 30 kHz in bandwidth to carry the frequency modulated signal on the assigned carrier frequency.

Both of these systems use narrowband analog FM modulation to send voice channels. When you turn *on* your handheld unit, it sends a signal to the base station telling it to go off-hook. This signal starts the sequence of operations that the public switched telephone system (PSTN) uses to process calls. See Chapter 16 for the entire sequence.

Once the base station gets the off-hood signal, dial tone and dialing proceed just like they would in a wired telephone. Because the handset uses dual tone multifrequency (DTMF) dialing, these frequencies are used to modulate the carrier frequency of the handset.

When someone calls you, the base station, which is wired to the telephone system, receives a ring tone from the local exchange. It then uses a narrowband pager channel to send its own ring signal to the handset. Again, once you press the *on* button and go off-hook; the sequence of operations for conducting a telephone call proceeds just as it would in a wired environment.

In comparing the two types of cordless telephones, both of the 900 MHz systems will perform better in most environments. Both systems use a set of channels in the assigned frequency bands to "choose" the best channel for the current communication. This can be observed by examining the display, featured in some models, that shows what channel pair is being used for the current communication. This will change as you move farther away from the base station or just change direction, altering the path loss and noise characteristics.

Finally, it is interesting to note that the some of the same frequencies used for the low-frequency cordless telephones are used for baby monitors. It is amazing what conversations can be heard from these devices by a neighbor or interested party driving down the street. Sometimes this is in total innocence, sometimes not.

Apparently, few realize that because they work just like a cordless telephone, including using the same frequencies, and similar powers, they have the same range as those devices. A word of caution to new parents; use these devices with caution, unless you want private conversations between you and your spouse becoming part of the lexicon of gossip in the neighborhood. These devices are valuable tools in helping manage the new addition to the household; just be aware of the implications of placing an open transmitter in your house.

■ CELLULAR RADIO

Cellular radio systems, more familiar to many as cellular telephone systems, utilize a large number of FM radio links, frequency division multiplexed (FDM), to accommodate a fairly large number of simultaneous calls on the same frequency. This is accomplished by splitting up the region, typically a city, into a number of roughly hexagonal cells. If you have ever seen a honeycomb, you know how the cells are configured into a grid so that the entire area is covered.

In each cell there is one base station with a transmitter capable of spanning the entire cell, but not much beyond. This means that each FM radio link, operating at one of the frequencies, is limited to a single cell and its adjacent partners. This might seem like a disadvantage, but instead it is the key to cellular telephones' wide acceptance. Because the power output of the base station is low, those frequencies can be used by another cell's base station to communicate with another user just a few miles away in another, nonadjacent cell.

This means that the same frequencies are used many times over in any cellular system. Recall the honeycomb pattern mentioned above; as long as no two sides of the honeycomb touch, a frequency can be used that has been used before. Figure 9.18, illustrates the concept. Note that although the cells are labeled as F1, F2, and so forth, each stands for a group of frequencies.

It is interesting to note that only four groups of frequencies are needed. This result is a general one; for any map, only four colors are needed to show the boundaries in such a way that no like color touches another. This is a famous, unproven, geometry problem, known as the four color problem. Four colors always seem enough, but no one has been able to prove it. Examine a map of the world where the countries are shown by color, and you will find that only four colors are used.

The central concept of cellular radio lies here, in the frequency reuse of channels in the same geographic area, for example a city. This was necessary because the allocation of bandwidth is very expensive for an industry to purchase, and as a result, any way to accommodate more users in the same frequency bands, here through reuse, is a big advantage. The number of users who may share the same frequency at the same time, in

Figure 9.18
Frequency reuse concept.

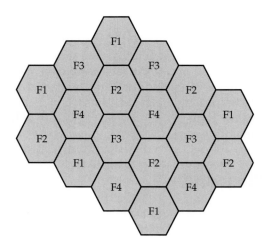

any small area such as a city, in nonadjacent cells depends on the number of cells but usually is about 10.

Each base station is connected to the wired telephone system through a switching center. In this way, calls from fixed telephone locations can be routed to a mobile subscriber and vice versa. As too many users try to access the system in any geographical area, congestion will occur and calls will be blocked because there are no free channels.

This expected growth in the system is accommodated by reducing the size of the cell and splitting it up into several cells, each with its own base station. This effectively allows more calls to be handled by the system as long as the cells do not get too small. The minimum size cell is set at a diameter of 2 km. If it was smaller than this, the base stations would interfere with each other and the frequency reuse concept that the system is based on would not work.

EXAMPLE 9.12

How many cells could Washington, D.C. accommodate?

Washington is a square 10 miles on a side; therefore its total area is 100 square miles. Because the area of a 2 km diameter circle is given by the formula πd squared, the maximum number of cells is

$$\text{maximum \# of cells} = \frac{\text{total area}}{\text{cell area}} = \frac{100 \text{ miles}^2}{\pi (1 \text{ Km})^2} = \frac{(100)(1.62 \times 10^3)^2}{\pi (1 \times 10^3)^2} = 83 \text{ cells}$$

There are, by law, 832 duplex channels in each geographical region, originally with two providers each allocated half of the channels to promote competition. Because there are four frequency groups to be split up, each frequency group represented in Figure 9.18 has one-quarter of that amount, or 208 duplex channels divided among two competitors. That means that each competitor can have a maximum of 104 calls going on simultaneously in each cell. (Actually, it is somewhat less than this, as is pointed out below.) It is interesting to note that the bandwidth allocated to the cellular telephone industry was previously used for UHF TV, channels 70 to 83. This spectrum ranges from 806 to 890 MHz and was seized in 1974.

The system currently installed in the United States is called the Advanced Mobile Phone Service (AMPS); in Europe and Japan, similar technology is used but with different names and number of channels. In Europe and Japan it is known as Total Access Communication System, (TACS), with more channels in Europe and fewer in Japan than in the United States. The frequencies used are also somewhat different but are in the same general band, 820 to 960 MHz. Also, the TACS systems uses a slightly narrower channel bandwidth than the AMPS system. TACS uses 25 kHz, whereas AMPS uses 30 kHz, the narrower channel bandwidth allowing a TACS system to squeeze in more channels in the spectral allocation for the service.

This technology is also called 900 MHz technology. This is because there is an entire line of components manufactured specifically for this industry and operable over this frequency range. Because these systems are worldwide, very large economies of scale have worked to significantly reduce the cost of components designed to work in this frequency range. As a result, many related technologies use components manufactured for the cellular telephone industry because of the big cost advantage; hence the term *900 MHz technology* is used to imply wide availability of components at competitive pricing.

Next, we will examine how these channels are divided up and used by the cellular telephone system. First, each of the 832 channels mentioned above is a duplex channel. The actual number of simplex channels is twice this amount, or 1664. Each is 30 kHz wide and is good for only one-way communication (simplex), either from the base station to the mobile subscriber or vice versa. To actually carry on a telephone conversation, you need a two-way communication system (duplex). This is accomplished by using two of the 30 kHz channels, one for communication to the mobile subscriber from the base station and one for the reverse direction.

Originally, each region was split among two competitors, and as a result the 1664 simplex channels were divided into four groups. There were 416 simplex channels for competitor A to be used for the base stations to communicate to the mobile subscriber and 416 for competitor B for the same purpose. There were 416 simplex channels for competitor A to be used for the mobile subscribers to communicate to the base station and 416 for competitor B for the same purpose. Therefore, there were 416 duplex FM channels for each competitor, in each geographic region. It may interest you to know that competitor A was always the traditional telephone service provider for your region, and competitor B was open to competitive bidding among other companies that wanted to participate in this business in your geographic area.

This situation changed in 1995. A legal decision finalized in that year opened up all markets to multiple competitors, not just two. When this decision was made, no new frequency space was allocated, so newcomers to the market are allowed to lease bandwidth from the original two competitors. Today, it is not unusual to find up to six competitors in virtually every market of over 250,000 people. This has significantly altered the economics of providing this service to consumers and has resulted in intense competition among the various participants in each market. It is very common now to receive a "free" cellular telephone in exchange for signing an exclusive service contract with one of the providers. This telephone is a fairly high-technology piece of equipment, with a cost to manufacture of $100 or more. The giving away of this component is one indication of the intense competition in this market.

Again, as mentioned above each mobile telephone requires two simplex channels so you can both talk and listen at the same time. People differ about the number of channels; this difference lies in whether they are talking about simplex channels, one competitors duplex channels, and so forth. A large number of people are involved in the cellular telephone industry, each with an individual perspective on the situation.

Additionally, some of these channels are not used for conversations but are reserved for management, data, and a paging system to "ring" your portable telephone. Twenty-one are reserved for these uses. See Table 9.2 for a summary of the AMPS service as it was originally implemented.

Note that 12.5 MHz divided by 30 kHz is just 416, the number of simplex channels allocated in each direction to each competitor. The control channels, 21 for each com-

Table 9.2
AMPS Summary

	Competitor A	Competitor B
Base station TX frequency	869–880, 890–891.5 MHz	880–890, 891.5–894 MHz
Total BS TX BW	11 + 1.5 = 12.5 MHz	10 + 2.5 = 12.5 MHz
Mobile telephone TX frequency	824–835, 845–846.5 MHz	835–845, 846.5–849 MHz
Total MT TX BW	11 + 1.5 = 12.5 MHz	10 + 2.5 = 12.5 MHz
Number of simplex channels	416 + 416 = 832	416 + 416 = 832
Number of duplex channels	416	416
Channel spacing	30 kHz	30 kHz

petitor, are taken out of their total allocation of channels. This means that each competitor actually had only 395 duplex channels for customer use. Housekeeping tasks associated with the operation of the system are accomplished with the control channels.

EXAMPLE 9.13

Continue the Example 9.12 and find the maximum number of simultaneous calls that could go on in Washington, D.C. Assume that every available duplex channel is being used by a subscriber.

$$\text{maximum \# calls} = \frac{(\text{\# of cells})(\text{\# of duplex channels})}{4 \text{ frequency groups}} = \frac{(83)(832 - 42)}{4} = 16,392$$

Next, an examination of how the calls are handled and how the small size of the cells affects how the system stays with you when you move from cell to cell will be provided. This will be done by examining in detail each step of the process involved in a telephone call using the cellular system.

The very first thing that is required is that the cellular telephone be turned ON. Because the base stations are constantly transmitting on the management channels, when this happens, the handset scans the management channels mentioned above and looks for the strongest signal from a base station. When it finds this signal, it assumes that this is the base station the best signal will come from and locks onto that management channel. Therefore, the first thing that happens when someone tries to call your cellular telephone is that the base station looks to see if you are in its area. If you are, it then uses a pager channels to ring your individual handset and dedicates one of the duplex channel pairs to your conversation.

The system can find your individual telephone because each handset is equipped with a PROM that contains a unique code, which identifies your handset to the base station. The base station uses some of its management channels to get this number from your telephone when it first turns ON and finds the closest base station. This means that every time you turn ON your cellular telephone you are transmitting your unique code for anyone with the right equipment to hear it.

Because this code also determines who gets billed for calls that originate from your portable handset, once the code is found, it can be programmed into another PROM in another handset. Then when calls are made from that modified handset, they are billed to the code number, which is the telephone bill of the owner of the original handset. This is telephone fraud and is a major problem in many large cities with densely packed cells.

This management of the telephone call using the paging and management channels is implemented using a communications protocol. This protocol handles call origination, release, billing issues, and control of the channels both within a particular cell and across cell boundaries. It operates using data channels implemented with FSK signaling operating in a FDM manner. This means that it can carry on several simultaneous "conversations" with handsets at the same time and stay in touch with all the handsets being used at any one time in a cell.

One of the most interesting things about the cellular telephone system is how it works when you move from one cell to another, adjacent cell. This technique is called a hand-off. Adjacent cells cannot use the same frequency channels to communicate from and to the base station. Therefore the base station must switch the call from its connection to the central office, or another base station, and also find an open voice channel in the next cell.

Further, as the boundary is crossed, the switch to the new channel pair and transfer of ownership of the call to the adjacent base station must be accomplished. Additionally, this must all occur in a short enough period of time so that there is no noticeable loss of service during switching. The hand-off typically takes about 250 msec, or one-quarter of a second.

This is a complex process that must take into account a number of factors. Imagine that you make a U-turn just at the boundary of the cell. Or imagine that you are just strolling along, perhaps window shopping, and you stroll forth and back across the boundary every few minutes, all the time talking on your cellular telephone. Other complex switching scenarios exist.

As can be seen, the management of the telephone call in a cellular system requires a complex management scheme that takes into account many different factors and is distributed among the base stations in your area. This type of control is implemented in a combination of hardware and software, with the software following the general principles of a communication protocol. Here, the protocol manages the way the call is established, conducted, switched, released, and billed.

All cellular telephone systems, because of the complexity of the cell approach and frequency reuse, use some similar approach to that taken here in the United States. The name of the protocol used here is AMPS. The requirement for such a protocol to handle the communication system underlines the central difference between mobile radios and cellular telephones. Mobile radios use similar radio technology, namely, narrowband FM, which, because they are operated in a point-to-point manner on a single-frequency channel, require no such complex software to operate. Mobile radios are used widely in public safety applications and are similar to a walkie-talkie.

To conclude this discussion of cellular telephones, the distinction between analog and digital phones is described. An analog cellular telephone, such as AMPS, uses the analog modulation techniques described in this chapter. Following the approach in

Chapter 1, where the form of the modulated signal while in the channel defines the type of system, this would be an analog communication system.

The digital cellular telephones are distinguished by the PCM encoding of the voice prior to modulation. Instead of an analog modulating signal, they use a digital modulating signal. However, the modulated signal is still analog in form. Our definition for communication systems would then classify this as an analog communications system as well since the form of the signal while in the channel is analog. Both systems are implemented using a mix of analog and digital circuitry.

■ SUMMARY

This chapter discussed both FM and PM modulation and demodulation. Both types of angle modulation have several common attributes that differ from what was learned when studying AM. In angle modulated systems the amplitude of the modulating signal is carried by the amount of frequency shift and is measured by the frequency deviation. The frequency information is contained by the rate of frequency shifts.

The main difference between FM and PM is how the modulation index is defined; for PM, the modulation index is proportional to the amplitude of the modulating signal and inversely proportional to the modulating frequency. For the FM case, the same direct proportionality to the amplitude of the modulating signal exists, but there is no dependence on the modulating frequency.

Another way of expressing those facts is to talk about frequency deviation; for both FM and PM there is a direct relationship between frequency deviation and the amplitude of the modulating signal. A larger peak voltage for the modulating signal leads directly to a large frequency deviation and a larger bandwidth.

However, the dependence on the modulating frequency is different for FM and PM. For PM, an increase in modulating frequency leads directly to an increase in frequency deviation and larger bandwidth. For FM, however, the magnitude of the frequency deviation is unaffected by the modulating frequency. The only impact an increase of the modulating signal frequency is an increase in the rate of frequency deviation.

Additionally, the intimate relationship of PM and FM can be seen by recognizing that any PM modulator can provide a FM modulated signal. The FM modulated signal can be generated by having the PM modulator be driven by a modulating signal where the amplitude of the modulating signal is *inversely proportional* to the modulating frequency.

Finally, it is important to reiterate the commonalties and differences in amplitude modulation and angle modulation with the two familiar forms of both, AM and FM radio:

AM radio: Amplitude information is conveyed by the *amount* the envelope opens or closes (modulation index).

AM radio: Frequency information is conveyed by *how often* the envelope opens or closes (repetition rate).

FM radio: Amplitude information is conveyed by the *amount* the carrier frequency changes (frequency deviation).

FM radio: Frequency information is conveyed by *how often* the carrier frequency deviates.

PROBLEMS

1. Find the modulation index, peak modulating voltage, and frequency deviation for a frequency modulator with a deviation sensitivity of 5. The modulated wave is given by the equation, $m(t) = 10 \cos[100t - 8 \sin(20t)]$. Express your results in angular frequency.

2. Find the modulation index, peak modulating voltage, and frequency deviation for a phase modulator with a deviation sensitivity of 5. The modulated wave is given by the equation $m(t) = 10 \cos[100t + 8 \cos(20t)]$. Express your results in angular frequency.

3. Find the bandwidth required for a frequency modulator with a deviation sensitivity of 10. The modulated wave is given by the equation $m(t) = 25 \cos[200t - 2 \sin(40t)]$. Express your results in angular frequency.

4. Find the bandwidth required for a phase modulator with a deviation sensitivity of 10. The modulated wave is given by the equation $m(t) = 25 \cos[200t - 2 \cos(40t)]$. Express your results in angular frequency.

5. Find the average power for a frequency modulator with a deviation sensitivity of 2. The modulated wave is given by the equation $m(t) = 10 \cos[100t - 4$ $\sin(20t)]$. The load resistance is 100 Ω. Use equation 9-16.

6. Perform the same calculation as in problem 5 using Table 9.1.

7. Find the power in the unmodulated carrier for problem 6. Compare and contrast the results you obtained in problems 5 through 7.

8. How many simplex channels are used to carry on a telephone conversation using the cellular telephone system described? Give the frequency locations and bandwidths used. Also specify the transmit and receive frequencies from the cellular telephone *user perspective.* Is there only one way to answer the question? Try to find two answers that depend on something other than the specific frequency locations used.

9. Assume that a particular geographic area has six competitors providing cellular service. Taking into account the management channels, how many calls are possible in each cell simultaneously for each competitor?

10

Pulse Modulation

This chapter will form our study of pulse modulation. In the last several chapters, amplitude and angle modulation were explored. These modulation techniques varied a continuous sinusoid, sine, or cosine in amplitude, frequency, or phase. Those techniques are called continuous wave (CW) modulation. This is because the waveform varied was continuous in nature.

In the study of pulse modulation, ways to vary a pulsed waveform in amplitude, width, or position will be discussed. The focus of the chapter will be pulse amplitude modulation (PAM) and its close cousin, pulse code modulation (PCM). Pulse width modulation (PWM) and pulse position modulation (PPM) are only briefly surveyed because the bulk of economic interest is in PCM, for example, virtually every telephone call you make is digitally transmitted using PCM techniques.

Before going into detail about these techniques, some fundamentals that are needed to study this type of modulation will be reviewed.

■ SAMPLING THEORY

The first thing to realize about digital communications is that many times analog waveforms need to be sent digitally. The best example of this is telephone calls. One way this could be done is by using traditional A/D circuits at the source and D/A circuits at the destination. Most readers will have had a course that has introduced you to these circuits, but some important points will be briefly reviewed. An A/D converter digitizes, or samples, an analog signal at regular intervals and represents the original analog or continuously varying signal as a series of binary data points that correspond to the amplitude of the original signal. See Figure 10.1.

This series of binary values is an accurate representation of the original signal if certain criteria are met. The first of these is that the sampling must be regular. This means that the samples must be evenly spaced. This is shown in the sampling interval in Figure 10.1. The spacing must remain constant, which is a requirement of sampling theory. The second point is that the signal must be sampled often enough to accurately represent the signal. If it is too slow, the binary data points, when reconstructed, will not look anything like the original signal. Figure 10.2 illustrates the effect of varying the sample interval.

The third point that the more bits that are used to represent each sample, the more accurate the sampled quantities are. Any error due to this effect is called a quantization error. For example, suppose that you had an analog signal that varied from 0 to 10 V and tried to sample it with a 2 bit A/D. Two bits gives just four possible amplitude values, each about 2.5 V apart. The quantization error here could be as much as 1.25 V, or half the step size. On the other hand if you used an 8 bit A/D, 8 bits gives 256 possible amplitude values, each only about 0.04 V apart. It should be clear that the latter approach will give a lower quantization error and smaller step size. This is shown in Figure 10.3.

Figure 10.1
Sampling an analog signal.

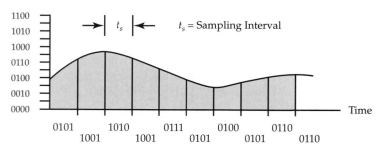

The series of binary data points.
Note that sample value is taken at the start of the sampling interval.

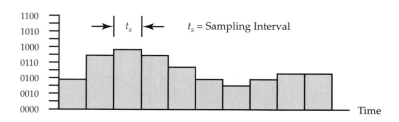

Figure 10.2
Effect of sampling interval.

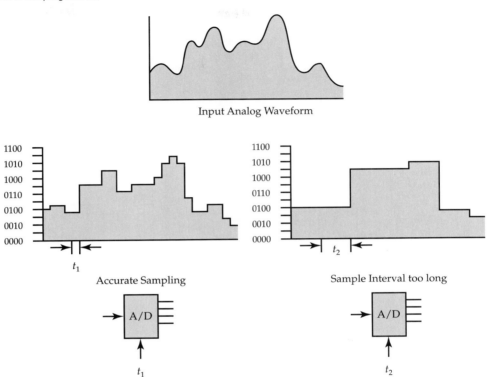

Note that in Figure 10.2, the number of bits was held constant and the sampling interval was varied. In Figure 10.3, the sampling interval was held constant and the number of bits was varied. Also, note that in Figure 10.3, the amplitude steps accommodated the same dynamic range. Both of these comparisons were made to help you understand how they interact. The sampling interval and the dynamic range will be held constant when discussing the number of bits needed for a specific performance level. In this way the comparisons are kept real and representative of trade-offs that occur in practice.

Figures 10.2 and 10.3 illustrate the effects of not following either point 2 or point 3. As can be seen, skimping on bits or clock speed will have bad effects. Remember, once the signal is digitized, or sampled, only the samples represent the information in the original analog signal. If the signal is not represented well, information is lost that can never be recovered. It is very important to set these parameters correctly. To summarize, there are three rules that must be obeyed to obtain an accurate sampling of the analog data:

1. The sampling interval is held constant.
2. The signal must be sampled often enough.
3. Enough bits must be used to represent each sample so the amplitude accuracy is correct.

Figure 10.3
Effect of number of amplitude bits used in sampling.

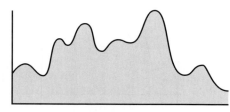

Input Analog Waveform

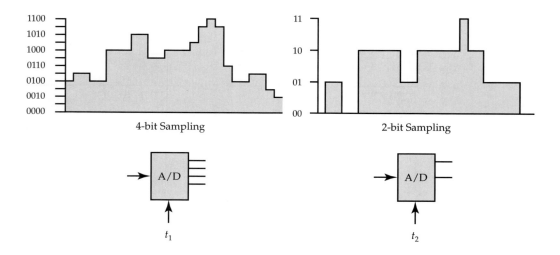

Now that you have good understanding of the practical issues, it is time to examine the second point above more carefully. This point is the real heart of sampling theory. The Nyquist theorem defines sampling theory. Theorems are usually a part of mathematics studies that most of us would rather forget, but here it has a very practical and easy to understand result: For any sampled data system, there is a minimum sampling rate that must be observed if the results are to be accurate. This minimum sampling rate is defined by the maximum frequency component present in the original analog or continuous waveform to be sampled. The sampling rate must be at least twice that frequency.

So rule 2 is very easy to follow. Just measure the input signal to determine the maximum frequency present using something like a spectrum analyzer or FFT module in a digital oscilloscope, multiply it by 2, and the minimum frequency of the sample clock is determined. This rule is expressed in equation 10–1:

$$f_{sample} \geq 2 * f_{signal} \qquad \text{(10-1)}$$

It is possible to sample more often and get more accuracy, but all that is necessary to recover the original signal is twice the highest frequency present in the original signal. Stated another way, the result of this rule is to make sure that *each* cycle of any frequency present in the original signal is sampled at least twice. This results in a mathematical guarantee (a theorem and proof) that the original waveform can be reproduced from the sampled data.

■ ALIASING

In practice each waveform is usually sampled between two and three times to make sure that this rule is not violated. If it is violated and the original waveform is not sampled at the rate of at least twice its highest frequency, a phenomenon known as aliasing will arise. Aliasing means that a frequency has folded over and is an alias, or false image, of the correct frequency. Aliasing always results in making the frequencies look lower in frequency than they should be.

This folding over is probably somewhat obscure. To understand, recall from Chapter 6 that any repetitive waveform can be represented as a series of sines and cosines and that these sines and cosines are all harmonically related to each other. By following rule 1, the sampling pulse is a repetitive waveform so can be represented as a group of sine and cosine waves.

Essentially what happens is that if the signal is not sampled fast enough, and hence the fundamental frequency is not high enough, due to the sampling process, the negative frequency image folds over and appears in the output spectrum. The sampling process itself is essentially amplitude modulation of the sampling waveform by the original analog waveform. (Please verify the above sentence for yourself; it is an important insight to how aliasing actually arises. Pay special note to which waveform is the modulating signal.) This signal that appears is an *alias* of the original analog frequency that should be in the output spectrum. Remember any alias is always lower in frequency than what should be seen, because it is always the sum of some multiple of the sampling waveform and the negative image of the analog waveform.

Figure 10.4 illustrates how aliasing arises. As stated above, if the signal is not sampled often enough, the negative frequency image of the sampling clock folds over and appears in the output spectrum.

As can be seen from an examination of Figure 10.4, the alias frequency is of a lower frequency than the signal frequency. Further, it has resulted from the sample clock not sampling each cycle of the input signal twice. Note that for the first cycle of the input signal the sample clock did sample twice, but it did not for the second cycle. Rule 2 says that for every cycle, the sample clock must be fast enough to sample it twice. Example 10.1 illustrates the effects of aliasing and how to calculate the alias frequency.

Figure 10.4
Illustration of aliasing.

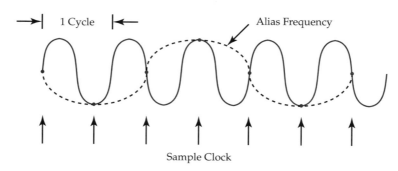

EXAMPLE 10.1

Sample an 8 kHz signal with a 12 kHz sample clock. This clearly violates rule two expressed in equation 10-1:

$$f_{sample} \geq 2 * f_{signal} \qquad 12 \text{ kHz} \geq 2 * 8 \text{ kHz} = 16 \text{ kHz}$$

Unless the sample frequency is at least 16 kHz, rule 2 has been violated. The sampling has not occurred often enough. Determine what the maximum frequency would be that could be sampled with the 12 kHz sample clock:

$$f_{sample} \geq 2 * f_{signal} \qquad 12 \text{ kHz} \geq 2 * 6 \text{ kHz} \rightarrow 6 \text{ kHz} = f_{signal,max}$$

To be sampled accurately by the 12 kHz sample clock, the maximum input frequency would have to be 6 kHz. Determine the alias frequency in the original problem:

$$f_{alias} = f_{sample} - f_{input} \tag{10-2}$$

$$f_{alias} = 12 \text{ kHz} - 8 \text{ kHz} = 4 \text{ kHz}$$

Equation 10-2 illustrates that to determine the alias frequency just subtract the input frequency from the sample frequency. As a further test, always check the answer to make sure that the alias frequency determined from equation 10-2 is always less than the maximum input sample frequency that would be accurately sampled with the sample clock. This test can be written mathematically as

$$f_{alias} < \frac{f_{sample}}{2} \tag{10-3}$$

$$4 \text{ kHz} \leq \frac{12 \text{ kHz}}{2} = 6 \text{ kHz}$$

As can be seen, the answer checks.

If the reasons for aliasing are not clear, do not worry. If you just follow the rule of always sampling fast enough, there is no need to be concerned. However, there are many everyday events where it is possible to see the result of insufficient sampling giving arise to aliasing. One of the most common is when watching a fan blade rotating. Once the blade is rotating fast enough, it appears that it is rotating in the opposite direction much more slowly. This effect is also often seen on stationary exercise bikes. You know that this cannot be true and correctly assume it is some kind of optical illusion. The cause of that illusion is aliasing.

Because the item is rotating faster than you can see it, your eye tries to "sample" the image and reconstruct it. However, it makes a mistake. Because your eye can only sample so fast, it violates the Nyquist theorem, and you observe an alias of the actual image. Note that the alias is always slower than the rotating blade, which emphasizes the statement that any alias frequency will be lower in frequency than the frequency it masks.

The last thing is to reiterate that aliasing, except for rare occasions, must be avoided. The easiest and surest way of guaranteeing this is to pass the input signal through a LPF before sampling the waveform. This LPF will attenuate any frequencies above its cutoff frequency. The cutoff frequency of the filter is set to less than half of the sampling rate on the A/D. This guarantees no aliasing.

Of course, the corner and cutoff frequency and the sampling rate must be chosen such that you get all the information needed from the original analog signal. This is a system design problem and is usually defined by the bandwidth of the signal. For example, in a voice frequency design, the upper frequency of interest is 3400 Hz. For an audiophile design, the upper frequency of interest is 20,000 Hz, and so forth. Low pass filters when used in this way are called antialiasing filters.

■ EXAMPLE 10.2

Determine the cutoff frequency of an LPF for a sampled data system. Also determine the sampling rate. You are told that the input signal is from a high-quality stereo system and you are to determine the antialias filter's cutoff frequency for a new type of compact disk product.

Although you search for a specification of the upper frequency, you cannot find any numbers. You conclude the information is not in the document and try to find another way to set the frequency. You ask your friend who is an audiophile what the maximum frequency of his stereo system is. He responds that his system response is flat up to 20,000 Hz. Because he has a reputation for excessive detail about his hobby, you imagine that if that frequency satisfies him, it probably will satisfy the person who wrote the document as well. (Perhaps part of the assignment was to determine what that frequency should be as well as find the cutoff frequency.)

Now that a maximum input signal frequency is determined, it is an easy matter to find the cutoff frequency for the LPF. You specify a LPF that is flat to 20 kHz, has a corner frequency of 22 kHz, and rolls off by 40 dB by 30 kHz. This sets the sampling rate to 60 kHz. You have no idea if such a filter is feasible or not at this point, but it should satisfy the sampling theory restrictions of which you are aware.

■ PULSE AMPLITUDE MODULATION

PAM is probably the simplest implementation of pulse modulation. In this scheme, the amplitude of the pulse train produced carries the analog information. Essentially, a sample and hold circuit samples the input analog waveform at regular intervals and holds that value for the sample interval. Then each pulse is an instantaneous (almost) sample of the input analog waveforms amplitude. PAM is illustrated in Figure 10.5.

The first waveform shown is the input analog waveform that is sampled. The second is the pulse clock that drives the sample and hold circuit. The third is the resultant PAM waveform; the amplitude of each pulse matches the amplitude of the input analog waveform at the moment of sampling. As can be seen from the figure, connecting the samples of the PAM waveform would reproduce the original input waveform. Note the zero amplitude sample and the negative amplitude sample. A typical analog circuit implementation of this type of modulator is shown in Figure 10.6.

Note that there are only two components, a sample and hold module and an oscillator to produce the sample timing. Because the sample and hold module uses a capacitor to store the voltage, there is no issue of amplitude quantization as with the A/D discussed earlier. This is a nice bonus of this inherently analog approach to measuring magnitude. Next, will this circuit work this simply to produce pulse amplitude modulation? The answer is Yes if the maximum frequency of the input analog waveform is less than twice the oscillator frequency to assure a sample twice each period.

Of course, there is always Murphy's Law that suggests that everything was not anticipated. Unexpected events happen all the time. So, be a good engineer and use a little precaution to make sure that no frequencies get into the sampled data system that are higher than expected. As suggested earlier, one simple way to do this is to put in a low-pass filter just prior to sampling the waveform. Figure 10.7 shows this modification. As mentioned above, an LPF, when used in this manner, is often called an antialiasing filter because that is the function it is performing.

Now that a PAM waveform is captured, and ready to send, the original signal is recovered at the other end with another low-pass filter. The second filter removes all the

Figure 10.5
Pulse amplitude modulation.

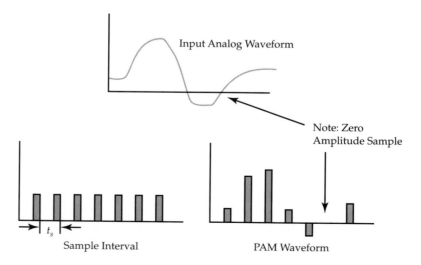

Figure 10.6
PAM circuit implementation.

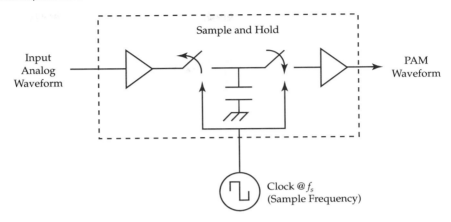

high-frequency harmonics of the pulse train, essentially connecting the dots, or in this case, the tops of the pulses to form a smoothly varying, continuous waveform that closely represents the original. Getting it as close as possible is a big part of the game, but nothing is absolutely perfect, so just make it as close as possible within the constraints of insight, time, and money. An illustrative PAM modulator and demodulator is shown in Figure 10.8. Note that the communications channel is not considered to contribute any noise or distortion to the signal as it passes through it from source to destination.

The only remaining question is How is the cutoff frequency for the second LPF chosen? To a first approximation, it is selected to be identical to the first LPF. If you think about it, this makes sense; if the first filter got rid of unwanted frequencies, it must have passed all the desired frequencies, so it will do the same thing on the other end.

Now a couple of caveats; first, the choice of the LPF is not so easy; the passband characteristics and corner frequency are also of interest and need to chosen carefully for best performance. Sometimes these are purposely altered to compensate for modulation

Figure 10.7
PAM circuit with antialiasing filter added.

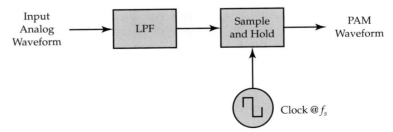

Figure 10.8
PAM modulator and demodulator.

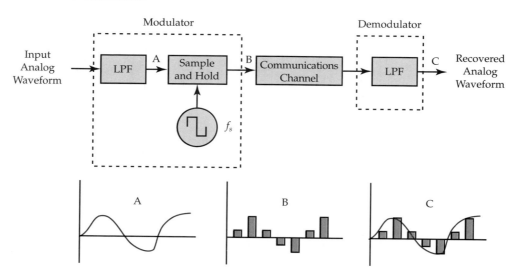

effects and channel degradations; almost certainly in any real system they will not be identical. Second, this system has no provision for noise; it assumes a perfect channel.

Third, the design of the sample and hold circuitry also has an impact. For example, just how instantaneous is that sampling anyway? Maybe more important, how instantaneous does it have to be to meet the specifications? Finally, you may choose to change the sample rate to improve the circuit, have more points to allow greater frequency coverage, but this usually costs money.

A good question to ask is where is the trade-off point where people will pay more for more performance, as compared to that point where the performance is acceptable, just make it as inexpensive as possible. This last concern is present in every system; it is not special to PAM. It is important to take the opportunity to point this out whenever possible; very often it determines success or failure in the marketplace. You might ask yourself, If the product line fails, just how secure is my paycheck?

■ ANALOG AND DIGITAL COMPARISON

The modulation of analog waveforms into digital pulses and recovering and reconverting them back into analog waveforms is the main focus of this chapter. This activity takes place in many digital communications systems. Remember, all real-life systems are analog in nature. Digital techniques may be used to move digitized replicas of them from one place to another, because digital techniques offer several advantages over analog techniques of transmission and reception, but in the end and at the beginning, analog waveforms are required. As you might have guessed from the above discussion on sampling theory, A/D and D/A converters are key components. However, a simple-minded approach of just doing the conversion does not yield the best overall system.

The first thing to capture here is that when a comparison between analog and digital is made, the subject is *not* analog inputs versus digital inputs. The difference of interest is in using analog modulation schemes such as AM, FM, and PM compared to digital modulation schemes studied in this chapter. These modulation schemes can be used to transmit digital or analog data from source to destination. The key item is the relative advantages and disadvantages of these two basic approaches.

Analog modulation and demodulation has only one real advantage today: It consumes less bandwidth for a given input bandwidth than digital techniques. Virtually every other advantage lies with digital transmission techniques. Much of this advantage is due to the technology available today. Thirty years ago, the story would have been much different, and it may be different again in 30 years if optical techniques evolve in certain ways. The technology that makes such a difference is the availability of digital ICs in large numbers and at low cost. These devices are very reliable as compared to analog components and lack the periodic tuning that many analog designs inherently require for optimum performance.

However, it is not only that cheap flip-flops and the like can be purchased. It is also that coding techniques work to help digital schemes and because the data is already in binary form, applying coding theory to improve signal-to-noise ratios is not cumbersome, and the designs mesh nicely. Additionally, coding can be used for encrypting, and making the transmission secure becomes for some applications a critical advantage. Coding will be discussed in a later chapter.

One other major advantage of digital techniques is that much larger dynamic ranges are possible when using large numbers of bits to store amplitude values. If you have a CD player and cassette player, you can compare the specifications between the two for dynamic range. The CD player, utilizing 16 bit PCM far outperforms the analog cassette player.

The only real disadvantage that digital implementations have that analog ones avoid is the requirement that for digital signals to be recovered accurately at the demodulator, the demodulator must accurately sample the signal. This accuracy means that it must sample the signal at the same time for each sample, relative to its position. Because the time delay between each sample can vary during transmission, synchronization is required at the demodulator. This generally means that of some kind of a PLL circuit being required.

Although analog systems *may* use some form of synchronous demodulation that also requires this type of circuitry, for digital modulation systems it is a definite requirement. This requirement adds cost and complexity to the receiver. On the other hand, because these circuits can now be implemented routinely in digital form, the cost factor is becoming less of an issue. Fundamentally, the bandwidth advantage is analog's hole card; it seems clear that analog modulation will predominate in channels where the signal is not confined to a wired or optical media (e.g., atmospheric channel). Because bandwidth is a shared resource in this environment, bandwidth utilization is a critical issue.

■ PULSE CODE MODULATION

PAM, although simple in concept, is not the best choice for modern implementations. It is an important step in understanding a very good system that is widely used: PCM. PCM uses PAM as a first stage; it makes use of PAM techniques to convert an analog waveform into a series of pulses. But PCM goes further; it actually sends a serial code word, a group of bits, for each sample. This group of bits is the output of an A/D that is sampling the waveform in just the way that the sample and hold circuit did for the PAM case. Now it is clear why the number of bits that determine the amplitude resolution are important. Did you wonder what happened to rule 3 in the previous discussion where we used a sample and hold circuit instead of an A/D?

Recall that in the sample and hold case, a capacitor was used to store the sampled voltage. To convert to an all digital design, you must carefully determine how many bits are needed to sample the amplitude accurately enough for the system objectives. PCM sends this group of bits, called a PCM code word, at every sampling interval. Typically, it first serializes the PCM code word and sends a stream of data bits at every sampling interval.

Furthermore, this group of bits, which is sent for every sample, gives a good way of accurately representing the amplitude of the pulse while sending pulses that are all the same amplitude. This is a critical point of understanding of why PCM works so well in the real world. Most communications channels work best for signals in a relatively narrow amplitude range; certainly there are preferred amplitudes that when used minimize distortion. So a big advantage of PCM over PAM, and for that matter for almost any analog system, is that all the signals sent are of the same amplitude. The varying amplitudes of the samples are represented as different PCM code words instead of pulses of different amplitudes. Table 10.1 illustrates this.

■ QUANTIZATION ERROR

Every PCM system that uses PAM techniques suffers from the same source of error. This source of error is called quantization error, and it results from the fact that an analog

Table 10.1
PAM Pulse Amplitude and PCM Code Word Representation

Input Analog Amplitude	PAM Pulse Shape	PCM Code Word	Input Analog Amplitude	PAM Pulse Shape	PCM Code Word
−3	⊓⌐	011	+0	──	100
−2	⊓⌐	010	+1	⌐⌐	101
−1	⌐⊓⌐	001	+2	⌐⌐	110
−0	──	000	+3	⌐⌐	111

waveform can take on an infinite number of values, whereas any digital approximation can take on only some fixed number of values. The number of values a digital approximation can take on is determined by the number of bits in the A/D converter.

As you may recall from your classes on digital systems, A/D converters give a stair-step approximation of the input waveform; the smaller the stair-steps, the better and the more expensive the A/D. Quantization error is defined as half of the step size of the converter. This is represented mathematically in equation 10-4:

$$\text{quantization error} = \frac{\text{step size of A/D converter}}{2} \qquad \textbf{(10-4)}$$

One always wants to minimize the quantization error in any system design. The quantization error is a key component in determining the signal-to-noise ratio of both linear and nonlinear PCM systems. A linear PCM system is one where the step size always stays the same; a nonlinear one is where the step size varies according to some rule.

For now, assume that all PCM systems are linear, later it will be discovered that most real implementations are not linear. These nonlinear systems are referred to as companded PCM systems. For any PCM system, better potential performance in the presence of noise is obtained as the quantization error is reduced. These calculations for companded PCM systems are complex and outside the scope of this text. However, to illustrate this concept a calculation for a linear PCM system will be performed.

■ EXAMPLE 10.3

The number of bits used in the A/D converter indicates the number of bits used for the magnitude portion of the PCM code word. It also indicates the amplitude resolution or step size. Any step voltage used is an approximation of the actual input to the A/D. That error is called quantization error. For a certain PCM system an 8 bit A/D converter is used with a step size of 0.2 V. What is the quantization error?

$$\text{quantization error} = \frac{\text{step size}}{2} = \frac{0.2}{2} = 0.1 \text{ V}$$

■ EXAMPLE 10.4

To further illustrate the relationship between step size and quantization error, suppose a 2 V peak analog waveform is to be sampled. The waveform has a 0 V dc offset, so a sign bit to represent the digital magnitude values that are of negative value will be needed. Assuming a 4 bit code word, size the A/D converter, compute the step size and quantization error.

Because 1 bit is used for the sign, 3 bits are used for magnitude. A 3 bit A/D converter is required. The sign bit will be detected in parallel with the converter; 3 bits means $2^3 = 8 - 1 = 7$ steps. A 2 V peak signal means a peak-to-peak voltage swing of 4 V. These two quantities are divided to obtain the step size. The quantization error is then easily obtained:

$$\text{step size} = \frac{V_{P-P}}{\text{\# of steps}} \qquad \textbf{(10-5)}$$

$$\text{step size} = \frac{4}{2^3\,2\,1} = \frac{4}{7} = 0.57$$

$$\text{quantization error} = \frac{\text{step size}}{2} = \frac{0.57}{2} = 0.285$$

A typical PCM modulator is shown in Figure 10.9. As can be seen, this is similar to the PAM design discussed earlier. The input antialiasing filter is still there, but instead of a sample and hold circuit, an A/D converter is present. Additionally, a parallel to serial converter is included that takes the parallel output of the A/D and serializes it for transmission in the communications channel. Again, the more bits in the A/D, the better the performance over any fixed range of input voltage values. More bits means lower quantization error, and better amplitude resolution.

The bottom part of Figure 10.9 illustrates how the PAM sampling of the input analog waveform converts the analog values to 4-bit digital output words. Once these are serialized, they become PCM code words. Essentially, the PCM process just takes the digitized amplitudes of the input signal and outputs them serially as digital words. Examine the digital word outputs, 0011, 1001, 0100, and compare them to the serialized code words. Note that the first sample, 0011, is sent first.

◼ NONUNIFORM QUANTIZATION

Although this design is straightforward, it is not complete. Consider how costs could be reduced while still accommodating a wide range of input voltage values. One way to keep the quantization error constant while accommodating a wider input voltage range

Figure 10.9
PCM modulator.

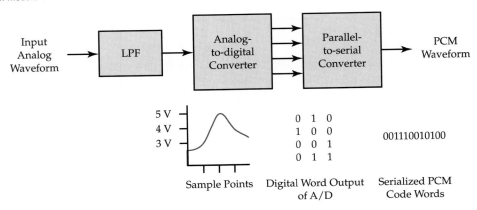

Figure 10.10
Three bit quantization.

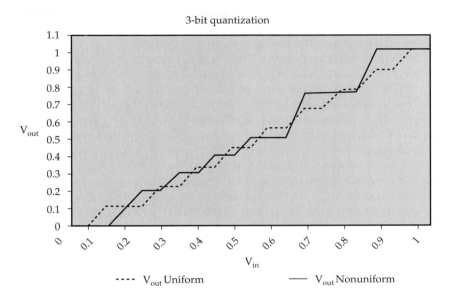

Table 10.2
Three-bit Quantization Values

V_{in}	V_{out} Uniform Quantization	V_{out} Nonuniform Quantization
0	0	0
0.05	0	0
0.1	0.11	0.1
0.15	0.11	0.1
0.2	0.11	0.2
0.25	0.22	0.2
0.3	0.22	0.3
0.35	0.33	0.3
0.4	0.33	0.4
0.45	0.44	0.4
0.5	0.44	0.5
0.55	0.55	0.5
0.6	0.55	0.5
0.65	0.66	0.75
0.7	0.66	0.75
0.75	0.77	0.75
0.8	0.77	0.75
0.85	0.88	1
0.9	0.88	1
0.95	1	1
1.0	1	1

would be to add bits to the A/D. However, this gets expensive quickly. A better way would be to compress the input signal in some way and then uncompress it on the other end. But how can this be done? It does not seem possible to compress an analog signal and still keep all the information necessary to recover it.

The answer lies in the particular application that we will investigate. Although PCM techniques are used widely in many devices and fields, virtually all telephone conversations are conducted by PCM encoding the voice waveforms and transmitting them digitally to the destination and then decoding back into an analog voice waveform. Maybe knowledge of how humans vary their voices can be used to save some bits.

Human beings generally talk in low voices on the telephone; although some scream, most telephone conversations are conducted using only about half of the dynamic range of human speech. Furthermore, people tend to expect that loudly screaming voices will be distorted and so tolerate a little amplitude distortion for very loud talking people.

Therefore, because apparently people will tolerate some distortion at high amplitudes of the input analog waveform, let's take advantage of that fact and increase the quantization error for large amplitudes. This is the central idea behind nonuniform quantizing. Traditional A/D devices always use uniform quantization; each stair-step is the same size. For the nonuniform case in this application, the steps are set small for small input voltages and large for large input voltages.

Figure 10.10 and Table 10.2 show the quantization in both the uniform and nonuniform case with the number of bits held at 3. This will allow a direct comparison of the output code words in the two approaches. As can be seen, the uniform quantization approximates a linear relationship between the input and output voltages. The nonuni-

Figure 10.11
Uniform and nonuniform quantization.

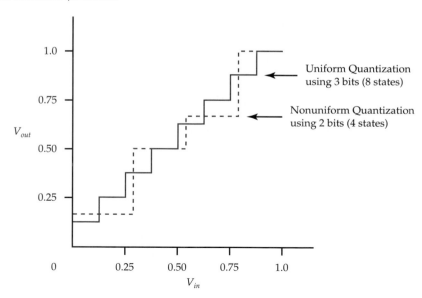

form quantization places most of its output steps at low values of the input voltage. This allows for more resolution at low input voltages.

In Figure 10.11, examine how the idea of moving to a nonlinear quantization can directly effect the number of bits that must be sent in each code word. In the figure, the two curves are approximately similar, but in the uniform case there are 8 states, whereas in the nonuniform case, there are only 4. Note that each series of stairsteps covers the entire dynamic range of the input signal but that in the uniform case 8 binary states are required, whereas in the nonuniform case, only 4 binary states are required. This results in a savings of 1 bit for each sample.

Notice in the nonuniform case that 3 of the 4 bits are used for amplitudes of less than 70% of the total dynamic range of the input signal. These amplitudes are approximately 0.15, 0.45, and 0.70 V in this example. This result gives good amplitude resolution for normal speech, close to the number of states in the uniform case. Notice that the entire upper 30% of dynamic range is represented by only 1 bit, or 25% of its states. This points out the difference between the nonuniform quantization approach and the uniform approach, which requires 50% of its states and, hence, bits to lie in that range.

Therefore good amplitude resolution or quantization is obtained for that portion of the dynamic range of the input that concerns us, with a significant cost savings. This is accomplished by changing the word size of the A/D. It is reduced by 1 bit, which in this example is a 33% savings in bits transmitted. On the other end we also save that same bit in the D/A required, another cost savings with little system impact.

EXAMPLE 10.5

Suppose one uses companding to reduce the PCM word size by 2 bits. What is the information flow impact on a system that originally used 8 bits but now requires only 6 bits? Assume an original data rate of 1 Mbps.

$$\text{original number of words transmitted} = \frac{\text{data rate}}{\text{word size}} = \frac{1 \text{ Mbps}}{8 \text{ bits}} = 125,000 \text{ words/sec}$$

$$\text{new number of words transmitted} = \frac{\text{data rate}}{\text{word size}} = \frac{1 \text{ Mbps}}{6 \text{ bits}} = 166,666 \text{ words/sec}$$

As can be seen, a significant improvement in amount of information flow occurs for the same data rate by using a shorter PCM code word. Clearly, companding is an important technique.

It is clear that one way to optimize a PCM system is to employ nonuniform quantization. One might ask Are there other ways to optimize as well? The answer is Yes, a choice was skipped over earlier and was not addressed. The A/D converter output was simply converted to a serial steam of bits. In that process it was assumed that no further optimization on the assumed binary output of the A/D would be exercised. The binary sequence would be directly serialized. Now this will work, of course, but in doing so a fundamental part of what makes PCM work so well is being overlooked.

Why not explore applying an alternate binary code? There are many transformations that could be made to a standard binary code that would improve the overall performance of the PCM system. Two that will be discussed are the folded Gray code and the code typically used in commercial implementations of CODECs, the folded binary code. Table 10.3 summarizes how these codes work.

There are a couple of things about Table 10.3 that are important to notice. The first column shows the input analog voltage thresholds where the digital output code will change. Note that there are two values for zero, $+0$ and -0. Most codes need to be able to handle both positive and negative input voltages, so every code needs a sign bit. Symmetry requires that if there is any output for zero input, there must be two versions of it, one with a positive sign bit and one with a negative sign bit. In all the codes shown, the first bit position is a sign bit, 1 for positive values and 0 for negative values.

The first code column, a traditional binary code, will output 000 for its most negative input and 111 for its most positive. The second column, the folded Gray code, has the property of only changing 1 bit between adjacent code positions. So 100 and 000 represent the smallest input magnitudes, sign respective, and the codes changes by 1 bit position as greater input magnitudes are seen. The third column, the folded binary code, has the same code outputs as the Gray code for the smallest input magnitude and just counts binary up as the magnitude increases.

Note that both the folded Gray code and the folded binary code are 100% symmetric about zero, whereas the binary code is not. (This symmetry about zero is what gives rise to the adjective folded. Any code that exhibits this property is known as a folded code.) This symmetry offers some cost savings not only when encoding the code in the transmitter but also when decoding the code at the receiver. The idea is to design a simple circuit to detect sign, strip it, and remember it, followed by a single circuit for decoding the magnitude portion. The magnitude is then inverted or not depending on the state of the sign bit. Virtually all real implementations use some form of folded code.

By not requiring the D/A converter to interpret the sign bit, one obtains a reduction in the complexity of the D/A converter required for each receiver. Simply by using a folded code and absorbing the expense of a simple circuit to detect the status of the sign bit, the cost of the D/A in every receiver is reduced.

Table 10.3
PCM Codes

A/D Input Voltage	3 Bit, Sign-Magnitude, PCM Code Words		
	Binary Code	Folded Gray Code	Folded Binary Code
$+3$	111 (7)	110 (+3)	111 (+3)
$+2$	110 (6)	111 (+2)	110 (+2)
$+1$	101 (5)	101 (+1)	101 (+1)
$+0$	100 (4)	100 (+0)	100 (+0)
-0	011 (3)	000 (−0)	000 (−0)
-1	010 (2)	001 (−1)	001 (−1)
-2	001 (1)	011 (−2)	010 (−2)
-3	000 (0)	010 (−3)	011 (−3)
Position of sign bit	|	|	|

■ CODE WORD LENGTH

The number of bits chosen to use to encode the A/D output has several important consequences. It determines the resolution of the PCM system, its performance in noise, and its bandwidth. So the number of bits used or, as it is referred to, the length of the PCM code word or even just PCM word, has a big impact on system performance. Generally, the longer the code word, the better the system performance both in precision and performance in noise, but the wider the bandwidth required, the greater the cost. So understanding how these change with the code word is an important step in understanding how PCM systems work.

Quantization Error

Although quantization error has already been discussed, it is prudent to include a short discussion here in the context of all the factors that influence the choice the number of bits in a PCM code word. First, the number of bits used in the code word is determined from the number of bits output by the A/D converter. As has already been discussed, the number of bits output from an A/D determine its amplitude resolution, or step size. Typically, the same output step voltage results from a range of values of the input signal. So, any step voltage used is an approximation to the actual value input to the A/D. The error that results from this approximation is, as you already know, called quantization error, and the process of assigning the code to the input value is called quantizing. See Figure 10.12.

Figure 10.12
Quantization error.

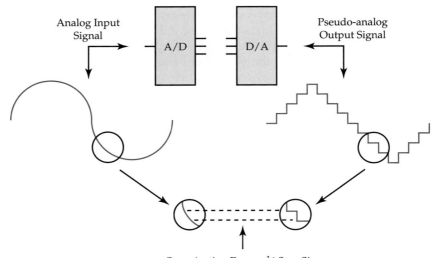

Quantization Error = $\frac{1}{2}$ Step Size

As can be seen from the figure, the quantization error does not appear until the A/D in the receiver converts the digital code back to an analog signal. Therefore, this error is not an effect of the channel but of the actual PCM encoding and decoding process. This means that it will add to whatever other sources of error that might creep in through filtering, transmission, and so forth. It is a fundamental component of error in any PCM system.

Quantization Noise

The second impact that code word length has is that the longer the code word, the better the performance in the absence of noise. As discussed in the last section, every PCM system has one source of error, the quantization error. The other main source of error *not* due to the channel environment, which introduces bit errors in the PCM code word and hence amplitude error at the output is a relationship between signal to noise ratio (S/N) and word length. This second source of error is known as quantization noise.

There is a special rule called the 6 dB rule that applies to PCM systems. It says that for each additional bit you add to the code word, you get an additional 6 dB S/N performance improvement at the reproduced analog output. That means that for a 2 bit code word, the S/N performance would be 12 dB, for a 3 bit word, 18 dB, and so forth. So only using a few bits, good S/N performance results.

Why S/N is being discussed when it has been stated that this effect is not due to channel effects, and is usually described as some kind of noise? Well, S/N ratios have theoretical maximums, and if you do not provide for sufficiently large theoretical S/N ratio, you can never get them big enough once they start being degraded by the noisy channel. The 6 dB rule allows calculation of the maximum S/N that can be expected in a perfect environment. Channel effects will always reduce this.

PCM Bandwidth

The third major effect that code word length has on PCM systems is the relationship between word length and bandwidth required for transmission. This is actually a relationship between bit rate and bandwidth, but because the longer the code word, the faster the bit rate, everything else held equal, it can be talked about in either way. The bit rate is just equal to the number of bits in the code word times the sampling rate of the converter because each sample will produce one code word output from the A/D encoder circuit. It is known from the discussion on sampling theory that the sample rate must be at least twice the maximum frequency component in the input signal. So, the minimum bandwidth required by a PCM signal is defined as shown below:

$$\text{PCM bandwidth} = \text{bit rate} \geq N * f_{\text{sample}} \qquad \textbf{(10-6)}$$

$$\text{PCM bandwidth} \geq N * 2 * BW_1 \qquad \textbf{(10-7)}$$

where N = number of bits in PCM code word
f_{sample} = sampling rate $\leq 2 * BW_I$
BW_I = bandwidth of input analog signal

This is an important result that shows that the bandwidth of the PCM signal is always at least twice (and usually more) the bandwidth of the input analog signal. This is one of the only reasons not to use digital transmission. It is always true that a digital transmission takes up more bandwidth in the channel than an analog one if the modulating signal is held constant. However, the other benefits of digital transmission usually outweigh this single disadvantage. The benefits are the cost saving from using digital components, performance improvements possible through coding techniques, and no accumulation of noise because of analog repeaters almost always dominate for wired media.

■ EXAMPLE 10.6

Find the minimum PCM bandwidth for a system with an analog signal maximum frequency of 10 kHz and using an 8 bit PCM word. Then determine the maximum theoretical signal to noise ratio using the 6 dB rule:

$$\text{PCM BW} \geq N * 2 * \text{BW}_I = (8)(2)(10 \text{ kHz}) = 160 \text{ kHz}$$

Before the signal to noise ratio is computed, think a moment about the result obtained above. Recall earlier when digital transmissions were discussed and compared to analog. At that time the only real disadvantage of digital techniques of modulation was given as the amount of bandwidth they required as compared to analog modulation techniques.

For a DSB AM modulation the bandwidth required would be only 20 kHz, and for a SSB modulation choice, only 10 kHz. For any reasonable modulation index an angle modulated waveform would also require less bandwidth. In some applications this bandwidth advantage is critical and should not be overlooked. It is almost always true that bandwidth is a critical issue for systems designed to work in atmospheric or unguided channels, especially those like cellular telephone or satellite television. On the other hand, a system designed to work on a guided channel like twisted pair wiring it does not make so much difference. An example is the telephone system. These results are summarized Table 10.4, where the modulation frequency is taken to be 10 kHz.

The signal-to-noise ratio is given by the number of bits in the PCM code word:

$$\text{S}/\text{N}_{\text{max}} = N * 6 \text{ dB} = (8)(6 \text{ dB}) = 48 \text{ dB}$$

Table 10.4
Bandwidth Comparison of Modulation Techniques

Modulation Technique	Bandwidth Comparison (kHz)
AM-DSB	20
Narrowband FM (2 sidebands)	40
PCM	160

■ COMPANDING

The next thing to discuss about PCM systems is companding. Actually, this was touched on briefly above when nonuniform quantization and its usefulness in enhancing resolution in a portion of an input dynamic ranges were pointed out. The United States, Canada, and Japan have agreed to use one rule for this nonuniform quantization, called the μ-law. In Europe and most of the rest of the world, they have standardized on a slightly different rule for this called the A-law. Both are very similar and the practice of applying them is known as companding.

Companding is nonuniform quantization, and it results in the compression and then expansion of the input signal. The word is formed from *com*pressing and then ex-*panding*, producing yet another term formed from an expression of the physical processes that it describes. Essentially, larger amplitude signals, the loud voices discussed above, are "amplified" less than those of lower amplitude. This variable "amplification" effect is accomplished by applying fewer code decision points in the large amplitude input range and making use of the extra resolution offered for low-amplitude signals. Figure 10.13 shows how this works; it illustrates both the μ-law and A-law standards. They are very close.

These figures are just simple V_{in} versus V_{out} types of graphs. The values of μ and A are set by agreement but of course can take on any value desired. In the United States, Canada, and Japan μ is set at 255. In Europe and most everywhere else, A is set at 100. In a way, this points out just how profound the difference in unit preferences between the United States and Europe is. Note the number used in the United States is odd and has no relation to anything except that it is easily implemented in an 8 bit counter. On the other hand, the European quantity was set at 100, a nice even, metriclike number, and the equation was adjusted so that good performance would result with A set equal to 100. The two equations are shown below. Both approaches closely emulate a logarithmic response curve.

Figure 10.13
The μ-law and A-law standards.

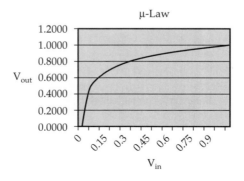

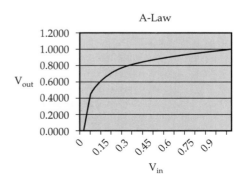

$$\mu\text{-law} \qquad |V_o| = \frac{\ln[1 + \mu\,|\,V_i\,|]}{\ln[1 + \mu]} \qquad 0 \le |\,V_i\,| \le 1 \tag{10-8}$$

$$\text{A-law} \qquad |V_o| = \frac{A\,|\,V_i\,|}{1 + \ln A} \qquad 0 \le |\,V_i\,| \le \frac{1}{A} \tag{10-9}$$

$$|V_o| = \frac{1 + \ln[A\,|\,V_i\,|]}{1 + \ln A} \qquad \frac{1}{A} \le |\,V_i\,| \le 1 \tag{10-10}$$

Note that the input voltage is always taken as its absolute value, or is always positive. This is because the only concern is with magnitude because the sign bit is always added to the code word after the companding. This retains the sign of the input signal. Additionally, note that the crossover point for the right expression to use for the A-law is V_{in} equal to 0.1 V.

■ **EXAMPLE 10.7**

Find the output voltage for a μ-law companding if the input voltage is 0.5 V and $\mu = 255$:

$$|V_o| = \frac{\ln[1 + \mu\,|\,V_i\,|]}{\ln[1 + \mu]} = \frac{\ln[1 + 255\,|(0.5)|]}{\ln[1 + 255]} = \frac{4.86}{5.54} = 0.875 \text{ V}$$

Figure 10.14
Curves for μ-law.

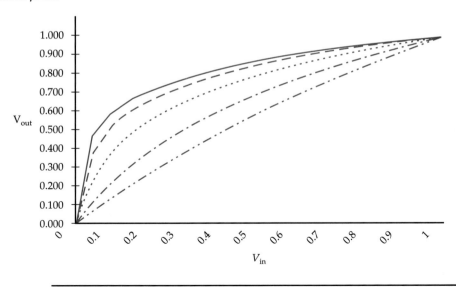

Now do the same problem but set the input voltage to -0.5 V. Note that the result is the same. The values given by these equations always have a positive magnitude. Negative values are generated by applying a negative sign bit to the positive magnitude:

$$|V_o| = \frac{\ln[1 + \mu \,|\, V_i \,|]}{\ln[1 + \mu]} = \frac{\ln[1 + 255 \,|(-0.5)|]}{\ln[1 + 255]} = \frac{4.86}{5.54} = 0.875 \text{ V}$$

Figure 10.14 illustrates what the μ-law curves look like for various values of μ. These curves were generated by using the equations presented above. The linear "curve" that is the lowest shown is for $\mu = 1$, the next $\mu = 5$, then $\mu = 25$, 100, and 255, respectively. Note the large output values for small input voltages and the little change in the output for larger input values.

■ DYNAMIC RANGE

The next thing about PCM systems to be discussed is how the number of bits is selected for a given input dynamic range. The dynamic range of a signal is the logarithmic ratio of the maximum divided by the minimum amplitude level that the signal can obtain. Because dynamic range is an easily measured quantity, it would be nice to be able to calculate how many bits the minimum PCM code word would require to accommodate it. This would let us estimate the bandwidth and bit rate from the input dynamic range specification, which is typically supplied or easily measured.

The calculation is straightforward. For example, to keep the quantization error constant if the dynamic range of the input range doubles, you must double the number of "steps." This adds one to the number of bits in the code word. Additionally, equation 10-11 will give the number of bits required for the magnitude variation of the input signal to be sampled.

$$V_{DR} = \frac{V_{max}}{V_{min}} = 2^N - 1 \tag{10-11}$$

where $V_{DR} = $ voltage dynamic range of input analog signal. If the use of a sign bit is required, it must be added. Sometimes you may see dynamic range defined as a logarithmic ratio of voltages. The voltage dynamic range is related to the dynamic range in the following way:

$$DR \text{ (dB)} = 20 \log \frac{V_{max}}{V_{min}} = 20 \log V_{DR} \tag{10-12}$$

Therefore, be careful when applying these formulas; make sure you know whether one is talking about dynamic range as a ratio of voltages or as a decibel value. If one expresses the dynamic range as a ratio of voltages, a nice relationship for the number of bits required can be developed from equation 10-11 and is shown in equation 10-13:

$$V_{DR} = 2^N - 1$$

$$\log(V_{DR} + 1) = \log(2^N) = N \log(2)$$

$$N = \frac{\log(V_{DR} + 1)}{\log(2)} \tag{10-13}$$

■ EXAMPLE 10.8

For a dynamic range of 15 dB, how many magnitude bits are needed in a PCM code word? First, find the voltage dynamic range to apply equation 10-12 and then use equation 10-13 to find the number of bits required:

$$DR \text{ (dB)} = 20 \log(V_{DR}) \rightarrow V_{DR} = 10^{(15/20)} = 5.62$$

$$N = \frac{\log(V_{DR} + 1)}{\log(2)} = \frac{\log(6.62)}{\log(2)} = 2.73 \rightarrow 3 \text{ bits}$$

It should make sense to you that one always rounds up in this type of calculation. To see this ask yourself the question: If there are between three and four cups of water in a container, how many cups are required to hold all the water in the container? The answer is, of course, four.

■ EXAMPLE 10.9

Continuing the above example, how many quantization levels would there be for 3 bits? The answer is just the power of 2 for both uniform and nonuniform quantization:

$$\# \text{ of steps} = 2^{(\# \text{ of bits})} = 2^N = 2^3 = 8$$

Next, what would be the step size of the A/D if we assume linear quantization?

$$\text{step size} = \frac{V_{DR}}{2^N - 1} = \frac{5.62}{(8 - 1)} = 0.8 \text{ V}$$

An interesting observation comes about when one realizes that the V_{min} in equation 10-11 is often the step size or resolution of the A/D converter. When this fact is combined with the observation that the V_{max} in the same equation is the peak-to-peak voltage of the input analog signal, the following result can be found by rewriting equation 10-12. This result is not so useful for calculations, but it illustrates a couple of import results.

$$V_{DR} = \frac{V_{max}}{V_{min}} = \frac{\text{peak-to-peak voltage of input analog waveform}}{\text{step size or resolution of the A/D converter}} \qquad \textbf{(10–14)}$$

This tells us that if the peak voltage doubles, the voltage dynamic range is also doubled. If the step size is halved to get more resolution, the voltage dynamic range is again doubled. The voltage dynamic range is related to the number of bits needed for the code word size. As a result, a direct relationship between peak voltage of the input waveform and number of bits needed for a particular resolution is found. The relationship also indicates an indirect relationship between the step size and the number of bits needed for a particular code word size.

■ PCM POWER

PCM is unique among the modulations studied thus far because the power is not linearly related to the spectrum, or bandwidth, of the input analog signal. That is because there is no direct relationship between the input signal and the output pulse waveform. Always before, the input analog signal could be traced through the circuitry to see how it was represented in the output waveform.

For PCM, the analog input is first changed to PAM, the last place where the relationship to the input signal is clear. When the encoding and compression are performed, the input waveforms "shape" is lost, and only a digital representation of the signal remains. The frequency content of a digital code has no relationship to the frequency content of the original sampled waveform.

For example, a PAM outputs a pulse of amplitude 5 for an input sample of the analog waveform that had amplitude 5. After the additional steps in a PCM, the code might be 1101 or 101101 or almost anything depending on the code choice and the number of bits used in the code word. The frequencies produced by these bit sequences have no relationship to the input analog signal; they only contain the information. Therefore, the shape of the waveforms produced depends only on that information, not on the original shape of the input analog signal.

So where does this leave us in determining the power? It does not depend on the analog waveshape of the input signal, but it must depend on its own pulse shape and, not unreasonably, on the bit rate. As the bit rate increases, the bandwidth required should also increase because more information is contained in the signal. Unless the way that information is represented is changed, more information means more bandwidth required. Remember, PCM uses code words, so for each sample, the number of bits used in the code word must also be considered.

Now, you may be wondering where the dependency of the pulse shape comes in because there are many different kinds of pulses that could be used. The result presented below is only valid for rectangular, polar (Non-return to zero) pulses. These are commonly used and will be assumed in all pulse modulation analyses. Refer to Chapter 6 for more information on the two pulse shapes that were discussed.

Figure 10.15
A 50% duty cycle pulse.

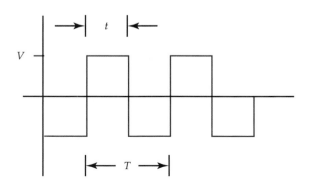

The power in a PCM signal depends on the same things that it does with the CW modulation techniques we have already discussed, such as voltage and load resistance. After all, it is just a signal like any other, and Ohm's Law holds for square waves and pulses, just as it does for analog waves. However, there is one interesting distinction when determining the power of a pulsed waveform, and that is the duty cycle of the pulses themselves. Recall the discussion in Chapter 6.

Clearly, a pulse train with a 90% duty cycle has a higher average power than a pulse train with only a 10% duty cycle. Now in PCM signals, the duty cycle is influenced by two things, the actual shape of the pulses and how many of them are 1s and how many are 0s. The first effect is illustrated in Figure 10.15 and expressed in equation 10-15.

$$P_{pcm} = (\text{pulse duty cycle})\left(\frac{V^2}{R}\right)$$

$$P_{pcm} = \frac{t}{T} * \frac{V^2}{R} \tag{10-15}$$

where $\frac{t}{T}$ = duty cycle of individual pulse.

The variables in equation 10-15 are illustrated in Figure 10.15. The expression for power in a PCM waveform is then given by the relationship shown above. If the pulses are all 50% duty cycle,

$$\text{at 50\% duty cycle, } T = 2 * t \qquad \text{and} \qquad P_{pcm} = \frac{V^2}{2R}$$

The next factor, the number of 1s and how many 0s, will be accounted for in the same way as the pulse shape factor. It is shown in equation 10-16. The use of these two equations is illustrated in the next two examples.

$$P_{pcm} = \left(\frac{\text{total \# 1s} - \text{bits}}{\text{total \# bits}}\right)(\text{pulse duty cycle})\left(\frac{V^2}{R}\right) \tag{10-16}$$

EXAMPLE 10.10

A PCM pulse train uses an 80% duty cycle pulse. The bit pattern of the pulse train is 50% 1 bits and 50% 0 bits. The peak voltage of the waveform is 5 V and the load impedance is 100 Ω. What is the power?

$$P_{pcm} = \left(\frac{\text{total \# 1 bits}}{\text{total \# bits}}\right)\left(\frac{t}{T}\right)\left(\frac{V^2}{R}\right) = \left(\frac{1}{2}\right)\left(\frac{8}{10}\right)\left(\frac{5^2}{100}\right) = 100 \text{ mW}$$

EXAMPLE 10.11

A certain PCM pulse train has been analyzed and found to contain, on average, three 1 bits for every single 0 bit. The duty cycle of each bit is 40%. The peak voltage of the pulse train is 5 V and the load impedance is 100 Ω. Find the power in the PCM waveform.

$$P_{pcm} = \left(\frac{\text{total \# 1 bits}}{\text{total \# bits}}\right)\left(\frac{t}{T}\right)\left(\frac{V^2}{R}\right) = \left(\frac{3}{4}\right)\left(\frac{4}{10}\right)\left(\frac{5^2}{100}\right) = 75 \text{ mW}$$

where the shape factor of 3/4 results from the fact that 3 out of every 4 bits were a 1 bit. This illustrates how to combine the two effects on power: just find the product of the two shape factors and insert this into the appropriate equation.

Just to be absolutely clear about the pulse duty cycle factors, examine Figure 10.16. It illustrates various shape factors or duty cycles for the bits themselves. Each of the waveforms was generated from the same logical pattern of bits.

It is also possible to use the Fourier series techniques that were explored in Chapter 6 to calculate the power spectrum. The above approach gives us an average power, but with a Fourier analysis the power spectrum can be found. The example below uses the waveform shown in Figure 10.15. The peak voltage of the waveform will be set to 5 V, the duty cycle to 50%, and the period to 1 msec. The Fourier series is as shown below:

$$\text{FS} = \frac{20}{\pi} \sin(2\pi 1 \times 10^3 t) + \frac{20}{3\pi} \sin(2\pi 3 \times 10^3 t) + \frac{20}{5\pi} \sin(2\pi 5 \times 10^3 t) + \cdots \quad \textbf{(10-17)}$$

■ PCM INTEGRATED CIRCUIT NAMING CONVENTIONS

This encoding and decoding process used by PCM gives commercial implementations the common name they are known by, CODEC. Just like modem, CODEC is a word formed by combining parts of two words that are fundamental to the operation of the device. Here the words combined are *co*ding and *dec*oding; hence CODEC. Also, newer implementations of these devices also feature the word COMBO, and just to keep you

Figure 10.16
Duty cycle and shape factor.

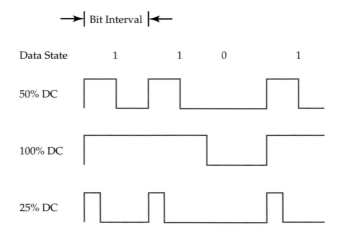

guessing, increasingly, the word CODEC is being dropped and one is left with just the name combo chip. The combo chip is just a CODEC *combi*ned with the antialiasing filtering built into the integrated circuit.

■ DIFFERENTIAL PULSE CODE MODULATION AND ADAPTIVE DIFFERENTIAL PULSE CODE MODULATION

An interesting refinement of the PCM system discussed so far is called differential pulse code modulation (DPCM). This scheme makes use of the fact that many types of analog signals do not change rapidly from sample interval to sample interval. As a result, the amplitude change must be small and the code words very "close." When this is the case, as it is for most voice and some video applications, a lot of redundant information is present in adjacent PCM code words.

Therefore, if there was a way to only represent the differences between the analog values at the sample points, amplitude resolution and hence bits could be reduced by sending only the difference from the last sample. This is where the name comes from; DPCM, sends only the differences between successive samples. Because differential is defined as "showing a difference" the name differential pulse code modulation results.

The idea is that if the range of amplitude values needed to accommodate our PCM code word shrinks, the number of bits needed to accurately represent it also shrinks. This means that the same amount of information can be sent with fewer bits with DPCM than with PCM. (Look back to the discussion on how the step size or resolution is related to code word size.) The implementation of such a system is very similar to the PCM systems already described, but the A/D conversion process only outputs a code word that represents the difference in amplitude from the last sample. Note that the circuitry must be able to sense a positive or negative difference independent of the actual magnitude of the sample.

Adaptive differential pulse code modulation (ADPCM) is a further refinement of DPCM. ADPCM is used in many telecommunications speech applications. It also works by calculating the difference between consecutive voice samples. The adaptive part comes with the use of a filter, called an adaptive filter, that allows transmission of the data at a lower rate. Typical voice systems use a 64 kbps data rate. This is arrived at by taking the product of the sample rate, 8 kHz, and the number of bits sent. ADPCM systems have similar performance at half that data rate, or 32 kbps. Instead of sending 7 bits of amplitude information, they send only 3 or 4. The savings in bandwidth explains the popularity of this method in many telecommunications voice applications.

■ DELTA MODULATION, ADAPTIVE DELTA MODULATION, AND CONTINUOUS VARIABLE SLOPE DELTA MODULATION

Three variations of delta modulation, or DM, will be briefly discussed. The first of this family is DM. This technique yields good results for slowly changing signals. In DPCM, the modulator output a code word that only depended on the difference in amplitude from the previous sample. Although the code word shrunk due to the decreased dynamic range it was required to represent, there were still several bits sent.

DM takes this same idea a step backward and ignores the actual amplitude difference. It just sends a single bit, 1 or 0, depending on whether the current sample is larger or smaller, respectively. This shrinks the PCM code word to a single bit, and for that reason this approach is sometimes not discussed as a variant of PCM but rather as a completely different technique.

This makes a certain sense because there is no attempt to gauge the absolute amplitude or, for that matter, the relative amplitude differences between successive samples. DM just outputs a 1 if the input signal is larger than the previous sample and a 0 if it is smaller. One way to look at this system is to think of it as sending only a special sort of sign bit that indicates the sign of the slope and contains no magnitude information.

Another reason why it is sometimes viewed as an alternate technique is that delta modulation in all its forms samples at the bit rate, not the Nyquist rate. This means that the sample clock used to sample the input is running at the same clock rate as the D/A. Because there is no sampling theory limitation, many view this as a completely different class of pulse modulation. Figure 10.17 illustrates a typical DM signal.

This system relies on the fact that the changes are slow and quite regular from sample instant to sample instant. If the input analog signal changes too fast, the stair-step approximation cannot keep up and will seem to lag the input analog waveform. This lagging is viewed as a distortion component and has a special name, slope overload distortion. This name comes from the observation that if the slope of the input analog waveform is too large, DM will not be able to keep up and will distort. See the Figure 10.18 for an illustration of this. What happens when the signal is changing too rapidly to be a good candidate to represent using DM is illustrated.

As can be seen, the output does not track the input well; it misses the fast rise and falling components of the input analog waveform. It also does not do a very good job of tracking the peaks and valleys of the amplitude variation. A good question is what does an input signal with a slope that is too large actually represent? It represents a signal with higher-frequency components than the sampled system was designed to handle.

Therefore, depending on the dynamic range of the input analog signal, the rate at which samples are acquired in a DM system must be altered. It should be clear to you that for large input amplitude variations, the sampling rate must be increased to avoid

Figure 10.17
Delta modulation.

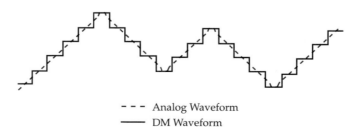

- - - Analog Waveform
——— DM Waveform

Figure 10.18
Delta modulation showing slope overload distortion.

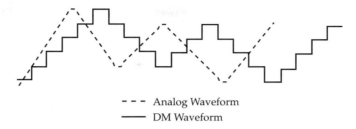

$- - -$ Analog Waveform

——— DM Waveform

slope distortion. Let's see if a simple equation can be developed that estimates when the step size will be too small for the input signal to delta modulate.

To begin this analysis, recall how slope is defined:

$$\text{slope} = \frac{y}{x}$$

$$y = \text{step size}$$

$$x = \text{sample interval} = \frac{1}{\text{sample frequency}}$$

$$\text{slope} = \frac{\text{Step size}}{\text{Sample interval}} = (\text{step size})(\text{sample frequency})$$

To go further, assume that the input analog waveform that is to be sampled is a sine wave of amplitude A, A sin(*ft*). Then the slope is just the first derivative, or *Aft* cos(*ft*). This function has a maximum value of *Af*, because the maximum value a sinusoid can have unity. Inserting this value into the equation developed above, it is found

$$\text{slope} = (\text{step size})(\text{sample frequency})$$

$$Af_i \leq (\text{step size})(f_s)$$

$$\text{step size} \geq \frac{Af_i}{f_s} \qquad \qquad \textbf{(10–18)}$$

where f_i = input signal frequency
         f_s = sample frequency

For best results keep the step size close to equality in the above relation. Also note that with DM and its variations discussed below, the first few samples are usually garbage. Because no absolute amplitude information is ever sent, until the input analog signal hits one amplitude rail or the other, the code is not valid. Once it hits a rail, the code, or bit in this case, typically synchronizes, and you have an accurate tracking.

Adaptive delta modulation (ADM) tries to overcome this by changing the rules with regard to how an A/D operates. Instead of keeping the amplitude step size con-

Table 10.5
PCM and DM Variants Comparison

Type	Concept	Restriction
DPCM	Send difference, arbitrary # bits	Slowly changing signals
ADPCM	Send difference, fewer # bits	Slowly changing signals
DM	Send difference, only 1 bit	Slow and smoothly changing signals
ADM	Send difference, arbitrary step size	Slowly changing signals
CVSDM	Send difference, arbitrary step size	Algorithm dependent

stant, the step size is varied in amplitude to track the input analog waveform. Note that there is still only 1 bit sent for each change, but the value of this bit is changed. For example, when a larger step size is required to track the input signal accurately, the code word output is still just a single bit, but it represents a larger step.

Most implementations keep track of the most recent few code word outputs, and if they stay all 1s or all 0s for a predetermined number of samples, the step size is increased or decreased, respectively, by about 50%. The number of samples before a step change is made, and the amount of the step size change varies from implementation to implementation. The typical number of consecutive samples increasing or decreasing before a step size change would be made varies from 3 to 5, and 30% to 50% is a typical percentage adjustment.

Continuously variable slope delta modulation, CVSDM, or more typically, CVSD, is a further refinement of ADM, discussed above. It is exactly similar to ADM, except that there is no predetermined number of intervals before the step size is varied, and there is no fixed amount by which the step size is varied in amplitude. This allows sophisticated algorithms to be utilized to accurately track input signal variations when the input signal is accurately characterized. For speech waveforms this analysis has been done due to its wide application in the telephone industry. Most implementations keep the 3 to 5 step rule that is typical in ADM systems.

Table 10.5 summarizes the concept and limitation of the various forms of PCM and DM discussed.

■ PULSE WIDTH MODULATION (PWM) AND PULSE POSITION MODULATION (PPM)

Pulse width modulation is closely related to its cousin, pulse position modulation. Both are further refinements of PAM. PWM is implemented by using the amplitude value of the PAM signal to vary the pulse width to transmit the amplitude information from source to destination. The larger the amplitude of the PAM pulse, the larger the duty cycles of the pulse or the larger the ratio of the high state to the low state.

PPM is also derived from the PAM waveform, except in this case, the relative position of a narrow pulse is changed depending on the amplitude of the PAM pulse. The larger the amplitude, the later in the period of the pulse does the spike occur. See Figure 10.19 for a comparison of all three of these pulse modulation techniques. It illustrates how the three basic pulse modulation types would appear if seen synchronized on an oscilloscope; note the timing relationships shown.

Figure 10.19
PAM, PWM and PPM.

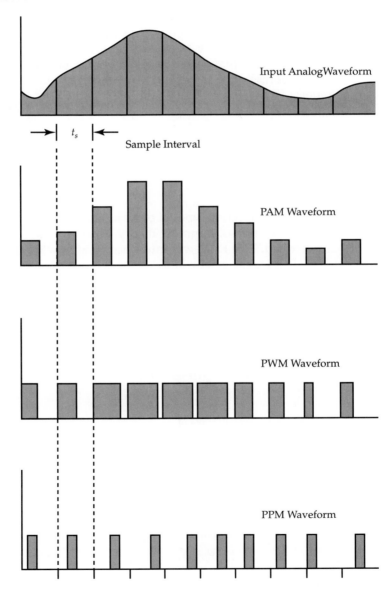

For PWM, the pulse always starts at the rising edge of the sample interval. It then stays high for a proportional amount of time corresponding to the amplitude or voltage of the input analog wave. What results is a series of pulses of constant amplitude and varying duty cycle. For PPM, the pulse starts at a proportional amount of time later in the total sample interval, again corresponding to the amplitude or voltage of the input analog wave. Here, a series of pulses of constant amplitude and duty cycle are obtained, but with varying position. The higher the amplitude, the later the pulse is positioned within the sample interval.

PWM and PPM are not widely used for transmission because they require a larger bandwidth to operate than equivalently performing PCM systems. This is because the varying width of pulses in the PWM case and the varying frequency elements produced by the change in fundamental period in the PPM case. Both require additional harmonics to accurately represent the signal and hence require more bandwidth with no payoff in signal to noise. They are presented here to illustrate more than one example of digital signaling, not as real choices as compared to PCM. As a rule of thumb, if you need to do digital transmission, use PCM and vary the number of bits to meet cost requirements. This will usually get you a system that meets the performance targets.

■ SUMMARY

In this chapter several different types of pulse modulation schemes have been explored. Following an introduction of sampling theory, an evolution of pulse modulation techniques was described. First PAM was introduced and how this was modified into PCM was illustrated. PCM is the most widely adopted type of pulse modulation. How quantization error comes about and how it effects both uniform and nonuniform or companded approaches to PCM were discussed. Power and bandwidth relationships were developed. Two variants of basic PCM and three types of delta modulation were introduced. Finally, PWM and PPM were briefly discussed.

PROBLEMS

1. For a signal with a maximum frequency component of 10 kHz, determine the minimum sampling period.

2. For an amplitude resolution of 1% how many bits would an A/D converter have to be?
  (a) A sign-magnitude converter
  (b) A magnitude only converter

3. For a sample rate of 8 kHz, determine the maximum input frequency a sampled data system could support.

4. For the following input frequencies determine if aliasing is occurring and at what frequency the alias will be seen. Assume a sampling clock speed of 20 kHz.
  (a) $f_{signal} = 8$ kHz
  (b) $f_{signal} = 10$ kHz
  (c) $f_{signal} = 12$ kHz
  (d) $f_{signal} = 16$ kHz

5. List three reasons why digital systems have an advantage over analog systems.

6. Sketch a 1 kHz sinusoid and identify the sample

points assuming a 6 kHz sample rate. Show two cycles.

7. For the same waveform as in problem 6, sketch the PAM waveform that would result. Show two cycles.

8. What is the dynamic range for an 8 bit sign magnitude A/D converter?

9. For an input dynamic range of 60 dB, find the number of bits needed in the PCM code word.

10. What is the dynamic range capability for a 16 bit sign-magnitude PCM code?

11. If the resolution of a PCM system is 1.0 V, determine the output voltages for the following 4 bit sign-magnitude PCM codes. The codes are all expressed as folded binary.
   (a) 1100   (c) 0111
   (b) 0101   (d) 1000

12. If the resolution of a PCM system is 0.5 V determine the output voltages for the following 3 bit sign-magnitude PCM codes. The codes are all expressed as folded Grey codes.
   (a) 110   (c) 011
   (b) 001   (d) 100

13. Determine the output voltage of a μ-law compander with $\mu = 255$ for the following input voltages.

Assume a maximum input voltage of 1.0 V.
   (a) 0.01   (c) 0.2
   (b) 0.1   (d) 0.6

14. Determine the output voltage of an A-law compander with A = 100 for the following input voltages. Assume a maximum input voltage of 1.0 V.
   (a) 0.01   (c) 0.2
   (b) 0.1   (d) 0.6

15. Repeat problem 13 with $\mu = 100$.

16. For a PCM system using a 6 bit code word and a sample frequency of 10 kHz, find the bandwidth of the PCM signal.

17. For a PCM system designed to operate to accomodate an input analog signal that has a dynamic range of 45 dB and a maximum frequency component of 8 kHz, find the bandwidth of the PCM signal.

18. For a PCM code word length of 6 bits, find the power in a PCM signal for a high voltage level of 5 V and a low voltage level of 0 V. The load resistance is 50 Ω. Assume a 50% duty cycle for the pulses and a bit pattern of 50% 1 bits.

19. Repeat problem 18 assuming a 25% duty cycle for the pulses.

20. Repeat problem 18 assuming a bit pattern of 75% 1 bits.

11

Multiplexing

Multiplexing has a root word, *multiple,* meaning many. The act of multiplexing is the act of combining multiple signals into a single channel or wire. This is done because the total length of wire needed to connect two places together drops dramatically if the data source is serialized rather than connecting one wire for each data source from point to point.

Imagine the number of wires needed to connect each telephone to every other one. The number and length of wire required would be tremendous. Can you imagine what it would be like if every time someone ordered a new telephone number, the telephone system would have to wire that phone directly to every other phone in the United States? What about if you wanted to call Europe or Asia? It quickly gets absurd. This is what drove the early invention and application of multiplexing, or as they are implemented in the telephone system today, switching techniques. Essentially, the need was to carry a large number of conversations on a single pair of wires; the solution was applying multiplexing, just as had been done by the telegraph system, which had faced the same problem but on a smaller scale.

Today, this same problem is very common is such fields as data acquisition and all kinds of communications. Multiplexing is one of the most powerful concepts in use today to reduce the cost of the system while maximizing the data flow. It is used very widely in the communications field in many different types of devices. The computer industry commonly uses this principle to implement advanced processing features such as parallel processing and double-width data busses, now appearing in desktop PCs. Many other examples exist.

There are several ways to implement multiplexing; the five that will be explored here are

1. Time division multiplexing, (TDM)
2. Statistical time division multiplexing (STDM)
3. Frequency division multiplexing, (FDM)
4. Code division multiplexing, (CDM)
5. Space division multiplexing (SDM)

How these different techniques are accomplished depends on how each one is done, and also on how the signals themselves are presented. For example, if all the signals to be multiplexed, or combined, were synchronous with each other, one type of system would result, whereas if they are asynchronous, another approach may be required. Although both analog and digital implementations are possible, both operate with the concept of a group of signals entering a group of switches that connect each input to the common channel in some pattern. These switches can be made using analog or digital technology. FDM approaches are commonly analog, whereas PCM/TDM approaches are commonly digital. This rule is not absolute, but it is a good guide, especially for products being designed today. The table below summarizes this situation:

	TDM	**FDM**
Signal source	Digital	Analog
Channel nature	One-time shared channel	Several exclusive mini-channels

■ TDM AND FDM

The primary difference between the two traditional approaches to this problem, TDM and FDM, is that in the TDM approach *each signal utilizes the entire bandwidth of the common channel for short periods of time.* In the FDM approach *each signal utilizes a small portion of the bandwidth of the common channel but continuously.*

Effectively, a TDM approach switches a big pipe to each source for short periods of time, and a FDM approach divides up the pipe into lots of little pipes and permanently attaches each to a single source.

One good way to understand the difference between TDM and FDM is to examine closely the television broadcast system used in the United States. One can clearly see the FDM nature of this system by recalling that each different channel has a different carrier frequency. If you receive television on cable, each of these channels rides on the same cable, divided up in frequency. That is an example of FDM. Each channel is multiplexed onto the same cable by separating them in frequency. Think again about the analogy above: The FDM approach divides up the pipe into lots of little pipes and each little pipe is a different channel.

Television also demonstrates TDM quite clearly. All programs are divided up into multiple sources. One source is the television program, and one is the commercials that are interspersed regularly throughout the same channel. Recalling the analogy above, the TDM approach switches a big pipe to each source for short periods of time. The pipe is the channel your TV is tuned to and the switching is between the program content and the commercials.

■ TDM

The simplest conceptual multiplexer is the standard TDM switch. As mentioned above, a TDM approach switches the entire bandwidth of the channel to each source for a short period of time, then goes on to the next source, and so on, until it comes back to the first one again. TDM approaches are inherently digital and work with digital data sources. Of course, analog data, such as voice, can be digitized using PCM and then can be multiplexed onto a single channel using TDM.

In this discussion, it will be assumed that any analog sources are digitized in a form similar to PCM. PAM signals can also be time division multiplexed, and it is possible to argue that PAM is not digital but analog. Here, PAM will be regarded as a multilevel digital signal because it has a finite number of output states. Therefore, when the multiplexing occurs, the data is in digital form. Figure 11.1 shows how a simple TDM system might work.

In Figure 11.1, there are three data sources connected to a rotary switch that connects to each source for a time period of 1 bit duration, so each data source contributes 1 bit to the common data source every third time slot. In modern systems, the rotary switch is implemented using digital circuitry that implements the rotary switch as an array of ON/OFF switches that, in turn, connect one input to a common bus. Many times the switches are implemented using simple transistors that are turned ON and OFF by a clock source driving a counter that has a modulus number equal to the number of data sources. The counter output is then connected to an address decoder to activate each switch in turn.

Figure 11.1
Conceptual TDM system.

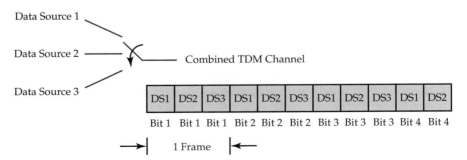

Note that there is a new item, a frame, in the Figure 11.1. A frame is usually defined as that period of time that it takes to multiplex onto a single common channel 1 bit from each data source. The frame time is an important specification of all multiplexing systems. Sometimes a few bits are added to the frame time, as defined above, to allow for special signaling to the other end of the channel where demultiplexing is usually going on. Often these extra bits are used to mark the beginning of a frame or send other synchronization data to the receiving end.

Careful examination of the diagram above will reveal that the amount of time each data source is connected to the common channel is determined by the frequency of the clock source. No set amount of time is used. Sometimes it is as in the above example; 1 bit from each data source is passed in turn. Other systems might require an entire group of bits or a word to be passed to the common channel on each clock cycle. Assuming each data source sends only one bit each period, multiplying the bit length by the number of data sources sets the clock frequency. To be sure that an accurate set of data is gathered, the state of each data source should remain static for the entire time it is connected to the common channel. This is shown in Figure 11.2.

Figure 11.2
Clocking for TDM.

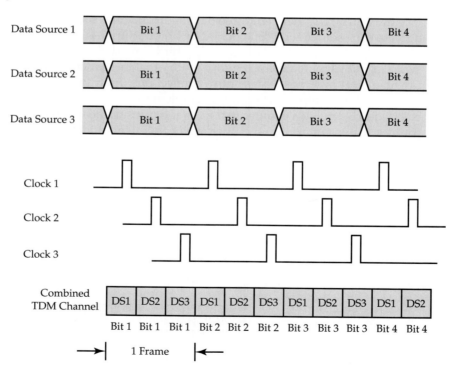

This approach would not work with analog data sources if they were not sampled first with the PCM approach. So again, TDM systems work with digital data sources. Note that in a PCM system providing the data source, the bit time in the above discussion would probably be the code word time, or the bit time multiplied by the code word length. This illustrates another important concept, that the time each source is connected to the common channel is dependent on the content of the data source. This distinction is often described as byte interleaving, as compared to the example in Figure 11.2, which shows bit interleaving. This distinction is usually a system design issue and is preset to a value that is determined from the application domain in which the device is designed to operate. Note that this assumes that the data sources are all synchronized.

■ TDM IN THE TELEPHONE SYSTEM

Perhaps the most common application of TDM is in the telephone system. There it is coupled with the PCM of analog voice signals, or analog modem signals, to concentrate the conversations of many people or data sources into a common channel or wire. How this works will be explored using real-world examples of data source multiplexing in the modern telephone system. The first of these will be the digital service level 1, (DS-1) framing on the T-1 carrier. Most telephone conversations are at some point in the transmission from source to destination in this TDM frame format.

Many times the two names T-1 and DS-1 are used interchangeably, depending on the background of the speaker. To be technically correct, refer to the particular TDM time slicing that the public switched telephone system (PSTN) has standardized on as the DS-1 format and the actual wires that carry this combined data source as a T-1 line.

So, what exactly is this DS-1 format? It is a grouping of 24 PCM encoded voice-band signals or channels. Each of the channels is represented by an 8 bit PCM code and is sampled at a rate of 8 kHz. This results in a data rate for each channel of

$$\text{data rate} = (\text{word length})(\text{sample rate}) \qquad \textbf{(11-1)}$$

$$64 \text{ kbps} = 8 \text{ bits} * 8 \text{ kHz}$$

If 24 of these are combined, the aggregate data rate on the T-1 line is

$$\text{aggregate data rate} = (\text{number of channels})(\text{channel data rate}) \qquad \textbf{(11-2)}$$

$$1.536 \text{ Mbps} = 24 \text{ channels} * 64 \text{ kbps}$$

This is the *actual* data transfer rate of a T-1 line using the DS-1 format. However, it is not the *total* data rate because for each frame an additional framing bit is added. This framing bit is used to ensure synchronization at the receiving end. The number of bits in a frame is calculated by recognizing that there are 8 bits from each channel representing one PCM word and there are 24 channels; therefore,

$$\# \text{ bits} / \text{frame} = (\text{number of channels})(\# \text{ bits} / \text{channel}) \qquad \textbf{(11-3)}$$

$$192 \text{ bits} = 24 \text{ channels} * 8 \text{ bits} / \text{channel}$$

Add one framing bit and you end up with 193 bits per frame. Now to determine the total data rate, just multiply the number of bits in each frame by the sample rate for each channel, or

$$\text{line rate} = [(\# \text{ of channels})(\#\text{bits/channel}) + \text{frameing bit (s)}](\text{sample rate}) \quad \textbf{(11-4)}$$

$$\text{line rate} = (\# \text{ bits/frame})(\text{sample rate}) = (\# \text{ bits/frame})(\text{frame rate}) \quad \textbf{(11-5)}$$

$$\text{line rate} = 193 \text{ bits/frame} * 8 \text{ kHz} = 1.544 \text{ Mbps}$$

This total data rate is usually referred to as the line rate or line speed (less accurately) of a T-1 line.

Note that there are other ways of referring to the data rate of a T-1 line using DS-1 format. One way is to talk about the frame rate. The frame rate is the same as the sample rate of each channel, or 8 kHz. It may not be immediately clear why the frame rate is always the same as the sample rate of each channel.

When analyzing this, it may be helpful to think about it by realizing that because each channel is sampled at the same rate, it samples for the same length of time, here 8 bits. Then combine that observation with the fact that each channel is sampled only once each pass. This demands that the frame rate be identical to the sampling rate of each channel, because each frame is built by sampling each channel at the sampling rate of that channel. This is the reason why frame rate is often used to describe multiplexing systems of this type. The frame rate is a direct reading of the sample rate of each channel and is a fundamental descriptive component of any sampling system. Figure 11.3 shows a detailed breakdown of the DS-1 format.

The times shown are calculated by recognizing that the frame rate is 8 kHz, so the frame time is just the inverse of that number, or 125 μsec. This result applies equation 11-1:

$$\text{frame time} = \frac{1}{\text{frame rate}} = \frac{1}{\text{sample rate}} = \frac{1}{8 \text{ kHz}} = 125 \ \mu\text{sec}$$

Dividing that by 193 bits gives the bit time, or

$$\text{bit time} = \frac{\text{frame time}}{\# \text{ bits/frame}} \quad \textbf{(11-6)}$$

$$\text{bit time} = \frac{125 \ \mu\text{sec}}{193 \text{ bits}} = 0.647 \ \mu\text{sec}$$

■ CLEAR CHANNEL CAPACITY

Clear channel capacity is a term used to describe how much of the DS-1 frame can actually be filled with customer data. Although the calculations above accurately describe the bit times and number of bits in a DS-1 frame, they do not give a clear indication of how much data can actually be sent from source to destination. It turns out that the eighth bit in each PCM word that represents the voice conversation is not always representing voice.

Figure 11.3
DS-1 format.

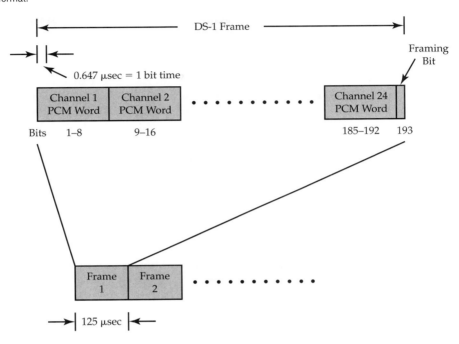

Each sixth frame's least significant PCM bit is "robbed" and used to signal the on or off-hook status. A 1 value for this bit signals on-hook, and a 0 value for this bit signals off-hook. This status tells the telephone system if the call is still in progress. It is called robbed bit signaling and although it theoretically results in some distortion for the unfortunate caller who is using that particular frame, the distortion is not noticeable. The robbed bit signaling data rate is easily calculated:

$$\text{Robbed bit data rate} = (1 \text{ channel})(8 \text{ kbps}) = 8 \text{ kbps} \qquad \textbf{(11-7)}$$

It does have an important consequence if a DS-1 frame is being used for transmitting data. Because it is generally desirable to have each frame contain the same amount of data, in reality there are only 7 bits of data capacity in each PCM word. This means that the clear channel capacity of each data frame is only 56 kbps. This result modifies the aggregate data rate calculation performed earlier for the DS-1 frame format. The clear channel aggregate data rate is given by

$$\text{clear channel aggregate data rate} = (24 \text{ channels})(56 \text{ kbps}) = 1.344 \text{ Mbps} \qquad \textbf{(11-8)}$$

Note that this effectively reduces the data transfer rate by 24 times the robbed bit data rate, or 192 kbps per DS-1 frame. This clearly shows how appropriately named robbed bit signaling is, it robs bits from the customer channel to the signal.

■ SUPERFRAMES

There are several formats used here and abroad. Table 11.1 summarizes the standards in the United States. The nomenclature for T carrier and F carrier is just that if a T precedes the physical line type, it is a copper line. If an F precedes it, it is a fiber line. The DS level sets the data rate and frame format. The carrier type, T or F, sets the type of line.

Note that the DS level data rate does not rise as an exact multiple of the number of channels. For all DS levels additional framing characters are inserted, just as they are for the DS-0 to DS-1 bundling. The only constant across all DS frames is that each contains some integer multiple of DS-0 frames. This is because the DS-0 frame represents one telephone call and is the worldwide standard for digitizing one voice conversation using a 8-bit PCM word sampled at 8 kHz, resulting in a 64 kbps data rate.

It is also useful to understand how these DS-1 frames are combined. Two groups of frames will be discussed. The first is the D-4 frame called a superframe, which is a group of 12 DS-1 frames. The D-4 format is the most popular version of these formats and is used widely in the United States. This frame format is shown in Figure 11.4. The superframe is made up of 12 individual frames, with the 193rd bit of each frame used as a control bit. In the discussion above it was called the framing bit; both names are in common use. These 12 bits, one from each individual frame, are combined and used to synchronize and manage the T-1 line signals.

As can be seen from Figure 11.4, the D-4 frame consists of 12 DS-1 frames arranged into what is called a superframe or sometimes a superframe format. The superframe is useful because of synchronization advantages that come about due to how it is constructed. This synchronization is important because it allows the receiver to synchronize from the incoming bit stream.

To understand this, it is important to know that the 12 framing bits, 1 per each frame, are not arbitrary when the DS-1 frames are combined into a D-4 superframe. Instead, each frame's framing bit is specified to a particular value. This creates a recognizable bit pattern, embedded in the incoming bit stream. The pattern that is used for

Figure 11.4
D-4 framing.

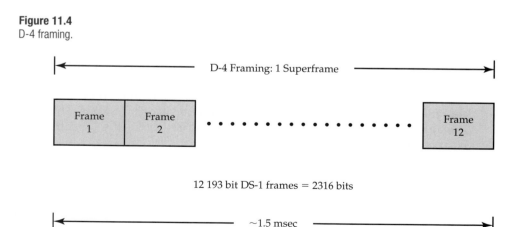

12 193 bit DS-1 frames = 2316 bits

~1.5 msec

Table 11.1
DS Level Summary

DS Level	T/F Carrier	Data Rate	Number of Channels
DS-0	N/A	64 kbps	1 DS-0
DS-1	T-1	1.544 Mbps	24 DS-0
DS-2	T-2	6.312 Mbps	96 DS-0
DS-3	T-3	44.736 Mbps	672 DS-0
DS-4	T-4	274.176 Mbps	4032

D-4 framing is 100011011100. When this pattern is recognized by the receiving station, it can easily synchronize to a bit and frame boundary by matching this pattern. Without this type of synchronization contained in the bit stream, the multiplexing described could not be synchronized and the full duplex, synchronous nature of voice telephone calls would not be possible.

The other frame format that will be discussed is another version of the superframe. This format is replacing the D-4 superframe in many wide area network (WAN) applications today because it offers some enhanced performance capabilities for data sources other than voice. Additionally, it provides a better way for T-1 providers to measure overall system performance. It does not address the clear channel capacity issue. This evolved superframe is known as the extended superframe format (ESF). ESF extends the superframe to twenty-four 193 bit frames. Just like the D-4 framing, the 193rd bit of each frame is reserved for control. But other differences exist; ESF is not just twice D-4.

The 24 control bits, one from each of the 24 frames, are now redefined. These 24 bits, one from each frame, have an aggregate data rate of 8 kbps. Of this data rate, 6 kbps, or 18 of the 24 control bits, are redefined. This is best understood by looking at the 24 bits as a kind of control frame. Then the three groups of bits are described as follows:

1. Two kbps (6 bits) is dedicated for framing and signaling. This provides the same functionality present in the D-4 frame format and provides backward compatibility. These are the bits that stayed the same.
2. Two kbps (6 bits) is dedicated for a CRC-6 code to accomplish error detection and correction due to any of a number of sources, including equipment errors, lightning, and so forth.
3. Four kbps (12-bits) is dedicated for a data link. This link is used to provide all kinds of enhanced functionality in the areas of diagnostics, remote switching, control, and many optional feature groups that are constantly being redefined by manufacturers.

To summarize, 24 frames contribute 24 control or framing bits. All these are not used to provide the management and synchronization of the frames like the D-4 case. In ESF framing, 18 out of the 24 bits are used to evaluate circuit performance. Six keep their traditional function. Six are used to detect and allow correction of error in the data. These 6 bits function as a 6 bit cyclic redundancy check (CRC) code; Chapter 12 explains

Figure 11.5
ESF.

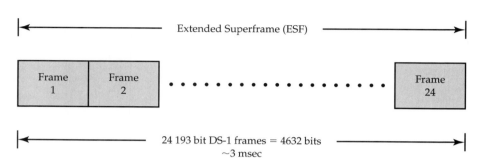

how this works. The other 12 bits are used to implement a 4 kbps data link for communicating between the two ends of the communication link. Typically that is between two D-4 channel banks or specialized TDM multiplexers. The construction of the ESF is shown in Figure 11.5.

Do not confuse D-4 framing with D-4 channel banks; D-4 framing is a technique to combine PCM frames on a T-1 line for use with channel banks. There are several types of specialized TDMs that are called channel banks, and at least one type is specifically designed to work with the D-4 framing, so it is often called a D-4 channel bank. This is a misuse of terminology that confuses more than it helps. For professionals in the field, it is a convenient form of shorthand and so understandable.

Before examining a particular type of TDM multiplexer, the critical importance of PCM to TDM techniques must be emphasized. For TDM to work, it must have digital data sources to multiplex. Any digital data sources, synchronous or asynchronous, can be handled. PCM is the technique to digitize, with arbitrary accuracy, any analog signal that needs to be multiplexed. This extends the application of this multiplexing technique to virtually any signal source, analog or digital. As a result, TDM is widely used in all kinds of applications, not just the telephone system.

■ ADD/DROP MULTIPLEXING (GROOMING)

Now that it is clear that telephone calls are digitized and combined into frames, the question arises. How do these frames, containing individual calls, add or subtract individual calls? As you might imagine not all calls in a frame necessarily come from the same location and go to the same location. So, if the calls are combined into frames to travel around the telephone system, how does any specific call get put on the right trunk and pulled off the right trunk when it arrives at the correct switching office?

The answer is that a type of time division multiplexer, called an add/drop multiplexer, is used. Using such a multiplexer to extract and add calls to a frame is called grooming (as in, He is being groomed for the chairmanship). One would groom a portion of the frame to point the way for the call location.

Figure 11.6
Add/drop multiplexing.

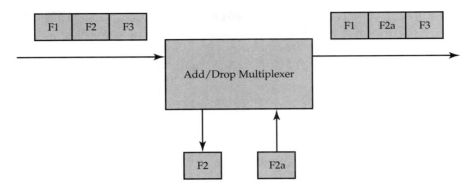

An add/drop multiplexer allows one to extract or add individual DS-0 or DS-1 frames out of a superframe structure. Although the functionality of add/drop multiplexing was described using the concept of a single call or DS-0 frame, these devices are usually designed to also work at the DS-1 level or higher. Add/drop multiplexers are primarily used by organizations to extract a DS-1 frame designated for a particular location. This allows the extraction of the information desired without demultiplexing the entire frame, extracting the information required, and then remultiplexing the remaining information. This results in significant cost savings as well as no additional delay in the circuit. This delay can become critical in a synchronous operating environment. The operation of an add/drop multiplexer is shown in Figure 11.6.

Extending TDM

In discussion so far, there were constraints on the data sources to make the concept clear. Let's now examine them and see how they can modify the TDM approach. The first assumption made was that each of the data sources was switching at the same data rate. This led us to just divide the frame up into equal slices and apply one slice to each input. But suppose one data source, say data source 2, is running at twice the data rate of the others.

Figure 11.7
TDM.

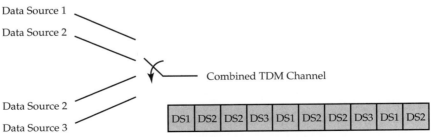

Figure 11.8
Timing relationships.

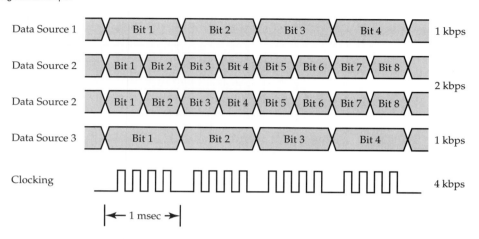

Could this be accommodated? The answer is Yes, and it would be done by just pretending that data source 2 is two data sources running at half the rate. The idea would be to just sample data source 2 twice as often as data source 1 and 3. This is shown in Figure 11.7.

This approach can handle almost any data rate as long as the various rates of the data sources have an integer relationship to each other. An integer relationship between signals just means that if the larger is divided by the smaller, a whole integer results. For example, if in Figure 11.7, data sources 1 and 3 were 1 kbps and data source 2 was 2 kbps, these two data sources have an integer relationship with each other. In this case it would be 2. The timing relationship between the data sources and the clocking rate are shown in Figure 11.8.

As can be seen from Figure 11.8 the clocking rate is just the sum of the original individual data rates from each source. For this example, the frame rate can be found by applying equation 11-9 and the clock rate by applying equation 11-10.

$$\text{frame rate} = \text{slowest data source} = \frac{1}{\text{frame time}} \tag{11-9}$$

Where

$$\text{frame time} = \text{time it takes to transmit 1 sample from each data source}$$

$$\text{clock rate} = \text{sum of data source rates} \tag{11-10}$$

In the situation shown in Figure 11.4, the frame rate is equal to the slowest data source rate or 1 kbps and the frame time is that reciprocal, or 1 ms. The clock rate is be 4 kbps. These calculations are illustrated in Example 11.1.

■ EXAMPLE 11.1

Find the clock rate, frame rate, and frame time for a TDM system with five inputs. The inputs are detailed below:

Figure 11.9
Diagram for Example 11.1.

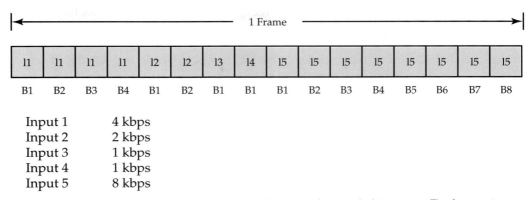

Input 1	4 kbps
Input 2	2 kbps
Input 3	1 kbps
Input 4	1 kbps
Input 5	8 kbps

The clocking rate is found by just adding up the data rates from each data source. The frame rate can be found by multiplying the number of original data sources times the slowest data source rate. The reason for this can be seen by examining Figure 11.8; each data source with a higher integer multiple of the data rate appears just that integer multiple of times. Therefore, the frame rate can be determined by the product of the slowest data source rate times the number of original data sources.

$$\text{clock rate} = 4 + 2 + 1 + 1 + 8 = 16 \text{ kbps}$$
$$\text{frame rate} = \text{slowest data rate} = 1 \text{ kbps}$$
$$\text{frame time} = 1 \text{ msec}$$

Figure 11.9 depicts this situation and is helpful in understanding the general situation.

It is also possible to make this approach work with data sources that are close to synchronous. If the sources are just a few bit times apart from being synchronous, a technique called bit stuffing is employed to make them appear synchronous to the multiplexer. Essentially, a few bits are stuffed into one or more data sources to ensure that all data sources entering the multiplexer are synchronized.

Sometimes this is done by the multiplexer itself, sometimes by the application or device sourcing the data. At the other end, the demultiplexer must be able to identify the stuffed bits and strip them before passing the data source, or the application using the data source must recognize the stuffed bits as invalid data and discard them. Depending on the application, either technique may be used.

Although bit stuffing works if the data sources are close to synchronous, situations arise where this is not the case. Usually, new designs are synchronous because it is inherently more efficient. This can be seen by realizing that bit stuffing consumes bandwidth without conveying any information.

Where the sources are not close to synchronous (e.g., each data source is not tied to the same clock source), a different approach is called for. Instead of taking 1 bit from each data source, take one character from each data source. Although this might seem similar to taking a group of bits from each data source in a synchronous environment, it has a critical difference.

In the synchronous case, the group of bits is required to have an integer relationship to any other data source. In the asynchronous case, there is no requirement that all characters be the same length or have any specific relationship to the data from another source. This results in taking a variable number of bits from each data source during each time slice.

This in turn requires that the data sources have a way of identifying to the multiplexer where the character starts and ends, usually with start and stop bits. These extra bits, 2 for each character, result in decreased efficiency for the system, so synchronous is often better because fewer bits need to be transmitted for each character of actual data. This observation together with the recognition that there are many examples of asynchronous data sources form the basis for the next refinement of TDM, STDM.

To summarize this discussion of TDM, the data sources must be digital. The data sources can be synchronous or asynchronous. If synchronous, the data sources can be all the same speed or integer related. If asynchronous, the time they are connected to the common channel is set to an arbitrary length depending on the nature of the data source. This can vary from 1 bit time to, typically, one word time.

In the asynchronous case, start and stop bits are required to determine where the character begins and ends to ensure an entire word is connected to the common channel. TDM of asynchronous data is less efficient because of the bandwidth consumed by the start and stop bits. In both the synchronous and asynchronous situation, once the sampling of each data source is completed, the group of bits that result on the common channel is called a frame. Frames can be any size, and the sizes are usually determined by systemwide design issues.

■ STDM

A related form of TDM is often used to enhance the overall data rate when the data sources are asynchronous. In many industries it is common for several computer terminals to be connected together and used as data entry terminals. This is an example of asynchronous data sources. People are not robots, connected to a common clock source, and the people operating these terminals take breaks, answer the telephone, or for some other reason stop entering data into the data source for significant periods of time. The goal with STDM is often to maximize the data transfer rate for those stations where data entry is actually going on. This means some way of turning OFF the stations that are idle is needed so more time slots can be allocated to those stations that are being used.

The character-based asynchronous multiplexing, as discussed earlier, provides an easy way to do this; if no start bit is seen for some period of time, that data source is skipped and the multiplexer moves on to the next one. Because start and stop bits are being used to mark the data sources, if no start bit is seen, there is no data to be transmitted and that time slot can be assigned to the next terminal in line.

This is called STDM and is often used to effectively concentrate the data and save considerable resources. At any time some of the operators will be occupied doing something else, and so many more lines can be connected to the multiplexer than could strictly be allowed if the data sources were all synchronous. The name STDM comes from the statistical nature of the connections to the common channel or wire. This is because for each frame the data sources present are statistically determined depending on the presence or absence of new data to be transmitted. Over the entire day, all stations experience approximately the same data transfer rate, but in any short period of time, some will be transmitting more than others will. Example 11.2 illustrates how STDM compares with TDM in a situation such as that just discussed.

■ EXAMPLE 11.2

A certain operation has four data sources sharing a 56 kbps line. How does the average data rate each can expect change if all are active compared to when just three are active? Draw a timing diagram for each and compare using TDM and STDM approaches.

$$\text{average data rate} = \frac{\text{aggregate data rate}}{\text{number of data sources}} \qquad (11\text{-}11)$$

$$4 \text{ Users: average data rate} = \frac{56\text{kbps}}{4} = 14\text{kbps}$$

$$3 \text{ Users: average data rate} = \frac{56\text{kbps}}{3} = 18.6\text{kbps}$$

Note that this calculation is only true if STDM is being applied. The illustration shown below shows why this is true. Note how in the TDM situation, part of the bandwidth is wasted, since that time slot is dedicated to the absent user.

In the second case, note how one part in four of the data rate of the line is wasted, since that source is not present and TDM cannot adapt to that situation without a reconfiguration. Also, note how the frame time for all situations stays the same, however the average data rate to each data source does not. In the last case, since STDM will skip the third source if it is not present, the average data rate each data source can utilize changes. Again, the frame time stays the same since the data rate on the line stays the same. The average data rate is now shared among three in the last case.

■ FDM

As was briefly addressed in the introduction, FDM operates by assigning a small slice of bandwidth to each signal source continuously rather than switching the entire bandwidth among many signal sources. FDM is an analog approach to multiplexing. It multiplexes in frequency rather than time. Prior to the adoption of PCM, if analog signals needed to be multiplexed, FDM was the only game in town.

FDM multiplexes in frequency by taking several data sources, all of which typically occupy the same frequency channel, and shifting them such that they are adjacent in frequency. By combining the bandwidths of each channel and adding them together, a rough idea of the total bandwidth of the shared common channel can be arrived at. This channel is used to send the entire multiplexed group of data sources. This calculation is not exact because a little room, called guard bands, must be left between each channel so that the signals will not interfere with each other, and also so that filters on the receiving end can break them apart and separate them out. This is illustrated in Figure 11.10, which shows how three voice channels, 300 to 3400 Hz, are frequency multiplexed onto a single wider bandwidth channel of about 10 kHz.

In Figure 11.11, pay special attention to the fact that the sources are now labeled signal sources rather than data sources. This is to underline the fact that FDM is an analog multiplexing scheme and makes use of analog signal sources. TDM, on the other hand, is a digital multiplexing scheme and makes use of digital data sources.

FDM makes use of the fact that if you have a wide bandwidth channel, you can frequency division multiplex many narrow bandwidth channels into it. A familiar FDM system is cable TV. The coaxial cable that comes into the home has a usable bandwidth of about 500 MHz at the distances and frequencies used in that industry. Each television channel is about 6 MHz wide, so many television channels can be carried by one coaxial cable.

Figure 11.10
Diagram for Example 11.2.

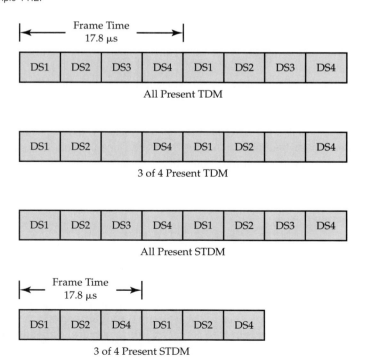

Figure 11.11
FDM, spectrum analyzer view.

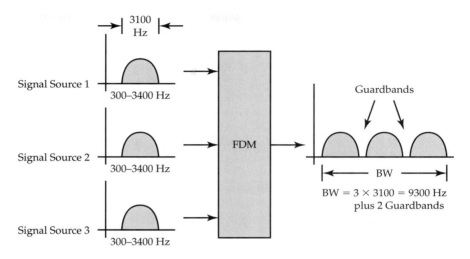

Each television channel is frequency division multiplexed onto the coaxial cable at a slightly different frequency than was used for broadcasting. This provides two benefits: First, it reduces interference with the television transmitters that are broadcasting through the air and might be picked up with a standard antenna on the roof or set top. Second, it allows small modifications of the television tuner, cable mode versus broadcast mode, to pick up the signals just as if they were transmitted in the traditional manner. The television tuner is switched to cable mode and the television will adjust its channel selector about 250 kHz and pick up the channels from the coaxial cable.

Note that because the cable company gets to choose what channel is frequency shifted where, different cable companies have different channels assigned to different stations. This means the same channel may carry different stations in different cable systems. This has nothing to do with the FDM technique; the frequency slots chosen are entirely up to the designer of the system. It is often used as a way for cable companies to differentiate their product offerings. To be fair, there are sometimes technical reasons for leaving a particular frequency slot open or closed depending on what other frequency slots are occupied. This is due to mixing of the carrier frequencies and can introduce distortion in the signals once demultiplexed.

Interestingly, FDM is actually accomplished by the use of DSB-SC modulation. See Chapter 7 for review of that method. Recall that the primary use of this modulation technique was frequency shifting. Here one large commercial application for this function is seen. The same reason that made it a poor choice for broadcast AM makes it a good choice for frequency shifting application in FDM. The absence of any carrier energy in

Figure 11.12
Relay towers.

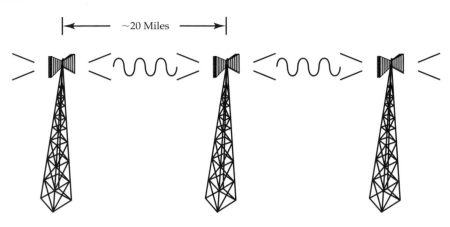

the output spectrum means that the modulation did not add any energy to the output spectrum; it just shifted it in frequency. Cable TV does not want to alter the video channels it is sending you; it just wants to be able to send them to you on cable rather than through the atmosphere.

Finally, the telephone system has historically used modulators operating in the microwave band to frequency division multiplex telephone voice channels without going through the PCM encoding step. This allows total analog transmission, a big advantage before PCM systems became cost competitive. Essentially, a group of towers would be arranged in a line-of-sight pattern, because the microwave band uses line-of-sight (LOS) propagation mode, and voice channels would be combined using FDM techniques and transmitted over long distances using a relay approach. See Figure 11.12.

The distance between relay towers is about 20 miles. These systems, although still common in rural areas, are being replaced in most parts of the country with fiber optic TDM systems. In the FDM approach, there was a hierarchy to grouping the voice channels that is different than that used in the TDM technique. There were at least three levels to this hierarchy. The *basic group* aggregated 12 voice channels, the *supergroup* was 60 voice channels, and the *master group* was 600 voice channels. Other, larger groupings were also possible and were occasionally implemented where traffic was concentrated enough.

■ WAVELENGTH DIVISION MULTIPLEXING (WDM)

WDM is a technique that has been developed to take advantage of the properties of fiber optic cables. Recall that wavelength and frequency are related through the equation

$$c = \lambda f$$

From this it can be seen that WDM is just a specialized form of FDM used in optical systems. This technique is being used by sophisticated fiber systems to carry a virtually infinite amount of bandwidth. You may have heard of tests various telephone companies perform that are usually expressed in the popular media as how many sets of encyclopedias can be transmitted per second. These systems are typically using WDM to achieve these very high data rates.

Essentially, because the bandwidth of a fiber optic cable is very wide, typically over 20,000 GHz, many channels operating at a few gigahertz can, in principle, be multiplexed onto a single fiber cable. This can result in tremendous aggregate data rates. To get some sense of just how much bandwidth can be carried over a single optical cable with this approach fully realized, examine the calculation below.

Take a data rate of 1 GHz and assume that 10,000 channels can be accommodated and modulated by different lasers operating at slightly different wavelengths. If the bandwidth of the optical cable is 20,000 GHz wide, this leaves a guard band of 1 GHz between each transmission. The aggregate data rate of this system would then be 10,000 GHz. (That's a lot of data.)

But what does a data rate of 1 GHz really correspond to? Take this chapter as an example. It contains, excluding figures, about 6000 words. If there are 8 bits per character and 7 characters per word, a total data size of about a third of a million bits results. Adding the figures, it has maybe 1 million bits. (Is each picture really worth a thousand words?)

Therefore, each 1 GHz channel can send 1000 chapters each second. Multiply that by 10,000 channels, and the system described above could send the equivalent of 10,000,000 chapters each second. Or, perhaps more suitable to its actual application, one chapter could be sent to each of 10,000,000 subscribers each second. That's how the claims of sending the encyclopedia 1000 times a second over a fiber cable are arrived at.

Some of these systems are in use today as fiber rings in large, metropolitan areas or as cross-country trunks. They are expensive to implement but are becoming increasingly common in most carrier networks. Today, these systems feature up to perhaps 20 lasers operating simultaneously as channels, but the trend is clear. As the demand for bandwidth rises, these systems will increase in channel density and roll out as economic situations require them.

The current trend in telecommunications is to combine the properties of WDM with TDM to achieve larger bandwidths of information transfer without changing the fiber pathways already existing. When these fiber bundles were first laid out, several extra fibers were placed to allow for future growth. At that time there was no real appreciation of how fast the growth of telecommunications would be.

Historically, the growth of voice telephone calls was well established, about 8% per year. Using this data, planners forecast enough bandwidth to last well into the twenty-first century with the extra cables laid but not used. (A fiber cable that is laid but not used is referred to as a "dark" cable. The act of bringing it into use is called "lighting" the cable, and fiber cables in use are referred to as "lit" fiber.)

What the planners did not anticipate was the explosive growth of data communications such as that associated with the Internet. Internet growth rates are on the order of 100% per year. Further, business data communications other than Internet traffic are also growing much faster than voice traffic, on the order of 40% per year. These growth rates swamped the planner's numbers, and although just 10 years ago people were wondering how all that fiber laid would ever be used, now the question is how can the usable bandwidth on each fiber be increased to accommodate the traffic growth.

The way this is being done is to combine TDM and WDM techniques. Increasing the TDM nature of the systems requires larger and larger data rates. These can get very expensive as the state of the art is pushed to the limit. For example, a multiplexer designed to operate at 1 Gbps is more than twice as expensive as one designed to operate at 500 Mps. Additionally, the existing unit must be replaced with an entirely new one. That also gets expensive very quickly.

However, if the approach of adding another wavelength to the existing fiber is taken, to double the bandwidth all that is needed is another multiplexer operating at the same rate as the existing one but running with a laser tuned to a slightly different wavelength. This is much more cost effective and still effectively doubles the bandwidth of the fiber. As you might imagine add/drop multiplexers operating at slightly different wavelengths have a happy home in this environment. This is due to their ability to extract tom wavelength without disrupting the other wavelengths operating on the same fiber. Functionally the system would work as in Figure 11.13.

Synchronous optical network (SONET) systems are being implemented in this way around the world to increase the bandwidth utilization of the existing fiber cables installed. By the end of 1999, systems in place will feature bandwidths of 160 Gbps on a single fiber strand. That means that for a typical fiber bundle of 16 pairs, for full-duplex, cable data rates approaching 2500 Gbps will be implemented.

■ CODE DIVISION MULTIPLE ACCESS (CDMA)

The above discussions have focused on ways to partition signals in time and frequency (and wavelength). The third major way of partitioning signals, that of code division, will now be briefly examined. Recall that the way TDM and FDM were distinguished was to say TDM divided up the entire bandwidth of the channel into little time slots, and each data source had the entire bandwidth to itself for some slice of time. FDM was described

Figure 11.13
WDM and TDM combined application.

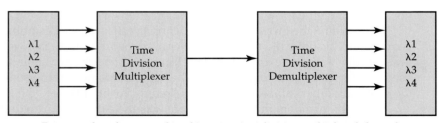

Four wavelengths are combined into one time division multiplexed channel.
Once received, they are demultiplexed into four separate wavelengths again.

as allocating a little slice of bandwidth to each data source for the entire time of transmission. CDM makes no restrictions on bandwidth or time. Many code divisioned signals can exist in the same bandwidth at the same time. The different codes would distinguish between them.

The title to this section is CDMA and not CDM, following the pattern used so far, because code division multiplexing, which means the division of messages by code, does not really tell much about how it would work. This does not mean that each message is tagged with a header featuring a different code. CDM means to multiply the signal by something called the code polynomial, essentially masking the transmission to a receiver unless the code is known. Only a receiver that knows the code can receive the signal correctly.

For these reasons, CDM techniques have traditionally been intimately associated with spread spectrum techniques and used to hide the transmitted waveform in the noise. When filtered by the correct digital sequence, it appears. This can provide considerable antijamming capability to deliberate interference. The basic idea of spread spectrum systems was to spread the signal over a very large bandwidth, typically at least a 100 to a 1000 times larger than required.

An alternate approach uses the code pattern to implement frequency hopping according to a nonpredictable pattern (the code), which resulted in making synchronous receivers, required in digital modulated systems, virtually impossible to use unless you knew the code. Hence the name CDMA, because access was what you were restricting through the use of the code. These two approaches were the only application for CDM techniques and so have become inherently associated with CDM.

The whole concept of the code selection was to find special code sequences that had low correlation with each other, and hence, many users could listen to simultaneous messages. If the codes were too "close" to each other, it was hard for the receiver to distinguish them and the receiver ended up jumping between them too fast to understand anything.

Originally, CDMA was considered for use in the cellular radio industry because it provided slightly better performance efficiencies; it could easily capitalize on the pauses in speech to provide additional message space. For most vendors cost issues overrode this slight increase of spectral efficiency, although if it had been implemented, the theft of phone time discussed in Chapter 9 would not be the problem it is today.

The newest version of cellular telephones makes use of this CDM approach and provides a much greater level of security from not only the theft of phone time, but perhaps just as important, from eavesdropping. Eavesdropping is essentially impossible when using CDMA. The emerging technology of satellite telephones will also use CDMA techniques. This is why the military used it exclusively for years, and it is why commercial companies are moving to it today to respond to the widespread and technologically simple eavesdropping possible with the typical cellular telephone in use today.

A detailed analysis of how CDMA works is outside the scope of this book; however, a few pointers can be made for interested readers. Essentially the input data source to be modulated is first modulated by the code word itself. This is manifested as a binary sequence. The new data stream resulting from this multiplication or first-pass modulation is then modulated again using one of the digital modulation techniques covered in Chapter 13 before it is transmitted.

On the downlink side of the transmission, the received signal is demodulated in the same way as studied earlier, appropriate to the modulation technique used and is then correlated with the original code word. *Correlated* or *correlation,* as used here, describes a mathematical technique that yields a measure of how similar two number sequences are. If the two code words do not match, the correlation step yields a zero value and the received signal has zero signal strength for the receiver with the wrong code word. Thus the signal is hidden from receivers other than the one it is intended for.

This explains why there are no restrictions on the band used to transmit or the time slot used. If the code word does not correlate with the code word embedded in the receiver, the signal strength of the message received is virtually zero. Hence, a CDMA telephone will hear many calls but will only ring when the correlation requirement is satisfied. Because the code is never transmitted in the clear, as in the cellular telephone discussed earlier, there is no danger of someone just listening and picking up the correct code to steal calling time. This is not to say that it is impossible to receive a CDMA signal not intended for you, but it takes very sophisticated equipment and is not possible in real time.

■ SDM

The last access technique that will be explored here is the one least discussed, but perhaps the most common one. It is not usually considered a form of multiplexing in the strictest sense, but it has been in use for centuries and is really just one example that is often overlooked because it is so simple. For a moment, consider the individual wires in a parallel ribbon cable or the two wires in the twisted pair cable that connects your telephone to the wall socket. Each of these cable assemblies is utilizing an access method called SDM to keep the lines distinct.

Some common examples of SDM applications not involving electronics include checking out at the supermarket, sorting papers on your desk by in and out boxes, any road where travel in each direction is spatially distinct, expressways with more than one lane, and so forth.

Although the above paragraphs made the concept of space division multiplexing clear, the focus was not on communications multiplexing, but on space division without the multiplexing part. A better illustration of how this technology works in the field of communications is a crossbar switch. The crossbar switch utilizes a matrix of connections where each column and row cross but are separated in space, hence, the designation space division switch.

At each crossing of column and row a potential connection can be made. For example, row 2 could connect to column 5. The nice thing about a crossbar switch is that any input (row) can be connected to any output (column) without connecting to any other column if desired. This means that any input can be connected to any output with a single switch closure.

However, the real power of a crossbar switch becomes clear when you realize that there is no reason why many different inputs and outputs cannot be connected simultaneously and completely flexibly. Again, any number of inputs (row) can be connected to any number of outputs (columns) simultaneously. This type of switch is widely used in telephone systems as a means of connecting calls flexibly. Figure 11.14 is a simple diagram of a crossbar switch.

Many times in actual systems there is a calculation made that takes into account that not all telephones are in use at any one time. In Figure 11.14, any input can be connected to any output, and this illustrated the basic operation of such a switch. In Figure 11.15, a more representative situation is shown. Here the callers are all connected to individual horizontal lines. To make a connection, two horizontal lines are connected to one circuit, shown as the vertical lines.

For a call to proceed, there must be a circuit available. Instead of building a matrix large enough to accommodate all telephones in use at any moment in time, a decision is made based on calling statistics about how many telephones will be in use at any moment in time. Then only that many circuits are implemented at the exchange. Calls made when no circuit is available are blocked. You hear a distinctive ring tone on your telephone, sometimes known as a "fast" busy signal. As can be seen from Figure 11.15 if telephone 7 or 8 tried to make a call, no circuit would be available.

Interestingly, the current cellular telephone system makes use of space division access methodology. If you think about it, you can see how the cells in a region act like separate cables in a bundle to keep the signals from interfering with each other. This is the

Figure 11.14
Crossbar switch (space division switching).

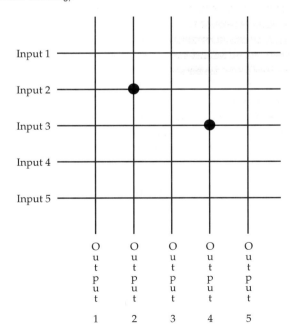

Figure 11.15
Practical implementation of crossbar switch.

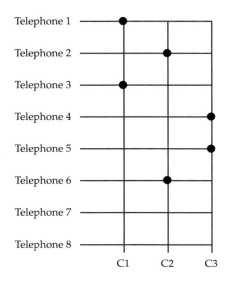

multiplexing principle behind the technique of frequency reuse. Review the section on cellular telephones in Chapter 9 and think about it in terms of a multiplexing system. You will discover how that system can be viewed as an example of SDM. It is typically discussed as an FDM system, as was done earlier.

This situation is not uncommon in engineering or, for that matter, in any science. Often, systems can be viewed from many different perspectives, all of which have their own particular uses in understanding how the system works. Perhaps this perspective will help you understand an aspect of cellular telephones that you did not earlier.

■ SUMMARY

This chapter has introduced various types of multiplexing approaches possible and given a few examples of actual implementations and how they work. TDM is by far the most common technique, and with the continuing movement to all digital technologies, this should continue. Traditional FDM techniques have a limited life span and will grow with application to fiber through the maturation of WDM. CDM techniques, traditionally were the exclusive province of the military, but this technique is now moving into the commercial marketplace, as security becomes more of an issue.

Appendix F gives a short description of the E-1 framing pattern used throughout Europe. Translation between this format and the DS-1 format described earlier is common when transatlantic calls must be exchanged between the two systems.

PROBLEMS

1. A particular PCM/TDM system multiplexes 36 voice channels using 8 bit PCM code word size and adds a framing bit to each frame. The sampling rate is 10 kbps. Find the line rate in bits per second.

2. A particular TDM system multiplexes two high-speed data sources operating at 1 Mbps and three lower-speed data sources operating at 250 kbps. Draw the frame showing sufficient bit positions for the first 2 bits from each low-speed data source. What is the frame rate? What is the frame time? What is the clocking rate?

3. Another possible format for telephone system framing is the following:
   32 channels
   16 bit PCM sampling
   2 framing bits
   44 kHz sampling rate
   Find the line rate, bits per frame, the frame rate, frame time, and bit time for this system.

4. Five voice channels are required to be transmitted on a single FDM transmission. If each voice channel has a bandwidth of 3100 Hz and guardbands of 2 kHz are required between each channel, what is the total bandwidth of the FDM common channel?

5. Design a crossbar switch intended to accommodate four inputs and four outputs. Show connections at input 1 to output 2 and input 3 to output 3.

6. Assume that instead of just 1 bit per frame being used for framing, 2 bits are used in the superframe format. What is the clear channel aggregate data rate?

7. Calculate the clear channel aggregate data rate for the E1 standard discussed in Appendix F. Assume that 1 bit per frame is used for signaling.

8. A certain PCM/TDM system multiplexes 10 voice channels with a word size of 8 bits with 20 data channels using a word size of 12 bits. Assume each frame uses 1 framing bit and sampling rate is 10 kHz. What is the line rate?

12

Coding

The first thing to understand about coding is that the word *code* is used in many different ways when discussing communications. It is used to describe things such as ASCII, or Morse, block, and variable length. It has many more uses, and the terminology can be confusing. Another thing to recognize about codes is that anytime a code is used to improve the error rate of transmission, overhead is added to the transmission, and a cost is paid. Every extra bit transmitted that does not actually contain information lowers its efficiency. Therefore, improving the error rate must be traded off with the extra bandwidth taken up by the code.

Not everything referred to as a code is used to improve the error rate. Some codes actually reduce the bandwidth sent, but these tend to be specialized systems for specific applications and are not the primary subject here. One example is a code that represents an entire message, for example, when the telegraph industry uses a single code to represent Happy Birthday or Happy Holidays or other commonly sent phrases.

For this study of coding, the discussion will break into two broad categories, channel coding and source coding. This first categorization of codes makes the distinction between those codes designed to represent the data input most effectively, as compared to representing the data most efficiently. Here *efficient* means minimizing the number of bits transmitted and *effective* means maximizing the performance in noise. Note that this implies that in many cases the two techniques are combined to yield the greatest advantage.

In this chapter, it should become apparent why communications systems with a digital data source benefit more from coding than those with analog inputs. This is because the digital nature of the input naturally lends itself to the formation of a code alphabet. To implement a source code there is a need to quantify the code alphabet. Any modulation scheme can be made more effective by improving its performance in noise, and so channel encoding is widely used in many communications systems. This means that of the two broad classes of codes to be explored, one of them is only applicable to digital communications systems. Because channel codes are more generally applicable, that will be discussed first.

■ CHANNEL CODES

Channel encoding is a way to represent the data transmitted from the source in such a way that they are "different enough" so that in the presence of small variations of noise one can discover any errors caused by the noise and attempt to fix them. This is also referred to as forward error correction (FEC). The terms *channel encoding* and *FEC codes* are often used interchangeably. This is usually not a problem; their differences will be discussed later. Channel encoding is concerned with error detection and correction. Error detection is the process of detecting errors in the received transmission; error correction is the process of fixing those detected errors. (If you do not know it is broken, how can you fix it?) There are many ways to approach channel encoding, and in some approaches, all the information necessary, or available, is contained in the encoding itself. Therefore, to correct an error two steps must take place: error detection and error correction.

There are two main subgroups to channel coding, those where all the information to both detect and correct an error is contained in the message itself, FEC codes, and the other main group of channel codes known as automatic repeat request (ARQ) protocols where this is not the case. This subclassification is where the interchangeability of the terms *FEC* and *channel codes* break down: All FEC codes are channel codes but not all channel codes are FEC codes. For example, ARQ protocols are not classified as a FEC code, but are a type of channel code.

ARQ techniques require the receiver to request retransmission of any frame of data where it detects errors. Therefore, the distinction between these two groups is *where* the information is to correct the errors. In the first case, FEC codes, it is contained in the code itself; in the latter case, ARQ protocols, it is held by the transmitter in the sense that the receiver requests the frame of data be sent again. Therefore, both code types contain the information necessary to detect an error, but only FEC codes also can correct it.

Many Layer 2 (Data Link Layer) Open Systems Interconnection (OSI) protocols use some form of the latter type, usually implemented with the ARQ protocol utilizing CRC codes to detect errors. Once the CRC code detects the error, the ARQ protocol requests a retransmission. This chapter will show how a CRC code works to detect errors. In Chapter 14 the protocol elements that are necessary to support the requests for retransmission where error(s) were detected will be described.

Be sure to recognize the distinction between those channel codes that stand by themselves, FEC codes, and those approaches that require retransmission from the source to operate, ARQ protocols. The first group requires no additional support from the transmitter once the message is sent. The second group requires coordination between the source and destination and a way of messaging between them, from either direction.

This is why channel encoding of the type known as ARQ protocols is referred to as protocols; a protocol must exist to communicate about errors that are detected and request retransmissions of data already sent. These are more complex than simple FEC codes where once you have sent it, you can forget it. Again, ARQ protocols are often encountered in local area network (LAN) and wide area network (WAN) environments.

Any modulation technique can be used to transmit either type of channel code just as they can be used to transmit any type of data; the codes are just a few additional bits sent with each message.

As will be apparent when source codes are explored, any source or channel code has an additional subclassification; it may be a block or variable code. Block codes are those where the length of the code stays fixed. Variable codes are those where the length is variable. The next sections will introduce three channel codes, two block codes (parity and Hamming) and one variable length code (rectangular). The discussion of channel codes will conclude with an explanation of how CRC codes used in ARQ protocols for error detection operate.

Block Codes

Block codes are those codes where the number of bits of the output is constant for any input. Another way of saying this is that a block code is a mapping of j input bits onto k output bits, where $j < k$. Parity is an example of a block code. Seven bits represent the input data and 8 bits represent the output, (e.g., $j = 7$ and $k = 8$). For any 7 bit ASCII code the output is 8 bits, 7 bits plus parity, for a total of 8 bits. In the next section this simple example of a FEC block code, parity, is explored.

Parity

Probably the best known FEC code is parity. It satisfies the definition of a channel encoding technique; it represents the data in some way that allows detection and potential correction of errors. Parity is one of the oldest and simplest methods of error detection. A single bit represents the oddness or evenness of the number of 1s. Note that parity is independent of the number of 0s and is not sensitive to the number of paired 1s. For even parity the parity bit is a 0 if the number of 1s is even and is a 1 for an odd number of 1s. Similarly, for odd parity, the parity bit is a 1 if the number of 1s is even and it is 0 for an odd number of 1s. Typically, a single XOR gate can be used to detect errors once the number of 1s has been determined.

Parity implemented as a single bit error detection scheme is quite simple and primitive. One parity bit can detect 1 error and will not detect 2 errors, thereby passing bad data to the receiver. Parity will only detect an odd number of errors. Parity should never be used unless there is a very low probability of error in the channel. The only real advantage of parity is that it is very simple to use and implement. The value of the parity bit is determined by adding up the total number of 1s present in the word. Again, for even parity, a parity bit of 1 is added if it is odd, and a parity bit of 0, if it is even. The idea is after adding the parity bit, the total number of 1 bits is even for even parity.

If only one parity bit is added, only one single bit error can be detected and double bit errors, such as when a 10 is switched to a 01, cannot be detected. In the latter case, the number of 1 bits remains the same. This illustrates an interesting property of FEC codes in general. FEC codes must include enough extra bits to detect the maximum number of errors expected in each group of data. These groups of data are referred to as frames or blocks. One would say a frame of data or a block of data was FEC coded. It can be seen that for large blocks of data in noisy channels, the number of parity bits could grow quickly and represent a large overhead to the actual message traffic. Example 12.1 summarizes both even and odd parity. The next FEC code introduced. Hamming codes, uses even parity.

■ EXAMPLE 12.1

Data:	1001010	Parity: Even number of 1 bits implies parity bit $= 1$ for even parity.
Data:	1001010	Parity: Odd number of 1 bits implies parity bit $= 0$ for odd parity.
Data:	1101010	Parity: Even number of 1 bits implies parity bit $= 0$ for even parity.
Data:	1101010	Parity: Odd number of 1 bits implies parity bit $= 1$ for odd parity.

Hamming Codes

As crude as single bit parity is as a FEC code, a nice extension to the same concept renders it much more useful. This type of block FEC code is the family of Hamming codes. These are those block codes where bit error(s) are not only detected at the receiver but also, if the length of the code is long enough, corrected. Hamming codes give the best code for single bit correction when performance in a white noise environment is considered. Richard Hamming developed not only the code that bears his name but also two terms that are used to define the performance of all block FEC codes. These terms are *Hamming weight* and *Hamming distance*.

Hamming weight is the number of binary 1 bits in a code word. The Hamming distance between two code words is the number of bit positions by which they differ. A bigger Hamming distance is desirable. The more differing positions that exist, the higher probability that the code words can be distinguished in the presence of noise. Remember, a channel code represents the data so that it is different enough so that any errors introduced in the channel can be discovered at the destination. The minimum Hamming code length is generated by adding some number of bits, m, to a source data transmission determined by the inequality below:

$$2^m \geq m + n + 1 \tag{12-1}$$

where

$$n = \text{original data word length}$$

$$m = \text{\# of Hamming bits required}$$

So the new length of the data transmission, when you include the Hamming bits would be $m + n + 1$, for an original data word of length n. The number of Hamming bits added is given by m. The background for this relationship is given below, but first let's look at a quick example of how equation 12-1 is applied. Note that the terms *parity bit* and *Hamming bit* are commonly interchanged because a Hamming bit is really just a parity bit. When you group several of them together, they implement a Hamming code.

■ EXAMPLE 12.2

Determine the number of parity bits required for a 4 bit message. Because Hamming codes are groups of 1 bit parity codes, the value of *m* that will satisfy the inequality in equation 12-1 must be found. Thus,

$$2^m \geq m + 4 + 1 \rightarrow m = 3$$
$$2^3 = 8 \geq 3 + 4 + 1 = 8$$

For this example, the number of parity bits required is 3 bits; adding that to the original message length, the new length of the message will be $4 + 3 = 7$ bits. The next job is to place the bits in the original data word.

The placement of the series of 1 bit parity bits, or Hamming bits, is not arbitrary. This is because the resultant number generated at the receiver must indicate the positions of the errors, and the coding technique guarantees this will be the result. The number generated that indicates the positions of the errors is known as the syndrome. One way to think about why the bit positions are crucial is each parity bit must cover one and only one parity bit location. Because parity can only detect a single bit error, it is critical that only one parity bit location be covered by each parity bit.

The Hamming code is a series of 1 bit parity checkers. *Hamming's insight was to recognize that every binary representation that has a 1 in the last bit position must be in the first parity check. From the same reasoning, the second parity check must be for those binary representations that have a 1 in the second from the last bit position, and so forth.* For this reasoning

Table 12.1
Binary Representations

Bit Position	Binary Representation
1	0001
2	0010
3	0011
4	0100
5	0101
6	0110
7	0111
8	1000
9	1001
10	1010
11	1011
12	1100

to work correctly, the positions of the check bits are predefined. They occupy the positions 1, 2, 4, 8, ... In general, the check bits occupy the positions.

$$2^m$$

This means that the first parity check covers bit positions 1, 3, 5, 7, 9, 11, . . . , the second parity check will cover bit positions 2, 3, 6, 7, 10, 11, . . . , the third parity check will cover bit positions 4, 5, 6, 7, 12, . . . , and the fourth parity check will cover bit positions 8, 9, 10, 11, 12, ... Table 12.1 should help make this clear.

Notice the first parity check catches all those binary representations with a 1 in the least significant bit (LSB). The second parity check catches all those binary representations with a 1 in LSB + 1, and so forth. Example 12.3 continues Example 12.2 and illustrates the proper placement of the parity bits.

■ EXAMPLE 12.3

The original code word of length 4 bits is 0101. The parity or check bits occupy the positions 1, 2, and 4 for a word of this length. After encoding the new data word becomes __0_101, where the _ represents where the check bits will be inserted.

To determine the check bits to enter at which positions, compute the parity check at all open positions, here bit positions 1, 2, and 4. The first parity check, which goes into bit position 1, checks 1, 3, 5, and 7 from Table 12.1. Looking at the new data word, __0_101, there is an even number of 1 bits, so to keep even parity, the check bit in position 1 must be set to a 0. Therefore, a 0 is entered into bit position 1. The new data word now becomes 0_0_101.

The second parity check is over positions 2, 3, 6, and 7. Again examining the new data word, there are an odd number of 1 bits in those positions. This means that to keep even parity across the bit position checked the parity bit must be set to a 1. The new data word now becomes 010_101. The third parity check is over bit positions 4, 5, 6, and 7. Here an even number of 1 bits occur in those positions, so to keep even parity, the parity bit is set to a 0. Inserting this into the new code word results in 0100101. This completes the Hamming encoding process.

■ EXAMPLE 12.4

For an original data word length of 8 bits, how many parity checks are required? Additionally, what are the bit positions that these bits occupy? Finally, is there any advantage to regarding the message as one 8 bit message over two 4 bit messages?

The number of parity checks required for any message length is given by equation 12-1. For $n = 8$, the number of bits required is 4 bits. The bit positions are given by the positions defined by evaluating increasing powers of 2:

$$1:2^0 = 1 \qquad 2:2^1 = 2 \qquad 3:2^2 = 4 \qquad 4:2^3 = 8$$

Because only 4 bits required, these are the four locations of the parity bits.

The effect of treating the message as two 4 bit words would be to require 3 parity bits for each 4 bit message. This means that the overhead in the message due to the Hamming coding would be a total of 6 bits, two messages, each with 3 parity bits. For the single 8 bit message, only 4 parity bits would be required. It seems clear that it is more desirable to send a single long message rather than two short messages. However, as will be shown later, for this additional message overhead, more potential checks on the data stream for errors do occur. Nevertheless, in all but the most severe noise environments, it is better to not break up the message into smaller sections and code each individually. Usually, the primary concern is message overhead due to coding.

■ **EXAMPLE 12.5**

Now introduce a single bit error and see if the Hamming code worked out above can find it. If the first bit position is changed from a 0 to a 1, the corrupted code word from Example 12.3 is now 1100101. Apply the parity checks in the same order at the receiver that was done at the transmitter.

Figure 12.1
Hamming code example.

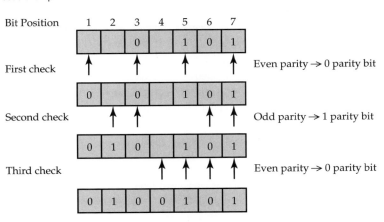

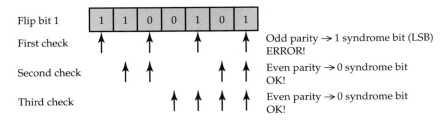

Syndrome is 001 → bit position 1 in error.
Flip bit one back.

Strip off parity check bits → 0101.
The original data sequence is recovered.

Parity check 1 yields an odd number of 1 bits, so the LSB of the syndrome becomes a 1. Parity check 2 yields an even number of 1 bits, so the LSB + 1 of the syndrome becomes a 0. The last parity check counts an even number of 1 bits, so the LSB + 2 of the syndrome becomes a 0. This completes the check.

The checks performed at the receiver indicate that there was an error and it is in bit position 1. This is determined by taking the checks and writing down a 1 if the parity is odd and a 0 if the parity is even. Then read the binary number out, and its decimal equivalent indicates the bit position in error. The result here was 001, with only the first parity check yielding odd parity. The first parity check occupies the LSB and subsequent checks move 1 bit position to the left for each check.

Therefore, by flipping back the bit in position 1, which corrects the error in transmission, the result is a corrected received word of 0100101. Then strip off the Hamming bits to recover the original message. The result is 0101, the original 4 bit word.

This set of calculations is very easy for digital logic circuits to perform, and Hamming codes have found many happy homes in silicon. The entire operation is contained in Examples 12.2, 12.3 and 12.5 and is summarized in Figure 12.1.

Note that the Hamming code syndrome indicates the position of the bit in error, regardless of the message content. If a different original data message had been chosen, the Hamming bits might be different, but if bit 1 were flipped, the syndrome would still be 001. Also note that a syndrome of all zeros indicates a message received with no errors. The Hamming code uses a variety of 1 bit parity codes to identify the bit position of the error. This error then can be corrected at the receiver.

A code with 3 Hamming bits has a Hamming distance of 3, $n = 3$. It detects a double bit error or corrects a single bit error. Generally, the larger the Hamming distance, the more (bits − 0) in error are detected or the more (bits − 2) are corrected. These must be viewed as a whole. A Hamming distance of 2 means a single bit error detection, a Hamming distance of 4 means single bit error correction *plus* double bit error detection, or triple bit error detection, and so forth. A Hamming distance of 5 is the minimum for double bit error correction.

Finally, the overhead ratio for this example was high; 3 bits were needed to find a single bit error in a 4 bit message. A 75 percent overhead is not the general case. By examining equation 12-1, it can be seen that for reasonable message lengths encountered in the real world, the Hamming code is quite efficient. This is illustrated in the next two examples.

■ EXAMPLE 12.6

Find the number of Hamming bits needed for a message length of 1000 bits. At first glance, it is difficult to solve equation 12-1 when the number of Hamming bits is unknown. An alternate approach is to find out how long a message can be encoded given a certain number of bits. The first guess is 9 bits. This implies a message length of 1001 bits plus m. The value of 2 raised to the tenth power is 1024. Inserting that into equation 12-1.

$$2^m \cdot \geq m + n + 1 \rightarrow 2^9 \geq 9 + 1000 + 1 \rightarrow 512 \geq 1010$$

The result is not quite enough bits for a message length of 1000 bits, but by adding 1 Hamming bit, it can be seen that the message length that could be covered would be 1024 bits. Therefore, 10 bits are required for an original message length of 1000 bits. Note that after adding the Hamming bits, the new message length is 1010 bits.

$$2^{10} \geq 10 + n + 1 \rightarrow 2^{10} \geq 10 + 1000 + 1 \rightarrow 1024 \geq 1011$$

■ EXAMPLE 12.7

Find the number of detection and correction bits possible for 10 parity bits.

Because 10 bits are added, 10 errors could be detected at 1 bit per error. It is also possible to correct some bits. Each bit corrected takes two additional bits over the detection bit. Any bit to be corrected must first be detected. Therefore, the following combinations are possible:

10 detection bits and 0 detection + correction
7 detection bits and 1 detection + correction
4 detection bits and 2 detection + correction
1 detection bit and 3 detection + correction

Another way to look at this is to take the Hamming distance, which is just the number of parity check bits applied to the original data word, and calculate what would be possible.

Hamming Distance	Possible Checks
1	1 bit error detection
2	2 bit error detection
3	1 bit error detection + correction
4	1 bit error detection plus 1 bit error detection + correction
5	2 bit error detection plus 1 bit error detection + correction
6	2 bit error detection + correction

In these examples, an original data word length of 4 bits was used, which required 3 Hamming bits. This meant, as can be seen from the listing above, that 1 bit in error could both be detected and corrected in the message. This bit could be a part of the original message or a Hamming bit itself; it makes no difference. With longer data words, more Hamming bits are required, increasing numbers of errors can be detected and potentially corrected. The overhead of a Hamming approach to error detection and correction grows in a predictable fashion with the data word length.

Summary of Hamming Method. The four basic steps in constructing a Hamming code are summarized below:

1. Use equation 12-1 to determine the number of Hamming bits required for the message length.
2. Determine the location of the Hamming bits using the 2^m rule.
3. Write the new message including the blank spaces for placement of the Hamming bits.
4. Perform parity checks to determine the value of the Hamming bits, and insert them into the message at the placements found in step 3.

In CRC codes, which are block error detection codes used in ARQ protocols, the overhead is fixed, independent of the message length, CRC codes provide a good detection capability. On the other hand, CRC codes have no built-in correction capability.

A retransmission is always required if errors are detected when using CRC codes. If the number of errors in a message is small enough to be both detected and corrected by a Hamming code, a retransmission is never required. This capability is one of the key reasons why Hamming codes are so useful in low error rate environments.

It is also interesting to realize that the fundamental difference in how the bit(s) in error are fixed results in these two codes finding applicability in two fundamentally different types of communications systems. ARQ protocols using CRC codes require a full-duplex channel, often found only in LAN and WAN environments. Hamming codes require no such complexity and work well in simplex channels such as broadcast networks or situations where responding to a message might reveal something about the message recipient. CRC codes will be explored after an introduction to variable-length channel codes is given.

Variable-Length Channel Codes

A variable-length code is just a code where the message length, once the coding is added to, it is variable with message content. It is easy to think of some variable-length source codes such as the Morse code, where the length of the code varies with the letter or message content. It is not so easy to think of a variable-length channel code. A few examples are provided.

The first example of a variable-length code is an example of a triplication code. These codes have been around for a long time. To illustrate, take an imaginary example from ancient times. Suppose you are a leader in a war against the neighboring kingdom. You have just lost a big battle and desperately need to send home for reinforcements or rescue. Because your enemy now surrounds you on all sides, you cannot just tell somebody to jump on a horse and ride like the devil to the King's castle to get help. All you have are three carrier pigeons that can find the castle from here. You are desperate. How can you improve the probability of the message getting through?

Why not try channel encoding and send three messages to increase the probability that one will get through? This is a simple example of channel encoding; the sending of three pigeons to make sure that one will get through. In data communications it usually means sending a message more than once and using the partial information you get from each to make sure you got the entire contents of the original message. The variable length is determined by how many pigeons are available.

In a triplication code, each message is sent three times, and at the destination a vote is taken, with the majority opinion being taken, about the content of the message prevailing. This allows one of the three messages to become corrupted in transport and yet the message still gets through. A triplication codes allows an error rate of 33 percent, without loss of message.

Another everyday example of triplication codes used as a channel encoding is seen in letter writing. The old adage Tell them once, tell them again, and tell them a third time makes the point. Often writing classes stress the need to make the main point more than once to make sure the reader understood it. This is channel encoding as well. You send the same information, usually stated a little differently or in a different context, three times to make sure the reader will remember the main point of the letter. Every repeated attempt changes the length of the code required to successfully communicate the message. Unlike letter writing, where there is a need to slightly change the message each time to retain the reader's interest, in data communications the message is sent exactly the same way each time.

These two examples of triplication codes illustrate variable-length channel encoding. More generally, these types of codes are known as rectangular codes. These codes all use the same principal, voting. The signal is sent over multiple channels or multiple times and when received, the majority wins. A more modern example of this is in the Space Shuttle. This system uses five computers to vote on alarms; whichever three have a majority on what action to take, that's what gets done.

An ARQ Protocol Error Detection Code, CRC Codes

This section will examine CRC codes that are commonly implemented as error detection codes in ARQ protocols. Again, the protocol aspect of channel coding will be examined in Chapter 14.

Every data communications system is concerned with moving bytes or frames of data from one location to another without error. CRC codes are a popular way to identify if an error has occurred in the frame of data being sent. What happens is a group of bits is added to the end of a frame of data. These bits are added in such a way that the received frame of data including the CRC code will be exactly divisible by some number. If this division is exact, with no remainder, the message has no errors. If the division is not exact, and some remainder is evident, the transmission is assumed to be in error.

The division described above is done in a special way. That special way is modulo-2 arithmetic. If you know how an exclusive-OR gate works, you know how modulo-2 arithmetic works. To summarize, modulo-2 arithmetic is binary addition *with no carries.*

For example, if 1101 and 1001 are added modulo-2, the following answer is found:

$$
\begin{array}{r}
1101 \\
+\ 1001 \\
\hline
0100
\end{array}
$$

The same result would be found if both these numbers were applied bit by bit to an exclusive-OR gate. That is what is meant by modulo-2 arithmetic.

CRC codes are block codes that are implemented by performing the following steps:

1. Shift the original data word the same number of bits left as the highest-order exponent of the generating polynomial P. In the example below the generating polynomial is given by $P = 110101$.
2. Divide the shifted data word by the generating polynomial. Discard the quotient Q (the result) and keep the remainder R. The remainder should have the same number of bits or less than the highest-order exponent of the generating polynomial. This remainder is the CRC code for the original data word.
3. To form the transmitted data word, take the original data word and append the CRC code found in the last step. This is what is transmitted over the communications channel.

4. At the receiver, divide the received data word by the generating polynomial. If the remainder is zero, no error occurred. If the remainder is nonzero, error occurred in the transmission.
5. In the case where no error occurred, just strip the bits appended in step 3, and pass the correctly recovered data out of the receiver. Where error occurred, either request retransmission or apply a method of error correction.

■ EXAMPLE 12.8

The original message to be sent is given by $M = 10101100$:

$$P = x^5 + x^4 + x^2 + 1$$

The generating polynomial is represented by $P = 110101$, where there is a 1 in the binary representation of P if the generating polynomial is nonzero and a zero if it is zero. This particular generating polynomial is known as a CRC-5. The highest power of the generating polynomial is given to the name.

The remainder to be calculated in this example will be 5 bits or less because the highest power of the generating polynomial is 5.

To illustrate how CRC encoding works in detail, this message will be worked through step by step. Appendix G contains table versions of the long divisions shown below. This allows an easy check of the bit positions, which is useful when first learning about this type of modulo-2 division.

First, shift the message by the highest power of the generating polynomial P. This shifts it by 5 bits:

$$\text{new message} = 1010110000000$$

Next, divide the new message by the generating polynomial and discard the quotient. Keep the remainder. Pay careful attention to how the division is carried out, remember, it is modulo-2 arithmetic. This means that you ignore which number is bigger, and just apply the two numbers as if they were connected to an exclusive-OR gate.

```
                        11011110
             110101)1010110000000
                   -1101010000000
                    0111100000000
                    -110101000000
                     001001000000
                      -1101010000
                       0100010000
                        -110101000
                         010111000
                         -11010100
                          01101100
                          -1101010
                           0000110
```

The quotient is 11011110 and is discarded. The remainder is 110 and is retained. The next step is to add the remainder to the new message:

$$1010110000000$$
$$+\underline{110}$$
$$1010110000110$$

This sum is the message that is actually transmitted. Two cases will be explored, first one with no errors in transmission. In this case, when the message above is divided by the generating polynomial P, the reminder should be zero:

```
                    11011110
         110101)1010110000110
                -1101010000000
                 0111100000110
                 -110101000000
                  001001000110
                   -1101010000
                    0100010110
                    -110101000
                     010111110
                     -11010100
                      1101010
                     -1101010
                            0
```

The answer is exactly what one would expect. Now, flip 1 bit and see if the answer changes. The LSB is the bit that is flipped from a 0 to a 1.

```
                    11011110
         110101)1010110000111
                -1101010000000
                 0111100000111
                 -110101000000
                  001001000111
                   -1101010000
                    0100010111
                    -110101000
                     010111111
                     -11010100
                      1101011
                     -1101010
                            1
```

where the last bit was flipped. Note that again exactly what one would have anticipated is found: a nonzero remainder indicating an error in transmission. Note that the CRC method does not give any indication of where the error occurred, only that it did occur.

Table 12.2
CRC generating polynomials

CRC 4	$x^4 + x + 1$
CRC-5	$x^5 + x^4 + x^2 + 1$
CRC-12	$x^{12} + x^{11} + x^3 + x^2 + x^1 + 1$
CRC-16	$x^{16} + x^{15} + x^2 + 1$
CRC-CCITT	$x^{16} + x^{12} + x^5 + 1$

For a better idea of just where the bit positions line up, see Appendix G, where these three modula-2 divisions are shown in table form. This explicitly points out the alignment for each step in the division. To illustrate how the number of bits in the remainder is determined by the order of the CRC polynomial, a fourth-order division is also illustrated in Appendix G.

The increased number of data bits required to be transmitted when using any CRC-XX code is dependent on the length of the data word. Like any code, how the length increases with the length of the data word is an important subject in determining the applicability and efficiency of the code. For this reason, the CRC-XX type codes are used with long data words to minimize the overall bandwidth increase required to use them. This is especially true when the communication channel is well known and does not contribute too many errors.

Many generating polynomials have been defined. Table 12.2, gives four of these CRC polynomials. The CRC-5 is the least used in practice and the most used to illustrate the concept.

Finally, it is of interest to note how this algorithm is implemented in circuitry. Figure 12.2 illustrates this. As can be seen, only two types of components are required. Each of the rectangular boxes represents 1 bit of delay, usually implemented with a D-type flip-flop. The other is the exclusive OR gate, which performs the modula-2 addition required.

The chief distinction of CRC codes is that they are used widely with ARQ protocols as the mechanism to detect errors. ARQ protocols require that a full-duplex channel exist for this type of approach to work. Remember, CRC codes cannot correct an error, they can only detect them. There must be a protocol in place for the destination to request retransmission when a message was received in error. CRC codes are widely used in LAN environments where a full-duplex channel exists naturally.

Figure 12.2
Implementation of the CRC-5 polynomial.

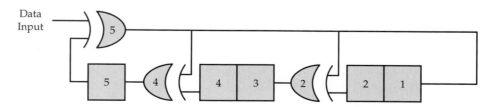

CRC codes are preferred over Hamming or any type of parity code when used in a full-duplex environment where an ARQ protocol can operate because they are only concerned with error detection. Although both Hamming and parity codes can be used as error-detection codes only, they are not the most efficient approach because most full-duplex LAN environments experience very few errors. Typical error rates for a LAN environment is one error in 1 billion bits of transmission. In many cases there will be no errors in a message at all.

On the other hand, when the errors occur, they are likely to occur in a group, or a burst. An error burst begins and ends with an error, but not necessarily all bits in between are in error. The bottom line is that parity or any scheme based on parity such as a Hamming code does not do a good job of detecting error bursts. Although the reasoning for this is outside the scope of this book, this is why CRC, or polynomial codes, as they are sometimes known are used for error detection. CRC codes are the preferred choice when the overall error rate is low and the errors that occur are likely to occur in error bursts.

Summary of Channel Encoding

Channel encoding is a way to represent the data from the source so that it is either different enough or redundant enough to be successfully reproduced at the destination. To wit, they are effective. There are two broad classifications of channel codes: FEC codes and CRC codes used as an error detection in ARQ protocols. In the sections above, examples of both were considered.

In FEC codes there are again two broad subgroupings: block and variable length. Block codes are those where the length of the code remains fixed; the examples of parity and Hamming codes were used to illustrate this type of code. This class is by far the most commonly used channel code in broadcast type systems.

In considering variable-length codes, a couple of examples of rectangular codes were briefly reviewed. These were an early historical fantasy, an example from general education discussions on good practices in letter writing, and how computers can vote to implement a channel code.

■ SOURCE ENCODING

Source encoding is a way to represent the data or symbols being transmitted from the source such that they are represented as efficiently as possible. The term *source code* is used in two different ways. The first way this term is used when the data must appear differently at one end of the communication than they did at the other. For example, a computer wishes to print out a message to a user. To the computer, the message is contained in a series of bits; to the user, the message is a sequence of alphanumeric symbols. Often these applications of source coding are not considered source coding at all but rather are discussed as character codes. Examples include ASCII and the Morse code.

The second use of the term *source codes* is as an information theoretic concept or tool to maximize the information rate from source to destination. Examples of these that will be explored are code trees and Huffman codes. There are many more, and they can get mathematically complex very quickly. This class of codes also clearly satisfy the above definition.

The term *symbol* in the definition above is probably a bit unclear. In all the modulation techniques studied so far, an input transition implied an output transition. In these cases, a bit is equivalent to a symbol. More advanced modulation techniques often group many input bit transitions into a single output transition. In these cases, the group of input or output bits that result in a transition is called a symbol. Until these are discussed in Chapter 13, you can read *symbol* as *bit* with no loss of understanding.

Historically, many codes have been used to represent the source data. Examples include the Baudot code, which was used as far back as the nineteenth century in early telegraph systems and continues to be used in the telex system. Because it was designed to work with mechanical typewriters as the printing mechanism, it integrated the typewriter's design principles in the code design.

Specifically, the Baudot code utilized a single control character, up-shift, to signify pressing the shift key on the typewriter keyboard. This indicates that all characters to follow are uppercase, the next transmission of a control character, down-shift, indicates that all characters to follow are lowercase.

It should be apparent how a single bit error in one of these control characters would produce a potentially large number of errors at the receiver. Note that this code type offers no error-detecting bits. Additionally, subsequent data depends on the correct reception of earlier data. For this reason this type of code is known as a sequential code.

Another familiar code used for source encoding is the ASCII code. This code uses 7 bits to represent all letters, punctuation, and numbers on a keyboard. It was the first computer code and has been in use since the early 1960s. The first 7 bits of the code are assigned as discussed and shown in Table 12.3. In ASCII, the LSB is always transmitted first; this can be initially confusing.

The ASCII code as it is usually envisioned is an 8 bit code. The last bit is used as an FEC error-detection bit and is a parity bit. As discussed earlier, it detects the number of 1s in the word. It can be used to detect an even or odd number of 1 bits, hence, the name even parity or odd parity. Both are used, but odd parity is more common because it detects the message of all 0s and marks it as in error. Even parity would detect the all 1s case, but loss of signal, (all zeros) is clearly an error and is only detected by odd parity. As a result, 8 bit ASCII combines source and channel encoding into one code. This sometimes causes confusion. In this discussion, ASCII will be discussed as a 7 bit block source code.

Therefore, in practice, ASCII is sometimes used as a 7 bit code, and other error detection schemes are applied to improve the probability of correct reception. If the DTE equipment requires 8 bit ASCII, typically this parity bit is stripped before transmission and added back after reception. This saves that bit position and reduces the bandwidth required for the channel, where the even rate of the channel is very small.

ASCII is a block source code. Like any source code it is used to represent the source data. Since the advent of binary computers, which use 1s and 0s rather than the alphabet and the decimal system, there has been a need to represent letters and numbers in a different base while still using the computer to process them. The ASCII code has become this code.

Table 12.3
7 Bit ASCII Code

1	2	3	4	5-0 6-1 7-1	5-1 6-1 7-1	5-0 6-0 7-1	5-1 6-0 7-1	5-1 6-1 7-0	5-0 6-1 7-0	5-0 6-0 7-0	5-1 6-0 7-0
0	0	0	0	\	p	@	P	0	SP	NUL	DLE
1	0	0	0	a	q	A	Q	1	!	SOH	DC1
0	1	0	0	b	r	B	R	2	"	STX	DC2
1	1	0	0	c	s	C	S	3	#	ETX	DC3
0	0	1	0	d	t	D	T	4	$	EOT	DC4
1	0	1	0	e	u	E	U	5	%	ENQ	NAK
0	1	1	0	f	v	F	V	6	&	ACK	SYN
1	1	1	0	g	w	G	W	7	'	BEL	ETB
0	0	0	1	h	x	H	X	8	(	BS	CAN
1	0	0	1	i	y	I	Y	9	)	HT	EM
0	1	0	1	j	z	J	Z	:	*	LF	SUB
1	1	0	1	k	{	K	[	;	+	VT	ESC
0	0	1	1	l	:	L	/	<	'	FF	FS
1	0	1	1	m	}	M	]	=	−	CR	CR
0	1	1	1	n	~	N	^	>	.	SO	SO
1	1	1	1	o	DEL	O	_	?	/	SI	SI

Again, some would argue that a code such as ASCII is not strictly a source code at all and should be referred to as a character set or character code. Because this code satisfies the definition of a source code, it is both unnecessary and confusing to add a further classification. Nevertheless, it is talked about in both ways among practitioners of the craft, so be prepared for both ways of referring to this code.

ASCII Code, a Block Source Code

ASCII is the standard code for source coding the alphanumeric character set that human beings like to use and computers don't understand. When computers communicate with human beings, they need a way to represent the data in the files they transfer, so they source encode the data using the ASCII code to communicate more effectively.

Again, the ASCII code uses 7 bits, which are actual code representations of different characters. Interestingly, the ASCII code was developed in such a way that subsets of the code are very useful for some applications. This is shown in Table 12.3. The form of the table might be a little unfamiliar because it is designed to bring out this point.

This presentation clearly demonstrates that ASCII is properly regarded as a source encoding, the encoding being variable for efficiency depending on the source data set. Because the lowest order bit position is sent first, this will be represented in the first column. The next three columns represent the next three bit positions. The seven bit positions all have the first four bit positions in common, only bit positions five through seven change. As a result, in each of these columns only the fifth, sixth, and seventh bit positions are shown, respectively. Also, note that the order of the bit positions is not in normal binary sequence. This was done to emphasize the fact that this code is reducible if the source data set is reducible. Note that there are a few characters that are represented more than once.

Variable-Length Source Codes

Variable-length source codes are a type of source encoding that is very similar to block codes except that the code is not a fixed length. In other words the length of the code varies from symbol to symbol. As mentioned earlier, the Morse code is the most familiar example of a variable-length source code. Because the usual idea in data communications is to express the most data in the least bandwidth, variable-length codes typically analyze the data alphabet to be sent and use short codes to represent those symbols that occur most frequently.

The Morse code gives an example; E in the Morse code is "dot," and T is a "dash." Both are very common letters and both use the shortest code length possible. Letters like H, V, F, L, P, J, B, X, C, Y, Z, and Q use code lengths of some combination of four dots and dashes.

For a good mnemonic to remember Morse code, see Figure 12.3. This diagram shows several interesting things about the Morse code. First, it clearly demonstrates the

Figure 12.3
Morse code mnemonic diagram.

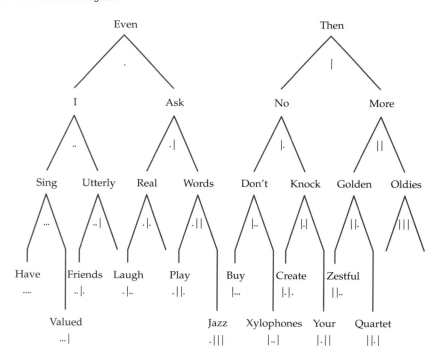

idea of a variable-length code, with the shortest code lengths on the top of the pyramid. In any good design, the codes the shortest length should correspond to the most frequently used letters of the code alphabet. Second, this diagram is a useful mnemonic to recall the code for people who are familiar with the binary code because it sorts the codes by a binary sequence. Note that if you regard a dot as a 0 and a dash as a 1, the diagram proceeds to count in binary from the top down and from left to right. Finally, note that there are code groups that do not correspond to a letter of the alphabet.

The choice of the code representation of each symbol to be transmitted depends on statistics. If every data symbol to be transmitted occurs with the same frequency, there is generally no advantage to using a variable-length code. This is because there is no reduction in data sent, and the complexity of the receiver is increased. This is because with a variable-length code comes the problem of knowing at the receiver where the code starts and stops for each transmitted symbol. This may seem like a complex problem, but with the right insights it becomes straightforward, recall the discussion of start and stop bits in Chapter 11. The use of stop and start bits is one approach, but as will be pointed out in the next few paragraphs, other ways exist.

When it is appropriate to use a variable-length code, apply the following approach to determine where the data stops and the code begins. First, find some way to tell what a symbol is at the receiver. This is straightforward with block codes; just count bits. With a variable-length code this approach will not work because the length of each data code is variable. Forget about the start and stop points at first and concentrate on making a decision tree that will allow the selection of the right symbol with no knowledge of the length of the transmitted code word.

The key is to make sure that *no code word has the prefix of any other code word*. The length of the shortest code determines the length of the prefix that must be examined. For example, in Table 12.4, the shortest code length is 1 bit. In code one, no code of any length has a prefix of 0. In code two the shortest code length is 2 bits. In code two, no code of any length has a prefix of any of the 2 bit codes shown (00, 01, 10). This allows the receiver to determine the length of the code because each code is unique, and no code is a shortened version of another. This avoids the clumsy process of inserting start and stop bits.

Table 12.4
Example of Variable Length Codes for Different Alphabet Frequencies

Letter or Code Symbol	Frequency One (%)	Code One	Frequency Two (%)	Code Two
1	45	0	20	00
2	20	10	20	01
3	15	110	20	10
4	10	1110	16	110
5	5	11110	12	1110
6	5	11111	12	1111

If you think about it, those in large families that get together on the holidays use this same method. If you and your grandparents, parents, sons, daughters, brothers, sisters, cousins, aunts, uncles, nephews, and so forth, get together, many will have the same last name. However, all have different first names or at least different nicknames used when the family gathers. Each person can be identified uniquely by just using the unique prefix of his or her full name. This is just the same as what is done here, except the prefix is not a first name but some number of bits.

It is interesting to compare this situation to Morse code, which, although also a variable-length code, does not have the unique prefix feature just mentioned. As a result, Morse code requires special signaling to determine the start and stop of transmitted code words. Typically this is done with a short pause between letters. Additionally, the entire transmission is typically started (CQ) and terminated (SK) with a special code word.

Code Trees

Code trees are a way to form a variable-length code that will not require the special type of start/stop signaling that codes like the Morse code do. To illustrate, assume an alphabet of six symbols that a variable-length code is used to represent. This use of the term *alphabet* is a way to refer to the set of symbols to be coded, just like the 26 letter alphabet that is used to write with is referred to. In coding the term *alphabet* is used to describe the n letter set of symbols to be coded. The frequency of the letters in the particular alphabet being used to illustrate the principle is listed in Table 12.4. The frequency of a letter in an alphabet is just how often it occurs.

Both codes shown in Table 12.4 have the property that no code word has the prefix of any other code word. To determine how good a particular code is for a particular alphabet, use the average-length calculation. The calculation takes the probability of each letter of the alphabet and multiplies it by the length of the code. The next example illustrates this for the two codes shown in Table 12.4.

■ EXAMPLE 12.9

$$\text{frequency one average length} = 1(0.45) + 2(0.20) + 3(0.15) + 4(0.10)$$
$$+ 5(0.05) + 5(0.05) = 2.20$$

$$\text{frequency two average length} = 2(0.20) + 2(0.20) + 2(0.20) + 3(0.16)$$
$$+ 4(0.12) + 4(0.12) = 2.64$$

Note that code one is better suited to the data alphabet with frequency one, and similarly code two is better suited to the data alphabet with frequency two. Also note that the choice of a single bit to represent the letter A in code one required the use of up to 5 bits to represent two of the letters. Although in code two, where the minimum code length for any letter is 2 bits, a maximum of 4 bits is required to represent two of the letters.

Example 12.9 shows an expression of a general rule; when constructing a variable-length code and minimal-length codes are chosen early, a penalty must be paid later in the code. Essentially, what happens is that many choices are eliminated from the code tree by that early choice. In code one, only *one* code can start with a 0 because it is a representation by itself of a letter in the alphabet. In code two, because no single bit represents a letter in the alphabet, two codes can start with zero.

It comes down to statistics. How frequent is each letter transmitted? This will guide you in determining the best code for a particular application. To illustrate further how this works, the decision tree diagrams for each of the above codes are shown in Figures 12.4 and 12.5. Note how the early choice of a single bit for a code word in code 1 caused the code tree to branch in one direction only. Contrast this with code tree 2, where branches occur in both directions.

Again, the best guide for deciding to choose how to branch the code tree is the statistics of the alphabet. The frequency of the letters in code 1, with code symbol 1 comprising 45% of the data, led us to a nonbranching tree. Contrast this with code 2, where the code symbol 1 comprises only 20% of the data leads us to chose a branching structure. In summary, the "flatter" the alphabet percentages are, the more likely the better code will occur with a branching structure.

Always remember that if the transmitted data is represented with more than the minimum number of bits, the data bandwidth necessary to transmit a random collection

Figure 12.4
Code tree one.

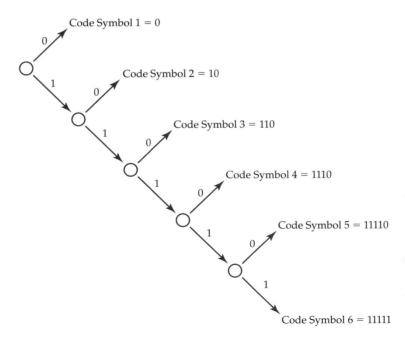

Figure 12.5
Code tree two.

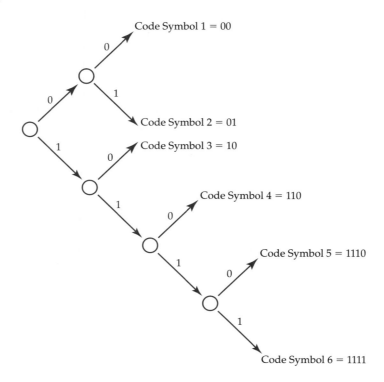

of the data will increase. Virtually all variable-length codes end up requiring this overhead. Therefore, make sure that the bandwidth gains achieved by using variable code lengths more than compensate for the increased bandwidth required to send the infrequently occurring letters of the alphabet. There is a way around this, and that is using something called trellis-coded modulation, or more generally, signal space coding. This subject will be briefly described later. Signal space coding extends coding theory into modulation theory and in some limited sense gets you the bandwidth required for the extra coding bits without cost.

Many popular telephone line modems, for example, the CCITT V.34 and V.90 standards, use this technique because the bandwidth of the plain old telephone system (POTS) telephone line is very limited and fixed across the system. For the last 10 years, this approach has been the primary method of increasing the data rate of modems used in PCs. Of course, this also increases the complexity of both the transmitter and receiver. Because the receiver is more susceptible to amplitude variation in the channel, except for these costs, the bandwidth increases that might be expected from the increased data rate can be minimized.

Huffman Codes

Another good example of a variable-length source code is Huffman codes. Huffman codes make use of the probabilities of the various symbols being sent. As in the Morse code, it is desirable to have the most frequently used symbols have the shortest encoding. Huffman codes are classified as variable-length source codes.

Building a Huffman code is straightforward. As will be seen, this type of code has many similarities to the code that would result by applying the code tree algorithm discussed above. To construct a Huffman code, a set of symbols, along with the probabilities that they occur, are provided. It is then a process of reduction and splitting to find the Huffman code. Huffman codes are not unique but do have unique prefixes. It is possible to end up with different codes depending on the initial choices of assignments. However, all Huffman codes for the same alphabet are the same average length *if you always select the lowest probabilities to combine at each step*. That is, if you multiply the probability of each symbol times its length and add them up, the total is the same for any Huffman code of the same alphabet, generated in the manner shown in Table 12.5.

To illustrate, take a five letter alphabet with the probabilities shown in Table 12.5. This table will also illustrate the first step in forming a code, the reduction process. As can be seen, the probabilities of each symbol are combined to reduce the number of states required for the code, essentially moving to a shorter code at each reduction step. At the first reduction, the code length was four codes, after the second, three codes, and after the third and final reduction, just two codes were required.

This is done by combining the *two least-probable symbols of the source alphabet into a single symbol* whose probability is equal to the sum of the two probabilities corresponding to the combined symbols. Therefore, the source alphabet to be encoded consists of one less symbol. No matter how many symbols are in the source alphabet, just continue this process until there are just two symbols in the alphabet to encode. Naturally, a 0 is chosen for one of them and a 1 for the other. Also, note that at each step of reduction, the codes were reordered so that the highest probability stayed on top.

This reduction process results in a very short encoding but there is no way to send the symbols that have been combined uniquely. Therefore, this process must be reversed and one of these two symbols must be split into two parts, typically by adding a second digit 0 for one and 1 for the other. In the next stage, one of the now three sym-

Table 12.5
Huffman Code Reduction Process

Symbol	Probability	First Reduce	Second Reduce	Third Reduce
S1	0.4	0.4	0.4	0.6
S2	0.2	0.2	0.4	0.4
S3	0.2	0.2	0.2	
S4	0.1	0.2		
S5	0.1			

Table 12.6
Huffman Code Split Process

Symbol	Third Split		Second Split		First Split		Choice	
S1	1	0.4	1	0.4	1	0.4	0	0.6
S2	01	0.2	01	0.2	00	0.4	1	0.4
S3	000	0.2	000	0.2	01	0.2		
S4	0010	0.1	001	0.2				
S5	0011	0.1						

bols is split into two symbols in just the same way. See the Table 12.6. The process is now moving backward, so read the table from right to left.

To determine the average length of any code, do the same procedure as was demonstrated earlier. Add up the code generated and determine the average length. To do this, multiply each code length in bits by the probability of each symbol:

$$\text{average length} = (0.4)(1) + (0.2)(2) + (0.2)(3) + (0.1)(4) + (0.1)(4) = 2.20$$

■ EXAMPLE 12.10

Find the Huffman code for the alphabet shown in Tables 12.7 and 12.8. Perform both the reduction and split processes. Then, find the average length of the code developed:

Table 12.7
Example 12.10, Reduction Process

Symbol	Probability	First Reduce	Second Reduce
S1	0.4	0.4	0.6
S2	0.2	0.4	0.4
S3	0.2	0.2	
S4	0.2		

Table 12.8
Example 12–10, Split Process

Symbol	Result	Second Split		First Split		Choice
S1	1	0.4	1	0.4	0	0.6
S2	00	0.2	00	0.2	1	0.4
S3	010	0.2	01	0.4		
S4	011	0.2				

$$\text{average length} = (1 \text{ bit})(0.4) + (2 \text{ bits})(0.2) + (3 \text{ bits})(0.2) + (3 \text{ bits})(0.2) = 2.0$$

This calculation shows that the average length of a code word will be 2 bits.

It is also of interest to see how a Huffman code would look and how to decode it. The next example illustrates this for the code developed in Example 12.10.

■ EXAMPLE 12.11

Suppose the message to be sent is S2,S2,S3,S1,S4,S3. The code string would look like the following:

$$00000101011010$$

To decode this, just read across the bits and when a match is found, immediately write it down, and start searching again. Because each code has a unique prefix, this approach will always work.

$$00 - S1, 00 - S1, 010 - S3, 1 - S1, 011 - S4, 010 - S3$$

Summary of Source Coding

In this section, two types of source coding were discussed. These were block source codes, such as ASCII, and variable-length source codes, such as the Morse or Huffman code. Again, source codes are those codes that are used to represent the data being transmitted as efficiently as possible. How to use a decision tree and statistics of the data alphabet to design codes for efficiency were explored.

■ COMBINED EXAMPLE

To further illustrate the two types of coding, channel and source, a combined example will be provided. Of course, as discussed, the 8 bit ASCII code is already a combined example. However, it is interesting to look at another. Most readers are very familiar with the binary code used to represent decimal numbers: Seven in base 10 is represented as 111 in base 2. This is a very simple example of coding, using no additional bits to enhance the reliability of the code (channel encoding) and just using a different number system to act like a source code. Strictly speaking, number representations are not considered codes, but for illustration, this consideration will be overlooked.

In this example, assume that the most significant (MSB) is distorted in transmission. First, understand that without channel encoding, the error could not be detected. Both potential MSB values, 0 and 1, are valid representations of decimal numbers 3 and 7. So channel encoding would be first used to detect errors.

If the entire message length was known to be 3 bits, (if you knew that the source encoding was 1:1), you could guess, with a 50/50 chance of success, that it was a decimal 3 or 7. This is a higher rate of error than might at first be realized. To see this, note that although only 1 bit in 3 was received in error, the entire block of data was in error when

Figure 12.6
Code relationships.

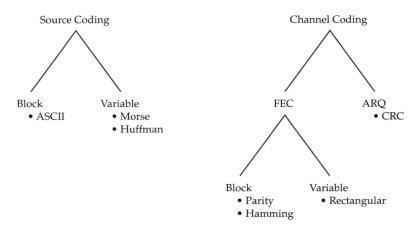

translated by the receiver. Therefore, a single bit error in transmission caused a 3 bit error in the receiver. This phenomena is usually referred to as frame error rate as compared to bit error rate and underlines the need for some type of coding to detect errors. It should be clear that with large frame sizes, the important error rate is the frame error rate.

If 1 bit parity code was used as a channel code, in this case you could reasonably expect to fix the error by knowing whether the number of 1 bits was odd or even. Note that this 1 bit parity code only detects single bit errors. If 2 bits were in error such that a 10 translated to a 01, a 1 bit parity would not detect the error. This is another illustration of the general principle that FEC coding requires enough bits to detect the maximum number of errors expected in each block or frame of data sent.

In a full-duplex environment, where the channel encoding variant, ARQ signaling, was permitted, if some additional error detection mechanism such as CRC codes was used, error detection could be determined. Once this was accomplished, a retransmission could be requested. Because the likelihood of the same error decreases the more times it is sent, eventually the message would be received correctly unless the noise was so high as to distort every message to the point of unintelligibility.

Alternately, if the message had been sent three times, (variable-length channel encoding at 3:1), just vote for the right message. Of course, the noise environment must be low enough so that it could be predicted with confidence that at least two of the three messages would get through without error. The idea is that whatever message content at least two out of three agree on, that must be the correct message. Figure 12.6 illustrates how the various codes discussed are related to each other.

■ SCRAMBLING

A related topic to coding, in the sense that it preconditions the data stream prior to transmission, is the subject of scrambling. This term is used in two ways in communication systems; the first is perhaps the better understood one. To scramble a signal is to hide it unless you know the decode sequence. This is not the intent of the use of the word in this section. Although the second meaning of *scramble* also includes this result, it is only circumstantial and in no way is message actually made secure. The main result of the scrambling discussed here is the smoothing the spectral shape. This means distributing the power smoothly across the entire transmit bandwidth.

To understand why this is useful, recall that in most cases the data set to be transmitted is "sort of" random in nature. This sort of random quality results because data that is interesting to transmit usually represents some economic value. Most of the time, things made for human beings are not random; they feature long strings of 1s or 0s. These strings might represent the white space on the edge of a piece of paper or the blue sky in a picture. Additionally, most realistic data sets have patterns that emerge quite frequently. A good example is the space between the state and zip code or the regularized pattern inherent in the two letter designation of state and five number zip code, all surrounded with spaces. To get around these nonrandom patterns of data, scrambling controls the spectral shape of the transmitter, basically to make it as smooth and random as possible.

To illustrate, imagine a string of data like 10101010, or '00000000', or '11110000'. In the process of modulation, these data patterns will generate spectral lines at the frequency associated with the data pattern. These spectral lines will have much greater energy than a truly random pattern. Many subsections of a receiver make implicit assumptions about the nature of the data pattern. One is that it will not feature strong spectral lines. This concern is real, because these can cause radio frequency interference in adjacent channels, violating the law.

To make sure that the spectral envelope is relatively smooth, a scrambler is inserted in the modulation scheme. This scrambler pseudorandomizes the data to reduce the probability of long transmitted sequences of identical data and randomizes spectral components of the transmitted data. All modern CCITT modems use some kind of scrambling in their modulators and, of course, the inverse scrambling in the demodulators.

This is accomplished in the same way as the polynomial function approach discussed above in the section on CRC codes. This generator polynomial has as its highest power 32, which is often described as the generator polynomial of order 32. This is widely used in LAN systems. The scrambler works by dividing the input data sequence by the generator polynomial. The descrambler in the receiver then multiplies the scrambled sequence by the same generator polynomial, hence, performing the inverse operation done at the transmitter.

■ TRELLIS CODED MODULATION (TCM)

Trellis coded modulation is a method whereby additional redundancy is placed in the alphabet to overcome errors in the channel. It is not often considered a channel code but is instead referred to as a type of digital modulation. Usually, this is discussed as an enhancement of a type of digital modulation known as QAM and designated TCQAM. QAM will be discussed in Chapter 13. Although the introduction of this section at this point may be premature, it is a coding technique and therefore is included in the chapter on coding.

Figure 12.7
Convolutional encoder used for TCM.

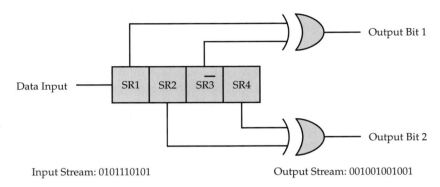

Input Stream: 0101110101 Output Stream: 001001001001

TCM uses a variation of FEC coding called convolutional coding that sends some number of redundant bit(s) in each symbol or code word. *Convolution* means to fold one part over another. Here, the value of the previous bits are used to determine the value of the additional bit(s) inserted; they are folded over. Effectively, at the receiver each bit in the data stream is compared with some number of previous bits. Because the convolutional encoder sets the state of the nth bit depending on the state of the previous few bits, if an error occurs due to noise in the channel, the previous bits can sometimes be used to correct the bit in error.

All dial line telephone modems, V.32, V.34, and V.90, that operate at data rates of 9.6 and higher use some form of TCM. The name *trellis* comes from the diagrams used to determine the value of the additional bit(s) inserted. The diagrams appear similar to trellis fences, which are exemplified by an overlay or lattice of boards. The actual algorithms used to determine the value of the additional bits inserted into the data stream are complex and outside the scope of this section. However, a brief example will illustrate the concept.

Typically, these systems are implemented as shift registers. The value of bits sent is determined through a truth table of the value of the input bits. In this example a shift register of 4 bits will be used; the value of the shift register contents will be applied to two exclusive-OR gates to obtain a modulo-2 value of the shift register contents. Both output bits will be sent. Figure 12.7 illustrates the circuit diagram. Assuming the shift register is loaded with all zeros to begin a bit pattern such as shown in Table 12.9 would result.

■ CODES USED TO ENHANCE SECURITY AND CRYPTOGRAPHY

In this section the way the word *code* is usually used in everyday language is explored. There are many codes used today. Interest is growing as more critical business and financial information is being transmitted over the Internet. Historically, this subject has been of interest to a wide variety of people and institutions.

Table 12.9
Input and Output Sequences for Figure 12.7

Input Data	SR1	SR2	SR3	SR4	Output Bit 1	Output Bit 2
0	0	0	0	0	0	0
1	1	0	0	0	1	0
0	0	1	0	0	0	1
1	1	0	1	0	0	0
1	1	1	0	1	1	0
1	1	1	1	0	0	1
0	0	1	1	1	1	0
1	1	0	1	1	0	1
0	0	1	0	1	0	0
1	1	0	1	0	0	0

My own initial contact with the subject was in a box of cereal where one could find a special decoder ring to get "secret" messages from a children's TV show. This is an example of a substitution code. This ring used a letter-to-letter substitution code. Such a code works by shifting the entire alphabet by the same offset. This renders it very easy to break; one only has to find a single letter match and the rest of the code is obvious. To illustrate, imagine a code message like RFGQ AMSPQC GQ DSL.

At first glance, this seems very cryptic, however, once it is known that the code is a simple substitution code and you are given one hint, the message is very easily determined. The hint is that the offset is two letters; an A in the code or cipher text is actually a C in plain text. This means one can construct a decoding table very easily, as is shown below. The actual decoding is left as an exercise for the reader.

Plain text: ABCDEFGHIJKLMNOPQRSTUVWXYZ

Cipher text: YZABCDEFGHIJKLMNOPQRSTUVWX

Later, a radio station issued a similar "official identification and decoder ring" to be used for a similar purpose. This ring used a number-to-letter substitution code. The ring consisted of two concentric dials. The center one could rotate and had the numbers 0 to 29 in equal graduations. The outer ring, which did not rotate, had the letters of the alphabet around it in equal graduations. However, the alphabet was not just A, B, C, . . . , but was in the following order: WABXFMDETROITZGNUVKSHEFMPLCSQY. Note that some letters are used more than once and that just knowing one letter number match, it is impossible to determine the next because the letters are in no particular order.

This is actually a pretty advanced code; it is called a multialphabetic substitution code because different numbers can map to the same letter, F, for example. However, if you need to send the letter J, you are out of luck. If the plain text and cipher text are both 26 letters long and each letter of the alphabet appears just once, the code is referred to as a monoalphabetic code. Many historical codes used this principle of just substituting one letter for another.

Another form of code that is related to the substitution codes above is where different substitutions are made for each occurrence of each letter. For example, the first time a letter A is encountered, it is replaced with a C in the cipher text. The next time the letter A is encountered in the plain text to be coded, it is replaced with a G, and so on. This can be extended to several layers and was and is a common method to encode secret messages. Today, powerful computers can easily decode these codes if enough messages are assembled so a pattern can be determined. This approach also requires a secret key.

Another class of code is the data encryption standard (DES) code. This is a code adopted and standardized by the United States as an official standard for use by all but the government. DES codes require a secret key to decode them. Because of modern computing techniques, the standard DES code is no longer secure. Essentially, the key can be determined by examining the message. This technique is called substitution permutation. Additionally, if the key itself is not at least as secure as the message, a DES code can be broken with the key.

For all the codes discussed above, keeping the key secret is critical. In the decoder ring example, the key was the order of the letters and their mapping to the numbers. About 20 years ago, the idea of public key cryptography was conceived. In this approach, the encryption key was different from the decryption key. Additionally, one could not be determined from another. At one stroke of insight, the secret key problem went away.

In this scheme, the encryption and decryption algorithm is distributed widely. Then the table of encryption keys assigned to each person who wants to get a secret message is distributed widely. Only the decryption key is private, and it is different for each person. This means that it is very easy to send anyone a secret message and only the intended recipient has the appropriate key to decode it.

This means that one principle way that secret messages were decoded is lost; it is not possible to just decode one message, or steal one key, to know how to decode all messages. Instead, the key for the particular recipient to whom the message was sent must be known. Additionally, there is nothing that says that each person's key stays the same or that each only gets one key. As can seen, this is a very secure system.

Today, most codes in practical use are of the class of codes known as RSA codes. These codes are specific examples of public key systems using specialized algorithms. There are several algorithms that will satisfy the public key model and each is usually named after the discover(s) or some idea central to the algorithmic approach. The RSA code uses the difficulty in factoring very large numbers to make it hard to break.

Finally, all cryptography suffers from advances in computing power. As computers get faster, the algorithms that generate the codes become more susceptible to being broken by sophisticated computers. Public key cryptography offers some special security here, but it also is susceptible to advances in computer speed and power. Recently, the Internet has been used to add to this power by linking hundreds of PCs together to break a code instead of using a single large computer. Even more recently, just a few more powerful workstations were used to break a similar code. As this book went to press, one of the authors of the RSA code published a design algorithm for a single specialized computer to break the RSA cod quite quickly.

PROBLEMS

1. Determine the Hamming code length for data word lengths as shown below:
   - (a) 10 bits
   - (b) 8 bits
   - (c) 16 bits
   - (d) 4 bits

2. Draw code trees for each of the following alphabets. Make sure that no code word has the prefix of any other code word. Compute the average length of each code:
   - (a) (1) 33 percent
     - (2) 33 percent
     - (3) 33 percent
   - (b) (1) 10 percent
     - (2) 20 percent
     - (3) 30 percent
     - (4) 40 percent
   - (c) (1) 25 percent
     - (2) 25 percent
     - (3) 25 percent
     - (4) 25 percent
   - (d) (a) 10 percent
     - (b) 45 percent
     - (c) 45 percent

3. Explain why 1 bit parity codes are useless for double bit errors.

4. Generate the Hamming code words of 7 bits for each of the following 4 bit data words. Assume that the Hamming bits are inserted in the correct positions as in the example in the text.
   - (a) 1010
   - (b) 1100
   - (c) 0001
   - (d) 1110

5. For each of the 7 bit code words developed in problem 4, flip bit 3, and verify that the syndrome correctly predicts the bit error location.

6. Which technique would be preferable to use, source or channel coding, if the problem was that people were listening in on your conversation? Why?

7. Which techniques would be preferable to use, source or channel coding, if the problem was that many of your conversations were being lost in transmit? Why?

8. Classical cryptographic codes such as a substitution code can be fun. Develop such a code for the 26 letter alphabet and show a sample message of at least five words both in plain text and cipher text.

9. Find and read an article on public key cryptography. Discuss in a paragraph or two if you think it would be a good system to use to keep secret credit card numbers on the Internet and why.

10. Perform the Huffman code generation process for the following alphabet. Also, find the average length of the code generated.

    S1:0.4 S2:0.2 S3:0.2 S4:0.2

11. Find the code tree for the following alphabet. Compute the average length of the code. See how efficient you can make it.

    S1:0.2 S2:0.2 S3:0.15 S4:0.15
    S5:0.1 S6:0.1 S7:0.1

12. Write a software program to take an arbitrary data word input of 8 bits and find the CRC code, using the generating polynomial shown below.

$$x^5 + x^4 + x^1 + x^0$$

13. Write a software program to check received data words that have been CRC encoded from problem 12. Verify that it correctly recovers the original transmitted data word when no errors in transmission occur and identifies when an error occurred.

Digital Modulation

In this chapter several methods of combining modulation types to produce effective modulation techniques for communicating digital signals will be explored. Much of what has gone before when discussing analog modulation techniques was in preparation for this chapter. These digital techniques are in wide use for data communications today. These digital communications techniques are used almost universally in the both terrestrial and space-based data communications.

An examination of how information capacity and bandwidth interact in digital communications systems will begin the chapter. Following the three basic types of digital modulation, amplitude shift keying (ASK), frequency shift keying (FSK), and phase shift keying (PSK) will be introduced. These three types come directly from the discussions of AM, FM, and PM modulation techniques and much of what was learned there will apply. Extrapolating from these basic techniques to more advanced modulation techniques that combine elements of both amplitude and angle modulation will follow. Emphasis will be on bandwidth and spectral issues. Brief presentations of representative modulators and demodulators are shown. Constellation diagrams, carrier-to-noise, and E_b/N_o calculations conclude the chapter.

Communications systems that use the principles of digital modulation go by the general name of digital radio. Digital radios, like modems, use pulsed waveforms as the modulating signals and utilize analog modulation techniques, sometimes implemented digitally, that result in the information being carried on a carrier signal. To be clear about where the techniques that are discussed in this chapter fit with what has already explored, examine Figure 13.1.

Figure 13.1
Classification of communication systems.

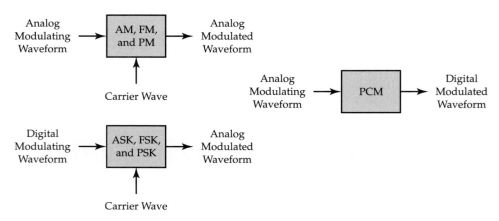

INFORMATION CAPACITY

Although Chapter 1 discussed in a general way how bandwidth and information capacity are related, there was no explicit development of a relationship between the two. The relationship known as Hartley's Law was developed to give a to expresses this relationship. Hartley's Law says that as the bandwidth or duration of a transmission increases, the amount of information communicated also increases.

$$I \propto BT \tag{13-1}$$

where I = information capacity
          B = bandwidth
          T = time or duration of transmission

The unfamiliar symbol in equation 13-1 means proportional to. This statement of Hartley's illustrates that just as distance equals rate times time, information capacity equals bandwidth times time.

It would be nice to be able to use Hartley's Law to estimate the data rate one could expect to achieve for a given channel bandwidth and duration of transmission. This will be done, but first it must be clear how hertz and bits per second are related. This will have an important impact on how the bandwidth of a digital signal is determined.

BANDWIDTH OF DIGITAL SIGNALS

This section examines how bandwidth of a digital signal is determined. Recall from Chapter 6 that the fundamental frequency of any pulsed waveform is given by its fun-

Figure 13.2
Frequency calculations for analog and digital waves.

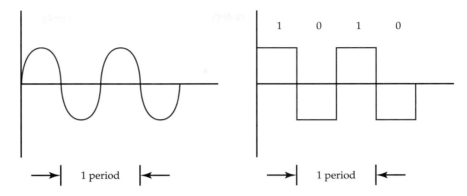

damental sinusoidal component. This was demonstrated for square waves and a number of pulsed waves of arbitrary shape and leads to the conclusion that the minimum baseband bandwidth of any pulsed wave must be just that fundamental frequency. This is often referred to as the pulse repetition rate.

To take the next step, think about how digital data is expressed and compare it to how an analog signal's frequency is determined. Figure 13.2, should make this clear.

As is well known, when the frequency of a sinusoidal wave is calculated, the period is just inverted. However, note that with digital signals, an alternating 1 and 0 combine to create one "period." To think about this, consider what the fastest digital signal change would be. Alternating 1s and 0s, like 10101010, is as fast as it can get. The frequency this alternating 1–0 pattern produces is just half of the bit rate. In other words, there are 2 bits in every square wave period. This result means that the baseband bandwidth of a digital signal is half the bit rate for any binary modulation scheme. This is expressed by the following equation:

$$f_m = \frac{\text{DR}}{2}$$ (13-2)

where f_m = equivalent modulation frequency = $\dfrac{w_m}{2\pi}$

DR = modulating signal binary data rate

A brief example will make this clear.

■ **EXAMPLE 13.1**

A binary signal is to be amplitude modulated. The data rate of the binary modulation signal is 10 kbps. What is the baseband bandwidth and the double-sided transmit bandwidth of the signal?

$$\text{baseband BW: } f_m = \frac{\text{DR}}{2} = \frac{10 \text{ kbps}}{2} = 5 \text{ kHz}$$

$$\text{transmit BW: BW} = 2f_m = (2)(5 \text{ kHz}) = 10 \text{ kHz}$$

When bandwidth is referred to, it will be taken to mean the double-sided transmit bandwidth unless specifically noted otherwise.

From now on the modulating data rate will be assumed to be converted to a frequency if stated in hertz and assumed to be in binary if stated in bits per second. Be careful in converting between them, or your bandwidth calculations will always be in error.

This maximum rate of change in the binary modulating waveform is referred to as the Nyquist rate. In this text, except where explicitly noted otherwise, the binary waveform is at this rate. This means that in all bandwidth calculations the maximum bandwidth will result. Because the modulating signal, the binary waveform, will usually have an arbitrary data pattern, if we use the Nyquist rate for the bandwidth calculations, sufficient bandwidth will always be enough to pass all information. Example 13.2 further illustrates the relationship between binary waveforms and frequency.

■ EXAMPLE 13.2

A binary waveform is formed of the 8 bit words shown below. Determine the frequency components and verify that by using the Nyquist rate for bandwidth calculations that all frequency components of the original data pattern are of a lower frequency than the Nyquist rate. Assume that the data rate of the binary modulating waveform is 1 kbps. The patterns are

$$10101010 \qquad 11001100 \qquad 1111000$$

Figure 13.3 should make the relationship clear. If the first pattern is used for finding the baseband bandwidth by applying equation 13-2, all other patterns will be of a lower frequency. Note that data rate is expressed in bits per second and frequency is expressed in hertz.

Now Hartley's Law can be reevaluated with this fact in mind. Essentially just multiply the bandwidth by an additional factor of 2. This rewriting of the relationship for digital signals is shown below:

$$I \propto 2BT \tag{13-3}$$

■ SHANNON'S LIMIT

Hartley's law gave us a relationship between information capacity and bandwidth depending on time of transmission. Shannon's limit will extend this concept to include the

Figure 13.3
Example 13.2

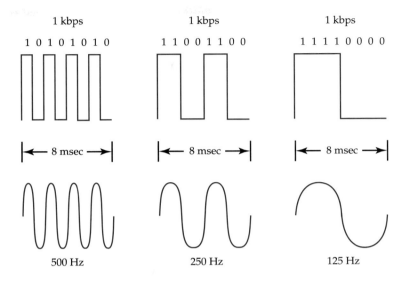

signal-to-noise ratio of the channel as well. This was a critical insight and opened the door to many modern modulation techniques. Equation 13-4 expresses the Shannon Limit:

$$I = 3.32BT \log\left(1 + \frac{S}{N}\right) \tag{13-4}$$

where S/N is the familiar signal-to-noise ratio that has been discussed for each modulation technique discussed so far, and the logarithm is the common or base 2, logarithm.

The really interesting thing about the Shannon Limit is that it says that if each symbol transmitted represents more than 1 bit, information capacity is limited only by the signal-to-noise ratio of the channel. Our study of modulation to this point has always assumed that each output transition was the result of an input transition. The Shannon Limit allows the consideration of representing more than one input change with one output change. This is a powerful concept and is at the basis of all modern digital communications.

Once it is rejected that one input change can only result in one output change, the linear relationship of information capacity and bandwidth shown by Hartley's Law is also rejected. In this chapter, the combination of modulation techniques that are used to produce these so-called M-ary modulators will be introduced. The M in M-ary, is short for multiple, and it takes its name from binary, conceptualized, as only an engineer could, as bin-ary.

■ EXAMPLE 13.3

What is the information capacity predicted by Hartley's Law and the Shannon Limit for a bandwidth of 3100 Hz and a signal-to-noise ratio of 30 dB? First, find the signal level that is implied by the logarithmic value of signal to noise:

$$\frac{S}{N}(dB) = 10 \log\left(\frac{S}{N}\right) = 30 = 10 \log\left(\frac{S}{1}\right) \rightarrow S = 10^{30/10} = 1000$$

As expected, 30 dB corresponds to a power ratio of 1000. Hartley's Law says that the S/N does not matter and if there is 3100 Hz of bandwidth, 6200 bps of information can be transmitted in 1 sec. This does not leave too much room for innovation. The factor of 2 comes from the observation that 2 bps corresponds to 1 Hz. This is shown below:

$$I = 2\,BT = 2(3100 \text{ Hz})(1 \text{ sec}) = 6200 \text{ bits}$$

The Shannon Limit says that much more information capacity is available if something other than binary modulation is applied:

$$I = (3.32)(3100 \text{ Hz}) (1 \text{ sec}) \log(1 + 1000) = 30.88 \text{ kbits}$$

The result is that by not restricting consideration to binary modulation techniques, a large increase in the maximum information capacity is achieved for this signal-to-noise ratio. For larger signal-to-noise ratios, the difference would grow larger. This should provide an incentive to begin the study of how to accomplish this.

Basic digital modulation schemes will be introduced before applying Shannon's Limit. There are also a couple of new terms to be introduced to talk about this idea. As you might imagine, knowing something is possible is only the first step to achieving it. However, you can get some idea of it by imagining a situation where 1 V is needed to distinguish between two logic states. It is as easy to tell 0 V and 1 V apart as it is to tell 1 V and 2 V apart. By combining these two cases, you are actually distinguishing between three levels, 0 V, 1 V, and 2 V, all with the same sensitivity or signal to noise of 1 V.

■ ASK

ASK is that modulation technique where the amplitude of the carrier wave is switched between two or more amplitude states. In the most basic implementation, this is referred to as ON-OFF keying (OOK). OOK is a binary modulated waveform with the presence of the carrier corresponding to a binary state of 1 and the absence of the carrier corresponding to a binary state of 0. Figure 13.4 shows an example waveform, the digital modulating signal that produced it, the resultant modulated signal after filtering, and two sample modulators. Note that these are equivalent; in the second modulation, the mixer is just acting like a switch controlled by the baseband-modulating signal.

As can be seen in Figure 13.4, ASK is very straightforward. An implementation con-

Figure 13.4
ASK, oscilloscope view.

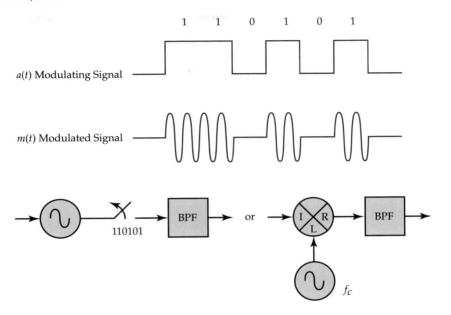

sists of an oscillator, a switch controlled by a binary modulating signal, and a bandpass filter to restrict the bandwidth prior to transmission. This OOK implementation is just the old telegraph system sending dots and dashes. The 0 binary input represents the spaces between dots and dashes, whereas the dots are single binary 1s and the dashes are two adjacent binary 1s. In the figure, it would be read as, dah-di-dit and in international Morse code it would represent the letter D.

The power spectrum of ASK is centered at the carrier frequency and, on each side of the carrier frequency, has the same shape as the baseband modulating signal. This means the resultant bandwidth will be twice that of the modulating signal bandwidth. This is the same result as for the DSB modulators discussed in Chapter 7. This should not be a surprise because nothing has changed except the form of the baseband-modulating signal. It is still AM, just driven by a digital waveform rather than an analog one. This is the general case for all of the first three digital modulation techniques we will discuss. See Figure 13.5.

Note that to make comparisons easy, the peak voltage of the modulating signal will always be said to be E_m. This will allow power comparisons without reference to the peak voltage of the modulating waveform. This is why the peak voltages shown in Figure 13.5 above are divided by 2 and is the same result found earlier with DSB AM. A DSB spectrum is centered on the carrier frequency. The bandwidth of the DSB spectrum is twice that of the baseband modulating signal. The only tricky part is remembering that the bandwidth of the modulating signal is half the binary bit rate or data rate.

Figure 13.5
ASK, spectrum analyzer view.

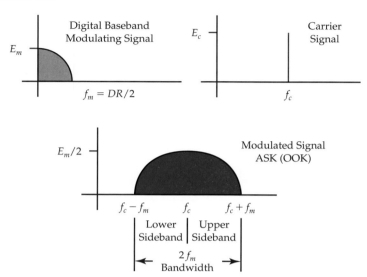

■ FSK

FSK is that modulation technique where the instantaneous frequency of the carrier wave is shifted, or switched, between two frequency states. Binary FSK implies two frequency states and is referred to as BFSK. Before exploring in more detail how BFSK and its variations work, the bandwidth of FSK modulators is discussed. This will also be an opportunity to further discuss the concept of Nyquist bandwidth.

Bandwidth of FSK Signals

The same situation holds with regard to the bandwidth of FSK modulators as was seen in the ASK case. The baseband bandwith will be half of the Nyquist binary data rate. This can be shown by extending what was learned about the bandwidth of FM signals in Chapter 9. To begin, recall that in the discussion about FM the bandwidth depended on the value of the modulation index. The same thing is true here; after all, FSK is just FM with a binary modulating signal. The formula for modulation index developed for FM is reproduced below:

$$m = \frac{K_2 E_m}{f_m} = \frac{\text{FD}}{f_m} = \frac{2\,\text{CS}}{f_m}$$

where FD stands for frequency deviation and CS, for carrier swing. Modifying these terms to the form used in this chapter, we have equation 13–5. Observe that what was discussed as frequency deviation in the analog modulation scheme is called the bandwidth, or more properly the Nyquist bandwidth, for a digital modulation scheme.

$$m = \frac{\text{BW}}{f_m} \qquad \text{(13-5)}$$

The Nyquist bandwidth is the minimum bandwidth that the modulated signal has while in the channel. This is because in a binary modulation environment the frequency deviation is equal to the frequency shift caused by the modulating signal. Each signaling frequency is offset from the carrier rest frequency by the carrier swing.

BFSK has special names for these two signaling frequencies: mark and space. Mark is the signaling frequency corresponding to a modulating signal value of a logical 1 and space corresponds to a modulating signal value of a logical 0. It will always be assumed that the mark frequency is the lower frequency of the two.

The modulating frequency, as always, is equal to half the binary modulating signals bit rate. Although it is possible to develop an equation for the modulation index for FSK from these observations, it really does not apply. Of course, once the modulation index is found, it is possible to find the bandwidth by using the Bessel table, just as was done in analog FM. However, as stated earlier, only those systems where the bandwidth is set at its maximum bandwidth will be considered here. This is the Nyquist bandwidth and results in a modulation index where only the fundamental component is used.

The modulation index is really only of interest when several harmonics are needed. Recall the Bessel table, which was indexed by the modulation index, was used to determine how many harmonics were needed to achieve good fidelity. Fidelity has no meaning in a data application. The only thing that is important is that at the destination, a logical 1 can be differentiated from a logical 0. In BFSK, and FSK generally, this is done by recognizing which signaling frequency is being received, mark or space.

BFSK systems are always narrowband systems. By considering only those systems where the minimum bandwidth required to pass the fundamental component of any data pattern is used, comparisons between various modulation schemes and density of modulation become straightforward. To see that this must result in a narrowband system, explore equation 13-5 a little further. Just observe that for a Nyquist bandwidth, BW always equals twice the modulation frequency. Then substituting, it is found that the modulation index always equals 2, indicating a narrowband system.

$$m = \frac{\text{BW}}{f_m} = \frac{2f_m}{f_m} = 2$$

There are two broad classifications of FSK techniques, coherent modulation and demodulation and noncoherent modulation and demodulation. Coherency has implications for both the modulator and demodulator for FSK. If the modulator is coherent the switching between two frequencies is accomplished in a very specific way. Noncoherent modulators do not have this restriction and for that reason are far more widely implemented. Coherency for the demodulator means demodulation of the modulated signal using knowledge of the phase of the carrier wave. Noncoherent detection does not require knowledge of the phase of the carrier wave and, hence, requires less complex circuitry and consequently costs less.

Since the 1970s, many commercial and military systems have utilized FSK techniques. This is due primarily to the relative simplicity of implementing noncoherent modems, most significantly the demodulator, because no carrier synchronization is required. Additionally, at least conceptually, the modulator design is simpler as well. In practice, virtually all FSK modulators are constructed using the coherent approach, even if the demodulator is constructed following the noncoherent approach. This is because the noncoherent method produces all kinds of undesirable transients, significantly complicating the transmitter. However, for reasons that will be explored throughout this chapter, FSK is not the preferred technique for most new designs. This does not mean that it is not of interest to study; many systems in the field today still use FSK techniques.

Before getting into more detail on the various forms of FSK, it is useful to summarize the concept of coherency versus noncoherency and to illustrate them. A BFSK modulator switches between two frequencies based on a digital modulating signal. This is shown in Figure 13.6. Both a coherent modulated waveform and noncoherent waveform are shown.

In both cases, one can clearly see that one output frequency is produced for one binary state and another frequency is produced for the other binary state. As stated above, this figure shows an example of both a coherent and a noncoherent FSK modulator. Note that only the noncoherent modulated waveform has the identified phase discontinuities.

Figure 13.6
BFSK waveforms, oscilloscope view.

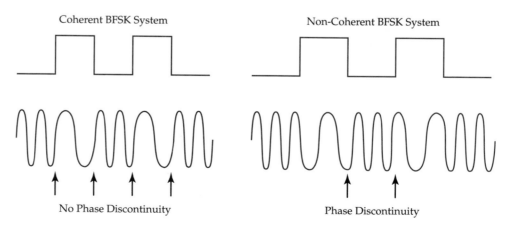

Coherent BFSK System   Non-Coherent BFSK System

No Phase Discontinuity   Phase Discontinuity

Noncoherent FSK Modulation

Sometimes these techniques are called incoherent instead of noncoherent; the choice is merely a matter of language preferences; use whichever you are more comfortable with. Both the modulators and demodulators are different in the noncoherent and coherent designs.

Any binary FSK system shifts the carrier frequency between two distinct frequencies. Noncoherent designs do it most straightforwardly. The modulated signal would look exactly like the FM modulated signal when modulated with a binary modulation signal. The waveforms are shown in Figure 13.7.

In Figure 13.7, the first signal is the binary-modulating signal. The second signal, FSK, is the binary FSK modulated signal; note it is just shifting between two frequencies. However, look at the next pair of signals, ASK1 and ASK2. These are just the two frequencies of the FSK modulated signal broken apart. If you add ASK1 and ASK2, you get FSK. Also, note the phase discontinuities shown again.

However, ASK1 and ASK2 are just individual ASK, or OOK, modulated signals. So BFSK modulation can be viewed as just two ASK modulated signals, added together.

Figure 13.7
Noncoherent FSK, oscilloscope view.

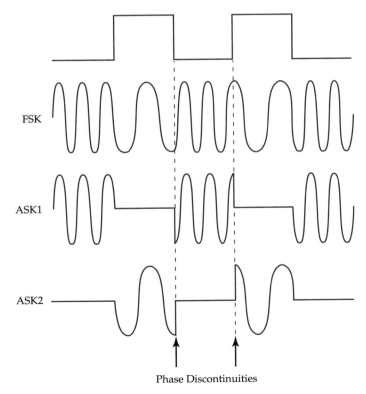

Phase Discontinuities

Figure 13.8
BFSK modulated waveform, spectrum analyzer view.

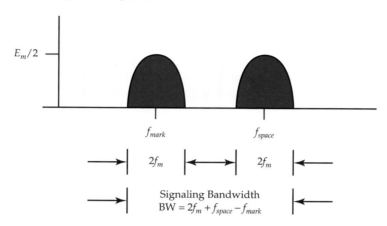

This means that the ASK modulator design illustrated in Figure 13.4 is also part of a BFSK modulator, with a few additions to generate two ASK signals and then add the signals together before transmission.

A good question would be What would the spectrum of such a signal look like? Because it is just the addition of two ASK signals, that fact will be used to describe the spectrum. Each individual ASK waveform looks just like a DSB spectrum centered at its carrier frequency. However, in this case there is no carrier frequency, just the mark and space frequencies. In BFSK, these two frequencies replace the concept of a carrier frequency used in the discussions on AM. In all other aspects the individual envelopes are similar.

Therefore, the FSK signal is just two DSB spectrums centered at the mark and space frequencies. The frequency difference of the two frequencies that the modulator switches between is determined by the application. In principle, any two frequencies could be used. Figure 13.8 illustrates what the signal would look like in frequency space.

Only one of these spectral envelopes exists at any one time because the modulator is switching between the two of them. This means that only one piece of the total bandwidth that the modulator requires is in use at any one time. This points out the major disadvantage to this technique. These systems require more bandwidth than equivalent PSK systems, and this limits their application. Most systems designed today use PSK or a related form of modulation. This form of digital modulation will be introduced after completing the discussion on FSK.

■ EXAMPLE 13.4

The total bandwidth of the BFSK waveform is very dependent on the choice of the signaling frequencies. In Figure 13.8, if the baseband signal data rate is 1 kbps, what is the bandwidth of *each* envelope?

$$f_m = \frac{\text{DR}}{2} = \frac{1 \text{ kbps}}{2} = 500 \text{ Hz} \rightarrow \text{BW} = 2f_m = (2)(500) = 1 \text{ kHz}$$

The answer is twice the baseband bandwidth, or 1 kHz. Further, what is the total spectrum bandwidth shown in Figure 13.8? The answer depends on the choice of the signaling frequencies and cannot be determined without more information.

■ EXAMPLE 13.5

If in Figures 13.7 and 13.8 the signaling frequencies are 20 kHz for the space frequency and 10 kHz for the mark frequency, what is the signaling bandwidth?

$$\text{BW}_{\text{bfsk}} = 2f_m - f_{\text{space}} + f_{mark} \tag{13-6}$$

$$= 1 \text{ kHz} + 20 \text{ kHz} - 10 \text{ kHz} = 11 \text{ kHz}$$

These two examples and Figure 13.8 point out that the minimum bandwidth required by an FSK system is 4 times the modulating frequency. This is twice the bandwidth of ASK and is expressed in the relationship below:

$$\text{minimum bandwidth BFSK} = 4f_m \tag{13-7}$$

A modulator could be constructed using the ASK approach described above, but this is not a good idea. As noted above, noncoherent modulators produce unwanted transients that complicate the transmitter and add cost. This is because when the switch between two frequencies occurs abruptly; there is no guarantee that the two waves will be synchronized in phase. This noncoherent shifting occurs unless the frequencies are chosen carefully and aligned with the bit transition times exactly. These switch points are shown as the phase discontinuities in Figures 13.7 and 13.8. Go back and review the oscilloscope views; notice that the noncoherent waveforms are switching at points where the signaling frequencies are not crossing the zero axis.

Coherent modulators implemented in the above manner are possible but require specific pairs of frequencies to be used as the mark and space choices. Although this approach is sometimes possible in hard channel design, in most cases it is not. The requirement for choosing the signaling frequencies for a coherent design implemented in the above manner is illustrated by the following discussion.

Because frequency is the first derivative of phase, if the phase change is not zero at the transitions between frequencies, a clean change between two frequencies will not occur. Other frequency components arise as transients occur due to the mismatched phase. See the relationships below for an explanation:

$$f = \frac{d}{dt} p \qquad f_1 = \frac{d}{dt} p_1 \qquad f_2 = \frac{d}{dt} p_2$$

For a clean change between f_1 and f_2, p_1 must equal p_2 at the moment of change. The most general way for this to be true is if

$$p_1 = p_2 = 0$$

Because f_1 does not equal f_2, the only general way for p_1 to equal p_2 is for the following relationship to be true:

$$p_1 = \int f_1 dt = p_2 = \int f_2 dt$$

This can only occur generally when $f_1 = f_2 = 0$. Obviously, it is possible to pick certain frequencies where $p_1 = p_2$ and f_1 does not equal f_2, but only specific cases. These cases are all like $f_1 = n * f_2$, where $n =$ integer.

In summary, it is possible to implement a noncoherent modulator using two distinct frequency sources and switching between the two. However, this is not a good idea in general because of the transients generated due to no phase coherence between the two frequency sources. Coherent FSK modulators offer a way to get around this limitation of having to pick special frequencies to avoid this kind of "spectral splash." However, we will first explore the demodulation process of noncoherent BFSK systems.

Noncoherent FSK demodulators directly demodulate the received signal in a very similar way to that of the simple envelope AM demodulator that we studied in Chapter 8. It is hard to imagine a simpler, or less-expensive, demodulation circuit, hence, the attractiveness and wide adoption of noncoherent FSK demodulators.

Noncoherent FSK Demodulation

Figure 13.9 illustrates how a noncoherent demodulator is constructed and operates. As mentioned above, the noncoherent demodulator is one of the key reasons why FSK is in wide use. Reasoning from the fact that a noncoherent FSK modulator can be viewed as two ASK modulators summed together, it is possible to construct a noncoherent demodulator out of two ASK demodulators, and that is just what is done.

The first component is just a summer hooked up as a splitter, splitting the modulated signal evenly into two paths at half power. Occasionally power amplification is required after the filtering step to provide enough voltage swing to turn the diode ON and OFF effectively; this is not shown. The envelope detector is already familiar from Chapter 8. The threshold detector is just a device that will square up the two analog states' output from the summer to standard voltage levels and switching times.

The performance of this type of design is not optimum, and as a result errors will occur in the presence of noise. It is, however, very inexpensive and is implemented widely where the additional error rate can be tolerated because of the cost advantages. If all else is held equal, a coherent design will always be superior when measured by performance in the presence of noise but will always cost more to implement.

Before going any further, realize that one can talk about an optimum design for anything. Has any other class you have taken ever talked about optimum design? Much of the attraction of the design principles involved in digital communications comes from the appeal of this concept.

Being able to measure a design against a standard that is judged the best possible

Figure 13.9
Noncoherent BFSK demodulator.

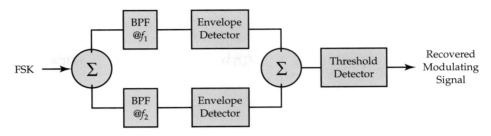

can be very appealing. In many situations, people feel the need to measure themselves against some independent standard. In sports, it is the record at the local, state, national or world level. There are many other examples. In engineering, it is nice to have a standard as well; digital communications techniques offer this. Although the detailed techniques used to design optimum modems are outside the scope of this text, general principles will be pointed out. Later in this chapter you will learn how to perform calculations that will indicate how close to optimum the particular implementation being measured is.

Coherent FSK Modulation (MSK)

Coherent modulator design is similar to noncoherent design in what it needs to accomplish, but it has the additional requirement that the phase change when switching between frequencies remain continuous. Signals that exhibit this property are called continuous phase waveforms. From this observation, coherent FSK modulation is often referred to as minimum shift keying, or MSK. The idea is that the frequency is shifted the minimum amount required to guarantee a continuous phase shift when shifting frequencies.

There are two ways to interpret that; the first would be to assume that the only way an MSK system could be implemented is by having the two signaling frequencies synchronized to the data rate. This is using the two ASK modulator approach and was demonstrated in a previous section. Another way to interpret that, and the more general one, is to realize that one important result that flows from the continuous phase shift requirement is that the frequency shifts are not all the same.

This means that each frequency shift must depend on the previous frequency shift. Each shift of the frequency must be just enough, the minimum, until the new frequency phase exactly matches that of the existing one. This is sometimes difficult to visualize, and it is more difficult to imagine how to implement it. It seems the phase of the first frequency must be computed. One way might be to keep track of its phase state until it comes time for a frequency shift and then immediately choose a frequency that will phase match the original one and shift to it. At first glance, this approach seems unlikely to succeed.

The key idea here is that because the frequency shift is not always the same, it is not easy to tell where the data shifts occurred by just examining the modulated waveform.

This has some important consequences; the most important is that MSK performs much better than noncoherent FSK. This is due to the continuous phase shift when moving between mark and space frequencies as compared to the abrupt phase shifts that occur in noncoherent FSK at the same transitions. It is also interesting to note that there is some amplitude modulation on the MSK waveform because of these continuous phase shifts.

Returning to the imaginary MSK modulator design, Why not try implementing it in a primarily digital design? That is, instead of using a pair of oscillators and a switch between them, Why not use a memory, counter, D/A, and filter to generate the frequencies? Then when the need to switch frequencies occurs, the counter is jumped the appropriate number of states to get a new frequency that phase matches the old one.

The central idea is that if pieces of the two frequencies are stored in memory, and read out into an D/A, it is possible to intelligently choose which piece to read out at any moment in time. This gives a result where there are no appreciable phase shifts when the frequency is shifted. Just pick the piece needed to satisfy the criteria. This piece depends on the phase of the frequency at time of choice, and it in turn is determined by the data sequence modulating the carrier.

The resultant MSK signal must have the following characteristics to be considered MSK:

1. The frequency deviation is exactly $\pm \frac{1}{2} w_m$, where w_m is the frequency version of the bit rate.
2. As already mentioned, the modulated signal is phase coherent at the switching instant.

Although presenting this design in detail is outside the intent of this book, these systems are clearly possible to implement. Similar methods that rely on the digital generation of waveforms are also possible. Note that item (1) above defines the choice of the mark and space frequencies. Actually, any odd multiple of this fraction will work. Any method must satisfy the above two criteria to be considered coherent FSK or more simply, MSK.

Coherent FSK (MSK) Demodulation

The coherent demodulation of MSK modulated waveforms is more complex than that shown for the noncoherent case, as was mentioned earlier. The most popular choice for this demodulation is shown in Figure 13.10.

As shown, this demodulator makes use of a PLL to detect the phase shifts that occur as the frequency shifts. Because the phase shifts are continuous, there is no chance that the PLL would become unlocked. This prevents this approach from being applicable to demodulate noncoherent FSK. The PLL free-running frequency is set to the midpoint between the mark and space frequencies. It is important to make sure that the lock range is wider than the difference between the mark and space frequencies. The dc error voltage produced by the PLL as it tracks the signal to the two frequencies yields a binary output signal. This is then cleaned up by a one-shot or similar device to square up the corners and restore correct voltage levels. Note that this is very similar to the FM demodulators that were discussed in Chapter 9.

Figure 13.10
Coherent FSK (MSK) demodulator.

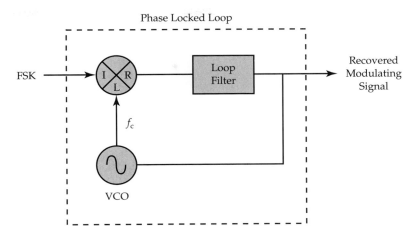

Coherent FSK modems perform better than their noncoherent cousins, but the overall performance is still significantly less than what can be achieved with the approaches that will be considered next. For this reason, most new designs are done using those techniques, and FSK in both its forms is disappearing from the marketplace except for narrowband signaling applications like pagers. Even up to 1990, it had dominant niches in data communications; these are now all but gone. As stated earlier, FSK is not the preferred choice for new designs.

■ PSK

Phase shift keying is that modulation technique where the phase of the carrier wave is switched between two or more phase states. It is just like the angle modulation systems where the phase was changed, except PSK requires the modulating signal to be pulsed in two or more amplitude states, binary or M-ary. PSK is the most dominant modulation technique in use today for implementing digital communications.

Recall that in the study of continuous modulating waveforms it was found that frequency modulation and phase modulation could be lumped together and studied as angle modulation. In the study of PSK, there will be analogy to amplitude modulation systems rather than frequency modulation systems because the performance of several PSK systems are identical to that found in similar AM systems.

Binary PSK (BPSK)
BPSK modulators take a binary modulating signal, switching between two amplitude states, and output a modulated signal where a carrier switches between two-phase

Figure 13.11
BPSK waveforms, oscilloscope view.

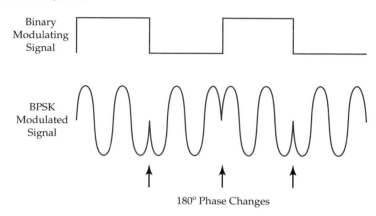

states, usually 0 and 180°. The waveforms are shown in Figure 13.11. Mathematically, the bandwidth of a BPSK modulated waveform is found by the following expression:

$$BW_{\text{bpsk}} = 2f_m \tag{13-8}$$

The spectrum is shown in Figure 13.12. This is the same spectrum that resulted from DSB-SC AM. Looking again at Figure 13.12, notice how the spectrum looks exactly like that of Figure 7.4. In theory, the waveforms of AM DSB-SC and BPSK are identical. There is no carrier signal present in the output waveform, a surprising result given that the modulated signal is just the carrier wave switching between two phase states.

One way of understanding this is to think about constructive and destructive interference. A BPSK modulated waveform is a carrier switching between two states that constitute 100% destructive interference, 0 and 180°. In a certain way of thinking, is it not possible that the two carrier waves would cancel each other out and all that would be

Figure 13.12
BPSK modulated waveform, spectrum analyzer view.

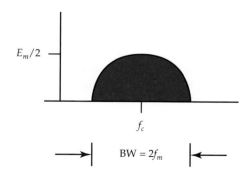

left is the switching information? That is not a very rigorous analysis, but it can help you become more comfortable with the result.

This means that all the results that we obtained in the analysis of DSB-SC will apply here. The bandwidth is just twice the modulating frequency, and no carrier is present. Also, just like the ASK situation, the modulating frequency equals half the bit rate. Example 13.6 illustrates these ideas.

■ EXAMPLE 13.6

For a BPSK modulator with a 1 Mbps binary modulating signal and a 10 MHz carrier frequency, find the upper and lower sidebands and the bandwidth of the resulting modulated signal. Remember to convert from a binary data rate to a baseband modulating frequency.

$$f_m = \frac{\text{DR}}{2} = \frac{1\,\text{Mbps}}{2} = 500\,\text{kHz}$$

$$f_{\text{usb}} = f_c + f_m \tag{13-9}$$

$$f_{\text{usb}} = \text{upper side band frequency} = 10.5\,\text{MHz}$$

$$f_{\text{lsb}} = f_c - f_m \tag{13-10}$$

$$f_{\text{lsb}} = \text{lower sideband frequency} = 9.5\,\text{MHz}$$

BPSK Modulator
An illustrative BPSK modulator design is shown in Figure 13.13. Its design is very straightforward. It consists of a binary modulating signal applied to a mixer, a carrier oscillator at the carrier frequency, and a BPF to filter out any unwanted harmonics generated by the mixing process. The spectrum would look like that shown in Figure 13.12.

BPSK Demodulator
The design of a BPSK demodulator is a bit more complicated. This is shown in Figure 13.14. There is a BPF to filter out any unwanted noise, centered on the carrier frequency, a mixer, and an LPF. These components are quite familiar by now, and you should expect them. The new piece is a coherent carrier recovery circuit. This circuit will be explored shortly.

Figure 13.13
BPSK modulator.

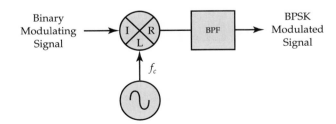

Figure 13.14
BPSK demodulator.

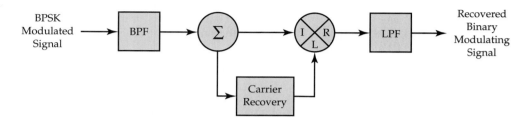

■ BANDWIDTH CONSIDERATIONS OF BFSK AND BPSK

Earlier it was stated that BFSK is not widely adapted in the field and that PSK is. The bandwidth relationship between the two forms of modulation is the most fundamental reason for this. As was developed earlier, the signaling bandwidth of BFSK is often dominated by the choice of the mark and space frequencies. This led to a calculation of bandwidth that depended on two things, the signaling frequency choices and the modulating signal data rate. This was expressed in equation 13-6. For BPSK, we found that the bandwidth of the modulated signal depended only upon the modulating signal data rate, as expressed in equation 13-8. Both of these are reproduced below:

$$BW_{bfsk} = |f_{space} - f_{mark}| + 2f_m \qquad BW_{bpsk} = 2f_m$$

As can be clearly seen, for any given data rate the bandwidth of the BPSK modulated waveform will be less than the BFSK signaling bandwidth. Even if the mark and space frequencies are chosen in such a way as to minimize the bandwidth, the difference must be at least twice the modulating frequency. This is shown in the next equation:

$$BW_{bfsk}(min) \geq 2f_m + 2f_m = 4f_m \qquad \textbf{(13-11)}$$

That means that BFSK is always at least half as efficient a user of bandwidth as BPSK. Realistically, the above minimum could never be reached because some kind of BPF is needed to separate the two spectra centered on the mark and space frequencies. Allowing for filter roll-off, this means that for all real systems, BPSK is likely to be at least 3 times as efficient a user of bandwidth as BFSK. This result is at the heart of why FSK systems are disappearing from the marketplace. This concept of bandwidth efficiency will be explored further in the next section.

■ BANDWIDTH EFFICIENCY

Bandwidth efficiency is a measure of how efficient the modulation technique is in terms of how much bandwidth it requires. Up until now all the digital modulation techniques were binary in nature, and all were equally bandwidth efficient. All had an efficiency of

1. This meant that for every hertz of bandwidth occupied by the double sided modulated signal, 1 bps was transmitted.

The modulation schemes discussed next no longer obey this restriction. To determine the bandwidth efficiency of a modulation technique, simply divide the input data rate by the bandwidth of the resultant modulated signal. This is shown in equation 13-12 and illustrated in Example 13.7.

$$BW_e = \frac{BW_{binary}}{BW} \qquad (13\text{-}12)$$

■ EXAMPLE 13.7

Find the bandwidth efficiency of a BPSK modulator. This system has a input binary data rate of 1 Mbps. Find the double-sided transmission bandwidth and the bandwidth efficiency.

$$f_m = \frac{DR}{2} = \frac{1\ \text{Mbps}}{2} = 500\ \text{kHz} \rightarrow BW = 2f_m = (2)(500\ \text{kHz}) = 1\ \text{MHz}$$

$$BW_e = \frac{DR}{BW} = \frac{1\ \text{Mbps}}{1\ \text{MHz}} = 1\ \text{bps/Hz}$$

It is also possible to talk about this concept of bandwidth efficiency by using the concept of number of input changes required to produce a single output change. This is explored next.

M-ary, as stated earlier, comes directly from the word *binary*. It can be defined as the power of 2 of the number of input changes required to produce a single output change. It could also be defined as the number of states of the output modulated signal. For example, in BPSK there are two phase states, 0 and 180°, so they are said to be 2-ary systems. A system with four amplitude levels would be said to be 4-ary. A system with four phase states in its output spectrum would also be said to be 4-ary.

The essential idea here is to capture a way of speaking about the number of input signal changes required for a single output change. To see how this is captured by this expression, look at the mathematical definition for M-ary in terms of the number input signal changes that are required for a single output change:

$$M = 2^N \qquad (13\text{-}13)$$

where M = measure of the density of signal states
N = number of input changes to produce one output change

where for BPSK, which is 2-ary, a single input change, from a logical 0 to a logical 1, results in a modulation signal that changes once. For quadratude PSK (QPSK) which is 4-ary, two changes, $N = 2$, are required for each output change. This is twice as efficient as BPSK.

Bandwidth efficiency is a measure of the number of input changes required to produce an output change. M is a measure of the density of signal states. Sometimes this is called information density. This is not the same as Hartley's concept of information capacity. The higher the density, the higher the efficiency of the modulation technique. Additionally, the higher the density, the less bandwidth required for a given input signal rate. These ideas are related in Example 13.8.

■ EXAMPLE 13.8

Relate the bandwidth efficiency and signal state density of BPSK and BFSK.

In Figures 13.8 and 13.12, both BFSK and BPSK have a modulated bandwidth that is exactly equal to the input modulation frequency. The signaling bandwidth required by BFSK is larger than this; however, the amount of bandwidth that is occupied at any instant of time is the same as in the BPSK case. Remember that in BFSK, each spectral envelope only exists for half the time.

Therefore, their bandwidth efficiencies both equal 1. Because both BFSK and BPSK are 2-ary, the number of input changes required for an output change, or N, is equal to 1. The number of input changes required to produce an output change, N, is the same as BW_e, the bandwidth efficiency. These two numbers can be used interchangeably.

$$N = BW_e \qquad\qquad\qquad \textbf{(13-14)}$$

$$M = 2^N$$

$$\text{BFSK: } M = 2^1 \rightarrow M = 2 \qquad \text{or 2-ary}$$

$$\text{BPSK: } M = 2^1 \rightarrow M = 2 \qquad \text{or 2-ary}$$

Therefore, for binary frequency or phase shift keying, bandwidth efficiency and the number of input changes required for an output change are equal. Either way of talking about how efficient or dense a modulation technique results in the same situation.

■ SYMBOL AND BAUD RATE

In the previous section a way to express the bandwidth efficiencies of M-ary modulation was defined. It is clear that they can be classified according to the number of input changes required for an output change. One can think of this as the difference between the source-to-destination information transfer rate and the actual signaling rate in the communications channel. For 2-ary systems, these are always the same. However, as higher information capacities are moved to, this will no longer be true.

One way to talk about this is with the baud, which is used to define the number of symbols per second in the communications channel. When one talks about baud rate, one is only talking about how the actual signal in the channel changes. Baud rate is only defined for the analog signal in the communications channel. For example, a BFSK system that has a modulating data rate of 1 kbps and a QPSK system that has twice the modulating data rate, or 2 kbps, would both have the same baud rate, or 1 kilobaud.

Most modern system descriptions have dispensed with the term *baud* and instead use either the M-ary designation or talk about symbols per second explicitly. We will follow this trend.

◼ DI-BITS, TRI-BITS, AND M-ARY ENCODING

When levels of modulation where M grows greater than 2 are discussed, a couple of new terms are used. It will prove useful to describe them in terms of M-ary encoding. For 4-ary systems the binary bit streams are encoded as di-bits. That means that they are accepted by the modulator in pairs. For 8-ary systems the binary bit streams are encoded as tri-bits. That means that they are accepted by the modulator in threes, and so forth. Figure 13.15 illustrates the concept of how di-bits and 4-ary encoding are coupled.

Tri-bits and 8-ary encoding proceeds in exactly the same way except there are eight amplitude levels instead of four. Additionally, it is important to note that all the encoding values have the same voltage difference, here 2 V. This is done to ensure the decision threshold always works with the same minimum noise margin for any di-bit code transition. In the following sections the modulating waveform will always be referred back to its binary bit rate. However, because it is traditional to show a single bit stream into the modulators, Figure 13.15 shows how these are distinguished. As can be seen, the di-bit groups are assigned an amplitude that is used by the modulators to generate the individual bit streams applied to the individual mixers.

◼ QPSK

QPSK is a 4-ary modulation technique. It is very similar to BPSK; in fact, it is generally made by just adding two BPSK modulated signals 90° out of phase. Because it is 4-ary, the number of changes in the input signal required to produce a change in the output signal is 2. As you might expect, the bandwidth efficiency of QPSK is also 2.

The Q in QPSK stands for quadrature. The first part of this word, *quad* (from quadrant, meaning one-fourth of circumference of a circle, or quadraphonic, meaning stereo with two extra "channels") is probably familiar. Actually, quadrature means the process

Figure 13.15
Four-ary encoding and di-bits.

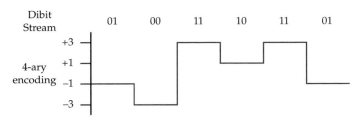

of making something square. Before going any further, how a quadrature signal is generated will be shown. This is done by examining a QPSK modulator.

QPSK Modulator

QPSK modulators are implemented in practice by adding two BPSK modulators together, 90° out of phase. The 90° phase shift is accomplished by simply driving one BPSK modulator with a cosine wave at the carrier frequency and the other by a sine wave. A sample QPSK modulator is shown in Figure 13.16.

Figure 13.16 shows a few unfamiliar things. First, the serial-to-parallel converter takes the input data, which is running at the bit rate of the modulator, and breaks it into two parallel streams of data each running at half the bit rate. This rate is called the symbol rate. For QPSK, it is 2. The symbol rate always expresses the bandwidth efficiency and signal state density as well, another way to talk about the same idea.

The labels P and Q in the figure represent the in-phase and quadrature phase symbol pairs. It might make more sense to label them I and Q for in-phase and quadrature-phase, and this is sometimes done; both practices are in use. These are the two quadrature signals. They are combined in a way that is sometimes referred to as quadrature mixing. The mathematical expression of the signal at the output of the summer is easy to find. It is shown below. $P(t)$ represents the in-phase data line and $Q(t)$ represents the quadrature-phase data line.

$$\text{summer output} = P(t)\sin(w_c t) + Q(t)\cos(w_c t) \tag{13-15}$$

For the first time, a LPF in line with the binary symbol data streams is seen. These filters are used to control the bandwidth of the baseband symbol lines. In advanced systems, they are also used to shape the spectrum of the modulating symbol lines to improve performance. After this preconditioning, the signals are applied to mixers, each LO port being driven by cosine or sine at the carrier frequency. The signals are then summed together and passed through a BPF to get rid of unwanted harmonics generated by the mixing process.

Figure 13.16
QPSK modulator.

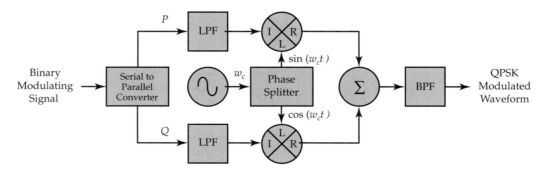

Note how similar this is to the design shown for a BPSK modulator. It looks just like two of them combined, with the addition of a few extra components to accomplish the combining. The only real difference other than that needed to add the signals together is the LPF. These are often used in BPSK systems as well but were not shown to enhance clarity of the basic operation of the BPSK modulator.

The bandwidth required by such a modulator is less than might be expected. This arises because what is important is not the input bit rate but the symbol rate. This is always true of M-ary modulators. For BPSK and BFSK, the symbol rate and bit rates were the same, so this relationship was not apparent. When other than binary modulation is considered, this relationship becomes clear. To see why the bandwidth is less than twice the bit rate, think about the symbol rate: It is really one half the 8 bit rate. In Figure 13.16, the baseband signal that is being modulated by the mixers is half of the input bit rate. Because the baseband bandwidth of the symbol rate is half, the bandwidth of the resultant signal is also half.

A look at the constellation in Figures 13.17, 13.18, and 13.19 should make clear why the word *quadrature* is used to describe what we see. Note that by adding the second BPSK pair of phasors, we take a constellation diagram that was "flat" and make it square. A constellation diagram is introduced in the next section.

Constellation Diagram

A constellation diagram is the most commonly used diagram to discuss M-ary modulation. It can be produced on an oscilloscope by taking the two outputs of the modulation circuit and attaching them to the *x* and *y* inputs of the oscilloscope. This must be done before the signals are added together to produce the modulated signal at the same relative place in the demodulator. It is helpful for some to think of these as phasor diagrams. They are very similar except there is no vector representation, just a dot on the screen where the typical phasor arrowhead would terminate. They show just where in amplitude and angle the modulation energy is placed.

Note that in actual practice, both of the BPSK signals that are produced by the modulator are also shifted 45° during the process of adding them together. Therefore, the actual constellation diagram becomes as illustrated in Figure 13.19. The reason for this comes out of the mathematics and is worked out below. Note that for Figures 13.18 and

Figure 13.17
BPSK constellation diagram.

Figure 13.18
QPSK constellation diagram.

Figure 13.19
Actual QPSK constellation diagram.

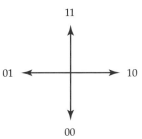

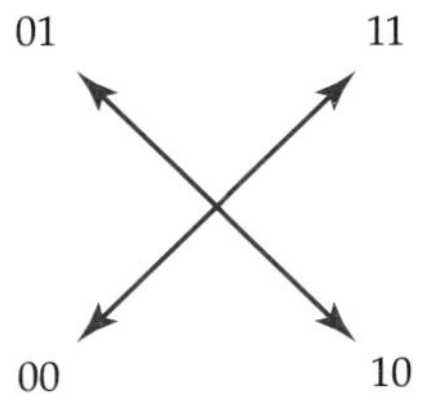

13.19, to confuse one state with another, an error of $\pm$ 45° must be made in the demodulator. That is the difference between each phase state.

Example 13.9 illustrates just how the signals are combined in a QPSK system. This will demonstrate how the extra 45° of phase shift come about during the process of combining the signals. Note that now the values of $P(t)$ and $Q(t)$ are explicitly broken out.

■ EXAMPLE 13.9

To facilitate this example, refer to Figure 13.16, where a QPSK modulator design is shown. The binary data input to the serial to parallel converter splits pairs of the binary modulating signal into two paths. Each possible 2 bit pair, or di-bit, will be examined and the signal phase at the output of the summer calculated. The mathematics of adding a sine and cosine wave are not instructive and so will not be presented here; only the results will be shown. Those interested can consult the function sum and function difference formulas used in trigonometry.

$$00: P = -1 \quad Q = -1 \rightarrow P = (-1)\sin(w_c t) \quad Q = (-1)\cos(w_c t)$$

$$P + Q = -1.414 \cos\left(w_c t - \frac{\pi}{4}\right) = +1.414 \sin\left(w_c t - \frac{3\pi}{4}\right)$$

$$01: P = -1 \quad Q = +1 \rightarrow P = (-1)\sin(w_c t) \quad Q = (1+)\cos(w_c t)$$

$$P + Q = -1.414 \sin\left(w_c t - \frac{\pi}{4}\right) = +1.414 \sin\left(w_c t + \frac{3\pi}{4}\right)$$

$$10: P = +1 \quad Q = -1 \rightarrow P = (+1)\sin(w_c t) \quad Q = (-1)\cos(w_c t)$$

$$P + Q = 1.414 \sin\left(w_c t - \frac{\pi}{4}\right)$$

$$11: P = +1 \quad Q = +1 \rightarrow P = (+1)\sin(w_c t) \quad Q = (+1)\cos(w_c t)$$

$$P + Q = +1.414 \cos\left(w_c t - \frac{\pi}{4}\right) = -1.414 \sin\left(w_c t - \frac{3\pi}{4}\right) = +1.414 \sin\left(w_c t + \frac{\pi}{4}\right)$$

Figure 13.20
QPSK with di-bit locations shown.

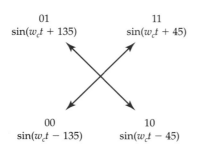

01	11
$\sin(w_c t + 135)$	$\sin(w_c t + 45)$
00	10
$\sin(w_c t - 135)$	$\sin(w_c t - 45)$

Table 13.1
QPSK Output Phase Truth Table

Binary Signal P bit	Binary Signal Q bit	QPSK Output Phase
0	0	−135
0	1	+135
1	0	−45
1	1	+45

where each term is expressed as a positive function of sine to illustrate exactly how the constellation diagram is tilted by 45° in the process of summing. Figure 13.20 shows the di-bit locations. From this diagram and the mathematics above a QPSK truth table, Table 13.1, can be constructed.

■ EXAMPLE 13.10

What is the bandwidth required for a QPSK modulated signal? The bandwidth required by such a modulator is just half of the bit rate, or the symbol rate.

The bandwidth efficiency for any binary input was given by equation 13-12, reproduced here:

$$BW_e = \frac{BW_{binary}}{BW} \qquad \textbf{(13-12)}$$

Using this relationship, the bandwidth efficiency can be calculated. However, when this equation was examined earlier, it was assumed that the input bit rate was what was applied to the mixers. However, in M-ary modulation schemes where M is not equal to 2, what is actually on the top of this equation is the symbol rate. This means that this equation must be rewritten with this new information in mind:

$$BW_e = \frac{SR}{BW}$$

$$SR = \text{symbol rate} \qquad \textbf{(13-16)}$$

Now for *QPSK only*, the symbol rate is just half the binary data rate, so equation 13-16 can be evaluated as

$$BW_e = \frac{DR/2}{BW} = \frac{DR}{2BW} \qquad \text{QPSK only} \qquad \textbf{(13-17)}$$

Therefore, the bandwidth efficiency is twice that of a 2-ary modulator. Applying this to an actual example, for a bit rate of 1 kbps, the following results:

$$BW = \frac{DR}{2BW_e} = \frac{1 \text{ kbps}}{(2)(1)} = 500 \text{ Hz} \qquad \text{QPSK only}$$

This illustrates the result for a QPSK modulator that the bandwidth required is just half of the input bit rate. Rearranging the above results and recognizing that the symbol rate is always the same numerical result as the transmit bandwidth gives us a general relationship between the bandwidth, or symbol rate, binary data rate, and bandwidth efficiency. *Use equation 13-18 for all calculations relating bandwidth efficiency and symbol rate for the various modulation types:*

$$SR = BW = \frac{DR}{BW_e} \text{ symbols/sec} \qquad \textbf{(13-18)}$$

QPSK Demodulator

QPSK demodulators start to get a bit complex and contain components that will require examination. The problem is to detect four distinct phase states and associate them first

Figure 13.21
QPSK demodulator.

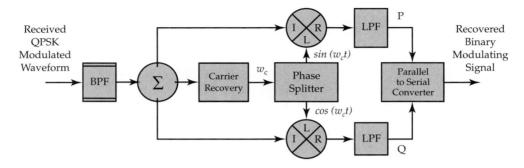

with the symbols that produced them and then convert those received symbols into the binary input stream that was originally applied to the QPSK modulator. To distinguish these four phase states from each other, it is critically important to recover the phase of the original carrier wave when the phase shifts were applied. Remember, a sine wave looks just like a cosine wave unless you know the original phase state at $t = 0$. (Refer to Chapter 9.)

Because of this requirement, a special circuit, called a carrier recovery circuit, is required to detect this phase. Note that this same circuit component was shown in Figure 13.14 in the BPSK demodulator. A discussion of it was skipped until now for clarity. Carrier recovery circuits have many implementations, but only one will be discussed. To begin, a block diagram of a QPSK demodulator is shown in Figure 13.21.

In this figure, the received QPSK modulated waveform is first passed through a BPF to limit the noise bandwidth to that of the received signal. The signal is then split into three identical paths. The top and bottom are fed into mixers, which demodulate the broadband signals and restore the original P and Q symbol data streams. The baseband symbol streams are passed through a LPF just as they were on the modulator side and for the same reasons. Then the two data streams are put into a parallel-to-serial converter, which combines the two symbol signals into a single recovered binary signal at the original bit rate.

The center path is fed into the carrier recovery circuit, which recovers the original carrier wave and its phase state. This signal is then fed into a phase splitter, which generates the cosine and sine phases of the recovered carrier wave that were applied to the mixers mentioned above.

To conclude this analysis of QPSK, the mathematical relationship that describes the signal that appears at the output of the two mixers will be developed. The top one is the P line and the bottom one the Q line:

$$P \text{ line} = [P(t) \sin(w_c t) + Q(t) \cos(w_c t)] \sin(w_c t)$$

$$= P(t) \sin^2(w_c t) + Q(t) \cos(w_c t) \sin(w_c t)$$

$$= P(t) [1 + \cos^2(w_c t)] + Q(t) \left[\frac{\sin(2w_c t)}{2} \right]$$

$$= P(t) \left[1 + \tfrac{1}{2} + \frac{\cos(2w_c t)}{2} \right] + Q(t) \left[\frac{\sin(2w_c t)}{2} \right]$$

$$= \frac{3P(t)}{2} + \frac{P(t) \cos(2w_c t)}{2} + \frac{Q(t) \sin(2w_c t)}{2}$$

$$Q \text{ line} = [P(t) \sin(w_c t) + Q(t) \cos(w_c t)] \cos(w_c t)$$

$$= P(t) \sin(w_c t) \cos(w_c t) + Q(t) \cos^2(w_c t)$$

$$= P(t) \left[\frac{\sin(2w_c t)}{2} \right] + Q(t) [1 - \sin^2(w_c t)]$$

$$= P(t) \left[\frac{\sin(2w_c t)}{2} \right] + Q(t) \left[1 + \frac{1}{2} - \frac{\cos(2w_c t)}{2} \right]$$

$$= \frac{3Q(t)}{2} - \frac{Q(t) \cos(2w_c t)}{2} + \frac{P(t) \sin(2w_c t)}{2}$$

The double-frequency terms in both expressions can be easily filtered out by the low-pass filters that follow the mixers, and the remaining signal is just the modulating binary signals $P(t)$ and $Q(t)$. These are then fed to the parallel to serial converter and the original modulating bit stream is recovered.

■ CARRIER RECOVERY

The carrier recovery circuitry shown in Figures 13.14 and 13.21 can be implemented in different ways. The two most popular and traditional are the Costas loop, and the X2 and X4 loops. Variations of both of these exist.

For BPSK, an X2 loop is implemented, and for QPSK an X4 loop. Both types will be briefly examined to see why this difference exists. The X2 loop, shown in Figure 13.22, works by multiplying the received BPSK waveform by 2; this signal is then filtered at twice the carrier frequency, so only the double-frequency component is passed on to the mixer.

Critical to understanding of this approach is the fact that the X2 process removes the modulation and produces a clean carrier signal at twice the original carrier frequency. Because the VCO free-running frequency is originally set to twice the carrier frequency, the result of the mixing is that a baseband signal is generated that acts like an error signal for phase differences. This signal is applied to the VCO after passing through a LPF to introduce delay. The output of the VCO is then a replica of the original carrier signal with the same phase.

It is possible to regard the boxed-in components as a PLL. This would simplify the diagram but not offer as good an explanation of how it actually worked. To review this, look back in the section where PLL operation was described. The X4 loop works in ex-

Figure 13.22
X2 loop.

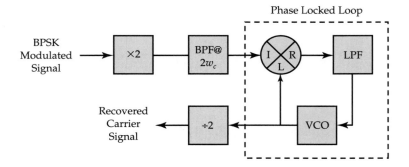

actly the same way except it multiplies and divides by 4 instead of 2. This is shown in Figure 13.23.

The double- and quadruple-frequency terms are easily generated by passing the modulated signal through a frequency doubler and then filtering for the desired carrier frequency component. The circuit implementation of such a design always filters out all but the required XN term through a narrow BPF. The other popular means of carrier recovery, such as the Costas loop and remodulator designs, yield the same performance results if the filters are equivalent in design and ideal components are assumed.

Figure 13.23
X4 Loop.

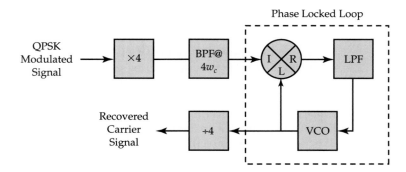

EIGHT-ARY PSK

Eight-ary PSK is the next level of signal state density from QPSK. Eight-ary PSK uses eight phase states, each $\pi/4$ apart. This results in a bandwidth efficiency of 3 bps/Hz. This also means that the symbol rate will be one-third the bit rate. This process can go on and on and is limited only by the effectiveness of the result in a noisy environment. Sixteen-ary PSK and above systems are in common use today.

Table 13.2 summarizes the relationships between the various concepts introduced for PSK systems. It relates the quantities of baseband bandwidth, transmit bandwidth, symbol rate, signal state density, and bandwidth efficiency. For ease of comparison, the binary modulation data rate is assumed to be 1 kbps for all four cases.

QUADRUPLE AMPLITUDE MODULATION (QAM)

After a while it doesn't make much sense to just keep adding additional phase states; the difference between them gets smaller and smaller, and the performance in a noisy environment doesn't get any better for the additional cost of implementation. Eventually, the requirement must be dropped that all the phasors have the same amplitude. Most modems designed today for use over the telephone system use a combination of amplitude and phase modulation. This means that there are multiple phase states, each one with two different amplitudes.

Before getting into systems that are more complex, the simplest form of modulation, QAM, where both amplitude and phase are combined, is examined. QAM uses four amplitude states. The interesting thing about this is that four amplitude states are exactly like four phase states. Look back at Figure 13.20. Why not regard the phasor values as amplitudes instead of phases? Moving clockwise from the top, you would read $(1, 1)$ $(1, -1)$ $(-1, -1)$ $(-1, 1)$. This is just as valid of an explanation as thinking of it as angles of 45, 315, 225, 135°, respectively.

If the constellation diagrams of two different ways of talking about modulation are the same, the two different modulation techniques are the same. Therefore, QPSK is identical to QAM. This is a special case and relies on the fact that the baseband symbol streams of both modems are shaped in the same way. A discussion of this situation is beyond the scope of this book.

Table 13.2
PSK Relationship Table

Modulation	W_m (Hz)	BW (Hz)	Symbol Rate Symbols/sec	Signal Density	BW_e (bps/Hz)
BPSK	500	1	1000	2-ary	1
QPSK	250	500	500	4-ary	2
8-PSK	166.7	333.3	333.3	8-ary	3
16-PSK	125	250	250	16-ary	4

In conclusion, there are two interesting results with phase modulation: BPSK is identical to DSB-SC AM, and QPSK is identical to QAM, which is just the combination of two DSB-SC AM signals itself. As mentioned in the paragraph above, this seeming pattern does not hold up for higher M-ary rates. Once higher values of M than 2 or 4 are considered, this equivalence of PSK to DSB-SC breaks down. The last modulation technique that will be examined will illustrate this.

Sixteen-ary QAM

Sixteen-ary QAM is a popular implementation choice, and it can be implemented in a couple of different ways. The approach examined here will illustrate how advanced M-ary modulators arrange the amplitude and phase states such that they achieve maximum performance in noise. One obvious way to implement this modulator would be to just generalize from 8-ary PSK and add another phase state between each existing one. That would reduce the phase difference between states from $\pi / 4$ to $\pi / 8$. That is a maximum phase difference of only about 45° between phasors.

This might seem like a lot, and it can be implemented and can work effectively. However, it is interesting to ask if there is a different way of looking at it that would maximize the difference between phasors. Remember from Chapter 12 that the goal of source coding is to make the states "different enough" to tell them apart. Is there something that could be done to make these more different from each other?

The answer is to combine amplitude and phase modulation, resulting in a constellation diagram that has larger "distances" between each phasor. Look at Figure 13.24 for a comparison of what can be accomplished using amplitude and phase as compared to using just phase. The distances between the phasors are important because as noise is added to the signals, the effect is to render the nice points represented in Figure 13.24 into noisy "smudges." For this reason, these regions centered about each point are called decision regions. The effect of noise on this process is shown in Figure 13.25. As can be clearly seen, when the addition of noise is added to the figure, errors in determining which state is which become more probable. The noise is shown by the light gray regions surrounding the signal state. Clearly, QAM is more robust than PSK as the number of signal states grows.

Figure 13.24
Sixteen-ary QAM and 16-ary PSK.

16-ary QAM

16-ary PSK

Figure 13.25
Noise added to constellation diagrams illustrating decision regions.

16-ary QAM   16-ary PSK

■ CARRIER-TO-NOISE RATIO

The carrier-to-noise (C/N) ratio is a commonly used method of describing the amount of power that the transmitter is putting out as compared to the amount of noise in the channel. It makes up one key component that is used to relate the performance of various systems. The carrier power is given by the simple equation that was introduced in Chapter 1, reproduced below:

$$P_c(\text{dBm}) = 10 \log \left(\frac{\text{power (watts)}}{10^{-3}} \right) \tag{13-19}$$

In discussing this subject, it is normally rewritten as follows:

$$C(\text{dBm}) = 10 \log \left(\frac{C \text{ (watts)}}{10^{-3}} \right) \tag{13-20}$$

where C is used to represent the power in the unmodulated carrier wave. The noise in any channel is given by the following relationship:

$$N = KTB \tag{13-21}$$

where N = thermal noise power (W)
K = Boltzman's constant
T = temperature (K)
B = bandwidth of channel (Hz)

In Chapter 1, noise was always expressed as a power, and it can be seen here that in communications noise power is talked about as temperature. This has a solid basis in physics as can be seen by recalling that the hotter a gas is, the more rapid the molecules move. This more rapid movement is indicative of more energy; the energy comes from the additional heat.

In communications studies, amplifiers, channels, and so forth, will often all have their noise contributions characterized by a temperature in kelvin. Recall that kelvin is just centigrade plus 273°.

Equation 13-21 relates the noise power to the bandwidth of the channel because the wider the bandwidth, the more noise that cen enter, just like the thicker the hose, the more water that can flow. Temperature is included for the reasons just stated, and Boltzman's constant is just a constant of proportionality that makes the numbers agree. It is equal to 1.38×10^{-23}.

To find the carrier-to-noise ratio in decibels,

$$\frac{C}{N} \text{ (dB)} = C \text{ (}dBm\text{)} - N \text{ (dBm)} \tag{13-22}$$

■ **EXAMPLE 13.11**

Find the C/N ratio in decibels for a communications system where the carrier power is measured at 1 μW and the noise power is measured at 0.2 μW. Both powers are measured in a bandwidth of 10 MHz

$$C = 10 \log \left(\frac{1 \times 10^{-6}}{10^{-3}} \right) = -30 \; dBm$$

$$N = 10 \log \left(\frac{0.2 \times 10^{-6}}{10^{-3}} \right) = -37 \; dBm$$

$$\frac{C}{N} = -30 \; dBm - (-37 \; dBm) = 7 \; dB$$

As can be seen from the above example, increasing the power increases the C/N ratio. Also, note that increasing the bandwidth decreases the C/N ratio. Therefore for best C/N ratio, have high power in narrow bandwidths at as low of a noise temperature as possible.

Table 13.3

Modem	Data Rate	Modulation	Bandwidth Efficiency
Bell 103	300 bps	BFSK	0.1 bps/Hz
Bell 201	2400 bps	QPSK	0.75 bps/Hz
CCITT V.32	9600 bps	TCQAM	3 bps/Hz
CCITT V.34	33.6 kbps	TCQAM	11 bps/Hz
CCITT V.90	56 kbps	TCQAM	18 bps/Hz

■ **E_b/N_o CALCULATIONS**

E_b/N_o calculations give a way to characterize all different kinds of digital modulation techniques by relating the energy per bit (E_b) transmitted to the noise power density. In this way curves can be drawn for performance for each type of modem with out concern about how fast the modem is, how powerful the transmitter is, or how noisy the channel is. This is an important result. E_b/N_o calculations extend the C/N ratio to independence of bandwidth.

Imagine you are asked to determine which type of modulation technique is best applied to a particular problem. It would be nice to be able to talk about different modulation techniques without worrying about how big the transmitter is or how fast the input data rate is. These calculations allow these comparisons. The energy per bit transmitted is given by the product of the carrier power times the bit duration. This can be written as

$$E_b = CT_b \tag{13-23}$$

where E_b = energy per bit
          C = Carrier power (W)
          T_b = bit duration (sec)

It should make sense that the energy per bit transmitted is just the carrier power, which is what is modulated, multiplied by the amount of time it is modulated. This is just like saying that the power used by a system is the amount of power multiplied by the time it is applied.

Because this measurement is intended to be independent of bandwidth, the noise term, given by N_o, must be ratioed to a fixed bandwidth. The bandwidth that was chosen was 1 Hz. The noise term can be found by just dividing the noise power measured in any channel by the bandwidth of the measurement. Again, the analogy with a hose may help: The thicker the hose, the more noise; to get a hose thickness independent measurement, divide the amount of noise by the thickness of the hose.

$$N_o = \frac{N}{B} \tag{13-24}$$

where N_o = noise spectral density
          N = thermal noise power (W)
          B = bandwidth of receive channel filter (Hz)

Although calculations can be made using the above relationships, typically they are converted into decibel form for easy comparison. The resulting equations are

$$E_b(\text{dBm}) = 10 \log\left(\frac{CT_b}{10^{-3}}\right) \tag{13-25}$$

$$N_o(\text{dBm}) = 10 \log\left(\frac{N}{B \times 10^{-3}}\right) \tag{13-26}$$

$$\frac{E_b}{N_o}(\text{dBm}) = 10 \log\left(\frac{CT_b}{10^{-3}}\right) - 10 \log\left(\frac{N}{13 \times 10^{-3}}\right) = 10 \log\left(\frac{CT_b}{10^{-3}}\right) - 10 \log\left(\frac{KT}{10^{-3}}\right) \tag{13-27}$$

Finally, it is possible to relate C/N and E_b/N_o ratios as is shown below:

$$\frac{E_b}{N_o} = \frac{C}{N} + 10 \log(BT_b) \tag{13-28}$$

The following examples illustrate how to apply these formulas.

■ EXAMPLE 13.12

Find the Eb/No ratio for a 2 Mbps QPSK modem operating at the power levels used in example 13.11.

$$E_b = 10 \log \left(\frac{CT_b}{10^{-3}} \right) = 10 \log \left(\frac{(1 \times 10^{-6})(5 \times 10^{-7})}{10^{-3}} \right) = -93 \, dBm$$

$$N_o = 10 \log \left(\frac{N}{B \times 10^{-3}} \right) = 10 \log \left(\frac{0.2 \times 10^{-6}}{(10 \times 10^6)(10^{-3})} \right) = -107 \, dBm$$

$$\frac{E_b}{N_o} = -93 \, dBm - (-107 \, dBm) = 14 \, dB$$

■ EXAMPLE 13.13

Using equation 13-28, what relationship between bit rate and bandwidth will yield the same result for both the C/N and Eb/No calculations?

$$\frac{E_b}{N_o} = \frac{C}{N} + 10 \log (BT_b)$$

Since

$$\log(1) = 0 \rightarrow B = T_b$$

Therefore, when the bit rate and receive channel filter bandwidth are identical, the two ratios are identical.

■ EXAMPLE 13.14

Find the equivalent noise temperature exhibited by the Eb/No ratio calculated in Example 13.12

$$\frac{E_b}{N_o} = 10 \log \left(\frac{CT_b}{10^{-3}} \right) - 10 \log \left(\frac{KT}{10^3} \right) \Big]$$

$$14 \, dB = 10 \log \left(\frac{(1 \times 10^{-6})(5 \times 10^{-7})}{10^{-3}} \right) - 10 \log \left(\frac{(1.38 \times 10^{-23})T}{10^{-3}} \right)$$

$$14 \, dB = -93 \, dBm - 10 \log \left(\frac{1.38 \times 10^{-23}}{10^{-3}} \right) - 10 \log (T)$$

$$14 \, dB = -93 \, dBm - 199 \, dBm - 10 \log (T)$$

$$10 \log (T) = -306 \, dB$$

$$T = 10^{-30.6} = 2.5 \times 10^{-31}$$

As can be seen, this temperature is extrememly low and for this reason is not often calculated. The intent of this example is to make very clear that the temperature in these equations is not the temperature of the receiver. Rather, it is an artificial temperature that is used to relate the quantities of interest in these types of calculations.

■ EXAMPLE 13.15

This example will explore the relationship between carrier power, bandwidth of the receive channel filter, and data rate. Specifically, what effect does doubling any one of them have on the E_b/N_o ratio? For this example, assume a C/N ratio of 10 dB, a filter bandwidth of 1 MHz and a data rate of 500 kbps.

$$\frac{E_b}{N_o} = \frac{C}{N} + 10 \log (BT_b) = 10 \, dB + 10 \log ((1 \times 10^6)(2 \times 10^{-6})) = 10dB + 3 \, dBM = 13dB$$

$$Double \, \frac{C}{N} : \frac{E_b}{N_o} = 13 \, dB + 3 \, dBm = 16 \, dB$$

$$Double \, B : \frac{E_b}{N_o} \, 10 \, dB + 10 \log ((2 \times 10^6)(2 \times 10^{-6})) = 10 \, dB + 6 \, dB = 16 \, dB$$

$$Halve \, T_b : \frac{E_b}{N_o} = 10 \, dB + 10 \log ((1 \times 10^6)(1 \times 10^{-6})) = 10 \, dB + 0 = 10 \, dB$$

As you might have expected, when the carrier to noise ratio is doubled, representing more signal to noise, the E_b/N_o value doubles. Similarly, when the bandwidth of the channel is doubled, representing a less efficient system, the E_b/N_o value doubles. Finally, when the data rate is doubled, causing a halving of the bit duration, the E_b/N_o value reduces by 3dB or halves. Since this represents a more efficient system, the E_b/N_o ratio drops.

Therefore, larger E_b/N_o values indicate a better channel environment, either more power, wider bandwidth or lower bit rate. Reducing the E_b/N_o ratio requires increased peformance from the modem for the same error rate. These calculations are illustrated in the next section for a variety of modulation types.

■ BIT RATE ERROR (BER) CALCULATIONS

Bit error rate calculations tell how many bits will be in error, on average, for a given E_b/N_o ratio. BER is a probability function, and it makes assumptions about the channel characteristics. The primary assumption is that the noise in the channel is just thermal noise. This is the only type considered here. Other noise sources, especially those with spikes in their spectrum, will result in lower BER numbers for a given E_b/N_o ratio. The mathematical analysis of BER requires knowledge of statistics that is outside the scope of this text. However, BER is drawn as a curve, and these diagrams will be reproduced to allow calculations to proceed.

The first graph, in Figure 13.26, is for ASK or OOK systems. There is only one curve because all ASK systems work in the same way. For any ASK system the probability of error in a transmission is given by the above curve. Example 13.16 illustrates how this type of graph is used.

Figure 13.26
BER graph for ASK systems.

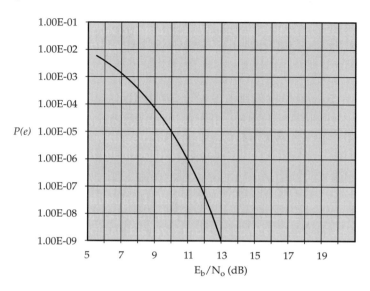

■ EXAMPLE 13.16

Find the BER for an ASK system operating at an E_b/N_o ratio of 11 dB. Examining the above curve, the E_b/N_o ratio corresponds to a BER of 1E-6. That means that for every million bits sent, on average, one will be in error.

The next graph, in Figure 13.27, is for FSK systems. As you know, all FSK systems can be divided up into two classes, those that use coherent detection and those that use noncoherent detection. In Figure 13.27, the curve to the right is the one for noncoherent detection. As you might expect, that curve represents a higher error rate for the same received power, or E_b/N_o ratio.

■ EXAMPLE 13.17

Compare the error rate performance of coherent and noncoherent FSK systems. For a BER of 1E-4, what are the E_b/N_o requirements of the two systems?

For the coherent FSK system, the E_b/N_o required is about 11.9 dB. For the noncoherent system the E_b/N_o required is about 12.8 dB. For this error rate, almost an additional 1 dB of power is required at the receiver for the same performance. Note that this additional power gives nothing in terms of increased message or information density. On the other hand, for the additional expense of adding coherent recovery to the receiver, the

Figure 13.27
BER graph for FSK systems.

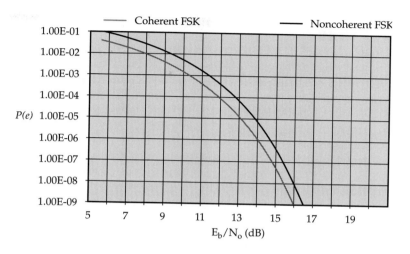

transmit power requirement can be reduced by almost 1 dB. Unless there are a lot of receivers, it probably does not make sense to make this trade-off.

The next graph, in Figure 13.28, is for M-ary PSK systems. The first line is used for both BPSK and QPSK, which have virtually identical error rates. The next line to the

Figure 13.28
BER graph for PSK systems.

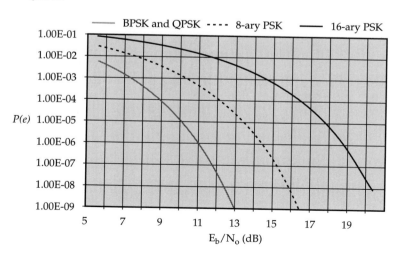

right is for 8-ary PSK, and the line to the far right is for 16-ary PSK. As can be seen, as the bit density grows, more power per bit is required for the same error rate.

■ EXAMPLE 13.18

Compare the BER performance of QPSK and 16-PSK systems for a E_b/N_o received power of 11 dB. For QPSK, a BER of 1E-6, or 1 bit in a million, is read. For 16-PSK, a BER of about 8E-2, or about 1 bit in 80, is read. Although more bits per symbol are achieved by using a 16-PSK system, the BER soars for this power level. How much power must be received for the 16-PSK system to have equivalent performance to the QPSK system?

Looking at the graph in Figure 13.28 for a BER of 1E-6, a 16-PSK system requires an E_b/N_o value of 19 dB. That means that 8 dB more power is required. That is a power ratio of about 2.5:1. For this extra power requirement, what does one get? The BER is the same, so no increased performance will be gained in that area. E_b/N_o graphs like the one in Figure 13.28 remove any dependency in data rate, so no more data is passing through the system.

The only thing left is bandwidth considerations. A 16-PSK system is much more bandwidth efficient. It features a bandwidth efficiency of 4 bps/Hz, or stated another way, four input state changes are required for one output change. A QPSK system has a bandwidth efficiency of 2 bps/Hz. Therefore, for this increase in power requirements, transmission bandwidth is reduced.

A 16-PSK system uses half the bandwidth of a QPSK system. Looking carefully at Figure 13.28, observe that to a first approximation, if you halve the bandwidth, you double the power. (Recall that 3 dB is double the power.) For each of the three curves shown, as one moves to the right, each curve uses half the bandwidth of the previous one. Additionally, each curve is roughly 3 dB higher than the previous one for the same error rate. Nothing is free; for a reduction in bandwidth, an increase in power is required.

The net result is that the bandwidth requirement is halved, but at a large price. The received power must be at least twice as great. This is the general case with higher-ary transmissions. The bandwidth savings always grow slower than the power requirements. In many cases, bandwidth is so valuable that this penalty is gladly paid.

Figure 13.29
BER graph for QAM systems.

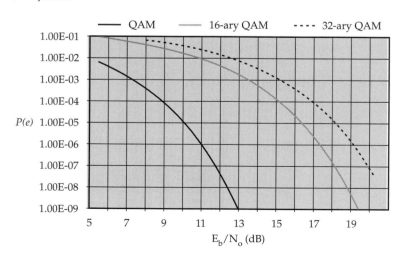

The last BER graph, in Figure 13.29, is for M-ary QAM systems. This graph shows three curves for 4-ary QAM, 16-ary QAM, and 32-ary QAM. Most new designs utilize the QAM approach, for the reasons shown below. The error rate performance is better than any other technique considered here.

■ EXAMPLE 13.19

To illustrate that QAM and QPSK are equivalent systems, find and compare the BER of the two modulation techniques for an E_b/N_o of 11 dB.

For the QPSK system, the BER is 1E-6, and the QAM curve shows the identical result. QAM and QPSK are equivalent systems. Under the same conditions, they will perform identically. This is because if one examines the constellation diagrams, the distance between each signal state is identical.

Compare the performance of 16-PSK and 16-QAM. It is interesting to note how the difference in the constellation diagrams affects the error performance. Because both have the same bandwidth efficiencies, both will take up the same bandwidth. This is a clear indication of how the distances between each amplitude and phase state affect the performance of a modern in the presence of noise.

Here, the comparison is dramatic. The performance at an E_b/N_o value of 18 dB is very different. For 16-PSK, an error rate of about 1E-5 results, whereas for 16-QAM the error rate is only about 8E-7. That is almost 2 orders of magnitude better performance for the same received energy per bit.

The final example in this chapter will illustrate how these graphs are used in industry to characterize the performance of a particular modem. In any manufacturing environment, the actual performance of any individual manufactured system will vary due to many factors. What is important is that the device meet the published performance specifications prior to being shipped to a customer. Very often BER graphs are used to characterize the performance of modems prior to shipment.

■ EXAMPLE 13.20

For a standard QAM, modem determine if the modem is functioning within tolerance or not. For this product the tolerance is defined to be within 1 dB of theoretical. The theoretical curve is shown in the BER graphs. All real modems operate to the right of, or above, the curve for that modulation type. If a modem shows a BER to the left of, or below, the curve, something is wrong. This would be better performance than theory predicts, an impossible situation unless the theory is wrong.

Table 13.4 lists three points from Figure 13.29. Examine them yourself and verify that the entries in the table are correct.

Table 13.4
QAM Performance Measurements

Modulation	E_b/N_o (dB)	Measured $P(e)$	Pass/Fail/Comment
QAM	11	1exp-5	Pass
QAM	11	1exp-4	Fail
QAM	11	1exp-7	Not possible

Note that the first data point is to the right of the curve, but within 1 dB. The second data point is also to the right of the curve, but 2 dB off, which fails the test of 1 dB. The third data point is to the left of the curve, so something is wrong. Either the modem is mislabeled or the test was performed incorrectly.

■ SUMMARY

The relationship between the bandwidth required for a particular modulation method and the trade-off in increased power for the same error rate has important implications for what types of modulation are preferred for certain channel types. If the application is a dedicated wired one, like a LAN, it does not make much sense to increase the signal density and add complexity to the modem. The only thing one gains by this approach is less bandwidth used for any bit rate. If the channel is a dedicated one, it makes little sense to pay the complexity costs of the design and the cost of a higher power signal as well.

On the other hand, for channels where the bandwidth must be shared among competing services, like a satellite system, or where the bandwidth is strictly limited by the technology, like the telephone system, it can make a large difference. Here, one is ready to pay for complexity and amplification to get increased throughput from an existing, limited channel allocation. This is because people will usually pay more for increased throughput; the only effective means of increasing throughput when the bandwidth is limited is increased signal density, and therefore the project is often self-funding.

Most LAN systems, when they make use of a digital modem, use binary or 4-ary modulation techniques, whereas telephone modems and satellite systems often use 16-ary and above modems. This choice is driven by the considerations discussed above.

PROBLEMS

1. Using the modified Hartley's Law, find the information capacity in bits of the following bandwidths. Assume a time of transmission of 10 sec.
   (a) 10 Hz   (c) 100 kHz
   (b) 1 kHz   (d) 10 MHz

2. For each of the above bandwidths, find the information capacity if the S/N ratio is now defined to be 10 dB. Use the expression for Shannon's Limit. Are the answers what you expected?

3. Describe briefly the difference in traditional FSK and MSK modulation techniques.

4. Find the bandwidth required for a BPSK modulator operating at 1 kbps.

5. Find the bandwidth required for a QPSK modulator operating at 1 kbps.

6. Find the bandwidth required for a QAM modulator operating at 1 kbps.

7. Find the C/N ratio for a carrier power of 10 μw and a noise power of 1 μw

8. Find the E_b/N_o ratio for problem 7. Assume a 100 kbps data rate in a 200 kHz channel.

9. If the bandwidth is doubled, what effect will this have on the E_b/N_o ratio? Why?

10. A certain modem has a transmit bandwidth of 10 kHz. The binary data rate is 20 kbps. What is the symbol rate?

11. Another modem has a transmit bandwidth of 20 kHz. Without knowledge of the binary data rate, can you find the symbol rate? Assume it is a type of PSK modem.

12. For an 8-PSK modem, if the binary data rate is 2 kbps, what is the transmit bandwidth?

13. For each of the following modulation types, determine from the measurements taken if the modem is functioning within tolerance or is not. Also check to see if the data you were supplied about the modulation type are correct. Assume that if the performance is within 1 dB from theoretical, it is operating correctly. Use the BER graphs to make these determinations.

Modulation	E_b/N_o (dB)	Measured $P(e)$	Pass/Fail/ Comment
ASK	11	1exp-4	
ASK	11	1exp-5	
QPSK	11	5exp-6	
8-PSK	11	1exp-4	

14. Assume a channel with a lower limit of 1 kHz and a BFSK modulator. Find the signaling frequencies, (mark and space) that would minimize the upper limit of the bandwidth of the transmission; also find the transmission bandwidth. Assume a modulating signal of 10 kbps. Find these values for each of the guardband options shown below:
(a) No guardband
(b) Guardband of 10 kHz.

15. Draw out a tri-bit encoding diagram and relate it to 8-ary amplitude assignments similarly to that done in the text for di-bit and 4-ary assignments.

14

Open System Interconnection Model

In this chapter, a model that can be used to define the protocol piece of any modern network will be examined. A network is really made up of two parts, the underlying physical network topology and hardware, along with the protocol that runs on the network. The protocol is what the application running on the device attached to the network uses to communicate over the physical topology. Protocols can be quite complicated when viewed as a whole, and so a standardized approach to analyze and explain them will be used. This approach breaks the protocol up into sets of specific responsibilities. Most protocols in use today can be discussed in terms of a model based on this approach, the model is called OSI.

OSI stands for Open System Interconnection. OSI is a reference model that, if followed, offers a way for products manufactured by different vendors to communicate in a standard way. That means that if vendor A makes a communications product and vendor B makes a communications product and they need to communicate, if both vendors have followed the OSI model, they can communicate without a custom gateway. The only thing that OSI or any reference model designed for communications is concerned with is the exchange of information between end systems. If both end systems follow the OSI model, there is a special term for them; they are called open systems (e.g., they are open to communications).

For the reason just stated, OSI is an excellent way to classify communication products. Because OSI has all the terms and nomenclature for how products communicate and the architecture of that communications functionality, it makes for an excellent way of sorting them out and for knowing what can work and what cannot.

OSI is not the only reference model that exists; there are several including Systems Network Architecture, (SNA), Integrated Services Digital Network (ISDN), and Transmission Control Protocol/Internet Protocol (TCP/IP). In this chapter OSI will be explored. ISDN will be discussed in Chapter 16 and TCP/IP in Chapter 17.

OSI is an international standard that is recognized by the International Organization for Standardization (ISO). As stated earlier, the goal of the standard is to give end systems manufactured by different vendors a way to share information seamlessly. The OSI model does this using a concept called layering, which is a way to talk about and design pieces of the functionality that will allow internetworking between different end systems. Essentially, the idea is to divide up the job into several, seven or fewer, subtasks and then define what each subtask does and how it communicates with the other subtasks.

In the discussion that follows, the OSI layered approach will be examined, each subtask will be explored separately, and its communications with other tasks briefly described. Although there are seven layers to the OSI model, these seven layers are really broken up into two groups. These are Layers 1 through 4, having to do with communications functions, and Layers 5 through 7 having to do with user-oriented functions. All traditional communications services use the Layers 1 through 4 to accomplish their tasks; for example the entire telephone system can be described using only the first four layers. Figure 14.1 illustrates the seven-layer OSI model.

There is actually one more layer associated with communications. This layer is Layer 0. Layer 0 is that layer that would correspond to the actual physical media that is being used, metallic, optical, or atmospheric. It defines the physical topology of the network. The introduction to topology in Chapter 15 and Chapters 3, 4, and 5, which discuss metallic and optical media and antennas, outline the characteristics of this layer to the extent they will be studied.

It is also important to understand that the Application Layer is not where the application programs that run on a computer connected to the network lie. These reside above the communications structure. The OSI model is a way to talk about communications, not define application software. The Application Layer just provides services to the application program, just like any layer does to the layer above it.

The focus of this chapter will be on the lower three layers of the OSI model because we are primarily concerned with how the communications functionality works, not on how the user-oriented functions work. Further, much of what happens in the Transport Layer is actually redundant to what should go on in the Network Layer if all real networks were flawless and all had the same service primitives.

For this reason, the Transport Layer will receive brief treatment. In the real world, the Transport Layer isolates the upper layers from the technology and imperfections of the subnet. For this reason, the distinction mentioned above is made between Layers 1 through 4 and Layers 5 through 7. In OSI, the terminology is as shown in Figure 14.1; for TCP/IP, the lower group is the transport service provider and the upper group is the transport service user.

Figure 14.1
OSI model.

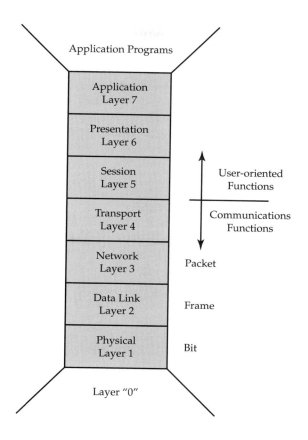

■ LAYERING

Today's computer and communications networks are designed in a highly structured way. To reduce the design complexity, most networks are organized in a series of layers each built on top of the former. The number, operation, and content of each layer is different for each network. *In all networks the function of each layer is to provide services to the next highest layer, insulating those layers from concerns of how the lower layers are actually implemented.*

This idea is at the heart of the OSI model. By separating the functionality into several specific tasks or layers, it becomes possible to define each layer as a set of operations that stands alone. If these layers are designed in the correct way, all interaction between the layers in a single and system is performed at the layer boundaries. This greatly simplifies the interaction between layers that is necessary to accomplish the larger job of defining the overall protocol. The set of layers is called the network architecture.

This is exactly like dividing up a job into a series of subtasks. For example, imagine that you have just bought a race car and want to enter it in a race. Although it is possible to do all the jobs yourself, it would be much better to divide up the jobs among various specialists. You might hire a driver to drive it, a mechanic to repair it, a marketer to obtain sponsors, and so forth.

This is the same idea that is applied to the task of building a communications protocol. For a communications protocol, what is divided up is the job of getting messages from the source to destination. Each layer has its own specialization and expertise, just like each individual of the race team has. The driver would be in the position to tell if something might be not quite right with the engine but would not be the best person on the team to fix the engine, so the driver would inform the mechanic of the problem and ask the mechanic to fix it.

■ SERVICE ACCESS POINT (SAP)

In the OSI model, each layer has its own specialized functionality, and when it needs the functionality of another layer, it requests it. It does this at the layer interface that exists between each pair of layers. It is important to realize that this interface defines which operations and services the *lower layer offers to the upper one.*

In protocols, which are really software programs, the responsibility for different tasks is divided up into separate subroutines. Although there are many subroutines in each layer, the idea of a layer as a subroutine of the entire communications task is a good one. When you write a program to add two numbers and print out the result, it is usually a good idea to separate the tasks. You might write a subroutine to add two numbers and another subroutine to print out the results. It would not make much sense to have both subroutines be able to print out the results.

This is the central idea behind a SAP. At each layer boundary, there is at least one SAP. It is at the SAP(s) that all communications between layers occurs. Further, it is always the upper layer that requests services from the lower one, never the other way around. Each layer has one or more services that it can offer to the layer above.

One can think of the service access points as a kind of counter where the customer, the layer above, comes to order lunch. The counter has many things on its menu and the customer, reviewing this menu, requests a specific item. Making an analogy with your computer, the service access point for the modem (layer 1) to send a message is the plug to the telephone line (layer 0). Figure 14.2 illustrates the layer interface, or boundary, and the location of the SAP.

■ SERVICE

As you may have realized from the previous discussion, OSI terminology has a special use for the word *service.* A service is a function provided to the layer above by making use of the services of the layer below. An OSI protocol functions by each layer providing service to the layer above by utilizing the services available from the layer below.

Figure 14.2
SAP interface.

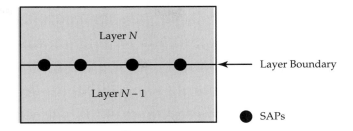

Each layer does this by passing special units of exchange called Interface Data Units, or IDUs, across the layer boundary at SAP locations.

The layer above is called the service user and the layer below is called the service provider. In Figure 14.2, the layer N would be the service user and the layer $N - 1$ would be the service provider.

It is important to make four key points about services and how layers communicate using them:

1. Although layers request services from the layer below, each layer communicates with its companion layer. For example, the source location Network layer communicates with the destination location Network layer through the services provided by the layers below each of them. This communication is called virtual communication. Two communicating layers are known as peer entities or layers, and each communicates with its own protocol; in the example cited this is the Network protocol.
2. Services are made up of operation primitives of which there are four classes: requests, responses, indications, and confirmations.
3. Services and protocols are *not* the same thing. Services are made up of operations; protocols are the set of rules for exchanging information between the source and destination. The source and destination systems use protocols to implement their services.
4. There are two broad types of service a layer can offer to the layer above it. These are connection-oriented service (COS) and connectionless service (CLS).

■ VIRTUAL COMMUNICATIONS

Suppose there are two computers at two different locations. Each one has a layered OSI protocol that it is using to exchange information with the other. Here, the only thing that is of concern is the communication network, not the ultimate program running on each system. The communications system is broken up into layers, with the functionality of each layer distinct from any other layer. It stands to reason, then, that only that similar layer at the other end of the communication would understand the message from its

Figure 14.3
Virtual communication at the Network Layer.

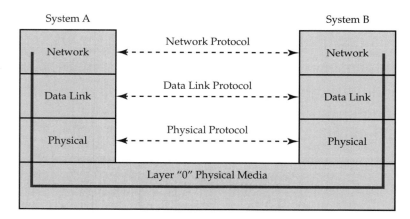

counterpart. This is the virtual communication between similar layers called a layer protocol.

Each layer has its own protocol. For example, the Network layers of two systems conduct a conversation using the services of the Data Link layer. The physical path that the information follows is made possible by the communicating layers requesting services from the layer below it. This is true for each successive layer as one proceeds down the network model. At each layer, the peer entities communicate with each other and use the services provided by the layer below to implement that communication.

There is a protocol communicating with a virtual communication between each similar layer at both source and destination. In Figure 14.3, the service boundaries and virtual communications are shown for two systems using a layered protocol to communicate. The physical path is shown as the dark line, and the virtual communication, as the dotted line.

As can be seen, there are three protocols illustrated in this figure. The layer 1 protocol, Physical; the layer 2 protocol, Data Link; and the layer 3 protocol, Network. The SAP locations are at the boundaries of the boxes delineating the layers of the two network architectures. It is also important to note that in this example not all seven layers of the OSI model are implemented. This is often the case. As must be clear once one thinks about it, different levels of sophistication of the communications implemented between source and destination require a different number of layers.

■ OPERATION PRIMITIVES

As was stated earlier, services are made up of four classes of primitive operations, referred to as primitives. These are summarized in Table 14.1. Requests and indications are paired along with responses and confirmations. When one system makes a request, the other system first indicates that it has heard the request. When one system generates

Table 14.1
Service Primitives

Service Primitive	Action
Request	Request service
Response	Response to Request
Indication	Indication of some action in response to a Request
Confirm	Confirmation of a Response

a response, the other system may confirm that response, depending on the type of service being offered by the layers below it.

An example from daily life may make this clearer. Suppose you wish to initiate a conversation with another person. The first thing you might do is to make eye contact. This is an example of the service primitive Request. It is confirmed by the other person by when he or she meets your eyes, an example of the service primitive Indication. Indication is some action in response to a request. The action is meeting your eyes.

The next step would normally be for one or the other person to say "Hello," acknowledging the request and the action of an indication. Which party would first say Hello is usually dependent on social convention and is a clear analog to protocol. The statement Hello is an example of a Response service primitive and is generated as a response to the implied request to have a conversation first initiated by making eye contact. Finally, to confirm the intention to have a conversation, the other party also says "Hello." This is an example of a Confirmation service primitive generated in response to the other person's response.

There are various levels of reliability in these responses and confirmations. Sometimes, silence rather than some active response or confirmation, is taken as the response or confirmation. When the two classes of services that all layers provide are examined, this distinction will become clear.

Additionally, these service primitives must pass across the layer boundaries at the SAP locations. These transfers are always done by units of data known as Protocol Data Units (PDUs). The convention for naming the units of data exchanged between each layer and the one immediately above it is the layer name coupled with the term (PDU). Essentially, each layer appends the notation to its name. For example, the transport unit of exchange is the Transport Protocol Data Unit (TPDU).

It is also true that these units of data were passed to facilitate communications systems long before the OSI model was developed with its specialized terminology. The lower three layers of the model, as indicated in Figure 14.1, have traditional names associated with the PDUs exchanged. The terms *packet*, *frame*, and *bit* are applied, respectively, to the lower three layers: Network, Data Link, and Physical.

As mentioned earlier, there is a conceptual boundary at the interface between the Session and Transport layers. The names packet, frame, and bit refer to the traditional names of PDUs in wide area networks where the lower three layers are run by the carrier; for most, these are the local and long-distance carrier providers to whom you subscribe. In these systems, users have no control over the subnet, so the need to be able to define a set of primitives that will work independent of the communications subnet make this layer distinction important.

■ SERVICES VERSUS PROTOCOLS

As was stated earlier, services and protocols are *not* the same thing. Services are made up of operations, and protocols are the set of rules for exchanging information between the source and destination. The source and destination systems use protocols to implement their services.

This means that the thing that one actually requests of another system is the service that system provides. As can be seen by the following example, the service can transcend changes in the protocol. Taking the example of the telephone system, the *protocol* for connecting to someone for whom you do not have the telephone number has changed with the evolution of the system. The *service* aspect associated with the need for connecting to someone for whom you do not have the telephone number remains the same.

In earlier days, when you wanted the telephone number of a friend, you called the operator and asked to be connected to the called party by name, for example, "Please connect me to Mr. Garland." The operator, a human being, would physically connect your telephone with the telephone circuit that was wired to Mr. Garland. Later, as technology improved, the operator searched a database and read off the number listed for the party you wanted to connect to. Later still, the human being still searched for the number, but the response was replaced by a computer voice providing you the correct telephone number.

As can be seen from this example, the service aspect remained and the protocol changed. This is one of the great advantages of separating these two concepts. Technology is changing faster than ever, and the way of doing something, the protocol, may change quickly. However, the need for the service remains. As long as the service is decoupled from the protocol, this evolution can proceed naturally. Where it is not, systems are quickly outdated and disappear. The reasons for this are complex but are captured by the idea that when the service and protocol are tightly coupled, when one changes, the other changes. Many times this changes the very nature of the service, and it becomes unattractive to many users of the service.

■ PROTOCOL DATA UNITS

Each layer communicates to the peer layer adjacent to it by passing a PDU. These PDUs contain the data and other information that is necessary for the destination peer layer to interpret the actions of the source peer layer (e.g., the virtual communication). However, the physical path of the data is down a network architecture, across a physical medium, and up a network stack.

Figure 14.4
PDU construction.

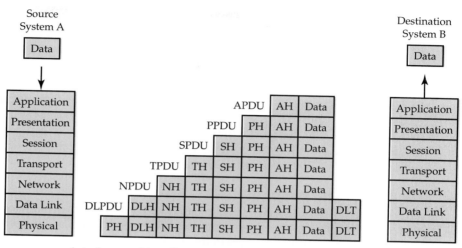

Actual composition of bits transferred through the physical medium

At the source each layer, upon receiving a PDU from the layer above, adds a header to it and passes it down one layer. Similarly, at the destination, each layer strips the header applied by its peer counterpart at the source and passes the remaining PDU up one layer.

At each layer, the PDUs have specific names that are derived from the layer where the header is applied. As stated earlier, the PDU exchanged between Transport layers in their virtual communication is called the TPDU. The PDU names at each layer are shown in Figure 14.4.

As can be seen, the PDU exchanged between each similar layer is composed of the information passed down to it from above at the source station. Each layer adds a header, except for the Data Link layer, which adds a header and trailer. The headers and trailers are denoted by the terms *DLH* and *DLT* for the Data Link layer and similarly for the other layers. The data come from the application running on the source station and are destined for the application running on the destination station.

■ SERVICE CLASSES

In the following sections, pay careful attention to the use of the words *communication* and *connection*. They have different meanings and it is important to keep the distinction clear. A communication can occur using either of the two broad types of service classifications. A connection is a specific type of service classification. There are two broad types of service that a layer can offer to the layer above it, COS and CLS.

COS

The most sophisticated service any layer can provide to the layer above it is COS, which is modeled after the telephone system. To talk, you pick up the telephone, dial the number, talk, and hang up. In data communications, the service user, the layer above, establishes the connection, uses it, and then terminates the connection.

Conceptually, the connection acts like a tube; the source places messages in at one end, and the destination takes them out at the other end. Therefore, with COS, the source and destination machines establish a connection before any data is transferred. With COS, first-in-first-out (FIFO) is guaranteed. COS provides the upper layer with a reliable data stream.

Because COS is the most sophisticated service that a layer can provide, its implementation is also the most complex. The more complex the implementation, the more service primitives that are required to implement it.

CLS

The other main class of service a layer can offer is CLS, which is modeled after the postal system. To send a message you individually address a letter and drop it into a mailbox. Suppose you dropped two letters in the mailbox, one after the other. CLS does not guarantee which letter arrives first. Each letter is individually addressed and each follows its own path to the destination. In data communications, the service user, the layer above, never establishes a connection. Instead the message is sent and either arrives at its destination or not. Only the destination can tell if the message arrives.

Conceptually, the communication has none of the attributes of a connection. It does not guarantee FIFO; each part of the message must be individually addressed, and each part may follow a different path to the destination.

There are two types of connectionless services. The first is the next step down in reliability from COS and is called acknowledged CLS. The analogy here is with sending a registered letter and requesting a return receipt. When the receipt comes back, the sender is absolutely sure the letter was delivered to the intended party. When this service is used, there are no connections established, but each message sent is individually acknowledged. In this way, the sender knows whether or not a message has arrived safely. If it has not arrived within a specified time interval, it can be sent again.

The least reliable service is the unacknowledged CLS. This service is often called datagram service in an analogy with the telegram service, which does not provide an acknowledgment back to the sender. This service consists of having the source send messages to the destination without having the destination acknowledge them. No connection is established beforehand or released afterward.

If part of a message is lost for any reason, no attempt is made to recover at the layer. This class of service is only appropriate when the error rate is very low and recovery is left to the higher layers. However, sometimes the delay associated with reliable messaging is unacceptable. It may be appropriate for real-time traffic applications where late data is worse than bad data. One example is digitized voice service; here bad data is preferable to late data.

To review, there are actually two "levels of effort" for CLS, acknowledged CLS and unacknowledged CLS. Both forms require each message that the source sends to the destination to carry the full destination address, and each is routed through the system independent of any other. Normally, the first to be sent arrives first; however, this is not guaranteed.

This creates a unique problem for both forms of CLS. There must be a mechanism that makes sure that the destination can make out what message was sent first so it can order them correctly. This is accomplished by numbering each frame that is sent and the layer providing the service guarantees that each frame is received exactly once and is received in the correct order.

A message might be received more than once when using CLS if an acknowledged CLS is used. The delay in sending the acknowledgment must be considered. If this delay takes too long, because each message travels through the communications system independent of any other, the source might assume that the message never arrived and send another copy. The destination must have a mechanism for sorting this kind of thing out.

For example, suppose you are having a conversation with someone and suddenly, in the middle of it, the person stops acknowledging your statements. No more casual nods of the head or short comments like Yes, OK, and so forth. Once the acknowledgments stop, most people will stop and repeat the last few sentences to make sure they were heard before continuing the conversation. Essentially, the acknowledgment did not arrive and so part of the message is sent again.

If an unacknowledged CLS is used, this problem with delayed acknowledgments goes away. The problem of what to do when the destination does not receive the entire message or parts of the message are received out of order remains. Therefore, the destination must still have some way to make sure it got all the parts of the message sent by the source. Because only the destination can know if all the parts of the message arrived, it must specifically request retransmission of any parts that it missed. Remember, because all this is occurring as a protocol between peer layers, the higher layers have no knowledge of these operations. All they know about is that there was a message requested from the layer below and now it has arrived, identified as complete by the layer below.

As should be clear, different services have different reliability factors, called quality of service (QOS) parameters. These are summarized in Table 14.2. Each of these services can be characterized by such a QOS parameter. Usually, a reliable service is characterized by having the receiver acknowledge the receipt of each message so the sender is sure it arrived. One example would be a file transfer. Clearly, such a transfer would

Table 14.2
Service Reliabilities

Service Type	Common Analog	Reliability
Connection-oriented	Telephone	High
Acknowledged CLS	Return receipt	Medium
Unacknowledged CLS	Telegram	Low

be unacceptable if a random byte or two is misplaced. It is generally true that message reliability can be traded off with end-to-end transmission delay. Acknowledged service always takes longer than unacknowledged service, all things being equal.

To see how the layer protocols combine to implement communication in a network, a running example of stations on a LAN network will be used. In the sections below be sure to clearly separate the physical path the communication takes from the virtual path.

■ PHYSICAL LAYER (LAYER 1)

The Physical layer provides the physical transfer of data bits between adjacent nodes. It focuses on electrical engineering and technology issues almost exclusively. This layer specifies such things as the bit rate, modulation technique, pin-out of interfaces and other similar issues. The Physical layer deals in bits. Because a lot of time has already been spent talking about different modulation techniques, connector specifications, and so forth, there will be no further discussion here. The important idea is that *any* of the modulation techniques can be used as a Physical layer. Additionally, as mentioned above, *any* media can be used for the so-called Layer 0. The only requirement is that the modulation technique and the media and topology be compatible.

At Layer 1, the virtual communication occurs between the moderns that implement the Physical layer. The Physical layer makes use of the service provided by the layer below to physically transfer the communication between stations. The SAP between the physical layer and the media is the modem's attachment to the media. Only the two physical layers can understand and demodulate the information being sent from the other. Here, modulation and demodulation are the service primitives of the Physical layer protocol.

The information to be sent is transferred to the physical layer by the layer above, the Data Link layer. This layer makes use of the SAP between the Data Link layer and the Physical layer to request the Physical layer to send the information. This is shown in Figure 14.5. The information transferred between the two Physical layers does not have any

Figure 14.5
Physical layer virtual communication.

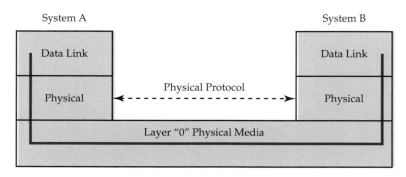

special name and is just referred to as bits. As was described earlier, there is a convention for all other layers units of exchange, called PDUs.

■ DATA LINK LAYER (LAYER 2)

The Data Link layer (DLL) of the OSI model concerns itself with the transfer of frames between adjacent stations. Pay special attention to the word *adjacent*. In this context, *adjacent* means any two stations on the same LAN segment. A segment is a unit of a network where all stations share a common address set. A good example of a segment from daily life might be all the houses on a street; because all have the same street name, all that is really needed to find one is the house number. To illustrate this concept Figure 14.6 shows how the frame is passed up to each DLL because it is the only layer that can recognize the house addresses. The Physical layer cannot tell if the message is destined for its upper layers or not; its functionality is confined to modulating and demodulating.

In the three link layer protocols that will be explored in this chapter, the Data Link layer performs three main tasks:

1. It insulates the Physical layer from the Network layer.
2. It defines how the bandwidth of the Physical layer is shared out among the stations connected to it.
3. It transforms a transmission facility into a line that appears free of transmission errors to the Network layer.

In three of the four access methodologies that will be explored, this is the origination of any acknowledgments that are sent back to the sender indicating that the message was received. In some other protocols, this is not the case. In these situations, this functionality is placed at the Network layer. The reasons for this will be discussed later.

As mentioned above, four types of access methodologies will be discussed. This approach will break up the discussion of the Data Link layer into three sections, each of which will build on the previous one:

1. A description of the access methodologies that the Data Link protocol can use. In a fundamental way, the access methodology chosen defines the Data Link

Figure 14.6
Message path showing DLL virtual communication.

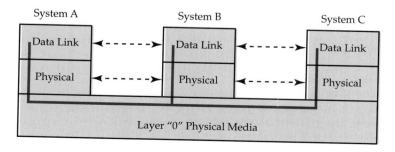

protocol. The access methodology defines how the bandwidth of the network is shared out among the stations connected to it.

2. A description of the Medium Access sublayer, which implements the access methodology portion of the Data Link layer.
3. A description of the Logical Link sublayer, which implements the services potion of the Data Link layer.

The first step is to provide a description of four access methodologies. Second, an overview of the components of a frame and their functionality is provided. Concluding the section is a brief description of the other half of the Data Link layer, the Logical Link sublayer.

In Appendix H details of the frame formats of the three IEEE project 802 access methods, Carrier Sense Multiple Access/Collision Detection (CSMA/CD), Token Passing Bus, and Token Ring, are provided. All are very similar and based on the High-Level Data Link Control (HDLC) frame structure. The commercial names of the implementations of these are, respectively, Ethernet, Token Bus, and Token Ring.

In the IEEE project, the Data Link layer was broken into two sublayers; these are the two sublayers mentioned above. The first specified the Medium Access Control (MAC) sublayer, and the second the Logical Link Control (LLC) sublayer. This was done to separate two distinct functionalities that the Data Link layer has.

The first is that functionality that has to do with accessing the particular Physical layer specified in the various standards. This section was particular to the Physical layer specified. It talks almost exclusively about such things as frame formats. Most of the differences arise from the physical topology chosen and how bandwidth is shared out among various stations on the LAN.

The second part is that section of the Data Link layer that is independent of the Physical layer, the LLC. This portion specifies the services that are provided to the Network layer, independent of the particular MAC utilized.

As can be seen from this description, the Data Link layer truly does insulate the Network layer from any contact with the Physical layer. This is because the LLC is common and is the source of all services provided to the layer above. Because the only interface between the layers occurs at SAP locations, and SAPs are where services are passed, the combined activities of the MAC and LLC effectively isolate the upper layers.

■ DATA LINK ACCESS METHODOLOGIES

As stated earlier, the access methodology a DLL protocol uses fundamentally defines its operation. Often, the access methodology is used as the definition of a particular DLL protocol; for example, sometimes Ethernet is defined as CSMA/CD. Ethernet is the commercial name of the IEEE 802.3 DLL protocol that uses an access methodology called CSMA/CD.

The access methodology defines how bandwidth on the network is shared out among the stations connected to it. This fundamental distinction is important to users, operators, and managers alike. Consider that Ethernet, 802.3, and CSMA/CD are all used to define a particular LAN, yet all these talk only about the access methodology used at the DLL.

CSMA/CD

The first access protocol, CSMA/CD, is best known as the Ethernet way of allocating the bandwidth resource of the LAN. Each station is free to transmit whenever it has data to send (multiple access) and listens for a collision with another station's transmission (carrier sense/collision detection). When this condition is sensed, each station backs off for a random period of time and retransmits its message. CSMA/CD has the potential to be the least fair in allocating the bandwidth resource. Under high-load conditions, it can exhibit unbounded time for message delivery.

What is a collision and how does it have anything to do with communications on a LAN? Think about how CSMA/CD actually works; from the above paragraph, "Each station is free to transmit whenever it has data to send." That sounds a little like anarchy. Imagine a room full of people, each with permission to speak freely and whenever they chose to; it is very likely that some are going to be talking at the same time others are. In some social situations, this makes no difference, but on a LAN network, only one message can be transported at a time. What happens when a second station starts talking before the first is finished? The answer is that a collision occurs.

Because both stations are on the same LAN, they both pretty quickly hear that another is "talking" at the same time they are. Because each knows that this will result in a garbled message, they both back off, or cease transmitting, for some random amount of time. Then each station listens for this period of time, and if it hears nobody talking, it starts transmitting again. Because each station is at a different physical location on the network, it takes different amounts of time for each station to hear another station's transmission(s). As a result, collisions are not uncommon. However, if the network is lightly loaded, in other words, if few stations want to "talk" at the same time, CSMA/CD works well. Average load for this access method to work well is less than 50 percent.

To make clear why it takes different amounts of time for different stations to realize that another station has already begun a transmission, recognize that the cable is a broadcast medium that can be quite long in practice. A length of 500 m is not unusual in large installations. Taking into account the velocity of propagation of any electromagnetic wave along a conductor, a time lapse of several μsec might elapse before a distant station recognized another station was transmitting. It is quite likely that in this amount of time, its own back-off timer has expired, and, if it has, data waiting to be sent will already have begun transmitting.

Sometimes the station is successful; sometimes it is not. This situation is at the heart of why CSMA/CD has unbounded message delivery time under high-load conditions. To better understand this, think about a network where every station wants to talk at the same time. Only very infrequently will a station have a clear channel to "talk." The constant cycle of starting to send, only to hear a collision, and then being forced to wait and retransmit, makes it very likely that the time to send a message can grow enormously. How long a particular station will have to wait to transmit grows exponentially with the amount of message traffic.

CSMA/CD is a good choice as an access protocol as long as three conditions are met. The first is that the number of messages on the network is small relative to the bandwidth of the network. A good number to use is less than 40 percent of the bandwidth of the network is in use at any one time. This will avoid excessive message delivery times that can be a problem in heavily loaded networks using the CSMA/CD access protocol.

The second condition is that there is no message priority. If every message has the same priority, CSMA/CD works well. However, because of the way the bandwidth of the network is allocated, shout first and listen later, there is no way to identify any message as most important (e.g., Be quiet while I transmit; my message is more important).

Third, and this is related to the first point, is that time of delivery is not important. Because circumstances can arise where a message might get blocked for some amount of time, there is no way to guarantee of how long a message will take to get through from source to destination. This means for certain systems where it is critical to know if a message has been sent, CSMA/CD is not a good choice. These last two points lead to the next two types of access protocols and provided much of the motivation for their development. Multiple access protocols came first, and the others were developed later.

Before going on to the next access protocol, it may be of interest to spend a bit of time examining how CSMA/CD was developed. Like most protocols, it grew from more humble beginnings. Most would say that CSMA arose from ALOHA, developed at the University of Hawaii. The problem they had was that Hawaii was a bunch of islands with one big computer on one island. They wanted to share access to the computer and needed a way to allow all the islands access to it through a satellite system. The satellite had one channel that was used for communication to the big computer, and everyone had to share this in some fair way. The ALOHA system was what emerged from this dilemma.

ALOHA works by letting each station or island transmit whenever it needs to. When only one island transmitted, and no one else did for the entire message length, this system worked fine. However, as you can imagine occasionally two islands wanted to use the big computer at the same time, and a collision occurred. When this happened, both messages were corrupted, just like what happens in CSMA/CD. Again, just like CSMA/CD, each station could wait for some random amount of time and then try again. Whether they actually did wait at all was not determined or required in a pure ALOHA environment.

This type of access only works well if the channel is not used very often. The fewer messages sent, the fewer collisions. Again, just like CSMA/CD, in high-load conditions, few messages get through. ALOHA only works well if the channel utilization is less than about 25 percent. That means that the big computer can only be "talked" to about 25 percent of the time; perhaps it is busy the rest of the time working on big problems. Still, for the time, about 1970, ALOHA was a revolution in access protocols.

Token-Passing Bus

Although the commercial acceptance of Token Bus as implemented in IEEE project 802.4 is lackluster in the extreme, it still represents a useful instructional tool for discussing various forms of access to a media that could be applied. Further, the idea of a token-passing scheme is implemented in other protocols; a specific example is FieldBus, which will be described in a later chapter.

Token-Passing Bus is the fairest methodology for splitting up the bandwidth resource. Each station has a fixed time slot to transmit its data and no more. Token passing is the arrangement of stations into a logical ring with each station knowing the address of the station on either side. Most physical topologies can support logical rings; for example, bus, star, or ring topologies are all possible. Each station accumulates its data until its turn to transmit. Topologies are discussed in Chapter 15.

When initialized, the highest-number station sends its first frame. After it is done, it passes permission to its immediate neighbor by sending it a special frame, called a token. The token propagates around the logical ring with only the token holder being able to transmit frames. Because only one station holds the token at any time, collision does not occur. However, error recovery and ring initialization are more complicated. This resulted in complex implementations in the IEEE project 802.4.

Token passing is just like in class where you raise your hand to speak and the instructor passes you the token. You then have the exclusive right to speak until the instructor tells you that your time has expired and either recognizes another, (passes the token to another) or holds on to it and begins talking. Token passing is an example of a logical ring accommodating a variety of physical topologies. Continuing the analogy, there is nothing that says that the token must pass to the person sitting next to you; the instructor may choose to recognize anyone in the class to pass the token to. This is an example of a logical ring. The idea of a logical ring in a physical topology other than a ring is sometimes not clear. Figure 14.7 illustrates this for a bus topology, the usual topology when a token-passing access methodology is used. The dotted line shows the logical ring.

Although in Figure 14.7 some stations adjacent physically are adjacent logically, this is only happenstance. The logical ring order for passing the token can be set by the user or by the protocol automatically. In practice, real systems have the token times and

Figure 14.7
Logical ring and physical bus.

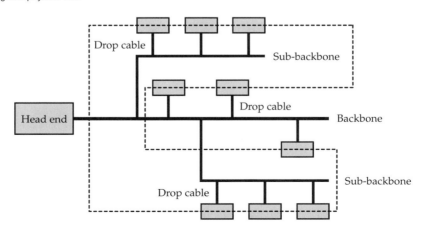

passing order preconfigured. This means that each station is guaranteed to have an opportunity to transmit in turn. There is no chance that a station will not get the token in order. This means that each station knows how long it will be until it can send another message, and systems can be designed with the maximum delay figured in.

Now the situation is a little different from the classroom analogy above might lead you to believe. As said above, in most situations a token-passing access methodology will have set times for each station to transmit. For example, station 1 might transmit for 1/4 sec, whereas station 2 has 1/2 sec. The token passes around the logical ring, but the time it is held by each station is preconfigured. The total of all the individual station's token-holding times is called the token rotation time. It sets an upper limit on how much time can pass before a station is guaranteed an opportunity to send a message. Examples 14.1 and 14.2 will make this clear.

■ **EXAMPLE 14.1**

Suppose a token-passing bus network has four stations connected to it. The token-holding times are set as shown below. How much time can pass before any station is guaranteed access to the network and can use its share of bandwidth to send a message?

Station 1:   3 sec
Station 2:   2 sec
Station 3:   8 sec
Station 4:   5 sec

The answer is found by adding up the token-holding times for each station. Here, $3 + 2 + 8 + 5 = 18$ sec is the token rotation time.

■ **EXAMPLE 14.2**

Once the token-holding times are known, it is possible to calculate how much bandwidth each station actually has. If we assume a 1 Mbps network with the station token-holding times as used in the previous example, what is the guaranteed data rate for each station?

$$\text{Station 1:} \quad \frac{3}{18}(1 \text{ Mbps}) = 166 \text{ kbps}$$

$$\text{Station 2:} \quad \frac{2}{18}(1 \text{ Mbps}) = 111 \text{ kbps}$$

$$\text{Station 3:} \quad \frac{8}{18}(1 \text{ Mbps}) = 444 \text{ kbps}$$

$$\text{Station 4:} \quad \frac{5}{18}(1 \text{ Mbps}) = 277 \text{ kbps}$$

Therefore, with Token-Passing Bus as the access methodology, a guaranteed absolute maximum time exists that can pass before any station can access the network and send its message. Additionally a guaranteed data rate for each station is provided. Compare this with the CSMA/CD approach. Because it is essentially a statistical approach to access, neither of these numbers can be calculated. Given the variable of location of the station on the network and how long its messages are, combined with the unknown number of other stations that want to transmit at the same time, it is conceivable that long periods of time might pass before the station had an opportunity to transmit its data.

This presents no problem in most situations, especially as data rates increase and network managers learn to not put too many stations on a segment. However, imagine that you are in a manufacturing environment, and the station that needs to transmit is a robot that rivets parts of cars together. The station discovers through its own diagnostics that it is riveting in the wrong place; perhaps a data file has been corrupted. It tries to send a signal that it is broken and the production line needs to be halted until it is fixed.

In the CSMA/CD environment, the time until it can send its transmission is unknown. It depends on the other traffic, how many stations, and so forth. In the token-passing environment, there is a fixed time until it can transmit. The number of damaged cars is limited to the time it takes for the station to get its turn to transmit. As you can imagine, this has important economic implications.

This situation and others like it explain why manufacturing and process control systems often prefer a token-passing access method or in some cases the scheduled operations approach described below. In an office environment, it usually makes no difference if one message is sent a bit late. In a manufacturing or process control environment, this unpredictability can mean anything from loss of production to critical safety issues not being transmitted in a timely manner.

To illustrate the same situation in a process control environment, imagine a pump filling a container with toxic stuff. For some reason, the relay that tells the pump that the container is full has broken. Just as before, the internal diagnostic of the relay circuitry has discovered this fact and is trying to tell the pump to stop, but the message takes too long to get through. Toxic stuff spills over the container and onto the floor. As a consequence, the plant is shut down by the safety officer after it is determined that the toxic stuff that spilled over the container cannot be removed from the floor. The entire plant must be shut down and the poisoned floor removed and rebuilt. The company decides that it is not worth it to rebuild there, shuts down the plant, and you and all your coworkers lose their jobs as a result of the wrong choice of an access protocol.

On the other hand, CSMA/CD systems are much less expensive because it has no requirements to maintain a common clock to schedule the token. Additionally, inserting a new station into a precisely calculated sequence is harder and more time consuming than inserting a new station into a scheme such as CSMA/CD. For these reasons and others, primarily cost, Token-Passing Bus access methodologies have been confined to narrow niches in the networking environment.

Token Ring

Token Ring access methodology is very similar to the Token Bus except that it is always implemented in a physical ring and messages can have priority. Just like in the token-passing situation, the token is passed from one station to another; it just rotates around the ring. When a station wants to transmit, instead of having a fixed time slot and waiting for it to occur as in token passing, the stations just seizes the token. It then talks as long as it wants. Once it is done with its message, the station regenerates the token and transmits it along the ring to the next station.

Token Ring systems are very efficient, even more so than token passing because instead of a predetermined amount of time that each station can send its message, each station can transmit as long as it holds the token. This means that if the message length varies for each transmission, the time the token is held also varies.

Message priority is implemented by having the token that is retransmitted after transmission of the message set to the priority of that message. The token then moves around the ring as described. However, for a station to take the token and start its transmission, it must have a message of at least that priority level. This acts to constantly increase the priority of the token, and low-priority messages can wait a long time to see a token with a low priority. This problem is alleviated somewhat by requiring the station that sets the priority of the token higher to also set it back when it next sees the token if it has no more high-priority messages.

Therefore, each station on the ring sends any high-priority messages first. If a large number of priority messages are waiting at most stations, low-priority messages might wait a long time to get passed. In practice, this is not a real problem; however, most commercial implementations of Token Ring systems are disappearing due to their inability to compete in cost with CSMA/CD-type systems.

Token Bus on the other hand will always have a niche in the manufacturing and process control industry because of the guaranteed maximum delay time for any message. Note that the priority mechanism and arbitrary length of time a station might hold the token combine to not give the Token Ring approach the same ability to guarantee maximum message delivery time.

Scheduled Operations

The last access protocol, scheduled operations, is useful when there are operations that only need to communicate when specific conditions either internal or external to the network become true. Upon the conditions becoming true, the communication occurs. To share out the bandwidth resource, scheduled traffic relies on a master station or predetermined time slots.

These time slots can be configured on-line with some protocols and are hardwired with others. This technique, at least in the latter case, is best used when each station's traffic is predetermined. An example might be a level switch on a tank to shut off flow. These messages only occur occasionally, and the devices do not need the extra processing and cost associated with being a token passer. Some protocols will allow a mixture of different access protocols to coexist; others, including most available today, do not offer this flexibility.

Scheduled operations is a very inexpensive type of access protocol. Many times, a simple timer or level switch is all that is used to initiate a transmission. The software required to implement such an access methodology is very simple. For this reason, scheduled operations are often used for inexpensive devices where the cost of a more complex scheme would outweigh its advantages.

Efficiency

Finally, it is of interest to discuss the relative efficiency of each of these four access methodologies, or protocols. This is a complex subject about which much has been written. This section will only touch on a single aspect of efficiency, that related to token-holding time and the amount of information a station has to transmit. CSMA/CD depends on a statistical determination of how many stations are trying to transmit at one time to determine its efficiency; it will not be included. A good rule of thumb is to expect no more than 50 percent.

Scheduled operations is a trivial situation in which the station transmits based on some event or clock. Clearly, the efficiency is totally dependent on the type of scheduling that is used. The other two, both token schemes, will illustrate how a token-passing scheme with fixed time slots for transmission compares to a token-passing scheme with data-dependent time slots for transmission. It will be shown that the later approach is much more efficient.

Suppose that there are four stations on each network. The first network uses Token-Passing Bus model, the second uses the Token Ring model. We will look at two cases. In the first case the amount of data to be sent from each station is predetermined and never changes. In the second, this amount of data is variable. For both cases the requirement is that all data be sent each time a station gets the token. Imagine that it is high-priority data that cannot be delayed. This situation is summarized in Table 14.3.

For the first case, both schemes exhibit close to 100 percent efficiency, if the time slots on the Token Bus are optimized. However, in the second case, the Token Ring system can modify its token-holding times to accommodate the variable amount of data, whereas the Token Bus system cannot. That means that the Token Bus system must set the token-holding times to the maximum that could be expected, resulting in lost efficiency when that maximum is not used. This is shown in Figure 14.8.

◼ MEDIUM ACCESS CONTROL SUBLAYER

As was discussed earlier, Data Link layers in the IEEE 802.x project are composed of two components, the MAC sublayer and the LLC sublayer. Although these are properly referred to as sublayers of the DLL, for the rest of this discussion and in the LLC section, the prefix sub will be dropped, and they will be referred to the MAC Layer and LLC layer.

From the name of the layer one can get a good idea of what it does: It controls the access of the network to the physical layer. Literally, it controls the access to the media in use by the network. This layer stands between the Physical layer implementation, which is usually determined from the medium or layer 0 that the network uses and the media-independent software and hardware implementation that lies above it. The MAC Layer controls the way the bandwidth of the network is shared out among the stations attached to it.

You should already have a good idea of these access methodologies by reading the above paragraphs. *The part of the DLL that implements the access methodology is called the MAC.* It does this by exchanging frames of data called MAC frames. The MAC frame is

Table 14.3
Efficiency Data

	Case 1	Case 2
Station 1	2	1–2
Station 2	3	1–3
Station 3	4	1–4
Station 4	5	1–5

the basic unit of exchange between devices on the network. Other frames are formed by building on the MAC frame, but this frame is the core of all data frames exchanged between devices.

Each different protocol has its own frame format or definition, but because they have to do the same kind of thing in each protocol, they are pretty similar. Additionally, because the three that will be explored were all developed under the same IEEE project, 802.X, they also have many other similarities. The functional components of the frames used in the three protocols 802.3, 802.4, and 802.5, or Ethernet, Token Ring, and Token Bus, will be briefly described. A more detailed frame breakdown is provided in Appendix H. All these frames are based on the HDLC format.

Each of the three frames in Appendix H follow this model with small variations. Some omit or change the use of one or more of the fields or differ in small details of interpretation. In each of the formats, the frame is transmitted in byte order from left to right.

The HDLC frame format used in these MAC frames is shown in Figure 14.9. Not all protocols use a MAC layer. For example, if the protocol is designed to only run on one

Figure 14.8
Token access scheme efficiency comparison.

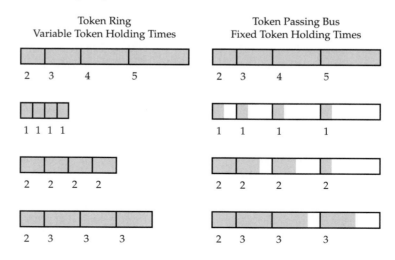

Figure 14.9
HDLC frame structure.

Start Delimeter	Source Address	Destination Address	Frame Control	Data	CRC	End Delimeter

type of physical layer and is only point to point, there is no need for a MAC layer. A good example of a protocol that may not use a MAC layer is TCP/IP. This is the protocol used by most stations on the Internet. Because TCP/IP often uses X.25 for the lower three layers, and X.25 is designed for point-to-point communications in a twisted pair physical layer, there is no MAC layer.

At the Data Link layer each protocol uses a different frame format. Having an understanding of the structure of this format can be very useful when diagnosing problems on a network. Many of the most powerful tools manufactured for this purpose, protocol analyzers, take this approach.

There are four key functions that must be implemented by the MAC frame structure used in a protocol:

1. Synchronizing the destination station clock to the source station clock for accurate demodulation
2. Determining the start and end of each frame
3. Determining the source and destination address for the frame
4. Checking for errors in the frame

Each frame format, in principle, consists of two distinct portions, the first to accomplish the first function listed above and a second to hold the data in the frame. In the 802.3 and 802.4 formats, this first portion is called a preamble. This is an alternating series of bits, several bytes long, that the station modem uses to synchronize its timing to that of the source station. In the 802.5 format, no preamble is needed because there is a constantly rotating frame, called a token, that maintains a common clock for each station.

The second function, determining the start and end of each frame, can be broken up into two separate tasks; the start flag and end flag can be treated differently. The start flag, called a Start Delimiter, is implemented in each of the 802.X MAC Layers in the same way. There is a unique pattern of bits, 1 byte long, that is used to signify the beginning of the data portion of the frame.

The end flag, called the End Delimiter, is also 1 byte long but is only required in two of the formats. The 802.3 format uses a length field placed in the data portion of the frame so that the end of the frame is determined by counting the number of bytes in the frame.

The third function, determining the source and destination station addresses is accomplished in each format in the same way. There are 2 bytes, 6 with extended addressing, that are used to uniquely identify the station address. Extended addressing is universally used. These addresses are called MAC addresses and are widely used in many Network Operating Systems (NOS) to enhance security.

The last function, checking for errors in the frame, is done with a field that implements the CRC, which was introduced in Chapter 12. In all three frame formats, the length of the CRC code is 32 bits.

Logical Link Control Layer

The other part of the DLL is that which implements the services. As mentioned earlier, there are a couple of things unique about the LLC Layer that are implemented in all 802.X networks. The first is that because it is common across all three IEEE 802.X protocols, Ethernet, Token Bus, and Token Ring, at the LLC Layer all three protocols look the same to the next layer up the stack. Essentially, the LLC Layer insulates higher layers from the differences between the various standards.

The second thing is that the LLC Layer offers a way to ensure a reliable data stream from source to destination station at the DLL. This capability allows layer 2 to offer a reliable data stream service to the Network layer (NL) above it. This capability is not widely implemented outside the IEEE 802.X protocols.

The third thing that the LLC layer does, and this again is something that is implemented in the NL and Transport layer (TL) as well, is to provide some method of flow control. Flow control is a procedure for the destination station to inform the source station that it needs to slow down. There are many ways for this to be accomplished, and a very basic approach will be explored after the services that a DLL can provide the NL are described.

The three primary service classifications that the DLL provides the NL should be familiar to you from the introduction to service types earlier. Sometimes these three services are known as LLC types. The three types are

1. Connection-oriented service: Type 1
2. Acknowledged connectionless service: Type 2
3. Unacknowledged connectionless service: Type 3

As can be seen the second two types of service are really two "flavors" of the same connectionless-type service. The type 1 service implements the reliable data stream service mentioned above. Type 1 services also are explicitly prevented from using acknowledgments, although why one would want to is not clear. Type 2 is the only DLL service where acknowledgments are permitted.

Remember, OSI has a special meaning for the word *service*; a layer always provides services to the layer above it and uses the services provided to it by the layer below it. Although in this section, these two service types are discussed as DLL services, all layers provide services based upon these two models of service, namely, connection-oriented and connectionless.

Just like the MAC layer, the LLC Layer has a frame structure that is used. LLC frames are constructed by building upon the frame structure that is present for the MAC frames. Essentially one just adds a header to the MAC frame. This is shown in Figure 14.10.

Frames are used to send messages over the DLL. Usually the entire message cannot be held in one frame; the size limits of the frames prevents this. So most messages con-

Figure 14.10
LLC frame structure.

DSAP Address	SSAP Address	Control	Information
1	1	1 or 2	MAC Dependent

sist of a large number of frames. A number of protocols use relatively small frame sizes, which increases the importance of the various acknowledgment mechanisms present in the DLL. The more frames sent from source to destination, the greater the probability that one or more will arrive garbled or not arrive at all.

The four fields are defined as follows:

Destination Service Access Point (DSAP). This is the address representation for the SAP(s) located at the destination. Although each SAP address is restricted to 1 byte, it may identify one or more SAPs for which the LLC information field is intended to be delivered.

Source Service Access Point (SSAP). This is the address representation for the SAP(s) located at the source. Just like the DSAP, each SSAP address is restricted to 1 byte but may identify one or more SAPs from which the LLC information field is originated from.

Control. The control field is where certain command and response data are contained and is the place where sequence numbers, if needed for each frame, are located. For any connectionless service, sequence numbers are required.

Information. The location where the MAC frame format for the particular MAC layer is placed. These are defined in Appendix H and were briefly discussed earlier.

As mentioned above, flow control in the DLL is a critical function. Not all stations can operate at the same speed, so a slower station must have a way to tell a faster station that is sending it data, that it needs to slow down. A basic approach that is used is the stop-and-wait protocol. In this approach the source station sends one frame of data and then waits for an acknowledgment. Until the destination station responds to the source station, no further data is sent.

Although this approach has the merit of never overloading the destination, it does require an acknowledged service option, or LLC Type 2. Additionally, there is the severe limitation of alternating, or half-duplex, communication. Although virtually all metallic and fiber channels are capable of full-duplex communication, this procedure is limited to half-duplex communication. As can be seen, each station must wait for receipt of a message from the other before it can transmit one of its own. Finally, it provides no means to recover from a network where the occasional frame may be lost. Clearly, if any frame is lost in this procedure, the communication stops because each station is locked into a procedure that requires it to wait for a response from the other station before transmitting again.

There are many advanced protocols for implementing the concept of flow control. Exploration of these approaches is outside the scope of this book. Many modern protocols use a variation of an approach called a sliding window protocol. These approaches to flow control allow full-duplex communication, have a procedure for recovering from a lost frame, and other advantages.

■ NETWORK LAYER (LAYER 3)

The NL is concerned with how to route messages between communicating applications. Because the NL is concerned with getting packets from the source all the way to the destination, it must know about the topology of the network and choose a path or paths through it.

As part of its function, it must count the packets to avoid overloading sections of the network it is trying to route through. If the network is one that is associated with a public utility such as the telephone system, this is where packets are counted and billing information originates. Protocols at this layer must be consistent or at least communicate for proper operation of a network.

The NL is the first layer in the model where the messages, or packets now that layer 3 is being discussed, must be routed all the way from the source to destination. Getting packets all the way through the communication system involves a lot of detail about how the communication system works. For example, is it reliable? If the communications system is reliable, it makes sense to not take a lot of time at this layer to check to make sure the packet actually was received at the destination when sent from the source.

On the other hand, if the communications system is not reliable, this layer must include sufficient complexity to take care of the various methods of ensuring reliable message transfer. These are exactly the same as the three levels of service identified above in the LLC Layer discussion. Recall that it was said there that there are three broad classes of service *any layer* can offer the layer above it. The NL is just another layer.

Therefore, the NL is implemented in various places in all three ways. Many networks are designed to use the telephone system as a major part of the communications channel. Because the modern telephone system is quite reliable, many networks use an unacknowledged connectionless protocol at this layer. This means they leave the error recovery for the few packets that get lost to the next layer up in the OSI model, the Transport Layer.

The other major action of the NL is to route messages through the network. Just like any layer, the NL uses service primitives and SAP addresses to accomplish this task. Again, there is a virtual communication between the source and destination network layers and a physical connection using the entire network.

It is important to emphasize that the NL is a source-to-destination layer. This means that it maintains a virtual communication from the original source to the ultimate destination. Contrast this with the DLL, which maintains a virtual communication only between adjacent systems on the same segment. This is shown in Figure 14.11. It is instructive to compare this figure with Figure 14.6. For example, the underlying network between systems A and B might be a low error rate system, whereas the underlying net-

Figure 14.11
NL virtual communication versus DLL virtual communication.

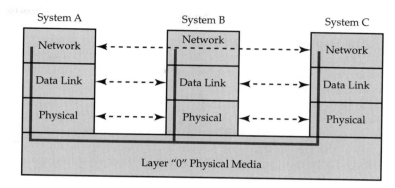

work between systems B and C might be very error prone. Recalling that in an unacknowledged CLS environment, only the destination system can know if the message gets through and that the DLL can only communicate between adjacent systems, one can see the importance of the NL.

To further illustrate, ask yourself the following question. If there is a need for retransmission of a portion of the data received by system C, how does it communicate that to system A, the original source system, without some kind of virtual communication from A to C? The answer is that this would not be possible without an NL.

The primary task of the NL is to route the message through many segments to the destination. To perform routing, a routing algorithm is needed. An algorithm is just a specific approach to solving a problem. For example, to add two numbers, one always adds the second to the first. It could be done the opposite way, but this is the algorithm that we all use. Similarly, there are algorithms that network layers use to plan out how to route messages (packets) from source to destination.

There are two broad ways this is done. First, if the source NL already has a virtual communication open to the destination NL, it just uses that one. Second, if the destination is a new one, a new virtual circuit is set up. Routers keep tables of virtual communications so that once they determine a path, they can use it again and again. This subject will be explored in more detail in Chapter 15; refer to that section for more detail.

■ TRANSPORT LAYER (LAYER 4)

The Transport layer (TL) accepts data from the Session layer and insulates it from changes that occur in hardware and technology at the lower layers. The Transport layer is also a true source-to-destination layer. Here, a program at the source carries on a conversation with a similar program at a destination. Again, in the DLL, the protocols are between each system and its immediate neighbors. At the NL, communications between source and destination systems are managed.

At the TL, the virtual communication is also between the ultimate destination and original source. Just like the NL the virtual conversation is between the TL on the initial source and final destination. These two systems may be separated by many intermediate segment and hops, each comprising a unique segment or internetwork.

The TL provides another layer of virtual communication to that of the NL. This virtual communication may be connection oriented or connectionless. Many times in real systems, either the network or transport layer will be null, and the functionality of both will be folded into one layer. There is not much difference between carrying on an e-mail chat conversation with your neighbor across the street, where you both use the same telephone system, and carrying on a conversation with a distant friend who uses a different telephone system. With your neighbor, you both use the same underlying internetwork, the carrier provider to whom you both subscribe. No foreign systems are required. To communicate with a distant friend in another country, at least two underlying internetworks must communicate. The equivalence of the NL and TL from this perspective is shown in Figure 14.12.

However, because the NL may not be a reliable service provider, for example, it may be implemented with an unacknowledged connectionless service, the responsibility for error recovery is passed up to the next layer. This is the TL. Without a TL, there would be no way for the source and destination stations to communicate across a segment that is not recovering errors. In the example above, if a telephone system between you and your foreign friend was not performing well, without a TL the two end systems could not communicate reliably. The TL would request retransmissions that were in error from the intermediate system. Figure 14.13 illustrates how the TL virtual communication stays in existence even if the NL-to-NL virtual communication breaks down. Here, the NL has failed between systems B and D.

This is the conceptual break discussed earlier. Think about the definitions of the first four layers and see if it makes sense to you that these functions described are all that is necessary to move data from one end system to another. In layer 1 all electrical engineering issues are settled. Layer 2 settles the way stations get a turn to talk and how communication between system on the same segment are done. In layer 3 communications, the ultimate source and destination are settled. In layer 4, errors in communications between the ultimate source and destination are addressed.

Figure 14.12
TL virtual communication, part 1.

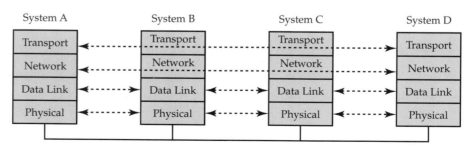

Layer "0" Physical Media

Figure 14.13
TL virtual communication, part 2.

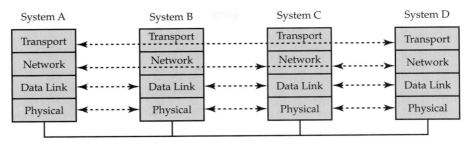

Layer "0" Physical Media

The three layers above the transport layer concern themselves with using the capability provided by the services of Layers 1 through 4 to carry on a conversation. These contain the user-oriented functions rather then the communications functions. This is just like the way you make use of a telephone (the communications functions) to carry on a conversation (the user-oriented functions) with a friend.

Finally, there is debate about whether the TL is the fourth communications-oriented layer or the first user-oriented layer. For this chapter, the first definition has been used, because how an OSI protocol works is being described. When TCP/IP is discussed, the definition will shift. This is because TCP/IP uses a universal addressing scheme that allows all internetworks across the globe to share a common NL. Because all share a common NL, they all share a common error-recovery mechanism. This means that there is no need to be able to patch across a badly performing internetwork. Therefore, the "TL" of TCP/IP is regarded as the first of four user-oriented layers rather than the last of four communications-oriented layers.

■ SESSION AND PRESENTATION LAYERS (LAYERS 5 AND 6)

The Session and Presentation layers are concerned with the enhancement of transport services and the syntax and semantics of the information transferred. A session might be used to allow a user to log into a remote time-sharing system or to transfer a file between two machines. A typical example of a presentation function would be to transform the source code used in the two end systems (e.g., ASCII or EBCDIC), thus making computers with different representations for the same data able to communicate.

■ APPLICATION LAYER (LAYER 7)

The Application layer is the ultimate source and sink for data transfer. It provides the actual user information processing function and application-specific services by translating user requests into specific network functions. It provides basic functions to a user or user program. An example might be, Read_File, Open_File, Get_Voltage, or Turn_Off_Switch. This layer also handles the responsibility for agreeing on which system is responsible for error recovery and the responsibility for authority to communicate.

The Application Layer differs from the other layers of OSI in several important ways. As the highest layer of OSI, it does not provide communications within the Application layer. This layer hosts the application programs that make use of the user-oriented and communications-oriented services existing below. For example, the Manufacturing Message Specification (MMS) protocol is an application program. As an Application layer protocol, it provides the conceptual interface for programs running on devices such as cell controllers or programmable logic controllers (PLCs). X.400 is also an application program in wide use; this application program forms the basis of many e-mail programs.

The services of the MMS protocol are generic and are intended to be referenced by Companion Standards. A Companion Standard is written for a specific class of applications. It is possible to utilize only the services of the base MMS standard. As suggested above, a Companion Standard has been developed for programmable logic controllers. Other Companion Standards include a Process Messaging Service for the process control industry and Numerical Control Semantics for MMS, a standard designed for the NC control industry. Companion Standards work most efficiently when coupled with the MMS communications capability.

There are many OSI protocols that have been developed and standardized. Some of the more common ones include GOSIP, MAP/TOP, and ISDN. GOSIP is the Government OSI Protocol. All federal agencies were at one time required to make any purchases of networking equipment in light of this standard. Manufacturing Automation Protocol/Technical Office Protocol MAP/TOP was a joint effort between General Motors and Boeing to develop an OSI standard suited for both controlling manufacturing processes and enabling advanced integration of design processes. Although neither have been widely adopted, both serve their respective sponsors well.

Both of those efforts utilize the entire seven-layer OSI model. As you can imagine, each communications node is expensive due to the complexity. For example a sensor does not need the capability to parse large files to report, once a day, that the temperature is x degrees. Protocols for these applications use this idea to significantly reduce the complexity of a communications standard while still basing it on the OSI model and obtaining the cross-vendor advantages that flow from its use.

■ SUMMARY

This chapter provided an overview of the concept of the OSI model and how it is used to describe how a protocol would work. The idea of a service has been introduced and the distinction between services and protocols has been made. Four fundamental ways of dividing up the bandwidth on a network have been described.

It has been shown how a layer may be divided up into two logical sections, here the Data Link Layer into the MAC and LLC portions. The way this can allow several access methodologies to be accomodated with a common set of service primitives, as was done in the IEEE 802.X project, has also been described.

Although not discussed specifically, one should see that the OSI model allows new layers to be made in response to changes in technology without altering the other layers. All that is important is that the service interface stay the same. This is a key advantage of protocol developed under the OSI model. It also points out one very valuable advantage, namely, that *one important consequence of applying the OSI model to a communications protocol is high-layer compatibility with low-layer diversity.*

This means that an upper layer of an OSI protocol may remain constant when lower layers change. For example, a common Application Layer can be used throughout a product line. This has many benefits to the customer, user, and support staffs due to only having to support one way of doing things. However, many of these products will have different connection requirements. In this situation, a common user interface to the customer of an organization" products is kept while still accommodating the differences in product line requirements.

It is important to understand the central idea that peer layers in a communications architecture communicate by a virtual communication through the exchange of PDUs. These PDUs travel down the network architecture at the source and back up the network architecture at the destination. The bits that are transferred through the physical medium are composed of all the headers and trailers appended at each layer. These surround and guide the application data from the source to the destination. This may include passing through many intermediate systems. Communications between and across these systems is coordinated by the appropriate layer.

The Physical layer handles all electrical engineering questions and the interface to the physical medium.

The Data Link layer handles the way stations get a turn to talk and how communications between adjacent systems on the same network segment is conducted.

The Network layer handles the communication between the original source and destination systems.

The Transport layer handles error recovery between the original source and ultimate destination systems.

These four layers are the communication-oriented layers and were discussed in some detail. Layers 5 through 7 are user-oriented layers and were only briefly touched on. The lower four layers of the OSI model are all that is necessary to describe any communications system.

PROBLEMS

1. Describe why the interface between Layers 4 and 5 of the OSI model is so important. What is the difference in services provided above and below this interface?

2. What are the two primary pieces of the Data Link layer?

3. Give a brief description of how CSMA/CD works.

4. Give a brief description of how token passing works.

5. What are the two types of services that any layer can offer to the layer above it?

6. Give a brief description of how COS works.

7. Give a brief description of how CLS works. What are its two variations?

8. What is the primary activity of the Network layer?

9. Why is flow control important?

10. What are the four key functions of a MAC frame?

11. What is the primary activity of the Transport layer?

15

Networking Hardware

This chapter will introduce many common pieces of networking hardware that are in use. Recall that the network hardware is only one piece of what is common referred to as a network. Although one piece is the underlying physical network, the second is the software, or protocol, that runs on the network. Sometimes the protocol determines the network type, sometimes not. Usually, almost any protocol can be run on almost any network, but again, sometimes the network type determines the protocols that can be run. This chapter will only concern itself with a description of the underlying hardware that makes up the physical network.

It is also important to understand that the descriptions of implementations in this chapter only concern those elements that comprise the communications portion of the device. Typically in PC and other microprocessor-based commercial and industrial applications, there is an application that is *using the services* supplied by the communications protocol that in turn makes use of the underlying network to communicate.

To begin that discussion, all networks will be divided up into two groups by their size and data rate or speed in bits per second.

■ SIZE AND DATA RATE

Like all things, networks are classified by their distinguishing characteristics. The first of these that will be defined is size. There are two primary classifications for networks according to how big they are. The first and smallest is a LAN. A LAN is usually confined to a single floor of an office, a single department, a subassembly area of a manufacturing center, and so forth. The number of individual users on any single LAN segment varies with the type of LAN protocol and architecture but usually is in the range of 10 to 50 users. By definition, a LAN is a local activity, not designed to extend outside a set of users with a common activity.

Sometimes, *LAN* is used to describe a series of LANs linked together. In this case, the activities of the group of users may vary widely. The term is used in both ways, sometimes referring to a single LAN and sometimes referring to a group of LAN segments connected together in such a way that communications flow between workgroups.

Although most LANs that you probably have come into contact with are networks of PCs hooked together to send and receive e-mail, share a printer, and so forth, many LANs are used in other ways. Two prominent uses include a LAN to network several dumb terminals to a mainframe computer, or PCs set up to "look" like dumb terminals, and manufacturing or process control instrumentation connected together to monitor and/or control a process.

Data rates on a LAN can vary widely. Today, most LANs operate at data rates of at least 10 Mbps, with most between 10 and 100 Mbps. One hundred Mbps LANs installed in the last several years are now relatively common. Many times you will find them in a mixed configuration with lower-speed segments kept distinct by some kind of joining device such as a bridge, switch, or router.

The next largest grouping of networks is the Metropolitan Area Network (MAN). It is designed to be a high-speed citywide or campuswide network that links multiple locations together at high data rates originally envisioned to be 200 Mbps. The MAN protocol and services, which include voice, data, and real-time video, are defined in the IEEE 802.6 standard. MANs never really took off, primarily because LAN speeds have gotten so high and the ability to use the telephone system to link LANs together avoided the need for a separate protocol. Today, networking is usually divided up into two size groupings, LANs and WANs.

The largest size network is a Wide Area Network (WAN), which is any network that links LANs together. Most often today, these links are implemented with dedicated T-1 lines or some other wide bandwidth data service offered by the telephone system. WANs range in size from a few offices of a small organization to worldwide integrated networks that service hundreds of locations.

Some organizations do not use the public networks for their WAN links but use dedicated systems of their own. The biggest example of this approach is the U.S. military, which has its own WAN that spans the globe. A critical component in any WAN/LAN networking approach is a component called a router. These form the links between the various LANs joined together into a WAN. Routers will be discussed further a little later.

An important note about LAN data rates or speeds is that the data rate used to characterize a LAN network is the maximum data rate on any segment. It is not the data rate that each user experiences for any reasonable period of time. The maximum data rate is divided among all the users on the network. Each user may experience a significant fraction of this rate for brief periods of time. However, on average the data rate for each user is the maximum data rate divided by the number of users transmitting or receiving from the network in any time period, plus some overhead depending on the protocol and topology being used.

■ EXAMPLE 15.1

To illustrate that each user only experiences a fraction of the data rate of the network we will use the example of an Ethernet 10Base-T network, operating at 10 Mbps with 20 users. What is the average data rate that each user can expect?

$$\text{average data rate} = \frac{\text{data rate}}{\text{number of users}}$$

$$\text{average data rate} = \frac{10 \times 10^6 \text{ bps}}{20} = 5 \times 10^5 \text{ bps} \tag{15-1}$$

This type of calculation works as long as the average data rate does not exceed some percentage of the total data rate of the network. Different protocols handle this situation differently, as was pointed out in the previous chapter. This is one of the primary ways that networks and protocols interact. For example, for Ethernet this calculation would be valid for average data rates up to about 50% of the total data rate. On the other hand, for Token Ring networks this type of calculation would be valid up to 99% of the data rate. Now that this is understood, a check that our previous result was valid can be performed. Taking 40% as a conservative estimate,

$$(\text{data rate})(40\%) \geq \text{average data rate}$$

$$(10 \times 10^6)(0.40) = 4 \times 10^6 \geq 5 \times 10^5 \text{ bps} \tag{15-2}$$

Interestingly, we find that our calculation holds with significant margin. Usually this type of concern is only important if the number of users grows large or the expectation of throughput is high. In networks where a common server is servicing large numbers of clients, this calculation breaks down. Often, in such situations, the server is the bottleneck, not the average data rate.

Because LANs are intended to be local, the second concern usually is the significant factor. For example, a workgroup that is largely exchanging e-mail, word processing, and spreadsheet files has a relatively low expectation of performance, whereas a similar group that is involved in complex simulations, graphic art, WWW downloads, video, or other types of applications requiring large and/or timely file deliveries has a relatively high expectation of performance. Without proper selection of the networking hardware used to build the underlying network, a surprisingly large impact can be made by a few users with high data rate expectations.

This illustrates why the choices of network and protocol and how they will service the user or application of the combination need to be considered as a whole. The critical element is always the application and how many users need access to it simultaneously.

This indicates the demands that are to be placed on the network and in turn allows an understanding of how networks, really networking hardware, and protocols interact to make the right choices to meet the stated expectations.

■ TOPOLOGY

Although all networks feature some topology, LANs are the only networking grouping level that illustrates all five primary topologies. The *topology* of something is just the physical or logical arrangement of that something. For example, a typical city intersection is an example of a star topology of streets. Four streets come together in a star configuration. The rays of the star are the streets as they radiate out from the intersection, and the hub of the star is the intersection. If you imagine a tree with each leaf as a user, you have an example of a tree topology, with all users connected to the common trunk. Join hands in a circle with a few of your friends and you are arranged in a ring topology, each joined to your nearest neighbor.

These examples are of physical topologies. Topologies can also be logical. A logical topology is where the physical connection may appear in any number of ways, but logically one always proceeds in a given way through all members of the network. To illustrate, suppose that you and a few of your friends are still in a circle with joined hands. If you count off in clockwise order around the circle, the physical order is the same as the logical order, or topology. If each of you now takes a number at random and then count off in numerical order instead of physical, you have an example of a logical ring topology that is different from the physical ring topology. In the discussion that follows when the word *topology* is used, it is understood to mean physical topology. Whenever a logical topology is being discussed, it will be explicitly stated so by the use of the term *logical topology*.

Star Topology

A star topology is probably the most common physical topology in use today for grouping PCs together into a LAN. If you recall the discussion in Chapter 3 you will remember the recommendation that all users be connected to a central wiring closet in a star topology. This is how most LANs are wired in an office setting. In most situations the individual wires radiating out to the PCs are connected together in a device called a hub. We will talk more about hubs a little later; for now just imagine them as the hub of a wheel, with spokes radiating outward.

Another major application of star topology is to connect PBX systems together. PBXs are described in Chapter 16. As will be seen there, all the telephones in an organization are connected to the PBX in a star topology. Each telephone call must pass through the PBX before entering or exiting the telephone system. Figure 15.1 illustrates a physical star topology.

Star topologies have a few advantages, which are the reason for their wide acceptance. First, and probably most important, because each station is connected directly to the hub by its own wired connection, if any station fails, other stations' traffic does not pass through that station and so is unaffected by another station's failure. The other big

Figure 15.1
Star topology.

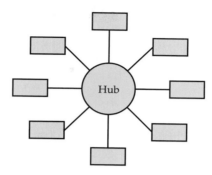

advantage is that stations can be added or deleted without affecting the traffic to any other station.

The big disadvantage with a star topology is that if the hub fails, all stations connected to that hub also fail. Hubs that have a tendency to fail are quickly eliminated from the marketplace. When an entire workgroup is brought down by a single point of failure, no one wants to explain to his or her boss why a reliable hub was not purchased. Most hubs today are very reliable. The other disadvantage with a star topology is that a separate cable is required for each station.

One example of how important reliability can become in the marketplace is a line of hubs designed to be used with fiber optic connections. Because reliability is often inversely related to power use, a manufacturer came up with a hub design that was 100% passive. This meant that there were no active components, and so the reliability was very high. To see this, ask yourself the question, Which will fail first, the electric can opener or the manual one? Similarly, which is more reliable, a battery powered watch or a sundial?

Ring Topology

The next topology is the ring topology. Most ring topologies are in place due to requirements of the protocol being run on the LAN. A ring topology is where each station is connected to its nearest neighbor on both sides, thus forming a ring. Messages are passed between stations by passing around the ring from station to station until they arrive at their destination.

A big advantage of this approach is increased security. It is very difficult to insert a message between stations without notice. Another advantage is that ring topologies lend themselves to a fair allocation of bandwidth. A big disadvantage is that if any one station is disabled, all traffic between stations is disrupted. Another disadvantage to ring topologies is that it is necessary to disable the entire network to add or remove stations. This is never a problem with star topologies, and given the rapid way networks evolve in most situations, it is a major disadvantage.

Some modern implementations of ring topologies get around the problem of one station's failure bringing down the entire ring by using two physically separate rings with message traffic rotating in different directions simultaneously. These may be implemented as mentioned above or concealed inside a specialized hub design. Then if any one station is disabled, all stations can still communicate with each other by using one ring or the other. The general term for this second type of ring is a *counter-rotating ring*; it is far less common than the traditional ring and is usually only implemented when the protocol being used is Fiber Distributed Data Interface (FDDI). Both types of rings are shown below in Figure 15.2.

Bus Topology

The third topology that is in wide use is the bus topology. If you think about how the seating in a city or school bus is arranged, you have the idea. There is a central backbone or aisle where all entrance or exit from seating must pass. The same idea is used in networks. There is a central cable, or backbone, to which all stations are directly connected through another cable, called a drop cable. The term *drop cable* comes from the fact that to drop in another station to the bus, just attach a new drop cable.

Communications on the bus are bidirectional and therefore physically full duplex but usually not logically full duplex. This means that although communications can run in both directions along the bus at the same time, any single station on the bus communicates in a half-duplex fashion through its drop cable.

The big advantages for a bus topology are that stations are very easy to add or delete, and broadcast or multicast transmissions are very bandwidth efficient as compared to other topologies. Another advantage is that bus topologies generally require less overall cable length than star or ring topologies. The major disadvantage to bus topologies is that they can be expensive and bulky to implement. Part of this reason is that bus topologies do not lend themselves to optical media due to the problem of manufacturing optical taps.

Figure 15.2
Single and dual counter-rotating ring topologies.

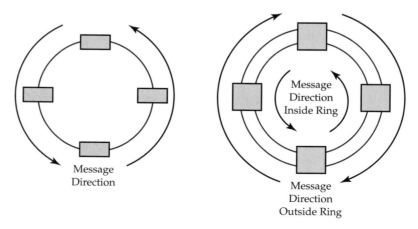

The classic example of a bus topology when discussing LANs is the combination of networking and protocols called the Ethernet 10Base5 standard. The Ethernet 10Base5 standard is configured as a bus topology with stations attached to a transceiver cable, the drop cable, which are in turn attached to the bus. This configuration is shown in Figure 15.3.

Although Ethernet 10Base5 is a good example of a LAN bus, it is rapidly disappearing due to the adoption of Ethernet 10Base-T and its faster cousins. These systems do not utilize this topology and instead make use of a star topology implemented with hubs.

The largest commercially important application of a bus topology is the cable television system. This is arranged in a bus configuration with each household connected to the backbone with a drop cable. The coaxial cable that is plugged into the back of your television, if you have cable television, is a drop cable.

The next time you are outside, try to follow the drop cable to the backbone. You should see a rectangular metal box with six to eight tap locations up on the telephone pole that has subscriber drop cables attached to it. For those of you who live in areas where there are no telephone poles and the telephone lines are buried, so are the cable television lines. Most cities have at least some areas where elevated telephone lines are the rule. Look around and you should be able to locate some. Figure 15.4, illustrates a typical bus topology.

Tree Topology

A tree topology is actually a more sophisticated version of the bus topology discussed immediately above. Instead of just one backbone and all stations connected directly to that backbone with a drop cable, a tree topology has several subbackbones, each with

Figure 15.3
Ethernet 10Base5 network.

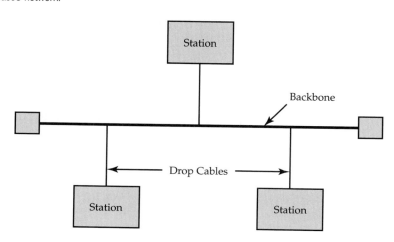

Figure 15.4
Bus and Tree topology.

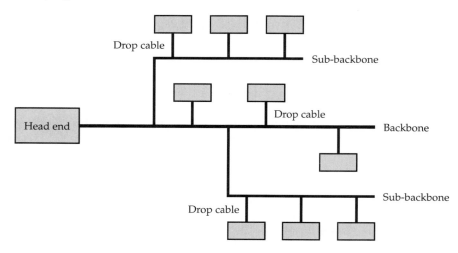

drops connected to it. As with a tree, there is a single trunk, several main branches, and leaves attached to smaller branches. The trunk is the primary backbone, the main branches are the subbackbones, and the individual stems are drop cables with the leaves attaching them to the stations. Most cable TV systems are actually tree topologies because of the large service area.

Daisy Chain Topology

The daisy chain topology is probably the most straightforward topology of all. In it each station is connected to the last station connected. The stations form a chain, one link after another, each link a station. This is just a method of attaching devices in a series configuration. This is simple, perhaps as simple and noncomplex as stringing flowers in a chain. The name must have come from this analogy. After all, what simpler topology is there than just hooking the stations up in series?

Sometimes daisy chain topologies are a little more complex in that any new station can be attached to any existing station, sort of a hybrid between daisy chain and a tree topology with no backbone or bus. A good example of this is the IEEE 1488 or HP-IB standard for connecting laboratory equipment to a common master station. In this protocol, any station, or link in the chain, can be configured as the master; usually it is a PC, but this is not required. Because in this alteration a daisy chain is really any topology, any type topology will work with the HP-IB standard.

The question of when to use what topology is usually determined by the application. Chapter 3 gave a brief outline of how LANs in a building are generally laid out. There were star topologies for each floor or wiring closet and a backbone connecting each star to another. Usually, if the LAN is large enough, there will be several topologies at different locations. This is especially true if different protocols are running on selected portions of the network.

■ LAN HARDWARE

Metallic and optical media, and their respective connectors, have already been discussed in Chapters 3 and 4; refer to those chapters for review. In this section, several classes of networking hardware will be examined. These are taps, hubs, repeaters, bridges, switches, protocol converters, routers, gateways, and communication processors. Each of these device classes will be discussed in terms of what layer of the OSI protocol they operate at, starting with layer 1 devices and finishing with layer 7 devices.

Tap

A tap is a coaxial connection device. Tap is used in two ways when talking about LANs. It refers to a group of taps enclosed in one physical container and to any particular tap in that group. To keep this distinction clear in the following sentences, a group of taps enclosed in one physical container will be referred to as a tap placement. The individual taps themselves will be referred to as tap locations. Each tap placement usually features from three to eight tap locations, usually implemented with F-type connectors. Each tap placement is made to the backbone or subbackbone of the cable network. These must be preplanned and designed in the original installation of the coaxial network.

To these tap locations a drop cable, coaxial in construction, is run to the particular device to be attached to the LAN. The number of tap locations makes no difference in how attachment is made; any open tap can be used. When designing the network, there is a difference in how many tap locations you select for each tap placement. The more tap locations, the higher attenuation for each connection. From a user standpoint, if there is an open tap location at any tap placement, go ahead and use it. If there is a problem, it is very rare that the design of the network is the source of the difficulty.

Taps have one peculiarity that is not shared with other connection devices. Unused tap locations at every tap placement need to be terminated in the correct impedance. This will minimize any reflections back onto the cable due to mismatched impedance. Because taps are only used in coaxial networks, and most of these are cable TV networks, this impedance is 75 Ω. A good practice is to always ensure that all tap locations are terminated. For networks that use fiber optic or twisted pair cable as media, taps are not used. Instead one of several types of hubs are used to terminate the media run from the LAN attached device.

Basic Hubs

A hub is the point in a fiber optic or twisted pair media network where all the circuits are connected together. Basic hubs come in two flavors, passive and active. A passive hub forwards all packets received on any port to all other ports. It is ideally suited to work with star topologies, where the hub is located at the center of the star. However, hubs can be wired in several ways; some implement a stars core and others, a bus or ring.

Beyond how they are internally wired, there are two kinds of basic hubs. One was already briefly discussed earlier, the passive or wiring hub. The other is an active device, called an active hub. A wiring hub is a purely passive device, just a wiring diagram enclosed in a box with connectorized attachment locations for easy hookup. Although these are inexpensive and very reliable, the reliability of today's active hubs together with the dominance of the Ethernet 10Baset-T and 100Base-T standards combine to eliminate the purely passive wiring hubs as a consideration. Most new installations will use some form of the active hub, a layer 1 device.

The active hub is powered and can provide a variety of services including regeneration of the signals, error correction, and so forth. Some hubs amplify the entire signal plus noise, whereas others just regenerate the signal alone. Manufacturers are continually expanding the capabilities of this widely used device. One very common networking scheme is the Ethernet 10Baset-T and 100Base-T standard. This type of hub is always active because it contains the transceiver.

Repeaters

A repeater is a device that takes the data signal, receives it, does any error correction it can, and regenerates the signal for retransmission. Active hubs combine the functions of a passive hub with a repeater. As a stand-alone unit, it is used whenever a long drop cable or backbone run must be accomplished and the length of the run exceeds the specifications of the media and physical layer used in the network. Again, the regeneration of signals that was referred to in the description of an active hub is the repeater function. A good way of thinking about an active hub is to regard it as a passive hub coupled with a repeater.

Repeaters are inexpensive devices that can be used whenever the signal-to-noise ratio of the intended signal becomes too degraded. Make sure the repeater is bidirectional if the signal flow on the cable is bidirectional. This is true for most topologies except ring topologies, where the signal flow is in only one direction on any physical ring. Both types of hubs and all repeaters are also referred to as physical, or layer 1, devices. This is because they ignore information at Layer 2 and above.

Port Switching Hub

A port switching hub is an interesting device that combines the technologies of an active hub with multiple internal LAN segments. Sometimes this device is called an intelligent hub. The combination of regeneration of the signal and the ability to selectively route messages has several advantages, and this device is finding wide application in LANs. These however, are *not* the same as the so-called LAN switches. LAN switches are more sophisticated devices and will be explored later.

Port switching hubs are designed to replace both classes of basic hubs. They feature a number of input ports on the front and a few output ports on the back. The front ports are just like the ports on a basic hub. Each connects to one of the internal LAN segments. The output ports on the back are connected to one of the internal LAN segments that exist inside the device. The number of internal LAN segments is the same as the number of output ports.

These devices work by performing a load balancing function on the data streams as they arrive at the front ports. Essentially, the hub counts the frames arriving at each of the input ports and automatically switches the front ports to one of the internal segments based on the total frame count of all ports connected to that internal segment. In this way, the load on each of the internal segments is kept about the same. This is the load balancing function.

For example, suppose one station, which is normally a low-usage station, suddenly starts downloading a large file. Because it is normally a low-usage station, it is probably connected to an internal segment where other stations account for most of the data flow. Because there would be little bandwidth available for this station, one would expect the download to take a significant amount of time.

However, with a switching hub, the hub itself notes the increased traffic and switches this station to an internal segment that is not as busy. Thus, the file can download more quickly. After the download, the switch will place the station on a segment in such a way to balance the load across all its segments.

This approach offers a significant increase in perceived performance for the user without any upgrade in the basic operating rate of the LAN itself. This is a very cost effective way to improve service. Typically, these switching hubs are placed between the users and either a LAN switch or directly to the server. The PC connections are made to the front ports, and the LAN switch connections are made to the back ports. Although we have not yet discussed the LAN switch, for now just think of it as another layer of load balancing before reaching the server. Figure 15.5 shows the port switching hub in a direct connection to a multiple server configuration.

In the scenario shown in Figure 15.5 the first four PC's shown are light users and the fifth is a heavy user. The switch has accommodated this load situation by balancing the load between the two servers. In this example, the heavy user has the full bandwidth of the network to speed the response time. The light users, not stressing the network at

Figure 15.5
Port switching hub.

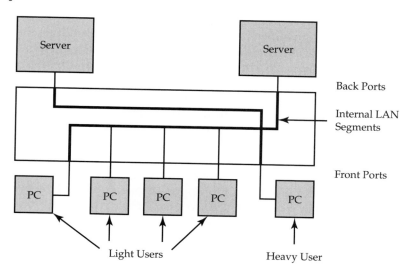

that same time, see no reduction of service, yet if they demand more bandwidth, the switching hub can reallocate resources of the two servers automatically.

As stated above this is a very cost effective means of enhancing service. A port switching hub costs virtually the same as an active hub. Most port switching hubs come with between 16 and 32 front ports and 2 to 8 rear ports. Finally, it is important to recognize that a port switching hub is a layer 1 device. Since it only counts frames and does not examine the frame contents, it operates on layer 1 of the OSI model and is a physical layer device.

Bridges

The next most complex piece of gear is the bridge. This is the first of the Layer 2 devices explored. Just as the name suggests, it bridges data between two segments on a network. The most common application for bridges is to break up networks into segments to balance the load. Port switching hubs are rendering this device obsolete. Port switching hubs are less expensive than bridges and have greater functionality in one traditional application area for bridges: load balancing through layer 2 filtering. This is a more sophisticated and traditional, but also slower, approach to load balancing; as a result, port switching hubs feature faster . . . throughput for frames and higher port densities in one device.

A bridge is the first internetworking device introduced. An internetworking device is any device that allows communications between network segments. There are three basic types of internetworking devices that will be discussed, the bridge or switch, router, and gateway; each is distinguished by the layer of the OSI model that it operates in. All bridges and most switches forward frames and operate at layer 2.

A bridge is a piece of hardware coupled with software that is often used to extend a network running a single protocol. In this situation, it acts like a logical break in the network, functionally creating two separate logical networks in one physical network. This serves to reduce the load on both segments by reducing the number of stations on each segment and performing the filtering function that only passes messages from one segment to the other that actually need to go there.

A bridge implements the filtering function by examining the destination MAC address of each message and forwarding it to the appropriate segment based on that destination address. Since a bridge knows what station addresses are on what segments, it can make an informed decision as to whether to forward a frame to another segment or not. However, it must examine each frame that arrives at its ports. This introduces delay or latency in the passing traffic. Although this delay is small in human terms, generally this is an undesirable attribute in a networking device where some traffic might be very time sensitive. One example is video traffic.

This filtering function is illustrated in Figure 15.6. Note that a message from station A to station C needs to pass through the bridge to reach its destination. In this case, the bridge does pass this message through to the second hub. However, a message from station A to station B does not need to pass through the bridge to reach its destination. In this case, the bridge does not pass this message through to the second hub. Note that the hubs in this diagram are passive. Additionally, note that a single port switching hub could accomplish a similar load balancing functionality without the additional latency introduced by examining the frame content and just switching based on frame count.

Figure 15.6
Bridge and passive hub operation.

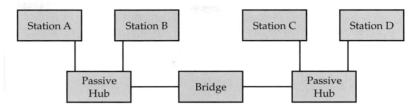

There are three primary types of bridging:

1. Transparent bridging, used exclusively in Ethernet networks
2. Source-route bridging, used exclusively in Token Ring networks
3. MAC bridging, used exclusively to bridge between Ethernet and Token Ring networks

Because both of the first two types of bridges are being replaced by switching, only MAC bridging is explored in its own section. MAC bridges are specialized devices that rely on the unique situation of both Ethernet and Token Ring having the same LLC Layer protocol. The first two types of bridging are named for the bridge-to-bridge protocol that each uses. They are transparent, originally developed by DEC, and source route, originally developed by IBM.

The first two classes of bridging rose out of the difference in philosophy of forwarding messages. The first approach, transparent bridging is a network where each bridge knows all the addresses of every station attached to the network. Transparent bridging is called transparent because the bridges exist independently from the stations on the network. They learn the node addresses in any attached segments on their own and use an algorithm called a spanning tree to select paths to forward frames.

The second approach, source-route bridging, is a network where the bridges just forward the message according to the path the source of the message specified. Source-route bridges do not exist independently of the network: The entire source-to-destination route is defined by the source node and is placed in the frame by the source node.

These are very different visions of how nodes and bridges should interact. The first approach requires that each station on the network must be known to the bridge. This is because only the bridge can make the decision on how to forward any messages to the addressed station. If the station is not known to the bridge, the message will never arrive because the bridge will not know how to get it there. In the second approach, the bridges are less sophisticated devices that just look at the address path specified by the source node and pass the message according to that specification.

In the end, the transparent bridging philosophy won the day. There was no need to make every station capable of forwarding a message when this functionality could be lumped into the bridge and not duplicated in every station. Today, virtually all bridges and their replacements, LAN switching hubs, work on the transparent approach. Again, used in this way, *transparent* means that the bridging and forwarding function is transparent to the station.

A way to understand the difference between source route and transparent bridging is to imagine yourself getting into a taxi at the airport. You are equipped with an address, 1234 Michigan Avenue. If this is all you need to get where you are going, the taxi driver supports transparent routing. All information about the path to take to get to the address is part of the taxi service. If, on the other hand, you not only need the address but also the way to get to Michigan Avenue, the taxi driver supports source-route bridging.

Figure 15.7, illustrates how the bridge device works and also reminds us of an important point about how protocols communicate. Each layer protocol carries on a virtual communication with its counterpart. For example, in this figure, the Transport layer on network A is carrying on a communication with the Transport layer on network B. *This single example is shown in Figure 15.7 by a double-headed arrow; actually there is such a virtual connection between each layer of each protocol.*

The actual physical path that the communication follows flows as is shown by the dark line. That is, each layer communicates with its peer layer, as illustrated by the single virtual communication shown at the NL. The path that the units of exchange, the PDUs, that each peer layer uses to implement their virtual communication flow up and down the protocol stack. Therefore, there are many virtual communications happening on a single physical path.

Figure 15.7
OSI perspective of a bridge.

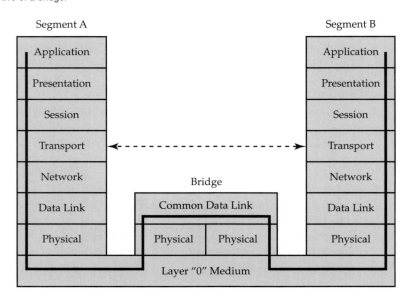

MAC Bridge.   A MAC bridge is a device that connects two or more 802.X networks and forwards frames between them. Bridges connect at the common LLC Layer, so only networks with a common LLC Layer can make use of MAC bridges. By translating between different MAC frames, MAC bridges can allow a protocol to switch media types. This is accomplished by placing a bridge between two different media running the same protocol. For example, it is common to have a MAC bridge placed between two Ethernet segments, one running on twisted pair wiring and the other on a fiber optic segment.

Another niche for MAC bridges is when they are used to bridge between two networks when the two networks are running very similar protocols, like Ethernet and Token Ring. This means that these devices can translate between the frame formats that are specified by the MAC Layer. It is this type of bridge that is shown in Figure 15.8.

This concept of bridging between two different protocols, if both protocols treat the MAC/LLC boundary in the same way, has been extended outside the IEEE 802.X environment in the same way one can build a bridge called a protocol converter within a product family. This device will be described later. In both these situations the bridge must know what stations are on what network. This is a basic requirement to be able to forward frames from one network to another.

Essentially, the information needed to understand how a bridge works in the IEEE 802.X environment is contained in the frame formats defined in Appendix H. A MAC bridge that translates from 802.3 to 802.5 would have to be able to change the 802.3 frame received into a valid 802.5 frame. Due to the differences of how each protocol sends groups of frames, this is not as easy as it sounds. Also complicating the issue is the fact that each of the 802.X protocols uses a different maximum frame length.

For a basic understanding of how a MAC bridge works, study Figure 15.8, which shows how a frame would be bridged between two protocols. In this example the bridge

Figure 15.8
MAC bridge operation.

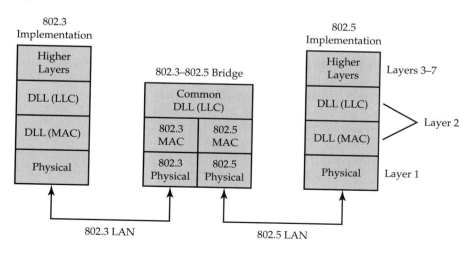

is designed to forward and receive frames to and from an 802.3 LAN and to and from an 802.5 LAN.

The important point is that the MAC bridge comprises the PHY and MAC layers from each protocol and a common LLC layer. This is because for MAC bridges to work, the LLC layer must be the same for both protocols being bridged. That is why bridges and protocol converters are only designed to work within a family of protocols such as 802.X or a specific product line, as is the case with protocol converters.

Both situations tend to require a common LLC layer or its equivalent. Again, as is indicated in the figure, a bridge is called a layer 2 device because the connection between the two protocols occurs at layer 2.

LAN Switches and Layer 2 Switches

The next type of Layer 2 device is the so-called LAN switch or layer 2 switch. Because most of these are designed for Ethernet 10Base-T or 100Base-T networks, they are also sometimes called Ethernet switches. These are often mistakenly referred to as switching hubs. They are not the same.

The critical difference is that a port switching hub does not examine the MAC address; it switches, based on traffic loading only, the load balancing described earlier. A LAN switch operating at layer 2 forwards frames between users based on a table containing the MAC addresses of the frames. This means that it can filter the frames based on the MAC addresses that are unique to each station. This is a much more powerful technique.

The table that the LAN switch uses to route frames is constructed in one of two ways. These two ways serve to classify all LAN switches into two classes. The two approaches are the cut-through and store-and-forward types.

The cut-through approach is the more basic of the two types. A cut-through LAN switch works by examining the MAC address in each frames header, and it just forwards the frame to the segment that connects to that station. The store-and-forward LAN switch buffers the entire frame in, and performs error checking on, the frame prior to forwarding it to the segment that connects to that station that corresponds to the MAC address in the frame header.

This means that the store-and-forward switch tends to be slower than a cut-through switch because it must buffer and examine the entire frame before forwarding it. This slows the process of frame transport, is referred to as latency, and is generally not desirable. Although all devices feature some latency, it should be clear that a device that just strips the MAC address off the header, the cut-through approach, is faster at passing frames than one that must read in the entire frame, the store-and-forward approach.

However, the store-and-forward LAN switch does gain an advantage from this process. Because it reads in the entire frame, it can throw away any frame that is in error. Thus, frames in error do not pass the switch and do not consume network resources. Generally, it is best to use cut-through LAN switches except where the probability of frames in error is significant. One might place a single store-and-forward LAN switch where it connects to the backbone and cut-through LAN switches for each workgroup.

It is important to note that a LAN switch, using MAC addresses in the frames, actually forwards layer 3 packets. This means that this device has some similarities to both bridges, layer 2 devices, and routers, layer 3 devices. This similarity is captured by the observation that LAN switches can provide a means to filter and forward packets between network stations.

Many LAN switches also feature advanced network management capability through the use of the Simple Network Management Protocols (SNMPs). These systems allow remote configuration, monitoring, and management of these devices through a PC console. Some allow network administrators to monitor and check the status of the entire network from their own station. This fact alone can make the investment in these devices worthwhile.

In summary, switches are a powerful new tool to enhance the performance of any LAN. They can significantly increase the perceived performance as seen by individual users or stations on the LAN without a large capital investment. Specifically, there is no great cost penalty in using switches instead of bridges, and the user-perceived data rate of the LAN increases significantly with no change in the underlying data rate.

VLAN (Virtual LAN)

A VLAN uses the technology of LAN switches to work. It is important to emphasize that LAN switching is applied exclusively to Ethernet type layer 2 protocols which use a CSMA/CD type access methodology.

The reason these devices are exclusively applied to the Ethernet family of networks; 10Base-T, 100Base-T, and others, is because the performance of networks that use a CSMA/CD access protocol are limited by collision statistics. Here, performance is taken to be the timely delivery of frames from other stations on any connected LAN segment. Allow anything over about a 40% collision ratio and performance will begin to significantly degrade. Layer 2 switches minimize the flow of frames on any LAN segment with destination addresses other than stations connected to that segment. This acts to maximize useable bandwidth on any segment and with more usable bandwidth, fewer collisions occur.

LAN switches have the same basic functionality as a traditional bridge, connecting LAN segments and using a MAC lookup table to route frames to that segment for which the frame is intended. As discussed in the previous section, the first benefit that layer 2 switches bring is that they significantly speed up this routing process. Most LAN switches do this by using cut-through routing where only the header of the frame is examined. Traditional bridges and a few layer 2 switches use store and forward routing where the entire frame is buffered before forwarding. Since cut-through allows the frame destination to be determined more quickly, the latency in the joining device is reduced, thus improving performance.

Therefore, just like a bridge, a LAN switch can improve bandwidth utilization on a segmented network by separating collision domains. If the traffic is not intended for a station on any particular segment, it is not forwarded to that segment, thereby freeing up that bandwidth.

To see the full advantage of VLAN technology it is necessary to think more deeply about how stations are connected to a traditional bridge as compared to a layer 2 switch. In a bridging environment, since each bridge has only two ports, all stations in a particular physical work area are connected on a single segment. Any frame traffic that has a source or destination on that segment consumes bandwidth on that segment.

Since most traffic in any environment tends to stay inside a work group or department, as long as the entire work group was located in the same physical work area, no penalty is observed with this arrangement. However, in most modern work environments today, work groups are dispersed throughout departments. Therefore, traffic within the work group does not stay on a single segment, but rather travels along the backbone to other segments. In a traditional bridging environment, this situation creates traffic congestion, since a single message now traverses several collision domains. To avoid this excess traffic, either work groups must be confined to a particular physical area or multiple bridges for each area must be used. Neither is an acceptable solution.

VLAN technology using layer 2 switches provides a way to respond to this dilemma and meet the goal of confining traffic in such a way that most traffic in any work group stays inside that work group. Since layer 2 switches feature multiple ports, several logically distinct virtual LANs can exist in any physical area. A layer 2 switch has multiple card slots, each of which can be designated as a VLAN segment. Traffic routing is performed by card slot, thereby minimizing excess traffic. In other words, LAN traffic is segmented by virtual LAN identification, allowing logical as well as physical segmentation of collision domains.

Figure 15.9 illustrates the two situations; here it is assumed that departments are segmented by floors. In Figure 15.9, E1, P1 and M1 represent the engineering, production and marketing teams assigned to work group 1; E2, P2 and M2 the teams assigned to work group 2, and so on. In case A, a traditional bridging structure is shown, with the LAN segmented by department. Assuming work groups to be composed of individuals among all three departments shown, this frame traffic moves through all segments, along the backbone. However, departmental traffic stays on a segment, since the department is confined to a single segment irrespective of work group.

In case B, work group traffic stays inside the VLAN and departmental traffic stays on the first level switch. In this manner, only that traffic to/from those stations outside both the work group and department travel along the backbone to other segments. This minimizes the excess traffic on both individual segments and the shared backbone.

Other advantages to VLAN technology include security, performance optimization, and network management. Security is increased because all traffic in any VLAN group stays on segments where that group is attached; if no router or similar device is attached to that VLAN, there can be no communication outside that group. It is hard to imagine a better security precaution without the cumbersome and difficult to manage physical separation of various LAN segments from the organizational network.

Performance optimization is possible by reducing the number of users on any particular VLAN to offer increased bandwidth to those users left. For example, an engineering group with very high traffic requirements might be allocated several small VLANs, each with only a few users, essentially dedicating an entire LAN bandwidth to each small group.

Finally, and perhaps most importantly, network management is significantly easier and more flexible. Since the VLAN assignment is performed by software, assignment to change connectivity is done via console rather than physical recabling. For example, ref-

Figure 15.9
VLAN.

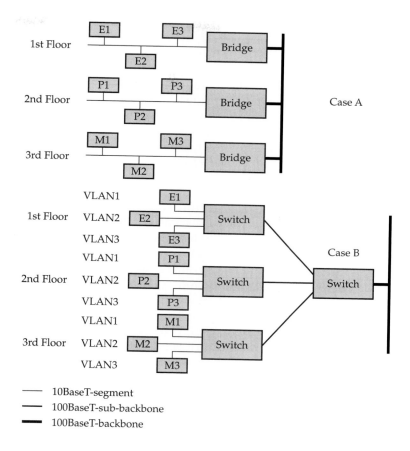

1st Floor — E1 — E3 — Bridge

2nd Floor — P1 — P3 — Bridge — Case A

3rd Floor — M1 — M3 — Bridge

Case B

—— 10BaseT-segment
—— 100BaseT-sub-backbone
━━ 100BaseT-backbone

erencing Figure 15.9, suppose the engineering work group 2 (E2) joins work group 1 (E1), doubling its size. The only change necessary is to re-assign VLAN2 on the engineering floor to VLAN1.

Protocol Converter

The last layer 2 device to be described is the protocol converter. That means it has similar functionality to a bridge. A protocol converter can convert between two similar protocols. In mainframe or legacy systems, the term *bridge* is almost never used, but the term *protocol converter* is widespread. When a legacy systems person uses the term *protocol converter,* what is usually meant is a device that will change from asynchronous to synchronous operation. Virtually all PC and PC type devices operate asynchronously, and virtually all legacy systems are designed to operate synchronously. Protocol converters are the devices that stand between these two protocol conventions and allow communications to pass across this boundary.

A concrete example may help make this clear. Virtually all modern LAN protocols use some variant of HDLC as the Layer 2, or Data Link, protocol. HDLC is a bit-oriented protocol. Some IBM mainframe systems use a byte or character-oriented protocol called Binary Synchronous Communications (BSC). Although this is an older protocol, there are many devices and systems using it in the field today.

To communicate between these two protocols, the basic structure of the messages must be translated. Bit-oriented protocols transmit 1 bit at a time, whereas byte-oriented protocols transmit 1 byte, or character, at a time. Further, byte-oriented protocols require an acknowledgment from the receiver after each character. Generally bit-oriented protocols send lots of bits, and variable amounts of bits are sent before an acknowledgment is required from the receiver. Clearly, these two systems of representing data are incompatible. A protocol converter would change the data representation and provide the acknowledgments that are necessary for each end system, thereby allowing communications across incompatible protocols.

A protocol converter is made up of hardware and software, different vendors making different choices. Each protocol converter is designed to interface to a different type of protocol. Most are designed to work with ASCII, but all of them are designed to interface with an IBM type mainframe protocol, typically BSC or Synchronous Data Link Control (SDLC). Some are even available to translate between the two IBM Data Link protocols, BSC and SDLC. In summary, protocol converters are bridges that are designed to work in an environment where one of the two protocols being converted to or from is a mainframe protocol. For example, an IBM-manufactured device that falls into this category is the IBM 3708, ASCII to SNA/SDLC protocol converter.

A subclass of protocol converters is a group of devices known as code converters. These devices are less complex than a true protocol converter and are used to translate one source code to another. (See Chapter 12 for a definition of source code.) The most common convert ASCII to or from EBCDIC. For example, an IBM-manufactured device that falls into this category is the IBM 7171, ASCII to EBCDIC converter. These devices have limited capability. They are often constructed of two universal asynchronous receiver transmitters (UARTs) coupled with a ROM lookup table for the code conversion. They are limited in that a true code converter cannot handle the synchronous-to-asynchronous aspect of protocol conversion that a protocol converter can. They can only change the source code, not the timing.

Routers

A router can be used to connect two networks running different protocols together, or extend a single network, so it has all the functionality of a bridge. However, its real power comes from its additional intelligence and switching capabilities. In fact, one definition of the term *router* is a device that selects the correct path for a message. Routers are layer 3 devices; that means that they connect networks with a common Network layer. Therefore, there are two activities that a router does:

1. Find the best path, or link cost, to route packets using a routing algorithm
2. Switch packets through an internetwork using the MAC address, (bridging functionality)

Because we have already discussed the second activity, this section and the ones that follow it will focus on the first. The task of how to choose a path for a packet to route it to its destination in the shortest time or most reliable manner can be very complex. Imagine that you are at your PC in San Francisco and are sending an e-mail to your friend in Hawaii. As you send your message, a router must decide to send it across the undersea trunk to Hawaii or perhaps route it through New York, London, and Tokyo to get to Hawaii. Obviously, it is going to make a difference which path your message takes. Routers examine every message they receive and make a decision about which pathway to the destination is best or has the lowest link cost. A router is always between you and your e-mail friend unless you are both on the same LAN.

Routers are used in virtually every LAN/WAN interface, and Figure 15.10 will help illustrate how they are attached. Each router has several interface ports. These always include at least one WAN port and one LAN port, as shown in the figure. Here the LAN port is assumed to be Ethernet 100Base-T; in principle, any LAN can be attached. Usually several ports of both types are available, or card slot(s) are provided for user configurability.

Additionally the router often provides for a serial interface to link serial devices such as a CSU/DSU to the router. The router stands between the address space on the LAN and the address space on the WAN. Its routing table contains the information on how to route messages from one LAN through the internetwork, or WAN, to the other LAN. As discussed below, this routing decision can be arrived at in several ways.

There are many fundamental ways a router could make a routing decision on which path to take. However, they all can be sorted by classifying them according to three basic algorithmic approaches:

1. Static or dynamic
2. Flat or hierarchical
3. Link state or distance vector

Routers also feature extensive network management capabilities. *Network management* is a term used to describe the statistics of the traffic flow on the network and the status of

Figure 15.10
Router LAN-WAN-LAN hookup.

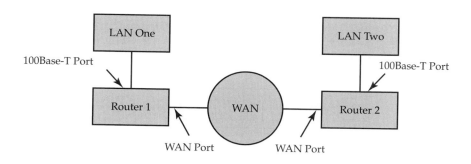

its components. The router gathers this information and can present it to a user through a PC or terminal interface. By examining this data, skilled practitioners can identify trouble spots and use sophisticated approaches to predict potential trouble spots before they occur. Routers can also be used facilitate network security by blocking certain routes from users. Network management is critical to the reliable operation of a network. Figure 15.11 illustrates the router functionality from an OSI perspective. Note that a router operates at OSI layer 3. Compare this figure with Figure 15.7, showing the layer 2 functionality of a bridge. Before exploring the three routing algorithmic approaches, two fundamental concepts relating to routing will be introduced first. The first issue, link cost, drives the selection and development of routing algorithms because it is the measure of how they select between paths. The second issue, flooding, is the basic approach that every router uses to determine what paths are available to it.

Link Cost.   Basically, link cost is what you would think it would be from the name. A link cost is defined between source and destination. This link cost is measured and then sorted among all other paths between the same source and destination. The smallest link cost wins, and all messages from a particular source use that path to a particular destination.

What defines link cost? There are at least three ways link cost is usually measured. Probably the most primitive technique would be to go to a map and note the number of miles between source and destination and enter that as the link cost. For example, a path from Detroit to Chicago that routes through Atlanta would have a larger link cost than one that proceeds directly between the two cities.

Figure 15.11
OSI perspective of a router.

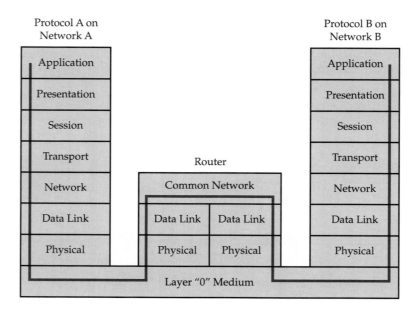

Another way would be to count the number of hops between source and destination. Each hop is a router node and can be easily counted. This assumes that the number of routers between the source and destination is representative of the magnitude of the link cost. This is not always the case, but to a first approximation is a pretty good assumption.

Another way would be to measure the time it takes for a packet to complete the path. If done only once, it is an example of static routing. If regular tests are carried out and the routing table updated on the completion of each test, this type of algorithm can mutate into a dynamic approach. When done in this way, the smallest link cost is defined as the shortest time. A nice consequence of this approach is that the table tends to reflect actual conditions on the network if the testing is carried out on a regular basis. To many users, especially on the Internet, the shortest time is the metric of interest.

The most sophisticated approaches to link cost computations combine elements of two or more of the above basic approaches. Some are very complex, but all strive to achieve some measure of smallest link cost and use that idea alone to fill in the router table.

Flooding. Flooding is just what you might expect from the name. Flooding is way to find out paths on the internetwork. Each router floods the network with test messages, and each message counts the number of hops. This is a brute force method of determining the shortest path between any particular source and destination. Flooding always finds the shortest path because it tests each and every path due to the flooding of the network.

An obvious disadvantage of this approach is that a lot of excess traffic is produced that has no value to any user. Each router on the network sends out test messages on every line it has to every other router. It is possible to limit the excessive nature of flooding by applying the random walk idea from statistics. In this refinement each router sends a *single random destination message* to search out unknown paths at random. This can be effective and limits the number of messages sourced by each router in the network, getting around the main problem with the idea of flooding.

Routing Algorithms. To perform routing, a routing algorithm is required. An algorithm is just a specific approach to solving a problem. A routing algorithm is used to build a routing table that lists the paths to all nodes to which it is connected. It constructs this table by determining a path to a particular destination and then noting several things about that path. The two most important things are the link cost and the address of the "hop" to the next network on the way to the destination. The hop address is just the address of the next router between the source and the ultimate destination. There may be many hops between the source and the destination. At each hop, the packet is routed to the next hop until it ultimately reaches its destination. There are many ways to determine the link cost; although the basic idea was introduced, the specifics for a few representative cases will be explored later.

As discussed earlier, all routing algorithms can be sorted according to three ideas. We will examine each of these individually. The first idea, static or dynamic, is very straightforward.

Static or Dynamic Algorithms   Static algorithms always use the same path independently of any special situations. Dynamic algorithms take into account the time-varying nature of the path and try different paths in an attempt to find the best one in real time. In an analogy with automobile traffic, the dynamic algorithms try alternate routes, sometimes cutting through subdivisions, and so forth. The static algorithms just get on the expressway like always, regardless of how congested it is. In a static algorithm the routing never changes once the routing table is built. This means that once a path is found for a message, it never changes until the routing table is changed, usually manually.

A table constructed with a static algorithm is predetermined and the router does not attempt to change them or react to changes in the network. Typically, this table of routes is computed once when the network is first turned on and then ignored. This is a good example of how a purely static router would work.

The dynamic approach requires the router to figure out on its own which path is best in some dynamic way that reacts to the real-time status of the network. The router does this job by periodically sending out messages to other routers and asking them for any "good" paths they might have found to any destinations that this router needs. It also sends out test messages and times how long different paths take and stores this information, typically in a routing table. This is a good example of a dynamic router. Used in this way, "good" is usually defined by some concrete parameter or combination of parameters such as best quality, least cost, shortest path, and so forth. The general way to refer to this is link cost.

Therefore, static algorithms do not respond to changes in the network, and dynamic ones do. They both need a way to determine the paths and this method depends on how the network is set up. This is the domain of the second idea, flat or hierarchical structure.

Flat or Hierarchical Algorithms   A router can assume that networks are interconnected in one of two ways, flat, like lines on a piece of paper, or hierarchical, like in a pyramid. In a flat architecture, all routers must be aware of all other routers, because all routers are considered belonging to one domain. A domain describes a group of nodes. Flat algorithms assume every domain can communicate directly with every other domain. Because of the complexity of the paths determined by this approach, most algorithms today use a hierarchical approach.

In a hierarchical approach, routers are grouped into domains, hierarchically. That is, not every router can communicate with every other router but instead must follow a route constructed of a group of backbone routers that interconnect domains. A good way to think of this is that the backbone routers are wide and fast expressways, and domains are exit ramps from the expressway. At each exit ramp a router connects from the backbone routers to the router connected into the domain.

The biggest advantage of hierarchical routing is obvious; it minimizes the traffic that occurs inside a domain. Because all traffic not destined for a node inside a particular domain does not pass through it, "cross-town" traffic is minimized. Similiarily, because most traffic in a domain never goes outside it, the traffic on the backbone is minimized as well. There may be several layers of domains constructed hierarchically.

Additionally, in a hierarchical approach, the routers connected in that domain only need to know about the other routers inside that domain, making the routing tables relatively small and simple. This is a another major advantage of hierarchical routing.

A domain is usually an organization, for example, the network that connects the workstations of everyone in a particular office or school. Most of the traffic generated stays inside the domain; it is e-mail to associates or fellow students and so forth. The congestion on that network is due to just the traffic generated by users of the network if the routing is done hierarchically. In the case of a flat algorithm, messages that are trying to find their way through to some ultimate destination would also be present.

Hierarchical routing is further subdivided into two subsections, called interdomain and intradomain algorithms. As can be imagined, the routing that must be accomplished by the backbone routers is of a different order of complexity than the routing accomplished inside a domain. Backbone routing is usually done with an algorithm that is most efficient in routing packets interdomain. Inside a domain, routing is accomplished most efficiently with an algorithm most efficient in routing packets intradomain.

Distance Vector or Link State Algorithms   The last idea in classifying routing algorithms is an examination of the actual method of constructing the routing table. There are two ways this is done, distant vector or link state algorithms. Link state routing is the more widely used today, but many networks, including major portions of the Internet, still use distance vector. A widely used distance vector algorithm is called Routing Information Protocol, or RIP. A widely used link state algorithm is Open Shortest Path First, or OSPF. Because these protocols are widely known and are often used as the definition of the two approaches, the discussion below refers to the two implementations, RIP and OPSF.

In a nutshell, RIP *floods the network connections to only those routers to which it is directly connected,* sending the information contained in its routing table defining the link cost of *all paths* it knows about. RIP sends its entire routing table in each message. OSPF does a similar thing, however; it *floods the entire network* with the information contained in its routing table defining the link cost of the *directly connected paths* it knows about. OSPF only sends that portion of the table that reflects its directly connected paths, a much smaller message than the entire routing table. Another way of looking at this is that RIP sends out small numbers of large messages, whereas OSPF sends out large numbers of small messages. Both of these algorithms will be discussed in more detail in the following sections.

Routing Information Protocol   RIP uses a concept known as distance vector routing to find the shortest path to each attached network. Each attached router maintains three vectors. The first vector represents a link cost value to every other router it is directly connected to. In this way, each router maintains a cost to reach every other attached network. The two other vectors that are maintained represent the distance, or delay, from the router to the attached network and a vector that keeps track of the current minimum delay route from the router to the attached network.

Thus, the router has three pieces of information called vectors:

1. Cost to any attached network
2. Delay to any attached network
3. Current best path to any attached network

About every minute, each router exchanges its distance/delay vector with only its directly attached neighbors. On the basis of the incoming vectors each node receives, it updates its distance/delay and current link cost vectors in such a way to minimize the distance/delay to those directly attached neighbors. These updates are then used to update the cost vector.

This approach has a problem in use on the Internet because TCP/IP operates asynchronously. Implicit in the idea of RIP is that all incoming vectors arrive effectively simultaneously. In an asynchronous network such as TCP/IP this is not possible. Additionally, some vectors may be lost in transmit. RIP does not do any error recovery at the Transport layer.

If a router does not respond after three exchanges of vectors, RIP assumes that path is gone. The fact of vectors arriving at different times, or not at all, can cause the protocol to keep an inaccurate link cost routing table due to the changing conditions on the network. By adding additional complexity to the basic approach outlined above, these difficulties are minimized.

The real problem with RIP is that it responds very slowly to changes in the network topology because the routing table is distributed throughout the attached networks. This results in messages not being sent over the least link cost (typically least delay) path. Additionally, RIP allows only 16 levels of link cost, resulting in a granularity inappropriate to the highly interconnected and large networks of today. These two concerns led to OSPF.

Open Shortest Path First   OSPF uses a simple method of determining the delay to any other attached network. This method is called link state routing. In this approach, each router is responsible for finding out the location and delay to each of its neighboring routers. Once this data is assembled, each router sends out a link state message packet to each of its identified neighbors informing them of what it has found out. Each router that receives such an information packet forwards it to all of its neighbors, and so on. In this manner, a table is gradually built up *in each router*, indicating the shortest path to every other router on any attached network. Each router in the configuration knows the shortest path to any other router.

When a router is first turned on, it determines a cost/delay value to each attached network by sending out the link state message packet to all attached routers and measuring the round-trip delay. Once this delay is divided by 2, it provides a good measure of path length to the router. By doing this periodically, it provides a way to measure variations in path delay. Like any routing protocol, OSPF uses flooding to search out paths.

Flooding always finds the shortest path to any router because all paths are tried. As the message packet is received at each router, each router then sends out the message again to all its attached routers except the one from which it received the message. This has the potential of creating a large amount of excessive traffic for two reasons. First, a geometrically increasing number of messages are retransmitted after each hop, and second, many packets will find their way back to the retransmitting node along some other path.

This raises a concern of when to update, similar to that experienced in RIP. Link state routing labels each link state message packet with an age value. Each router at which the message packet arrives decrements the age value by 1 and then sends it on in the manner described above. Once the age value reaches zero, the link state message packet is discarded. In this manner old routing information, contained in young link state packets, is automatically discarded. This limits the number of packets being generated, and the problem of when to update the routing table goes away because old information never replaces newer information.

Once the router has constructed its table, it sends out its set of costs to all routers on any attached network, not just those to which it is directly attached. This information is not sent out again until the periodic measurements it makes reveal a significant change in path delay or cost. This typically happens only when the topology changes through a router going down or a new path being established in the topology. This tends to minimize excess traffic on the network. Therefore, each router has a table that lists the cost to every other router in any attached network. Additionally, each router must respond to each update it receives.

Although the costs determined are defaulted to delay, represented well to a first order by number of hops, it is possible for a network administrator to set the cost on any specific link by configuring the router appropriately. Essentially, a cost number is associated with each port on the router. These link costs are maintained in several different ways, each representing cost from a different perspective. These are known as types of service (TOS). Each router maintains at least one of these cost structures and may maintain all five. The message packet sent out to determine the link cost indicates which TOS it is requesting.

1. TOS 0.   Minimum number of hops to destination; this is the default approach.
2. TOS 2.   Minimum monetary cost, usually funny money used for internal administration.
3. TOS 4.   Maximum reliability of network segments, usually error rates driven.
4. TOS 8.   Maximum throughput, data rate of network segments.
5. TOS 16. Minimum propagation delay.

Other protocols exist to route packets through the internetwork. In addition to the two already discussed, other protocols used include the following:

1. Interior Gateway Routing Protocol (IGRP)
2. Exterior Gateway Protocol (EGP)
3. Border Gateway Protocol (BGP)
4. Intermediate System to Intermediate System (IS-IS)

Congestion and Fairness   Once the choice of algorithm is made, a routing table is constructed according to that algorithm. Then there are two situations: First, if the source NL already has a virtual connection open to the destination NL, it just uses that one. Second, if the destination is a new one, a new virtual circuit is set up. Routers keep tables of virtual connections so that once it determines a path, it can use it until, in a dynamic environment, a better path is found. In a static environment, the router just uses the identified path for every message to that destination.

This is why if a router table gets corrupted, the entire communication between source and destination can be corrupted. It explains why some prefer static routing; if the routing table cannot be updated it cannot get corrupted. In a corrupted environment, the router keeps trying the same path to send the messages; if that path is wrong, it can take some time to discover it. This is further complicated by the fact that only rarely does the source-to-destination communication take place directly.

Usually several intermediate hops are taken. For example, if e-mail is sent to a friend on the other side of the world, the message goes through several internetworks that connect to others that finally connect to the LAN your friend's station is connected to. If one of the routers were to get confused about how to route to the next router in line, not just your message but all others going through that switching point would be disrupted.

All routing protocols are rated according to how fair they are. Fair routing protocols consider not only the end-to-end efficiency of the routing path but also the message traffic between hops. This is usually controlled by a factor called congestion; the more congested a path is, the less desirable it is to use to route traffic through. For example, when the expressway is congested, some people try to find an alternate path.

The expressway, when uncongested, is the shortest path from source to destination; however, when it is congested, sometimes by local traffic, it no longer is the shortest path. An example is a special local event, like a ball game letting out; the additional local traffic overwhelms the efficiency of that path. The router's job is to find the optimum route for any traffic that it is responsible for forwarding, taking into account the local situation. It is not just local traffic that can alter the efficiency of a particular path. For example, long distance traffic patterns change dramatically on a holiday weekend. Congestion on a network, just like on a highway, increases the time the message takes to get from source to destination. In communications it would be said that the performance of the network degrades.

To review, routers are used to route messages from source to destination and operate at layer 3 of the OSI model. The operational characteristics of how a particular router performs this function is best understood by examining the routing algorithm used. All routing algorithms use some link cost to find the best paths, and algorithms are ranked based on their capability to react to congestion and forward packets in some fair manner based on the congestion of intermediate links. If you think about it carefully, the only real differences between RIP and OSPF are in how they determine link costs and how they react to congestion and changes in the physical network architecture. Future enhancements to routing will include increased security at the network layer and ways of constraining the path selection for high priority, or latency-sensitive, traffic.

Gateways

The most sophisticated device that can be used to interconnect two incompatible protocols running on two networks is the gateway. A gateway can interconnect any two protocols running on any two networks. This is its primary advantage. The primary disadvantages to gateways are the cost and slow transfer rate, or latency, between the two protocols. Because of the way a gateway works, messages being translated by a gateway take a while to pass through them. This means that a message sent from one user to another will take significantly longer to be delivered if the two users are on opposite sides of a gateway.

Many gateways are used to translate between SNA and OSI protocols or between two LAN protocols. Another popular use for gateways is as packet assemblers and disassemblers (PADs). These are discussed in Chapter 16. A PAD is classified as a gateway because it operates above Layer 4.

Every two protocols you want to interconnect require their own gateway. Each gateway is customized for the two protocols it will translate between. Gateways are expensive devices but are necessary when communication between two networks running different protocols is required. Gateways are often used to connect PC users on one network running one protocol to a mainframe running a different protocol. This allows the PC users to work as they normally would when not needing the mainframe resource, and it also provides a seamless path into the mainframe when that is required. A gateway is a layer 7 device and is illustrated in Figure 15.12.

Communication Processors and Controllers

This class of devices is best represented by the family of products known as front end processors, or FEPs. A FEP is designed to work with a mainframe computer and function as its communications processor. A FEP attaches directly to the mainframe and performs all communications overhead associated with communicating with any device not designed to work with a mainframe. These devices also provide concentration of several low data rate communications into a high data rate channel for the mainframe. Additionally, they handle all the handshaking with these devices necessary to make the concentration transparent to the end devices. Concentration is like statistical time division multiplexing with a little extra handshaking thrown in.

A FEP's primary purpose is to off-load any communication-related translation

Figure 15.12
OSI perspective of a gateway.

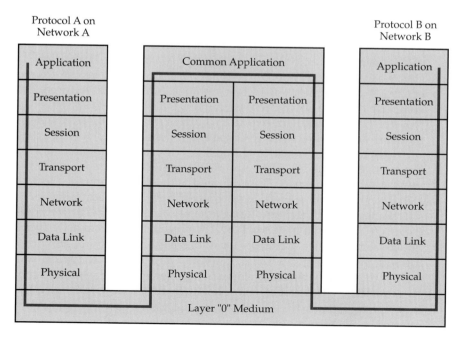

tasks from the central processing unit of the mainframe. This means it buffers all data into and out of the mainframe and provides a variety of interfaces and a variety of speeds for device attachment. FEPs are powerful devices that have allowed mainframe computers to bridge into the PC-oriented LAN world. The most common FEP is an IBM device, IBM 3745. It comes in several flavors, each representing additional interface port options and port quantities.

A FEP device has one major disadvantage; it is a very complex and expensive device. Additionally, because of the way it is designed, any changes to accommodate new protocols is a very expensive and time-consuming process. This means that FEPs are slow to adopt to new technologies appearing in the communications marketplace, which rapidly changes.

Because of all this, FEPs are slowly being replaced with router technology. A router already knows all about how to make most of the source code conversions necessary and, with the addition of one extra card, can communicate with the mainframe in the same manner as a FEP. Because a router is an order of magnitude smaller and is half the cost, the days of the FEP are numbered. However, due to the special, very conservative way that mainframe and legacy systems undergo evolution, it is likely that devices such as FEPs and protocol converters will be around for years, perhaps decades to come.

■ LAN ATTACHMENT

A basic goal of any student learning about networks and protocols is to understand how to mechanically attach a PC or other device, such as those we just discussed, to a particular LAN. Most attachments are similar and depend on the type of physical layer used.

Just as there are different types of physical media, metallic and optical, there are different ways of attaching to a LAN. Metallic media are generally of two types, twisted pair and coaxial. Optical media, if infrared LANs are excluded, are all fiber. Because the various types of connectors have already been discussed in earlier chapters, this discussion is a system-level one. Three types of networks will be considered, the many different types of Ethernet, Token Bus, and Token Ring. These three IEEE 802.X networks comprise most LANs you will encounter, with Ethernet types the most popular.

For LAN attachment a network interface card (NIC) is always required. NICs are modems designed to work with the type of media used and have software loaded that provides the higher-layer functionality. For example, to attach a PC to a LAN, the appropriate NIC and cable are required. The NIC is inserted into the backplane of the PC, and the cable is attached. The other end of the cable is attached to a tap for Token Bus, a hub for Ethernet, or a MAU (a specialized hub) for Token Ring.

Sometimes the technical term *Ethernet transceiver* or *Token Ring Attachment User Interface* (AUI), is used instead of NIC. *NIC* seems to be primarily applicable in the Ethernet marketplace as a substitute term for *transceiver,* but it is growing as a catch-all term for both groups. Figures 15.13, 15.14, and 15.15 illustrate typical LAN attachments for each of the three types of networks mentioned above. Each figure shows a PC as the device; obviously, this can be any intelligent device. As can be seen from examination of the three figures, each LAN uses the same basic approach to attachment. Some kind of interface card, here shown as a NIC card, is placed in the DTE device. The interface card

Figure 15.13
Ethernet 10Base-T or 100Base-T attachment.

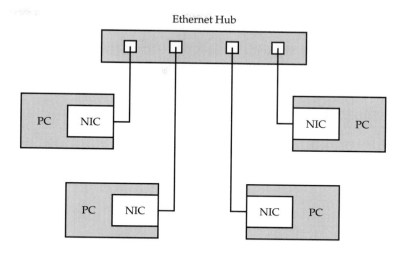

acts as the DCE device and communicates with other DCE devices on the network. Usually, these are other PCs and servers.

Installing a NIC card to an Ethernet 10Base-T or 100Base-T network is simplicity itself. All one needs to do is insert the card in the proper slot in the PC and attach the cable. The PC will usually automatically configure itself for the network card. There is no special activity to be done to the network, although if a network operating system (NOS) such as Novell is running, the user must be configured and an password assigned.

Figure 15.14
Token Bus or cable TV attachment.

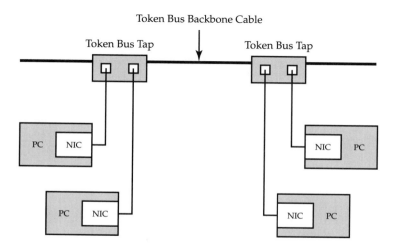

Figure 15.15
Token Ring attachment.

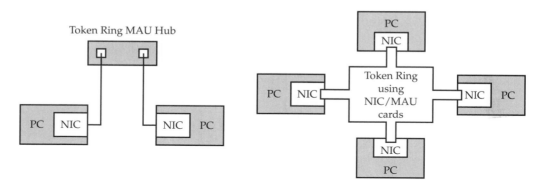

■ TYPICAL 10BASE-T AND 100BASE-T LANS

Although it is desirable to have a good sense of how each type of LAN is attached to the network, it is also good to have a sense of how a typical office LAN might be laid out. In the example discussed below, the Ethernet 10Base-T and 100Base-T standard is used. The rules listed below should be applied. Some of these are from standards established by the EIA/TIA and were briefly referenced Chapter 3. Some of these rules are just good practices to ensure a flexible and adaptive approach.

1. Horizontal cable run no more than 90 m between repeaters.
2. Backbone cables run no more than 500 m between repeaters.
3. All cables are run with four-pair CAT-5 cable.
4. No more than 25 stations on any segment.
5. LAN switches are used to filter the network traffic between main horizontal service areas.

In such a design often the individual PCs are attached to the wall with drop cables constructed of the cable specified above and connectorized with RJ-45 jacks. These plug directly into both the NIC cards inside the PCs and on the other side of the wall, into the hubs. Fiber could also be substituted for any of the backbone or horizontal cable segments. If this is done, the distance any individual run can go before a repeater is needed greatly increases, to approximately 2000 m. A typical client/server approach to networking is shown in Figure 15.16.

■ TROUBLESHOOTING

There are two main areas where trouble can arise from. These are electrical problems (hardware) and viruses (software).

Hardware Problems

Most problems in a network arise from noise being impressed onto the network cabling. This can be addressed by using shielded cables. Many 10 Base-T and 100 Base-T networks use unshielded twisted pair (UTP) wiring. If you encounter noise problems that are caus-

Figure 15.16
Typical client/sever 10Base-T and 100Base-T LAN.

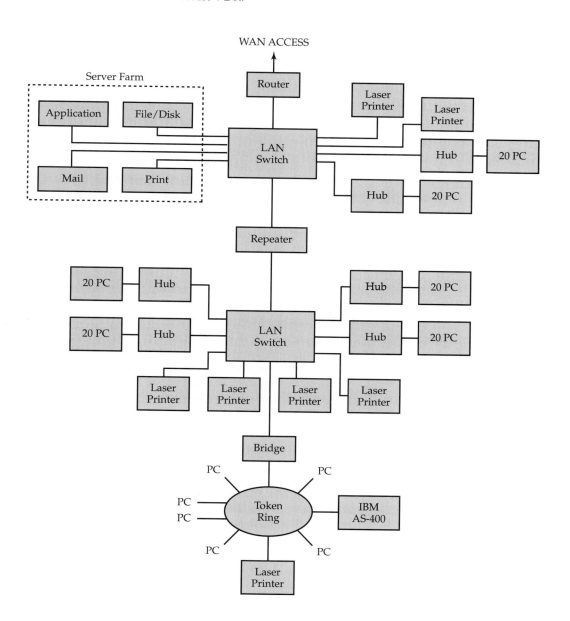

ing packets to be corrupted, a shielded cable can be one good solution. The idea is not to replace the entire network's cable, but just that section from which the noise is originating.

One can also replace the metallic cable with fiber optic cable. Fiber optic cable is naturally immune to electromagnetic interference (EMI) and radio frequency interference (RFI). (RFI is just EMI at a higher frequency.) The noise from low-frequency devices such as lights, engines, and so forth, is EMI, and the noise from higher-frequency devices such as microwaves is RFI. The problem with replacing metallic cable with fiber optic is that devices that attach to that segment will have to have their adapters and interface cards replaced as well to be compatible with the fiber.

Probably the best solution is to avoid the problem in the first place. To do this, take care when choosing the route the cable will take. Avoid areas where the cable is likely to pick up interference. Use shielded cables in any areas where you cannot avoid such a noise source. Even better, originally install the network using fiber optic cables. Although fiber looks more costly at first glance because the cable is more expensive than metallic cable, the significant cost in any network is in the labor cost when installing and the maintenance cost once the network is in place. Choosing fiber cable at the outset can be an important contributor to minimizing the long-term support costs.

If you do decide to use metallic cable, pay careful attention to grounding issues. These were discussed earlier and will not be revisited here. Also, be aware that low humidity breeds electrical problems. Low humidity, less than 70%, makes it much more likely that you will experience failures due to electric static discharge (ESD).

Software Problems

Everybody has heard of viruses. These are software programs that will invade the computers on the network and attach themselves (hence, the name virus) to other executable programs. Once attached, they may attack immediately, wait for some specific date to attack, or even wait for some specific action, such as a warm boot, to attack.

Typically they corrupt data or system files when triggered. Once this has occurred often the only solution is to erase the effected disk and reinstall the software. This is a good example of why it is important to back up all software and data files regularly.

There are two approaches to preventing this type of problem. Both should be used whenever possible. The first, and most important piece, is to buy antivirus software and install it on each station on the network. It is also possible to purchase antivirus software to install on a server and avoid the cost of placing it on each station. Antivirus software will detect the arrival of a virus on a disk and either automatically erase it or ask you what you want to do.

The problem with antivirus software is that is needs to be updated regularly. Devious people are always coming up with new ways to attack. Installing the software and not updating it regularly buys you only a few months of protection.

The second approach is to avoid the attack in the first place. In many installations the primary source of viruses are from the users themselves, who bring in an infected floppy disk. Once this disk is loaded into a station, the virus moves out from there. Some organizations avoid this problem by not installing floppy drives on the computer stations. This is not always an acceptable solution.

Other times, the virus comes into the local network from the outside network, typically the Internet. Use of an effective means to filter incoming messages with some kind of firewall will help block this access. Again, although approaches can be devised to avoid the attack in the first place, always install antivirus software and keep it updated.

NIC Card Troubleshooting

Because virtually every station on a PC network will have a NIC card, it is useful to spend some time discussing specific troubleshooting approaches that are applicable to that component. One is the short-cut method to find out if the NIC card is operating. Troubleshooting a NIC card in an Ethernet 10Base-T or 100 Base-T network is very simple. First, there is always an LED placed on the card edge that will light up if powered. If the card sees any traffic on the network, the LED will blink.

There are two signs that the network connection is malfunctioning. The first and most obvious is that the LED is dark. Usually the situation here is that the card is not seated properly in the PC. Of course, one must make sure the PC is powered up. The second sign is an LED that is not blinking. If the LED is not blinking, it means that no traffic is being seen by that NIC card. Here the usual culprit is a bad drop cable. Typically, it is best to replace the drop cable and check to see if the LED starts blinking. If you still do not see any activity, the next most likely situation is that the NIC card itself is malfunctioning. The best procedure is to swap this out with a known good card. One of these two steps will usually get the station up and running.

Other problems arise when the card is not installed properly. These will appear only the first time the PC is powered up after installation. The problems usually arise because the addresses (IRQ and I/O) have not been set correctly. Often this is because the wrong driver is loaded. Always use the drivers that come with the NIC card, not the ones already present on the computers hard drive. Modern NIC cards installed on Windows 95 and later operating systems are very easy to install. Just install the card, load the appropriate software driver, and let the operating system do the rest.

If an older card is being installed, you may have to manually configure the IRQ address that the card will use. This is typically done by installing the correct jumpers on the card. Whatever IRQ address you select, you must make sure the OS knows about it and uses the same address to access the card.

The last thing is very basic but is sometimes overlooked. NIC cards come designed for use with many different networks. It is important to specify a card that has the same network interface that you need. For example, if you are using a 10 Base-T network, make sure the NIC card uses an RJ-45 plug.

HUB Troubleshooting

Because many networks today use hub technology to build the network, a few words on troubleshooting the hub is appropriate. Most hubs use LEDs to indicate when the status of the port is okay. If the LED is not lit, the problem is between the hub port and that station.

If the indicator lights are all fine, and you are still experiencing trouble routing though that port on the hub, you might want to consider resetting the hub. Resetting the hub is done by cycling the power. However, when you do this, all stations attached to the hub will have service interrupted. Some hubs feature a reset switch. When this is available, it is usually better to reset instead of cycling the power.

■ SUMMARY

The goal of this chapter was to introduce you to many common, and a few not so common, pieces of network hardware that you may encounter at school or work. The descriptions here were designed to give a basic understanding of how the technology worked and where it fit into the OSI model. There has been no attempt to describe specific pieces of equipment manufactured by a particular vendor. It is always best to obtain the operation manual for any piece of equipment and review it for particular details of its operation.

However, if you can learn to fit the new piece of equipment into the OSI model by knowing what layer it operates on, you can get a good start in understanding just what the particular piece of technology can do. For this reason, the description of each device was prefaced with what layer it operated on. Many times it is necessary to be able to identify very quickly if there is a potential replacement for a particular piece of equipment that has failed. This approach may help you develop this skill.

Finally, several sections on installation and troubleshooting concluded the chapter.

PROBLEMS

1. What is the distinguishing difference between a LAN and a WAN?

2. Describe the difference between a logical and physical topology and give an example of each.

3. For a LAN network with 100 users, operating at 10 Mbps, what is the average data rate each user will experience?

4. Give one advantage and one disadvantage to a ring topology.

5. Explain why bus topologies can often be considered as both full and half duplex.

6. Describe the two types of basic hubs.

7. Describe the difference between a repeater and a bridge.

8. Describe the difference between a bridge and a router.

9. Describe the differences between RIP and OSPF.

10. Describe the difference between a layer 2 switch and a port switching hub.

11. Describe how flooding is used to determine link cost in a network.

16

Telecommunications

This chapter provides an introduction to the telecommunications system, beginning with a discussion of how various companies combine to provide both local and long distance telephone service. This is followed by the basics of telephone operations covering voltages, dual-tone multifrequency (DTMF) dialing and call progress tones. The traditional switching station hierarchy and basic components of a switch are then touched on, followed by feature groups and dialing procedures.

After that introduction to the system as a whole, four types of circuits and their relative performance and pricing are defined. After this discussion, examples of major components that would be encountered on customer premises are introduced, and their operation and application are summarized. This is followed by a short discussion of T-carrier line coding and an overview of ISDN as an example of a circuit-switched system. The chapter concludes with an overview of Signaling Service Seven (SS7) and X.25 as a point-to-point circuit-switched packet protocol.

■ LOCAL AND LONG DISTANCE PROVIDERS

There is no longer just one carrier in the United States. After the breakup of the Bell System, there were seven large pieces of the old telephone system. These were the Regional Bell Operating Companies, or RBOCs offering local service along with many smaller carriers that operate in specific regions of the country such as GTE. These companies have not directly competed with each other in their respective regions, and so consumers were never offered a choice for local telephone service. This will almost certainly change in the next few years. The seven original RBOCs are listed below:

Ameritech Corporation, Chicago

Bell Atlantic Corporation, Philadelphia

BellSouth Corporation, Atlanta

NYNEX Corporation, New York

Pacific Telesis Group, San Francisco

Southwestern Bell Corporation, St. Louis

US West, Incorporated, Englewood, Colorado

At this time, several of these have merged together to form larger "local" service areas. As of this writing, there are four left; SBC Corp. is the largest, followed by the combination of NYNEX and Bell Atlantic.

Bell Atlantic Corporation

BellSouth Corporation

Southwestern Bell Corporation (SBC Corp.)

US West, Incorporated

In the United States, there are about 180 local area and transport areas, or LATAs, with the number slowly increasing. Each original RBOC is licensed to operate in about 20 to 25 LATAs, depending on size. Just a short time ago that meant that inside each LATA there was only one licensed operator of local wired telephone services. *Local exchange carrier* (LEC) is the general term used to refer to the company offering local wired telephone service in any LATA. Today, inside each LATA the LEC or other carrier is the only licensed supplier of local wired telephone service.

In the near future, local service competition will become a reality. This competition is permitted by the ruling that followed the breakup of the telephone system, is the Telecom Reform Act, passed in 1996. Due to cost considerations of installing a local wire to each local service location, this competition has not yet occurred. It now seems clear that the cable TV line will be used to provide this service alternative in the near future. When that happens there will be multiple LECs in some service areas. As a result, the naming convention for local exchange carriers has changed. The existing local company is now referred to as the incumbent local exchange carrier, or ILEC. The competitors to come will be referred to as competitive local exchange carriers, or CLECs. For now, assume there is only one local service company and refer to it as the LEC.

That covers how local calls are handled, but what about long-distance calls? There are several providers of long distance service as well, but unlike the local situation, these are free to compete anywhere they choose. The general term for referring to a long dis-

Figure 16.1
POP.

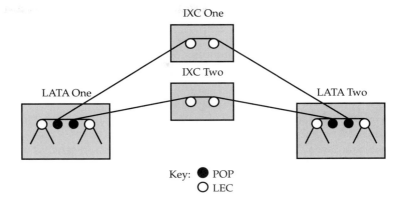

tance provider is *IXC*, standing for interexchange carrier. Some examples include the long-distance part of the old Bell network, AT&T, MCI, Sprint, and so forth. There is robust competition in this field, with new competitors emerging regularly.

Before the 1996 act, the LECs were prohibited from offering long-distance service outside a LATA, and the IXCs were prohibited from offering local service inside any LATA. The old Bell system was broken into two main segments, local service monopolies and long-distance competition. With the passage of the 1996 act, this changed as well. Today, either type of call can be carried by either type of carrier.

It is of interest to see how a new IXC that wants to offer long-distance service into a LATA gets started. A basic thing such a company would need is a point of presence (POP) inside the switching hierarchy to connect into one LATA inside a LECs service area. A POP is usually some form of a TDM connected to SONET or copper backbone that is owned or leased by the IXC and provides the pathway for the long-distance service the IXC is offering. Figure 16.1 illustrates how two LATAs are connected by two competing IXCs using POPs.

The POP is the point at which an IXC enters the hierarchy of switching described above. It is the place where the IXC must terminate its long-distance lines just before they are connected to your local telephone system, or LEC. Most IXCs have several POPs in each LATA. Each IXC also has some switching hierarchy itself to route and switch calls across the country and world. The hierarchies differ but are all similar to the old Bell system; they are just not as interconnected and do not have as many layers.

■ TWO-WIRE AND FOUR-WIRE INTERFACES

A voice telephone can be wired to the telephone system in one of two ways. For most, this is the two-wire interface. The two wires are signal and ground. These two wires are used to both transmit and receive. The four-wire interface is just two pairs of wires, signal plus ground for each transmit and receive. Four-wire circuits are normally used by the telephone system in trunk or long-distance circuits. This is because they use *balanced signaling* to achieve better performance in the presence of noise. This is important for the long distances that trunk circuits usually run. Refer to Chapter 3 for more on balanced and unbalanced circuits.

In some special circumstances, four-wire circuits can be brought into the user location if there is a need for increased performance. Many dedicated lines are implemented in this way. Bringing in a four-wire circuit costs more, but if a performance improvement is required, it may be achieved in this way.

Four-wire lines are often referred to as trunk lines, and two-wire lines are often referred to as subscriber lines. Although in most cases these two terms can be interchanged, there are circumstances where the correspondence is not perfect. One example was mentioned in the above paragraph; shortly, another will be illustrated when feature groups are discussed.

The twisted pair wiring used in the telephone system is commonly implemented with 24 gauge wire. Additionally, there is a standard for how many twists per foot are required. This standard is at least 10 twists per foot.

■ VOLTAGES

We will distinguish between the traditional telephone system, by referring to it as the plain old telephone system (POTS) and the modern environment using digital telephones, by ISDN. Most of us use POTS with traditional wired analog telephones, sometimes making use of enhanced services such as call forwarding. This discussion on voltages assumes an analog telephone in this environment.

It is fundamental to understand what various voltages exist on the POTS line in a typical household. Assuming that the telephone uses a two-wire interface, these two wires have special names, tip and ring. In installations, these wires will always be colored red and green corresponding to the tip and ring lines, respectively.

These are the only wires into the telephone and they are used to ring the telephone *and* to carry conversations. Tip is the wire that is connected to the positive side of the battery, and the ring wire is connected to the negative side. This terminology is a historical way of saying plus and minus. The names came from the original plug the operator used to connect telephone calls. The tip wire connected to the tip of the plug and the ring wire connected to the ring that surrounded the jack.

When a telephone rings, a −48 V ringing voltage is applied on the ring line, and the tip line is grounded. This −48 V runs at a current of between 20 and 80 mA. In modern telephones this is converted to a well-regulated 5 V and is used to power the telephone. The −48 V is generated by large banks of 24 V battery packs at the local switching station. These battery packs are continuously charged by the power grid. When the power grid goes down, your telephone operates with this battery backup. This is an important point: POTS systems power the telephone through the telephone system exclusively. As will be seen later, ISDN does not.

The last two voltage sources the telephone must work with are the voltage generated by the speaker calling you, about 1 V, and the voltage you generate when speaking into the telephone, about 20 mV. All these signals are carried over the same two wires, tip and ring. It is interesting to think about the circuit details of an interface that must work over this entire voltage range. This should give you some sense of the complexity of even so commonplace a thing as a telephone. The dialing or tones generated to dial another telephone are in the same frequency and amplitude range of the voice signals and will be discussed next, after a short digression into why the telephone system uses −48 V instead of 5 V.

All power distribution systems use large voltages to transfer power across the grid. The telephone system is no different. Although this is not a book on power system engineering, it is instructive to examine why large voltages are used to transfer power.

$$P = VI$$

If a current of 50 mA is assumed, the power is $P = (48)(50) = 2400$ mW. What would be the current flow if 5 V was transferred and the power requirements stayed the same?

$$P = VI \qquad 2400 = 5I \rightarrow I = \frac{2400}{5} = 480 \text{ mA.}$$

To see why this approach is not used, calculate the power loss due to resistance drop of the transmission line. This can be written in two forms:

$$P = I * \frac{I}{R} = E * E * R$$

Remembering that the resistance of wire or any metallic transmission line is very small, it can be seen that 480/(small) is much larger than (48)(small). Therefore, significantly lower power loss occurs using high voltages and small currents. This is much more efficient for the power generation facilities. Electronic systems can easily regulate down the voltage to that required in an efficient and cost effective manner.

■ DUAL TONE MULTIFREQUENCY

DTMF is how one "dials" a telephone number today. Some telephones come with a switch that says pulse-tone. This switch changes the way the telephone dials, switching between a pulse, the old fashioned system, and a tone, or DTMF system.

The POTS used pulse dialing only. Pulse dialing essentially was the output of a number of pulses that was the same as the number dialed. Note the use of the word *dialed*. When you rotate the dial on a pulse telephone to the proper number, as it rotated back, a pulse was generated for each number passed, essentially outputting the same number of pulses as the number that was dialed.

As POTS evolved, the pulse dialing equipment at the switching station became a relic of the past. Everything was moving toward digital and so did the telephone system. The result was a change to the touch-tone telephone. This system uses DTMF dialing. DTMF works by outputting two single-frequency tones for each number pressed.

Parenthetically, it is curious that everyone still refers to dialing a telephone number, when many have never even experienced this. The terminology today is to touch a number, although some prefer to say press.

An interesting thing about the frequencies chosen for use is that they are all in the same frequency band as human speech, 300 to 3100 Hz. Is there a chance that a random sound made by human speech would be interpreted by the telephone system as a valid tone? The design of the DTMF system makes this very unlikely. As mentioned above, each key pressed outputs two distinct frequencies. The harmonic mixing resulting from these two frequencies produces sum and difference frequencies that are also present. Using this information, the telephone system can readily determine which is a valid tone resulting from a pressed key and which is not.

Another interesting thing is the cleverness of choosing the pairs of tones. Because DTMF required two tones for each number, a quick calculation yields a total of 24 tones, 10 numbers plus * and #, two tones per number. That seems like a lot of tones, and the engineers thought so too. Implementation techniques at the time DTMF was first introduced were such that generating a tone was a task for analog circuitry and to implement 24 such circuits would require more space than there was inside a traditional telephone casing. By pairing the tones in a column-row configuration, it was seen that only seven tones, three vertical and four horizontal, were required.

Examine a tone telephone keyboard; the keys are arranged in a grid pattern with three columns and four rows. Each column and row has its own frequency. The tones are listed in Table 16.1. As can be seen from the table, when a 2 is pressed, the tone telephone generates two frequencies, 697 and 1336 Hz. It also produces the sum and difference frequencies, 2033 and 639 Hz. These are also unique for each column-row pair.

Because this scheme has been implemented widely, the cost of such keyboards using DTMF is very low. As a result, these keyboards are now used in all kinds of applications. The other key reason for the wide applicability of this scheme is that all the signaling frequencies used lie in the voice band. All sorts of communication equipment has been and is being made to transmit frequencies in this band.

This make retrofits very easy. No new special equipment is required to send data over a radio or communications system designed to transmit voice frequencies. Many remote control applications linked by radio or telephone systems use this. One common example is navigating through a "telephone maze" using the keyboard of your telephone to control automatic switching equipment. No operator is needed.

Table 16.1
DTMF Tones

1	2	3	697 Hz
4	5	6	770 Hz
7	8	9	852 Hz
*	0	#	941 Hz
1209 Hz	1336 Hz	1477 Hz	—

CALL PROGRESS TONES

Because DTMF is used to dial, other frequencies might also be used to control the operation of the telephone system. These special frequencies are called call progress tones. The tones selected for the DTMF system were carefully chosen to make sure they did not interfere with the previously established call progress tones.

The philosophy of using two tones instead of one to ensure that voice conversations do not trigger telephone equipment inadvertently is not unique to DTMF. All the call progress tones are also dual-frequency combinations. Unlike the DTMF tones, however, the call progress tones also switch ON and OFF to simulate ringing, and so forth. Even dial tone is only turned ON for a specific length of time, usually about 20 sec, although here it does not truly switch until one goes on-hook and off-hook again.

The tones used for these activities are presented in Table 16.2. Note that the busy and the no circuits available tones use the same frequency pairs. The only difference is that the busy signal switches half as quickly as the no circuit available signal. If you recall the last time you got such a signal, you may have described it as a fast busy signal. As can be seen from Table 16.2, you were correct.

SWITCHING STATION HIERARCHY

The switching system used by all carriers is structured hierarchically to some degree. However, different organizations implement different numbers of layers in the structure depending on many factors. This section will describe the switching station structure as it was when there was a monopoly and will serve as an introduction to the basic structures that all systems must use.

When the telephone system was a monopoly, there were five classes of switching stations, then called central offices. A switching station is a location where users lines are connected to switching equipment that connects to other switching stations. These other switching stations may be local or long distance, depending on whom the caller is contacting. The lower the number of office class, the more sophisticated the switching.

Table 16.2
Call Progress Tones

Tone Designation	Frequency (Hz)	Switching Frequency (sec)
Dial	350 and 440	20
Ring back	440 and 480	2
Busy	480 and 620	1/2
No circuits available	480 and 620	1/4

Switching stations are connected by trunks, which are four-wire circuits carrying PCM-coded data in the T-carrier hierarchy described in Chapter 11.

The traditional hierarchy of central offices was broken up into five classes of switching stations. Class 5 offices are where the local and long-distance calls enter or exit the hierarchy. It was the local switching station. If the calling and called parties are connected to the same local switching station, the call never goes outside that switching station. The computers running the switching equipment route the call right there. These computers are either special-purpose machines or generalized computers. The computer runs the software that is used to operate a crossbar switch or similar equipment that makes the connection between the two calling parties.

As the distance between the calling parties grows, or the traffic on the network grows, calls are not switched inside the local switching station but are passed up the hierarchy to lower-level offices. The lower the level of the office, the higher the bandwidth lines that connect to it. All switching stations are connected to all others.

Class 1 offices were the top of the pyramid. Again, note that traditionally, each class office can complete calls to any other class office. The telephone system at that time tried to use the office class of the highest number possible to connect your call because if the call can be completed without passing it up the hierarchy, the "cost" of the call to the service provider is less because it moves through less switching gear.

This is not always possible due to congestion on the telephone system. As congestion increases, more calls are passed up the hierarchy to lower and lower class offices. For example, at 1 A.M. on Sunday night, virtually any call made would be passed directly between class 5 offices. On the other hand, at 1 P.M. on Mother's Day, it is very likely that a call will be passed up at least one level in the hierarchy. The traditional hierarchical architecture is shown in Figure 16.2.

Figure 16.2
Traditional telephone switching hierarchy.

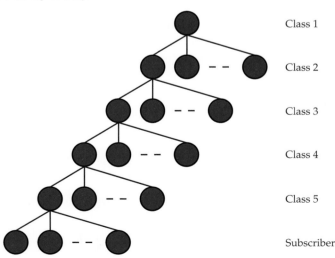

Class 1

Class 2

Class 3

Class 4

Class 5

Subscriber

Today, the modern telephone system does not rely on this strict hierarchy to route calls. A more modern approach using a dynamic routing algorithm to route calls efficiently through the network is used. Dynamic routing is discussed briefly in Chapter 15. Additionally, the system today uses a technology called SONET to physically carry calls from one office to another. SONET is an advanced optical network that features much higher maximum bandwidths than that obtainable with the T-carrier system.

■ SWITCHING STATION SWITCH

The digital switches that are in use today were first introduced about 1980 and are made by several manufacturers including Siemens, Northern Telecom, Fujitsu, and Lucent. Lucent and Northern Telecom dominate the industry. Lucent switches all have names like 4ESS and 5ESS, and Northern Telecom switches have names like DMS and S/DMS.

Figure 16.2 shows that each level of the hierarchy must be able to communicate other switching stations of the same level and above to route calls. As discussed above, the idea is to route the call from source to destination as efficiently as possible. Just as in routing, usually this means that it should go through as few switching stations, or hops, as possible. Each switching station may have from one to several switches. There may be old analog switches designed to handle dial telephones, switches from different manufacturers, and switches of different capability and integration. This comes about not only through technological evolution but also due to the need to support existing line types.

The oldest of these switches, now removed from service, are the crossbar switches. These switches consisted of a grid of 10 horizontal wires and 10 vertical wires. At each intersection, a switch is placed. This allows these devices to make up to 10 separate connections from 100 contact points. Additionally, the 100 contact points are controlled by 5 horizontal bars and 10 vertical bars operated by electromagnets. The great size of these units per call switch is surprising by today's standards, and the speed of switching was very slow.

The next generation of switches was electrical in nature but still analog in operation. These devices have also disappeared from the field today. In their day, the most common was the AT&T 1AESS. This switch was widely used and worked with the AT&T 3B line of computers. It consisted of three major components:

1. Switching network
2. System control
3. Input-output units

The switching network included signal receivers, ringing circuits, maintenance circuits, and the circuitry used to count the coins inserted in pay telephones.

The system control included all the call handling instructions, control of the switching network, and timing of calls for billing. The programming for these functions is called program store. The terminology used was a stored program-controlled system. The idea, now commonplace, but at the time innovative, was that because the switching was controlled by a program, written in software, great flexibility would result from this approach.

Changes in service offerings could be accomplished through a software update flexibility rather than requiring a new hardware configuration in the switch. Additionally, the facility of a software environment allowed diagnostic and management software routines to be written and used as never before. Finally, an electronic analog switch, usually a transistor, was much faster than an electromagnetic switch, so TDM could be implimented due to the faster switching speeds now available.

The input-output units are just the units that provide a communications path into and out of the switch, usually to other switching stations.

The next revolution was the digital switch using PAM-PCM coding to intermix voice and data lines flexibly. These devices are in wide use today, with Lucent models carrying the numbers 4ESS and 5ESS. The 5ESS switch is the most widely installed switch and can accommodate a wide variety of digital services and technology including ISDN, SONET, and so forth.

■ FEATURE GROUPS

Four levels of switching are still used. These are called feature groups. A feature group is the switching arrangement that the IXC and LEC use to allow users to make long-distance calls across LATAs and to access the correct LEC on each end. The four feature groups are known as A, B, C, and D.

Feature group A is used by the LECs to offer connections to an IXC using local subscriber lines rather than trunks. This means that the quality of the connection is lower than the other feature groups and so the cost is less. Long-distance calls within a LATA use feature group A. If more than a 1 is dialed to reach your IXC, the carrier is using feature group A and passing some of the savings on to you.

Feature group B is widely used by companies to establish long-distance connections using IXC leased lines. It is also the feature group that is used by the local switching station to connect to IXC trunk lines when the call goes outside the LATA. It features a trunk connection and so is of higher quality than feature group A.

Feature group B is implemented very simply. If a user, for example a company, wants to use a long-distance trunk line for some period of time, a technician calls a seven-digit telephone number of the form, 950-XXXX. This connects to the IXC that has been selected to provide the long-distance service. The last four digits of the telephone number vary among different IXCs. For example, MCI might be 950-1234 and Sprint might be 950-6789. Once the connection has been made, a personal identification number (PIN) is required to authorize the billing just as for your ATM card. Once the PIN has been correctly entered, the long-distance connection is established and billing begins.

It is not always true that the number is actually dialed and PIN entered manually. Specialized equipment is often implemented as PC software that does this from a point-and-click-type interface. There also are smart phones and dialers that can accomplish this task automatically, hiding this interface from the user.

Feature group C is a holdover from the days when the Bell System had a monopoly on both local and long-distance services. If the call stays entirely inside the elements of the old Bell System, for example a RBOC and AT&T long distance, the connection may be made with feature group C. This group has the same functionally as B but does not have the capability of dialing multiple IXC service providers. It is gradually being phased out, and if you live in a large city, it has probably already gone.

Feature group D is the standard for today. You have probably already used feature group D without realizing it. If you have had the opportunity to select your long-distance carrier or IXC and have it automatically used when a long-distance call is placed, you have used feature group D. This group is implemented by the user dialing a 1 prior to the long-distance call, and the call is automatically routed to the IXC previously selected. When you see advertisements for alternate long distance service, usually offering savings, if you have to dial anything other than a 1 to reach that provider, it is using feature group A, not B, C, or D.

■ DIALING AND NUMBER PLANS

As already discussed, a prefix, 1, is dialed for feature group D to access an IXC to carry your long-distance call. The rest of the familiar 10-digit telephone number breaks down as follows.

The first three digits dialed after the feature group is selected are the area code, a three digit number which represent a geographical area. In the past every area code had a 0 or 1 as the middle digit. This was used by the local office to identify that the number was an area code and not a switching station code, or as it used to be known, an exchange. Today, this restriction on area codes no longer holds. Due to the proliferation of new devices that need telephone numbers, fax machines, pagers, cellular telephone numbers, and so forth, this pattern could no longer be followed; the numbers just ran out.

The last four numbers are referred to as the customer number and define the connection from the local switching station to the telephone. As can be seen, there must be many local switching stations in any significant area because each exchange can only connect to a restricted number of customer numbers or telephones. An area that shares an exchange is referred to as a numbering plan.

As alluded to above, historically the seven-digit telephone number was broken up into two subgroups, the exchange and the customer number. The exchange was the three-letter or three-number prefix and the four-digit number that follows was the customer number. In the past, word *exchange* was in common usage and was usually defined as two letters, pronounced as a word and a number. For example, one might say, the number was Elgin 7-4117. Where the exchange was EL7, or Elgin 7, and the customer number was 4117.

Additionally, international calling must be accommodated and so each country has a unique prefix code that is dialed first. You are probably not surprised to discover that the country code for North America is 1. To dial a call where the destination is not part of the North American numbering plan (e.g., not area code-exchange-customer number), one uses the international numbering plan to reach the rest of the world. This numbering plan from the United States is defined as follows: 011-country code-city code-subscriber number, where 011 is the access to international service.

All countries do not have the same number of numbers in any particular telephone number. For example, a subscriber outside a city may have a shorter city code than a subscriber living inside the city. Thus, unlike the United States where every telephone has 10 numbers, when dialing internationally, even in the same local area, different telephones will have a different number of numbers. Each country, just like the United States, has its own number plan, but they all can fit into the international dialing scheme outlined above. The country codes for anywhere in the world are easily obtained from operator assistance.

Switched Lines

There are two main types of circuits that offer choices of connectivity to users of the telephone system. The first is the traditional dial-up line. This is exactly like the traditional telephone line. Often in data communications, this term will be used as a short way to refer to telephone lines dedicated to modem use. The idea is that the modems dial up their connection. However, there are many types of dial-up lines and not all of them are the same as a voice telephone line. Two prominent types are switched 56 and T-1 lines configured to be dialable. These are wider bandwidth lines configured so that a modem can dial them up when the connection is needed.

These higher bandwidth lines are also switched services and are really no different from dial-up access. The terminology *switched* comes from the fact that the service is switched ON or OFF by the telephone system. Essentially, what one does is dial up an access number and switch on switched service. Sometimes when organizations need high bandwidth connections only periodically, they will arrange to have dial-up lines available. The service provider then only charges them for time the line is actually in use, along with a basic monthly charge for the access or opportunity to use.

The second circuit type is known as a dedicated, or leased, line. This dedicated circuit is leased from the service provider and dedicated to a specific organization. In many cases, the company will pay a premium for specific performance levels, such as a maximum error rate for traffic on the line. In large companies, these dedicated lines are replacing traditional analog voice lines. For example, a company would bring in a dedicated T-1 line into its PBX and share its 24 channels among many more users. The analog voice lines are then removed, and the company pays one line charge for the T-1. Often this results in cost savings for the company.

When a dedicated line is leased from a service provider, that line is charged 24 hours a day, 365 days a year. Telephone line charges are computed from the basic model

$$\text{cost} = (\text{bandwidth})(\text{distance})(\text{time})(\text{profit margin}) \qquad \textbf{(16-1)}$$

This means that if a dedicated line is leased, it is advisable to be able to use it most of the time at most of its bandwidth. If this is not the case, dedicated lines are not cost effective, and it would make more sense to stay with dial-up or usage-based lines. These calculations will be illustrated in the next sections.

Representative numbers are shown to illustrate the cross-over points. It is important to understand that although the costs shown in the following tables are representa-

Table 16.3
Voice-Grade Calling Band Charges

Band	Distance (miles)	First Minute Charge (cents)	Average Minute Charge (cents)
A	0–8	3	1
B	9–16	7	2
C	17+	10	5

tive of those encountered today in one state from one carrier, they vary widely with location and carrier. Additionally, as competition grows in the local markets, these costs will alter.

A related switched line is ISDN service. ISDN service offers 144 kbps of data bandwidth. Although ISDN is not widely adapted, it will be included for a cost comparison. Note that ISDN requires a significant expense for specialized equipment at the user site. This component of cost will not be considered.

Voice-Grade Line (Analog). The charges for a traditional voice-grade line are a fixed cost and a usage charge that depends on the distance of the link and the time it is connected. There are three local distance bands, as they are called, the A, B, and C bands. These are summarized in Table 16.3. Each has a different cost per minute of use, with a first minute charge that is slightly higher; both are shown in the table.

The fixed cost is about $20 per month, per line. Probably the largest advantage to using an analog voice-grade line to pass data is the low cost and wide availability of the termination devices, modems, the most familiar DCE device.

ISDN (Digital). ISDN lines are charged out very similarly to voice-grade lines except that specialized end equipment must be paid for. Additionally, as mentioned above, special end equipment is required at each end of the link. You should plan on about $200 per end to account for this equipment cost. This end equipment is required for any digital service. Since the line data is already in digital form, there is no need for a modem; however, a specialized interface is required to change the voltages and line codes to something suitable for interfacing into your computer.

ISDN pricing is usually structured into three components: installation, monthly service charge, and a usage charge. The usage charge is based on the same band distances as voice-grade lines, but the charges are higher. Typical numbers for the first two components are

Installation	$150
Monthly service	$40

Table 16.4
ESDN Calling Band Charges

Band	Distance (miles)	First Minute Charge (cents)	Average Minute Charge (cents)
A	0–8	7	2
B	9–16	15	4
C	17+	20	20

Because ISDN is a two-channel service, once it is installed, data transmission on both channels must be paid for. This means that all the usage charges shown in Table 16.3 for voice-grade bands are roughly doubled. This is shown in Table 16.4.

Switched 56 (Digital).   A switched 56 service is digital in nature and does not use a modem. Switched 56 is perhaps the most cost effective way of purchasing bandwidth from a service provider. Essentially, switched 56 uses a CSU/DSU to access time division multiplexers that offer access to multiple 56 kbps DS-0 lines. (See Chapter 11 for a definition of DS levels.) This allows the user to access one or more 56 kbps lines on demand, depending on the CSU/DSU capability.

As a user, you only pay a fixed monthly charge for the right to access a switched 56 line and, when accessed, pay according to a line change formula similar to that shown in equation 16-1. These lines are used in two ways; first, they are often combined with a statistical multiplexer that accesses lines when the traffic requires it. As the users need more bandwidth, additional switched 56 kbps lines are switched ON. As the bandwidth reduces, the lines are switched OFF.

The second way these lines are used is as backup lines to dedicated lines. If a circumstance occurs where the dedicated line is severed or broken in some manner, the data transfer can still be accomplished by switching to backup switched 56 line(s). This is an inexpensive insurance policy for critical data services. Today, it seems that all data services are becoming critical data services.

Switched services are no longer confined to just 56 kbps lines. Virtually any combination of DS-0 lines can be purchased for switched 56-type service. Additionally, DS-1 and DS-3 lines are also being sold in this manner. As competition increases among service providers, the customer benefits from the flexibility offered for line access methods.

Switched 56 service is a 56 kbps data link that allows it to be turned ON and OFF with a simple telephone call. This service is designed to link two ends of a data circuit. The usage charge is based on a kilobyte count of the data that is transferred over the link; usually a megabit-packet count is used. There are two fixed charges and one variable charge. The fixed charges are

Set up	$450
Fixed monthly charge	$100

The variable charge is priced per megabit of data transferred; typically this is about $0.01 per million bits transferred. The setup charge is one time only, but the monthly charge must be paid every month, independent of the actual usage of the link.

■ EXAMPLE 16.1

As a telecommunications specialist you are asked to recommend a cost-effective solution to the following situation. The company has a need to link two of its sites with a line that would be used 4 hours a day, 20 days a month. The bandwidth needed is 56 kbps. Given the cost numbers in this chapter, which solution is best for the company? Assume that both locations are in band B. Additionally, ignore all setup and end equipment costs. Round all charges to the nearest dollar.

1. Voice-grade line: A dial-up line needs to be associated with a modem to determine the data rate. Suppose that the modem that will be used functions at a data rate of 28.8 kbps. That means that two dial-up lines will be needed to support a 56 kbps link.

$$(2 \text{ lines})[(\$20.00) + (20 \text{ days})(4 \text{ hr})(60 \text{ min})(\$0.02)] = \$232.00$$

2. ISDN line:

$$\$40.00 + (20 \text{ days})(4 \text{ hr})(60 \text{ min})(\$0.04) = \$232.00$$

3. Dedicated 56 kbps:

$$\$10 + \$10 + \$250 = \$270$$

4. Switched 56:

$$\frac{\$100.00 + (20 \text{ days})(4 \text{ hr})(60 \text{ min})(60 \text{ sec})(56 \text{ kbps})(\$0.01)}{1,000,000} = \$262.50$$

■ EXAMPLE 16.2

You recommended using two voice-grade lines with modems and it was accepted. Now, however, the company's usage has grown. Instead of just 4 hours a day, accounting is now using this link to update its payables schedules every evening for an additional 6 hours. Has the situation changed?

1. Voice-grade line:

$$(2 \text{ lines})[(\$20.00) + (20 \text{ days})(10 \text{ hr})(60 \text{ min})(\$0.02)] = \$520.00$$

2. ISDN line:

$$\$40.00 + (20 \text{ days})(10 \text{ hr})(60 \text{ min})(\$0.04) = \$520.00$$

3. Dedicated 56 kbps:

$$\$10 + \$10 + \$250 = \$270$$

4. Switched 56:

$$\frac{\$100.00 + (20 \text{ days})(10 \text{ hr})(60 \text{ mins})(60 \text{ sec})(56 \text{ kbps})(\$0.01)}{1,000,000} = 503.00$$

As can be seen, the increased usage now makes the dedicated 56 kbps line the clear winner. A dedicated line is usually a good choice where additional traffic growth is expected as this growth will come at no cost.

Example 16.02 illustrates an important lesson. Usage changes in an organization over time, and the telecommunication links need to be reevaluated regularly as this usage changes. Additionally, in todays unregulated market, rate changes and new product offerings also will change the parameters used to find the best solution for any particular situation.

Dedicated Lines
Dedicated 56 (Digital).   Dedicated 56 kbps links are more complex than traditional lines. This service is often referred to as DDS service. DDS services, because they are already digital in nature, do not require a modem at each end. Instead, a DSU is used to terminate the line. A DSU is more expensive than a modem. To trade off this cost, a digital line offers increased performance over an analog line at the same data rate.

To compute the cost for a dedicated 56 kbps link, one needs to know a few extra things about the application. First, where the exchange is and where the service originates and terminates must be known; this determines the variable distance-related element of the charge for the service. For the numbers presented below, a 10 mile distance is assumed. Usually, the distance is between the originating site and the local switching station; and on the other end, the distance between the destination site and its local switching station is small enough that it is treated as a fixed mileage charge.

There is also usually a small charge for actual termination of the circuit at each end. This accounts for the physical hookup that the telephone system does to implement each end of the circuit. It is referred to as the termination charge.

It is important to understand that the charges quoted depend on the length of the contract signed for the service. For example, the numbers presented below might correspond to a 1 year contract; if the contract was extended to a 3 year term, you should plan on saving about 10% in both the usage and fixed elements of the cost. Representative values are presented below for each component:

Fixed mileage charge	$10
Termination charge	$10
Variable mileage charge	$250
Installation	$700

The first three charges are month in and month out. The installation charge is one time only. These charges can vary a lot depending on how many circuits you subscribe to, for how long, and whether you purchase them directly from the LEC or through a third party.

56 kbps of Data in a 64 kbps Channel

The data rate for each of the digital services was 56 kbps. How is this data rate compared to the DS-0 rate defined in Chapter 11? The DS-1 frame is composed of twenty-four 64 kbps DS-0 frames. If the 56 kbps channels are formed from 64 kbps DS-0 frames contained in a DS-1 frame, what happened to the other 8 kbps in the examples above? This is the effect of clear channel capacity that was introduced earlier and is revisited here.

Clear channel capacity describes how much of the DS-1 frame can actually be filled with customer data. The eighth bit in each PCM word that represents the voice conversation is not always representing voice. Each sixth frame's least significant PCM bit is robbed and used to signal the on-hook or off-hook status. A 1 value for this bit signals on-hook, and a 0 value signals off-hook. This status tells the telephone system if the call is still in progress. This is called robbed bit signaling, and although it theoretically results in some distortion for the caller who is using that particular frame, the distortion is not noticeable.

It does have an important consequence if a DS-1 frame is used for transmitting data, as has been done here. Because it is generally desirable to have each frame contain the same amount of data, in reality only 7 bits of data capacity exist in each PCM word. This means that the clear channel capacity of each data frame is only 56 kbps. This result also modifies the clear channel DS-1 aggregate data rate to

$$\text{DS-1 clear channel aggregate data rate} = (24 \text{ channels})(56 \text{ kbps}) = 1.344 \text{ Mbps}$$

Multidrop Line

The last type of telephone line is a multidrop line. It was not considered in the pricing models because it is only used for very low-rate communications where cost is a primary factor and each user on the line only needs it for short periods of time.

Multidrop lines are used whenever a single user needs to communicate simultaneously with some number of other users. One of the lines on a multidrop circuit is designated the master. All other users who wish to communicate to other users on that multidrop line must first pass their message to the master, which then relays it to the appropriate user.

These lines are often used in data transfer situations where one location is configured as data central and all remote stations send their data to that station. One example might be a company with several data-logging sites in a small area. Each data-logging site would be connected to the company's data center and would be slaved to a master terminal on a multidrop line. The data center could poll each data-logging site for its information or just wait for a site to request access to the line to send data to the center.

Multidrop lines, although still available, are becoming obsolete as the cost advantages are outweighed by the need for more than one communication to take place simultaneously. In a multidrop line environment, only one conversation takes place at a time, and all conversations must be routed through the master site. If the data has a value related to its timeliness, for example, a stock quote, a multidrop solution would not be a good one. Increasingly, this is the case in data traffic, and multidrop lines are disappearing. Figure 16.3 illustrates the two-wire multidrop line. Four-wire multidrop lines are also available.

Figure 16.3
Two-wire multidrop.

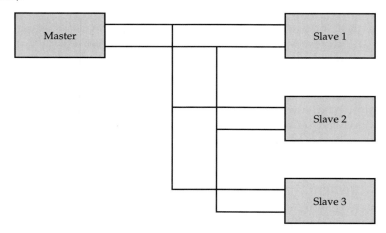

Multipoint DDS line

There is also type of line called a multipoint DDS line. This is usually a 56 kbps DDS service that is configured as a master-slave setup. This is done by configuring the CSU/DSU attached to each link as either a master or slave. The master CSU/DSU controls the destination path by individually addressing the slave DSU/CSU when information is to be transferred between the two. Only one path is selected at one time. This is shown in Figure 16.4. This arrangement accomplishes the same thing as the traditional multidrop but at a higher cost. The compensation for this cost penalty is a greater data transfer rate.

Figure 16.4
Multipoint DDS line.

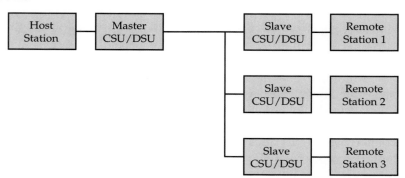

■ COMPONENTS

In the following sections, common components used in telecommunications are defined. Much confusion can result from not understanding what functionality a particular component can provide.

Modem

A modem is the most familiar type of DCE device. It is now installed with virtually every PC purchased and is used by large numbers of people to surf the Wide World Web. Conventional modems convert a digital modulating signal into an analog modulated signal. Earlier chapters described the three basic types of modulation: amplitude, frequency, and phase.

The facsimile machine also uses a modem to dial and/or answer the telephone line to which it is connected. Facsimile machines use a special handshaking sequence for their modems that allows another modem to distinguish between another facsimile machine calling and a modem not designed for a facsimile. In this way, a single telephone line can be used for both traditional modem-to-modem transmissions and facsimile-to-facsimile transmissions.

Modems designed for different applications come in a wide range of data rates. Those designed for use on an analog voice-grade telephone line are normally now shipped featuring maximum transfer rates of 53 kbps.

Limited-Distance Modem

A limited-distance modem, also called a short-hand modem, is not a modem at all in the traditional sense. There is no modulation or demodulation. It is just a line driver for a digital line. A typical application is to take a digital stream and regenerate it for retransmission. This regeneration function cleans up the signal by removing any noise accumulation and retransmits the signal at full voltage levels. Because the signal is already in digital form, the regeneration is accomplished by just reclocking the received signal and passing it to another line driver. These devices are pure physical layer devices.

CSU and DSU

The next component examined is the CSU/DSU. Many times these terms are used interchangeably, possibly because although they have separate functions, very often they are packaged into the same physical box. Additionally, many times a CSU has DSU functionality as well. These devices come in three forms, stand-alone CSUs and DSUs and combination CSU/DSUs. At least one of these devices is required for any digital line termination.

A CSU is used to connect a switched digital line to a DCE device. Switched lines include T-1, and fractional T-1, switched 56 service. It sits between the telephone system and a DSU. A CSU protects the switched line from electrical damage, like lightening, and provides a way for the telephone system to test the circuit through loopback. This allows the telephone system to query the status of the line by querying the CSU. This same conversation ability is what allows switched line access with a CSU connected to a DTE. The CSU always connects to the switched telephone system.

A DSU is exactly like a line driver or repeater. It is also referred to as a digital modem and is very similar to a limited-distance modem. It is the digital interface between a DTE device and a digital phone line. A DSU is all that is needed when connecting to a dedicated 56 kbps DDS line. It is a physical layer device that performs voltage-level and line code conversion. An example is from V.35 or RS-232 on the customer side to alternate mark inversion (AMI) encoding on the telephone system side. If the telephone line is switched, it must be combined with a CSU to work. In a combination CSU/DSU the DSU always connects to the customer equipment, typically a RS-232 or V.35 interface/LAN interface.

Because it is more common today to have switched services rather than dedicated line access, most of the time both traditional DSU and CSU functionality are needed. Manufacturers recognized this and have responded by making a box containing both a DSU and CSU, which is called a DSU/CSU or CSU/DSU.

Usually the best approach is to purchase a DSU for the dedicated lines speed and characteristics required and then a CSU containing DSU functionality for all digital switched lines. For most standard line rates there is a CSU available that will also provide the DSU functionality. Figure 16.5 illustrates the applications where each is used and the type of DTE devices that are associated with that type of service. Note that the

Figure 16.5
PBX.

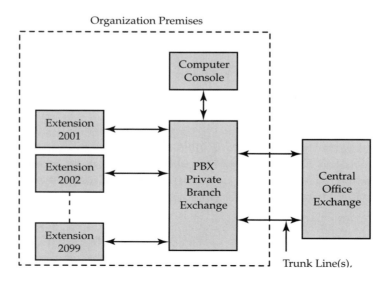

combination DSU/CSU is the most used and in most cases will be what is needed for modern switched service access. Note that the DSU in the top of the figure is optional if the signaling is the same on both sides (D4-AMI, etc).

The other interesting thing a CSU/DSU can do is to set the timing source for the switched digital service, usually a T-1 line. In all T-1 networks, *only one timing source is allowed.* All the equipment connected to the line needs to use the same clock. Typically, there are two choices. The first, and most common, is to use the timing derived from the network. In this case, the CSU/DSU gets its timing signal from the telephone system directly or sometimes from another piece of equipment at the other end of the line, such as another CSU/DSU.

In the second case, the other CSU/DSU must be configured to provide this timing. This is usually simply done by setting a switch to internal timing source. When this occurs, the CSU/DSU sends a timing signal out to the other equipment attached to the link. The problem with this approach is that this timing does not take into account the delay in the cable that attaches the CSU/DSU to the link. Because of this, timing errors occur due to this phase error. In most situations, it is better to allow each CSU/DSU to derive its timing directly from the network.

Each CSU/DSU must be configured in one of these two ways. It is very important that only one timing source on each link be used. If you do not control both ends of the link, it is important to work this out with the other party and the telephone system.

PBX

A PBX is in effect, a miniature telephone system. It is also known as a private automatic branch exchange, or PABX. Both terms are used interchangeably and mean the same thing. A PBX uses one or more trunk lines of the telephone system and breaks up that bandwidth among a large number of users. These are often used by organizations to economically install large numbers of telephones in a building.

It is much cheaper in the long run to purchase or lease a PBX and use that to connect to each telephone than it is to bring in a separate circuit for each telephone. With the PBX approach, a caller dials a main number and then presses an extension for the particular telephone desired. Sometimes a caller dials a main exchange, the first three numbers of a telephone number, and the last four numbers directly connect to a telephone. It depends on how the system is set up and how many telephones are connected to the PBX.

When dialing out using a PBX, one DS-0 segment is switched to the telephone. This is indicated by the presence of a dial tone. The PBX has a certain number of these to partition out. These are switched to users as needed. Because all telephones are not in use at any one time, many fewer DS-0 segments are needed than the number of telephones. As a result, less bandwidth must be leased from the telephone system. This is why PBX systems are economically attractive to organizations.

PBX systems are controlled from a PC or similar computer console. This computer controls the PBX switching that was discussed above. It also provides the interface for managing the PBX. Examples include

1. Designating the code to dial an outside line; for example, dialing 9 for an outside line
2. Setting area code restrictions by extension
3. Keeping track of outgoing call destinations by extension
4. Breaking out billing by department or extension
5. Changing extensions, adding new extensions, deleting old extensions, and so forth

Figure 16.6 shows how a PBX connects into and out of a promise.

66-Block

A 66-block is also commonly known as a punch-down block or sometimes as a quick-connect block. It is a piece of plastic that is about 2 ft 8 in. tall and $2\,^1/_2$ inches wide with metal clips that are designed to be used to connect two or four wire circuits to. These quick-connect clips eliminate the need to strip the wire when installing standard 20 to 26 AWG wire. When used with the appropriate tool as the conductor wire is pressed down into the clip slot, the spring action of the clip effectively strips the wire and makes a good connection. This tool is known as a punch-down impact tool. It is a spring-loaded device with replaceable blades for stripping the wire and placing it into the clip slot. It is an essential tool for working with punch-down blocks.

It is important not to confuse quick connect clips with bridging clips. A bridging clip is designed to complete the circuit across quick-clip locations. A bridging clip is the demarcation point discussed in the next paragraph. Sixty-six-blocks are usually mounted on a 4 × 8 ft sheet of plywood in arrays arranged in horizontal rows. All cir-

Figure 16.6
CSU and DSU.

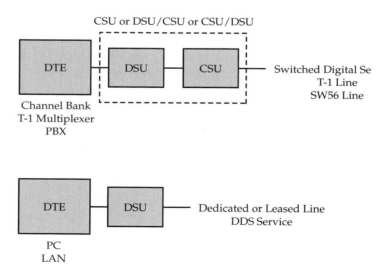

cuits, whether they be subscriber (two-wire) or trunk (four-wire) when they enter the building are terminated here. Then any internal connections inside the building are made. Any connections designed to go outside the building are also connected at this location. Each 66-block is designed to terminate 50 pairs of wire.

This arrangement provides a location where the telephone companies responsibility ends and the organizations begins, known as the demarcation point. On one side of the bridging clip are the lines that connect to the switching station, and on the other side are the lines that connect to telecommunication equipment, for example, a PBX, modems, telephones, and so forth. The importance of the demarcation point is that when problems are reported with a circuit, the telephone system only holds responsibility up to the demarcation point. If the company check the line to that location and nothing is wrong, it goes home.

This illustrates why it is important to know where this point is. Check the wiring inside your building from the DCE equipment to the demarcation point. If this is okay when you have a problem, do not waste time waiting for the telephone system to tell you that the problem is on your side. Quite often, the telephone system will bill you if it is called out and the problem is not on its side of the demarcation point. The bridging clip is easy to place and remove, allowing an easy way to isolate one side of the circuit from the other. This can prove very useful when debugging circuit problems and can save time and money spent on wasted service calls.

The name 66-block holds on even though both other names provided here are more descriptive. It is a proprietary name of a specific product manufactured by the Western Electric Company. Because it for many years was exclusively used by the Bell System for this purpose, the name has stuck. This is in much the same way as the proprietary name Kleenex has stuck as the common name for facial tissue, even though many brands are available today. Figure 16.7 illustrates the connection of half of a two-wire circuit using quick-connect clips and bridging clips across the demarcation point.

There is also a similar system to the 66-block system called the 110 cross-connect system. It also is a method for terminating twisted pair circuits. However, the 110 system is designed primarily for voice-only lines due to the increased density of the wire pairs in the block and the decreased accessibility. These 110-blocks are best used when the wiring is not subject to change and demarcation issues are not likely to arise. Therefore, they are ideal for large installations of 2-wire subscriber circuits and should not be used for data circuits.

Channel Banks

Channel banks are specialized T-1 multiplexers. They work in exactly the same way a standard TDM would, with some special limitations, because they are designed for use with voice channels of a fixed bandwidth, 3100 Hz.

A channel bank is designed to carry 24 channels of voice over a digital line. Each channel is fixed at 3100 Hz bandwidth. Because these devices are designed for voice, the clear channel data rate is only 56 kbps. By far, the most common channel bank is the D4 channel bank introduced in the 1970s. It is a dual 24 channel terminal; these groups of 24 channels are called di-groups when talking about channel banks. A di-group is de-

Figure 16.7
Bridging clip illustration.

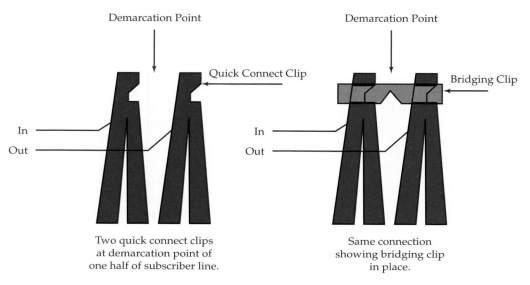

fined as a pair of 12 channel groups that are combined to create a single 24 channel group of data.

Each di-group has 24 slots for channel cards. A channel card is a card that provides an interface for whatever data or voice is to be inserted in that 3100 Hz slot. There are a wide range of channel cards, about 50, available in two broad groups, voice and data. There are cards for four- and two-wire circuits, and there are cards for a variety of physical connector types and data rates. Some cards occupy more than one slot, yielding interface data rates as high as 672 kbps. Other cards operate as low as 2.4 kbps but still require a full 3100 Hz bandwidth slot.

Both T-1 multiplexers and channel banks are generally intended to interface a group of data channels to a T-1 line. They both must work with the line coding types described in the next section. However, although T-1 multiplexers can handle an arbitrary number of inputs, for example, 96 circuits at 9600 bps, a channel bank can interface a maximum of 24 individual inputs. Additionally, T-1 multiplexers frequently offer sophisticated and flexible software bandwidth allocation; again, channel banks have 24 channels of 56 kbps. Channel banks are designed to work well with voice or analog inputs, T-1 multiplexers, or for that matter, any TDM that will require a digital input.

Channel banks are essentially outdated equipment and will probably disappear at the same time that the last analog telephone disappears and ISDN becomes universal. Because that will not be for some time, expect to see channel banks in use for the foreseeable future.

■ LINE CODING

In Chapter 6 line codes and pulse shaping were briefly introduced. You may recall that the preferred line coding was polar NRZ. The multiplexing framing that takes place in the telephone system was described in Chapter 11 on multiplexing. Here the line codes used for DS-1 type frames will be described. The codes used are all polar, but feature return to zero, (RZ) states. Such polar RZ codes always feature three code states, $-1, 0, +1$.

The first code, AMI, is used in most channel banks. It was developed to ensure the dc component of the binary code averages out to 0 V. AMI codes do a good job of breaking up any consecutive string of 1 bits, common in voice transmissions. The name tells you how it works, once you realized that a mark is another name for a 1 bit. Every other, (alternate) 1 bit (mark) is inverted (inversion). So, consecutive 1 bits are coded as $1, -1$.

The second code Bipolar 8 Zero Substitution (B8ZS), was developed to improve upon the AMI code, which like any standard line code does not change state for long strings of the same bit state. The B8ZS code explicitly substitutes for any continuous string of eight 0 bits that occur. Four of the eight 0 bits are replicated, and four are substituted to yield at least two zero crossings during the 8 bit times. This means that a frame encoded according to the B8ZS scheme will feature a maximum of seven consecutive 0 bits.

This substitution for long strings of zero bits is important because all clock synchronization techniques rely on periodic zero crossings to maintain synchronization. The solution was to change the line code so that this could occur. In normal voice transmissions, once they are PCM encoded, regular transitions occur. This, however, is not the case when raw data is being transmitted. One cannot predict what the form of the data might be. Long strings of 1 bit state could easily occur, presenting a problem for synchronization circuitry.

Either AMI or B8ZS line codes can be used for voice frames. However, for data frames it is advisable to specify B8ZS coding to get around the synchronization problem identified above. Figure 16.8 illustrates how the AMI and B8ZS line codes work. Note

Figure 16.8
AMI and B8ZS line codes.

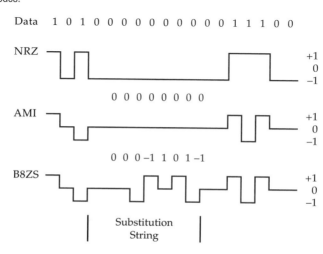

that there are two variations of B8ZS coding. The choice of the substitution code depends on the state of the last 1 bit prior to the substitution. If the last 1 bit was a +1, the code $000+1-10-1+1$ is used. If the last 1 bit was a −1, the code $000-1+10+1-1$ is used. In the figure, the latter substitution is shown.

Careful analysis of figure 16.8 shows that AMI is really a subset of B8ZS. To see this, examine the first few bits of each encoding: They are the same. The only difference in B8ZS is that any strings of 8 bits that are all zero are substituted for.

Note that an entire string of 8 bits must be substituted for; this means that one must look ahead to see if there really are eight 0 bits before beginning the substitution. Also, note that it is possible for the receiver to know that a substitution has taken place because the substitution string is one that cannot exist using the AMI encoding.

AMI requires that each alternate 1 bit be encoded as a 1 bit of opposite sign. In the B8ZS substitution string, this rule is violated by the substring $+10+1$. Therefore, it is impossible for a receiver to not notice a B8ZS substitution. Additionally, note that the B8ZS substitution string used depends on the state of the last AMI bit; this also violates the AMI rule.

Therefore, the first bit of the B8ZS substitution will alert the receiver that a B8ZS substitution has been made. Additionally, each substitution string preserves the alternate nature of each consecutive 1 bit following the substitution. When the receiver sees a B8ZS substitution, it replaces the substitution string with a series of eight 0 bits. Then the data string passed out of the receiver circuitry matches the original data stream. Example 16.3 illustrates the substitution.

■ EXAMPLE 16.3

Find the B8ZS substitution string for the 16-bit string of data. See Figure 16.9. Note that the substitution string selected depends on the state of the last 1 bit. In this example, it is a +1 after the AMI encoding.

■ TELEPHONES, PBXS, AND TRUNK BANDWIDTH CALCULATIONS

It is interesting to use knowledge of the bandwidth of telephone calls and an understanding of how a PBX works to calculate how many telephones a trunk of a specific size can handle. This depends to a large degree on how users use their telephones. In this section, a couple of examples will be worked out that will illustrate how this type of calculation is performed for users of a PBX.

In performing this type of calculation, there are two classes of calls that need to be considered. The first is those calls that never go outside the PBX. As can be seen from Figure 16.6, when a call is made that stays inside the building, no outside line is needed. In this case, none of the bandwidth of the trunk line to and from the switching station is used.

The second class of calls is those that use the outside trunk. These include both outgoing and incoming calls. It is this class of calls that determines the trunk utilization and bandwidth requirements.

Figure 16.9
Example 16.3

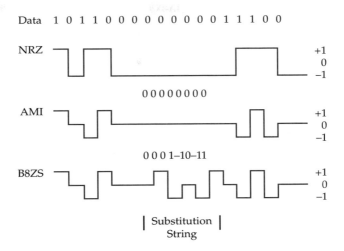

Before beginning the first example, it is important to note that this section is not intended to be used as a substitute for telephone system voice traffic engineering calculations. Rather, it is to give an intuitive approach to readers to address a small organizations needs that might be encountered in a typical work environment.

This is illustrated by the simplicity of the statistical model used. In this section, the average use of the telephones will be assumed to be the same for each hour of the day. Further, each call will be assumed to be of the same length. As must be clear, this is rarely the case; the number of calls during the lunch hour will not be the same as the number of calls in the hour before lunch. It is these statistical variations in the number of calls each hour and their duration that are the central difference between the approach below and real-world traffic engineering.

■ EXAMPLE 16.4

Imagine a company with a single PBX and a trunk consisting of a single T-1 line. Assume the average telephone makes and receives a total of 10 calls a day. Of this number, six are to or from outside numbers. If the average length of each call is 5 min, how many telephones can this trunk line support?

Begin with the observation that each working day, each telephone needs bandwidth on the trunk to support six calls that are 5 min long. Observing there are 8 hours per workday, the following utilization of each circuit results:

$$(6 \text{ calls})(5 \text{ min}) / (8 \text{ hr}) = \text{each telephone uses circuit 3.75 min/hr}$$

This number indicates how many telephones can share a single circuit. Because each telephone uses the circuit for 3.75 min each 60 minute hour, the following number of telephones that can share each circuit:

$$\frac{60}{3.75} = 16 \text{ telephones share circuit}$$

Because each circuit is a single 64 kbps DS-0 channel, and there are 24 per DS-1 trunk, the following number of telephones can be supported on a single DS-1 trunk line:

$$(16)(24 \text{ circuits}) = 384 \text{ telephones}$$

Now as must be clear, this calculation is only valid if just as each call is completed, another call is placed. This is an unrealistic assumption; in fact what would happen is that calls would regularly be blocked. This results when no circuit is available for the call. However, it would only be those calls that either were being placed to a number outside the office or those originating outside that would be effected by this. Calls from one extension to another, because they make no use of the trunk line, would be unaffected.

■ EXAMPLE 16.5

In this example, assume a purely analog communication system is being custom designed to connect two buildings with a private telephone system. Instead of the PCM/TDM system used in the last example, this one will use the FDM principle for dividing up the bandwidth. This example will illustrate the bandwidth efficiency of a purely analog approach.

Just as in the last example, there are an average of six calls in an 8 hour day, of average duration of 5 minutes, that must pass along the trunk between the two locations. Assume a bandwidth of 4 kHz per call, a 1 kHz guardband between calls, and a trunk bandwidth of 1.5 MHz. Find the utilization of each circuit in the same way as before:

$$(6 \text{ calls})(5 \text{ min}) / (8 \text{ hr}) = \text{each telephone uses circuit } 3.75 \text{ min} / \text{hr}$$

The calculation of how many telephones can share a circuit is also exactly the same:

$$\frac{60}{3.75} = 16 \text{ telephones share circuit}$$

However, a much different utilization of the bandwidth of the channel results. You may recall that the big disadvantage of a pulse modulation scheme such as PCM was the amount of bandwidth it requires. The impact of that will become very clear as the number of telephones per trunk is calculated. Remembering that each call will use 4 kHz of bandwidth in each direction for full duplex and 1 kHz of guardband, the following calculation for the number of channels per trunk results:

$$\frac{1.5 \text{ MHz}}{(2 \text{ circuits})(4 + 1 \text{ kHz})} = 150 \text{ circuits} / \text{trunk}$$

150 circuits per trunk result instead of just 24. This will greatly affect the total number of telephones a trunk can hold:

$$(16 \text{ telephones} / \text{circuit})(150 \text{ circuits} / \text{trunk}) = 2400 \text{ telephones} / \text{trunk}$$

As is illustrated by this example, sometimes the older FDM analog techniques of combining signals have a few surprises left in them. Note that if a half-duplex arrangement where each circuit shared a single 4 kHz channel were implemented, the number of telephones per trunk would double.

■ SWITCHING

To make a connection between two users of the telephone system, some kind of switching must take place inside the system to connect the two users. There are two main types of switching:

Circuit switching, connection oriented; the connection defines the path.

Packet switching, connectionless; no connection, arbitrary path for each packet.

Circuit Switching

Circuit switching involves the process of setting up and keeping open a connection between two users, hence, the classification connection oriented. It is the traditional method of connecting two users of the telephone system. The important thing about circuit switching is that the circuit is dedicated to those two users. This is the traditional conceptual way of connecting two telephone calls. This means that a dedicated wire is used to connect the two users, and all traffic flows between those two users will always be over the same wire or physical circuit. Every user has a dedicated circuit to the other user.

Circuit switching as used in the modern telephone system has not been that primitive for a long time. Today, circuit switching uses what are called virtual circuits. A virtual circuit is a physical circuit that is dedicated to the two users only so long as the telephone call persists. Once both parties hang up, the virtual circuit is released and the physical circuit they used becomes available for another call. If the same two users then immediately reconnect with each other, there is no assurance that they will use the same physical circuit. In all likelihood, it has already been switched to another call, and although the same two users are conversing, they are using a difference physical circuit but the same virtual circuit.

Packet Switching

Packet switching also involves the process of setting up and keeping open a communications path between two users, but with an important difference. Packet switching switches packets of data over a variety of circuits. For most packet switching protocols, there is not *a* dedicated physical or virtual circuit between the two users, hence, the term *connectionless*. Instead, each packet of data has a destination address, and the telephone system uses that address to route the packet to the correct destination, with an arbitrary physical path using many virtual circuits. At the end of this chapter how the original packet protocol, X.25, does use virtual circuits in a connection-oriented manner is discussed. Other than this exception, packet switching protocols are always connectionless.

Two by-products of packet switching that tend to limit its applications to data traffic only are that because the packets travel different paths, there is no guarantee they will arrive in the same order as sent. Secondly, because packets sometimes arrive out of order, some types of signaling are not well suited to traditional packet switching. For example, real-time voice and video messages sent in packet form need to arrive in the same order as sent. Many packet switching protocols cannot support this timeliness requirement. Those that do are not yet well accepted in the marketplace due to their high cost. Packet switching will not be explored further.

■ ISDN

There are two versions of ISDN, the narrowband ISDN (N-ISDN) and broadband ISDN (B-ISDN). N-ISDN is what is examined here; B-ISDN is often implemented via packet switching technologies and will not be discussed further.

N-ISDN is offered to subscribers in the United States in two versions, basic rate ISDN and primary rate ISDN. Both offerings of N-ISDN are commonly referred to as just ISDN. Basic rate ISDN is designed for individual use; it offers 2B + D service. This means two 64 kbps bearer channels, (2B), and one 16 kbps data channel (1D).

The 64 kbps size of the bearer channels in ISDN was chosen to accommodate a 64 kbps PCM voice channel. The data channel is a 16 kbps command and control signaling channel and is not designed for use by the user. However, a user can implement a low-speed data channel that takes second place to whatever control signaling is required by the connection.

Primary rate ISDN offers the user 23 64 kbps bearer channels (23B) and one D channel, 23B + D. This is a full T-1 line minus one 64 kbps channel used for the same functions as the D channel in basic rate ISDN. This service is intended for large users, typically with a digital PBX to break out the bearer channels into individual users.

It is important to understand that each of the B channels can be used independently. For example, there might be a data link to a computer on one B channel, whereas the other is used for voice communications. The third channel, the D channel, is designed primarily for use by the telephone system for connection management. Again, if proper equipment is purchased, this channel can be used as a low rate data connection using a packet protocol such as X.25. All three channels are carried on the same pair of twisted pair lines now used for an analog voice grade line.

Service Characteristics versus Architecture

As the last point indicated, it is important to not confuse ISDN with some kind of new circuit architecture that the telephone system has implemented. ISDN is identified by its service characteristics. Service characteristics are capabilities that allow new product offerings to become real. ISDN runs over the same physical network that POTS does. Of course, there are some new components to handle the advanced features offered, but the long-line network remains the same. Once the PCM pulse train is encapsulated into a DS-1 frame, you cannot tell the difference.

The three primary new features that ISDN offers are

1. True 64 kbps clear channel data rate on each B channel
2. End-to-end digital connectivity allowing service transparency (voice, data, video, etc.)
3. Standard terminal interface

An additional feature that looks like a failure is the fact that if you lose power, you lose your telephone connection. We will examine each of these features in turn. However, because feature 1 was discussed earlier, it will be omitted here.

End-to-End Digital Connectivity

End-to-end digital connectivity is a big advantage for some users. These are not the traditional users of the telephone system, who converse on it but are data users. For them it can offer significant advantages. With an all-digital connectivity, there is no conversion from or to analog signaling. This means no modem. With no modem bottleneck, each user can utilize the full bandwidth of the ISDN line. For a basic rate interface (BRI), this means at least 128 kbps of bandwidth. This is at least 3 times faster than any voice-grade analog line with a modem can provide over any reasonable time period.

Not having to convert to analog and then back again saves the cost of the modem on each end. This used to be a bigger deal than it is today and may partly explain why ISDN is only slowly gaining market acceptance. Modems for voice-grade lines are very inexpensive and seem to be getting cheaper every year. Avoiding this cost does not seem like a good trade-off because an ISDN hookup has a significantly higher monthly charge. True, more bandwidth is gained, but you pay for that. Any saving that may be realized by avoiding the cost of a modem is more than compensated by the requirement to purchase a terminal adapter, discussed below.

Service transparency means that because the line is all digital, any digitized data source can be multiplexed into it transparently. Recall that for TDM all inputs must be digital data, so if video is digitized, it can be combined and sent along with a PCM-encoded voice transmission and ISDN will not know the difference. Therefore, ISDN offers TDM channels directly to the user. Once a terminal adapter is purchased, what it is connected to makes no difference to how ISDN operates. Remember that ISDN is distinguished by its service offerings not by technology. A user with an ISDN connection could carry on a simultaneous voice, facsimile, and World Wide Web session. Further, the throughput of the World Wide Web session would have a higher performance than would be typical using a dedicated voice-grade analog line with a 53 kbps modem.

Standard Terminal Interface

There are three interfaces defined for ISDN terminal adapters. A terminal adapter is a device that connects an analog or digital source to the four-wire S-interface. In the United States, the terminal adapter is owned by the user and must be purchased before connection to an ISDN line is possible with non-ISDN equipment, like a standard telephone.

There are two classes of terminal adapters, those intended for use in the consumer and small business market and those intended for larger organizations. The smaller one is discussed first. This terminal adapter is made up of two primary parts, the terminal adapter (TA) itself and a network termination (NT), which acts a lot like a CSU/DSU. The TA uses an R-interface to the user equipment. Between the TA and NT is an interface called the S-interface. Between the NT and any ISDN equipment, like an ISDN telephone,

Figure 16.10
ISDN interface.

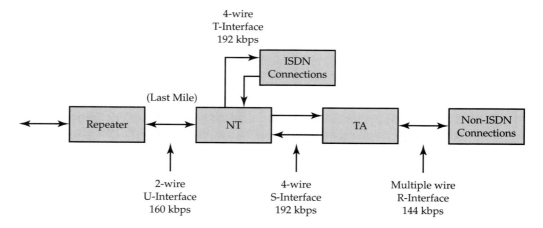

is the four-wire T-interface. The NT uses a U-interface to the service provider. See Figure 16.10 for a diagram of an ISDN connection to the network.

The U-interface is just a standard two-wire connection to the service provider, just as would occur with a standard analog voice line. However, because it uses pulse modulation, it is called a digital local loop or digital subscriber line (DSL). The data rate over this connection is 160 kbps: the two 64 kbps B channels, a single 16 kbps D channel, and 16 kbps used by the service provider to manage and frame the data. Because of the relatively high data rate, the distance where good transmission can be guaranteed is limited. In telecommunications terminology this is called the last mile. In fact, it can be up to about 3 miles, but the line must reach a line repeater within this distance. The line repeater may or may not be located in the switching station.

One of the limiting factors that has prevented ISDN from becoming widely adapted is this restriction. Most of us do not live less than 3 miles from a switching station. This means that to offer ISDN service the service provider must place a repeater every 3 miles or less from the switching station to every subscriber. This is not cheap and partly explains why ISDN rates are higher than voice-grade analog line rates. Any digital subscriber line has this requirement.

The interface that is intended to work with ISDN-type equipment is the T-interface. This is a four-wire interface that connects equipment designed to work with an ISDN connection directly to the ISDN line. It actually is a bus-type interface; several ISDN devices may be connected in parallel from this line in a drop cable-type arrangement. Although this number varies, the maximum number of devices is eight.

The next interface is the S-interface. The S-interface is actually two 2-wire pairs, each running at 192 kbps. It is important to note that all ISDN lines are configured as full duplex. So when line rates are discussed, the actual data rate between the adapters at the user site is twice that number. For example, an N-ISDN service is actually two 2B + D services, one for transmit and one for receive, but only between the TA and NT. This can be seen in Figure 16.10.

The data rate on the S-interface is 192 kbps. This is arrived at by adding an additional 32 kbps signaling between the TA and NT for control of the terminal equipment. Integrated units may combine the TA and NT into one box, and the S-interface is not exposed.

The last interface is the R-interface. The R-interface is actually a family of interfaces that depends on what type of DTE equipment the user plans on connecting to the ISDN line. It might include a telephone adapter for voice connections, several RS-232 connections for a PC and other DTE equipment, and so forth. A maximum of eight different devices can be multiplexed into a single ISDN TA. This illustrates the TDM capability of ISDN and underlines the advantage of an all-digital connection, allowing multiple services over a standard connection.

In some installations, usually those for larger organizations, the NT component is broken up into two pieces, NT1 and NT2. When this is done, the T-interface connects the two NT devices. In this situation, no ISDN equipment is connected to the T-interface. Both the NT1 and NT2 reside at the user site, and all user equipment is connected to the NT2 through S-interfaces or an S-interface through a TA to a R-interface. When a NT2 is used, it is usually a digital PBX, LAN, or even a terminal controller.

In Europe, all ISDN networks use the NT1 and NT2 distinction. This is because the European LEC was granted permission by the regulatory agencies to provide the NT1 functionality. The consumer, large or small, only purchases the NT2. In the United States this was prohibited and both sets of functionality can be purchased by the consumer. To better understand this distinction of functionality, the separate roles of the NT1 and NT2 will be briefly explored.

In the same way the 66-block is the demarcation point for analog lines into a building, the NT1 is the demarcation point for DSL lines. It is the point where the customer and the LEC providing the service shake hands. The NT1 provides the termination for the two-wire DSL line, the U-interface. As will be seen in the next section, DSL lines in general use some kind of rate reduction code and the U-interface makes use of a specific type of line code. The NT1 must translate this line code back into standard AMI line encoding used on the S-interface and the T-interface. The NT1 also provides some maintenance and synchronization functions that are normally considered the network provider's job. For this reason in Europe the LEC provides the NT1 functionality. In the United States this decision went the other way.

The NT2 device is only used when the connection to the LEC is a primary rate interface (PRI) ISDN link, 23B + D. When this is required, the NT functionality is broken up into the NT1 and NT2. The NT2 then provides a refinement of the interface point between the TA and NT functionality. The NT2 stands between the NT1 and the ISDN connections to the T-interface. This is the demarcation point in Europe. In the United States regardless of the bandwidth of the connection, BRI or PRI, the U-interface is the demarcation point between the customer and the service provider.

To conclude this section, the data rate, coding, and use of each of the four interfaces defined in Figure 16.10 are summarized:

Interface	Coding	Data Rate (kbps)	Comments
U-Interface	2B1Q	160	2B + D + 16 kbps
T-Interface	AMI	144	2B + D + 16 kbps + 32 kbps
S-Interface	AMI	192	2B + D + 16 kbps + 32 kbps
R Interface	AMI	144	2B + D

If You Lose Power, You Lose Your Connection

The primary disadvantage, other than having to purchase the NT and TA components, to ISDN lines for use as a voice telephone is what happens when power fails. Traditionally, the telephone system maintains and powers your telephone from the line. This power is totally independent from the power supplied to your house through the power system.

People depend on the telephone when power is lost for many things, but ISDN will not work without a TA and an NT. Both of these devices draw power from the plug in the wall. If power fails, so does your ISDN voice connection.

This seems like a serious problem and before the advent of cellular telephones, it was. Now, many of the same people who would be interested in having an ISDN connection also have a cellular telephone in case of an emergency. For those people who do not need a digital connection into their home for something other than a voice connection, traditional analog voice connections are cheaper and more reliable.

■ ISDN LINE CODES

The U-interface is the longest running line in the ISDN connection. It must reach from the subscriber site to a repeater up to 3 miles away. The data rate on this line is 160 kbps. One way that this long distance is achieved at this high data rate is using a special line coding technique called rate reduction codes. A rate reduction code actually lessens the number of transitions, or zero crossings, for a particular data string. This looks like a lower data rate because fewer zero crossings mean less interference between the twisted pair lines. Anytime a transition occurs, it is an opportunity to generate interference or cross talk. Rate reduction coding is one popular way to reduce this interference without reducing the data rate. Figure 16.11 illustrates the 2B1Q code used on the ISDN U-interface lines.

A 2B1Q code makes use of five amplitude levels, 3, 1, 0, −1, −3. The use of additional amplitude levels allows amplitude shifts, indicating bit transitions, without zero crossings, hence, reducing interference. A shift in amplitude with change in sign, almost always generates more interference than an equivalent shift in amplitude with no change in sign. Essentially, what one gets when using such a code is longer "bit" intervals, defined by zero crossings, with amplitude changes during the bit period, more than 1 bit per bit.

The logic behind the bit transitions is shown in Table 16.5. For every 2 bits of input data a transition is defined. When the bit pair does not transition, for example, a 10 to 10, no transition occurs. As can be seen, this technique works by assigning an amplitude level to a particular bit pair. The transitions are governed by this assignment.

Figure 16.11
2B1Q ISDN rate reduction code.

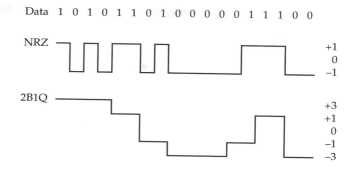

COMPARISON OF CIRCUIT-SWITCHED SYSTEMS SIGNALING PROTOCOLS

The two circuit-switched systems discussed were POTS and ISDN. Because most readers are more familiar with POTS, its operation will be described first in terms of an access protocol and then that will be compared to how ISDN operates. An access protocol is just a set of rules for the signaling that the system uses to work. All circuit-switched systems must go through some kind of calling control to initiate and manage a connection. There are three basic steps: call setup, data or voice transfer, and call termination.

In POTS, the signaling that accomplishes call control is done with a series of pulses for dial telephones and tones for touch-tone telephones. The steps are as follows:

1. The caller alerts the telephone system's local exchange that he or she wants to originate a call by transitioning from on-hook to off-hook. This is accomplished by lifting the handset off its cradle.
2. The local exchange acknowledges this request and provides a dial tone, indicating to the customer that the call can proceed.

Table 16.5
2B1Q Transitions

00	01	10	11
00–00 no change	01–00 −1 to −3	10–00 +3 to −3	11–00 +1 to −3
00–01 −3 to −1	01–01 no change	10–01 +3 to −1	11–01 +1 to −1
00–10 −3 to +3	01–10 −1 to +3	10–10 no change	11–10 +1 to +3
00–11 −3 to +1	01–11 −1 to +1	10–11 +3 to +1	11–11 no change

3. The caller sends the address of the person he or she wants to communicate with by dialing or pressing a telephone number.
4. The local exchange passes the request on to the local exchange to which the called party is connected and that local exchange attempts to make the connection by ringing the called party's telephone.
5. Simultaneously with ringing the called party, the calling party is let know that the connection is being attempted by the ringback signal heard by the calling party.
6. If the called party accepts the connection by going from on-hook to off-hook, both ringing signals are terminated. The called party's local exchange then sends a message to the calling party's local exchange that the connection is established and billing should commence.
7. The connection exists and the call proceeds.
8. Either party can terminate the connection by going from off-hook to on-hook and the connection is terminated and billing stops. Usually the telephone system rounds up to the next full minute of billing time.

As can be seen, the three basic steps are performed:

Call setup	Steps 1 to 6
Voice/data transmission	Step 7
Call termination	Step 8

For ISDN using a digital line, the situation is more complex and less familiar, but all the steps above must still be carried out. Probably the best way to do this is to refer to the CCITT standard, X.21. X.21 is an interface standard that defines the interface between DCE and DTE equipment synchronously operating over the public data network. It defines the signals conveyed over an EIA standard such as RS-232-D. There are eight signals defined, six of which concern us at this time. These are shown in Figure 16.12.

These six wires are used to accomplish the signaling necessary to accomplish call control for digital subscriber lines used by ISDN. Lines 1 to 4 are actually used for the data and control, and lines 5 and 6 are used for timing information. Notice that all timing information is sourced from the DCE device, whereas control is sourced from the DTE device. This is the typical situation. The ground and shield lines are not shown in Figure 16.12.

1. DTE ready is sent to each party's DCE device by taking line-1 high and line-2 low.
2. The calling party submits a call request by taking line-1 low and line-2 high.
3. The calling party sends the address of the called party on line-1; line-2 is high.
4. The called party hears ringing accomplished by line-3 high, line-4 low. The calling party hears a ringback signal while waiting for connection to be established. While waiting, numerous signals are passed to and from the local DTE-DCE interface.
5. Once the call is accepted, numerous signals are passed to and from the remote DTE-DCE interface.

Figure 16.12
X.21.

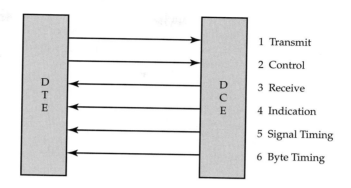

6. The call proceeds and data are transferred on line-1 and line-3.
7. One party decides to terminate the call, and a DTE clear request is sent, line-1 low, line-2 low.
8. The other party acknowledges the termination with a DCE clear indication, line-1 low, and line 4 low.
9. Both parties' DTE and DCE devices communicate locally with confirmation messages that confirm call termination.
10. Both parties' DTE devices signal to their DCE devices that they are ready, line-1 high, line-2 low.

As you can see, both mechanisms accomplish the same thing but in different ways that relate to how they were designed. For ISDN, the three basic steps were carried out as follows:

Call setup	Steps 2 to 7
Voice/data transmission	Step 8
Call termination	Step 9

In addition, because ISDN is a basically digital mechanism, the DTE devices need to announce the their status before they can proceed. This notification is established in step 1, prior to the calling process, and in step 10, after the calling process has concluded.

POTS uses traditional analog techniques on a single line pair to accomplish the call control necessary. In ISDN using a DSL, multiple lines of communication exist due to the essential TDM nature of the connection. This renders the signaling more complex, but it implements the same functionality.

■ SIGNALLING SYSTEM SEVEN (SS7)

SS7 was developed by the international community as an alternate means to pass the signaling that the telephone system uses. This is a superset of the same signaling that was discussed in the previous section. SS7 is a protocol through which switching elements of the telephone system exchange information to do call setup, routing, and control. This signaling is part of every call and every telephone system in every country needs it. Therefore, when it was clear that a transition from the traditional way of providing this signaling was needed, it was logical for a common system to be developed.

The first thing is to reemphasize what the term *signaling* means as used in this context: It means the procedure that is used to perform the three tasks that every call must have, call initiation, voice or data transfer along with the route it takes, and call termination. When a number is dialed, that can be seen as signaling the telephone system to connect to that number address. This is just what was explained in the calling control steps outlined in the POTS approach. The timer counting the minutes that the two parties are connected is the signaling, really monitoring, that is done during voice or data transfer. When one hangs up or goes off-hook, that can also be seen as signaling the telephone system to terminate the call.

As discussed in the previous section, POTS uses in-band signaling to perform these same three tasks, initiation, monitoring, and termination. *In-band signaling* refers to the situation where the signaling and the voice or data transfer shared the same telephone line. For example, in POTS, the dialing, dial tone, and off-hook condition all work over the same physical phone line that is used for voice or data transfer. This is an example of in-band signaling.

In-band signaling works as long as there is no need to add any kind of special services to the telephone system and keep them transparent to the customer. As described earlier, one of the evolutions that characterized POTS was the switch stored program control (SPC). This was a great solution for the time but constrained the number of different types of service that the telephone system could offer due to the way SPC worked. If the service offerings were not anticipated prior to the construction of the SPC, it could not easily be modified to accommodate them.

Essentially, the SPC's design approach did not allow the SPC to evolve to accommodate entirely new services that could not be built up from the existing service logic component blocks. This lead to the idea of using a separate system to carry the signaling necessary for this evolution to enhanced service offerings. This way the signaling system could evolve separately from the voice or data transfer system. This was a major revolution and significantly lowered the cost of changing the signaling because instead of every switch needing to be changed, for every evolution of service, just the signaling system needed to be changed.

Therefore, the decision was made to carry the information necessary to the call on separate physical lines from those used for voice or data transfer. *Out-of-band signaling* is the term used when the call control or signaling is done on separate physical lines from those used to transfer the voice or data between the caller and the called party. Functionally, the network uses the installed base of SPC switching systems for voice and data transfer and a separate network for service specific functions.

As was discussed in the last section, ISDN also uses out-of-band signaling. Reviewing the two signaling examples from POTS and ISDN, one can clearly see that in the POTS case it is done using the same line the voice or data transfer uses. In the ISDN case the X.21 interface is not the same line as is used to perform voice or data transfer.

Figure 16.13
Out-of-band signaling.

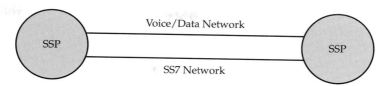

SS7 is also an out-of-band approach. In SS7 the entire facility that manages the calls is outside the network over which the traffic passes. The term used to discuss that portion of the telephone network that actually passes customer traffic is the *switching fabric*. It is composed of switches connected by a variety of lines. Today, these switches are often Lucent 5ESSs or some other vendors switch as discussed in the section on switches. The concept of out-of-band signaling is illustrated in Figure 16.13.

Out-of-band signaling also has advantages in efficiency and utilization of the voice/data network. The three primary benefits are

1. Support for the advanced features and services
2. Faster call setup times
3. Not using the voice/data network lines for nonrevenue tasks like signaling

The network used for managing calls is an entirely different physical network than is used for actually conducting telephone connections. This alternate network is referred to as the *interoffice network* (e.g., the switches are placed in a switching station, and the network that the switches use to communicate about how the traffic will be switched is the interoffice network). The signaling that this network uses is referred to as common channel signaling and the protocol that the signaling follows is called SS7. The original name of this system was Common Channel Signaling Network, or CCSN. Today, these ideas are merged, and this interoffice network is called the SS7 network.

SS7 uses an alternate physical network to carry its information. This network is a packet-switched network, whereas the voice/data transfer uses the circuit-switched network. SS7 itself is a software product that was developed using the OSI model. The protocol has seven layers, with three Message Transfer Parts, (MTPs,) that implement the lower three layers of the OSI model. Additionally, there is a layer 0, which defines the alternate physical network.

Layer 0 in the interoffice network is composed of full-duplex 64 kbps DDS lines. These lines are usually multiplexed up into DS-1 lines for transfer between offices and switches.

Layer 1 is also known as the signaling data link and in the United States is usually implemented with a packet interface. Interfaces that are included in the standard are DS-1, V.35, DS-0, and DS-0A; the latter is defined below. However, due to the modular nature of any OSI protocol, this layer is also implemented with satellite links. Layer 1 in the SS7 protocol is called Message Transfer Part Level 1.

Layer 2 corresponds to the Data Link Layer and like any Layer 2 protocol, the protocol concerns itself with two items: ensuring reliable communication between adjacent stations on a link and identifying frames types known as signal units. The structure of the signal units is patterned after the HDLC frame structure. The three signal units specified are the Message Signal Unit, (MSU), Link Status Signal Unit, (LSSU), and Fill-in Signal Unit, (FISU). Layer 2 in the SS7 protocol is called Message Transfer Part Level 2.

The MSU is used to carry all call control, database query (more on that later), and network management communications in its data field. Each MSU is routed according to its destination address. Because only MSUs cross link boundaries, only MSUs have source and destination addresses. The LSU is used to carry a byte or two of link status information between signaling locations on a single link. The FISU is a frame that is used to continuously monitor the link. Essentially, whenever a station does not have a MSU or LSU to send, its sends a FISU. These frames are continuously checked for errors by examining the CRC field in the frame. This allows the stations to be constantly aware of the current quality of the line and immediately detects any break or degradation. Fill-in frames are very appropriately named.

Layer 3 corresponds to the Network Layer, and the functionality here is similar to what would be expected of a Network Layer. Message Transfer Part Level 3 is concerned with routing the message signal units and providing network management. As mentioned earlier, the routing is based on the destination address in the MSU. The upper portion of this layer is called the Signaling Connection Control Part (SCCP) and is where the service aspects of the layer are contained. Just like any layer, it has two broad ways to provide communications. These are further subdivided into two subclasses of both CO and CLS services and are summarized below:

Class 0 service: Basic connectionless service

Class 1 service: Sequenced connectionless service

Class 2 service: Basic connection-oriented service

Class 3 service: Flow control connection-oriented service

When the MTP3 and SCCP are combined, they are referred to as the Network Service Part (NSP). The SS7 protocol is compared to the OSI model in Figure 16.14. The figure also shows the ISDN parts and the higher-layer components that are briefly touched on below.

Layer 7, the Application Layer, is where the Transaction Capabilities Application Part (TCAP) is located. This is where the protocol that supports application services that the system can offer are located. For example, there is a TCAP part for each of the following telephone system services; Enhanced 800 number service, Alternate Billing Service (ABS), Custom Local Area Signaling Service (CLASS), and others. Basically, TCAP is a set of protocol rules designed to make sure consistent messages are passed between the switching nodes. The actual application programs lie above this layer. A brief description of each of these services follows:

Enhanced 800 service.   This is 800 service that allows the portability of 800 numbers. In the traditional network, once an 800 number was assigned, it was tied to a specific area code. This service addresses that shortcoming.

Figure 16.14
SS7 protocol.

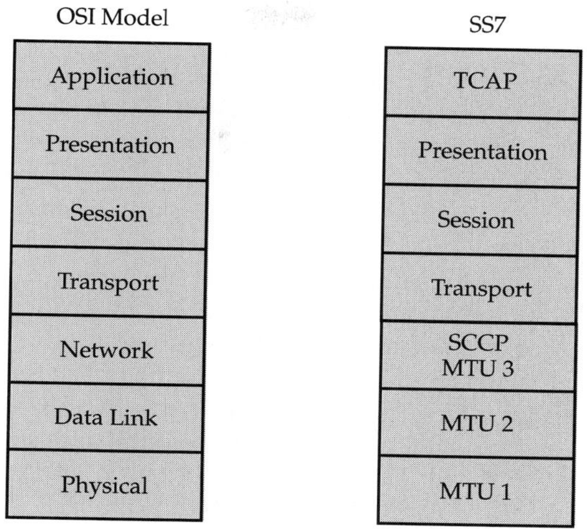

OSI Model		SS7
Application		TCAP
Presentation		Presentation
Session		Session
Transport		Transport
Network		SCCP MTU 3
Data Link		MTU 2
Physical		MTU 1

ABS.   These are the services that allow you to use a calling card to place a telephone call, to bill to a third number, and to place collect calls. Any time the calling party does not directly pay for the call, this service is used.

CLASS.   This is broad class of services including call blocking, automatic recall, call forwarding, call waiting, call tracing, and so forth.

■ INTEROFFICE NETWORK

As discussed above, SS7 is an internationally developed and recognized standard for interoffice signaling. There are four main components of the SS7, or interoffice, network; they are described below. The first three components are generically referred to as nodes. Additionally, there is a special way of referring to any switch that has SS7 capability; these are called signaling points, or SPs. For example, a Lucent 5ESS switch is an SP because it has SS7 capability.

SSP: Service Switching Point

SCP: Signal Control Point

STP: Signal Transfer Point

Link: Signaling Data Line

An SSP is a switching station that is connected directly to the SS7 network and has an SP. Not all offices are connected directly to the SS7 network. When an office is, it has a special designation of being able to launch an SS7 query; it is called a SSP office. A query is what the signaling is called when a call is originated from a telephone attached to the office. When an office is not connected directly to the SS7 network, it is designated a non-SSP office. When a telephone call is being originated from a non-SSP office, that office must use the SS7 network to route this call over the interoffice network to a SSP office for connection to the network.

An SCP is nothing more than a specialized computer that knows all about a certain database. This database is associated with some service that the telephone system can provide using SS7. For example, there are databases for processing 800 calls, 900 calls, ANI, call forwarding, local number portability (LPN), and so forth. Those elements of the SS7 protocol that comprise these databases are called parts. SCPs and SSPs communicate using the SS7 network. Essentially, when a particular service is needed, for example, when an 800 number is dialed, the switching system is alerted to the need for input from a particular database contained in a SCP (e.g., a particular "part" of the SS7 protocol).

Before going on the next two components, there are a few things to say about queries and databases. These form the heart of the SS7 network. The SS7 network is in place to pass queries and responses from and to SS7-capable switches. The queries are responded to from databases, and these databases generate the responses back to the switches. In SS7 terminology, an SSP with an SP switch sends an MSP to an SCP, which generates an MSP back to the SP located in the SSP. The MSPs are passed through the SS7 network through STPs, defined next.

STPs are the signal transfer points that pass the signaling around the SS7 network. The STPs are connected by 56 kbps DDS trunk lines and are really specialized packet switches. If these 56 kbps DDS lines are used to connect to or from STP and either SSPs or SCPs, they are called A links and are the primary traffic links used in the SS7 network. Each RBOC must have two STPs for each LATA and therefore two A links. One is used as an active backup for the other. There are several types of links used in the SS7 network; these will be discussed next.

There are actually six types of signaling data links used in the SS7 network. As mentioned earlier, all are bidirectional, or full-duplex, links. This means that the transmit and receive traffic pass in both directions at the same time and data rate. Each type of link is used to connect between specific types of nodes in the SS7 network. Again, a node is just a particular type of office or switch. Table 16.6 lists the six types of nodes and their

Table 16.6
SS7 Link Types

Link	Connection
A (access)	STP-SSP, same network
A (access)	STP-SCP, same network
B (bridges)	STP-STP, same hierarchy level; message traffic
C (crossovers)	STP-STP, same hierarchy level; administrative
D (diagonal)	STP-STP, different hierarchy level
E (extended)	STP-SSP, different networks
E (extended)	STP-SCP, different networks
F (fully associated)	SSP-SSP, same network, adjacent nodes

Figure 16.15
A, B, and C links.

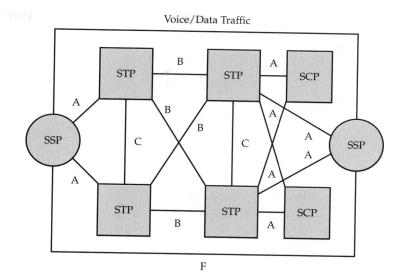

Voice/Data Traffic

use to connect between specific types of nodes. The term in parenthesis is the long name of each link. Some link types are used for multiple purposes. In the table, *hierarchy* refers to the class of office, and *different networks* captures the distinction between communicating between nodes in a single country or telephone system and between countries that would have different telephone systems.

How A, B, and C links are connected is shown in Figure 16.15. These three types of links form the primary paths for all message traffic. D and E links function primarily as secondary or alternate routes. F links are only used in networks without STPs. In Figure 16.15, the F link shown would function if the rest of the network was disabled. Note that the A links are redundant and that the B links are multiply interconnected to bridge across SSPs. The A and B links carry the message traffic that is used by the switch fabric to control the voice/data traffic. Note that the C links, which primarily carry administrative traffic, do not connect to the SSP offices at all. Finally, the voice/data traffic shown at the top of Figure 16.15 is not part of the interoffice network.

There are actually three types of links used in the United States. They are all DDS services, and we have discussed the first previously. All these links use either V.35 or RS-232 physical interfaces. Although the link data rates are at 56/64 kbps, they are multiplexed up into DS-1 frames for actual transport through the network. It is probably best to think of these as logical links rather than physical ones. They are listed below:

Digital signal level 0 (DS-0).   A single 64 kbps channel operating at its clear channel data rate.

Digital signal level 0 A (DS-0A).   A single 56 kbps channel operating at its normal data rate. As in the voice network, the other 8 kbps is used for clocking and frame checking.

Digital signal level 0 B (DS-0B).   A DS-0 channel that is composed of several multiplexed 9600 bps administrative links.

This combination of STPs, SCPs, SSPs, and links form what is also referred to as the Advanced Intelligent Network, or AIN. Sometimes this is shortened to just Intelligent Network, or IN. Both are used. This nomenclature comes from the observation that SS7 network takes the intelligence out of the switch and distributes it among the SS7 network (e.g., The SCPs contain the intelligence and are one element of the SS7 network, hence, Intelligent Network). As you can see from the last few paragraphs, the many names for very similar things is one of the most confusing aspects of learning about how the modern telephone system works.

Now that the terminology has been explained, it is important to reemphasize that the distributed intelligence and component parts allow the SS7 network to be rapidly configured to respond to changing customer requirements.

■ X.25 VIRTUAL CIRCUITS

X.25 has traditionally been the most widely adapted packet protocol. It is designed for use on the public data network. In fact, the long name for X.25 is Interface between data terminal equipment (DTE) and data circuit terminating equipment (DCE) for terminals operating in the packet mode and connected to the public data network by dedicated circuit. X.25 has been the most widely used protocol since about 1980. It is the only widely adopted example of a circuit-switched packet network.

Although X.25, like any packet protocol, transfers data in packets rather than in a continuous stream, it does make use of a virtual circuit in the same way a standard telephone call does. There is a specific call setup and call termination sequence that is very similar to that used for POTS or ISDN. The only difference is that instead of specific tones, or lines changing, specific packets are exchanged between devices called packet assemblers/disassemblers, or PADs. These packets have representative names like Call-Request, Incoming-Call, Call-Accepted, and Call-Connected. These are used by the DTE and DCE to facilitate call setup.

Like any circuit-switched system, the connection is established prior to any data transfer and terminates after transfer is completed. It functions in the same way as a tube. FIFO is guaranteed and packets are numbered, but the numbers are used for error recovery purposes or if the data to transfer is too large for a single packet, not to for out-of-order arrival because of path length differences.

To demonstrate that the packet exchange is very similar to the call setup operations used by POTS or ISDN, the sequence of these call setup packets is provided. Compare this approach to the two shown earlier. In the discussion below, the PADs are the DCE components, and the calling and called devices are the DTE components.

1. The calling terminal device alerts the telephone system that it wants to establish a virtual circuit by sending a Call-Request packet. This packet contains the address of the source and destination PADs.
2. The telephone system acknowledges this request and passes the packet to the destination address. This packet is accepted by the called device's PAD.
3. The called device's PAD sends an Incoming-Call packet to its terminal device.
4. The called terminal device accepts the call by sending a Call-Accepted packet to its local PAD.
5. The calling PAD receives the Call-Accepted packet and sends a Call-Connected packet to its local terminal device.
6. Data transfer occurs.
7. Either terminal device sends a Clear-Request packet to its local PAD. The local PAD then sends a Clear-Indication to the remote PAD.
8. The remote PAD sends a Clear-Confirmation to the other PAD.

Again, the call setup process accounts for most of the steps, here 1 to 5. The data transfer occurs in step 6 and call termination is contained in steps 7 and 8.

■ SUMMARY

This chapter has discussed several basic aspects of the modern telecommunications system that you are likely to encounter in an entry-level position. A single chapter cannot do justice to what has taken a century to build, but this introduction should get you started.

PROBLEMS

1. Using the basic formula for computing telephone line charges, equation 11–1, compare how the line charge would vary under each of the following conditions:
   (a) Twice the distance
   (b) Twice the time
   (c) Twice the distance for half as long
   (d) Twice the profit margin

2. Using the data provided in the chapter, compute the most economical solution, dial-up, dedicated 56, or switched 56, for each of the following conditions.

Compute the charges for 1 month of service, assume 20 working days a month. Use the cost data for band C.
   (a) Time: 16 hr/day   BW: 28 kbps
   (b) Time: 24 hr/day   BW: 56 kbps
   (c) Time: 3 hr/day   BW: 56 kbps
   (d) Time: 8 hr/day   BW: 100 kbps

3. Show the AMI line code for each of the following 16 bit data patterns:
   (a) 1100001010100111
   (b) 0000001100001110

4. Show the B8ZS line code for each of the following 16 bit data patterns:
   (a) 1100000000000000
   (b) 1100000110001000

5. Show the 2B1Q line code for each of the following 16 bit data patterns:
   (a) 1100101001000100
   (b) 1111111000101010

6. What is the biggest user disadvantage of ISDN?

7. Identify the sum and difference frequencies for each of the following DTMF keys:

   (a) 2   (c) *
   (b) 5   (d) #

8. A certain analog telephone system is being designed. If the average telephone is used to make four calls per 8 hour workday, and the average length of the call is 10 minutes, how many telephones may be connected? Assume that 20% of the calls need to use the trunk. The trunk bandwidth is 500 kHz. Assume a bandwidth of 4 kHz for each call and a guardband of 1 kHz.

17

Three Protocols

In this chapter three representative protocols, FieldBus, Ethernet, and TCP/IP, will be explored. FieldBus will illustrate how a protocol can be designed to be used with low-cost devices that may need to utilize multiple access protocols, such as Token Bus and scheduled operations. Ethernet is so widely adapted that every reader needs to be exposed to certain details of product offerings and more information than was provided when discussing CSMA/CD. TCP/IP is also so pervasive that it needs a section all its own. As many of you probably already know, TCP/IP is the protocol that the Internet uses.

■ FIELDBUS

FieldBus is a modern communications network, developed under the OSI model. FieldBus is designed to provide data transfer and device control services to applications where the devices are simple field devices such as sensors, process controllers, and process actuators. The way to determine if the FieldBus was designed for use with a device is to ask whether the device is configurable or programmable. FieldBus is designed for configurable devices, that is, for devices for which the function is determined by the rearrangement of its components, not the providing of a procedure for solving a problem.

FieldBus has been developed for time-critical applications, which are a subset of applications commonly known as real-time applications where the device requires service by the network within a critical time window. This time window although necessarily occurring at a precise moment in time, need not do so in a real-time manner. For example, a time-critical application might require service within a 1 msec interval every time a vat is filled with fluid, perhaps every 5 min. A real-time application might require service within a 1 msec interval every time a shaft rotated 360°, perhaps every 50 msec.

By reducing the number of layers and eliminating functionality that is not required in the applications envisioned for this standard, FieldBus can reduce the response time devices require. FieldBus can also service real-time applications; it can provide the communications necessary for both of the above examples. See Appendix I for a sample calculation.

From an operational viewpoint, FieldBus provides the flexibility of simple token passing while simultaneously providing as much prescheduled operation as the applications require. It provides a simple 4 to 20 mA replacement and is also designed to accommodate the media types becoming most important to the future of the automation industries. These include high-speed networks using low-cost twisted pair and high-performance coaxial cable. By allowing such flexibility in the physical layer, FieldBus can seamlessly integrate physical networks of different speeds and qualities. For example, networks using both high- and low-speed segments will require only a simple and reliable bridge for interconnection.

FieldBus fully supports the 4 to 20 mA direct wired path from the control room through a junction box to each field device. FieldBus also supports common process configurations in which the control room is wired to field controllers or multiplexers that, in turn, are separately wired to transmitters and valves. It provides this functionality through its bridging functions. Bridges allow the control room direct access to all devices including those connected to a controller. The control room can access the controller to obtain the data it needs indirectly, or it can access the device directly through the bridge function contained in the controller. This avoids the large delay introduced by a device such as a gateway.

For scheduled high-speed applications, a simple and precise (to 1/32 sec) scheduling mechanism is provided. Very short messages may be transmitted when short control cycles are needed. All messages have a priority: Urgent, Normal, or TimeAvailable. This permits urgent alarm traffic to be communicated before normal control traffic, with low-priority traffic such as downloads taking a back seat. Table 17.1 summarizes the main capabilities of FieldBus.

FieldBus Architecture

The FieldBus network architecture is shown in Figure 17.1. It is much simpler than that defined as the generalized OSI model but retains many of its characteristics. Only Layers 1, 2, and 7 are defined to simplify installation in low-cost devices.

Table 17.1
FieldBus Summary

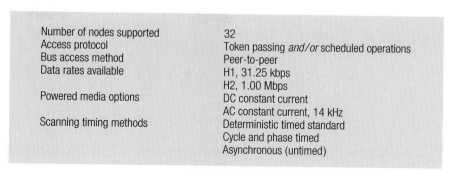

Number of nodes supported	32
Access protocol	Token passing *and/or* scheduled operations
Bus access method	Peer-to-peer
Data rates available	H1, 31.25 kbps
	H2, 1.00 Mbps
Powered media options	DC constant current
	AC constant current, 14 kHz
Scanning timing methods	Deterministic timed standard
	Cycle and phase timed
	Asynchronous (untimed)

Physical Layer.   The Physical layer of FieldBus, like any Physical layer, is concerned with the transmission of raw bits of data over a communications channel. The standard specifies three types of twisted pair wiring for the physical media. The FieldBus standard specifies two ways of providing power to devices via the medium and two data rates. The two options for power are ac and dc constant current. The ac frequency of operation is 14 kHz.

The network is designed to allow either type of device exclusively or a mixture of both. In the case of dc power, small ac communications signals are superimposed on the dc power. In the ac-powered case, the communications signal is superimposed on the ac power and is picked up as a current in the receiving device. FieldBus will support at least 32 device connections, but if devices are bus powered, power availability may limit this number.

Figure 17.1
FieldBus architecture.

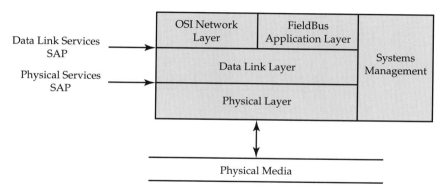

Table 17.2
Wired Media Types

Wired Media	Maximum Cable Length (m)
Type A	1900
Type B	1200
Type C	400

The two data rates that FieldBus supports are H1 at 31.25 kbps and H2 at 1 Mbps. Communications is bidirectional but in only one direction at a time (i.e., half-duplex). The three types of wire cable specified in the standard are shown in Table 17.2.

Type A cable is the preferred cable in new installations; it is specified to be a single or multiple, individual shielded, twisted pair cable. Type B will probably be used in both new and retrofit applications where multiple FieldBus networks are run in the same area of a user's plant. Type B cable is specified to be a multiple, twisted pair cable with an overall shield. Type C cable is the least preferred cable and should not be installed. Type C cable is specified to be single or multiple twisted pair cable without any shield.

Type C cable is included in the standard to cover existing plant networks installed before Types A and B become available and/or cost effective. Type C cable is much more susceptible to RFI/EMI degradations in a plant and may preclude operation when installed under inappropriate environmental conditions.

In general, two basic cable architectures are utilized with the copper wire networks. These are listed below:

1. A linear bus topology where the network contains one trunk cable terminated at both ends with spurs distributed along the length of the trunk
2. A tree topology again terminated at both ends but with spurs concentrated at one end of the trunk

Figure 17.2
FieldBus PDU.

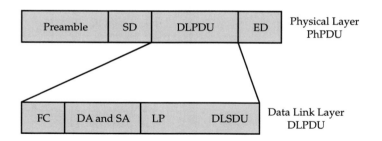

Table 17.3
Data Link Service Options

Service Type	Example	Reliability
Connection oriented	Telephone	High
Least Loss	Return receipt	Medium
Least Cost	Telegram	Low

H1 networks support either topology, whereas H2 networks, with their higher speed, require a linear bus topology.

The FieldBus PDU is constructed according to rules outlined in the FieldBus standard. Figure 17.2 illustrates the composition of this PDU from the Physical layer up to the Data Link layer. This is the conceptual construction of the bits as they go across the medium from one user to another. There is an implied time axis from left to right in the figure. The Physical layer Protocol Data Unit (PhPDU) is the result of this concatenation process. As can be seen, each layer appends additional information on the PDU as it goes through the protocol stack.

Data Link Layer.   As you are aware, there are two broad types of service that a layer can offer to the layer above it: COS and CLS. Table 17.3 summarizes the example and associated reliability of each of these approaches.

There are two levels of effort specified in the FieldBus DLS for CLS. These are Least-Loss, more generically known as acknowledged connectionless service, and LeastCost, more generically known as unacknowledged connectionless service.

The two access protocol methods that are utilized by FieldBus to provide service to the devices on the network are token passing and scheduled operations. These protocol options are shown in Table 17.4.

The Data Link layer used in FieldBus provides the support required for both token-based access control and scheduled operations. FieldBus defaults to only token passing. To provide service to those devices that are not token passers, when the specially designated LinkMaster gets the token, it services any outstanding scheduled requests. This

Table 17.4
Data Link Protocol Options

Data Link Access Protocol Options
Token passing
Scheduled operations

device also occasionally polls silent stations to determine if they require network support. If one or more devices requires centralized scheduling, the FieldBus protocol will automatically adapt to these requirements without any reconfiguration required. When these immediate requirements are met, FieldBus automatically reverts to token passing.

Token passing is the fairest methodology for splitting up the bandwidth resource. Each station has a fixed time slot to transmit its data and no more. Token passing is the arrangement of stations into a logical ring with each station knowing the address of the station on either side. Each station accumulates its data until it is its turn to transmit. When initialized, the highest number station sends its first frame. After it is done, it passes permission to its immediate neighbor by sending it a special frame called a token. The token propagates around the logical ring with only the token holder being able to transmit frames. Because only one station holds the token at any time, collision does not occur.

Scheduled operations are those operations that only need to communicate when specific conditions, internal or external to the network, become true. Scheduled traffic relies on a master station or predetermined time slots to divide up the bandwidth resource. These time slots can be configured on line with some protocols and are hardwired with others. This technique, at least in the later case, is best used when each station's traffic is predetermined. An example might be a level switch on a tank to shut off flow. These messages only occur occasionally, and the devices do not need the extra processing and cost associated with being a token passer.

Application Layer.   The Application layer in the FieldBus network architecture must also provide the services of OSI Layer 6, the Presentation layer. Services of this layer are called FieldBus Messaging Services (FMS). Above the FMS is a set of higher-layer services. This layer is known as the User Application layer (UAL). It is oriented toward providing data transfer and other services to a data acquisition and control system. In this section, discussion will focus on the UAL only. The UAL provides data transfer and device control services to applications using the FieldBus protocol.

The objective of the Application Layer is to achieve compatibility between conforming devices to the FieldBus standard. There are multiple levels of conformance to this standard that are generally tied to the degree of FMS and UAL implementation completeness. The levels range from field replaceable units to bus compatibility with no application compatibility; they are known as dynamic interchange, functional interchange, generic, open, and nonconforming, which correspond to interchangeable, interoperable, interworkable, interconnectable, and incompatible devices. These levels are shown in Table 17.5.

One important element of time-critical communications is database access. FieldBus has special database access mechanisms that are superior to conventional access controls for distributed databases. Another key requirement in automation and process control systems is that the dynamic behavior of the control system must be predictable and deterministic. Most process control systems perform cyclic calculations in well-defined time windows. These time windows must stay synchronous and consistent with the dynamics of the process under control. This requires the standard to specify the execution cycle so that functional control blocks (data) are interchangeable.

Table 17.5
FieldBus Conformance Levels

Level of Conformance	Phrasing Used in Standard
Dynamic interchange	Interchangeable
Functional interchange	Interoperable
Generic	Interworkable
Open	Interconnectable
Nonconforming	Incompatible

Scanning is the process used by controllers and other devices to acquire data from input/output (I/O). The FieldBus standard provides for three types of scanning methods: synchronous, report by exception, and broadcast update. The method used depends on the way the process operates; however, the FieldBus standard allows any system to use more than one method.

FieldBus also provides four timing models for function blocks: timed standard, cycle and phase timed, asynchronous (untimed), and undefined. Each logical node must select only one of these methods.

One important reason to use FieldBus is to allow distribution of the sensors, controllers, and actuators over a larger area than one network. Traditional approaches to facilitating communication among field devices often introduced significant delays or dead time into the control cycle over connection of all devices on the same network and can cause problems when trying to field replace units.

FieldBus anticipates this difficulty and allows exact specification of the scan cycle. The scan timing is independent of the method used by system devices to obtain data from the process. FieldBus provides a way to define the time slots in which control blocks will execute. In FieldBus, this is called timed standard processing of function blocks.

Cycle and phase scheduling allows each function block in a physical node to be on its own time schedule. As a result, there can be no exact time schedule when utilizing this timing mode. Because some function blocks must execute in the proper sequence, the phase method is provided to offset the timing of the individual blocks to guarantee the order of execution.

Finally, there is asynchronous scanning, for devices that cannot be scheduled for cyclic execution. Generally, this is due to uncertainties in the physical system. These devices include analyzers and scanning gauges. See Appendix I for an example scan time calculation.

■ ETHERNET

Ethernet is the most widely adopted LAN protocol, and it is now available in a wide variety of data rates and media choices. The format of the name for each flavor of Ethernet defines its capabilities and originally had the following form:

Table 17.6
Ethernet Options

Name	General Characteristics
10Base2	10 Mbps baseband network with a 200 m coaxial cable maximum segment length
10Base5	10 Mbps baseband network with a 500 m maximum coaxial cable segment length
10Base-T	10 Mbps baseband network with a 100 m twisted pair maximum segment length*
10Base-FL	10 Mbps baseband network with a 2 km fiber maximum segment length
100Base-T	100 Mbps baseband network with a 100 m twisted pair maximum segment length*

* Length depends on quality of the cable used.

⟨data rate in Mbps⟩⟨medium type⟩⟨maximum length * 100 m⟩

More recently introduced forms of Ethernet that do not make use of coaxial cable alter the naming convention such that the last term becomes a shorthand for media type. This can be seen in Table 17.6.

More detailed information relating to the cabling for the two coaxial standards is found in Appendix J. Refer to Chapter 3 for the various CAT categories of twisted pair cable. If the cable is at least CAT-3 or higher, these data rates are achievable for 10Base-T. If CAT-5 is used, they are achievable for 100Base-T.

The coaxial cable types for 10Base2 and 10Base5 are sometimes referred to as Thinnet and Thicknet, respectively, recognizing the fact that the coaxial diameter of the two media is significantly different. 10Base2 uses a variety of coaxial cable called RG-58, whereas 10Base5 uses RG-8. Both cables exhibit an impedance of 50 Ω, but the RG-8 was specified to be double shielded, making it very bulky. Additionally, 10Base5 requires expensive N-connectors to attach the device to the interface, whereas 10Base2 uses much less expensive BNC connectors.

For the original Ethernet, 10Base5, the coaxial adapter was of the vampire class. That meant that instead of using a connector or tap to connect a station to the network, one just stabbed it with the tap. The tap consisted of a needle that penetrated the outer jacket and shield and made contact with the center conductor, hence, the name vampire. This type of tap made addition or removal of stations very easy and contributed greatly to Ethernet's early adoption. Additionally, the fact that Ethernet stations did not require any special configuration of the network when added or removed also contributed to its early adoption by a wide variety of users.

This illustrates an important point about how communication products become adapted in the field. Ease of use is always a critical issue, along with cost. Performance, as long as the information gets through, is of lesser importance except in certain specialized applications. Ethernet's long suits are ease of use and cost. The performance, especially in a highly loaded environment, is a relative weakness. However, the first two factors outweighed the third, and as a result, Ethernet is almost synonymous with LAN technology for many people.

Ethernet is really just a description of the lower two layers of the OSI stack. The specification describes activities of the Data Link Layer and physical layer alone. This means that Ethernet, like Token Bus and Token Ring, may be used with a wide variety of higher layers. Probably the best illustration of this is to examine Novell networks. Novell is a piece of software that implements Layers 5 to 7. It is combined with a Transport and Network Layer component along with the Data Link and physical layer component, and is referred to as a Novell network. This is shown in Figure 17.3.

There are Novell networks that use 10Base-T, 100Base-T, Token Ring, and so forth. Therefore, when one talks about an Ethernet network, all that is described is the functionality of the Data Link Layer and Physical layer. This functionality also usually describes the underlying topology of the network as well due to the interaction of the physical layer and network media.

Like all but the most trivial networks, Ethernet networks are made up of segments. A segment is a group of LAN stations connected together. As described earlier, a LAN is defined to be a local activity, often a LAN is a segment. Segments are separated and joined by joining devices, such as those described in Chapter 15 on networking hardware. Examples include repeaters, bridges, routers, and the various switches that were introduced.

Although strictly speaking Ethernet segments would never need a router to join them due to the specification only extending up to layer 2, routers offer performance management capability that sometimes makes them a good choice for a joining device. Figure 17.4 illustrates a 10Base-T and 100Base-T Ethernet network with two segments. Each segment is running at a different rate, so the joining device must be a bridge or

Figure 17.3
Ethernet and Novell relationship to OSI model.

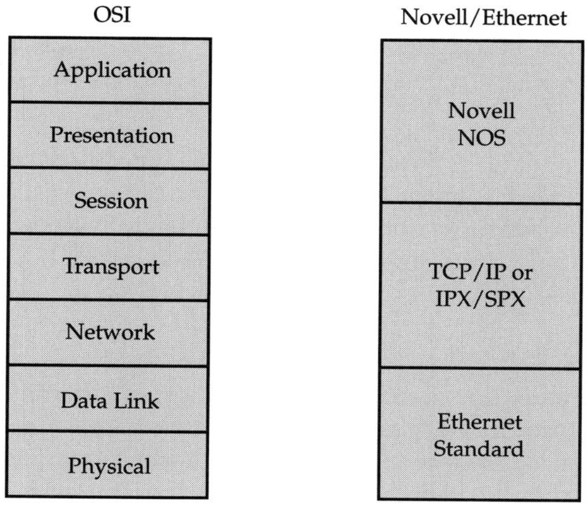

Figure 17.4
A 10Base-T and 100Base-T Ethernet network.

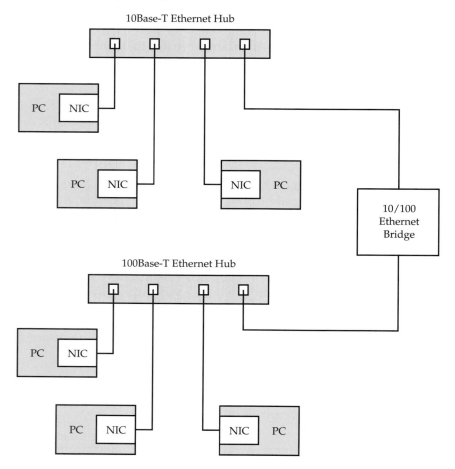

higher-level device. If each segment were running at the same data rate, one could use a simple repeater. In the next sections, the types of Ethernet listed in Table 17.6 are explored in a little more depth to illustrate the differences between them. Remember, Ethernet is a trade name, and what was defined by the IEEE as 802.3 is really what is being discussed.

10Base2

As was already discussed, the 10Base2 form of Ethernet is known as Thinnet, or when it was first introduced, Cheapernet. The two names came from a comparison with the original form of Ethernet, 10Base5, which was fatter, (used a thicker cable) and more expensive. From the naming convention, it is apparent that this type of Ethernet runs at a

Figure 17.5
10Base2 bus topology.

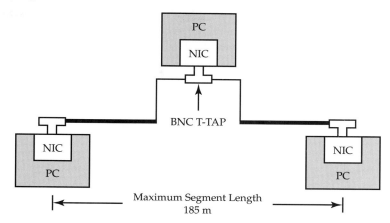

data rate of 10 Mbps, its modulation is baseband, and the maximum cable segment length is 200 m. Not explicitly stated, because there is no T or F in the name, the convention also tells us that the cable type is coaxial.

This type of Ethernet is intended to be laid out in a bus topology; an example is shown in Figure 17.5.

There are a couple of interesting things about this figure to note. First, the taps themselves are unique to this technology. They are BNC connectorized T-connectors, called BNC T-Taps. The taps are usually integrated onto the NIC cards. This means that there are no drop cables. Instead, the bus cable routes directly to the station that is to be physically attached to the network running this type of Ethernet protocol. Coaxial cable is used in this form of Ethernet is RG-58. It is also important to realize what is meant by segment length. This is the total length of the bus for a single LAN segment.

Recall that when the term *LAN* was introduced, it was said that LAN can mean a single LAN or multiple LANs tied together with some kind of segmentation or joining device. For a single Ethernet 10Base2 LAN, 185 m is the total length of the LAN. If multiple LAN segments are connected by a repeater or other joining device, multiple segments can be strung together. This effectively constructs a larger LAN composed of two or more LAN segments.

It is also true that in this case the naming convention for Ethernet breaks down. Because the convention only uses a single digit for the distance, the resolution is low. The actual specification for maximum segment length is 185 m. Due to the low speed as compared to other forms of Ethernet, this technology is disappearing except in those situations where cost is the only issue (e.g., don't replace it if it works and data rate expectations are very low).

10Base5

10Base5 is the original form of Ethernet specified by the IEEE. The naming convention indicates that the data rate is 10 Mbps, the modulation is baseband, and the maximum segment length is 500 m. Again, because there is no F or T in the name, it can be inferred that the cable is of coaxial construction, it is RG-8 cable, which is very rigid due to the construction of the shielding. This makes it heavy and difficult to route due to its large bend radius.

Although it has a bus topology just like 10Base2, there is a little difference. This technology uses special cable called a transceiver cable to connect a station to the coaxial segment. Therefore, instead of the coaxial cable being required to snake around to each station, it can be laid out in a central location, and each station is connected via the transceiver cable. This is a good thing due the very rigid type of coaxial cable used, RG-8. The length of the transceiver cables is limited to a maximum of 50 m. RG-8 cable is 50 Ω cable.

This type of Ethernet uses a taps called medium access units, or MAUs. As already discussed, these are commonly known as vampire taps but also include an active component called a transceiver. This is the reason why they are called MAUs instead of just taps. They contain more functionality than a simple tap. The MAUs combines the functionality of the transceiver and tap and is distinct from the NIC.

It is usually very interesting for students to realize that in this form of Ethernet the transceiver cable is not coaxial. This is because the transceiver, although physically adjacent to the tap, is logically distinct from the tap. The tap is a simple vampire design; it taps the center conductor of the coaxial line and then this single conductor is passed to the transceiver.

The transceiver is an active electronic component that transforms this signal onto a DB-15 connector. This 15 wire cable connects the transceiver to the NIC card and is best referred to as a transceiver cable. Following standard practice, the cable has a male end intended to be attached to the DTE device and a female end intended to be attached to the MAU. This means that the connector on the NIC card is female and the connector on the MAU is male.

10Base5 Ethernet networks, due to the way the protocol works, have special locations where the taps must be placed for proper operation. 10Base5 cable comes from the manufacturer marked with colored bands every 2.5 m. These identify the locations where the taps must be placed. This is of critical importance for this protocol.

Like any network in this family, segments can be strung together to form larger LANs. However, the standard recommends a maximum of 5 segments. It is also possible to string segments together with long lines where no stations are attached. One might imagine connecting two buildings together. The maximum length of the "no station segment" is 1000 m. This length must be included in the calculation of the total length of the entire network. It is also important that one end of each segment be tied to ground.

The actual rule for the total length of the network is 2500 m. This would lead one to expect a maximum of 200 stations per segment, (500 m/2.5 m = 200 stations) and a maximum of 1000 stations altogether on five segments. Neither result is correct; the specification calls for no more than 100 stations on any single segment. The protocol will still operate if these specifications are exceeded, but at decreasing levels of effectiveness. At some point the increased length or number of stations will cause the protocol perfor-

Figure 17.6
10Base5 attachment.

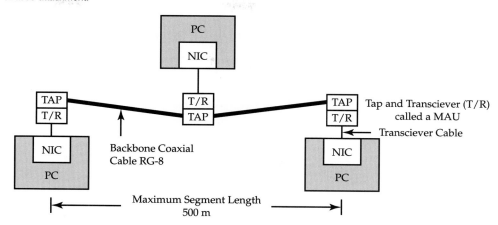

mance to break down, and only the occasional message will get through. Figure 17.6 shows how a station is attached in an Ethernet 10Base5 network.

10Base-T

10Base-T is the first type of Ethernet that does not use coaxial cable. Following the naming convention, when the cable type is not coaxial, the segment length is replaced by a single letter code identifying the cable type. Here, the T represents twisted pair cable. The data rate is 10 Mbps, and the modulation signal is baseband. 10Base-T was a revolution in LAN networking and is very widely adopted. The key advantage it has over its predecessors and competitors is a very simple and inexpensive cabling arrangement.

The twisted pair cable specified is four-wire unshielded twisted pair cable, or four-wire UTP, a very inexpensive choice. The connectors, instead of being coaxial or 15-wire DB-15 connectorized, are simple, inexpensive RJ45 jacks. Refer Chapter 3 for more information on this connector. To review, it is an eight-wire connector with only four wires used. The transmit pair is on pins 1 and 2, and the receive pair is on pins 3 and 6. The pin out is summarized in Table 17.7.

10Base-FL

The 10Base-FL standard is virtually identical to 10Base-T except for the media used. Instead of four-wire UTP, two simplex fiber optic cables are used for transmit and receive. The data rate is 10 Mbps, the signaling is baseband in nature, and the maximum length of the connection to the hub is 2 km. The topology is a star, just like 10Base-T.

Additionally, like 10Base-T, each link can make only one connection: the hub to the station. Like any optical system, no electrical charge is carried. This has big advantages in certain situations like linking buildings together and when ground loops manifest

Table 17.7
Connector Pin Out

Pin	Name
1	Transmit data +
2	Transmit data −
3	Receive data +
4	NC
5	NC
6	Receive Data −
7	NC
8	NC

themselves. A related advantage is that fiber links are not susceptible to taps, and because no electrical charge is carried, they radiate no electromagnetic field. Therefore, a more secure network is possible.

■ TROUBLESHOOTING 10BASE-T

The cable is specified to have of impedance 100 Ω. Some early implementations did not follow this rule, so if there are problems and the installation is older, suspect the cables and try replacing them with new ones, adhering to the impedance standard. It may be that easy to fix the problem. Also, make sure the hub is designed to the impedance standard as well. Again, this is not a problem except with devices and cables manufactured prior to formal adoption of the standard, 1991.

The maximum length of any segment is 100 m. Because 10Base-T networks are almost universally implemented with centrally located hubs and stations arranged in a star topology, the segment length is defined as the length of the cable segment from the hub to the station. Another big advantage to 10Base-T from the user perspective is that instead of both the tap and transceiver being a separate physical device as the 10Base5 version of the standard and called a MAU, the transceiver functionality is bundled into the hub. The tap is just the RJ45 jack. Hubs with the transceiver integrated into them are sometimes referred to as MAU hubs. Figure 17.7 shows how a 10Base-T network is hooked up.

Of course, the NIC card is still required in each station, but the ease of adding or removing stations is greatly enhanced with this arrangement and topology. The biggest problems with this arrangement are the sometimes confusing situation with the cable and hub wiring specifications and the confusion between straight-through and crossover cables, especially when one should be used instead of the other.

There are two specifications for the UTP. The first is the one that is always used in a normal configuration. This is a straight-through wired connection from the NIC card to the hub. A straight-through cable is one where pin 1 connects to pin 1, and so forth.

Figure 17.7
10Base-T.

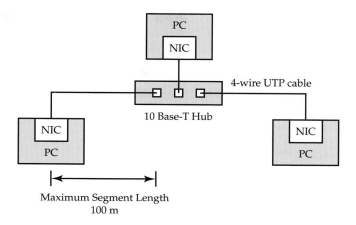

4-wire UTP cable

10 Base-T Hub

Maximum Segment Length
100 m

Inside the hub, a crossover is performed to accomplish the signal translation necessary for the connection a file server. This crossover is TD+ to RD+ and TD− to RD−. Table 17.8 shows how this cable is wired.

Many installations of 10Base-T are in an office environment where PC stations are connected through a hub to a server. To diagnose a problem hub, a crossover cable is used to connect the file server directly to the NIC card in the station. This cable bypasses the hub to see if the problem can be isolated to the hub or the cables used in the original configuration.

This is a useful troubleshooting technique, but one must make absolutely sure that there is only one crossover in the network path between the station and file server. In a normal situation this crossover is performed inside the hub itself. No crossover cable is used. However, when two cables exist that to a casual eye are the same, potential problems emerge. Use the tip in Chapter 3 to determine if the cable is a crossover or straight through.

Table `17.8
10Base-T Crossover Cable

Signal	Pin	Pin	Signal
TD+	1	3	RD+
TD−	2	6	RD−
RD+	3	1	TD+
RD−	6	2	TD−

If this was the only problem, it would not be severe; someone would mark the troubleshooting crossover cable in some way and no one would ever use it for a standard connection. However, sometimes portions of the cable plant are wired with crossover cable. In this case both types of cables exist in the network and must be combined in such a way that only one crossover exists in any path connecting the station and the file server.

To get at this problem, many hub manufacturers use an LED on the NIC card that will alert the installer that the cabling is wired correctly. If the LED is lit, the connection is correctly wired. If the connection features zero or an even number of crossovers, the LED will be dark. If it blinks, the cable is wired incorrectly, and intermittent functionality will rule the day. Replace any cables where the LED is blinking.

Fast Ethernet Family

100Base-T is a member of the Fast Ethernet family of protocols. All members of this family operate at a data rate of 100 Mbps. The topology is a star. There are actually two versions of the 100 Mbps standard using metallic conductors. The first, 100Base-T4, uses four-pair Category 3 or 4 cable. See Chapter 3 for a description of the various categories. The second, 100Base-TX, uses two-pair Category 5 cable and is more widely implemented. Both limit the hub to station length to 100 m.

Category 3 cable is widely installed in office buildings to accommodate telephone service to the office. Therefore, it makes a nice choice for a media option due to the lowered cost barrier to upgrade to Fast Ethernet (e.g., no new wiring is required). However, because of the relative low quality of this wire, all four wires are needed to accomplish this data rate. The second metallic standard, 100Base-TX, uses only two wires, but they must be newly installed for most buildings.

100Base-TX also uses a unique line code to reduce the data rate on the wire. It is another example of the so-called rate reduction line codes. The specific code used in 4B5B. It works very simply. Because the Category 5 wiring can handle higher data rates than the other types of wiring, the actual clocking rate used for 100Base-TX is 125 MHz. The line code acts to reduce this to 100 Mbps by sending only 4 bits for every five clock periods. This increases the reliability by adding a little redundancy, five-fourths and reduces the susceptibility to noise of the signaling on the wire. This same code is used in the standard FDDI. The 4B5B code is illustrated in table 17.9.

Table 17.9
4B5B Coding

4 bit data	5 bit code	4 bit data	5 bit code
0000	11110	1000	10010
0001	01001	1001	10011
0010	10100	1010	10110
0011	10101	1011	10111
0100	01010	1100	11010
0101	01011	1101	11011
0110	01110	1110	11100
0111	01111	1111	11101

This code works by taking each group of 4 bits and transforming them into a group of 5 bits. This translation is shown in Table 17.9. Because there are 32 possible combinations of 5 bits and only 16 possible combinations of 4 bits, there are some combinations left over after accounting for all possible data sequences. This fact is taken advantage of by using some of the leftover groups to send control codes. These control codes are not shown in Table 17.9 but eight are defined.

There is also a member of this family, called 100Base-FX, that uses fiber optic cable. As you might imagine, this uses two simplex single mode fiber links or a single duplex multimode fiber to conduct the transmit and receive signals in a similar way as 10Base-FL. The distance from hub to station is much longer for a fiber network. For the single-mode case, lengths of up to 10 km are recommended, whereas the multimode cable, because of its increased loss per kilometer, is limited to 2 km.

Fast Ethernet uses the same access methodology, frame format, and service offerings that Ethernet does so that it would be backward compatible with the large number of 10 Mbps Ethernet networks installed. The important distinction between these standards and a related one, 100VG, is that the former use the same access methodology as the lower-speed cousins, CSMA/CD. This means that interconnection between segments operating at different speeds can be done at the physical layer.

100VG uses a different MAC protocol called Demand Priority. This offers advantages in time-critical applications like voice and video but is not compatible with earlier forms of Ethernet. If you have an existing network based on traditional Ethernet, consider carefully before adding a segment of 100VG. On that segment, performance will increase for some types of traffic, but the cost of linking that segment to other segments will be much higher.

The last thing to mention about Fast Ethernet is that the hubs that it uses are not exactly the same as the hubs used for the lower-speed versions of this protocol. Usually, an older 10 Mbps hub can be upgraded to handle Fast Ethernet by swapping the individual cards used at each port. This is an inexpensive procedure and allows reuse of existing equipment when the data rate of the segment is upgraded.

■ TCP/IP

TCP/IP is used on the Internet. It is the most popular nonproprietary communications architecture in the marketplace. TCP/IP was developed as part of the ARPANET research project sponsored by the Department of Defense (DOD). Because TCP/IP was developed prior to definition of international standards for developing communication protocols (the OSI model), therefore, it does not conform to them. Although TCP/IP was not developed under the OSI model, a correspondence can be made. This correspondence is illustrated in the next section.

Relation to OSI Model
As can be seen from Figure 17.8, the Process layer functions as a transport user. Additionally, a correspondence exists between the Host-to-Host layer functioning as a transport provider. Finally, the Network Access layer provides the physical interface and performs the link control and access mechanism responsibilities.

Figure 17.8
TCP/IP model.

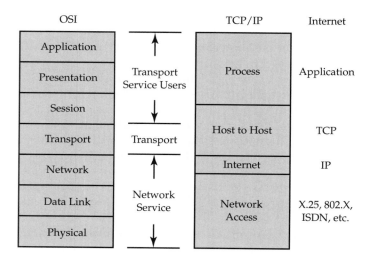

As will be seen in the following paragraphs, TCP/IP uses an entirely different nomenclature to talk about communications. Because it was developed before the days of networked PCs, the standard is closely associated with the idea of a host-to-host communication between mainframe computers servicing terminals.

TCP/IP is a communications architecture composed of three basic components: processes, hosts, and networks. Processes are the fundamental elements that communicate; examples are a file transfer operation and a remote login. Processes execute on hosts, and hosts are connected by networks that transfer data from one host to another.

This indicates that the transfer of data from one process to another involves first getting the data to the host in which the process resides and then getting it to the pro-

Figure 17.9
TCP processes.

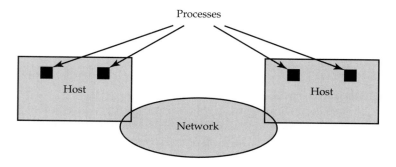

Table 17.10
TCP/IP Protocol Tasks

Layer Number	Layer Name	Function	Name
4	Process Layer	Protocols used to support the application	
3	Host-to-Host Layer	Reliability mechanisms	TCP
2	Internet Layer	Routing of data between networks	IP
1	Network Access Layer	Exchange of data between a host and a network	

cess within the host. Therefore, a communications network needs to be concerned only with routing data between hosts, and the hosts are concerned with directing data to processes. See Figure 17.9.

There are four separate tasks involved in the TCP/IP communications architecture; these are shown in Table 17.10. Therefore, TCP/IP is really composed of four protocols combined and named for the middle two. [Actually, there are five, the fifth being an additional Process layer Protocol. Both the File Transfer Protocol, (FTP) and Simple Mail Transfer Protocol (SMTP) are usually present in any implementation.] Also, as in any layer architecture, many different network access layers can be utilized, and the resulting protocol stack continues to be called TCP/IP.

This again illustrates the power of layered architectures. The Network Access layer uses the protocol appropriate to a specific network, for example, Ethernet, Token Ring, or X.25. The Process layer is also home to many different types of protocols such as FTP or SMTP. The result is that one term, *TCP/IP*, stands for many different communications options. As long as the Process layer protocols can communicate, all implementation variations of TCP/IP will communicate (with appropriate intermediate system, or IS, devices).

The next subject is how these protocols may be configured for communications. In this discussion, when the term *relay* is used, it will be used generically (non-OSI) to include devices of the bridge, router, gateway, and protocol converter classes. Note that in

Table 17.11
Non-OSI Definitions of Relay Devices

Layer	Name	Function
1	Repeater	Copies individual bits between cable segments
2	Bridge	Stores and forwards frames between LANs
3	Gateway	Stores and forwards packets between dissimilar network
4	Protocol converter	Provides interfacing in higher layers

Table 17.12
OSI Definitions

Layer	Name	Function
1	Repeater	Copies individual bits between cable segments (relay)
2	Bridge	Stores and forwards frames between LANs
3	Router	Stores and forwards packets between dissimilar network
7	Gateway	Provides interfacing between OSI and non-OSI networks

the non-OSI world, relaying can be done at any layer, whereas in the OSI world, relaying can only be done at the physical layer (Layer 1).

Because a non-OSI protocol, TCP/IP, is being described, this seemed the right approach. Tables 17.11 and 17.12 make the correspondence to the OSI equivalent device at the appropriate layer. Some statements will only apply to one or more of these devices, not all four. Generally, refer to the OSI model to determine whether a statement applies to a specific device.

In reading Tables 17.11 and 17.12, remember that the words *bit, frame,* and *packet* have historical meanings in communications terminology that were adapted by the networking community. Bits are talked about when discussing Physical layer issues; frames, for Data Link layer issues; and packets, for Network layer issues. The terms refer to the traditional names of PDUs in WANs where the lower three layers are run by the telephone system.

Each host contains software at the Network Access, Internet, and Host-to-Host layers and software at the Process layer for one or more processes. Relays between networks need the Network Access layer to interface to the networks that they attach to and the Internet layer to be able to perform the routing and relaying function.

Like any protocol, for successful communication, each entity must have an unique address. Actually two levels of addressing are needed. Each host must have a unique address on the network, and each process on a host must have an address that is unique on that host. This allows TCP, the host-to-host protocol, to deliver data to the proper address.

When any two processes need to communicate, they must somehow be able to identify each other. This is done via an addressing scheme. First, each network must maintain a unique address for each host attached to that network. This allows the network to route packets through the network and deliver them to the intended host. This is called the subnetwork attachment point address. The term *subnetwork* is used to identify a physically distinct network that may be part of a complex of networks interconnected by relays.

At the internet level, it is the responsibility of the Internet protocol to deliver datagrams across multiple networks from source to destination. Hence, the Internet protocol must be provided with a global network address that uniquely identifies each host.

Finally, once a data unit is delivered to a host, it is passed to the Host-to-Host layer for delivery to the ultimate user (process). Because there may be multiple users, each is identified by a port number that is unique to that host. Thus, the combination of port and global network address uniquely identifies a process within an environment of multiple networks and hosts. This three-level address (network, host, port) is referred to as a socket.

■ INTERNET PROTOCOL (IP)

This section will focus on the IP and addressing within it. First, the word *internet* as used here and in the above paragraphs has nothing to do with the familiar Internet and WWW. It is composed of hundreds of interconnected networks, most using TCP/IP, including the two unclassified segments of the Defense Data Network (DDN), MILNET and ARPANET. As the term is used here, an internet is nothing more that an interconnected set of networks, connected by relays. Also confusing to some is that the term *internet* is used to described the TCP/IP protocol stack.

IP provides a connectionless, or datagram, service between hosts. That is, IP does not set up a logical connection between hosts and does not guarantee that all data units will be delivered or that those delivered will be in the proper order.

Recall our earlier discussion on the differences between a connectionless and connection-oriented mechanism. A connectionless service is one that corresponds to the datagram mechanism of a packet switching network. On the other hand, a connection-oriented service is one that corresponds to the physical circuit mechanism of a circuit switching network.

The decision to have the Internet layer provide an unreliable connectionless service evolved gradually from an earlier connection-oriented service as the ARPA evolved into the ARPA internet. This network contains many networks, not all of them reliable. By putting all the reliability mechanisms into the Transport layer (TCP), it was possible to have reliable end-to-end connections even when some of the underlying networks were not very dependable. Recall that this was exactly the rational behind using a Transport layer in the OSI network architecture.

A major segment of IP is concerned with addressing. This is a complex subject, full of labels, where traditional distinctions are blurred. To illustrate, a distinction is generally made among names, addresses, and routes. A name specifies what an object is, an address specifies where it is, and a route indicates how to get there. On a single network, the name and address distinction is arbitrary; either can be used to uniquely identify any object.

Each protocol stack uses a different method to accomplish addressing of individual stations. For Ethernet networks, the MAC address is the unique identifier. Novell IPX has its own approach, as does Apple Talk. IP assigns a unique number to every station. This is in addition to any addressing that might exist in the layers below, such as the MAC address used in Ethernet networks. For the Internet, there is a governing body called the Internet Network Information Center, or InterNIC that assigns these numbers.

As will be seen shortly, the IP address is 32 bits long and is composed of two parts, the network and the host. Each is converted into a decimal number, which is referred to as an IP number. However, before going into that detail, terminology that is commonly used to talk about the subject of addressing in the internet is reviewed.

On an internet, the distinction between names, addresses, and routes is less clear. Applications continue to use names, and individual networks continue to use addresses and, if necessary, routes. To transfer data through a relay, two entities must be identified; the destination network and destination host. The relay requires the address of the network to perform its function. This address can be specified in a number of ways:

1. The application can refer to a network by a unique number; in effect the name and address are the same.
2. The internet logic in the host can translate a network name into a network address.
3. A global addressing scheme can be used. That is, there is a unique identifier for each host in the internet. For routing purposes, each relay would need to derive network addresses from host addresses.

For example, as discussed earlier, Ethernet uses the third approach, and so does the Internet. For Ethernet, the main advantage of this approach is that the network address can be hardwired into the device. The main disadvantages are that a central authority must manage the assignment of names and that unnecessarily long address fields must be carried across networks. Therefore, typically a relay will receive an internet packet with a reference in the form NET.HOST, where NET is a network address. The identifier HOST is usually a name and an address. To the higher-layer software that generated the packet, HOST is an address, translated from an application-level name.

When it becomes time for a relay to deliver a datagram to a host on an attached network, HOST must be translated into a subnetwork attachment point address. This is because different networks will have different address field lengths, as well as many other problems in mapping addresses. Hence, HOST is treated as a name by the relay.

This is an example of a two-level hierarchical addressing scheme. This is what was meant earlier about the IP address being broken up into two parts. Note that by appending an SAP address on the end, this can become a three-level addressing scheme, NET.HOST.SAP. This is what is used. The SAP is an individual Service Access Point in a host. Conceptually, *SAP* is a more general term for *port*. It has the same function as the SAP does in OSI terminology. With this identifier, the IP can be viewed as process to process rather than host to host.

This leads one to the observation that addressing and where it is performed has a correspondence with layer complexity. In the above example, with a SAP in the internet layer, the IP is responsible for multiplexing and demultiplexing datagrams for software modules that use the internet service. The advantage, of course, is that the next higher layer can now be simplified, a useful observation for vendors building products where cost and complexity are real issues.

How does the station software determine the NET.HOST identifier of a desired destination? This is provided by a directory service, generally located on a server. Each server contains part or all of the name and address directory for internet hosts. Note that a directory service here is a database for the local address span only. This is not a routing table for reaching outside of the locally connected hosts.

Routing is perhaps the most well-known responsibility of the IP. Note that for successful operation of a router between two networks, both networks must use the same IP. All routing strategies fall into the same classes as discussed previously, but they are referred to a little differently in the TCP/IP world. The terms *fixed* and *adaptive* map to terms used in the OSI discussion, *static* and *dynamic*. Routing has already been discussed in preceding chapters to the extent it will be.

Internet also provides some minimal error control. Basically, it discards datagrams when it deems that it is appropriate to do so. This error control always takes place at the relay points in the network. The router may discard a datagram for a number of reasons, including lifetime expiration, congestion, and bit error. Note that notification of the source is not guaranteed. For example, if the address field is damaged due to a bit error, identification of the source is not possible.

In this section, until now, most of what has been said could apply to any implementation of the IP. What follows is specific characteristics to the IP specified in MIL-STD-1777. As with any layer protocol, it is defined in two parts:

1. The interface to higher layers (TCP) specifying the services that IP provides
2. The actual protocol format and mechanisms, specifying in this case the host-router and router-router interactions

The first part is sometimes referred to as the IP services and is generally less precisely defined than the protocol itself. Its definition is biased toward a functional rather than an explicit and precise definition. This is because as the interaction between layers occurs within a single system, generally made by a single manufacturer, room is left for innovation to perform this interaction in the most efficient manner possible.

The inner workings of the IP can best be understood with a definition of the IP datagram. The figure shown in Appendix K illustrates this definition. The basic idea is that all services that a protocol can provide must fit into the datagram format. In any OSI forum, the packet defined in Figure K.1 is referred to as PDU or because it is operating at the OSI network layer, as a NPDU. As you probably have guessed by now, TCP/IP uses the term *datagram* for packets.

It is interesting to understand how the three IP address formats work on the Internet. The source and destination addresses are of one of four classes, A, B, C, or D. The idea is that the larger the local installation, (local address space), the more bits are needed in any address to accommodate the number of local stations. As can be seen from examination of Figure 17.10, class A addresses are designed for very large installations, class B is designed for large organizations, and class C is designed for smaller ones. Class D addresses are reserved for multicasting applications.

This structure allows a variety of network sizes to be accommodated with a uniform-length address field. This simplifies the IP address resolution problem and at the same time recognizes that there are many more small organizations that want an officially recognized address than there are large ones. These IP routing addresses can be

Figure 17.10
IP address formats.

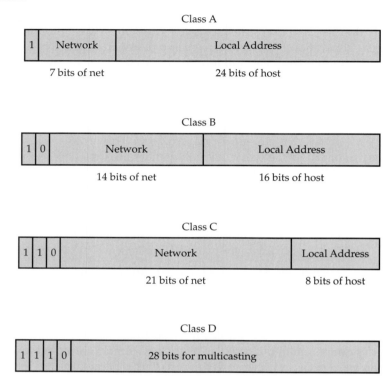

Class A

| 1 | Network | Local Address |

7 bits of net   24 bits of host

Class B

| 1 | 0 | Network | Local Address |

14 bits of net   16 bits of host

Class C

| 1 | 1 | 0 | Network | Local Address |

21 bits of net   8 bits of host

Class D

| 1 | 1 | 1 | 0 | 28 bits for multicasting |

purchased from the InterNIC for any organization. The price is about $500 a year. As you might imagine, it is much easier to obtain class C than class A addresses. The address formats are shown for each of the classes in Figure 17.10. These addresses are assigned by two different groups. The network portion is assigned by the group referred to earlier, the InterNIC. The host or local address portion is assigned by the local network administrator.

Such addresses are written in decimal form for the Internet and are used for POP addresses for ISPs. Each byte of the 4 byte address is written in decimal form to be more compact and easily recognized by human beings. Because the first byte is constrained by the status of the first few bits that are used to classify the addresses, a numeric range is defined for each class. These ranges exclude the first bit, which is always a 1. This is shown in Table 17.13.

You might like to see what your ISP address is and identify the class address it is using. Most ISPs are Class B or C, as are most large corporations and educational institutions. Class A addresses are often reserved for network providers or large subnets of which the Internet is composed. Subnets as used in IP addressing are described next.

Table 17.13
IP Address Ranges

Class	Starting Address	Ending Address	Number of Hosts
A	000.000.000.000	126.255.255.255	16,580,000
Not used	127.000.000.000	127.255.255.255	N/A
B	128.000.000.000	191.255.255.255	65,000
C	192.000.000.000	223.255.255.255	254
D	224.000.000.000	247.255.255.255	

Subnet Addressing

A subnet is a set of addresses used to identify a smaller portion of a network that makes up a large network. For example, when you are assigned an address from your ISP, you are essentially made a subnet of the ISP's network. The way this is done is by segmenting the Host portion of the address. The network portion of the address must not be altered. The approach used is to divide this range of addresses into two groups, subnet and host.

For example, for a class C address in a small company, one might break the 8 bit address range into two 4 bit groups. The first 4 bits or the 4 MSB bits would identify the subnet and the host address for the last 4 bits would be for the subnet. Usually this is done for ease of managing the address fields by the network administrator. It should be noted that any choice of host and subnet address lengths is possible as long as the total length adds to the host address length for the particular class address assigned.

A company might decide to set the host address ranges as departments within the organization. Administration, purchasing, engineering, production, and sales might all have specific 4 bit host addresses assigned to them. Then each department would take the individual stations in their departments and assign each one of them one of the 4 bit subnet addresses. For this example, 16 departments could be uniquely identified, each of which could have up to 16 stations attached to the Internet.

Routers would use these subnet masks to automatically route messages to and from individual stations. For example, assume engineering was assigned the host address of 1011 and the manager of that department assigned subnet address 0001. The router would know how to route a message to and from that station by routing all messages with 1011XXX addresses to engineering and the those with address 10110001 to the manager's station.

These addresses are also written in decimal form. For example, in our small company class C address, the network IP is set to 203.120.20.0. This indicates a broadcast to the entire network, because the host address is set to all zeros. The manager's department would have the address span 203.120.20.176 through 203.120.20.191. The manager's address would be 203.120.20.177, and the broadcast address for the engineering department would be 203.120.20.176.

You will also encounter the term *subnet mask.* This is just a way to specify how many bits are used to segment out the subnet in any particular network address. They are exactly the same format as the IP address. The only difference is that all bits except the subnet portion of the host address field are set to 1. For example, the subnet mask for our small company would be 255.255.255.176. This indicates that only the last four bits of the host address are available for subnet addressing.

■ PROCESS LAYER

Earlier in the discussion about IP, two protocols were briefly mentioned, FTP and SMTP. These will now be briefly described along with the two other applications commonly found in TCP/IP, TELNET and SNMP. TELNET is a piece of software that allows remote login on the host machine. Simple Network Management Protocol, SNMP, allows exchange of management information between network devices. The first three applications formed the basis of networking in the ARPANET environment. They shielded the user from the complexities of TCP and allowed them to transfer files, send and receive e-mail, and login remotely. SNMP will be the dominant Process layer protocol used by a network engineer or technician.

FTP

FTP is a piece of application software that uses the TCP services to exchange files between two hosts. FTP works quite differently from similar services in the OSI world. Because TCP/IP was designed before the OSI model was developed, it did not partition out parts of the job to other layers of the protocol stack. Everything associated with file transfer had to be performed in this location. Therefore, word size differences, bit order preferences, bit versus byte transfer procedures, and so forth all had to be accommodated in the FTP. As a result, the number of different types of files it can handle was quite limited.

SMTP

SMTP is a piece of application software that forms the basis for all e-mail sent on the Internet today. It was originally defined in a now famous document, RFC 822. This document in its original form was limited to sending text messages. Just like FTP, SMTP must contain all the particulars associated with any e-mail transfer. As many of you no doubt realize, this limitation of text only no longer exists and many updates to RFC 822 have occurred over the years. Just like FTP, SMTP uses TCP services to accomplish its mission.

The format for e-mail addresses is defined by this standard. All follow the same format, shown below:

NAME@DOMAIN

For example,

Godzilla@Downtown.Tokyo.Jpn

As can be seen from this example, the domain contains three parts. The first two parts are descriptive terms identifying the location. The third part is one of a few reserved abbreviations that are used throughout the Internet for routing mail. Although they form only a part of the domain, often just the last part is called the domain.

Using this terminology, several domains are now described. It is very probable that more will be defined in the near future. A change in the registration authority is now being considered. Currently, the bulk of the domain registrations are performed by one organization, licensed by the U.S. government. There are six domain types used in the United States:

.COM. This is for commercial organizations.

.EDU. This is for educational organizations.

.GOV. This is for government bodies.

.MIL. This is for military organizations.

.NET. This is for network organizations like your ISP.

.ORG. This is for non-profit organizations.

These domains are those used primarily in the United States. However, many organizations based outside the United States use a two- or three-letter abbreviation for their country name as the final field in domain name. For example, the United Kingdom uses .UK, Canada uses .CA, and Japan uses JPN.

Telnet

TELNET seems to be derived from the expression *terminal to remote host protocol.* However, this software provides a mechanism, again using TCP services, to remotely login to a host running TCP/IP. Because there are many different types of terminals, TELNET takes care of any differences in how the host represents data and how it must be displayed on the terminal.

TELNET complements this translation by a series of codes that it uses to both query and parse the data sent along the connection. One of the most revealing things about how the nature of computers and communications has changed over time is shown in one of these codes that TELNET provides. It is code 246, and its literal meaning is "Are you still there?" For most of the history of data communications, the line rate and the computer on the other end were so slow that a remote user, logged in using TELNET, might wonder if the connection still existed. In this case, one could send this code to get a "quick" response to this question.

SNMP

SNMP was originally designed only for TCP/IP networks but has grown into a standard for managing networks of many types. It is now a standard feature on many types of network devices such as hubs, switches, routers, and others discussed in Chapter 15.

Network management is the subject of how to use an automated tool to automate much of the effort involved in collecting statistics, querying status, remotely configuring devices, and the other activities involved in day-to-day operation of a network. For example, you might want to find out how many bits are actually being sent by a particular modem in any 24-h period and determine if at any time its power is cycled. Additionally, on Tuesday, you need to reconfigure the modem and want to do it from your desk. These are the kinds of things possible with any network management tool utilizing SNMP.

Network management is probably the most critical tool used in the day-to-day operation of networks. Clearly, as networks have grown, the availability of a tool to effectively manage, query, and control network devices is critical.

There are three core elements to SNMP in addition to the protocol definition itself:

1. Agents, present in the managed devices themselves
2. Network Management Station, or NMS, typically a dedicated computer for this task
3. The database of information called the Management Information Base, or MIB

The agents are small pieces of software that are placed in the network devices. The critical idea here is that they are small and do not burden the network device with excessive processing in the exchange of information between the device and the NMS. Essentially, the agent responds to requests from the NMS or based on some simple procedure independently forward information to the NMS.

The NMS is usually a fairly sophisticated computer, and a workstation-grade PC is the usual choice. Sometimes there will be more than one NMS on a network, but usually not. The NMS runs software that builds the MIB through querying network devices. It typically provides for a variety of graphical displays of the data it is collecting. It also allows a method for configuration of any managed network device.

The MIB is usually described as a collection of objects with unique identifing tags. What they really are is a collection of data items that are present in any managed object. Each class of network device has its own set of data items or objects. For example, all hubs have a similar set of data items. Sometimes this collection is called the hubs MIB.

SNMP has three basic operations, and for the most part it operates as a simple request response protocol using the first two operations. The NMS requests information exchange from a network device, and the network device responds with one or more of its data values. The NMS can also enable an agent to notify it upon some specific event using the third operation. In this situation, the NMS does not respond to the network device. These exchanges are carried out with the following three commands:

1. Get: The NMS retrieves the value of an object from a network device.
2. Set: The NMS sets the value of an object in a network device.
3. Trap: The network device informs the NMS of some event.

There are two versions of SNMP on the market, SNMP and SNMPv2. Version 2 is an improved protocol with greatly increased security functions. It is backward compatible to SNMP. The concern with implementing network management is that you must

be sure that only authorized people can configure and get information about network devices remotely. SNMPv2 provides for a way for the agent to verify that the authorized NMS is making a request and allows encryption of the data exchanged. In networks with multiple NMS devices, agents can be configured to grant different levels of access to different NMS devices.

■ SUMMARY

This chapter has introduced three very different protocols and related each to the OSI model. The first, FieldBus, is a very simply implemented protocol designed for inexpensive products that still require precise timing control. Several Ethernet specifications were summarized, and the distinctions between them were discussed with a focus on how stations are attached to the physical network. Ethernet specifies only the lower two layers of the OSI model, and all but one type discussed uses the same layer 2, so the real differences between them are at the physical layer. Finally, TCP/IP was introduced and terminology, addressing and process protocols were discussed.

PROBLEMS

1. Discuss which member of the Fast Ethernet family of protocols you would choose to use to add a segment in each of the following cases:

   (a) Existing 10Base-T network using CAT 5 cabling.
   (b) Existing 100Base-T network using CAT 5 cabling.
   (c) Existing 100Base-T network using fiber optic cabling.
   (d) New installation where voice and video requirements are critical.
   (e) New installation in a very large campus environment.
   (f) Existing 10Base-T network using CAT 3 cabling.

2. What were the basic reasons why Ethernet was adopted so widely?

3. Can two networks that use 10Base-T and Token Ring respectively, as their layer 2 protocols and Physical layer, and TCP/IP as a Transport and Network layer both be called TCP/IP networks? Why?

4. Can two networks that use 10Base-T and Token Ring respectively, as their layer 2 protocols and Physical layer, and Novell at layers 5–7 both be called Novell networks? Why?

5. Describe the difference between the Internet protocol, IP and the Internet as the term is commonly used to describe WWW access.

6. What are the three core aspects of SNMP and their responsibilities?

Fourier Series

To determine the amplitudes, A and B, solve the integrals and evaluate them at the end points. The numerical result gives you each amplitude.

$$A_n = \frac{w}{\pi} \int_0^{2\pi/w} y(t) \cos(nwt) \, dt$$

$$B_n = \frac{w}{\pi} \int_0^{2\pi/w} y(t) \sin(nwt) \, dt$$

(A-1)

The following example illustrates how to apply these equations and find the dc bias of the waveform, called in Fourier analysis, the dc constant, K.

EXAMPLE A.1

Note in Figure A.1 that the horizontal axis is shown in such a way that this diagram would work for any frequency square wave. This is true because for any angular frequency, the period is always just the angular frequency divided by 2π, or $w = 2\pi f$. This is the same thing as saying that the frequency is the inverse of the period. To see this examine the algebra below:

$$\text{period} = \frac{2\pi}{w} = \frac{2\pi}{2\pi f} = \frac{1}{f}$$

The constant is expressed as follows:

$$K = \frac{A_0}{2} = \frac{w}{2\pi} \int_0^{2\pi/w} y(t) \cos(0wt) \, dt$$

$$= \frac{w}{2\pi} \int_0^{2\pi/w} y(t) \, dt$$

(A-2)

Notice two things: First, one can always break an integral into two pieces if the function takes on discrete values for those pieces. Second, $y(t)$ is the square wave shown above and, as can be seen from Figure A.1, has a value of 1 for the first half of the period and a value of 0 for the second half. This means it is possible to write

$$K = \frac{w}{2\pi} \left(\int_0^{\pi/w} y(t) \, dt + \int_{\pi/w}^{2\pi/w} y(t) \, dt \right)$$

Because the value of $y(t)$ is zero for the second integral, and the integral of zero is just zero, and we are left with

$$K = \frac{w}{2\pi} \int_0^{\pi/w} dt = \frac{w}{2\pi} \left(\frac{\pi}{w} \right) = 1/2$$

As mentioned above, this constant expressed a dc bias. If you look more carefully at Figure A.1, you will see that the waveform shown is shifted up 1/2 V. It is not symmetric about the x-axis but moves between 1 and 0 V; this means it has a 1/2 V dc bias. Because any dc bias

Figure A.1
Arbitrary frequency square wave.

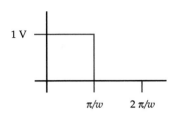

must be expressed by the constant, so far our mathematics agrees with what one would expect.

The next task is to evaluate the cosine amplitudes. Because there is only one cycle of the square wave shown in Figure A.1, the integral is evaluated over one cycle. Also, because the square wave is zero over the second half of the period, just like when we evaluated the integral for the constant, the second half will be zero.

$$A_n = \frac{w}{\pi} \int_0^{2\pi/w} y(t) \cos(nwt)\, dt = \frac{w}{\pi} \int_0^{\pi/w} \cos(nwt)\, dt$$

$$= \frac{w}{\pi} \left(\frac{1}{nw} \right) \sin(nwt) \Big|_0^{\pi/w} \qquad \text{(A-3)}$$

$$= \frac{1}{n\pi} [\sin(n\pi) - \sin(0)] = 0$$

The surprising result is that for a square wave, all the cosine amplitudes are zeros. This happens because the square wave shown is an odd function. Recall that an odd function is not symmetric about the origin. Mathematically, this is expressed by

$$y(-t) = -y(t)$$

Anytime a function is odd, all the cosine amplitudes will be zero. This can be an important time saver, so make note of it and notice whether functions are odd or even before just plugging in the numbers and turning the crank. An even function is expressed mathematically as

$$y(-t) = y(t)$$

Sine waves are always odd, and cosine waves are always even. To evaluate the sine amplitudes proceed in the same way:

$$B_n = \frac{w}{\pi} \int_0^{2\pi/w} y(t) \sin(nwt)\, dt = \frac{w}{\pi} \int_0^{\pi/w} \sin(nwt)\, dt$$

$$= \frac{w}{\pi} \left(\frac{1}{nw} \right) \cos(nwt) \Big|_0^{\pi/w}$$

$$= \frac{1}{n\pi} [\cos(n\pi) - \cos(0)] \qquad \text{(A-4)}$$

$$= \frac{2}{n\pi} \qquad n = 1, 3, 5, 7, 9, \ldots .$$

$$= 0 \qquad n = 2, 4, 6, 8, \ldots$$

Here, some more simplification results when n is an even number; the sine amplitudes are all zero. You are left with only needing to calculate the sine amplitudes when n is an odd number, and these are given by the simple fraction shown above.

The reason why we need to calculate the sine and cosine amplitudes is because they express the amplitudes of the harmonics. Remember that the first harmonic is generally referred to as the fundamental because it is at the same frequency as the waveform being analyzed. The voltages given by this equation are expressed as peak voltage values. To convert them to peak-to-peak values, multiply them by 2. The frequency domain picture of this square wave is shown in Figure A.2. The figure shows the amplitudes of the first several harmonics. If the square wave in Figure A.1 was a 1 kHz square wave, the harmonics shown in Figure A.2 would occur at frequencies of 1, 3, 5, and 7 kHz.

The other way to find the amplitudes of the various harmonics is to measure them with either a spectrum analyzer or a digital oscilloscope with an FFT module. This is usually the case in the field. The latter type of device works using a mathematical trick explored briefly in Appendix B.

Figure A.2
Frequency domain of square wave.

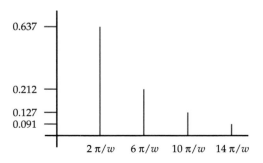

Sampling Theory and the FFT

For now there are two rules that must be obeyed to accurately sample a waveform:

1. The signal must be sampled often enough.
2. The sampling interval is held constant.

The Nyquist theorem defines sampling theory. Theorems are usually a part of mathematics studies that most of us would rather forget, but here it has a very practical and easy to understand result: For any sampled data system, there is a minimum sampling rate that must be observed if the results are to be accurate. It is defined by the maximum frequency component present in the original analog or continuous waveform to be sampled. The sampling rate must be at least twice that frequency.

So we see that rule 1 is very easy to follow. Just measure the input signal to determine the maximum frequency present using something like a spectrum analyzer or FFT module in a digital oscilloscope, multiply it by 2, and you have determined the minimum frequency of your sample clock. This rule is expressed in equation B-1:

$$f_{sample} \geq 2 * f_{signal} \qquad \text{(B-1)}$$

You can sample more often and get more accuracy, but all that is necessary is twice the highest frequency present in the original signal. It is interesting to note that this rule makes sure that each cycle of any frequency present in the original signal is sampled at least twice. This results in a mathematical guarantee (a theorem and proof) that the original waveform can be reproduced from the sampled data.

This rule of sampling the waveform at least twice each cycle is critical and must always be followed. If it is not, the entire approach will fail, and the wrong fundamental frequency and amplitude will result. This means that you must determine what the maximum frequency could be and then make sure you sample it at least twice.

Obviously, if you make sure you sample the highest frequency twice, all lower frequencies will be sampled at least twice and sampling theory will be satisfied.

Some of you may be wondering how to determine the highest frequency of an unknown signal. Well, the answer is often in the application. For example, if you know the unknown wave is, for example, a human voice or music, its maximum frequency is 20,000 Hz. If you know the unknown wave is from a telephone line, the maximum frequency is under 4000 Hz. If it is digital signal from a device running at 56 kbps, the maximum frequency is determined by how many harmonics of the fundamental frequency of 56 kbps you desire to keep.

Sometimes the signal is entirely unknown and yet you must apply sampling theory. In this case, the best approach is to take a good guess at the maximum and put the signal through a low-pass filter before sampling the waveform. The low-pass filter corner frequency is set at the highest frequency you expect in the signal. The minimum sampling rate is then determined by the low-pass filter's cutoff frequency. The low-pass filter will filter out any higher frequencies that might be there, and if you choose your cutoff frequency right, you will get a good solution.

If you guess too low, the analysis will still be good for that portion of the waveform that you let through the filter. For example, let's suppose that the waveform was a new music CD that you just purchased but that you guessed the maximum frequency at 5 kHz. (Audiophile frequency range is from 20 to 20,000 Hz.) This means that you will miss all the high frequency sounds in the analysis but that the analysis will still be good for that portion of the sounds you let through the filter. The resultant wave that you get by applying Fourier analysis will be missing the high frequencies and may sound like it is coming from a cheap speaker system, but it will sound surprisingly close to the original. There are many other examples. The key is that if it is a problem in a textbook, you must be provided with the maximum frequency. If it is in the real world, usually the maximum frequency can be determined from the application itself. Again, the bottom line is that you must be able to find the maximum frequency to set the sampling rate.

Once you have set the sampling rate, you must also ensure that it stays constant. This is the second rule; each sample must be evenly spaced in time. There is one more rule that we must follow so that the formulas presented below always work. This is not strictly a requirement of sampling theory, but it makes Fourier analysis easier if you follow it. We will require that the number of samples be even. That means no odd number of samples.

If you follow these three simple rules, your sampled data will be an accurate representation of the original signal. To use the terms that are common in the industry, the original wave is called a continuous signal and the sampled signal is called the sampled data. When you apply the integrals introduced earlier, you are performing a continuous Fourier analysis. When you apply sampling theory and use the series equations introduced earlier, you are performing a discrete Fourier analysis, discrete meaning made up of parts, here the sampled data. The series that results is called the discrete Fourier series.

Applying these ideas, new forms for the sine and cosine amplitudes can be written without using integrals. These are presented below. Note that the lowercase n represents the harmonic order, and the uppercase N represents the number of samples. Here are the new equations for the amplitudes:

$$y(k) = \frac{A_0}{2} + \sum_{n=1}^{N/2}\left[A_n\cos\left(\frac{2\pi nk}{N}\right) + B_n\sin\left(\frac{2\pi nk}{N}\right)\right] \quad \textbf{(B-2)}$$

$$A_n = \frac{2}{N}\sum_{k=0}^{N-1} y(k)\cos\left(\frac{2\pi nk}{N}\right) \quad \textbf{(B-3)}$$

$$B_n = \frac{2}{N}\sum_{k=0}^{N-1} y(k)\sin\left(\frac{2\pi nk}{N}\right) \quad \textbf{(B-4)}$$

The first equation is called the discrete Fourier series equation, and the second and third equations tell you how to calculate the sine and cosine amplitudes.

In the field, you may be equipped to find the Fourier transform of a signal with unknown frequency characteristics. For example, you might have a communications system that is not performing correctly at one particular location, and some signal seems to be interfering with the performance of the system. Your job is to locate the signal and determine its frequency components so you can design a filter to eliminate the problem. A device that can identify the interfering frequency by an examination of the output of the system can be a valuable tool. With a Fourier analysis tool like a FFT analyzer, such things are possible.

■ FFT

When the series formulas above are programmed into a computer in a special way, they are called a fast Fourier transform. The word *fast* just comes from the programming tricks used to speed up the calculation. Looking closely at equations B-2 through B-4, one can see that as N gets large, the number of multiplications needed to find the series solution gets very large. Therefore, some clever people figured out a way to speed it up. This way has become known as the FFT.

There is nothing different about an FFT from a standard Fourier transform carried out on paper, except the clever computer programming. To actually determine the frequencies as well as the amplitudes, complex exponential mathematics are needed. Here, the best approach is to get access to a FFT and use it to determine the signal characteristics. This introduction to FFT has essentially ignored the phase information contained in the waveform. Consequently, frequency information is not available to an analysis using the above equations. However, although the mathematical development of the correct equations is beyond the scope of this text, the correct equations will be presented. The full form of the equations is shown below. Capital F stands for the function's Fourier transform, and lowercase y stands for the function or waveform itself.

$$F(n) = \sum_{k=0}^{N-1} y(k)e^{-i2\pi nk/N} \quad \textbf{(B-5)}$$

$$= \sum_{k=0}^{N-1} y(k)\left[\cos\left(\frac{2\pi nk}{N}\right) - i\sin\left(\frac{2\pi nk}{N}\right)\right]$$

$$= \sum_{k=0}^{N-1} y(k)\cos\left(\frac{2\pi nk}{N}\right) - i\sum_{k=0}^{N-1} y(k)\sin\left(\frac{2\pi nk}{N}\right)$$

$$= A_n + iB_n \quad \textbf{(B-6)}$$

The amplitudes of the sine and cosine functions are now given by these equations. When these amplitudes are combined in the way shown above, the amplitude of either the sine or cosine is given by the respective $F(n)$. For example, $F(0)$ gives the amplitude of the dc bias. $F(1)$ gives the amplitude of the fundamental frequency, $F(2)$ gives the amplitude of the second harmonic, and so forth. The phase information is given by noting whether the A or B value is zero. If A is zero, the phase of the signal at that frequency is like a sine, and if B is zero, the phase of the signal at that frequency is like a cosine.

As mentioned above, further examination of the FFT is beyond the scope of this book. However, this is the basis for how the FFT modules you will encounter actually work.

Derivation of Transmission Efficiency

This appendix contains a derivation of the transmission efficiency, α, from the expression $m(t)$, where $a(t)$ represents the general form of the modulating signal:

$$m(t) = (a(t) + E_c)\cos(w_c t) = a(t)\cos(w_c t) + E_c\cos(w_c t) \tag{C-1}$$

Because it is clear that the load resistance cancels out in the relationship for α, the transmission efficiency, because it is a ratio of powers, shown in equation C-2, and the load resistance is present in both, and for this discussion $R = 1\ \Omega$. By definition,

$$\alpha = \frac{2P_{sb}}{P} \tag{C-2}$$

We start with the same definition for the power in a modulated waveform expressed slightly differently. It is given by the square of the average value modulating signal, representing the voltage, divided by the load resistance, which we have assumed to be zero. This is shown in equation C-3:

$$P = 2P_{sb} + P_c = \overline{m^2(t)} \tag{C-3}$$

where $m(t)$ = average value over time.

$$P = \text{mean square value of } m(t) = \overline{m^2(t)} \tag{C-3}$$

Where the bar over $m^2(t)$ means average over time. Now, from equations C-1 and C-2,

$$\overline{m^2(t)} = \overline{a^2(t)\cos^2(w_c t)} \\ + \overline{E_c^2\cos^2(w_c t)} + \overline{2E_c a(t)\cos^2(w_c t)} \tag{C-4}$$

Because the modulating frequency is much less than the carrier frequency and the modulating signal, $a(t)$, is a sinusoid with average value of zero, the last term in equation C-4 is zero. Again, this is because the average over time of $a(t)$ is zero. Both of these assumptions have been made before and are true for most DSB-LC applications. So,

$$\overline{m^2(t)} = \overline{a^2(t)\cos^2(w_c t)} + \overline{E_c^2\cos^2(w_c t)} \tag{C-5}$$

$$= \frac{\overline{a^2(t)}}{2} + \frac{E_c^2}{2} \tag{C-6}$$

So,

$$P = 2P_{sb} + P_c = \frac{\overline{a^2(t)}}{2} + \frac{E_c^2}{2} \tag{C-7}$$

Now, because $P_c = E_c^2/2$ for a $1\ \Omega$ load,

$$2P_{sb} = \frac{\overline{a^2(t)}}{2}$$

Rewriting α,

$$\alpha = \frac{2P_{sb}}{P} = \frac{\overline{a^2(t)}/2}{[\overline{a^2(t)}/2] + (E_c^2/2)} = \frac{\overline{a^2(t)}}{\overline{a^2(t)} + E_c^2} \tag{C-8}$$

591

Recalling that

$$a(t) = E_m \cos(w_m t) = mE_c \cos(w_m t)$$

$$\overline{a^2(t)} = m^2 E_c^2 \, \overline{\cos^2(w_m t)} = \frac{m^2 E_c^2}{2}$$

(C-9)

The relationship for α becomes

$$\alpha = \frac{m^2 E_c^2/2}{E_c^2 + m^2 E_c^2/2} = \frac{m^2 E_c^2}{2E_c^2 + m^2 E_c^2} = \frac{m^2}{2 + m^2} \quad \textbf{(C-10)}$$

α = transmission efficiency of DSB-LC transmitter

Note that this is the same result arrived at earlier.

Calculation of the Minimum-Value Time Constant in an Envelope Demodulator

In this appendix, the differentiation that lies between equations 8-17 and 8-18 will be shown. To begin, equation 8-18 is reproduced below:

$$RC \leq \frac{1}{w_m} \frac{1 + m \cos(w_m v)}{m \sin(w_m \tau)} \tag{D-1}$$

The first thing to recognize is that the minimum value of this expression needs to be found. Then the expression can be evaluated at that minimum value by substituting in the value of τ that gives the minimum value for the expression.

To find the minimum of any expression, one must find the critical points. The critical point for an expression that describes a real physical situation is a point where the derivative equals zero or the derivative fails to exist. Because both critical points involve the derivative, our next step is to find this. To do so, first break it into manageable parts. For ease of notation, the substitution of t for τ is done here:

$$\frac{d}{dt}\left[\frac{1}{w_m} \frac{1 + m \cos(w_m t)}{m \sin(w_m t)}\right]$$

$$= \frac{d}{dt}\left[\left(\frac{1}{w_m m \sin(w_m t)}\right) + \left(\frac{\cos(w_m t)}{w_m \sin(w_m t)}\right)\right] \tag{D-2}$$

$$= \frac{d}{dt}\left[\frac{1}{w_m m \sin(w_m t)}\right] + \frac{d}{dt}\left[\frac{\cos(w_m t)}{w_m \sin(w_m t)}\right] \tag{D-3}$$

The first derivative can be evaluated simply. The result is

$$\frac{1}{m w_m} \frac{d}{dt}\left[\frac{1}{\sin(w_m t)}\right] = \left(\frac{1}{m w_m}\right)\left(\frac{-1}{\sin^2(w_m t)}\right)$$

$$\times [w_m \cos(w_m t)] = \frac{\cos(w_m t)}{m \sin^2(w_m t)}$$

The second derivative is a bit more complex but still can be found by applying the straightforward rules of differentiation.

$$\frac{1}{w_m} \frac{d}{dt}\left[\frac{\cos(w_m t)}{\sin(w_m t)}\right] = \frac{1}{w_m}\left(\left[\frac{1}{\sin(w_m t)}\right]\right)$$

$$\times \left\{\frac{d}{dt}[\cos(w_m t)]\right\} - \left[\frac{\cos(w_m t)}{\sin^2(w_m t)}\right]\left(\left\{\frac{d}{dt}[\sin(w_m t)]\right\}\right)$$

The first term becomes simply

$$\left(\frac{1}{w_m}\right)\left(\frac{-w_m \sin(w_m t)}{\sin(w_m t)}\right) = -1$$

The second term becomes

$$\left(\frac{1}{w_m}\right)\left(\frac{\cos(w_m t)}{\sin^2(w_m t)}\right)[w_m \cos(w_m t)] = \frac{\cos^2(w_m t)}{\sin^2(w_m t)}$$

By adding the first result to these two terms, the derivative of original expression is found:

593

$$\frac{d}{dt}\left[\frac{1}{w_m}\frac{1 + m\cos(w_m t)}{m\sin(w_m t)}\right] = \frac{\cos(w_m t)}{m\sin^2(w_m t)} - 1 + \frac{\cos^2(w_m t)}{\sin^2(w_m t)}$$

Putting everything over a common denominator for convienent evaluation of where the expression's critical point lies,

$$\frac{d}{dt}\left[\frac{1}{w_m}\frac{1 + m\cos(w_m t)}{m\sin(w_m t)}\right]$$

$$= \frac{\cos(w_m t) - m\sin^2(w_m t) + m\cos^2(w_m t)}{m\sin^2(w_m t)}$$

To find the minimum, set the expression equal to zero and find a value of t for which that occurs:

$$\frac{\cos(w_m t) - m\sin^2(w_m t) + m\cos^2(w_m t)}{m\sin^2(w_m t)} = 0$$

$$= \cos(w_m t) + m\left[\cos^2(w_m t) - \sin^2(w_m t)\right]$$

The bracketed expression can be substituted for using the trigonometric identity:

$$\cos(2a) = \cos^2(a) - \sin^2(a)$$

Substituting,

$$\cos(w_m t) + m\cos(2w_m t) = 0$$

As can be seen by inspection, any time the cosine function equals zero, this expression will equal zero. The cosine function always equals zero for integer multiples of $\pi/2$. Now that the value of t for which the derivative equals zero has been determined, substitute it back into the original expression and find the result:

$$RC \le \frac{1}{w_m}\frac{1 + m\cos(w_m\pi/2)}{m\sin(w_m\pi/2)} = \left(\frac{1}{w_m}\right)\left(\frac{1 + 0}{m}\right) = \frac{1}{mw_m}$$

$$\text{(D-4)}$$

where it is recognized that the sine function is unity for the same integer multiples of $\pi/2$.

Relationship Between Phase and Frequency

As discussed, frequency and phase modulation are related to one another. This must be the case if they can be described by the same equation. However, one key term, the modulation index, had different definitions for PM and FM so, there is a difference between frequency modulation (FM) and phase modulation (PM). This difference lies in the relationship between frequency and phase. This section begins by exploring this relationship using an analogy with distance and velocity.

■ FREQUENCY, THE FIRST DERIVATIVE OF PHASE

Most of you already know that the first derivative of the sine is the cosine and that the first derivative of the co-

for derivative, and the angle is just the phase, or as it is sometimes called, the phase angle. See Figure E.1.

Now, take that analogy a step further by observing that just as the analogy was made above, an analogy can be made of the *slope of a function to frequency* and the *value of the function to phase*. Examining Figure E.1 at time 0 and $\pi/2$ will illustrate this correspondence. Remember, a zero slope is indicated by a horizontal line and a maximum slope is indicated by a vertical line.

For the first pair of signals in Figure E.1, the table above shows at time 0 the value of the sine wave is 0. For the analogy to hold, the slope of its derivative should be 0 as well and it is. At time $\pi/2$, the value of the sine wave is at its maximum, so for the analogy to hold, the derivative should have a slope that is at maximum as well, and again it is so. Further, it is interesting to note that because the slope of the sine wave near time 0 is positive, the

Time	Sine Wave (Phase)-(value)		Cosine Wave (Frequency)-(slope)	
0	0-phase	value = 0	1-frequency	slope = 0
$\pi/2$	1-phase	value = maximum	0-frequency	slope = maximum
π	0-phase	value = 0	1-frequency	slope = 0

sine is −sine. You should also know that the only difference in the sine and cosine waves is a 90° phase shift. Therefore, there are two waveforms of the same frequency whose phase difference is 90°, or $\pi/2$. Recall that the time rate of change of the distance traveled is the velocity. The analogy will be made that the frequency is equal to the time rate of change of the angle of the sinusoid, where the time rate of change has been substituted

value of its derivative or the cosine wave should be positive, and it is.

Note that looking at the second pair of sinusoids, where the value of the cosine wave at time 0 is at its maximum, one would expect the slope of its derivative or sine to be at a maximum as well, and it is. Additionally, note that because the slope of the cosine wave near time 0 is negative, the value of its derivative or sine wave

Figure E.1
Frequency and phase.

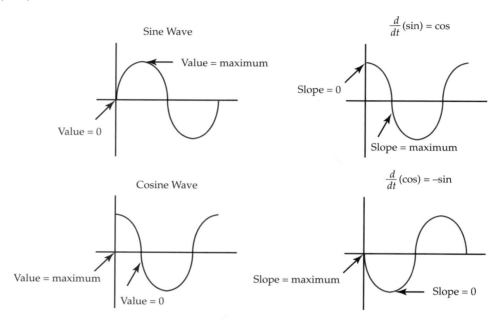

should be negative, and it is. Other points on the graphs can be verified by the reader to drive home the analogy that says frequency is the first derivative of phase, just like slope is the first derivative of the rate of change of a function over time.

The purpose of this analogy is to underline that the only difference between a sine wave and a cosine wave is the phase difference. If you took a snapshot of a sine wave or a cosine wave, without knowing the value at time $t = 0$, you could not tell them apart. If you are unsure of this, try it in the laboratory. Have a partner hook a signal generator up to an oscilloscope and switch between a cosine wave and a sine wave. Can you tell the difference? Can you even do this experiment? The answer is No, because the designer of a signal generator also realized that there is no real difference between a sine wave and a cosine wave and only offers a single sinusoidal selection.

Just like you cannot tell the difference between a sine wave and a cosine wave, which are the first derivatives of each other, you cannot tell the difference between a frequency modulated waveform and a phase modulated waveform. (One caveat, if you know about the modulating signal, you can.) This observational similarity is one key reason why it is helpful to recognize early that one result of the equivalence of PM and FM is that the modulated waveforms cannot be told apart without detailed knowledge of the modulating signal. When you examine these types of signals in the field or on the bench, usually you will have access to knowledge

of the modulating signal. However, it is helpful to keep this in mind when first learning about this type of modulation.

This illustrates the close relationship between FM and PM, or PM and FM, because frequency is the derivative of phase. From a certain point of view, phase is the more concrete concept of the two; after all, we talk about the slope of a function, not the other way around. Or even more oddly, do we talk about a function being the integral of the slope? Recall that the derivative and integral are inverse functions. This treatment will use a focus on phase as the core type of modulation for these two related modulation schemes, PM and FM.

Therefore, the result is that in PM, the phase angle of the carrier signal is modulated (changed) linearly with the *amplitude of the modulating signal*. In FM, the phase angle of the carrier signal is modulated (changed) linearly with the *integral of the amplitude of the modulating signal*. Because phase and frequency are so closely related, any change in phase will result in a change in frequency, and vice versa. As implied above, unless you know about the modulating signal, you cannot know what type of modulation it is. See Figure E.2 to picture this.

In the bottom part of the figure, both the modulating and modulated signals are shown, in the top part, only the modulated signal is shown. In both parts, the modulation signal is the same, namely, a slowly varying sinusoidal wave. For PM a slowly changing phase is expected as a result, which is seen. For FM a change in frequency with the integral of the modulating signal is ex-

Figure E.2
PM and FM.

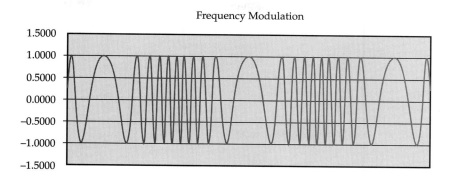

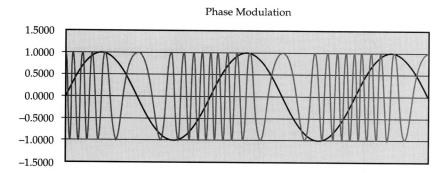

pected. To understand this, recall that the integral of a sine wave is a cosine wave. Both sine wave and cosine waves change at the same rate. Therefore one would expect a slowly varying frequency as a result, and this is what is shown.

Note how the two modulated signals would be impossible to tell apart if you did not know the phase relationship of the modulated signal to that of the modulating signal. The PM signal frequency shifts occur most rapidly when the modulated signal is passing through the x-axis, and, hence, the slope is greatest. The FM signal frequency shifts occur most rapidly when the modulating signal is at its maximum.

If you shift one modulated signal by 90°, or $\pi/2$, you cannot tell the difference. (Actually, there is an inversion that occurs due to the quadrant shift. This is apparent when the modulating signal is such a simple one. This has been removed from Figure E.2 to illustrate the concept.) Verify this to yourself from the figure.

This should now help you understand how these two modulation schemes can be viewed both as the same and as different, so don't be surprised if you read both assertions. Neither is truly wrong, they just partial statements of the truth. Recall the equation that is used to describe all three analog modulation types, AM, FM, and PM, which is as shown below:

$$m(t) = a(t) \cos[w_c t + \phi(t)] \qquad \text{(E-1)}$$

This looks a little different from the equation used for AM modulation; there is one new term. In Chapter 7, the focus was on amplitude variation of $a(t)$ and the modulation it produced. Because it multiplied the carrier wave directly, the amplitude variation resulted in amplitude modulation of the carrier wave. In this appendix $a(t)$ will reduce to just the amplitude of the carrier wave as shown below:

$$m(t) = E_c \cos[w_c t + \phi(t)] \qquad \text{(E-2)}$$

The new term is $\phi(t)$. This takes on different values depending on what modulation type is being used, two conditions will be treated separately;

1. $\phi'(t)$ varying to produce FM modulation
2. $\phi(t)$ varying to produce PM modulation

Note that $\phi(t)$ is a time-varying signal.

■ MODULATION

Because modulation is a basic concept and one you are already familiar with, it is helpful to describe exactly what is meant by phase and frequency modulation:

Phase modulation.   The phase change in the carrier wave due to varying the *amplitude* of $\phi(t)$.

Frequency modulation.   The frequency change in the carrier wave due to varying the *amplitude* of the first derivative of $\phi(t)$.

Now it becomes apparent why the first section of this appendix demonstrated that frequency is the first derivative of phase. This is because frequency modulation is defined by referencing the first derivative of phase modulation, which is the core reason why phase and frequency modulation are lumped together and called angle modulation.

Any change in frequency or phase changes the angle of the carrier wave. This can be expressed mathematically. Just as was done in chapter 9, describe $\phi(t)$ as a peak voltage multiplying a sinusoid. Note that this is also very similar to the approach taken to analyze amplitude modulation.

$$\phi(t) = E_m \cos(w_m t)$$

where
E_m = peak voltage of modulating signal
w_m = modulating signal frequency

Note that just as in the amplitude modulation situation, there is a modulating signal amplitude and frequency. It is critical that you realize that just because what is being studied is not called amplitude modulation, it does not mean that the amplitude of the modulating signal is not controlling the modulation. It is the *amplitude of $\phi(t)$ that matters*; this can be seen in the above equation.

Mathematically, phase and frequency modulation can be described as shown below:

$$\phi(t) = E_m \cos(w_m t) = \text{phase modulation}$$

$$\phi'(t) = \frac{d}{dt}\left[\phi(t)\right] = E_m \frac{d}{dt}\left[\cos(w_m t)\right]$$

$$= \text{frequency modulation}$$

These two equations tell us a lot about how these two types of modulation are really the same. You know what the derivative of the cosine function is going to turn out to be, and from the discussion in the first section, you know that you cannot tell a cosine wave apart from a sine wave. Before any more new terms are introduced, let's rewrite the equation for $m(t)$ with all its components:

$$m(t) = E_c \cos[w_c t + E_m \cos(w_m t)]$$

Combining these three equations, one can write expressions for a PM and FM signal when modulated by a sinusoid. These are shown below:

$$m(t) = E_c \cos[w_c t + E_m \cos(w_m t)] \quad \text{phase modulation}$$

$$\text{(E-3)}$$

$$m(t) = E_c \cos[(w_c t) - E_m w_m \sin(w_m t)]$$
$$\text{frequency modulation} \quad \text{(E-4)}$$

where the modulating signal in each case is $E_m \cos(w_m t)$.

■ MODULATION INDEX

Just as we did in Chapter 9, the modulation index will be defined differently for PM and FM. Recall that any change in frequency will produce a change in phase, and vice versa. This makes sense because one is the derivative of the other. So any attempt to modulate the frequency only will indirectly modulate the phase, and vice versa.

Although the modulation index is defined differently for PM and FM, the concept is similar to that used in discussing AM. The definitions of modulation index are summarized below for all three cases:

For the AM case it is the peak amplitude shift experienced by the carrier.

For the PM case it is the peak phase shift experienced by the carrier.

For the FM case it is the peak frequency shift experienced by the carrier.

Additionally, the latter two modulation indexes, just like the modulation index for the AM case, are also directly proportional to the amplitude of the modulating signal. This was not written above to stress the similarity of the concepts. The amplitude of the PM and FM modulating signals will be a constant to make easier our examination for this appendix.

This amplitude discussion sometimes creates confusion. It is only the amplitude of the modulating signal that causes the FM or PM modulation. The larger the amplitude, or modulation index, the more rapid the frequency or phase shifts will be. The amplitude of the resultant modulated waveform envelope will not change in either FM or PM.

Again, do not confuse amplitude modulation of the frequency or phase of a signal with amplitude modulation of the signal itself. The first changes the frequency or phase in some way, whereas the second directly multiplies the amplitude of the signal. The first is angle modulation, and the second is amplitude modulation and was discussed in Chapter 7.

So far, these definitions of modulation index seem logical; the commonalties and differences in the definitions above are predictable. However, there is a difference that emerges when you examine what the modulation index is independent of frequency and phase and how it behaves as a function of them.

Examining the derivative of the function shows the instantaneous peak shift of any function. When that derivative reaches a maximum, the instantaneous peak shift is a maximum as well. Frequency is defined as the derivative of phase. Therefore, the modulation index for PM involves the rate of change of the phase, or the second derivative of the frequency. Recall that the second derivative of a function is like the first derivative of the velocity, which is just the acceleration. Let's examine this with an analogy and then go on to discuss the FM case.

An example from daily life is used to make this clear. Pay special attention to the difference between the terms *rate* and *rate of change* in the discussion that follows. If you are in your car going a constant speed, you have a constant velocity but zero acceleration. It is not until you change the velocity that you can get a nonzero acceleration. Velocity tells you how fast you are increasing or decreasing your *rate* of travel, whereas acceleration tells you how fast you are increasing or decreasing your *rate of change* of travel. If you do not accelerate, your rate of change of travel cannot change. To accelerate, your *rate of* travel cannot be constant; it must curve up or down, and its rate of change, or alternately its slope, must change.

Because our focus is on communications, let's restate the above paragraph using communication terms. Try to imagine you are riding on a waveform, going a constant 1 kHz. You will have a constant frequency but zero rate of change in frequency or phase shift. It is not until you change the frequency that you get a phase change. Frequency tells you how many zero crossings you get per unit time, or how fast the *rate* of zero crossing transitions is, whereas phase shift tells you how fast you are increasing or decreasing the *rate of change* of zero crossing transitions.

If you do not change the *rate of change* of phase shift, your *rate* of zero crossing transitions cannot change. To change the rate of zero crossing transitions, the rate of zero crossing transitions cannot be constant; it must curve up or down; its rate of change or, alternately, its slope, must change. These are unfamiliar concepts to most and that was a tough paragraph or two. Go back and review the one about traveling in your car and make the analogy again; it should help before rereading the last couple of paragraphs again. Make sure you follow that discussion before going on to the next paragraph.

If there is no variation of the phase (e.g., the *rate of change* of the phase is constant), the modulation cannot depend on the frequency. In other words, it is impossible for the frequency to be effected by the rate of change of a phase shift unless the phase shift is changing itself and has a nonzero second derivative.

The result is that for PM, the modulation index, which represents the rate of change of the phase shift of the carrier signal, is independent of the frequency of the modulating signal. The only thing left to examine is the amplitude of the modulating signal, which must be directly proportional to the voltage swings of the modulating signal times some constant related to the gain of the modulator. Different implementations have different gains, so we must account for this by the use of the constant K_1 for PM.

Be careful; do not confuse the voltage swings in the modulating signal to be amplitude modulation. For PM, the expression for modulation index is given by equation E-5:

$$\text{PM modulation index: } m = K_1 E_m \qquad \text{(E-5)}$$

Again, to emphasize, the result for PM is that the modulation index, which represents the rate of change of the phase shift, is *independent of the modulation frequency*. For the PM case only, m is only dependent on the amplitude of the modulating waveform and the deviation sensitivity of the modulator.

Turning now to an examination of the modulation index for the FM case, the modulation index involves the rate of change of the frequency, which is just the second derivative of phase. So you can probably conclude that the FM case will turn out similar to the PM case. Because the rate of change of frequency must depend on the absolute frequency itself, the modulation index can almost certainly be predicted to depend on frequency. If that is so, what is the dependence? Because the approach taken above will not work here, a different tack must be found.

The modulation index is defined as the peak frequency shift of the carrier. Therefore, the greater the frequency shift, the greater the modulation index. But is there a dependence on the value of the frequency? If so, what frequency is being discussed, carrier or modulation? Because modulation index is defined as a frequency shift of the carrier, it cannot depend on the carrier frequency, or the definition would be absurd. So it must be the modulation frequency we are discussing.

This makes sense because the *modulation* index should depend on the *modulation frequency* for *frequency modulation*. Therefore, modulation index talks about the frequency shift of the carrier, which depends on the changes in the modulation frequency. The amplitude of the modulation signal will produce changes in the frequency of the carrier. Remember where it is in the equation, not outside the cosine term but inside, affecting the argument of the cosine, not its amplitude. So if the amplitude is producing the frequency shifts, what does the frequency of the modulation signal have to do with it? To help see this examine Figure E.3.

Figure E.3
w_m and w_c.

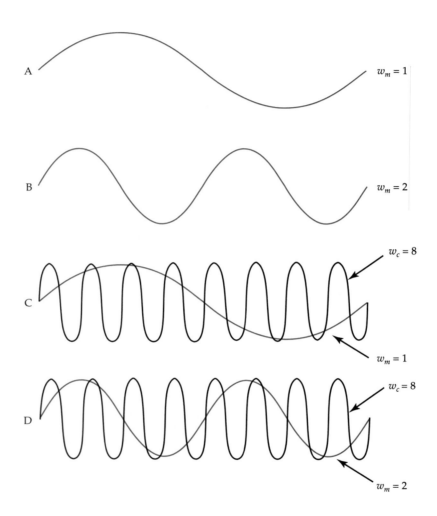

Figure E.3 shows two possible modulation signals, that shown in B is twice the frequency of the first, shown in A. The question we are trying to answer is What is the relationship of the carrier frequency to the modulation frequency? The carrier frequency is fixed, so a modulating signal that is, for example, 1% of its frequency will change from 0 amplitude to full-scale amplitude in 25 cycles of the carrier. If the modulation signal is 2% of its frequency, the change from 0 amplitude to full scale will occur in 12.5 cycles, and so forth. So, the higher the frequency of the modulation signal compared to the carrier frequency, the lower the *frequency difference* (or peak fre-

quency shift) for each cycle of the modulation wave. Now examine parts C and D of Figure E.3, where the modulation signals A and B are shown superimposed on a higher-frequency carrier signal.

Note that in the first case, C, twice as many cycles of the carrier wave are needed to go one cycle of the modulation wave as the second case, D. But the second case has the higher modulation frequency. So we are left with the result that modulation index for the FM case must be inversely proportional to the modulation frequency. This somewhat counterintuitive result is true. It can be verified by a mathematical treatment that is located in several sources. Recall that it is expressed mathematically in equation 9-3 (shown below as equation E-6):

$$\text{FM modulation index: } m = \frac{K_2 E_m}{w_m} \qquad \textbf{(E-6)}$$

■ POWER CALCULATION

Because the expression we have for $m(t)$ gives us the amplitude of the modulated wave in volts, it can be used to find the average power in an angle-modulated waveform. Recall equation 9-1, reproduced below:

$$m(t) = E_c \cos[w_c t + \phi(t)] \qquad \textbf{(E-7)}$$

To use this equation generally, a relationship that will give us the average power of the modulated waveform, or just average power, is needed. The average of anything can be obtained by measuring the value over some period and then dividing by the period. The value desired is the power, and dividing it by the period gives the average. Because the voltage of the waveform can be measured over one period, and power is given by squaring the voltage and dividing by the resistance, we have the relationship that is needed. Verify for yourself that it makes sense:

$$P_{\text{mod}} = \frac{1}{RT} \int_{-T/2}^{T/2} m^2(t) \, dt$$

where
P_{mod} = average power of $m(t)$ over period T
T = one period of $m(t)$
R = load resistance

This concept is introduced here because it gives a simple way to compute the average power of any modulated wave. Some of you will be wondering why the period of integration was chosen the way it was (e.g., why not from 0 to T, instead of from $-T/2$ to $T/2$). In principle, it makes no difference as long as one full period of the waveform is captured. However, in communications mathematics it is often easier to use an integral that is symmetric about the origin. The reason for this lies in the special properties of even and odd functions when they are integrated over a period that symmetric about the origin.

To illustrate why this is true and also just how straightforward the expression is to compute the average power of any modulated wave, let's substitute our expression for $m(t)$ into the above integral and work through the math:

$$P_{\text{mod}} = \frac{1}{RT} \int_{-T/2}^{T/2} \{E_c \cos[w_c t + \phi(t)]\}^2 \, dt$$

$$= \frac{1}{R} \int_{-1/2}^{1/2} E_c^2 \cos^2[w_c t + \phi(t)] \, dt$$

$$= \frac{E_c^2}{R} \int_{-1/2}^{1/2} \cos^2[w_c t + \phi(t)] \, dt$$

$$= \frac{E_c^2}{R} \int_{-1/2}^{1/2} \frac{1}{2} [1 + \cos^2(w_c t + \phi(t))] \, dt$$

$$= \frac{E_c^2}{2R} \int_{-1/2}^{1/2} dt + \frac{E_c^2}{2R} \int_{-1/2}^{1/2} \cos^2[w_c t + \phi(t)] \, dt$$

$$= \frac{E_c^2}{2R} + 0$$

Some of you are probably wondering why one could just set the definite integral to zero. The answer lies in what is known; because the cosine function is even, $\cos(-x) = \cos(x)$, and the definite integral is symmetric, it extends from $-1/2$ to $1/2$ of the period of the modulated waveform, $m(t)$, it must equal zero. Some readers might rather have seen a detailed evaluation of the integral, but this integral has no general solution unless you examine particular forms of $\phi(t)$. As a result, instead of examining a bunch of examples and then saying, "Gee, the result is always the same, so it must *always* be the same," it is better to argue in the above manner using what is known about even functions. This is much quicker and does not rely on assuming a result for which we have no proof.

So, we end up with the average power of the waveform just equal to the average power of the unmodulated carrier waveform. It did turn out to be simple. Unlike the general situation in AM, the power of the carrier signal is found to be *the same as the average power of the modulated signal*. This results because there is no amplitude modulation of the carrier wave, usually a good assumption when evaluating analog PM and FM systems. This will change when we discuss combining amplitude modulation with angle modulation, but for now it is an important result.

Again, in pure angle modulation, because there is no amplitude modulation of the carrier envelope, the average power of the unmodulated carrier wave is exactly equal to the total power. It is also possible to obtain the total average power by adding up the average power of all the harmonics that are produced by the modulation process. Each harmonic has a peak voltage value; this is squared and divided by twice the load resistance and summed with the value for the average power of the modulated carrier. Remember that each harmonic builds two sidebands at $w_c \pm w_m$.

Again, note that the average power in an angle modulated wave is a constant, independent of the modulation index. So, no matter what level of modulation is performed on an angle modulated wave that's both PM and FM, the power remains constant as long as there is no amplitude modulation. This result, and some of its implications, is one of the key factors that determine what modulation scheme to use for a particular application.

E-1 Framing and Wire Line Standard

The E-1 standard used throughout Europe and most of the rest of the world is standardized by the CCITT, an international standardization organization that is responsible for many communications standards used throughout the world. Telephone calls using this standard are PCM encoded. As described in Chapter 11, a slightly different companding curve is used, but in other ways, it is very similar. For example, each system uses 8 bit PCM words sampled at 8 kHz.

The major difference between the E-1 standard and the DS-1 standard is the number of voice channels in the frame, which leads to a different line rate. The E-1 standard allows 30 voice channels instead of the 24 used in the United States. However, there are not just 30 time slots in the frame. Two additional time slots, slot 1 and 17, are used for management of the TDM system.

Slot 1 is dedicated to alarm conditions and slot 17 is used for signaling associated with management of the 30 voice channels contained in the frame. Performing the same type of calculations we did for the DS-1 frame, we find for the data rate of each channel:

$$8 \text{ bits* } 8 \text{ kHz} = 64 \text{ kbps}$$

If 32 of these are combined, the aggregate data rate on the E1 line is

$$32 \text{ channels* } 64 \text{ kbps} = 2.048 \text{ Mbps}$$

Note that the two management channels contain the same number of bits as the voice channels. These management channels eliminate the need for additional framing bits in the E-1 standard.

The frame time is, just like any TDM system that samples each input only once, the same as the inverse of the frame rate, again 8 kHz, or inversely, 125 μs. To find the number of bits in a frame, proceed just as was done in Chapter 11, remembering that there is no framing bit:

$$\#bits/frame = (\# \text{ of channels})(\# \text{ of sample bits})$$

$$= (32)(8) = 256 \text{ bits/frame}$$

It is interesting to note that the frame time is the same for both standards because the sampling rate is the same. Because the number of bits per frame is different, there is a different bit time for each standard. The bit time is found by taking the frame time and dividing it by the number of bits in a frame:

$$\text{bit time} = \frac{\text{frame time}}{\# \text{ bits/frame}} = \frac{125 \times 10^{-6}}{256}$$

$$= 0.488 \times 10^{-6} \text{ sec} = 0.488 \text{ } \mu\text{sec}$$

Finally, it is possible to compute the bandwidth of the signaling or management channel. Because there are 16 bits of signaling spread across 256 bits, the signaling rate for the E-1 frame format is

$$\text{signaling rate} = \frac{(\# \text{ signaling bits/\# total bits})}{\text{frame time}}$$

$$= \frac{(16/256)}{125 \times 10^{-6}} = 500 \text{ bps}$$

Detailed Modulo-2 Division Used for CRC Calculations

Here are the table versions of the modulo-2 division that was performed in Chapter 11 in the section on CRC codes. The data and polynomial are given below.

$$D = 10101100$$

$$P = 110101$$

As can be seen in Figure G.1, the remainder is 00110. Note that the number of bits is the same as the order of the polynomial; this is always the case. The remainder must be added to the original data message and sent, so the transmitted message is

$$D = 1010110000110$$

At the receive end, the message is again divided by the polynomial and if there is no remainder, the message is assumed to contain no errors. This situation is demonstrated in Figure G.2.

As can be seen, for the above division, there is no error. To demonstrate what happens if an error occurs, we will change 1 bit and show how the division now predicts this by resulting in a nonzero remainder. The bit that has been changed is the last bit in the message. This is shown in Figure G.3.

Figure G.4 shows another example illustrating modulo-2 division as applied in CRC coding. The data and polynomials are given below. Note that this polynomial is of fourth order and so the remainder is 4 bits.

$$D = 1101101$$

$$P = 10011$$

As can be seen, the remainder is 1001. Note that the number of bits is the same as the order of the polynomial; this is always the case. This remainder must be added to the original data message and sent, so the transmitted message is

$$D = 11011011001$$

One can now proceed just as in Figure G.3.

Figure G.1

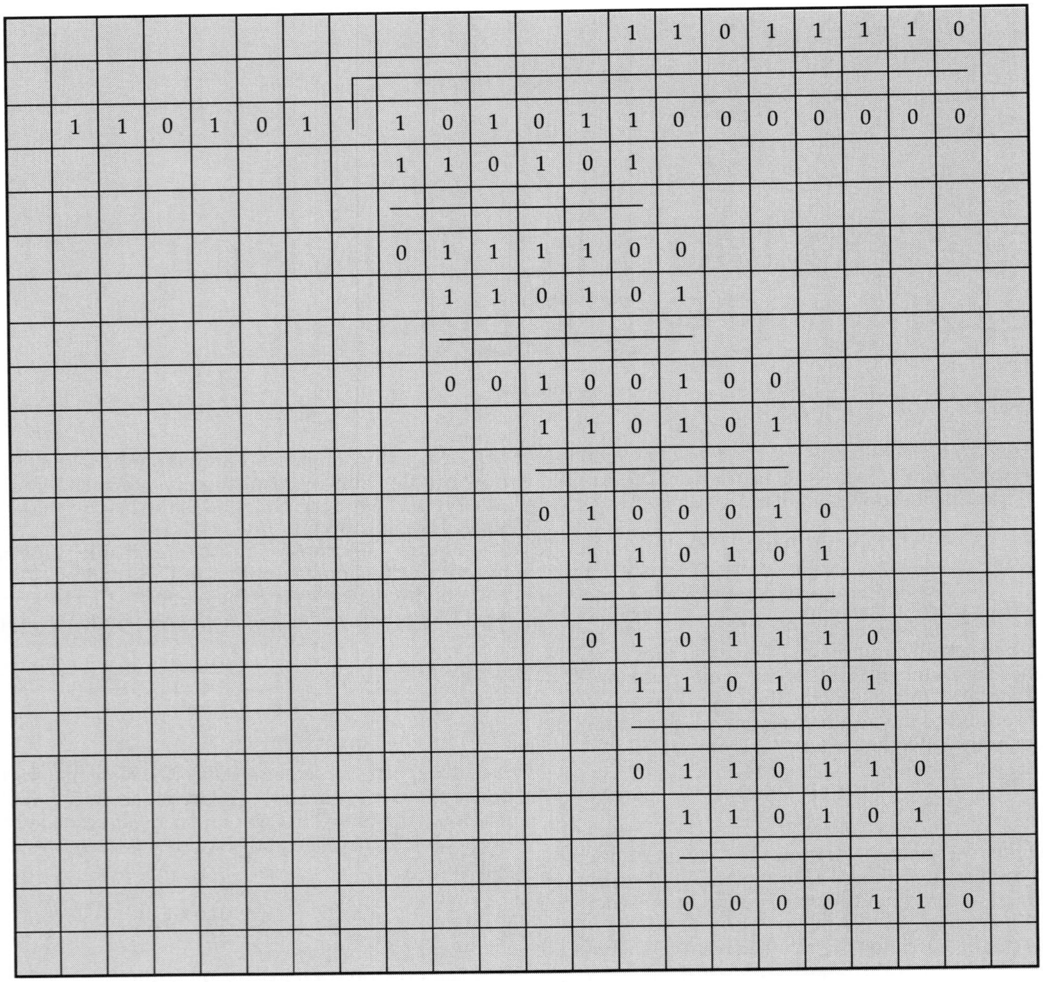

```
                                    1 1 0 1 1 1 0
          1 1 0 1 0 1 ) 1 0 1 0 1 1 0 0 0 0 0 0 0
                        1 1 0 1 0 1
                        _____
                        0 1 1 1 1 0 0
                          1 1 0 1 0 1
                          _____
                          0 0 1 0 0 1 0 0
                              1 1 0 1 0 1
                              _____
                              0 1 0 0 0 1 0
                                1 1 0 1 0 1
                                _____
                                0 1 0 1 1 1 0
                                  1 1 0 1 0 1
                                  _____
                                  0 1 1 0 1 1 0
                                    1 1 0 1 0 1
                                    _____
                                    0 0 0 0 1 1 0
```

Figure G.2

Figure G.3

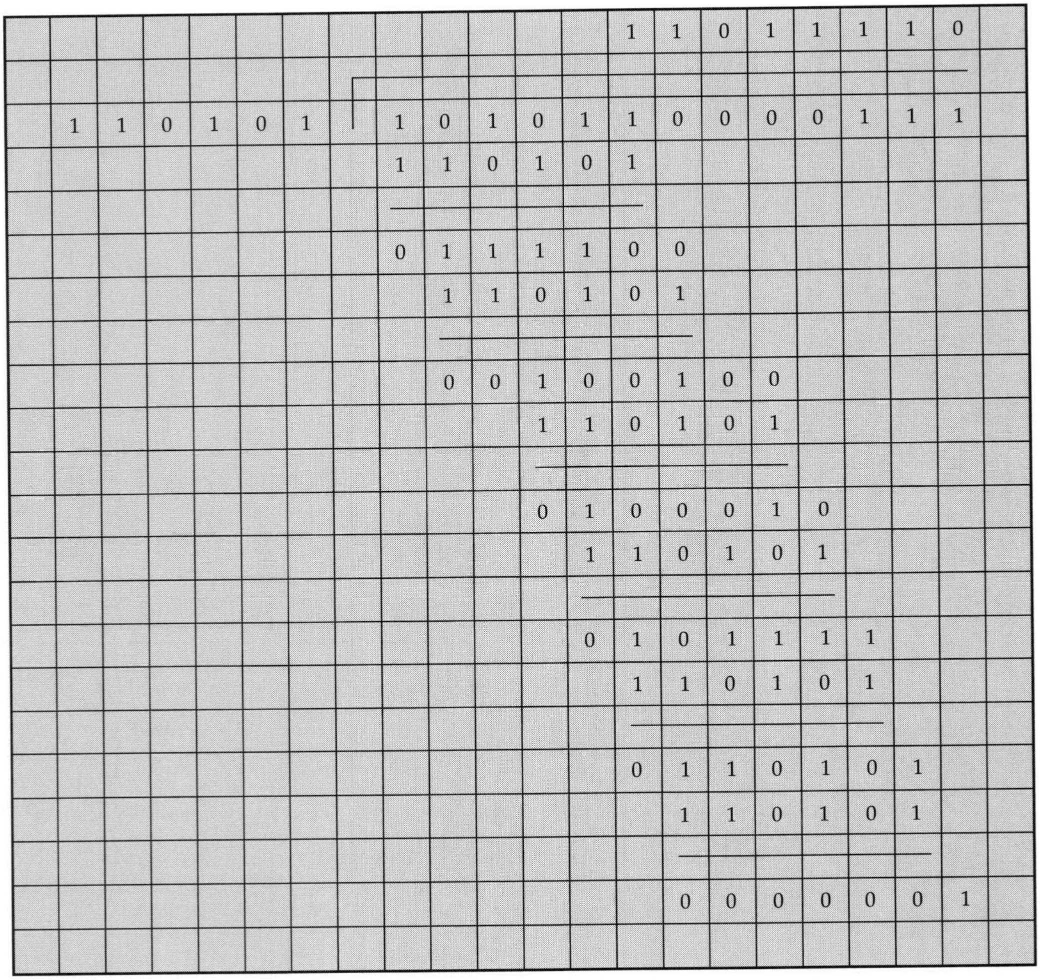

Figure G.3

```
                              1 1 0 1 1 1 1 0
    1 1 0 1 0 1 ) 1 0 1 0 1 1 0 0 0 0 1 1 1
                  1 1 0 1 0 1
                  _____
                  0 1 1 1 1 0 0
                    1 1 0 1 0 1
                    _____
                    0 0 1 0 0 1 0 0
                        1 1 0 1 0 1
                        _____
                        0 1 0 0 0 1 0
                          1 1 0 1 0 1
                          _____
                          0 1 0 1 1 1 1
                            1 1 0 1 0 1
                            _____
                            0 1 1 0 1 0 1
                              1 1 0 1 0 1
                              _____
                              0 0 0 0 0 0 1
```

Figure G.4

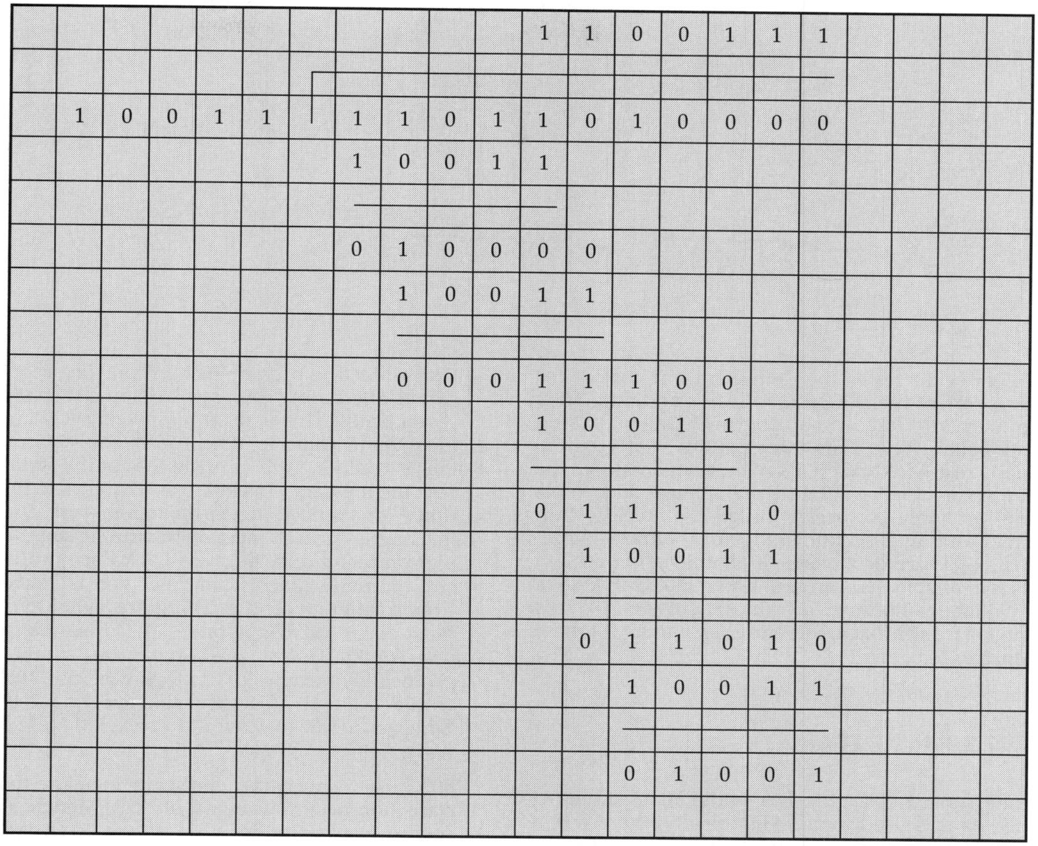

```
                              1  1  0  0  1  1  1
   1  0  0  1  1  |  1  1  0  1  1  0  1  0  0  0  0
                     1  0  0  1  1
                     ─────────────
                     0  1  0  0  0  0
                        1  0  0  1  1
                        ─────────────
                        0  0  0  1  1  1  0  0
                              1  0  0  1  1
                              ─────────────
                              0  1  1  1  1  0
                                 1  0  0  1  1
                                 ─────────────
                                 0  1  1  0  1  0
                                    1  0  0  1  1
                                    ─────────────
                                    0  1  0  0  1
```

802.X Frame Formats

This appendix describes the detailed frame format for three members of the IEEE 802.X LAN standards. They are commercially known as Ethernet, Token Passing Bus, and Token Ring. This information is very useful when analyzing a LAN with a tool that can break out the frame structure for you. There are several such tools available; probably the best is called the Sniffer. With such a tool and detailed knowledge of the frame structure of the DLL protocol being used, a level of problem analysis is available that can drill down into the value of individual bit positions of the frames themselves. This is a very powerful approach, therefore, a summary of these frame formats is presented.

■ 802.3 FRAME FORMAT

The frame format in Figure H.1 is the 802.3 standard (Ethernet) as it is used today. Historically, there was a difference between Ethernet and the IEEE 802.3 standard, but very few original Ethernets are still in operational use today. For all intents and purposes, Ethernet and IEEE 802.3 are synonymous.

Most of the components are common in each of the three frame formats we will explore, so we will not describe in the next sections any that are described here, except where significant differences exist.

Preamble: The preamble of a frame is a regular series of alternating data symbols 10101010 repeated seven times. This is used by the physical layer device, the modem, to synchronize the stations clock that is receiving the frame to that of the station that sent the message. The reasons why certain modulation formats need synchronization were discussed in Chapter 12 in the section that discussed the modulation technique. Because LANs are multiaccess environments, each frame received is likely to be from a different sender. Therefore, synchronization must occur for every frame. The preamble pattern used for 802.3 is a square wave at the data rate of the protocol. For example, 10 Mbps Ethernet, 10Base-T, would use a 10 MHz square wave, and 100 Mbps Ethernet, 100Base-T, would use a 100 MHz square wave.

802.3 uses Manchester encoding to ensure that a bit transition occurs in every bit cell. Manchester encoding just is another type of line code. It is very useful in environments where clock recovery from the data stream is important. The code was described in Chapter 6.

Start delimiter (SD): The start delimiter of a frame is a byte of data that always has the same form, 10101011, and is used to mark the end of the preamble and the start of the informational frame. Al-

Figure H.1
802.3 frame format.

Preamble	SD	DA	SA	Length	Data	Pad	CRC
7	1	2 or 6	2 or 6	2	0–1500	0–46	4

The number below each field is the number of bytes in that field.

though the preamble is considered part of the frame structure, it contains no information, only a pattern that the receiving modem needs to synchronize its clock to the sender. Therefore, it is not considered part of the informational frame. Sometimes it is referred to as part of the frame, and sometimes the SD is considered the start of the frame. It usually depends on the background of the speaker; engineers tend to consider it part of the frame, whereas computer scientists tend to ignore it.

Destination address (DA): This is a 2 or 6 byte field that defines the address of the destination. The MAC Layer uses this field to decide if the frame is intended for its station. The important thing with the DA is that all stations on any network must have the same address length, 2 or 6 bytes. You cannot mix these in a single network. A 2 byte field allows only 32K possible addresses. Extending this to 6 bytes greatly increases the possible number of devices. Because 802.3 addresses are centrally administered, the 6 byte address format is the norm. Both the DA and SA have a particular structure, with a small difference. The individual/group bit is always set to a zero for source addresses. For destination addresses, it is defined as shown in Tables H.1 and H.2.

Individual addressing is used when the destination station is on the same network as the source address. Group addressing is used to address a group of stations with a single transmission; this is called multicasting. There is a special bit sequence if the transmission is designed to be addressed to all station; this is called broadcasting.

Source address (SA): The address field of the sender. The same rules apply as for the DA, with the exception mentioned there.

Length: The length field is used to tell the receiving station the length of the data field that follows. This is important because 802.3 does not work correctly unless each frame is of a minimum size. If the data to be included is too short, the pad field is used to lengthen the frame length. For this reason, it is important for the receiving station to know how much of the "data" field is actual data and how much is pad appended by the transmitting station to meet the minimum-length frame requirement. This varies with the data rate of the implementation; however for 10 Mbps systems it is 64 bytes.

Data: The place where the data to be transmitted is placed. The amount of data can vary from 0 to 1500 bytes. The data always comes from the next layer up the stack, the LLC Layer. Only data segments of an integer number of bytes can be transmitted; partial bytes are not allowed here or for any of the three frame formats we will explore.

Pad: Where pad bytes are placed if needed. Up to 46 bytes of pad are applied. The rule is that the length plus data plus pad be at least 48 bytes.

CRC: The location of a 4 byte, or 32 bit, CRC field. This is often referred to as the Frame Check Sequence, or FCS. Because we have already talked about this as CRC coding, the diagrams show it as CRC. The official IEEE term is FCS. As you might guess, because the field is 32 bits long, the polynomial order is 32, and is shown in Equation H.1:

Table H.1
Two-Byte Address Format

Bit	Use
1	Individual/group address bit; 0-individual, 1-group
2–15	15 bit address

Table H.2
Six-Byte Address Format

Bit	Use
1	Individual/group address bit; 0-individual, 1-group
2	Universal/local address bit; 0-universal, 1-local
3–48	46 bit address

$$P = x^{32} + x^{26} + x^{23} + x^{22} + x^{16} + x^{12} + x^{11}$$
$$+ x^{10} + x^8 + x^7 + x^5 + x^4 + x^2 + x + 1 \quad \textbf{(H-1)}$$

The CRC checks everything after the SD and up to the end of the pad field. The polynomial used is reproduced in Figure H.2. All three 802.X frame formats use the same polynomial.

Finally, it is important to note that all fields are transmitted *byte by byte, low-order bit first*, except the CRC field, which is transmitted *bit by bit high-order bit first*.

■ 802.4 FRAME FORMAT

Most of the fields shown in Figure H.3 are the same as for the case just examined. The preamble can be much longer but must always be at least 3 bytes for the 10 Mbps implementation of Token Bus. As shown, typical ranges are from 3 to 30 bytes; most implementations transmit between 10 and 16 bytes of preamble. The upper limit is over 100,000 bytes. This maximum is never encountered unless the implementation is badly damaged. As in the 802.3 case, this field is designed to help the physical layer modem establish its receive timing. Most of the other fields are the same except we have no pad here and no length field. Although the SD and ED are still 1 byte long, they are different in structure. A new field is the FC field.

Start delimiter (SD): Just as in the 802.3 situation, this field immediately follows the preamble and signifies the start of frame. It is interesting to notice that the field does not just contain 1s and 0s but also a symbol known as N. This stands for nondata. Token Bus implementations use three data symbols, 0, 1 and N, or nondata. Nondata symbols are transmitted at half amplitude and are always sent in pairs. By placing them in the specific order shown, a unique representation for the start delimiter is established. In Figure H.4, both the SD and ED frames are shown.

Frame control (FC): In Token Bus, the FC field is a 1 byte field that tells the receiving station what kind of data or MAC control frame is being sent. There are many different types of frames, in addition to data frames.

Destination address (DA): For the 2 byte field this field is exactly like the 802.3 field described above. In the 6 byte case, there is a small difference; instead of an arbitrary field for the 46 bits of address, it is defined as a concatenation of a manufacturer's code with a serial number. The multicast and broadcast codes are similar to 802.3 as well, with broadcast defined as all 1s.

Data: The data unit field is where the data is placed. The FC field defines it as LLC data or MAC control frame. The length of this field is defined from 0 bytes to a maximum, depending on the length of the address fields. For 2 byte addressing, the maximum length is 8180 bytes. For 6 byte addressing, the maximum length is 8172 bytes. The governing rule is that the total length of the frame between SD and ED cannot exceed 8191 bytes.

End delimiter (ED): This is very similar to the SD for 802.4 in that it uses three data symbols, 0, 1, and N. However, the last 2 bits are unique. The I bit stands for intermediate; if it is set to a 1, there is more to

Figure H.2
IEEE 802.X CRC polynomial.

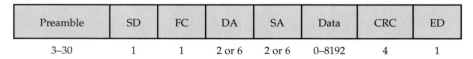

Preamble	SD	FC	DA	SA	Data	CRC	ED
3–30	1	1	2 or 6	2 or 6	0–8192	4	1

The number below each field is the number of bytes in that field.
Format for 10 Mbps option only.
Preamble can be much longer, but the range shown is typical.

Figure H.3
802.4 frame format.

Start Delimiter

End Delimiter

Figure H.4
SD and ED byte construction.

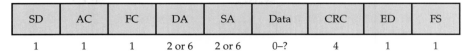

SD	AC	FC	DA	SA	Data	CRC	ED	FS
1	1	1	2 or 6	2 or 6	0–?	4	1	1

The number below each field is the number of bytes in that field.
Data field maximum length determined by token holding time.

transmit. This means that the data to be transmitted could not be fit into the data field and will continue in the next frame. If this bit is set to a 0, it indicates end of transmission. The E bit is only designed to be set by a repeater. If this bit is set to a 1, it means that the immediately preceding frame had an CRC error. This can be used to identify where the error occurred, and it indicates to the destination that the frame should be treated as invalid and retransmission should be requested.

Some other small differences exist from the situation for 802.3; for example, the CRC now covers everything from the end of the start delimiter to the end of the data field.

■ 802.5 FRAME FORMAT

The 802.5 frame has several differences from the first two discussed. There is no preamble used, and there are two new fields, AC and FS. 802.5 does not need to synchronize because there is always a special short frame rotating around the ring called a token. The token acts to keep all the stations in synchronization because they are always receiving timing information from the frame transitions. A token is a 3 byte frame composed of SD, AC, and ED.

$$P = x^{32} + x^{26} + x^{23} + x^{22} + x^{16} + x^{12} + x^{11}$$
$$+ x^{10} + x^8 + x^7 + x^5 + x^4 + x^2 + x + 1 \quad \text{(H-1)}$$

802.5, like 802.4, uses more than two data symbols. In the case of 802.5 there are four. Two of these, represented by J and K are nondata bits. Because 802.5 uses differential Manchester encoding, and this has not been discussed, we will not explore them further. Differential Manchester encoding is a more sophisticated line code than the Manchester encoding described in the section on Ethernet.

The other big difference is that this Token Ring network does not appear to impose a limit on the size of the data field. Actually, there is an upper limit determined by a variable called the token holding time. Practical upper limits usually are set at about 10,000 bytes.

Access control (AC): Only 802.5 of the three protocols discussed here has a notion of priority at this low level. The AC field is used to indicate the priority of the token in a token frame and the priority of the sender in a data frame. There are eight levels of priority allowed, from 000 to 111, lowest to highest. A higher priority allows a station to hold the token preferentially. Because only the station holding the token can transmit, having a high priority can significantly improve the data flow from a station.

Frame control (FC): This is very similar to the FC field used in 802.4. If the first 2 bits are 00, the frame type is a control frame; if they are 01, it is a data frame.

Destination and source address (DA and SA): These are very similar to both 802.3 and 802.4 with some minor variations in the 6 byte format.

Data: This field is often called the information field. It is of variable length and often is of zero length. It is used to send additional information that can be used for a variety of purposes usually concerned with management of the ring. If it is of nonzero length, it is broken up into five subfields each with an integer number of bytes. The detailed exploration of these fields is beyond the scope of this text; however, the size and contents are listed in Table H.3.

Frame status (FS): Frame status is also unique to Token Ring implementations. Because each station is constantly retransmitting frames intended for a station farther along the ring, each originating station needs a way to tell the next station if it originated the frame or is just retransmitting it. In other words, the status of these bits allows the sending station to determine if the frame it sent was actually copied by the intended destination station. It can distinguish among three conditions:

1. The destination station is not present on the ring.
2. The destination station is present but for some reason did not copy the frame.
3. The destination station is present and did copy the frame.

Only the last case indicates a successful transfer of

Table H.3
Information Field Makeup

Number of Bytes	Contents
2	Vector length (VL)
2	Vector identifier (VI)
1	Subvector length (SVL)
1	Subvector identifier (SVI)
Arbitrary	Subvector value (SVV)

data. Usually the first result happens because the station is not powered up. The second often occurs in times of high congestion when a station might not have time to copy the frame. The third condition is the normal acknowledgment.

A good question is Why does the originating station need to be able to tell the next station if it originated the frame or are just retransmitting it? Once the station that the frame was intended for has correctly received the frame, it reinserts it, adding the above code corresponding to its situation. When the originating station sees this frame with the bits set to indicate successful reception, it strips off the frame and reinserts the token. The network is then ready to pass the next frame. Of course, if the bits do not indicate reception, the frame is retransmitted with the bits set in the same way an original transmission would be and the process begins again.

FieldBus Timed Standard Scanning Example

Many FieldBus devices require an exact specification of the scan cycle. Often the requirement is for 1/2 cycle response times for devices operating at 60 Hz. The calculation below illustrates that FieldBus can support this requirement.

Assumptions:

H2 data rate or 1 Mbps

32 devices connected

All devices operating at 60 Hz

All devices requiring 1/2 cycle response time

Message size of 8 bytes or 64 bits

Protocol message overhead of 3 times the message size or 192 bits

Calculation:

1/2 cycle time at 60 Hz translates to 120 messages/sec
Total PhPDU size of 64 + 3*64 = 256 bits

To calculate bit-rate required,

(# devices)(PhPDU size)(# messages/sec)

(32)(256)(120) = 983,040 bit/sec

or just less than 1 Mbps

Having verified the data rate to be sufficient, calculate the resultant scan time. A 1 Mbps data rate translates into a bit time of $1 \mu s$.

(# devices)(PhPDU size)(bit time)

(32)(256)(0.000001) = 0.008192 sec

or just over 8 ms

This demonstrates that FieldBus can support typically encountered scan time requirements with a reasonable number of devices connected. Clearly, the scan time can be reduced by reducing the number of devices connected. A 5 msec scan time can be achieved for up to 19 devices. If a shorter message size is assumed or less protocol overhead, this also can serve to reduce the scan time further or increase the number of devices connected for a given scan time.

It should be noted that this example does not take into account hardware or software delays in the devices themselves. These delays are not possible to predict without actual measurements of working devices. This example attempts to account for these delays by assuming a message overhead of 3 times the message size. Some of that message overhead will necessarily not be available to account for these delays because significant message protocol overhead is anticipated in the standard. These estimates may or may not be a good assumption depending on the implementation choices made by a particular vendor.

Additional Cabling Detail for the Coaxial Ethernet Family of Standards

In some cases, specifications for a particular standard will conflict; always select the most stringent value that satisfies all relevant specifications.

Thinnet, 10Base2

Maximum segment length	185 m
Maximum number of stations per segment	30
Minimum transceiver spacing	0.5 m
Termination	50 Ω both ends
Maximum number of repeaters	2 per data pathway

Thicknet, 10Base5

Maximum segment length	500 m
Maximum number of segments	101
Maximum number of stations per segment	100
Maximum number of stations	1024
Minimum transceiver spacing	2.5 m
Maximum transceiver drop cable length	50 m
Termination	50 Ω both ends
Maximum number of repeaters	2 per data pathway

IP Datagram Format

This appendix describes the detailed frame or datagram format for the IP protocol. It is sometimes referred to as the IP datagram and is shown in Figure K.1. The presentation follows the same approach as Appendix H and for the same reasons. A detailed analysis of the value of the individual bit positions of a datagram can offer a level of problem analysis that is very powerful. For example, knowing the destination and source address locations will allow a determination of the destination station and sender of the datagram. Again, a protocol analyzer tool such as the Sniffer is required to break out the individual datagrams for this analysis.

Version: (4 bits) The version number of the protocol. This allows evolution of the protocol, meaning different definitions of the format, while still accommodating older version(s) on the network. The version number would be used to alert the network that this datagram needs to be handled according to the rules associated with the particular version denoted.

IHL: (4 bits) The length of the header field in bytes. The maximum length is 5 bytes.

Type of service: (8 bits) Specifies the quality of service parameters available with the protocol version. Includes such things as reliability and delay.

Total length: (16 bits) The total datagram length in bytes. Note that this includes the length of the header.

Identification: (16 bits) A unique datagram identifi-cation number. In theory, only one datagram on the network at any one time would have this number.

Flags: (3 bits) Primarily used to allow for fragmentation of datagrams and subsequent reassembly. Sometimes used to prohibit fragmentation.

Fragmentation offset: (13 bits) Indicates where in the logical datagram the particular physical piece in this datagram belongs.

Time to live: (8 bits) Used to measure the number of seconds, hops, and so forth, this datagram has before being erased.

Protocol: (8 bits) Indicates the next level protocol that is to receive the data in this datagram.

Header checksum: (16 bits) A FCS-type checksum used for error detection.

Source address: (32 bits) Address of the source of this datagram.

Destination address: (32 bits) Address of the destination of this datagram.

Options and padding: (variable) Used to fill in to ensure the datagram has an integer number of bytes.

Data: (variable) The content of the datagram. The total length of the datagram, including header is 65,536 bytes. The maximum length of the data in any datagram depends on the amount of options and padding inserted.

Figure K.1
Internet Protocol datagram format.

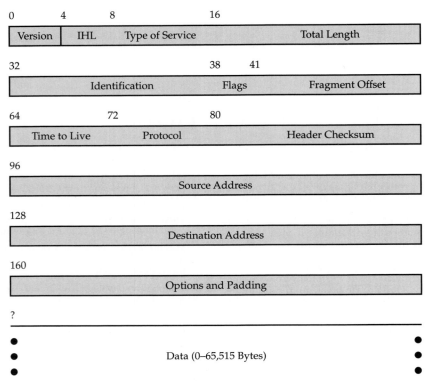

Note: Integer numbers show bit position, Data field indicates length in bytes.

Active element. An antenna element that is driven electrically.

Aliasing. An alias frequency is a false image, always lower in frequency than the correct frequency

American Standard Code for Information Interchange (ASCII).

Amplitude modulation (AM). The form of modulation where the information is carried in changes of the amplitude of the carrier wave.

Analog communications system. A communication system that transfers an analog or digital data source from source to destination. The signal stays continuous in nature while it is in the communications channel. Analog communications systems often require a carrier signal and most are broadband. Examples include broadcast radio transmitters and receivers, broadcast television transmitters and receivers, cable television transmission facilities, and receivers and modems.

Analog component. A component that operates with continuous signals applied to its input and produces a continuous signal on its output. Typically, any nonclocked component is an analog component. Examples include amplifiers, transformers, resistors, and capacitors.

Analog data source. An input signal where its values are continuous with no abrupt breaks. Virtually all naturally produced signals are analog data sources. A good example is a microphone.

Angle modulation. The form of modulation where the information is carried in changes of the angle, frequency, or phase of the carrier wave.

Angular frequency. The frequency expressed in radians per second (rad/sec). It is numerically equal to the frequency in hertz multiplied by 2π.

Anisotropic. Radiates or receives with more gain in a preferred direction(s).

Antenna. A device that efficiently radiates electromagnetic energy into free space. Antennas can be used to gather this energy or radiate it.

Antialiasing filter. A low-pass filter that cuts off any frequency component that is more than half the sampling frequency.

Asynchronous. Data that are not synchronized with the system clock.

Attenuation. The power loss of a system defined by the ratio of the input power over the output power.

Automatic gain control (AGC). A method of automatically compensating for the differences in received signal strength in a receiver.

Avalanche diode. Avalanche diodes combine the detection of optical energy like a PIN diode or photo diode with amplification of the light energy detected.

Balanced modulator. A common implementation is using a double balanced mixer.

Balun. A specialized transformer for connecting balanced and unbalanced signaling.

Bandwidth. Literally, a range of frequencies. Usually used to describe the range of frequencies used for a transmission of the modulated signal through a communications channel.

Baseband. A communications system where the signal while in the channel extends down to zero frequency.

Baudout code. An early code designed for use with typewriters.

Bessel function. A mathematical function that is used to evaluate the amplitude of angle modulation harmonics.

Bit. A single item of information, typically, a 1 or a 0.

Bit error rate (BER). A measure of the performance of digital modems.

BPSK. Binary Phase Shift Keying.

Broadband. A communications system where the signal while in the channel does not lie close to zero frequency. All broadband systems use a carrier signal.

C. The speed of light, 300 million m/sec.

Carrier. The specific frequency that is modulated or impressed with the information contained in the modulating signal. The carrier contains no information itself other than that contained in the modulating signal. All three aspects of the carrier may be modulated, amplitude (AM), frequency (FM), and phase (PM).

Carrier frequency. Same as carrier.

Carrier signal. Same as carrier.

Carrier wave. Same as carrier.

Carson's Rule. A rule used to estimate the bandwidth of large modulation index angle modulators.

Cellular radio. Same as cellular telephone.

Cellular telephone. A system using FDM techniques to allow wireless telephone connection to the switched wired network.

Center frequency. Usually the same frequency as the car-

617

rier. In all cases, either the average frequency of a modulated signal when the modulating signal is analog in nature or the frequency of the modulated signal when there is no modulation applied.

Characteristic impedance. That impedance that captures the impedance seen by a signal traveling down a line.

Coaxial cable. A type of metallic conductor where the signal line is enclosed by one or more shields.

CODEC. A shorthand concatenation of the words, coding, and decoding.

Code division multiple access (CDMA). A method of accessing signals that depends on matching the code used to spread the transmitted signal in the receiver.

Coding. A method of altering the information; there are two types, channel and source.

Coherent. All waveforms having the same phase relationship with each other. In other words, all waveforms rise and fall simultaneously or in some continuous way.

Communications channel (CC). The path along which the communication takes place. It may be a hard guided channel or a soft unguided channel.

Communication system. A system to send information from one place, the source, to another place, the destination.

Companding. Nonuniform quantization.

Constellation diagram. A way of representing the signal space locations of digital moderns.

Constructive interference. A variation of wave amplitude that adds two or more individual wave amplitudes, resulting in a greater resultant wave amplitude.

Continuous wave (CW). A carrier wave with no modulation.

Critical angle. That angle for which total internal reflection occurs.

Cross talk. Interference on one signal line from an outside source, usually a parallel wire.

Cycle time. Same as period.

Cyclic redundancy check (CRC). A term for using FEC error detection.

Data communications equipment (DCE). That piece of equipment in a communications system that stands between the DTE and CC. It connects the user device to the CC. A typical example of a DCE is a modem. The female connector is always used to plug into a DCE device.

Data terminal equipment (DTE). That piece of equipment in a communication system that is designated the user device. A DCE is used to connect it to the CC. A typical example of a DTE is a personal computer. The male connector is always used to plug into a DTE device.

Decade. Same as a factor of 10.

Decibel. A base 10 logarithmic measure that is a pure number. The decibel is the power of 10. It is used to represent the value of a ratio of powers.

Deemphasis. The process of compensating for the emphasis introduced in FM broadcasts.

Delta modulation. A method of pulse modulation where the output is dependent on whether the input is larger or smaller than the previous sample.

Demodulation. To recover the modulating signal from the modulated signal.

Destructive interference. A variation of wave amplitude that adds two or more individual wave amplitudes, resulting in a smaller resultant wave amplitude.

Diagonal clipping. A type of distortion exhibited by the time constant of an envelope detector.

Dielectric. A material with low electrical conductivity compared to a metal.

Dielectric constant. A ratio of a materials electrical permittivity to that of the permittivity of free space.

Digital communications system. A communications system that transfer an analog or digital data source from source to destination. The signal while in the communications channel is digital in nature but may be analog or digital at either end. Examples include PCM systems used in the telephone system and ISDN modems.

Digital component. A component that operates with digital signals on at least one of its inputs or outputs. Typically, the component will require a clock source. Examples include flip-flops, microprocessors and A/D and D/A converters.

Digital data source. An input signal where the values it takes on have "square-like" edges. In the ideal world, these would be discontinuous with a single point taking on more than one amplitude value. A good example is a computer keyboard.

Diode detector. Same as envelope detector.

Dipole antenna. A simple antenna where the length of the antenna is the same as the carrier wavelength.

Directional. Same as anisotropic.

Director element. A parasitic antenna element that is used to direct the energy into the active element.

Dispersion. The effect caused by exposure of a dielectric like an optical fiber when exposed to an electromagnetic field. Dispersion is also used to described the effect caused by multimode propagation down a fiber.

Double sideband suppressed carrier (DSB-SC). A method of AM modulation where no carrier is present in the modulated signal. Typically used for frequency translation.

Dynamic range. A way of expressing the amplitude range of a signal.

EIA-232. Interface between data terminal equipment and data circuit terminating equipment employing serial binary data interchange. A set of standards specifying the electrical and mechanical characteristics of this interface.

EIA-449. General-purpose 37 and 9 position interface for data terminal equipment and data circuit terminating equipment employing serial binary data interchange. A set of standards specifying the electrical and mechanical characteristics of this interface.

EIA-530. High-speed 25 position interface for data terminal equipment and data circuit terminating equipment. A set of standards specifying the electrical and mechanical characteristics of this interface.

Electrical permittivity. When divided by the permittivity of free space, the same as dielectric constant.

Electromagnetic interference (EMI). A general term that encompasses any interference by and source of electrical or magnetic fields. Includes all forms of RFI.

Electromagnetic spectrum. The range of frequencies from 0 Hz to 300 GHz and beyond.

Electromagnetic wave. A specific frequency wave that is part of the electromagnetic spectrum.

Envelope detector. A detector composed of a diode, capacitor, and resistor. Often used for demodulation of DSB-LC waveforms.

Extended binary coded decimal interchange code (EBCDIC). A code used by early computers.

Feedpoint. That location on an antenna where the electrical signal is applied or extracted.

Fiber optic cable. A light transmission path that depends on the principle of TIR to operate.

Fiber optics. The study of how light travels down a fiber optic cable.

Flywheel effect. An mechanical analogy used to explain the functioning of an oscillator.

Folded dipole. An antenna very similar to the half-wave dipole.

Forward error correction (FEC). The primary method of channel coding in simplex channels.

Fourier analysis. The study of signals using the Fourier series.

Frame. A group of data defined by taking one sample from each input source.

Free space. A term that defines space free of any perturbations that would effect the electrical or magnetic field strength.

Frequency. The number of repetitions of a periodic signal per second. The inverse of the period.

Frequency deviation. A measure of the extent a carrier shifts in frequency due to a modulating signal.

Frequency division multiplexing (FDM). A way of dividing up bandwidth based on frequency slots.

Frequency modulation (FM). One of two forms of angle modulation.

Frequency multiplier. A circuit where the output is a multiple of the signal frequency applied to it.

Frequency reuse. A way of using the same frequency sets in many distinct geographical areas.

Frequency shift keying (FSK). A method of digital modulation based on FM.

Full duplex (FDX). A communication system where information is transferred in two directions, but only in one direction at a time. A good example is a walkie-talkie.

Gain. The rise of power of a system defined by the ratio of the input power over the output power.

Graded-index optical fiber. A fiber where the index of refraction gradually changes across the diameter of the core. The index of refraction is not constant.

Gray code. A code where the output changes in only 1 bit position for each successive input step.

Ground wave. The mode of propagation of electromagnetic waves where the waveform follows the contour of the planet. For all electromagnetic waves below 3 MHz, this is the mode of propagation.

Guided channel. Those channels that you can touch and not get wet. Examples include any metallic or optical media. The signal travels along a repeatable, known, confined path; also known as a hard channel.

Half duplex (HDX). A communications system where information is transferred in two directions at the same time. A good example is the telephone system.

Half-wave dipole antenna. An antenna whose length is equal to half of the wavelength of the desired frequency.

Hamming Code. A block FEC code.

Hard channel. Same as guided channel.

Hard limiter. A device where the output is a fixed voltage over a wide range of input voltages.

Harmonic. A frequency with an integer relationship to the fundamental frequency.

Hartley's Law. A method of estimating the information capacity of a channel.

Helical antenna. An antenna that is constructed in a helically wound manner.

Hertz (Hz). The unit of frequency, defined as the number of cycles per second. Also defined as the number of zero crossings per second.

Hertz antenna. An antenna that does not use the ground as part of its resonant circuit.

Horn antenna. A specialized form of parabolic antennas.

Index of refraction. The ratio of the speed of light to that of a material.

Information bandwidth. Same as information capacity.

Information capacity. The amount of information that can be sent from source to destination. In normal usage, the information capacity of DCE equipment is the speed of that piece of equipment.

Information theory. The study of how coding can be used to increase the information capacity of a transmission.

Insertion loss. That loss that occurs simply due to the insertion of a signal into a system.

Instantaneous frequency. The time rate of change of the angle of a wave.

Interference. Any extraneous power interfering with the signal transmission or reception. Also a variation of wave amplitude due to the superposition of two or more waves.

Interlaced scanning. The method of line scanning used in broadcast television.

Intermodulation distortion (IM). That distortion that results from the mixing of two signals in a receiver.

International Telecommunications Union (ITU). A United Nations organization that sets telecommunications standards and frequency allocations. Representatives are from over 170 nations.

Isotropic. Radiates or receives with identical gain in all directions.

Lase. To function as a laser.

Laser (light amplification by stimulated emission of radiation).

This device converts electromagnetic radiation into a single frequency of amplified and coherent radiation.

Limiter. A circuit that limits the voltage swing of the output.

Line of sight (LOS). The mode of propagation used by frequencies above 30 MHz. Electromagnetic waves at these frequencies travel in a straight line from source to destination. LOS is used for all orbital communications from the planet.

Local area network (LAN). A network confined to a local activity.

Local oscillator (LO). The local carrier oscillator.

Log periodic antenna. An antenna made up of elements that increase or decrease in a log periodic way. This greatly expands the bandwidth of the antenna.

Loop antenna. An antenna that is constructed in a loop.

Lower sideband. That sideband that occupies the frequency just below the carrier frequency.

Magnetic permeability. A measure of the extent to which a material is susceptible to induced magnetization; related to magnetic susceptibility.

Manchester code. A coding technique that guarantees a transition every clock period independent of the form of the input data.

Marconi antenna. An antenna that uses the ground as part of its resonant circuit.

Mark. The lower of the two FSK output frequencies; represents a logical 1.

Modem. A concatenation of the terms *modulate* and *demodulate*. A device that performs some type of analog modulation.

Modulate. To vary the amplitude (AM), frequency (FM), or phase (PM) of the carrier. Usually, it means the product of the modulating signal with the carrier.

Modulated signal. The signal that results from the product of the modulating signal and the carrier. It is the signal that conveys the information from source to destination and is present in the CC.

Modulating signal. The signal that contains the information that is to be sent from the source to the destination.

Modulation. The act of varying one of the characteristics of the carrier. Examples are amplitude (AM), frequency (FM), and phase (PM). Also combinations of these such as QAM.

Modulation index. A measure of the depth of modulation.

Multimode optical fiber. An optical fiber where there are many paths (modes) of travel for the light rays to take as they propagate down the length of the fiber. This causes the distortion effect known as dispersion.

Multiplexing. A way of dividing up the bandwidth.

Narrowband FM (NBFM). A form of angle modulation where the index of modulation is 2 or less.

Network. The combination of hardware and protocols.

Noise figure. A measure of the noise contribution of a device.

Nonlinear device. A device where the output curve is nonlinear if a linear input is applied.

Non return to zero code (NRZ). A line code where the signal does not return to zero, independent of the data to be coded.

Numerical aperture. Defines the light gathering power of a device.

Nyquist bandwidth. The minimum bandwidth required to pass all possible frequency components of the input.

Open Systems Interconnection (OSI). A model used to define and classify communications architectures.

Oscillator. A circuit where the output has a regular zero crossing frequency.

Overmodulation. That modulation that results when the modulation index is greater than 1.

Packet. The traditional term used for Layer 3 PDUs.

Parabolic antenna. An antenna that is constructed in a parabolic shape.

Parasitic antenna. Same as Yagi antenna.

Parasitic element. An antenna element that is not driven electrically.

Parity. A simple form of error detection.

Peak-to-peak voltage. Twice the peak voltage.

Peak voltage. Half the peak-to-peak voltage.

Period. The time of one cycle of a waveform.

Percentage modulation. Same as modulation index.

Phase locked loop (PPL). A device that uses frequency differences to track an input frequency.

Phase modulation (PM). One form of angle modulation.

Phase Shift Keying (PSK). That form of angle modulation where the input is a digital signal and the output is a carrier with abrupt phase shifts.

Photoelectric effect. The process of converting optical energy into electrical current.

Photovoltaic effect. Same as photoelectric effect.

PIN diode. A faster switching diode developed for optical detection.

Pilot signal. A method of demodulation where the local carrier is synchronized to a transmitted carrier.

Polarization. The angle of the waveform. Typically, horizontal or vertical.

Preemphasis. A method of providing additional amplification to the high-frequency components of an FM transmission.

Private branch exchange (PBX). A minature telephone system.

Product detector. Using a mixer to demodulate.

Protocol. The rules by which two systems communicate.

Pulse amplitude modulation (PAM). The form of pulse modulation where the amplitude of the pulse represents the amplitude of the input signal.

Pulse code modulation (PCM). The form pulse modulation where a code word represents the amplitude of the input signal.

Pulse modulation (PM). That general form of modulation using pulses rather than continuous signals.

Pulse position modulation (PPM). That form of pulse modulation where the position of the pulse represents the amplitude of the input signal.

Pulse width modulation (PWM). That form of pulse modulation where the width of the pulse represents the amplitude of the input signal.

Quadrature amplitude modulation (QAM). A form of digital modulation equivalent to QPSK.

Quadrature phase shift keying (QPSK). A form of digital modulation where the input data is represented by a group of four phase states.

Quality factor (Q). A measure of the quality of a passive component. For antennas a measure of how narrow the receive or transmit band is.

Quantization. A measure of the resolution of a sampled data system.

Quarter-wave antenna. An antenna whose length is equal to one-quarter the wavelength of the desired frequency.

Radian (RAD). The unit of angular frequency.

Radiation resistance. The impedance of an antenna measured at the feedpoint of the antenna.

Radio frequency (RF). That band of electromagnetic energy that lies between the upper end of the low frequency band, 300 kHz, and the lower end of the optical band, 300 GHz. This band encompasses virtually the entire communications spectrum.

Radio frequency interference (RFI). The disruption of any radio frequency caused by interference generated by another source of radio frequencies.

Receiver. Any system that combines the demodulator with the necessary circuitry to both acquire the signal from the communications channel and present it to the user at the destination.

Reflector element. A parasitic antenna element that acts to reflect some energy back into the active element.

Refraction. The bending of waves.

Repeater. A Layer 1 device that amplifies a signal.

Return to zero code (RZ). A line code where the signal returns to zero between each bit.

RS-232. Recommended standard EIA-232. Same as EIA-232.

RS-449. Recommended standard EIA-449. Same as EIA-449.

RS-530. Recommended standard EIA-530. Same as EIA-530.

Sensitivity. A measure of how sensitive the input of a receiver is.

Signal-to-noise ratio (S/N). The ratio of signal strength, or power-to-noise power. Both quantities must be measured in the same bandwidth for the ratio to have meaning.

Simplex (SX). A communication system where information is transferred in one direction only, all the time. A good example is broadcast television.

Single-mode optical fiber. An optical fiber constructed in such a way that all rays of light entering the fiber travel the same path (mode) as they propagate down the length of the fiber.

Single sideband (SSB). A method of AM where only one sideband is transmitted.

Skin effect. The traveling of current only in a narrow region of a conductor.

Sky wave. The mode of propagation of electromagnetic waves between the frequencies 3 and 30 MHz. It makes use of the reflecting properties of the planet's atmosphere to propagate and, essentially, skips along. These skipped areas are referred to as skip zones.

Slope detector. A method of detecting frequency changes used in angle demodulators.

Slope overload. A type of distortion experienced in delta modulation.

Soft channel. Same as unguided channel.

Soft limiter. A limiter where the output is linear over a portion of the input range and hard limited over the rest.

Space. The higher of the two frequency shift keying output frequencies; represents a logical 0.

Spectrum analyzer. A device that displays signals on a horizontal axis of frequency. A way of viewing frequency space.

Spread spectrum. A method of modulation where the output spectrum is spread over a wide range of frequencies.

Standing wave. A term used to describe the reflected wave generated due to an impedance mismatch.

Standing wave ratio (SWR). A ratio of two impedances, the load impedance and the characteristic impedance of the metallic conductor. The larger in magnitude always is in the numerator. Therefore, the value of SWR is always greater than 1. A perfect match is defined as an SWR = 1.

Static. Nonchanging.

Step-index optical fiber. A fiber in which the entire core has the same index of refraction. The index of refraction steps or shifts abruptly at the core/cladding boundry.

Stereo. Two channel.

Superheterodyne receiver. A form of AM demodulation.

Surge impedance. Same as characteristic impedance.

Switching center. Any location where a switch is placed in the telephone network.

Synchronous. In phase.

Time division multiplexing (TDM). A way of sharing bandwidth.

Time domain reflectometer (TDR). A device for measuring reflections and locating faults.

Total internal reflection. The special case of reflection where there is no transmitted or refracted wave. All energy is contained in the reflected wave.

Transmitter. A system that combines the modulator with the necessary power amplification and circuitry to place the modulated signal into the communications channel.

Tuned radio frequency receiver (TRF). A simple receiver design consisting of only a radio amplifier, detector, and an audio amplifier. The detector must tune over the entire range of the receiver.

Unbalanced line. A line where the signal is not paired to a dedicated ground line.

Unguided channel. Those channels that you cannot touch, except for water. Examples include any communication that uses an atmospheric channel, including satellite, cellular telephones, broadcast radio, and television. The signal does not travel along a confined path but rather propagates from source to destination with varying paths; also known as soft channels.

Unidirectional. Same as anistropic.

Upper sideband (USB). That sideband that extends upward from the carrier frequency.

V.35. Data transmission at 48 kbps using 60 to 108 kHz group band circuits. ITU standard for a trunk interface between a modem or any network access device and a packet network. Group band means a modem that uses a bandwidth of several telephone circuits.

Velocity factor. The percentage of the speed of light in free space at which the electromagnetic wave travels in a material.

Velocity of propagation. The actual velocity at which an electromagnetic wave travels in a material.

Vertical antenna. An antenna that is placed vertically.

Vestigial sideband. A form of modulation where only a portion of one sideband is transmitted along with the entire other sideband.

Video signal. That portion of a television signal that contains the picture.

Voltage controlled oscillator (VCO). A device that outputs a frequency depending on an input voltage.

Voltage standing wave ratio (VSWR). Same as standing wave ratio.

Wavelength (λ). For any periodic wave, the distance between any two points where the phase difference is 2π.

Wide area network (WAN). A network that links LANs.

Wideband FM (WBFM). A form of angle modulation where the modulation index is 10 or greater.

Yagi antenna. An antenna that uses half-wave dipoles as the active element.